SIPRI Yearbook 2013
Armaments, Disarmament and International Security

www.sipriyearbook.org

Tilman Brück, Director, *Yearbook Editor and Publisher*
Ian Anthony, *Executive Editor*
D. A. Cruickshank, *Managing Editor*

Editors
D. A. Cruickshank, Joey Fox, Jetta Gilligan Borg,
David Prater, Caspar Trimmer

STOCKHOLM INTERNATIONAL PEACE RESEARCH INSTITUTE
Signalistgatan 9
SE-169 70 Solna, Sweden
Telephone: +46 8 655 97 00
Fax: +46 8 655 97 33
Email: sipri@sipri.org
Internet: www.sipri.org

SIPRI Yearbook 2013

Armaments, Disarmament and International Security

**STOCKHOLM INTERNATIONAL
PEACE RESEARCH INSTITUTE**

OXFORD UNIVERSITY PRESS
2013

OXFORD

UNIVERSITY PRESS

Great Clarendon Street, Oxford OX2 6DP,
United Kingdom

Oxford University Press is a department of the University of Oxford.
It furthers the University's objective of excellence in research, scholarship,
and education by publishing worldwide. Oxford is a registered trade mark of
Oxford University Press in the UK and in certain other countries

British Library Cataloguing in Publication Data
Data available

Library of Congress Cataloging in Publication Data
Data available

ISSN 0953–0282

ISBN 978–0–19–967843–3

Typeset and originated by SIPRI
Printed in Great Britain on acid-free paper by
CPI Antony Rowe, Chippenham, Wiltshire

SIPRI Yearbook 2013 is also published online at
<http://www.sipriyearbook.org>

Contents

Part I. Security and conflicts, 2012

Part III. Non-proliferation, arms control and disarmament, 2012

Annexes

Preface

It is with great pleasure and honour that I present the SIPRI Yearbook for the first time, having started as the eighth director of SIPRI in January 2013. SIPRI is, of course, one of the leading global think tanks analysing international security, conflict and peace. It is also a great team of dedicated researchers, and one of my biggest pleasures in the new job has been to get to know and to work with this outstanding group of experts. They work exceptionally hard to help many people, including the readers of the Yearbook, to identify and understand sources of insecurity, to prevent and resolve conflicts, and to sustain peace.

This concern for peace and security is what motivates and unites us in SIPRI. It is also what concerns our many friends and supporters around the world, who look to SIPRI to provide unbiased, reliable and timely information and analysis. SIPRI has a huge global network of friends: practitioners, experts, journalists and members of the general public. Meeting them over the past few months has been an inspiring and humbling experience. I see my role as SIPRI director as being to help build this community—for the benefit of SIPRI and our partners and for the benefit of a safer and more peaceful world.

This, the 44th edition of the Yearbook, is published initially in English in print and online, and will soon be translated in full into Arabic, Chinese, Russian and Ukrainian, and summarized in many other languages. It looks in turn at security and conflicts, military spending and armaments, and non-proliferation, arms control and disarmament.

In the field of security and conflicts, part I documents developments in 2012 in armed conflict (chapter 1) and peace operations and conflict management (chapter 2). Chapter 1 includes studies on armed conflict in the wake of the Arab Spring—illustrating how political instability and violence can spread across borders—and the long-running yet fragile peace in East and South East Asia. Alongside this is a presentation of comprehensive data on patterns of organized violence—state-based, non-state and one-sided—over the decade 2002–11 collated by the Uppsala Conflict Data Program (UCDP). Chapter 2, on peace operations and conflict management, not only provides full details of all multilateral peace operations in 2012, along with trends in peacekeeping over the decade 2003–12, but also looks at the establishment of the three operations that were launched in 2012, in Guinea-Bissau, Niger and Syria, and other developments around the world.

In part II, on military spending and armaments, the Yearbook once again provides a detailed account of global, regional and national military spending, the arms sales of the 100 largest arms-producing and military services companies, the volume of all international transfers of major conventional

weapons, and stocks of nuclear weapons. Chapter 3, on military expenditure, looks in detail at the continuing effects of budget austerity in Western
countries, not least the United States, and the impact on defence budgets of
the withdrawal of Western troops from Afghanistan. The chapter also analyses topics such as broader security spending in Central America in the
context of violent crime and the faltering steps towards improved transparency and good governance in military budgeting in Colombia and Indonesia. Chapter 4, on arms industry developments, shows how companies
are adapting to reduced military spending by, among other strategies, looking for new markets such as cybersecurity. Chapter 5, on arms transfers,
highlights China's emergence as a major arms supplier and declining arms
imports by states in Western and Central Europe, while one section looks at
where the parties to the conflict in Syria are getting their arms. Chapter 6
describes the nuclear forces of each of the nuclear weapon-possessing
states, and gives the total global stocks of fissile materials, collated by the
International Panel on Fissile Materials.

On non-proliferation, arms control and disarmament, part III covers controls on nuclear weapons (in chapter 7), chemical and biological materials
(in chapter 8), conventional arms (in chapter 9), and trade in arms and
dual-use goods (in chapter 10). Chapter 7 looks in particular at developments in Iran, North Korea and NATO, and at efforts to prevent acts of
nuclear terrorism. As well as monitoring developments in the chemical and
biological weapons conventions, chapter 8 studies the allegations that Syria
possesses chemical weapons and the security risks arising from academic
research on the transmissibility of avian influenza. Chapter 9 starts with a
survey of humanitarian arms control of weapons such as mines, cluster
munitions and the explosive remnants of war, then looks at the efforts to
control small arms being made at the subregional level in Africa and the
more troubled efforts to control arms in Europe, and finally surveys con-
fidence- and security-building measures in Asia and in the Americas. Chapter 10 opens with an account of the failed attempt to agree an arms trade
treaty in 2012, then surveys multilateral arms embargoes and other measures to restrict trade, developments in the informal export control regimes,
and related developments in the European Union.

Together, these contributions from 39 authors from 14 countries provide
the single most comprehensive annual compendium on developments in
international security, conflict and peace available. However, no such
account can be complete without an acknowledgement of what we do not
know. In the introduction to this Yearbook, I therefore sketch out my views
as an economist on which data and which knowledge fields are currently
under-researched. As an economist, I sense a need and an opportunity for a
comprehensive framework for measuring flows of peace and security. The
relationships between actors for peace and security could be mapped with

their interactions being measured and, in many cases, quantified. Akin to the system of national accounts in economics, a 'global system of security accounts' in conflict, peace and security studies could be developed that would place the data that SIPRI collects on, for example, military spending, arms transfers and peace operations in a comprehensive and logical framework, with data gaps being filled over time. Naturally, this is a tall agenda. However, SIPRI has consistently fulfilled the high expectations of our constituents, and I am confident that we will continue to make new and innovative contributions to the measurement and analysis of security, conflict and peace in the years ahead.

I would like to thank the team whose energy and enthusiasm has made possible this edition of the SIPRI Yearbook. I am grateful to all the authors, be they based at SIPRI or elsewhere, for their work on the many interesting chapters of this edition of the Yearbook. Many thanks are due to the external referees, whose support and feedback we greatly appreciate. Dr Ian Anthony provided an invaluable contribution as the SIPRI Research Coordinator and Executive Editor of the Yearbook. I also really appreciate the excellent work of the SIPRI editors: Dr David Cruickshank, Joey Fox, Jetta Gilligan Borg, Dr David Prater and Caspar Trimmer. Many other colleagues at SIPRI made the Yearbook and the good work of the institute possible: Göran Lennmarker as the Chairman of the Governing Board, all our valued Governing Board members, Elisabet Rendert, Chief Financial Officer, Nenne Bodell, Library and Documentation Director, Stephanie Blenckner, Communications Director, Gerd Hagmeyer-Gaverus, IT Director, Cynthia Loo, Senior Management Assistant, and all of SIPRI's great support and research staff. I am also grateful for the support provided by Jakob Hallgren, who joined SIPRI as its new Deputy Director in September 2012. He replaced Daniel Nord, who did SIPRI great service as SIPRI's longest-serving Deputy Director.

Last, but certainly not least, I would like to thank my predecessor, Dr Bates Gill, for his five years at the helm of SIPRI—he took excellent care of an impressive institution. I am very curious about where the journey will take us from here!

Professor Tilman Brück
SIPRI Director
Stockholm, May 2013

Abbreviations and conventions

ABM	Anti-ballistic missile
ACV	Armoured combat vehicle
AG	Australia Group
ALCM	Air-launched cruise missile
APC	Armoured personnel carrier
APEC	Asia–Pacific Economic Cooperation
APM	Anti-personnel mine
APT	ASEAN Plus Three
ARF	ASEAN Regional Forum
ASAT	Anti-satellite
ASEAN	Association of Southeast Asian Nations
ATT	Arms trade treaty
ATTU	Atlantic-to-the Urals (zone)
AU	African Union
BCC	Bilateral Consultative Commission (of the Russian–US New START treaty)
BMD	Ballistic missile defence
BSEC	Organization of the Black Sea Economic Cooperation
BTWC	Biological and Toxin Weapons Convention
BW	Biological weapon/warfare
CADSP	Common African Defence and Security Policy
CAR	Central African Republic
CBM	Confidence-building measure
CBRN	Chemical, biological, radiological and nuclear
CBSS	Council of the Baltic Sea States
CBW	Chemical and biological weapon/warfare
CCM	Convention on Cluster Munitions
CCW	Certain Conventional Weapons (Convention)
CD	Conference on Disarmament
CDS	Consejo de Defensa Suramericano (South American Defence Council)
CEEAC	Communauté Economique des Etats de l'Afrique Centrale (Economic Community of Central African States, ECCAS)
CFE	Conventional Armed Forces in Europe (Treaty)
CFSP	Common Foreign and Security Policy
CICA	Conference on Interaction and Confidence-building Measures in Asia
CIS	Commonwealth of Independent States
COPAX	Conseil de Paix et de Sécurité de l'Afrique Centrale (Central Africa Peace and Security Council)
CSBM	Confidence- and security-building measure
CSDP	Common Security and Defence Policy
CSTO	Collective Security Treaty Organization
CTBT	Comprehensive Nuclear-Test-Ban Treaty
CTBTO	Comprehensive Nuclear-Test-Ban Treaty Organization
CTR	Cooperative Threat Reduction
CW	Chemical weapon/warfare
CWC	Chemical Weapons Convention
DDR	Disarmament, demobilization and reintegration
DPKO	UN Department of Peacekeeping Operations
DPRK	Democratic People's Republic of Korea (North Korea)

DRC	Democratic Republic of the Congo	ICTY	International Criminal Tribunal for the former Yugoslavia
EAEC	European Atomic Energy Community (Euratom)	IED	Improvised explosive device
EAPC	Euro-Atlantic Partnership Council	IFS	Instrument for Stability
ECOWAS	Economic Community of West African States	IGAD	Intergovernmental Authority on Development
EDA	European Defence Agency	IGC	Intergovernmental conference
ENP	European Neighbourhood Policy	INDA	International non-proliferation and disarmament assistance
ERW	Explosive remnants of war		
EU	European Union	INF	Intermediate-range Nuclear Forces (Treaty)
FATF	Financial Action Task Force		
FMCT	Fissile material cut-off treaty	IRBM	Intermediate-range ballistic missile
FSC	Forum for Security Co-operation (of the OSCE)	ISAF	International Security Assistance Force
FY	Financial year	JCG	Joint Consultative Group (of the CFE Treaty)
FYROM	Former Yugoslav Republic of Macedonia	LEU	Low-enriched uranium
G8	Group of Eight (industrialized states)	MANPADS	Man-portable air defence system
GCC	Gulf Cooperation Council	MDGs	Millennium Development Goals
GDP	Gross domestic product		
GGE	Group of government experts	MIRV	Multiple independently targetable re-entry vehicle
GLCM	Ground-launched cruise missile	MOTAPM	Mines other than anti-personnel mines
GNEP	Global Nuclear Energy Partnership	MTCR	Missile Technology Control Regime
GTRI	Global Threat Reduction Initiative	NAM	Non-Aligned Movement
GUAM	Georgia, Ukraine, Azerbaijan and Moldova	NATO	North Atlantic Treaty Organization
HCOC	Hague Code of Conduct	NBC	Nuclear, biological and chemical (weapons)
HEU	Highly enriched uranium		
IAEA	International Atomic Energy Agency	NGO	Non-governmental organization
ICBM	Intercontinental ballistic missile	NNWS	Non-nuclear weapon state
		NPT	Non-Proliferation Treaty
ICC	International Criminal Court	NRF	NATO Response Force
		NSG	Nuclear Suppliers Group
ICJ	International Court of Justice	NWFZ	Nuclear weapon-free zone
		NWS	Nuclear weapon state
ICTR	International Criminal Tribunal for Rwanda	OAS	Organization of American States

OCCAR	Organisation Conjointe de Coopération en matière d'Armement (Organisation for Joint Armament Cooperation)	SALW	Small arms and light weapons
		SAM	Surface-to-air missile
		SCO	Shanghai Cooperation Organisation
ODA	Official development assistance	SCSL	Special Court for Sierra Leone
OECD	Organisation for Economic Co-operation and Development	SICA	Sistema de la Integración Centroamericana (Central American Integration System)
OHCHR	Office of the UN High Commissioner for Human Rights	SLBM	Submarine-launched ballistic missile
OIC	Organization of the Islamic Conference	SLCM	Sea-launched cruise missile
OPANAL	Organismo para la Proscripción de las Armas Nucleares en la América Latina y el Caribe (Agency for the Prohibition of Nuclear Weapons in Latin America and the Caribbean)	SORT	Strategic Offensive Reductions Treaty
		SRBM	Short-range ballistic missile
		SRCC	Sub-Regional Consultative Commission
		SSM	Surface-to-surface missile
		SSR	Security sector reform
OPCW	Organisation for the Prohibition of Chemical Weapons	START	Strategic Arms Reduction Treaty
		TLE	Treaty-limited equipment
OPEC	Organization of the Petroleum Exporting Countries	UAE	United Arab Emirates
		UNASUR	Unión de Naciones Suramericanas (Union of South American Nations)
OSCC	Open Skies Consultative Commission		
		UAS	Unmanned aerial system
OSCE	Organization for Security and Co-operation in Europe	UAV	Unmanned aerial vehicle
		UCAV	Unmanned combat air vehicle
P5	Five permanent members of the UN Security Council		
		UN	United Nations
PFP	Partnership for Peace	UNDP	UN Development Programme
PRT	Provincial reconstruction team		
		UNHCR	UN High Commissioner for Refugees
PSC	Peace and Security Council (of the African Union)	UNODA	UN Office for Disarmament Affairs
PSC	Private security company		
PSI	Proliferation Security Initiative	UNROCA	UN Register of Conventional Arms
R&D	Research and development	WA	Wassenaar Arrangement
SAARC	South Asian Association for Regional Co-operation	WMD	Weapon(s) of mass destruction
SADC	Southern African Development Community	WMDFZ	WMD-free zone

Conventions

. .	Data not available or not applicable
–	Nil or a negligible figure
( )	Uncertain data
b.	Billion (thousand million)
kg	Kilogram
km	Kilometre (1000 metres)
m.	Million
th.	Thousand
tr.	Trillion (million million)
$	US dollars
€	Euros

Geographical regions and subregions

Africa	Consisting of North Africa (Algeria, Libya, Morocco and Tunisia, but excluding Egypt) and sub-Saharan Africa
Americas	Consisting of North America (Canada and the USA), Central America and the Caribbean (including Mexico), and South America
Asia and Oceania	Consisting of Central Asia, East Asia, Oceania, South Asia (including Afghanistan) and South East Asia
Europe	Consisting of Eastern Europe (Armenia, Azerbaijan, Belarus, Georgia, Moldova, Russia and Ukraine) and Western and Central Europe (with South Eastern Europe); in discussions of military expenditure, Turkey is included in Western and Central Europe
Middle East	Consisting of Egypt, Iran, Iraq, Israel, Jordan, Kuwait, Lebanon, Syria, Turkey and the states of the Arabian peninsula

SIPRI Yearbook online

www.sipriyearbook.org

Full access to the SIPRI Yearbook online is free for individuals when you buy the corresponding edition of the Yearbook in print. This applies to editions since 2010.

Benefits of the online version include having the complete text of the SIPRI Yearbook on your desktop or handheld device; a simple but powerful search function; copious deep linking to authoritative Internet resources; and the authority of SIPRI whenever and wherever you are online.

If you have bought this edition of the SIPRI Yearbook, you can use the token printed on a detachable card inside this volume to create a user account that will allow you to login to the SIPRI Yearbook online.

More information is available at <http://www.sipriyearbook.org/>.

Introduction
An economist's perspective on security, conflict and peace research

TILMAN BRÜCK

The use of physical force is, unfortunately, one of the key elements in the repertoire of human behaviour. Given the persistence and prominence of the intentional use of force, or violence, for human interactions, group behaviour and state actions, it is surprising how limited the degree of understanding of this topic still is. Many of the policies dealing with potential or actual group-based violence therefore remain imperfect. For example, none of the Millennium Development Goals (MDGs), which have shaped the development aid discourse since 2000, refers to peace or security.[1] This silence on security, conflict and peace in the global development discourse was avoidable and is overdue to be remedied, especially as no conflict-affected country has yet achieved any MDG.[2]

The SIPRI Yearbook aims to remedy these knowledge gaps: it provides information on and endeavours to enhance understanding of security, conflict and peace, thereby enabling better policies to be made in the pursuit of a more peaceful, secure and equitable world. In this spirit, this essay identifies and discusses some research areas where a better understanding of violent conflict may pay dividends for practitioners. Violence creates dependencies, or cycles of violence, from which it is often difficult to escape. Stopping such cycles of violence requires peace- and security-enhancing institutions. But building such institutions in turn requires tightly aligned and closely coordinated policies.

Economics only started to acknowledge that violence may be part of human behaviour and interactions after the end of the cold war.[3] Related

---

[1] United Nations, General Assembly, 'United Nations Millennium Declaration', Resolution 55/2, 8 Sep. 2000.

[2] World Development Report 2011: Conflict, Security, and Development (World Bank: Washington, DC, 2011), p. 5.

[3] Stewart, F. and FitzGerald, V. (eds), War and Underdevelopment, vol. 1, The Economic and Social Consequences of Conflict (Oxford University Press: Oxford, 2000); Addison, T. and Brück, T., Making Peace Work: The Challenges of Social and Economic Reconstruction (Palgrave Macmillan: Basingstoke, 2009); World Development Report 2011 (note 2); Kaldor, M., New and Old Wars: Organised Violence in a Global Era, 3rd edn (Polity Press: Cambridge, 2012); and Justino, P., Brück, T. and Verwimp, P. (eds), A Micro-Level Perspective on the Dynamics of Conflict, Violence and Development (Oxford University Press: Oxford, forthcoming).

research fields in other social sciences include the psychology of aggressive and violent behaviour, the sociology of protest movements that can become violent, and political science and international relations, where the use of force between states has long been studied. In economics, in contrast, the only previous analyses of violence may have been in game theory modelling of the cold war and in the economics of crime.

Humans regularly apply force or coercion in daily activity, with or without instruments or tools. Some such uses of force are not morally reprehensible. Other uses of violence are illegal of course, for example in the cases of murder, robbery or domestic violence. In some cases, using force against other people in a purposeful way and doing so as part of a group or against a group is not illegal or may be made legal by ex post facto legislation (e.g. after a war or coup d'état). In yet other cases, even planning violent action for political means may be illegal (e.g. in forming a terrorist group). There are clearly multiple and overlapping forms of violent action whose legality is contested and which therefore trigger a substantial institutional response.

A major responsibility of democratic government is to define and control its monopoly on violence in order to prevent the use of violence by non-state actors. Any form of weakened governance leading to the emergence of competing manifestations of violence, or of fragmenting violence, represents a degree of fragility. In such a scenario, it is likely that multiple forms of violence will be expressed by and against different (groups of) actors with various motives spanning dimensions such as politics, religion, geography and gender. Examples of forms of competing violence include organized crime such as in Mexico, secessionist movements such as in Aceh, Indonesia, or terrorist organizations such as al-Qaeda. It is a government's inability or unwillingness to maintain its monopoly of violence in a legitimate way that characterizes a fragile country or territory. In the extreme, the entire state becomes ineffective, dysfunctional or non-existent (and hence failed), such as in Afghanistan, Mali or Somalia.

Peace and security require not just the absence of group-based violence but the presence of a legitimate state defining and enforcing its citizens' property rights and thereby regulating the expression of violence. Sustained and just peace is thus linked to both the absence of non-state violence and the existence of effective and legitimate governance of state violence—and both dimensions can show degrees of perfection. Furthermore, both dimensions are inherently measurable, either quantitatively or through iterative qualitative analyses using appropriate analytical frameworks.

Social science has identified at least four significant fields that exhibit, to varying degrees, knowledge gaps concerning the strategic use of force by groups in areas having weakened state institutions, including in undemocratic states. In declining order of knowledge and understanding, these four fields are the following.

1. *The drivers of insecurity, conflict and fragility.* While much is known regarding the drivers of violence, conflict and institutional failure (or poor governance and hence fragility), important gaps remain.

2. *Trends in security, conflict and peace.* While it has been relatively straightforward to list the states engaged in armed conflict in a given year, understanding the nature of a specific conflict is much more challenging.

3. *The consequences of violent conflict and insecurity.* There is little understanding of how violence has affected socio-economic and political outcomes. This is especially true at the individual, household and group levels, where outcomes are usually adverse ('costs'), although, of course, some people, groups or countries benefit from violent conflict.

4. *Interventions and institutions for security and peace.* No comprehensive understanding has yet been developed of the options for intervention in conflict settings, or for peacebuilding and reconstruction more generally.

Taken as a whole, these gaps imply the absence of a comprehensive system of security data tying together the different strands of peace research, which may be the most fundamental and systematic knowledge gap presented thus far. This lack of understanding greatly complicates peacebuilding and conflict prevention. It makes interventions in conflicts much more ideological (and therefore perceived as self-interested), much less an issue of actual common interests and ultimately less successful—leading to self-fulfilling prophecies or 'narratives' of failed interventions, seemingly demonstrating the limitations of such actions. It even reduces the opportunities for systematic and meaningful post-intervention assessments in all these areas. Poorly informed policy decisions rarely yield good outcomes. While the reverse (i.e. that well-informed policy debates yield enlightened political outcomes) may not be correct, it may be worth taking the chances to provide the evidence before decisions of life and death are made.

Each of the four gaps is considered in sections I–IV, which outline the nature of what is not known, what has been done recently and what remains to be studied. Each section identifies the ways in which advancing knowledge in these areas can help inform, evaluate and guide policy discussions and policymaking. In each case, the ways in which recent research at SIPRI has continued and will continue to shape the debate on these important issues in peace research is described. Naturally, there are other deserving research gaps to be addressed in security, conflict and peace research. This essay addresses a selection of these; future editions of the SIPRI Yearbook may identify further gaps.

I. The drivers of insecurity, conflict and fragility

Military spending, arms production and arms transfers are among the drivers of insecurity, conflict and fragility.

Government spending on the military is a necessary prerequisite for traditional armed conflict. Hence, the monitoring of military spending over time and across countries (as is done at SIPRI) permits the dynamic and comparative analysis of, among other things, arms races or of a build-up of military potential—thus providing a useful indicator of either a response to actual conflict or of incipient conflict.[4] However, new military technologies are constantly emerging, wars can be waged against non-state targets such as religiously inspired terrorist groups or in the pursuit of regime change in potentially fragile countries, while low-technology, localized and self-perpetuating intrastate wars continue in such places as Central Africa. Thus, counting spending on traditional armed forces may not be sufficient to track possible future insecurity. Instead, understanding security spending more broadly or spending on governance and the rule of law as well as understanding the values of the various components of traditional military spending may be needed to understand military capacities and future conflicts in the 21st century.[5]

It is not just military spending but also the production and trade of weapons (both licit and illicit) that can drive insecurity.[6] In the field of arms production, there are at least four main research challenges ahead. First is the study of the implications of a multipolar economic and security world for the global distribution of security-related goods and services. Specifically, it is hard to find information about arms producers in countries—such as China—that are increasingly becoming significant arms exporters but which are not subject to market scrutiny comparable to that of producers in Western countries. Second, the trend towards more military services (e.g. for maintaining complex weapon systems) changes the nature of procurement and the business of the security companies.[7] It is not just the provision of hardware that is profitable but also participation in ongoing conflicts. For example, the provision of information and communication technology (ICT) services and of privately contracted armed security personnel—as was pioneered by the United States and practised in the wars in Afghanistan and Iraq—changes the incentive structure that private sector firms face. This represents a dramatic shift in the involvement of the private sector in the provision (or undermining) of security, which deserves

---

[4] See chapter 3 on military expenditure in this volume; and the SIPRI Military Expenditure Database, <http://www.sipri.org/databases/milex/>.

[5] E.g. on security spending in Central America see chapter 3, section IV, in this volume.

[6] See chapter 4 on arms production and military services and chapter 5 on international arms transfers in this volume.

[7] Jackson, S. T., 'The military services industry', *SIPRI Yearbook 2012*.

further research. Third, the dominance of some large and well-known companies obscures the many small firms, especially in emerging fields of military technology, that may nevertheless be important. Thus, to the extent that military technology is increasingly network based and that military services in general are gaining in importance, observing the small producers and suppliers may be as relevant as watching the big companies.[8] Fourth, and of increasing importance, is that technological transformations change what can be considered arms. Similar to the development of chemical and later nuclear weapons, the recent development of cyberwarfare capabilities poses a new security challenge derived from technological change.

To track the flow of arms between states, SIPRI measures official and unofficial international arms transfers.[9] Naturally, given the opacity of how even official arms exports are handled, efforts to improve transparency are likely to be incomplete and inconsistent. For example, in some cases the value of the deal, the precise equipment shipped or the other conditionalities (or bribes) included in the agreements will be unknown. However, SIPRI provides comparable data of the volume, not just the financial value, of international arms transfers. While this causes much scope for disagreement and criticism, it is arguably the best method in a challenging research area. Areas for further research in the field of international arms transfers include measuring the volume of arms procured locally (rather than imported) and measuring equipment longevity.[10]

Another important driver of conflict and fragility is the trafficking of weapons, people, money or conflict goods and resources (e.g. drugs, timber, diamonds and rare metals), especially when shipped by sea or air.[11] SIPRI tracks flows of goods that are likely to undermine security and good governance.[12] For example, by identifying particular trafficking patterns, SIPRI has had success in detecting which ships are likely to repeatedly engage in illicit transfers. It can be shown, for example, that a majority of all ships identified as involved in destabilizing or narcotics-related transfers via sea in the period 1991–2011 were owned by companies in member

---

[8] On the example of the cybersecurity industry see chapter 4, section II, in this volume.

[9] SIPRI Arms Transfers Database, <http://www.sipri.org/databases/armstransfers/>.

[10] SIPRI tracks the status of nuclear and chemical weapons holdings and destruction activity, as well as strategic trade control measures to ensure that dual-use material, technology and expertise is not misused for chemical, biological or nuclear weapon activities. See chapter 6 on world nuclear forces, chapter 8 on threats from chemical and biological materials, and chapter 10 on dual-use and arms trade controls in this volume.

[11] On efforts to control financial flows see chapter 10, section III, in this volume; and Bauer, S., Dunne, A. and Mićić, I., 'Strategic trade controls: countering the proliferation of weapons of mass destruction', *SIPRI Yearbook 2011*, pp. 441–43.

[12] Griffiths, H. and Bromley, M., *Air Transport and Destabilizing Commodity Flows*, SIPRI Policy Paper no. 24 (SIPRI: Stockholm, May 2009); and Griffiths, H. and Jenks, M., *Maritime Transport and Destabilizing Commodity Flows*, SIPRI Policy Paper no. 32 (SIPRI: Stockholm, Jan. 2012).

states of the Organisation for Economic Co-operation and Development (OECD).[13] This raises critical implications for policies in developed countries about their contribution (even if implicit) in creating further fragility.

II. Trends in security, conflict and peace

An important trend in peace research has been the drilling down into the details of conflict dynamics below the national level. This has been achieved partly through the collection of conflict event data by first tracking events—such as shootings by one side or the other in a war—and then categorizing them and recording their exact date and location (i.e. time stamping and geocoding them). The resulting data sets—such as the Uppsala Conflict Data Program (UCDP) Conflict Encyclopedia and the Armed Conflict Location and Event Dataset (ACLED)—usually focus on violent events and usually use news reports in local or international media, with all the biases that this may entail.[14]

Two similar, but much less common, sources of related event data are truth and reconciliation commissions and digital technologies such as text messages or social media.[15] In many ways, each of these approaches risks systematically omitting certain types of event. For example, it could be that in areas with no mobile phone coverage armed groups feel less constrained from committing atrocities. Hence, a challenge is to validate the quality of the event databases generated (e.g. by combining multiple data-collection methods into a single meta-database).

Furthermore, conflict event databases have used restrictive definitions of what constitutes a conflict event, often focusing on violent events between people. Thus, it may instead be useful to combine traditional conflict event data sets with events related to interventions such as sanctions or broader drivers of conflict such as arms transfers. This would open the door to the study of conflict dynamics in a more detailed and nuanced way, learning about how, for example, weapon deliveries to the rebels in Syria or the

---

[13] Griffiths and Jenks (note 12), p. 20.

[14] On UCDP data on armed conflict and the data-collection and methodology, see chapter 1, section III, in this volume.

[15] On the use of data from the truth and reconciliation commission in Peru see Fielding, D. and Shortland, A., 'What explains changes in the level of abuse against civilians during the Peruvian civil war?', University of Otago Economics Discussion Papers no. 1003, May 2010, <http://www.business. otago.ac.nz/econ/research/discussionpapers/>; and Cibelli, K., Hoover, A. and Krüger, J., 'Descriptive statistics from statements to the Liberian Truth and Reconciliation Commission', Benetech Human Rights Program for the Truth and Reconciliation Commission of Liberia, June 2009, <http:// hrdag.org/publications/>. On the use of modern technologies in monitoring violence see Matheson, D. and Allan, S., *Digital War Reporting* (Polity Press: Cambridge, 2009).

displacement of people in such a war have an impact on the conflict dynamics.[16]

Conflict event data can help to track specific examples of violent conflict but it cannot actually help to measure how secure societies are. Societal security can be defined to encompass a balance between low incidents and threats of violence, appropriate protection for such a level of threat and a subjective perception of security (which may be independent of the actual levels of violence and protection thereof).[17] Many aspects of individual lives, in both the economic and the social domains, are already quantified in various ways. Inflation, exchange and growth rates are recorded, as well as poverty, literacy and birth rates, and infinite data on the weather. However, there has been no attempt to create a single measure expressing how secure, say, Somalia, Sri Lanka or Sweden is. Of course, the number of people killed in wars in each country and how much they spend on their militaries are generally known in broad terms. However, this is distinct from knowing how secure these countries are. If the relative degree of security between states were known, much could be learned about trends in security and possibly even about causal relationships—and security policies could hence be improved further.

What is needed, then, is an indicator of security that varies across countries and years at least, if not localities and months or even days.[18] Such a security indicator must differentiate between the underlying intentional threats or risks from human sources (such as terrorist groups, combatants or organized crime) as well as the protective and preventive steps taken by both governments and private sector actors such as firms and individuals. If there are high levels of threats, then there must also be high levels of protection. If, however, there is a low level of threat, then there can be correspondingly low levels of protection. It follows that security is neither a minimum of threat nor a maximum of protection, but the right balance between the two. This also means that there can be an overprotection of a country, which would be economically wasteful and could even be counterproductive.

The question arises of whether Europe, for example, suffers from such a degree of post-September 2001 overprotection from terrorism, while other, more lethal and more preventable risks are neglected by public policy.[19]

---

[16] On arms transfers to Syria see chapter 5, section III, in this volume. On people displaced by conflict see Cohen, R. and Deng, F. M., 'Mass displacement caused by conflicts and one-sided violence: national and international responses', *SIPRI Yearbook 2009*.

[17] Brück, T., de Groot, O. J. and Ferguson, N., 'Measuring security', eds R. Caruso and A. Locatelli, *Understanding Terrorism: A Socio-economic Perspective* (Emerald Publishing: Bingley, forthcoming 2013).

[18] Brück et al. (note 17).

[19] On such risks see e.g. Sköns, E., 'Analysing risks to human lives', *SIPRI Yearbook 2007*, pp. 252–56.

Such a situation could arise if perceptions of insecurity are out of balance. In other words, a societal optimum is unlikely to be reached where only threat and protection are in balance; perceptions of both factors also need to be aligned. A country with few or no incidents of terrorist violence can experience disproportionately high levels of fear of terrorism.[20] Obviously, fighting terrorism in a country that has low or no threat of terrorism may actually increase fear. Hence, an important public policy in regard to terrorism may be the management of fears and the education of the public about risks.

III. The consequences of violent conflict and insecurity

Group-based violent conflict can be viewed as a systematic challenge to a state's right and ability to define and enforce its citizens' property rights. Violent conflict aims to re-order a country's institutions, where 'institution' is broadly defined to include both formal structures and informal rules and norms. For example, rebels in the Basque country in Spain started a war of secession to dispute the right of the Spanish Government to enforce its sovereignty. Such a dispute may be about languages used in schools or about how the police are organized, but it may also be about the identity of a region and its inhabitants—that is, about informal traditions, which may have no direct legal or economic implications.[21] Some agents of violent conflict, the 'human drivers of insecurity', such as terrorist groups, may wish to weaken central state institutions directly. Others, such as organized criminal groups, which need a docile state that tolerates or at least ineffectively pursues the criminals, may wish to weaken the central state as a means to an end.[22]

Depending on its context, group-based violent conflict can be interpreted as an instance of a weakened institutional framework, in which people need to make decisions without the full recourse to the justice system to enforce contracts or to social networks for the informal enforcements of norms and agreements. In the extreme, such violence may lead to a complete breakdown of institutions and hence state failure. Under such circumstances, people will have to cope on their own, perhaps relying on violence or impromptu, ad hoc agreements and alliances.

The view of conflict offered here matters because it is not the occurrence of violence itself (e.g. deaths from war actions) that drives the effects of war but the changed institutional framework. There may of course be direct

---

[20] See e.g. Brück, T. and Müller, C., 'Comparing the determinants of concern about terrorism and crime', *Global Crime*, vol. 11, no. 1 (2010).

[21] Justino, P., Brück, T. and Verwimp, P., 'Micro-level dynamics of conflict, violence and development: a new analytical framework', eds Justino et al. (note 3).

[22] See e.g. Stepanova, E., 'Armed conflict, crime and criminal violence', *SIPRI Yearbook 2010*.

effects of violence, say on the witnesses of atrocities or on family members of those killed in war. But the indirect effects of conflict on the economy and society through the weakened institutions may have different and larger effects than the direct violence does.

A recent strand of research has studied the effects of violent conflict at the micro level.[23] For almost 10 years the Households in Conflict Network has provided a platform for this type of research. Its 140 or so working papers demonstrate the progress made and the gaps that remain. The research is starting to produce repeated and robust evidence on the negative effects of war on child health, for example, and on the destructive effects of group-based violence on asset endowments. It is also starting to pioneer ways to improve the methodologies available for measuring conflict in household surveys.[24] The specific challenge is to measure the conflict experience of each individual and to understand how people objectively and subjectively experience destruction, dislocation and despair. Human experience is likely to vary widely even within the same locality or household depending on gender, age, and political, economic or social status. Most strikingly, no data has been collected on individual perceptions of peace across time and space, which would seem a fruitful avenue of research and policymaking. The role of the private sector in building peaceful societies is also woefully under-researched.[25] There is therefore a lack of suitable data sets and no consensus is emerging on how violent conflict shapes livelihoods, migration or poverty.

Finally, how micro- and macro-level processes in a conflict interact is not well understood either. This suggests that rather than placing all financial resources at the macro or the micro level, an attempt should be made to build models that can bridge this dichotomy—or at least develop narratives that can account for multiple levels. Interestingly, there are also significant knowledge gaps in macro-level research on conflict, despite the fact that this is where the literature first took off after the end of the cold war. For example, there is still little research on estimating the total macroeconomic costs of conflict, a number which, if known, would presumably provide a powerful incentive for policymakers to reduce the incidence of violent conflict in the world.[26]

---

[23] eds Justino et al. (note 3).

[24] Brück, T., Justino, P., Verwimp P. and Avdeenko, A., 'Identifying conflict and violence in micro-level surveys', Households in Conflict Network (HICN) Working Paper no. 79, July 2010, <http://www.hicn.org/>.

[25] Brück, T., Naudé, W. and Verwimp, P., 'Business under fire: entrepreneurship and violent conflict in developing countries', *Journal of Conflict Resolution*, vol. 57, no. 1 (Feb. 2013); and Naudé, W., Brück, T. and Verwimp, P., 'Business and the barrel of a gun: understanding entrepreneurship and violent conflict in developing countries', UNU-WIDER Policy Brief no. 4, 2013, <http://www.wider.unu.edu/publications/policy-briefs/>.

[26] On the limited example of the economic cost of conducting 2 wars see Perlo-Freeman, S. and Solmirano, C., 'The economic cost of the Afghanistan and Iraq wars', *SIPRI Yearbook 2012*; and

IV. Interventions and institutions for security and peace

The final area for review is to consider what is known about interventions to overcome conflict and to build (or keep) peace and what roles institutions can play in this. This edition of the SIPRI Yearbook offers a wealth of evidence on efforts to build and implement international agreements to curtail stocks, use or trade of weapons—major conventional arms, small arms and light weapons, and nuclear, biological and chemical weapons.[27] While limited progress on the control of the production and use of certain types of arms have been made in recent years (especially concerning anti-personnel mines), aligning the interests of producing and using states for the tighter legally binding regulation of other convention weapons (such as mines other than anti-personnel mines or cluster munitions) has proved quite elusive, with probably significant though largely undocumented humanitarian costs.[28] Other challenges in humanitarian arms control, especially applicable to Africa, are that effective, functioning states are needed to implement international conventions when they are finally agreed, in part to control borders and prevent the circumvention of established rules by transnational armed groups.[29] Effective humanitarian arms control therefore needs effective states, not just more agreements on paper.

While it seems that the choice of the international community has been to either focus on regional multilateral (e.g. the North Atlantic Treaty Organization) or bilateral security arrangements (e.g. those between Russia and the USA) or to negotiate the lowest common denominator in genuine international agreements (e.g. in negotiations on an arms trade treaty), there are also encouraging efforts for comprehensive multilateral arms control agreements.[30] The 1972 Biological and Toxin Weapons Convention and the 1993 Chemical Weapons Convention are total disarmament treaties and the 1968 Non-Proliferation Treaty prohibits any spread of nuclear weapons and requires good faith disarmament efforts.[31] Not every state has joined these treaties and not every party complies with them, but the record of participation and compliance is generally good—or at least much better than in most treaties of a comparable nature.

At the same time, 2012 saw the systematic failure of the international community to prevent the emergence of a large-scale intrastate war in

---

Brück, T., de Groot, O. J. and Schneider, F.. 'The economic costs of the German participation in the Afghanistan war', *Journal of Peace Research*, vol. 48, no. 6 (Nov. 2011).

[27] See chapters 6 and 7 on nuclear arms and arms control, chapter 8 on threats from chemical and biological materials, chapter 9 on conventional arms control, chapter 10 on arms trade controls, annex A on arms control agreements, and annex B on security cooperation bodies in this volume.

[28] See chapter 9, section I, on humanitarian arms control in this volume.

[29] On the case of small arms control in Africa see chapter 9, section II, in this volume.

[30] On the negotiation of an arms trade treaty see chapter 10, section I, in this volume.

[31] On these 3 treaties see chapters 7 and 8 and annex A in this volume.

Syria, mostly as a result of the inadequacies of the existing legal and institutional framework for conflict management.[32] This is not to say that international policy coordination in other policy fields is necessarily better (areas like the management of macroeconomic imbalances or climate change spring to mind) but is instead to argue that the shortcomings of the current international security order have become particularly acute and costly when the issue of intrastate war is at stake. Below that threshold of violence, it is often accepted—however deplorable from a moral point of view this may be—that states are de facto at liberty to oppress their own people, as the case of North Korea illustrates. Far above that threshold, states must not be permitted to become international security risks, as Libya under Muammar Gaddafi and Iraq under Saddam Hussein were at times perceived to be. However, the international community is uncomfortably frozen when dealing with the warlike oppression of domestic political discontent, if only due to the institutional legacies of World War II such as the United Nations Security Council vetoes.[33]

It seems that a variety of tools for interventions have risen and fallen in popularity over time. Imposing sanctions, for example, is a signature intervention of the international community to express diplomatic discontent, while humanitarian assistance and peace operations are often used to demonstrate activities to domestic audiences. But these policy instruments appear increasingly to be applied in a reactive fashion, with European Union sanctions against Syria, for example, being repeatedly a response to news of atrocities rather than preventive measures of diplomacy.[34]

While progress is being made in mapping some interventions, there is a need to strengthen the knowledge base on what is really known about the effectiveness of these interventions and their impacts.[35] In doing so, there are interesting opportunities for combining databases on conflict dynamics, illicit shipments or peace operations to name some examples. How do sanctions have an impact on conflict dynamics? How do peace operations or illicit arms transfers change security? How do peace operations affect private sector reconstruction? These are large questions that are often hard to study empirically due to the lack of good data, to the practical and ethical

---

[32] On the conflict in Syria see chapter 1, section I, chapter 2, section II, chapter 5, section III, chapter 8, section III, and chapter 10, section II, in this volume. On broader developments in conflict management see chapter 2 in this volume.

[33] See e.g. Evans, G., 'Responding to atrocities: the new geopolitics of intervention', *SIPRI Yearbook 2012*.

[34] On developments in arms embargoes and other sanctions see chapter 10, sections II and III, in this volume. On developments in peace operations see chapter 2 in this volume.

[35] E.g. Seybolt, T. B., SIPRI, *Humanitarian Military Intervention: The Conditions for Success and Failure* (Oxford University Press: Oxford, 2007); and Wiharta, S. et al., *The Effectiveness of Foreign Military Assets in Natural Disaster Response* (SIPRI: Stockholm, 2008); and Fruchart, D. et al., *United Nations Arms Embargoes: Their Impact on Arms Flows and Target Behaviour* (SIPRI/Uppsala University: Stockholm/Uppsala, 2007).

challenges of fieldwork, and to difficulty of finding funds to support this type of research.

On numerous occasions, the research community has documented how interventions succeeded or failed after the event.[36] However, there is still a gap in providing respected, reliable advice on how to intervene successfully before, during and after violent conflict to the benefit of people and with a view to strengthening peaceful institutions. In other words, there is no conventional wisdom based on scientific evidence on how to make peace. Compared to the medical sciences, peace research still has a long way to go before the knowledge base will be sufficiently strong to make truly evidence-based policies in the fields of security, conflict and peace.

One tool to help learn from past experience is to design randomized control trials, just like in the medical sciences, in the context of interventions for peace and security or merely in standard development interventions (like strengthening education or employment) in conflict-affected or fragile environments.[37] While policymakers wishing to design an anti-poverty programme in a peaceful developing country have an abundance of empirical evidence and broad generalizations on which to build their design, in the fields of interventions and the design of institutions for peace this is not true at all—and it may be 10 or 20 years before that level of insight is reached. It will literally require hundreds of studies in dozens of settings before it can be said with confidence how to promote lasting peace. Hence, much hard work remains for researchers in this field, which is sobering and encouraging at the same time.

It would also help to have the numerical models referred to in section III above to facilitate estimating the costs and benefits of various types of intervention—this type of numerical policy modelling is common in other policy fields but is rare in security and peace research. Combining the various data sources that are available or that need to be constructed to undertake informative and useful policy simulations may be one way forward to guide decision makers.

V. Looking beyond 2015: developing new data and a global system of security accounts

The above discussion of selected recent trends in security, conflict and peace research assumes throughout that some aspects of these topics can be measured in a meaningful way (i.e. policy and operationally relevant). If so many other issues in an individual's life or in society can be measured, it should be possible to develop metrics for peace and security, at both the

---

[36] E.g. Seybolt (note 35).

[37] Bozzoli, C., Brück, T. and Wald, N., 'Evaluating programmes in conflict-affected areas', eds Justino et al. (note 3).

individual and the aggregate, national levels. One such example would enumerate the experience of conflict at the individual level, as argued above.[38] Another such example at the national level is the pioneering Global Peace Index.[39] However, neither measuring perceptions of insecurity, counting the war dead, tallying incidents of weapon smuggling, developing proxies for peace nor estimating a security indicator is good enough in itself. Despite these and many other developments referenced in the SIPRI Yearbook over the years, at least two important challenges remain.

The first challenge is to define the remaining data needs to advance the study of security, conflict and peace. Compared to many other scientific disciplines, the advances in data and knowledge in this field are much slower and less supported by national or international research infrastructures. Just as genome sequencing has dramatically altered knowledge about life and supports advances in medical treatments, generating more powerful data on peace and security would induce advances in knowledge and decision making. As the future of the Millennium Development Goals for 2015 are being debated, the time is right for researchers, decision makers and donors to come together and to decide on which metrics can help reduce fragility and conflict in the future.

The second challenge will be to develop a 'global system of security accounts', which brings together in a consistent framework the many variables measuring flows of security and peace. In economics, having a system of national accounts helps to ask and answer the right research questions and supports policymaking as there is an understanding of how the different parts of the economy may move in relation to each other. In the field of international peace and security, a similar overarching 'global system of security accounts' is currently lacking, which weakens analysis and policymaking alike. The SIPRI Yearbook has for almost five decades provided a narrative on global security developments, building on SIPRI's unique ability to gather, collate and interpret relevant trends. The time may be right to ask how this narrative can be formalized to further develop knowledge on and policies for security and peace.

[38] Brück et al. (note 24).
[39] See e.g. Schippa, C. and Morgan, T., 'The Global Peace Index 2012', *SIPRI Yearbook 2012*.

Part I. Security and conflicts, 2012

Chapter 1. Armed conflict

Chapter 2. Peace operations and conflict management

1. Armed conflict

Overview

In 2011–12 conflict continued to be a major concern for the international community, most notably in the Middle East, western Asia and Africa, but also with increased levels of interstate tension in East Asia. Nevertheless, deaths resulting from major organized violence worldwide remained at historically low levels.

At the same time, the decline in both numbers of conflicts and fatalities that has characterized post-cold war international security has largely levelled off, albeit with spikes in some years (see section III in this chapter). Indeed, there are indications of a possible reversal of some of the key trends of recent decades. These indications include rises in the numbers of state-based and non-state conflicts as well as fatalities in 2011, although it is too early to identify a trend.

A key issue in understanding the changing patterns of conflict over recent decades and their likely future evolution is the relationship of states, and notably the major powers, to armed conflict. Perhaps the biggest single factor that has shaped the significant global decline in the number of armed conflicts and casualty rates since the end of the superpower confrontation of the cold war has been the dramatic reduction in major powers engaging in proxy conflicts

However, the relationship between states and conflict may be changing once again. In recent years there has been an increase in the number of intrastate conflicts that are internationalized—that is, that have another state supporting one side or another. Such involvement often has the affect of increasing casualty rates and prolonging conflicts.

During 2011 there were several significant internationalized intrastate conflicts, notably in Africa, some of them long-standing conflicts. The Middle East, however, presented one of the most challenging environments as the civil war in Syria increasingly manifested the characteristics of a regional conflict in which neighbouring states became parties to the conflict (see section I). At the same time, the escalation of the conflict in 2012—against the backdrop of concerns about weapons of mass destruction, growing religious radicalism and sectarianism—threatened to draw in major extra-regional powers.

The growing international aspects of the Syrian conflict raised broader questions about the ability of the international community to contain, manage and end the violence in the country. Another key factor in the overall reduction in levels of armed conflict following the end of the cold war has been

*the rising incidence of intervention in conflicts and for post-conflict recon-
struction by the international community, in the form of peace and stabilization missions. The stalemate within the United Nations Security Council on
how to respond to the Syria conflict has raised concern about whether the consensus among leading powers necessary to respond to major conflicts can still
be found in an increasingly multipolar international security system.*

*The challenges represented by conflict in the Middle East also highlighted
the complex pattern of armed conflict found around the world. While the civil
war in Syria became one of the bloodiest conflicts in the world in 2011–12,
Africa continued to experience the vast majority of non-state conflicts, and
those in the Americas had the highest average number of deaths per conflict
and the highest proportions of non-state conflict between formally organized
groups.*

*Even though East and South East Asia were the sites of some of the most
destructive state-based conflicts from the 1950s to the 1970s, they have
become among the world's most peaceful regions (see section II). Only one
interstate conflict has been registered in South East Asia since 1989, and none
in East Asia. However, with important questions emerging about the global
distribution of organized violence and the role of regional and major powers
in conflicts, the situation in these regions has become a key issue. In recent
years, tensions associated with shifting power balances in East Asia, notably
involving China and the United States and its allies, have risen, sometimes to
potentially dangerous levels. In South East Asia a set of bloody localized conflicts remain unresolved and some even flared up in 2012. There are thus real
concerns that the East and South East Asian peace may evaporate.*

*With the increase in conflict numbers, evidence of an intensification of
armed violence in terms of fatality rates, rising interstate tensions in some
regions, and major disagreements among major powers about the appropriate
international response to key conflicts, international security may have
entered a period of transition. A central question in this context is whether
change will bring rising levels of interstate conflict.*

*Shifting interests and changing capabilities as a result of a weakening of the
unipolar post-cold war security balance and the emergence of elements of
multipolarity are clearly affecting the overall international order, even while
levels of conflict remain relatively low. Nevertheless, some developments in
2011–12 could be seen as warning signs that if the positive trends in conflict
that emerged in recent decades are to be sustained, new ways need to be found
to build cooperative international relations to manage the changing global
security order.*

NEIL MELVIN

I. Armed conflict in the wake of the Arab Spring

MARIE ALLANSSON, MARGARETA SOLLENBERG AND LOTTA THEMNÉR
UPPSALA CONFLICT DATA PROGRAM

The Arab Spring of 2011 represented a major upheaval in a region that had previously seen few open, mass-based challenges to its regimes. It brought radical political change in a number of countries, notably Tunisia, Egypt, Morocco and Libya.[1] In some countries, processes for regime change continued into 2012—in the case of Syria as a full-fledged civil war, whereas in other countries, such as Bahrain and Jordan, protests remained largely non-violent. In some countries where regimes did change in 2011, political instability continued, largely because of the unsettled nature of the political landscape. For example, in Egypt protests continued against the new military-led government, at times violently, and then also against the newly elected president, Mohamed Morsy; in Libya there were incidents of violence between the new regime and supporters of former leader Muammar Gaddafi.

The Arab Spring and subsequent developments in 2012 illustrate different ways in which political instability and violence can spread. The revolts initiated in 2011 can be described as contagious uprisings, through which protests and challenges against regimes spread through demonstration effects.[2] This type of contagion did not continue in 2012; no new mass revolts erupted. However, ripple effects of the Arab Spring were visible across a wider region in 2012.

This section focuses on the three state-based conflicts active in 2012 that were either a continuation of the Arab Spring (Syria) or exhibited direct links to those revolts (Yemen and Mali).[3] These cases illustrate some of the ways in which conflict in one country can contribute to instability and conflict in others through the diffusion of fighters, weapons, ideas and tactics. They also illustrate two patterns of escalation influenced by the events in the region in 2011: the intensification of fighting and the fragmentation of the opposition, with an increasing number of armed groups active.

---

[1] For an overview of events in the region in 2011 see Allansson, M. et al., 'The first year of the Arab Spring', *SIPRI Yearbook 2012*.

[2] See e.g. Bellin, E., 'Reconsidering the robustness of authoritarianism in the Middle East: lessons from the Arab Spring', *Comparative Politics*, vol. 44, no. 2 (Jan. 2012), pp. 127–49. 'Demonstration effect' is a process whereby political action by 1 group influences political action by other groups in pursuit of their own causes. See e.g. Kuran, T., 'Ethnic dissimilation and its international diffusion', eds D. A. Lake and D. Rothchild, *The International Spread of Ethnic Conflict: Fear, Diffusion and Escalation* (Princeton University Press: Princeton, NJ, 1998).

[3] See 'Sources and methods' in section III for a definition of state-based conflict.

Syria

Processes of both diffusion and escalation were evident in the Syrian conflict in 2012. There was a dramatic increase in the intensity of the fighting as well as in the number of opposition groups. Developments since the beginning of the uprising also included the diffusion of fighters, ideas and tactics into Syria from groups involved in other conflicts in the region and further afield.

The Arab Spring uprising in Syria began in March 2011 with a series of largely peaceful demonstrations. These were soon met with increasing brutality on the part of the Syrian state, leading in turn to a rising number of army defections. Many of the defectors joined the Free Syrian Army (FSA), which was formed in late July 2011.[4] The fighting in the initial stages was primarily between the government and the various militia groups fighting under the banner of the loosely organized FSA. The opposition then became increasingly fragmented as new armed groups formed and gained strength.[5] The common denominator for these groups was the goal of ousting the Baathist government of President Bashar al-Assad.

The second year of the uprising also saw the emergence of radical Sunni Islamist groups calling not only for the overthrow of the Assad government but also for the establishment of an Islamist regime.[6] Assad had claimed since the start of the uprising that the armed opposition consisted of criminal gangs and foreign-backed terrorists. The opposition rejected the claims and also downplayed the role of jihadist movements.[7] However, during 2012 it became increasingly clear that groups like the radical Islamist and jihadist Jabhat al-Nusra and Kata'ib Ahrar al-Sham, formed in January 2012, were growing in both strength and number.[8] There were also several reports of foreign fighters, for example from Jordan, participating in the Syrian conflict.[9]

What role these jihadist groups and foreign fighters played in the conflict in 2012 has been debated; analysts have argued that while they only made up a fraction of the armed fighters in the country, they had a significant impact on the conflict dynamics by introducing the use of, for example, sui-

---

[4] Flood, D. H., 'An overview of Syria's armed revolution', *CTC Sentinel*, vol. 5, no. 4 (Apr. 2012), p. 1; and the entry for Syria in the UCDP Conflict Encyclopedia, <http://www.ucdp.uu.se/database/>.

[5] Starr, S., 'A fight for the spoils: the future role of Syria's armed groups', *CTC Sentinel*, vol. 5, no. 8 (23 Aug. 2012), p. 2; and International Crisis Group (ICG), *Syria's Phase of Radicalisation*, Middle East Briefing no. 33 (ICG: Damascus/Brussels, 10 Apr. 2012), pp. 1–4.

[6] International Crisis Group (ICG), *Tentative Jihad: Syria's Fundamentalist Opposition*, Middle East Report no. 131 (ICG: Damascus/Brussels, 12 Oct. 2012), pp. 10–11.

[7] Flood (note 4), p. 4; and International Crisis Group (note 6), p. 1.

[8] International Crisis Group (note 6), pp. 10–19.

[9] See e.g. Al-Shishani, M. B., 'Syria emerges as a new battlefield for Jordan's jihadists', *Terrorism Monitor*, 10 Jan. 2013, pp. 4–5.

cide bombers and improvised explosive devices (IEDs).[10] The Syrian groups seem to have been influenced by other groups in the region. For example, Jabhat al-Nusra confirmed that it had gained bomb-making skills from jihadists who had fought in Iraq.[11]

One of the government's strategies to counter the growing armed resistance has been the use of local militia groups, commonly known as the shabiha (ghosts).[12] These militias have been blamed for brutal repression of civilians in opposition areas, including by massacres and torture.[13]

Both the shabiha and the fragmented opposition shared a common feature in 2012: the lack of a clear leadership structure. The FSA's official leaders, for example, resided in Turkey and it was argued that they had limited control over the different FSA factions.[14] This lack of cohesion and leadership is highly likely to affect a future peace process, and the risk of spoilers from both sides is high. Should the common goal of ousting Assad be achieved, divisions in the already factionalized armed opposition are likely to grow. In addition, it is unclear whether the shabiha would disarm and demobilize, should the regime fall.[15]

The involvement of external actors such as Turkey and the Lebanon-based non-state group Hezbollah further complicates the situation. Tensions along the Turkish–Syrian border ran high in 2012 and there was a massive influx of Syrian refugees to the country.[16] As for Hezbollah, it is unclear to what extent the group is active in Syria, but it continues to be a strong supporter of the Assad regime.[17] Given this context, where many countries and subnational groups have a stake in the outcome of the conflict, there is a potential risk of the Syrian conflict exacerbating tensions, and even sparking conflict, in other parts of the region.

Yemen

The case of Yemen in 2011–12 clearly illustrates escalation processes and how rebel groups on the periphery can benefit from a temporary power

[10] See e.g. Starr, S., 'Shabiha militias and the destruction of Syria', *CTC Sentinel*, vol. 5, no. 12 (28 Nov. 2012), p. 12.

[11] International Crisis Group (note 6), pp. 11, 15; Abouzeid, R., 'Meet the Islamist militants fighting alongside Syria's rebels', *Time*, 26 July 2012; and Abdul-Ahad, G., 'Al-Qaida turns tide for rebels in battle for eastern Syria', *The Guardian*, 30 July 2012.

[12] Starr (note 10).

[13] Starr (note 10).

[14] International Crisis Group (note 6), pp. 6, 22.

[15] Starr (note 10), p. 14; and Starr (note 5), pp. 2–3.

[16] 'Nato deploying Patriot missiles to Turkey–Syria border', BBC News, 4 Jan. 2013, <http://www.bbc.co.uk/news/world-europe-20911919>.

[17] Zambelis, C., 'Hizb Allah's role in the Syrian uprising', *CTC Sentinel*, vol. 5, no. 12 (28 Nov. 2012), pp. 14–17.

vacuum at the centre, in this case political turmoil following widespread anti-government demonstrations.

The demonstrations, which began in January 2011, were soon met with lethal violence from government forces. A rising death toll and a continuously weakening power base eventually forced Yemeni President Ali Abdullah Saleh to resign in late November. Vice-President Abdo Rabu Mansour Hadi was subsequently sworn in as interim president for a two-year period in February 2012. Although their number subsequently decreased, demonstrations continued throughout the year.[18]

Overshadowed by these developments, the conflict between the government and al-Qaeda in the Arabian Peninsula (AQAP), which began in 2009, escalated dramatically.[19] Benefitting substantially from the weakening of the Yemeni Government, which focused largely on retaining power and suppressing public unrest, AQAP launched a large-scale offensive mainly in the southern governorate of Abyan in March 2011.[20] The group captured seven towns and cities, including the capital of Abyan, Zinjibar. AQAP subsequently proclaimed the seven captured areas as 'Islamic emirates' and imposed a strict interpretation of Islamic (sharia) law.[21] Fighting in Abyan continued throughout 2011 and into 2012.[22] The large-scale capture of territory by a local al-Qaeda branch is unprecedented in Yemen. Up until 2011 the group had only been involved in relatively minor clashes with the government. Thus, the events in 2011 and 2012 marked a drastic escalation of the conflict as well as change in AQAP's tactics.

The Yemeni Army eventually managed to regain control of Abyan through a large-scale offensive during the spring and summer of 2012, with decisive help from local tribes in the form of so-called popular resistance committees. In both 2011 and 2012 government forces were also supported by the United States through attacks using unmanned aerial vehicles (UAVs, or drones).[23] As AQAP was pushed back it seemed to shift its stra-

---

[18] Allansson et al. (note 1); Raghavan, S., 'Yemen protests continue six months after Saleh's fall', *The Guardian*, 12 Aug. 2012; and Dawood, A., 'Efforts continue to seek justice for journalists who died in 2011', *Yemen Times*, 26 Nov. 2012.

[19] AQAP was formed in early 2009 through the merger of the local al-Qaeda branches in Yemen and Saudi Arabia. In 2011 the formation of an offshoot, Ansar al-Sharia, was announced. According to AQAP, Ansar al-Sharia was formed to gain popular support for the group in the southern region in which it operates. UCDP views AQAP and Ansar al-Sharia as 1 group. See the entry for Yemen in the UCDP Conflict Encyclopedia (note 4).

[20] 'Yemen militia besieges tribal leader: son', Agence France-Presse, 6 Nov. 2012; and International Crisis Group (ICG), *Yemen: Enduring Conflicts, Threatened Transition*, Middle East Report no. 125 (ICG: Brussels, 3 July 2012), pp. 10–11.

[21] Coombs, C. L., 'Hot issue: the Ansar al-Shari'a insurgency in Southern Yemen: the view from the ground', Jamestown Foundation, 9 May 2012, <http://www.jamestown.org/single/?no_cache=1&tx_ttnews[tt_news]=39348>.

[22] Yemen entry in the UCDP Conflict Encyclopedia (note 4).

[23] Carlino, L., 'Al-Qaeda in the Arabian Peninsula sets assassins loose in strategic shift', *Terrorism Monitor*, vol. 10, no. 19 (18 Oct. 2012), pp. 7–8; and Agence France-Presse, '8 Qaeda suspects dead in Yemen air strike: local official', *Lahore Times*, 25 Aug. 2011.

tegy from controlling strategically important areas to targeted assassinations and suicide attacks, even in the Yemeni capital, Sana'a.[24]

While AQAP was on the defensive during the latter half of 2012, there are concerns for the future. The initiation of the National Dialogue Conference (NDC), intended to revise the constitution prior to the 2014 elections, was repeatedly postponed.[25] Originally scheduled for mid-November 2012, the conference eventually opened on 18 March 2013.[26] There are fears that a failed process and potential power struggles will afford AQAP renewed space to operate in the country, leading to further conflict escalation.[27]

Mali

The case of Mali vividly illustrates how conflict in one place can be ignited by the diffusion of fighters and arms from a conflict elsewhere—specifically the 2011 intrastate conflict in Libya. The flow of resources from Libya was facilitated by the lack of government control in northern Mali as well as the porous borders in the region. The emergence and increased influence of Islamists groups that characterized the developing conflict in Mali in 2012 reflects a general trend in the Sahel that was also seen in Syria and Yemen.

When the Gaddafi regime began to crumble in 2011, a large number of Malian Tuareg fighters who had been involved in the Libyan civil war returned to northern Mali.[28] Carrying with them heavy and small arms taken from Libyan stockpiles, most of them withdrew to the hills of Tin-Assalak, north of the Malian town of Kidal and close to the Algerian border.[29] A few months later this flow of fighters and arms contributed to a sudden and dramatic flare-up of long-standing Tuareg resentment against the central government, setting off a chain of events that surprised analysts.

The returnees from Libya were a mixed group. Most had fought on Gaddafi's side in the 2011 conflict. While many had been in Libya for years, others had only been recruited during 2011. There was a long history of

[24] Shahbaz, A., 'Strategic and tactical shift keeps al-Qaeda insurgency alive in southern Yemen', *Terrorism Monitor*, vol. 10, no. 21 (15 Nov. 2012), pp. 4–5.

[25] 'Failure of national dialogue likely to help Al-Qa'idah expand in Yemen', BBC Monitoring Middle East, 27 Nov. 2012

[26] 'Yemen national dialogue conference begins', BBC News, 18 Mar. 2013, <http://www.bbc.co.uk/news/world-middle-east-21828527>.

[27] 'Failure of national dialogue likely to help Al-Qa'idah expand in Yemen' (note 25)

[28] There is no consensus on how many they were; estimates vary between hundreds and thousands. E.g. 'Mali: returning Touaregs—jihad or peace?', *Africa Research Bulletin*, vol. 49, no. 10 (Dec. 2011), p. 19 099; and 'Mali's Tuaregs demand self-rule for northern region, threaten military action', Text of 5 Nov. 2011 article by K. Mahmud on Al-Sharq al-Awsat Online, BBC Monitoring Africa, 6 Nov. 2011.

[29] Weapons ranged from rifles to small-calibre anti-aircraft cannons mounted on pick-up trucks. On the types of weapon leaving Libya see United Nations, Security Council, Consolidated working document on the implementation of paragraph 5 of Security Council Resolution 2017 (2011) 16 Mar. 2012, annex to S/2012/178, 26 Mar. 2012.

cooperation between Gaddafi and the Tuaregs of both Mali and Niger. Already in the 1970s large numbers of young Tuaregs migrated to Libya due to severe droughts in their home countries. Many received military training, as Gaddafi incorporated some into his regular military forces and others into a Libyan-sponsored 'Islamic legion', which was dispatched to fight in places such as Afghanistan, Chad, Lebanon and the Palestinian territories.[30] In the late 1980s economic conditions deteriorated and only those Tuaregs who had obtained Libyan citizenship were able to stay in Libya.[31] Others who returned to Mali launched a separatist rebellion there in 1990.[32] A few years later, some fighters, rejecting a 1992 peace accord, returned to Libya and became senior officers in the Libyan Army.[33]

When these well-armed and battle-hardened Tuaregs returned to Mali in 2011–12, they entered an already volatile situation. Northern Mali on the eve of the 2012 Tuareg rebellion was economically underdeveloped, with a limited presence of administrative structures and a general dissatisfaction with the central government; many of the same grievances that had bred earlier Tuareg uprisings persisted. Furthermore, northern Mali was highly insecure, serving as a haven for smugglers, traffickers and the transnational militant Islamist group al-Qaeda in the Islamic Maghreb (AQIM). Malian President Amadou Toumani Touré ruled the north through a network of alliances with competing and opportunist elites.[34]

The returning fighters quickly went on to form alliances with other groupings in the region. On 16 October, the Mouvement national de libération de l'Azawad (MNLA, National Movement for the Liberation of Azawad) was formed, under the banner of leaders such as Mohammed Ag Najem, a former professional officer in the Libyan Army.[35] The new organization was a merger of the Libyan returnees, a Tuareg political organization called Mouvement national de l'Azawad (MNA, National Movement of

---

[30] See e.g. Keita, K., 'Conflict and conflict resolution in the Sahel: the Tuareg insurgency in Mali' *Small Wars and Insurgencies,* vol. 9, no. 3 (1998), p. 111; and Schultz, R. H., 'Can democratic governments use force in the war against terrorism? The US confrontation with Libya', *World Affairs,* vol. 148, no. 4 (spring 1986), p. 208.

[31] International Crisis Group (ICG), *Popular Protest in North Africa and the Middle East (V): Making Sense of Libya,* Middle East/North Africa Report no. 107 (ICG: Brussels, 6 June 2011), p. 23.

[32] For more information on the conflicts in northern Mali in the 1990s and 2000s see Lecocq, B., *Disputed Desert: Decolonisation, Competing Nationalism and Tuareg Rebellions in Northern Mali* (Brill: Leiden, 2010); and the entry for Mali in the UCDP Conflict Encyclopedia (note 4).

[33] Pacte national conclu entre le gouvernement de la République du Mali et les Mouvements et Fronts Unifies de l'Azawad consacrant le statut particulier du nord du Mali [National pact concluded between the Government of the Republic of Mali and the unified movements and fronts of Azawad giving the special status of northern Mali], signed 11 Apr. 1992, Bamako. See Morgan, A., 'The causes of the uprising in Northern Mali', Think Africa Press, 6 Feb. 2012, <http://thinkafricapress.com/mali/causes-uprising-northern-mali-tuareg>.

[34] International Crisis Group (ICG), *Mali: Avoiding Escalation,* Africa Report no. 189 (ICG: Brussels, 18 July 2012), pp. 1–8; and Amnesty International (AI), *Mali: Five Months of Crisis: Armed Rebellion and Military Coup* (AI: London, 2012), pp. 5–6.

[35] Azawad is Tuareg separatists' name for the area of northern Mali to which they lay claim.

Azawad) and the remnants of the group fighting the 2007–2009 rebellion, Alliance Touareg Nord Mali pour le Changement (ATNMC, North Mali Tuareg Alliance for Change).[36]

Also formed at the end of 2011 and comprising large numbers of Tuareg returnees from Libya was the Salafist group Ansar Dine (sometimes referred to as Ansar Al-Din or Ansar Eddin). It was established by Iyad Ag Ghaly, a veteran of the Tuareg uprisings of the 1990s, who had grown increasingly devout and who attempted to join the MNLA leadership, only to be rebuffed.[37] While little was known of this group in the first months of 2012, they came to play an increasingly important role in the conflict.

On 17 January 2012 the MNLA launched an offensive and, with the Malian Army in a state of disarray, quickly made large territorial gains. Between January and mid-March the group, backed by an increasingly strong Ansar Dine, was able to capture nearly a third of the country's territory. These developments bred widespread protests in the capital, Bamako, culminating in a coup on 22 March, with a group of junior officers under Amadou Sanogo ousting President Touré. After this, the army became even weaker and the main northern towns fell to the rebels one by one in late March. On 6 April the MNLA declared an independent state of Azawad, comprising the three northern regions Gao, Kidal and Timbuktu.

As the MNLA, and to some extent Ansar Dine, carried out their lightning offensive across the north, reports of involvement in the fighting by AQIM and the Mouvement pour le Tawhîd et du Jihad en Afrique de l'Ouest (MUJAO, Movement for Unity and Jihad in West Africa), an AQIM splinter group, started to emerge. By early April these groups had become stronger than the MNLA. Pressing south, the rebels entered territory where the population was more favourable to the message of Ansar Dine—the imposition of sharia across a united Mali—than to the MNLA's separatist agenda, a fact that Ansar Dine used to its advantage. Furthermore, Ansar Dine started to receive reinforcement, both personnel and weapons, from AQIM.[38] AQIM, for its part, seems also to have come out stronger after the Arab Spring, gaining from the spillover of weapons and fighters from Libya.[39]

During April and May it became clear that the Islamists had created an alliance against the MNLA and the latter was pushed out of all the main towns that had been captured. In late June, the Islamists forcibly evicted the separatists from Gao, where they had set up their provisional govern-

[36] International Crisis Group (note 34), pp. 10–11.

[37] 'Mali: returning Touaregs—jihad or peace' (note 28); and International Crisis Group (note 34).

[38] 'Al-Qa'idah chief adopts Afghan Taleban model in Mali: paper', Text of Echourouk El Youmi website, 8 Aug. 12, BBC Monitoring Middle East, 9 Aug. 2012; and International Crisis Group (note 34), pp. 16–17.

[39] 'Al-Qa'idah's affiliate getting stronger in north Mali: US general', Transcription from Al-Jazeera TV, 21:30 GMT, 27 July 2012, BBC Monitoring Middle East, 28 July 2012.

ment. As the MNLA withdrew into the desert, the Islamists set about creating a de facto Islamic state in the captured territories, enforcing its strict interpretation of sharia.

Between the end of June 2012 and January 2013 positions were more or less deadlocked in Mali. The Islamists controlled the vast northern region; the MNLA, weakened and regrouping, attempted to launch an attack against MUJAO in November with little success; political wrangling continued in the south; and negotiations on an external military intervention, mandated by the UN Security Council and initially to be led by Africans, proceeded fitfully, without any impact on the ground.

All of this changed in early January 2013, when the Islamists launched a new offensive southwards, seizing the town of Konna and raising fears that they would push south all the way to the capital. In response, on 11 January France deployed troops to the country, opening a new phase of the conflict.

Conclusions

Syria, Yemen and Mali were ravaged in 2012 by armed conflicts related in one way or another to the Arab Spring. All three cases point to the importance of understanding the Arab Spring and its repercussions in order to fully grasp regional conflict developments. They are all to some extent defined and influenced by the major political upheavals in 2011. However, depending on the domestic contexts, the chain of events set in motion by the Arab Spring was different in each country.

In Syria, the conflict escalated and became increasingly complex. A growing number of groups became active, some of which were influenced by radical Islamist ideas and joined by foreign fighters who brought with them new technologies and tactics. In Yemen, the protests that took place in 2011 largely died out, whereas the armed conflict between the Yemeni Government and AQAP escalated dramatically. The group gained considerable momentum as the government was preoccupied with the ongoing demonstrations in 2011, but was pushed back in 2012 by the new government. Finally, in Mali the diffusion of fighters and arms from Libya ignited existing grievances in the northern part of the country. What started as a separatist rebellion was soon overtaken by groups with a different agenda, reflecting the spread of radical Islamist ideas in this part of the world.

While differing in many respects, Syria, Yemen and Mali also illustrate general phenomena central to peace and conflict research: conflict diffusion and conflict escalation.

Conflict diffusion is most clearly displayed in the case of Mali. The likelihood of conflict in a country is heavily influenced by the presence of armed conflict in a neighbouring state.[40] The means of diffusion vary, including the spread of arms and fighters (as witnessed in Mali) and ideas (which was also seen in Syria). Notable in all three cases is the spread of radical Islamist ideas. The presence of extremist agendas has been found to make compromise more difficult, which complicates the resolution of conflict.[41]

Conflict escalation is a widely researched field. Escalation commonly refers to an intensification of the fighting, which was seen in all three cases. It can also be understood in terms of an increase in the number of armed groups.[42] Witnessed in both Syria and Mali, escalation has been shown to have negative implications for the prospects for conflict resolution.[43]

There is a clear risk that conflict may spread and escalate further in this region. However, just as the present conflicts were difficult to foresee at the outset of the Arab Spring, the future paths of conflict are equally difficult to predict. In Mali, it is not yet clear where the events set in motion in January 2012 will lead, particularly after the French intervention.[44] As for Syria, the potential for conflict diffusion continues to increase in a region where many countries and subnational groups have a stake in the outcome. In Yemen, the strengthening of the local al-Qaeda branch in recent years made the country a key centre for radical Islamists. If the government fails to curb their activities, there is a risk that the groups' activities will spread beyond national borders.

[40] See e.g. Forsberg, E., *Neighbors at Risk: A Quantitative Study of Civil War Contagion* (Uppsala University: Uppsala, 2009); Salehyan, I., *Rebels without Borders: Transnational Insurgencies in World Politics* (Cornell University Press: Ithaca, NY, 2009); and Hegre, H. and Sambanis, N., 'Sensitivity analysis of empirical results on Civil war onset', *Journal of Conflict Resolution*, vol. 50, no. 4 (Aug. 2006), pp. 508–35

[41] Zartman I. W. and Faure, G. O. (eds), *Engaging Extremists: Trade-offs, Timing and Diplomacy* (United States Institute of Peace Press: Washington, DC, June 2011).

[42] Pruitt, D. G. and Kim, S. H., *Social Conflict: Escalation, Stalemate, and Settlement*, 3rd edn (McGraw-Hill: New York, 2004), pp. 88–91.

[43] See e.g. Nilsson, D., 'Partial peace: rebel groups inside and outside of civil war settlements', *Journal of Peace and Conflict Research*, vol. 45, no 4 (July 2008), pp. 479–95; and Cunningham, D. E., 'Veto players and civil war duration', *American Journal of Political Science*, vol. 50, no. 4 (Oct. 2006), pp. 875–92.

[44] On the discussions in 2012 regarding possible international deployments to Mali see chapter 2, section II, in this volume.

II. The fragile peace in East and South East Asia

STEIN TØNNESSON, ERIK MELANDER, ELIN BJARNEGÅRD, ISAK SVENSSON
AND SUSANNE SCHAFTENAAR*
UPPSALA UNIVERSITY

In the 1980s East and South East Asia went from being the world's bloodiest battleground to one of its most peaceful regions, and this era of relative peace has continued (see figure 1.1 and table 1.1).[1] In 2010, state-based conflicts, non-state conflicts and one-sided violence killed only an estimated 674 people, the lowest number recorded by the Uppsala Conflict Data Program (UCDP) in any year for this group of countries.

More than 30 years of relative peace have contributed to making East and South East Asia the world's main economic growth region. Yet the peace seems by no means secure. While states have avoided direct conflict with each other and have stopped supporting insurgent movements on each other's territory, decades-old suspicions linger and economic integration has not been followed up with political integration. Increasing tensions since 2008 have been underpinned by rapid military build-ups in several countries, notably in East Asia.[2] Meanwhile a number of intrastate armed conflicts remain active in South East Asia, and some of these have escalated in recent years.

This section presents the statistical evidence for the East and South East Asian peace and its historical development. It goes on to examine the ongoing intrastate conflicts in Myanmar, the Philippines and Thailand, and then looks at the recent upsurge in interstate tensions in East Asia, and the possible risks to peace.

The East and South East Asian peace

In the first three decades after World War II, East and South East Asia was the site of the world's deadliest wars: the Chinese Civil War in 1946–50, the 1946–54 First Indochina War, the 1950–53 Korean War, and the 1959–75 Viet Nam War. Eighty per cent of battle deaths worldwide in the period

---

[1] East Asia here includes China, Japan, the Democratic People's Republic of Korea (DPRK, North Korea), the Republic of Korea (South Korea), Mongolia and Taiwan. South East Asia here includes Brunei Darussalam, Cambodia, Indonesia, Laos, Malaysia, Myanmar, the Philippines, Singapore, Thailand, Timor-Leste and Viet Nam. The East Asian Peace programme at Uppsala University covers all of the listed countries as 'East Asia'.

[2] See chapter 3, section I, chapter 5, section I, and chapter 9, section IV, in this volume.

* The authors are the core group in a 6-year programme on the East Asian Peace at Uppsala University, funded by Riksbankens Jubileumsfond. See <http://www.pcr.uu.se/research/eap/>.

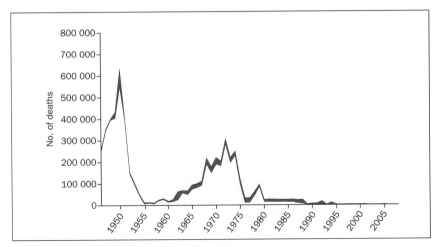

Figure 1.1. Battle-related deaths in armed conflicts in East and South East Asia, 1946–2008

Note: The figure is based on data from the Peace Research Institute Oslo (PRIO), using the UCDP definition of battle-related deaths. Because of methodological differences, PRIO estimates may be higher than UCDP estimates for the same conflicts. For those conflicts where PRIO provides a best estimate, that estimate is used; for other conflicts, the PRIO high and low estimates are used. The shading indicates the difference between the high and low estimates.

Source: Lacina, B. and Gleditsch, N. P., 'Monitoring trends in global combat: a new dataset of battle deaths', *European Journal of Population*, vol. 21, nos 2–3 (2005).

1946–79 were in East and South East Asia.[3] In the same period there were a number of massacres, genocides and man-made catastrophes: the 1958–60 Great Leap Forward and 1966–76 Cultural Revolution in China, the anti-communist massacres in Indonesia in 1965–66, the 1975–79 Cambodian genocide, and the massacres that followed the 1975 Indonesian invasion of East Timor.

In the 1980s, as battle deaths increased in other regions, they dropped off sharply in East and South East Asia, and the region's share of global battle deaths fell below 8 per cent. Since 1990 there has been an overall reduction in global battle deaths but East and South East Asia has remained ahead of the trend: its share in the world total has fallen to 3.5 per cent (approximately 27 000 of the 760 000 battle deaths worldwide in 1990–2011, according to UCDP best estimates).[4]

---

[3] Tønnesson, S., 'War and peace between nations since 1945', ed. N. Owen, *The Routledge Handbook of Southeast Asia History* (Routledge: London: forthcoming 2013), pp. 96–97.

[4] Data from the UCDP battle-related deaths data set, <http://www.ucdp.uu.se/>. On the global reduction see Pinker, S., *The Better Angels of Our Nature: Why Violence Has Declined* (Penguin: London, 2011); Goldstein; J. S., *Winning the War on War: The Decline of Armed Conflict Worldwide* (Penguin: London, 2011); and Gleditsch, N. P. et al., 'The decline of war', *International Studies Review*, vol. 15, no. 3 (forthcoming 2013).

Table 1.1. Number of conflicts and one-sided violence actors in East and South East Asia, 1980–2011

Year	State-based	Non-state[a]	One-sided[a]	Total fatalities	Year	State-based	Non-state	One-sided	Total fatalities
1980	11	..	..	15 000–25 000	1996	5	1	2	1 275
1981	13	..	..	15 000–26 000	1997	7	1	2	2 145
1982	9	..	..	14 000–27 000	1998	5	2	3	760
1983	9	..	..	14 000–26 000	1999	4	2	1	1 919
1984	10	..	..	15 000–26 000	2000	5	2	4	2 960
1985	8	..	..	14 000–26 000	2001	5	1	2	1 681
1986	10	..	..	14 000–27 000	2002	5	–	7	1 444
1987	11	..	..	9 000–24 000	2003	5	–	4	2 133
1988	10	..	..	7 000–26 000	2004	4	–	4	1 695
1989	7	–	2	5 860	2005	7	1	2	1 479
1990	9	1	1	2 636	2006	5	1	3	1 338
1991	7	1	3	3 589	2007	5	1	2	1 245
1992	8	–	4	2 469	2008	5	–	2	892
1993	4	1	1	890	2009	6	1	2	1 036
1994	6	–	1	2 038	2010	5	–	2	674
1995	5	1	3	2 357	2011	7	1	2[b]	1 504

Note: Figures for 1980–88 have been compiled from best estimates when PRIO provides such estimates, otherwise from both low and high estimates (rounded to the nearest 1000).

[a] Non-state conflicts and one-sided violence are recorded only from 1989.

[b] This figure excludes the alleged killing of 72 Hmong civilians by government forces in Viet Nam, due to insufficient corroborating evidence. This incident is included in table 1.7 in section III.

Sources: For 1980–88, Lacina, B. and Gleditsch, N. P., 'Monitoring trends in global combat: a new dataset of battle deaths', *European Journal of Population*, vol. 21, nos 2–3 (2005). For 1989–2011, UCDP 'battle-related deaths' data set, version 5-2012, <http://www.ucdp.uu.se/>; Eck, K. and Hultman, L., 'Violence against civilians in war', *Journal of Peace Research*, vol. 44, no. 2 (2007), pp. 233–46; and Sundberg, R., Eck, K. and Kreutz, J., 'Introducing the UCDP non-state conflict dataset', *Journal of Peace Research*, vol. 49, no. 2 (2012), pp. 351–62.

Although several states have persisted in using capital punishment and violent means of repression, the available statistics do not indicate that the decline in armed conflict has been offset by an increase in other kinds of organized violence.[5] East and South East Asia has simply become more peaceful (see figure 1.2).

Developments in Indochina (Cambodia, Laos and Viet Nam) account for much of the decline in battle deaths. For most of 1945–89, Indochina was the region's main battleground. The war that broke out between France and Viet Nam in 1946 became part of the cold war in 1950, with China helping Viet Nam win the battle of Dien Bien Phu in 1954, after which Viet Nam was temporarily divided into North and South Viet Nam. China, later

[5] Kivimäki, T., 'East Asian relative peace: does it exist? What is it?', *Pacific Review*, vol. 23, no. 4 (Aug. 2010), pp. 503–26.

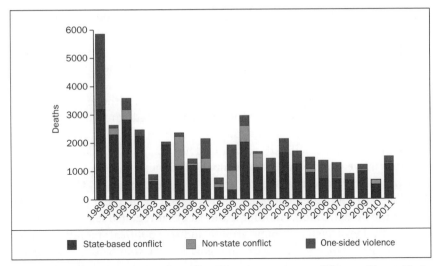

Figure 1.2. Fatalities in state-based conflicts, non-state conflicts and one-sided violence in East and South East Asia, 1989–2011

Numbers of deaths are UCDP best estimates except for 2011, where 72 Hmong civilians allegedly killed by Vietnamese Government forces are excluded due to insufficient corroborating evidence.

Sources: As for table 1.1.

joined by the Soviet Union, assisted North Viet Nam, the National Liberation Front (NLF) in South Viet Nam, and similar movements in Cambodia and Laos in their wars against the local United States-backed regimes in 1965–75. By 1976, Communist regimes had been established in all three countries of Indochina, bringing a precipitous drop in battle-related deaths—despite a short but very bloody war between China and the Soviet-backed Viet Nam in 1979. This war followed Viet Nam's invasion of Cambodia to remove the pro-Chinese and genocidal Khmer Rouge and install a pro-Viet Nam regime. In the late 1970s the strategic focus of the cold war rivalry shifted to Europe and the Middle East.

Battle-related deaths in East and South East Asia fell sharply again in 1989. A low-key insurgency against the Viet Nam-supported government in Cambodia, sustained by a broad alliance of China, the USA and the non-Communist South East Asian states—organized since 1967 in the Association of Southeast Asian Nations (ASEAN)—ended when Viet Nam withdrew.[6] Also in 1989 a long communist insurgency ended in Myanmar and the military government agreed ceasefires with several armed ethnic groups.

[6] For a brief description and list of members of ASEAN see annex B, section II, in this volume.

The 1990s and 2000s saw a decrease not just in communist rebellion but also in ethnic conflict. The main reasons for this decline were a strengthening of government capacities to control their populations, new infrastructure that made it harder to maintain guerrilla bases in the jungle, a reduction in available aid from abroad, and also a shift in the tactics of rebel movements from armed resistance to 'people power'. Although non-violent rebellions have at times been violently suppressed, they have also had notable successes, such as the ousting in 1986 of Philippine dictator Ferdinand Marcos, Thailand's return to democracy in 1992 and the fall of Suharto's 33-year-old New Order regime in Indonesia in 1998.

How can the trend towards regional peace be explained? One factor is the Sino-US rapprochement in the 1970s, which made them de facto allies against the Soviet Union. Another is the fact that regional leaders gave priority to market-driven economic growth and saw political stability as a prerequisite for realizing their economic goals. Most countries of the region have at some point shifted from ideological aims backed by military power to policies geared towards economic growth. The most important initiator of such change was Deng Xiaoping, China's de facto leader from 1978 to 1997. His pragmatism contributed significantly to regional stability and economic integration.

Yet there is little to indicate that East and South East Asia is becoming a 'security community'.[7] As described below, several armed conflicts remain active in the region, and in 2011 their number went up from five to eight.[8] There are also many unresolved militarized disputes.

Active armed conflicts

Despite significant interstate tensions, the UCDP did not register any interstate conflict in East and South East Asia between 1989 and 2010. The long-standing conflict between the Democratic People's Republic of Korea (DPRK, North Korea) and the Republic of Korea (South Korea) erupted into violence in 2010. In March the sinking of the South Korean warship *Cheonan*, which South Korea officially blamed on a North Korean torpedo caused 46 deaths.[9] Another 4 South Koreans and possibly some North Koreans were killed in November when North Korea fired against the

---

[7] Deutsch, K. W., *Political Community at the International Level* (Doubleday: New York, 1954); Deutsch, K. W. et al., *Political Community and the North Atlantic Area* (Greenwood: New York, 1957); and Acharya, A., *Constructing a Security Community in Southeast Asia: ASEAN and the Problem of Regional Order* (Routledge: London, 2001).

[8] Some figures given in this section differ from those given in section III due to methodological differences.

[9] South Korean Ministry of National Defense, Joint Civilian–Military Investigation Group, 'Investigation result on the sinking of ROKS "Cheonan"', 20 May 2010, <http://www.mnd.go.kr/webmodule/htsboard/template/read/engbdread.jsp?typeID=16&boardid=88&seqno=871>. See also Farrell, A., 'Behind the mystery of the Cheonan', *Metro Éireann*, 15 Aug. 2012.

nearby South Korean-held Yeonpyeong island.[10] However, because the cause of the *Cheonan* sinking has not been firmly established, it is not counted by UCDP as a conflict. In 2011 the only interstate conflict since 1989 was registered when fighting between Cambodia and Thailand in a disputed area near the Preah Vihear temple, which had been going on since 2009, killed 28 people.[11]

However, several intrastate conflicts have remained active in South East Asia (see table 1.2). While most have their origin in the process of decolonization, some countries have been more affected than others. There is a tendency for the more conflict-ridden countries to have a military that either evades control by the government or dominates it.[12] Laos and Viet Nam, like China, have armies tightly controlled by a Communist party. The Communist regimes established in those two countries in 1975–76 have gradually overcome resistance from ethnic minority groups so that in recent years there has been no armed struggle, only demonstrations and riots.[13] Malaysia and Singapore have been able to prevent internal armed conflict since the 1960s as both states have well-organized security forces under civilian control.[14] The countries where the military has been an independent political force are Indonesia, Myanmar, the Philippines and Thailand. It can be no coincidence that these are the countries where internal conflicts have been most persistent.

A notable characteristic of East and South East Asia's post-World War II history has been the scarcity of successful peace agreements. Significantly, the Korean armistice of 1953 has not been replaced by a peace agreement, leaving the two sides technically at war. The Geneva agreements on Indochina in 1954 and Laos in 1962 failed, as did the 1973 Paris agreement on Viet Nam. Most armed conflicts in the region have ended in the military defeat of one side, in a ceasefire, or have simply petered out. While this may mean that fighting has stopped, the underlying incompatibilities are often not addressed, leaving the potential for conflict to re-emerge. This fact does not, perhaps, bode well for the ongoing peace processes in Myanmar and the Philippines.

---

[10] 'China calls for emergency talks amid Korea crisis', BBC News, 28 Nov. 2010, <http://www.bbc.co.uk/news/world-asia-pacific-11856454>.

[11] See the UCDP Conflict Encyclopedia, <http://www.ucdp.uu.se/database/>.

[12] Mietzner, M. (ed.), *The Political Resurgence of the Military in Southeast Asia: Conflict and Leadership* (Routledge: London, 2011).

[13] For 2001 and 2004 see Hayton, W., *Vietnam: Rising Dragon* (Yale University Press: New Haven, CT, 2010), pp. 215–16. In May 2011 there were unconfirmed reports that up to 72 ethnic Hmong Christians had been killed in Điện Biên province. 'Vietnam: investigate crackdown on Hmong unrest', Human Rights Watch, 17 May 2011, <http://www.hrw.org/en/news/2011/05/17/vietnam-investigate-crackdown-hmong-unrest>.

[14] Slater, D., *Ordering Power: Contentious Politics and Authoritarian Leviathans in Southeast Asia* (Cambridge University Press: Cambridge, 2010).

Table 1.2. State-based conflicts, non-state conflicts and one-sided violence actors in East and South East Asia, number and fatalities, 1989–2011

Location	State-based		Non-state		One-sided violence		Total fatalities
	No.	Fatalities	No.	Fatalities	No.	Fatalities	
Intrastate conflicts							
Philippines	2	13 362	5	173	4	686	14 221
Myanmar	9	8 621	4	2 007	2	1 922	12 550
Cambodia	1	4 333	–	–	1	667	5 000
Indonesia and Timor-Leste[a]	2	2 461	3	2 053	4	2 230	6 744
Thailand	1	1 284	–	–	2	1 789	3 073
Laos	1	75	–	–	1	73	148
Interstate conflicts							
Cambodia–Thailand, 2011	1	28	–	–	–	–	28
Other							
China	–	–	–	–	1	2 651	2 651
Total fatalities		**30 164**		**4 233**		**10 018**	**44 415**

Note: UCDP best estimates are used for battle-related deaths and one-sided violence fatalities.

[a] The Uppsala Conflict Data Program (UDCP) treats Timor-Leste as having been part of Indonesia until 2002. Since then the number of fatalities in Timor-Leste has not reached the UCDP threshold of 25 deaths in one year.

Sources: As for table 1.1.

The only successful peace agreements in the region have been the 1991 Paris Agreement on Cambodia and the 2005 agreement between the Indonesian Government and the Gerakan Aceh Merdeka (GAM, Free Aceh Movement).[15] The Aceh agreement was part of a general shift to peace in Indonesia. After the election of former general Susilo Bambang Yudhoyono to the Indonesian presidency in 2004 the violent upsurge after the fall of Suharto in 1998 ended, except in West Papua. Indonesia has since been at the forefront of developing policies within ASEAN to address threats to peace both between and within states.

Since 1989 the Philippines has suffered more battle deaths in armed conflict than any other country of the region. Fatalities have been registered almost continuously in all three UCDP categories: state-based conflict, non-state conflict and one-sided violence. The government is engaged in two parallel conflicts. One is with the Communist Party of the Philippines (CPP), which fights for a general land reform, making the Philippines the only country in the region with an active communist insurgency. The other is with the Moro independence movement in Mindanao, where the strongest organization is currently the Moro Islamic Liberation Front (MILF).

[15] For details of these agreements see the UCDP Conflict Encyclopedia (note 11).

The smaller Abu Sayyaf Group has also engaged in armed fighting, kidnappings and terrorist acts but has become less active.

The fighting between the MILF and the government escalated in 2011 but stopped when a peace plan was agreed in October 2012, with Malaysian mediation. This seemed a breakthrough, as the parties agreed to an overall formula for resolving the conflict.[16] Uncertainty remains, however, about its implementation and the possibility that the rival Moro National Liberation Front (MNLF), which made its political settlement with the government in 1996, could undermine the process. The Philippine Government and the CPP are also engaged in long-running negotiations facilitated by Norway.[17]

Since 1989 Myanmar has had the second highest number of battle deaths of any state in the region. Its many protracted internal armed conflicts began immediately after it gained independence in 1948. The wave of ceasefire agreements between the government and armed groups after 1989 reduced the amount of fighting but did not lead to political settlements.[18]

Myanmar's transition to a constitutional government in 2011 brought mixed results. Many new ceasefires were agreed, including the first ever between the government and the Karen National Union (KNU).[19] However, a 1994 ceasefire with the Kachin Independence Organization (KIO) and its Army (KIA) broke down, leading to renewed fighting in June 2011, after which a series of attempts to agree a new ceasefire failed.[20]

In Rakhine State the new national constitution adopted in 2008 and elections in 2010 exacerbated conflict between the Buddhist Rakhine majority and the Muslim Rohingya minority, which many Rakhine see as immigrants from Bengal. This led to outbursts of communal violence in June and October 2012, and the internal displacement of tens of thousands of people.[21] The government has announced its intention to carry through a peace process and involve all armed groups in a national political dialogue before planned elections in 2015.[22]

Organized violence has also killed thousands of people in Thailand. In 2001 a new generation of Malay Muslim insurgents began a series of violent

[16] 'Philippines and Muslim rebels agree peace deal', BBC News, 7 Oct. 2012, <http://www.bbc.co.uk/news/world-asia-19860907>.

[17] International Crisis Group (ICG), *The Communist Insurgency in the Philippines: Tactics and Talks*, Asia Report no. 202 (ICG: Bangkok, 14 Feb. 2011). The CPP pulled out of talks in Nov. 2011 but agreed to a 26-day ceasefire from 20 Dec. 2012. Pagaduan-Araullo, C., 'The "special track" falters', Business World Online, 4 Apr. 2013, <http://www.bworldonline.com/content.php?section=Opinion&id=68185>.

[18] International Crisis Group (ICG), *Myanmar: A New Peace Initiative*, Asia Report no. 214 (ICG: Jakarta, 30 Nov. 2011), p. 3.

[19] South, A., *Prospects for Peace in Myanmar: Opportunities and Threats*, PRIO Paper (Peace Research Institute Oslo: Oslo, Dec. 2012).

[20] International Crisis Group (ICG), *Myanmar: Storm Clouds on the Horizon*, Asia Report no. 238 (ICG: Jakarta, 12 Nov. 2012).

[21] International Crisis Group (note 18), pp. 1–2.

[22] International Crisis Group (note 18), p. 20.

attacks in the Patani region of southern Thailand, which was part of a former sultanate annexed by Thailand (then Siam) in 1902. Malay Muslim insurgents fought against the Thai Government from the 1950s to the 1970s, but never with the intensity displayed since 2001. Strict security measures undertaken after the first attacks in 2001 provoked a spiral of violence from 2004. Loosely organized insurgent groups carried out a great number of killings and bombings. Under a state of emergency declared in 2005, the Royal Thai Army set up local militias and maintained a heavy presence.[23] Fighting continued throughout 2012.

While the Patani conflict escalated, a polarized political struggle also developed in the Thai capital, Bangkok, between the 'yellowshirt' movement seeking to oust the elected Prime Minister, Thaksin Shinawatra, and the 'redshirt' pro-Thaksin movement. The yellowshirts identify with the traditional elite and are backed by much of Bangkok's middle class, while the redshirt movement has its main support base in Thailand's highly populated north and north-east and among immigrants from those regions to the capital. Both before and after Thaksin was ousted in a 2006 military coup there were violent incidents in Bangkok. More than 90 people were killed in 2010.[24] Demonstrations have continued, but with little violence, under the government of Thaksin's sister, Yingluck Shinawatra, who was elected in 2011. Thai society remains polarized at a time when a possible conflict over the royal succession looms.

The yellowshirt movement also whipped up nationalist sentiment against Cambodia over a disputed area near the Preah Vihear temple. Weak governments were unable to handle the dispute diplomatically. Troops were deployed on both sides, and there were violent artillery exchanges in 2009, 2010 and 2011.[25]

Thus, although Thailand is a middle-income country with long-standing experience of democracy (albeit frequently interrupted by military coups), it has had three kinds of conflict in recent years: intrastate over territory; intrastate over government; and interstate over territory. The power struggles in the capital have impaired the state's capacity to prevent conflict with minority groups as well as foreign countries.

[23] International Crisis Group (ICG), *Thailand: The Evolving Conflict in the South*, Asia Report no. 241 (ICG: Bangkok, 11 Dec. 2012), pp. 1–2; and Melvin, N. J., *Conflict in Southern Thailand: Islamism, Violence and the State in the Patani Insurgency*, SIPRI Policy Paper No. 20 (SIPRI: Stockholm, Sep. 2007).

[24] International Crisis Group (ICG), *Bridging Thailand's Deep Divide*, Asia Report no. 192 (ICG: Bangkok, 5 July 2010), pp. i–ii, 1–3.

[25] International Crisis Group (ICG), *Waging Peace: ASEAN and the Thai–Cambodian Border Conflict*, Asia Report no. 215 (ICG: Bangkok, 6 Dec. 2011).

Rising tensions

Since 2008 interstate tensions have increased on the Korean peninsula and in China's relations with Japan, South Korea, the Philippines, the USA and Viet Nam. This has been due to a range of factors, including resource-related rivalries, arms procurements, contested historical memories, and the perceived rise of China and decline of the USA. The capacity of the USA to maintain its presence in regional geopolitics through alliances, naval bases and the permanent deployment of troops in Japan and South Korea has been questioned. In 2008, when the USA was hit by a financial crisis, China assumed a more assertive attitude towards its neighbours. This led to incidents and a strategic backlash, with several states asking the USA to reaffirm its commitment to regional security. US President Barack Obama responded by rebalancing the focus of US military planning, foreign policy and economic policy in what was termed a 'pivot' to Asia.[26]

The rising tensions have accentuated risks to the regional peace. While the internal armed conflicts in South East Asia are unlikely to escalate and threaten regional stability, the Korean situation and China's maritime disputes carry greater risk since the USA might become directly involved. The more cooperation there is between China and the USA, and the more the two sides appreciate their economic interdependence, the less likely they are to let serious risks arise. Yet there can be no certainty that the two governments are able to control events. The USA is bound by treaty to defend Japan, South Korea and the Philippines if they come under attack, and China may find it difficult to back out of a crisis if nationalist movements mobilize. Taiwan and Viet Nam are not US allies but Viet Nam has moved closer to the USA in recent years, and the USA continues to sell weapons to Taiwan.

Although Taiwan's unresolved status caused much tension in the mid-1990s and early 2000s, it has not done so recently. This is largely due to improved relations across the Taiwan Strait since Ma Ying-jeou was elected Taiwanese president in 2008.

In 2012 the Korean situation was particularly worrisome, however. The Six-Party Talks on North Korea's nuclear programme had stalled in 2007, and in 2009 North Korea restarted its nuclear programme.[27] It carried out its first nuclear test explosion in 2006, and a second in 2009. In late 2011 the young Kim Jong Un took over as leader following the death of his

[26] Manyin, M. E. et al., *Pivot to the Pacific? The Obama Administration's 'Rebalancing' Toward Asia*, Congressional Research Service (CRS) Report for Congress 7-5700 (US Congress, CRS: Washington, DC, 28 Mar. 2012).

[27] The 6-Party Talks began in Aug. 2003 as a Chinese diplomatic initiative aimed at resolving the controversy over how to address North Korea's suspected nuclear weapon programme. In addition to China and North Korea, the other parties are Japan, South Korea, Russia and the USA. See also chapter 7, section II, in this volume.

father, Kim Jong Il. He reconfirmed his father's *songun* (military first) policy and prioritized moving ahead with the nuclear programme. North Korea successfully test-fired a rocket in December 2012 and carried out a third nuclear weapon test in February 2013.[28] The USA urged China to use its leverage to persuade North Korea to abandon its nuclear weapon and missile programmes.[29] As North Korea's main trading partner and source of food and oil, China was believed to have influence in Pyongyang. Kim Jong Un, however, was recalcitrant. Since China's economic support to North Korea is motivated by fear of a regime collapse that could cause a flow of refugees into China and lead to Korean reunification on South Korea's terms, it seemed reluctant to exercise its enormous leverage.

China's maritime disputes carry less risk than the Korean situation. Maritime incidents sometimes serve as lightning rods for interstate tensions. Yet there is a real risk of escalation if the USA should decide to intervene on behalf of an ally or to defend the principle of the freedom of navigation. The USA is bound under the 1960 Treaty of Mutual Cooperation and Security to help Japan protect its sovereignty and keeps a controversial base at Okinawa. China and Japan have built close economic relations but have never gained mutual trust. Their suspicions are fuelled not just by territorial disputes but by resentment linked to Japan's colonization of Korea and Taiwan and the 1931 and 1937 invasions of China, and of Japan's failure to distance itself convincingly from its history of war crimes.

After a period of relative calm at sea following the adoption of a Sino-ASEAN Declaration on the Conduct of Parties in 2002, there was an upsurge of maritime incidents in the East China Sea and South China Sea from 2008.[30] These incidents were fuelled by fishing interests, prospects of finding oil under disputed parts of the continental shelf, certain ambiguities in the Law of the Sea, and the mere fact that few maritime boundaries have yet been agreed on.[31] Legal experts disagree over how much impact small islands can have on the delimitation of maritime zones. Their status as either 'low-tide elevations', with no maritime zone of their own, 'rocks', with a right to only 12-nautical mile (22-kilometre) territorial waters, or 'islands' that can sustain human habitation or an economic life of their own,

---

[28] See chapter 6, section IX, and chapter 7, section II, in this volume.

[29] Nakamura, D. and Harlan, C., 'Obama urges China to add to global pressure on North Korea over rocket launch', *Washington Post*, 26 Mar. 2012; and Quinn, A. and Blanchard, B., 'Clinton urges China to help on Iran, North Korea', Reuters 3 May 2012.

[30] Declaration on the Conduct of Parties in the South China Sea, signed 4 Nov. 2002, <http://www.asean.org/asean/external-relations/china/item/declaration-on-the-conduct-of-parties-in-the-south-china-sea>. See also Wezeman, S. T., 'The maritime dimension of arms transfers to South East Asia, 2007–11', *SIPRI Yearbook 2012*; and chapter 9, section IV, in this volume.

[31] See International Crisis Group (ICG), *Stirring Up the South China Sea*, Asia Report no. 223 (ICG: Brussels, 23 Apr. 2012); and Raine, S. and Le Mière, C., *Regional Disorder: The South China Sea Disputes* (Routledge: Abingdon, 2013).

with a right to a continental shelf and 200-nautical mile (370-km) exclusive economic zone (EEZ), remains contested in international law.[32]

Patriotic feelings have contributed to transforming these disputes over small islands into major issues. China, Taiwan and Japan claim the Japanese-controlled Senkaku/Diaoyu islets east of Taiwan in the East China Sea. In the South China Sea, China, Taiwan and the Philippines claim Scarborough Shoal, west of Luzon. China, Taiwan and Viet Nam claim the Chinese-held Paracel Islands. The Spratly archipelago is claimed in full by China, Taiwan and Viet Nam and in part by Malaysia and the Philippines. Brunei Darussalam also has a maritime zone claim in the area. While the South East Asian claimants agree that the Spratlys can have only 12-nautical mile territorial waters, China argues that they are entitled to a 200-nautical mile EEZ.[33]

All the states involved (except Taiwan, because of its unrecognized status) have signed and ratified the 1982 United Nations Convention on the Law of the Sea (UNCLOS) and are thus bound by it.[34] There is an increasing awareness that any boundary agreement has to be based on the Law of the Sea, but posturing is likely to continue for as long as states try to maximize their zone claims.

The most dangerous incidents in 2010–12 were related to the Senkaku/Diaoyu islands, where Japan arrested a Chinese fishing boat captain in September 2010, leading to several weeks of vigorous Chinese protests and nationalist mobilization before he was released. A new crisis arose in 2012 when the Japanese Government bought the Senkakus from a private owner, provoking not just protests from China (which could not recognize any such transaction as it claims sovereignty over the islands) but also the dispatch of Chinese naval ships and military aircraft.[35] There was also a standoff between Chinese and Philippine vessels in April–May 2012 at Scarborough Shoal, ending in a Philippine withdrawal. China then sealed off the entrance to the lagoon with a rope and has kept a more or less permanent presence.[36]

---

[32] International Court of Justice (ICJ), 'Maritime delimitation in the Black Sea' (*Romania vs Ukraine*), Judgment of 3 Feb. 2009, *ICJ Reports*, 2009, p. 110, para. 149; and International Court of Justice, 'Territorial and maritime dispute' (*Nicaragua v. Colombia*), Judgment of 19 Nov. 2012, *ICJ Reports*, 2012, p. 90, para. 238.

[33] Chinese Permanent Mission to the United Nations, Note verbale to UN Secretary-General Ban Ki-moon, CML/8/2011, 14 Apr. 2011, <http://www.un.org/Depts/los/clcs_new/submissions_files/vnm37_09/chn_2011_re_phl_e.pdf>.

[34] United Nations Convention on the Law of the Sea (UNCLOS), opened for signature 10 Dec. 1982, entered into force 16 Nov. 1994, *United Nations Treaty Series*, vol. 1833 (1994).

[35] Manyin, M. E., 'Senkaku (Diaoyu/Diaoyutai) Islands dispute: U.S. treaty obligations', Congressional Research Service (CRS) Report for Congress R42761 (US Congress, CRS: Washington, DC, 22 Jan. 2013).

[36] Perlez, J., 'In Beijing, Clinton will push for talks over disputed islands', *New York Times*, 3 Sep. 2012.

As of 2012, it was impossible to gauge how seriously the rising tensions were threatening regional peace. New leaders took power in several countries. The Chinese Communist Party elected Xi Jinping as its new leader in October 2012, shortly before Barack Obama was elected to a second term as US president. In late December 2012 Shinzō Abe took over as Japanese prime minister. Also in December, South Korea elected a new, conservative president, Park Geun-hye, who had spoken out in her campaign in favour of rapprochement and confidence building between the two Koreas.

It is not yet clear what factors have done most to underpin the relative regional peace since 1980—power balance, economic interdependence, economic growth priorities, or new values and discourses. Nevertheless, there sadly seem to be few grounds for considering the peace secure.

Conclusions

While there was a precipitous decline in organized violence in East and South East Asia in the period 1980–2010, the militarized disputes in the Taiwan Strait, the Korean peninsula, the East China Sea and the South China Sea have not been resolved. Furthermore, economic growth has allowed many states to acquire new weapon systems.[37] China and North Korea are nuclear powers, while Japan and South Korea operate under a US nuclear umbrella. China, Japan and South Korea have built efficient modern navies. The US Navy has boosted its presence in the region and conducted many joint exercises with its allies. Although there is not yet a regional arms race, the growth in military capabilities contributes, together with continuing intrastate armed conflicts in several countries, to the fragility of the East and South East Asian peace. The growing number of submarines is considered particularly destabilizing.[38]

The region may still have a chance to deepen the peace it has enjoyed for well over 30 years, but this will require improvement of several bilateral and multilateral relationships, notably between the two Korea states; China and Japan; China and ASEAN; and China and the USA. Unfortunately, there are presently no signs that the national leaders are ready to enter into regional security cooperation beyond the purely consultative frameworks of ASEAN+3 (ASEAN plus China, Japan and South Korea), the ASEAN Regional Forum, and the East Asia Summit, which since 2011 has included Russia and the USA.[39]

---

[37] See chapter 5, section I, in this volume.

[38] Till, G., *Asia's Naval Expansion: An Arms Race in the Making?*, Adelphi Papers nos 432–33 (Routledge: London, 2012), pp. 45, 89, 98, 124–26.

[39] For more on confidence-building mechanisms in Asia see chapter 9, section IV, in this volume.

III. Patterns of organized violence, 2002–11

LOTTA THEMNÉR AND PETER WALLENSTEEN
UPPSALA CONFLICT DATA PROGRAM

This section provides an overview of trends in the 10-year period 2002–11 in three categories of violent action used by the Uppsala Conflict Data Program (UCDP) in mapping organized violence around the world: state-based conflict, non-state conflict and one-sided violence. The overall number of incidents of organized violence resulting in the deaths of at least 25 people in a particular year (the threshold for counting by UCDP) was slightly lower in 2011, at 98, than in 2002, when it stood at 114. This was solely due to a decrease in incidents of one-sided violence; both state-based and non-state conflicts were more prevalent in 2011 than in 2002 (see figure 1.3).

Within the overall trend, each of the three types of violence has its own internal dynamics, while also being affected by the dynamics of the other types. The full picture is, of course, more complex, but there is no clear positive or negative correlation between the three types of violence.

State-based conflicts

State-based conflict is defined as a contested incompatibility between two parties—at least one of which is the government of a state—that concerns government or territory or both, where the use of armed force by the parties results in at least 25 battle-related deaths in a calendar year (see 'Sources and methods' below for more detail).[1] A state-based conflict that results in 1000 battle-related deaths in a year is classified as a 'war' in that year; other state-based conflicts are classified as 'minor state-based conflicts'.[2] This definition extends from low-intensity conflicts that are active for just one or a few years to high-intensity, protracted conflicts.

In the 10-year period 2002–11 there were 73 active state-based conflicts, including 37 that were active in 2011 (see table 1.3).[3] Over the decade, the annual number increased, albeit unevenly, and at 37 in 2011 it reached a level only seen in one other year of the period: 2008 (see table 1.4).

There was also an overall increase in battle-related deaths in state-based conflicts over the decade, with over 22 500 people killed in battles in 2011 (see figure 1.4), compared to just over 17 000 in 2002.[4] Again, the increase was uneven, with the lowest number (c. 11 500) recorded in 2005 while the

[1] This category is called 'armed conflict' in other UCDP data sets.
[2] The category minor state-based conflict is called 'minor armed conflict' in other UCDP data sets.
[3] Note that the UCDP counts fighting between different sets of actor over the same type of incompatibility (government or territory) in the same country as a single conflict.
[4] For the full definition of battle-related deaths see below.

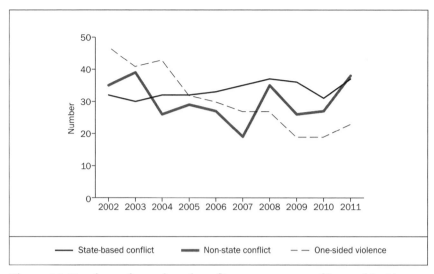

Figure 1.3. Numbers of state-based conflicts, non-state conflicts and incidents of one-sided violence, 2002–11

highest number (almost 31 000) was reached in 2009. This peak was largely due to the dramatic escalation of the conflict in Sri Lanka, which ended in that year with the defeat of the Liberation Tigers of Tamil Eelam (LTTE). Developments in Afghanistan and Pakistan also played a part. The conflict between the Afghan Government and the Taliban escalated in 2009 and a new, intense conflict erupted between the Pakistani Government and Tehrik-i-Taliban Pakistan (TTP, Taliban Movement of Pakistan).

UCDP data distinguishes between three types of state-based conflict: interstate, intrastate and internationalized intrastate. Interstate conflicts are fought between two or more governments of states. Intrastate conflicts are fought between a government of a state and one or more rebel groups. Internationalized intrastate conflicts are intrastate conflicts in which one or both sides receive troop support from an external state. Intrastate conflicts are by far the most common; in most years they account for more than 80 per cent of all conflicts, and never for less than 70 per cent. Interstate conflicts are the least common. In the 10-year period 2002–11 there were only four: between India and Pakistan (2001–2003), Iraq and the USA with its allies (2003), Djibouti and Eritrea (2008), and Cambodia and Thailand (2011). Although rare, interstate conflicts should not be neglected. Given the vast resources that can be mobilized by governments compared to rebel groups, conflicts between states may rapidly escalate and cause high numbers of fatalities.[5]

[5] See e.g. Lacina, B. and Gleditch, N. P., 'Monitoring trends in global combat: a new dataset of battle deaths', *European Journal of Population*, vol. 21, no. 2–3 (June 2005), pp. 145–66.

Table 1.3. State-based conflicts in 2011

For more detailed definitions of the terms used see 'Sources and methods' below.

Location[a]	Parties	Incompatibility	Start year[b]	Fatalities, 2011	Change from 2010[c]
Africa					
Algeria (Algeria, Niger)	Government of Algeria, Niger vs al-Qaeda in the Islamic Maghreb (AQIM)	Government	1998/ 1999	269	+
CAR	Government of CAR vs Convention des patriotes pour la justice et la paix (CPJP, Convention of Patriots for Justice and Peace)	Government	2009/ 2009	44	+ +
Côte d'Ivoire	Government of Côte d'Ivoire vs Forces de Défense et de Sécurité Impartiales de Côte d'Ivoire (FDSI-CI, Impartial Defence and Security Forces of Côte d'Ivoire)	Government	2011/ 2011	35	..
Ethiopia (Ethiopia, Kenya)	Government of Ethiopia vs Ogaden National Liberation Front (ONLF)	Territory (Ogaden)	1994/ 1994	25	– –
	vs Oromo Liberation Front (OLF)	Territory (Oromiya)	1974/ 1977	25	0
Libya	Government of Libya vs National Transitional Council (NTC)	Government	2011/ 2011	1 600	..
	vs Forces of Muammar Gaddafi	Government	2011/ 2011	328	..
Mauretania (Mali, Mauretania, Niger)	Government of Mauretania, Mali, Niger vs al-Qaeda in the Islamic Maghreb (AQIM)	Government	2008/ 2010	30	0
Nigeria	Government of Nigeria vs Jama'atu Ahlis Sunna Lidda'awati wal-Jihad (Boko Haram)	Government	2009/ 2009	324	..
Rwanda (DRC)	Government of Rwanda, DRC vs Forces démocratiques de libération du Rwanda (FDLR, Democratic Liberation Forces of Rwanda)	Government	2001/ 2001	116	–
Senegal	Government of Senegal vs Mouvement des forces démocratiques de Casamance the Democratic Forces of the Casamance)	Territory (Casamance)	1988/ 1990	25	..
Somalia (Kenya, Somalia)	Government of Somalia, Ethiopia, Kenya vs Al-Shabab	Government	2008/ 2008	1 917	0
South Sudan	Government of South Sudan vs South Sudan Defence Movement/ Army (SSDM/A)	Government	2011/ 2011	101	..
	vs South Sudan Liberation Movement/ Army (SSLM/A)	Government	2011/ 2011	111	..

Location[a]	Parties	Incompatibility	Start year[b]	Fatalities, 2011	Change from 2010[c]
Sudan	Government of Sudan				
	vs Justice and Equality Movement (JEM)	Government	2003/ 2003	98	– –
	vs Sudan Liberation Movement/Army (SLM/A)	Government	2003/ 2003	130	–
	vs South Sudan Defence Movement/ Army (SSDM/A)	Government	2010/ 2010	492	+ +
	vs South Sudan Liberation Movement/ Army (SSLM/A)	Government	2011/ 2011	312	..
	vs Sudan People's Liberation Movement-North (SPLM/A–North)	Government	2011/ 2011	217	..
Sudan	Government of Sudan vs Government of South Sudan	Territory (Abyei)	2011/ 2011	149	..
Uganda (DRC)	Government of Uganda, DRC vs Alliance of Democratic Forces (ADF)	Government	1996/ 1996	73	0
(CAR, DRC, S. Sudan, Sudan)	Government of Uganda, CAR, DRC, South Sudan, Sudan vs Lord's Resistance Army (LRA)	Government	1988/ 1988	64	+
Americas					
Colombia	Government of Colombia				
	vs Fuerzas Armadas Revolucionarias de Colombia (FARC, Revolutionary Armed Forces of Colombia)	Government	1964/ 1964	202	–
USA (Afghanistan, Pakistan)	Government of USA, France vs al-Qaeda	Government	2001/ 2001	190	–
Asia and Oceania					
Afghanistan (Afghanistan, Pakistan)	Government of Afghanistan, Multinational coalition[d] vs Hizb-i Islami-yi Afghanistan (Islamic Party of Afghanistan)	Government	1980/ 1980	44	– –
	vs Taliban	Government	1995/ 1995	7 184	+
Cambodia, Thailand	Government of Cambodia vs Government of Thailand	Territory (Common border)	1975/ 1977	28	..
India	Government of India				
	vs Communist Party of India–Maoist (CPI–Maoist)	Government	2004/ 2005	287	–
	vs Kashmir insurgents	Territory (Kashmir)	1984/ 1989	140	– –
Myanmar	Government of Myanmar				
	vs Kachin Independence Organization (KIO)	Territory (Kachin)	1961/ 1961	209	..
	vs Democratic Karen Buddhist Army Brigade 5 (DKBA 5)	Territory (Karen)	2010/ 2010	115	+ +
	vs Karen National Union (KNU)	Territory (Karen)	1966/ 1966	203	+ +
	vs Restoration Council of Shan States (RCSS)	Territory (Shan)	1986/ 1996	44	+
	vs Shan State Progress Party (SSPP)	Territory (Shan)	2011/ 2011	141	..

Location[a]	Parties	Incompatibility	Start year[b]	Fatalities, 2011	Change from 2010[c]
Pakistan (Afghanistan, Pakistan)	Government of Pakistan				
	vs Tehrik-i-Taliban Pakistan (TTP, Taliban Movement of Pakistan)	Government	2007/ 2008	2 599	–
	vs Baluchistan Liberation Army (BLA)	Territory (Balochistan)	2004/ 2004	42	..
Philippines	Government of the Philippines				
	vs Communist Party of the Philippines (CPP)	Government	1969/ 1969	205	0
	vs Abu Sayyaf Group (ASG)	Territory (Mindanao)	1993/ 1933	80	0
	vs Moro Islamic Liberation Front (MILF)	Territory (Mindanao)	1990/ 1990	83	..
Tajikistan	Government of Tajikistan				
	vs Islamic Movement of Uzbekistan (IMU)	Government	2005/ 2010	28	– –
Thailand	Government of Thailand				
	vs Patani insurgents	Territory (Patani)	1965/ 2003	142	+ +
Europe					
Russia	Government of Russia				
	vs Forces of the Caucasus Emirate	Territory ('Caucasus Emirate')	2007/ 2007	359	–
Middle East					
Iran (Iran, Iraq)	Government of Iran				
	vs Partî Jiyanî Azadî Kurdistan (PJAK, Free Life Party of Kurdistan)	Government	2005/ 2005	219	..
Iraq	Government of Iraq, USA				
	vs Ansar al-Islam (Supporters of Islam)	Government	2003/ 2004	27	..
	vs Dawlat al-'Iraq al-Islamiyya (ISI, Islamic State of Iraq)	Government	2004/ 2004	834	–
Israel	Government of Israel				
	vs Harakat al-Muqawarna al-Islamiyya (Hamas, Islamic Resistance Movement)	Territory (Palestinian territories)	1989/ 1993	25	..
	vs Harakat al-Jihad al-Islami fi Filastin (PIJ, Palestinian Islamic Jihad)	Territory (Palestinian territories)	1987/ 1995	31	+
Syria	Government of Syria				
	vs Free Syrian Army (FSA)	Government	2011/ 2011	842	..
Turkey (Iraq, Turkey)	Government of Turkey				
	vs Partiya Karkerên Kurdistan (PKK, Kurdistan Workers' Party)	Territory ('Kurdistan')	1983/ 1984	599	+ +
Yemen	Government of Yemen, USA				
	vs al-Qaeda in the Arabian Peninsula (AQAP)	Government	2009/ 2009	1 140	+ +

CAR = Central African Republic; DRC = Democratic Republic of the Congo.

[a] Location refers to the state whose government is being challenged by an opposition organization. If fighting took place elsewhere, all countries where fighting took place are listed in brackets. The location name appears once for each conflict in the location. There can only be 1 conflict over government and 1 conflict over a specific territory in a given location.

[b] Start year refers to the onset of a given dyad (i.e. the fighting between a government and a rebel group or another government). The first year given is when the first recorded battle-related death in the dyad occurred and the second year is the year when fighting caused at least 25 battle-related deaths for the first time.

[c] 'Change from 2010' is measured as the increase or decrease in the number of battle-related deaths in 2011 compared to the number of battle-related deaths in 2010. The symbols represent the following changes: + + = increase in battle-related deaths of >50%; + = increase in battle-related deaths of >10 to 50%; 0 = stable rate of battle-related deaths (–10 to +10%); – = decrease in battle-related deaths of >10 to 50%; – – = decrease in battle-related deaths of >50%; . . = the conflict was not active in 2010.

[d] The following countries contributed troops to the coalition in 2011: Albania, Armenia, Australia, Austria, Azerbaijan, Belgium, Bosnia and Herzegovina, Bulgaria, Canada, Croatia, Czech Republic, Denmark, El Salvador, Estonia, Finland, France, Georgia, Germany, Greece, Hungary, Iceland, Ireland, Italy, Latvia, Lithuania, Luxembourg, FYR Macedonia, Malaysia, Mongolia, Montenegro, Netherlands, New Zealand, Norway, Poland, Portugal, Romania, Singapore, Slovakia, Slovenia, Spain, Sweden, South Korea, Tonga, Turkey, Ukraine, UAE, UK and USA.

Source: UCDP Dyadic Dataset v. 1-2012 and UCDP Battle-related Deaths Dataset v. 5-2012b, <http://www.pcr.uu.se/research/ucdp/datasets/>.

Internationalized intrastate conflicts have become increasingly common. In both 2010 and 2011 there were nine such conflicts, the highest number in the period. This meant that in 2010, 29 per cent of active state-based conflicts had the involvement of an external actor. This is a very high proportion, not just for 2002–11 but also in comparison with a longer time period.[6] Since external involvement tends to prolong conflicts, this may not bode well for future peacemaking efforts.[7]

The internationalized intrastate conflicts active in 2002–11 can be divided into two broad (and sometimes overlapping) groups: (a) conflicts linked to the USA's 'global war on terrorism', such as the wars in Afghanistan and Iraq and the USA's conflict with al-Qaeda; and (b) cases of government intervention in internal conflicts in neighbouring countries, such as the conflict between Uganda and the Lord's Resistance Army (LRA), where the government in 2011 received support from the Central African Republic (CAR), the Democratic Republic of the Congo (DRC) and South Sudan.

Of the 73 state-based conflicts active in 2002–11, 29 (or 40 per cent) were fought in Africa, 27 (37 per cent) in Asia, 9 in the Middle East (12 per cent), 4 in Europe (5 per cent) and 4 in the Americas (5 per cent). While Africa started the decade with the highest number of conflicts, it was overtaken by

---

[6] See Themnér, L. and Wallensteen, P., 'Armed conflicts, 1946–2010', *Journal of Peace Research*, vol. 48, no. 4 (July 2011), pp. 525–36.

[7] See e.g. Cunningham, D. E., 'Blocking resolution: how external states can prolong civil wars', *Journal of Peace Research*, vol. 47, no. 2 (Mar. 2012), pp. 115–27.

Table 1.4. State-based conflict, by intensity, type and region, 2002–11

	2002	2003	2004	2005	2006	2007	2008	2009	2010	2011
Total	**32**	**30**	**32**	**32**	**33**	**35**	**37**	**36**	**31**[a]	**37**
Intensity										
Minor	26	25	25	27	28	31	32	30	27	31
War	6	5	7	5	5	4	5	6	4	6
Type										
Interstate	1	2	–	–	–	–	1	–	–	1
Intrastate	28	26	28	26	27	30	30	28	22	27
Internationalized intrastate	3	2	4	6	6	5	6	8	9	9
Region										
Africa	15	10	10	7	10	12	13	12	10	15
Americas	2	1	3	2	2	3	3	3	3	2
Asia and Oceania	12	15	14	16	15	14	15	15	12	13
Europe	1	1	2	2	1	2	2	1	1	1
Middle East	2	3	3	5	5	4	4	5	5	6

[a] One conflict has been added to the total for 2010 given in *SIPRI Yearbook 2011*, that between the Ethiopian Government and the Oromo Liberation Front, because newly available information indicates that it passed the threshold of 25 battle-related deaths in that year.

Asia and Oceania between 2003 and 2010, due mainly to a large increase in the number of conflicts in Central and South Asia. During this period Asia saw the resumption of the conflicts in Afghanistan and in Pakistan's Balochistan province, and the escalation of low-intensity violence between the Thai Government and insurgents in southern Thailand, which first crossed the threshold of 25 battle-related deaths in 2003. There were no state-based conflicts recorded in Oceania in 2002–11.

Simultaneously, a number of conflicts came to an end in Africa, although some only temporarily (CAR, Chad and Somalia) and others seemingly more permanently (Angola and the Republic of the Congo). This positive trend in Africa was sharply reversed in 2011. New conflicts erupted in Libya and Sudan as well as in the newly independent South Sudan at the same time as conflicts that had been dormant for many years once again turned violent (e.g. in Côte d'Ivoire and Senegal).

Over the decade, the number of battle-related deaths in African conflicts decreased somewhat, going from over 7100 in 2002 to under 6500 in 2011, although the lowest figure was in 2005 (see figure 1.4). Asian conflicts turned markedly more deadly, however, increasing by roughly 4500 fatalities (63 per cent) from almost 7100 in 2002 to just less than 11 600 in 2011, and reaching a peak of 21 707 in 2009. The pattern was mainly driven by developments in Central and South Asia, particularly the high-intensity conflicts in Afghanistan and Pakistan.

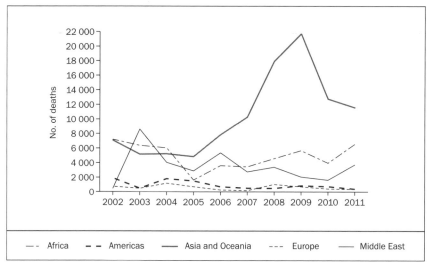

Figure 1.4. Battle-related deaths in state-based conflicts, by region, 2002–11

The number of battle-related deaths fell in both the Americas and Europe, despite similar numbers of conflicts in both regions at the start and end of the period. A peak of over 1000 battle-related deaths in Europe in 2004 was driven by an escalation of the conflict between the Russian Government and the self-proclaimed Chechen Republic of Ichkeria. Another, in 2008, was driven by the outbreak of renewed fighting between the Government of Georgia and the self-proclaimed Republic of South Ossetia, supported by Russia. Both of these conflicts terminated during the period, influencing the decreasing trend in the number of fatalities. The decrease in the Americas was largely related to the de-escalation of the conflict in Colombia, between the government and the Fuerzas Armadas Revolucionarias de Colombia (FARC, Revolutionary Armed Forces of Colombia), and the conflict between the US Government and al-Qaeda.[8]

The number of battle-related deaths in the Middle East rose from fewer than 500 in 2002 to more than 3700 in 2011, a nearly 700-per cent increase. This reflected dramatic developments in the region. In 2002 the deadly conflicts in Iraq and Yemen had yet to begin and in 2011, six conflicts were active and the Arab Spring had triggered the outbreak of the conflict between the Syrian Government and the Free Syrian Army.

---

[8] While the fighting in the conflict between the USA and its allies and al-Qaeda started on US soil with a series of terrorist attacks on 11 Sep. 2001, it then moved to other parts of the world. In 2002–11 fighting in this conflict mainly took place in Afghanistan and Pakistan.

Non-state conflicts

A non-state conflict is defined as the use of armed force between two organized groups—neither of which is the government of a state—that results in at least 25 battle-related deaths in a year. Non-state conflicts are divided into three subcategories according to the groups' level of organization: (*a*) conflicts between formally organized groups such as rebel groups and militias; (*b*) conflicts between informally organized supporters and affiliates of political parties and candidates ('informally organized supporter groups'); and (*c*) conflicts between informally organized groups that share a common identification along ethnic, clan, religious, national or tribal lines ('informally organized ethnic or religious groups').[9] Thus, non-state conflict relates to a broad spectrum of violence that tends to greatly affect the civilian population but often has fewer implications for international relations than state-based conflict. For example, the category includes conflicts between highly organized groups—such as the two factions of the separatist National Socialist Council of Nagaland (NSCN), NSCN–Isaac–Muviah and NSCN–Khaplang, which are fighting in the Nagaland region in north-eastern India—as well as conflicts between ethnic communities in the Horn of Africa such as that between the Toposa and Turkana in north-western Kenya.[10]

A total of 223 non-state conflicts were active worldwide in 2002–11, including 38 that were active in 2011 (see table 1.5). There was a slight increase in the number of active non-state conflicts over the decade, but as with state-based conflicts the rise was far from smooth (see table 1.6).

The increase in the number of conflicts was accompanied by a rise in the average number of fatalities (see figure 1.5). The 35 conflicts fought in 2002 caused a little over 5800 fatalities, making the average number of people killed per conflict 166; while the 38 conflicts in 2011 accounted for almost 6400 fatalities, with an average of 168 fatalities per conflict. However, trends in non-state conflict numbers and fatalities over the decade differ. This is most clearly illustrated by the change from 2008 to 2009, when the number of conflicts dropped by 9 but the number of fatalities increased by as much as 1700. This increase was mainly driven by the violent escalation

---

[9] There is a potential overlap between the types of non-state conflict. E.g. in many countries supporters of different political parties are almost by definition members of a specific ethnic group. During election years these groups are mobilized under a political banner, whereas they are mobilized as an ethnic group in conflicts occurring in other years. To be able to get a good overview and to follow a conflict even though it is reported in different ways in different years, UCDP has a coding rule that if there is a conflict between 2 ethnic groups in 1 year, and these ethnic groups are then involved in fighting mobilized along political lines (i.e. as supporters of a party) in another year, all conflict years are coded as part of the same ethnic conflict.

[10] See e.g. Baumann, J. et al., 'Organized violence in the Horn of Africa', *SIPRI Yearbook 2012*.

Table 1.5. Non-state conflicts in 2011

For more detailed definitions of the terms used see 'Sources and methods' below.

Location[a]	Side A	Side B	Organization level[b]	Start year[c]	Fatalities, 2011	Change from 2010[d]
Africa						
CAR	CPJP	UFDR	1	2011	60	..
Côte d'Ivoire	Guéré	Malinké	3	2011	33	..
DRC	FDC	FDLR	1	2011	27	..
Guinea	Kpelle	Malinké	3	2011	25	..
Kenya	Borana	Turkana	3	2011	29	..
Kenya	Dassanetch	Turkana	3	1997	55	..
Kenya	Toposa	Turkana	3	1992	26	..
Nigeria	Birom	Fulani	3	2010	100	+ +
Nigeria	Christians (Nigeria)	Muslims (Nigeria)	3	1991	830	..
Nigeria	Ezilo	Ezza	3	2011	50	..
Nigeria	Fulani	Tiv	3	2011	124	..
Nigeria	Hausa	Sayawa	3	2011	38	..
Nigeria	Supporters of ACN	Supporters of PDP	2	2008	26	..
Somalia	Al-Shabab	Shabelle Valley Alliance (SVA)	1	2011	36	..
Somalia	Forces of Shayk Muhammad Said Atom	Puntland state of Somalia	1	2010	33	– –
Somalia	Sa'ad subclan of Habar Gidir clan (Hawiye)	Suleiman subclan of Habar Gidir clan (Hawiye)	3	2004	40	..
Sudan	Atuot Dinka	Jur Beli	3	2011	43	..
Sudan	Bor Dinka	Murle	3	2007	44	..
Sudan	Dinka	Nuer	3	1997	133	–
Sudan	Gony Dinka	Thiyic Dinka	3	2011	95	..
Sudan	Lou Nuer	Murle	3	2006	1 415	..
Sudan	Misseria	Ngok Dinka	3	2011	212	..
Americas						
Mexico	CIDA	La Barredora	1	2011	105	..
Mexico	Gulf Cartel	Los Zetas	1	2010	345	–
Mexico	Jalisco Cartel New Generation (Cártel de Jalisco Nueva Generación)	La Resistancia	1	2011	33	..
Mexico	Jalisco Cartel New Generation	Los Zetas	1	2011	101	..
Mexico	Juarez Cartel	Sinaloa Cartel	1	2008	1 668	–
Mexico	La Familia Templarios (the Knights Templar)	Los Caballeros	1	2011	100	..
Mexico	Los Zetas	Sinaloa Cartel	1	2010	85	+ +
Asia and Oceania						
Afghanistan	Hizb-i Islami-yi Afghanistan	Taliban	1	1994	25	– –
India	NSCN–Isaac–Muivah faction	NSCN–Khaplang faction	1	2005	37	..
Pakistan	Lashkar-e-Islam (Army of Islam)	Lashkar (army) of Zakakhel tribe	1	2011	128	..

Location[a]	Side A	Side B	Organization level[b]	Start year[c]	Fatalities, 2011	Change from 2010[d]
Pakistan	Lashkar-e-Islam	TTP–Tariq Afridi faction	1	2011	41	..
Pakistan	Lashkar of the Kukikhel clan	TTP	1	2011	60	..
Pakistan	Lashkar of the Masozai Qaumi tribe	TTP	1	2011	79	..
Philippines	Bangsamoro Islamic Freedom Fighters (BIFF)	Moro Islamic Liberation Front (MILF)	1	2011	31	..
Middle East						
Egypt	Copts (Egypt)	Muslims (Egypt)	3	2011	31	..
Syria	Opponents of Bashar al-Assad	Supporters of Bashar al-Assad	2	2011	30	..

ACN = Action Congress of Nigeria; CIDA = Cártel Independiente de Acapulco (Independent Cartel of Acapulco); CPJP = Convention des patriotes pour la justice et la paix (Convention of Patriots for Justice and Peace); FDC = Forces de défense congolaise (Congolese Defence Force); FDLR = Forces démocratiques de libération du Rwanda (Democratic Liberation Forces of Rwanda); NSCN = National Socialist Council of Nagaland; PDP = People's Democratic Party; TTP = Tehrik-i-Taliban Pakistan (Taliban Movement of Pakistan); UFDR = Union des Forces démocratiques pour le rassemblement (Union of Democratic Forces for Unity).

[a] Location refers to the geographical location of the fighting.

[b] Organization level: 1 = formally organized groups; 2 = informally organized supporter groups; and 3 = informally organized ethnic or religious groups. See 'Sources and methods' for full details.

[c] Start year is the first year (since 1988) when conflict caused 25 fatalities.

[d] 'Change from 2010' is measured as the increase or decrease in the number of battle-related deaths in 2011 compared to the number of battle-related deaths in 2010. The symbols represent the following changes: + + = increase in battle-related deaths of >50%; + = increase in battle-related deaths of >10 to 50%; 0 = stable rate of battle-related deaths (–10 to +10%); – = decrease in battle-related deaths of >10 to 50%; – – = decrease in battle-related deaths of >50%; .. = the conflict was not active in 2010.

Source: UCDP Non-state Conflict Dataset, v. 2.4-2012, 1989–2011, <http://www.pcr.uu.se/research/ucdp/datasets/>.

of the conflict between the Lou Nuer and Murle ethnic groups in Southern Sudan and between Ahlu Sunna Waljamaca and al-Shabab in Somalia.

The most common type of non-state conflict in 2002–11 was conflict between informally organized ethnic or religious groups. Of the 223 non-state conflicts, 128 (57 per cent) were fought between such groups. Eighty-seven of the conflicts (39 per cent) were between formally organized groups. Conflicts between informally organized supporter groups were uncommon: only 8 (4 per cent) were recorded in the entire period. Non-state conflict involving informally organized supporter groups was the least common of the three subcategories in all years of the period.

Table 1.6. Non-state conflict, by subcategory and region, 2002–11

	2002	2003	2004	2005	2006	2007	2008	2009	2010	2011
Total	**35**	**39**	**26**	**29**	**27**	**19**	**35**	**26**	**27**	**38**
Subcategory										
Formally organized groups	13	15	13	11	7	10	13	9	16	18
Informally organized supporter groups	1	3	1	–	1	–	2	1	–	2
Informally organized ethnic or religious groups	21	21	12	18	19	9	20	16	11	18
Region										
Africa	30	34	20	22	21	11	23	18	13	22
Americas	2	2	3	3	–	–	3	3	7	7
Asia and Oceania	2	2	2	4	5	5	8	5	6	7
Europe	–	–	–	–	–	–	–	–	–	–
Middle East	1	1	1	–	1	3	1	–	1	2

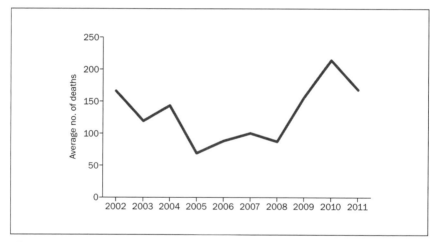

Figure 1.5. Average number of battle-related deaths in non-state conflicts, 2002–11

The vast majority of non-state conflicts in 2002–11 were located in Africa. Most of them were clustered in a few countries. Of the 165 non-state conflicts in Africa over the decade, 125 (or almost 76 per cent) were fought in Ethiopia, Kenya, Nigeria, Somalia and Sudan.

While most deaths in non-state conflicts occurred in Africa, the average 161 deaths per conflict there was well below the corresponding figure for the Americas, 524. This is to be expected, since most non-state conflicts in

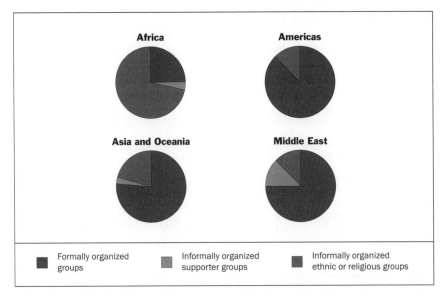

Figure 1.6. Subcategories of non-state conflict, by region, 2002–11

Africa involved ethnic, clan, religious, national or tribal groups (see figure 1.6), which cannot mobilize resources as effectively as formally organized rebel groups or militias, which accounted for the majority of non-state conflicts in other regions. The Americas, in contrast, is one of the regions with the highest proportion of non-state conflicts between formally organized groups. Over the period, most non-state conflicts in the Americas were fought between rebel groups and pro-government militias (e.g. FARC and the pro-government Autodefensas Unidas de Colombia, AUC), rival criminal gangs (e.g. Comando Vermelho and Terceiro Comando in Brazil) or drug cartels (e.g. the Juarez and Sinaloa cartels in Mexico). In 2011 all non-state conflicts in the Americas were located in Mexico and were fought between drug cartels. Many of these conflicts continued into 2013.[11]

One-sided violence

One-sided violence is defined as the use of armed force by the government of a state or by a formally organized group against unorganized civilians that results in at least 25 deaths. A state or group that kills 25 or more unarmed civilians during a year is registered as carrying out one-sided violence in the UCDP data. This includes a wide variety of situations, from

---

[11] On security spending related to the drugs war in Central America see chapter 3, section IV, in this volume.

Table 1.7. One sided-violence in 2011

For more detailed definitions of the terms used see 'Sources and methods' below.

Location[a]	Actor	Start year[b]	Fatalities, 2011	Change from 2010[c]
Africa				
CAR, DRC, Sudan	Lord's Resistance Army (LRA)	1989	145	– –
Côte d'Ivoire	Alliance des Jeunes Patriotes pour le sursaut national (AJPSN, Alliance of Young Patriots for National Revival)	2011	52	..
Côte d'Ivoire	Forces républicaines de Côte d'Ivoire (FRCI, Republican Forces of Côte d'Ivoire)	2011	49	..
Côte d'Ivoire	Government of Côte d'Ivoire	2000	277	..
Libya	Government of Libya	1989	152	..
Nigeria	Government of Nigeria	1990	32	..
Nigeria	Jama'atu Ahlis Sunna Lidda'awati wal-Jihad (Boko Haram)	2010	89	0
Somalia	Al-Shabab	2008	44	– –
Somalia	Government of Somalia	1989	36	..
Sudan	Government of Sudan	1989	174	..
Americas				
Mexico, Guatemala	Los Zetas	2010	268	+ +
Asia and Oceania				
Afghanistan	Taliban	2004	60	– –
India	Communist Party of India–Maoist (CPI–Maoist)	2005	184	–
Myanmar	Government of Myanmar	1992	107	+ +
Pakistan	Tehrik-i-Taliban Pakistan (TTP, Taliban Movement of Pakistan)	2007	198	– –
Pakistan, Afghanistan	Lashkar-e-Jhangvi (LeJ, Army of Jhangvi)	1998	121	–
Thailand	Patani insurgents	2004	116	–
Viet Nam	Government of Viet Nam	2011	72	..
Europe				
Russia	Forces of the Caucasus Emirate	2010	40	–
Middle East				
Bahrain	Government of Bahrain	2011	26	..
Iraq	Dawlat al-'Iraq al-Islamiyya (ISI, Islamic State of Iraq)	2004	322	– –
Syria	Government of Syria	2011	2 924	..
Yemen	Government of Yemen	2011	142	..

[a] Location refers to the geographical location of the one-sided violence.

[b] Start year is the first year (since 1988) when one-sided violence caused 25 fatalities.

[c] 'Change from 2010' is measured as the increase or decrease in the number of fatalities in 2011 compared to the number of fatalities in 2010. The symbols represent the following changes: + + = increase in fatalities of >50%; + = increase in fatalities of >10 to 50%; 0 = stable rate of fatalities (–10 to +10%); – = decrease in fatalities of >10 to 50%; – – = decrease in fatalities of >50%; .. = the conflict was not active in 2010.

Source: UCDP One-sided Violence Dataset, v. 1.4-2012, 1989–2011, <http://www.pcr.uu.se/research/ucdp/datasets/>.

Table 1.8. One-sided violence, by actor and region, 2002–11

	2002	2003	2004	2005	2006	2007	2008	2009	2010	2011
Total	**47**	**41**	**43**	**32**	**30**	**27**	**27**	**19**	**19**	**23**
Actor type										
Non-state actors	34	30	33	22	19	18	20	15	18	13
State actors	13	11	10	10	11	9	7	4	1	10
Region										
Africa	26	23	18	12	10	15	14	8	7	10
Americas	2	1	3	4	1	–	2	1	2	1
Asia and Oceania	14	12	13	8	14	9	10	7	8	7
Europe	1	1	3	–	–	–	–	–	1	1
Middle East	4	4	6	8	5	3	1	3	1	4

largely small-scale, day-to-day attacks, such as those by the Ivorian militia Alliance des Jeunes Patriotes pour le sursaut national (AJPSN, Alliance of Young Patriots for National Revival, commonly called the Young Patriots)—which supports former president Laurent Gbagbo—to large-scale cases such as the Syrian Government's attacks on civilians throughout 2011.

A total of 130 actors were recorded as carrying out one-sided violence in 2002–11, including 23 active in 2011 (see table 1.7). The annual number declined markedly in the period, starting at 47 in 2002 (see table 1.8).

This decline was matched by a drop in the number of fatalities in one-sided violence (see figure 1.7). Between 2002 and 2008 the number of fatalities decreased every year, falling by 43 per cent between 2004 and 2005, due in part to a decline in one-sided violence by the Sudanese Government and the Janjaweed militia in Darfur. There were widely oscillating figures in the last three years of the period: an increase by 63 per cent in 2009, as both the Forces démocratiques de libération du Rwanda (FDLR, Democratic Liberation Forces of Rwanda) and the LRA stepped up their campaigns against civilians in Central Africa, was followed by a 49 per cent drop the following year, as the activities of these two actors de-escalated markedly. In 2011 the number of fatalities increased dramatically again, this time by 81 per cent. An increase of this magnitude has not been recorded previously in the data, and it was largely driven by the actions of the Syrian Government, which caused almost 3000 fatalities during the year.

As with non-state conflicts, the trend in fatality numbers from one-sided violence can differ from the trend in actor numbers. For example, as the number of actors carrying out one-sided violence increased from 41 to 43 between 2003 and 2004, the number of fatalities decreased from approximately 10 800 to fewer than 7900. This type of discrepancy is most often due to a change in the behaviour of single actors. In 2003–2004 the drop was to a large extent due to developments in Liberia, where the govern-

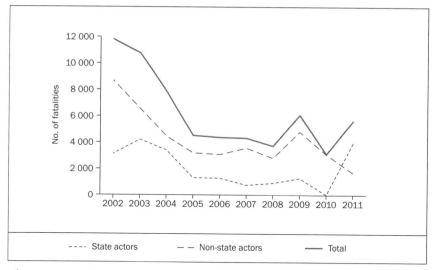

Figure 1.7. Fatalities in one-sided violence, by type of actor, 2002–11

ment carried out extensive one-sided violence in 2003, but none in 2004, when a peace deal had been reached between the warring parties. Furthermore, the Congolese rebel group Forces nationalistes et integrationistes (FNI, Nationalist and Integrationist Forces) and the Janjaweed militia in Sudan de-escalated their activities markedly.

Non-state actors tend to be the most common perpetrators of one-sided violence, as they were in all years of the period 2002–2011, and over the period as a whole, 95 of the 130 actors (73 per cent) were rebel groups or militias. It is interesting to note, however, that in 2011 this pattern was at its weakest, with only three more non-state than state actors registered. This at least partly reflects the developments in North Africa and the Middle East, where governments targeted peaceful demonstrators during the Arab Spring. It was also in part due a significant decrease in the number of non-state actors carrying out one-sided violence, which fell by more than 60 per cent over the period as a whole. Although one-sided violence by individual government actors can be particularly lethal, as illustrated by the actions of the Liberian Government in 2003 and the Syrian Government in 2011, taken together, non-state actors killed more civilians in all years of the period apart from 2011. Nevertheless, the two actors that killed the most civilians during a given year in 2002–11 were both governments: the Syrian Government in 2011 and the Sudanese Government, whose attacks in Darfur in 2004 led to the deaths of more than 2500 civilians. The third highest number of deaths was caused by the Sunni Islamist opposition group Dawlat al-'Iraq al-Islamiyya (Islamic State of Iraq, ISI), which killed almost 2000 civilians in 2007.

Nearly half of the 130 actors targeting civilians in 2002–11 were in Africa (63), followed by Asia and Oceania (38), the Middle East (17), the Americas (7) and Europe (5). Over the decade, Africa saw the highest number of one-sided actors in all but two years, when Asia and Oceania had more.

Africa was the region with the highest number of fatalities in all but four years of the decade. In 2006 and 2010 the highest number of fatalities was in Asia; in 2006 mainly due to a marked increase in the number of one-sided actors, and in 2010 due more to a dramatic decrease in fatalities in Africa. In 2007 and 2011 the highest number of fatalities was recorded for the Middle East, mainly due to attacks by ISI (in 2007) and the Syrian Government's targeting of unarmed civilians during the popular uprising that began in February 2011 and that escalated as the year passed.

Conclusions

There was little change in the rate of organized violence over the 10-year period 2002–11, both in terms of the numbers of actors engaging in these types of activity and the number of fatalities. One-sided violence exhibited a clear downward trend during the period, but this was counterbalanced by increases in state-based and non-state conflict.

Looking at the incidence of organized violence, it is clear that the three categories show markedly different patterns over time. The annual number of non-state conflicts can rise and fall sharply, displaying no obvious trends. In contrast, major changes in the number of state-based conflicts tend to happen slowly; while the number of state-based conflicts hovers around a mean value of 33 throughout 2002–11, this is well below the peak year 1992, when 53 conflicts were active.[12] Developments in the incidence of one-sided violence fall somewhere between these two extremes.

Another interesting difference between non-state and state-based conflicts is that the former tend to be more sporadic and short-term. Once again, the pattern for one-sided violence falls between the two, with numerous examples of actors only recorded in the data for one or two years while some other actors target civilians over long periods.

All three categories of organized violence were most common in Africa. However, while non-state conflicts were clustered in some countries and regions, notably the Horn of Africa and Nigeria, many of the larger state-based conflicts in Africa were located elsewhere, for example in Liberia and North Africa. However, the average number of fatalities in African non-state conflicts was lower than, for example, in the drug-related non-state

[12] Themnér, L. and Wallensteen, P., 'Armed conflict, 1946–2011', *Journal of Peace Research*, vol. 49, no. 4 (2012), pp. 565–75.

violence in South America, which in part reflects the level of organization of the actors involved.

The data for 2002–11 illustrate the difficulty of drawing direct links between patterns in the different categories of organized violence studied. There are some shared traits, but also many important differences. The different categories of violence can certainly influence each other (as shown in sections I and II above). However, the mechanisms are complex, and understanding them—let alone how to manage them—requires in-depth, case-based study.

Sources and methods

Definition of state-based conflict

The UCDP defines state-based conflict as a contested incompatibility concerning government or territory over which the use of armed force between the military forces of two parties, of which at least one is the government of a state, has resulted in at least 25 battle-related deaths in a calendar year. The separate elements are defined as follows.

1. *Incompatibility that concerns government or territory.* This refers to the stated generally incompatible positions of the parties to the conflict. An *incompatibility that concerns government* refers to incompatible positions regarding the state's type of political system or the composition of the government. It may also involve an aim to replace the current government. An *incompatibility that concerns territory* refers to incompatible positions regarding the status of a territory and may involve demands for secession or autonomy (intrastate conflict) or aims to change the state in control of a certain territory (interstate conflict).

2. *Use of armed force.* This refers to the use of armed force by the military forces of the parties to the conflict in order to promote the parties' general position in the conflict. Arms are defined as any material means of combat, including anything from manufactured weapons to sticks, stones, fire or water.

3. *Party.* This refers to the government of a state, any of its allies, an opposition organization or an alliance of opposition organizations. The *government of a state* is the party that is generally regarded as being in central control, even by those organizations seeking to seize power. If this criterion is not applicable, the party controlling the capital of the state is regarded as the government. An *opposition organization* is any non-governmental group that has announced a name for itself as well as its political goals and that has used armed force to achieve them. A state or a multinational organization that supports one of the primary parties with regular troops may also be included in the table. In order to be listed in the table, this secondary party must share the position of one of the warring parties. A traditional peacekeeping operation is not considered to be a party to the conflict but is rather seen as an impartial part of a consensual peace process.

4. *State.* A state is an internationally recognized sovereign government controlling a specific territory or an internationally non-recognized government controlling a specific territory whose sovereignty is not disputed by an internationally recognized sovereign state that previously controlled the territory in question.

5. *Battle-related deaths.* This refers to deaths directly related to combat between the warring parties and can include both deaths on the battlefield and civilians caught in cross-fire. UCDP defines a state-based conflict that has incurred at least 25 battle-related deaths during a calendar year as a minor state-based conflict and any with at least 1000 battle-related deaths during a calendar year as a war in that year.

Definition of non-state conflict

The UCDP defines non-state conflict as the use of armed force between two organized armed groups, neither of which is the government of a state, which results in at least 25 battle-related deaths in a year. The separate elements are defined as follows.

1. *Organized groups.* There are three levels of organization. *Formally organized groups* (*organizational level 1*) are rebel and other organized groups whose level of organization is high enough to include them in the state-based conflict category. These include rebel groups with an announced name, as well as military factions. *Informally organized supporter groups* (*organizational level 2*) are groups composed of supporters and affiliates of political parties and candidates. These are commonly not groups that are permanently organized for combat, but which at times use their organizational structures for such purposes. *Informally organized ethnic or religious groups* (*organizational level 3*) are groups that share a common identification along ethnic, clan, religious, national or tribal lines. These are not groups that are permanently organized for combat, but which at times organize themselves to engage in fighting.

2. *Battle-related deaths.* The definition of battle-related death varies according to the level of organization of the fighting groups. For formally organized groups (organizational level 1) the recording of battle-related deaths follows the same criteria as for state-based conflict, that is, the warring groups must target representatives of the other formally organized group. Targeting of civilians, even if those civilians are of, for example, the same ethnicity as a group's rivals, is coded as one-sided violence. For informally organized groups (organizational levels 2 and 3), the definition of battle-related death is extended to include both civilian and armed victims as long as there is a pattern of violent (lethal) interaction between the groups, with both parties carrying out attacks.

Definition of one-sided violence

The UCDP defines one-sided violence as the use of armed force by the government of a state or by a formally organized group against civilians, which results in at least 25 deaths in a calendar year. Extrajudicial killings in custody are excluded. The separate elements are defined as follows.

1. *Use of armed force.* This is the use of arms in order to exert violent force, resulting in death. Arms are defined as any material means of combat, including anything from manu-factured weapons to sticks, stones, fire or water.

2. *Government.* See above.

3. *State.* See above.

4. *Formally organized group.* This can be any non-governmental group of people that has announced a name for the group and that uses armed force. This corresponds to 'opposition organization' as defined for the state-based conflict category and to 'formally organized group' as defined for the non-state conflict category.

5. *Extrajudicial killings in custody.* This is the killing by the government of a state of a person in its custody. In custody is defined as when a person is located in a prison or another type of government facility.

Sources

The data presented here is based on information taken from a wide selection of publicly avail-able sources, both printed and electronic. The sources include news agencies, newspapers, academic journals, research reports, and documents from international and multinational organizations and non-governmental organizations (NGOs). In order to collect information on the aims and goals of the parties to the conflict, documents of the warring parties (govern-ments, allies and opposition organizations) and, for example, the Internet sites of rebel groups are often consulted.

Independent news sources, carefully selected over a number of years, constitute the basis of the data collection. The Factiva news database is indispensable for the collection of general news reports. It contains more than 25 000 sources in 22 languages from 159 countries and provides sources from all three crucial levels of the news media: international (e.g. Agence France-Presse and Reuters), regional and local.

The UCDP regularly scrutinizes and revises the selection and combination of sources in order to maintain a high level of reliability and comparability between regions and countries. One important priority is to arrive at a balanced combination of sources of different origin with a view to avoiding bias. The reliability of the sources is judged using the expertise of the UCDP together with advice from a global network of experts (academics and policymakers). Both the independence of the source and the transparency of its origins are crucial. The latter is important because most sources are secondary, which means that the primary source also needs to be analysed in order to establish the reliability of a report. Each source is judged in relation to the context in which it is published. The potential interest of either the primary or secondary source secondary source in misrepresenting an event is taken into account, as are the general climate and extent of media censorship. Reports from NGOs and international organizations are particularly useful in this context, complementing media reporting and facilitating cross-checking. The criterion that a source should be independent does not, of course, apply to sources that are consulted precisely because they *are* biased, such as govern-ment documents or rebel groups' Internet sites. The UCDP is aware of the high level of scrutiny required and makes great efforts to ensure the authenticity of the material used.

Methods

The data on organized violence are compiled by calendar year. It includes data on conflict locations, type of incompatibility, onset of the conflict, warring parties, total number of battle-related deaths, number of battle-related deaths in a given year and change in battle-related deaths from the previous year. See also the notes for tables 1.2, 1.4 and 1.6.

The data on fatalities are given the most attention in coding for the UCDP database. Infor-mation on, for example, the date, news source, primary source, location and death toll is recorded for every event. Ideally, these individual events and figures are corroborated by two or more independent sources. The figures are then aggregated for the entire year of each con-flict. The aggregated figures are compared to total figures given in official documents, in special reports and in the news media. Regional experts such as researchers, diplomats and journalists are often consulted during the data collection. Their role is mainly to clarify the contexts in which the events occur, thus facilitating proper interpretation of the published sources.

UCDP codes three different fatality estimates—low, best and high—based on the reliability of reports and the conflicting number of deaths that can be reported for any violent event. All of the data presented here are based on the best estimate, which consists of the aggregated most reliable numbers for all incidents of each category of violence during a year. If different sources provide different estimates, an examination is made as to what source is the most reliable. If no such distinction can be made, UCDP as a rule includes the lower figure in the best estimate. UCDP is generally conservative when estimating the number of fatalities. As more in-depth information on a case of organized violence becomes available, the con-servative, event-based estimates often prove more correct than others widely cited in the news media. If no figures are available or if the numbers given are unreliable, the UCDP does not provide a figure. Figures are revised retroactively each year as new information becomes available.

2. Peace operations and conflict management

Overview

The number of personnel serving with multilateral peace operations worldwide fell by more than 10 per cent in 2012, as the slight reduction in personnel deployments that started in 2011 gathered pace. The large drop was due to the withdrawal of troops from the International Security Assistance Force (ISAF) in Afghanistan (see section I in this chapter). However, the reductions followed almost a decade of rapid expansion, and the total for deployments, at 233 642, was still the third highest since 2003.

Excluding ISAF, a different pattern emerged, as personnel deployments rose slightly. A total of 53 missions were active during 2012, one more than in 2011. Three new operations were launched, in Syria, Niger and Guinea-Bissau (see section II), and four missions closed (including one of the new missions). The small increases in both personnel deployments (excluding ISAF) and active missions in 2012 suggest that the trend, which had been downward since 2009, may be starting to stabilize.

The withdrawal of forces from ISAF was part of the transition process under which ISAF is handing over security responsibilities, district by district, to the Afghan national security forces. The transition, and ISAF's drawdown, are scheduled to be complete at the end of 2014. This is likely to sustain the downward trend in troop deployments. Even if Western attention were to completely refocus on, for example, the troubled Sahel region or Syria, new missions were to be deployed in those regions and the number of North Atlantic Treaty Organization (NATO) forces that remain in Afghanistan were sizeable, it is unlikely that these would balance the withdrawal of the 102 052 forces deployed with ISAF.

Nevertheless, some of the forces withdrawn from Afghanistan will probably be redeployed elsewhere and therefore the number of military personnel deployed outside Afghanistan is likely to increase. If they are not redeployed, some governments, particularly in the West, might fear legitimacy problems for their national armed forces at a time when they are under pressure to cut spending as part of austerity measures linked to the 2008 global financial crisis. Austerity was certainly a factor in the decisions of many countries, especially the United States, to accelerate the withdrawal of their troops from ISAF.

Austerity also led some states to be more critical of spending on peace operations and to increase budget constraints on missions in 2012. The United Nations Security Council increasingly imposed benchmarks and indicators to evaluate existing UN missions' effectiveness and efficiency, and linked these to future mandate renewals. More missions were given narrowed mandates focusing on a core set of tasks achievable within a defined time frame. Cooperation between UN missions was also re-emphasized. For example, the UN Mission in Liberia (UNMIL) and the UN Operation in Côte d'Ivoire (UNOCI) cooperated in responding to instability in the border region between the two countries, and inter-mission cooperation facilitated the rapid deployment of the short-lived UN Supervision Mission in Syria (UNSMIS).

Doubts about the capacity and will for protection of civilians (POC) in peace operations were reinforced in 2012. The UN operations in Côte d'Ivoire, the Democratic Republic of the Congo (DRC) and South Sudan were the subject of outrage, both in their host countries and internationally, for perceived high-profile failures in the area of POC in 2012 (see section III). However, the problem may lie more in unrealistic mandates and expectations. Missions given civilian protection mandates are not given the forces necessary to control and dominate the territory under their responsibility. In addition, current and potential troop-contributing countries have little incentive to risk their troops' lives for POC as long as their national interests are not at stake.

With the international response in Libya and the early stages of the response to the Syria crisis in 2011, including the deployment of an Arab League observer mission, some had seen the possible beginnings of a firm actionable commitment to the concept of the responsibility to protect (R2P). These hopes were dashed in 2012 as the international community proved unable to agree on any action to halt the violence in Syria. Much of the debate concerned the balance between R2P and state sovereignty.

Divisions in the international community were also visible in the response to a military coup in Guinea-Bissau, where the African Union (AU), the European Union (EU) and the UN refused to recognize a transitional government set up through a controversial process mediated by the Economic Community of West African States (ECOWAS).

Despite these doubts, divisions and budget constraints, there is no reason to believe that the number of operations will decrease significantly in the near future, and the number of troops deployed outside Afghanistan is in fact likely to grow. How deep the dip in total personnel deployments will be after the drawdown of ISAF, and how diffuse the future picture, depend on three factors: the depth of future budget cuts in the West (and the extent to which they are allowed to affect the military and peacekeeping capacity); the number of troops that are eventually deployed in Mali, the broader Sahel and potentially Syria; and the extent to which countries are willing to put R2P and POC into practice rather than simply express outrage over the lack of responsiveness.

JAÏR VAN DER LIJN

I. Global trends in peace operations

JANE DUNDON

A total of 53 peace operations were conducted in 2012, one more than in 2011 but still the third lowest number in the period 2003–12 (see figure 2.1). The number of personnel deployed with peace operations in 2012 was the third highest in the period, at 233 642; however, it was a marked drop, of 28 487, from the previous year's figure of 262 129 (see figure 2.2).[1] This drop was due to reductions in the International Security Assistance Force (ISAF) in Afghanistan, by far the largest single mission in 2012; excluding ISAF, deployments increased by 847 personnel. This is the first increase in total personnel figures excluding ISAF since 2008.

Three new missions opened in 2012: the Economic Community of West African States (ECOWAS) Mission in Guinea-Bissau (ECOMIB), the European Union (EU) Capacity Building Mission in Niger (EUCAP Sahel Niger) and the United Nations Supervision Mission in Syria (UNSMIS). Four missions closed during the year: the EU Police Mission in Bosnia and Herzegovina (EUPM), the UN Integrated Mission in Timor-Leste (UNMIT) and two missions in Syria, the League of Arab States Observer Mission to Syria and UNSMIS, both of which were forced to close (the Arab League mission after a month and UNSMIS after four months) due to high levels of violence, hampering the ability of the missions to implement their mandates. The small increase in the number of operations between 2011 and 2012 suggests that the trend, which has been downwards since 2009 (see figure 2.1), may be beginning to stabilize.[2]

The significant decrease in personnel deployments in 2012 was due principally to the withdrawal of 29 334 ISAF troops from Afghanistan (see section III below). ISAF troops accounted for 44 per cent of total deployments in 2012 (down from more than half in 2010 and 2011). Non-ISAF personnel deployments increased slightly in 2012, from 130 743 to 131 590.

During the year several operations reduced their personnel numbers, including the EU Military Operation in Bosnia and Herzegovina (EUFOR ALTHEA), the African Union (AU)/UN Hybrid Operation in Darfur (UNAMID), the UN Stabilization Mission in Haiti (MINUSTAH) and the UN Interim Force in Lebanon (UNIFIL), while the International Stabiliza-

---

[1] The figures for personnel deployments given here are generally estimates as of 31 Dec. 2012 or the date on which an operation terminated. They do not represent maximum numbers deployed or the total number of personnel deployed during the year.

[2] The quantitative analysis presented here draws on data collected by SIPRI to examine trends in peace operations in the 10-year period 2003–12. It is limited to operations that meet the SIPRI definition of a peace operation (see section IV below). The data presented provides a snapshot of ongoing peace operations in 2012 and is meant to serve as a reference point to enable comparative analysis between 2012 and previous years.

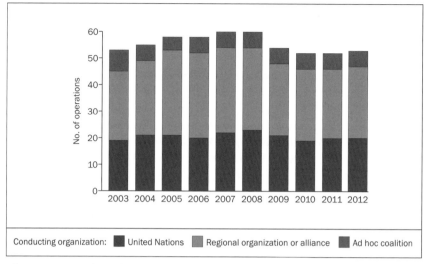

Figure 2.1. Number of multilateral peace operations, by type of conducting organization, 2003–12

tion Force (ISF) in Timor-Leste began its drawdown in November in preparation for a planned complete withdrawal in April 2012.

The three new operations launched in 2012 accounted for 921 personnel in total. In addition, several existing missions increased their personnel numbers. The UN Mission in South Sudan (UNMISS), which started in 2011, came close to reaching its authorized personnel figure of 7000 in 2012. The AU Mission in Somalia (AMISOM) almost doubled its troop numbers to 16 970 following a UN Security Council resolution in February that expanded the mission's operational scope and capacity.[3]

The UN, which was responsible for 20 of the 53 peace operations in 2012 (38 per cent), remained the main conducting organization (see figure 2.1). However, almost half of the total personnel deployed to peace operations worldwide—107 186 personnel (46 per cent)—were deployed to operations conducted by the North Atlantic Treaty Organization (NATO), mainly ISAF (see figure 2.2). This made NATO the largest conducting organization, in terms of personnel deployed, for the third consecutive year.[4]

ISAF, with 102 052 troops deployed, was the largest operation in 2012, for the fourth year running. The second and third largest missions were the UN Organization Stabilization Mission in the Democratic Republic of the Congo (MONUSCO) and UNAMID. Ten operations deployed more than

[3] UN Security Council Resolution 2036, 22 Feb. 2012.
[4] United Nations figures include peace operations led by the UN Department of Peacekeeping Operations, the UN Department of Political Affairs and UNAMID.

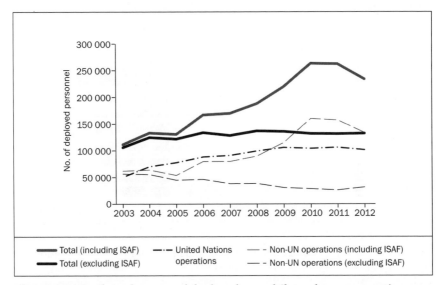

Figure 2.2. Number of personnel deployed to multilateral peace operations, 2003–12

ISAF = International Security Assistance Force.

5000 personnel: seven under UN command, two led by NATO and one AU mission (see table 2.2 in section IV).

Including ISAF, the largest contributor of troops to multilateral peace operations in 2012 was the USA. The top 10 troop contributors included only two European countries—the United Kingdom and Italy—compared to four in 2011 (see figure 2.3), a drop that is mainly due to the ISAF drawdown. Excluding ISAF, the picture changes: Pakistan becomes the largest contributor, followed by Bangladesh; the top 10 contributors are all South Asian and African countries. More than two-thirds of troops deployed with UN missions came from countries in the top 10 (excluding ISAF). Uganda, Burundi and Kenya contributed more troops to AMISOM than they did to UN missions. The top 10 contributors of civilian police in 2012 were also from South Asia and Africa, along with two Middle Eastern countries (see figure 2.4).

The total known cost of peace operations in 2012 was $9 billion. The UN accounted for the largest portion of this known cost—$7.2 billion (80 per cent). However, the reported costs of most non-UN operations do not include personnel costs, which are generally borne by personnel-contributing states; the actual costs of NATO operations, in particular, are likely to be much higher than those of UN operations.[5] This is due to the UN mostly

[5] United Nations, Department of Peacekeeping Operations, 'Background note: United National peacekeeping', June 2012, <http://www.un.org/en/peacekeeping/documents/backgroundnote.pdf>.

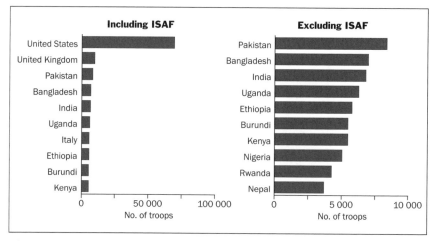

Figure 2.3. The top 10 contributors of troops to multilateral peace operations, including and excluding the International Security Assistance Force (ISAF) in Afghanistan, 2012

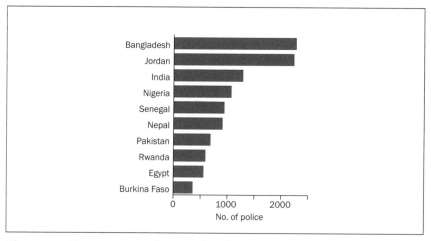

Figure 2.4. The top 10 contributors of civilian police to multilateral peace operations, 2012

using less expensive non-Western forces and to several measures in recent years to rationalize the use of UN peacekeeping resources, including a greater emphasis on cooperation between missions.[6]

---

[6] Gowan, R. and Gleason, M., 'UN peacekeeping: the next five years', New York University, Center on International Cooperation, Nov. 2012, <http://cic.nyu.edu/content/un-peacekeeping-next-five-years>, p. 8; and 'Peacekeeping and inter-mission cooperation', *Security Council Report: Monthly Forecast*, Dec. 2012.

II. New peace operations in 2012

JANE DUNDON AND JAÏR VAN DER LIJN

Three new multilateral peace operations opened in 2012: the United Nations Supervision Mission in Syria (UNSMIS), the Economic Community of West African States (ECOWAS) Mission in Guinea-Bissau (ECOMIB) and the European Union (EU) Capacity Building Mission in Niger (EUCAP Sahel Niger). EUCAP Sahel Niger was part of broader attempts by the international community to respond to growing instability in the Sahel region. Hence, this section also discusses progress in 2012 towards the deployment of a multilateral operation in Niger's neighbour, Mali, where an internal conflict broke out in 2012.[1]

Syria: the United Nations Supervision Mission in Syria

In early 2012 the year-old intrastate conflict in Syria showed little sign of abating. International condemnation of the violence in Syria was widespread. Following the closure of the League of Arab States Observer Mission to Syria in January, after barely a month's deployment, the UN took on a central role in mediating the conflict. Kofi Annan, a former UN Secretary-General, was appointed Joint Special Envoy of the United Nations and the Arab League on the Syria crisis on 23 February.[2]

Annan submitted a six-point peace plan to the Syrian Government, which included a proviso that the government should cease troop movements to, stop the use of heavy weapons in, and pull back troop concentrations in and around population centres.[3] The government accepted the proposal and Annan succeeded in brokering a ceasefire between the government and opposition forces in late March.[4] The government undertook to withdraw its military forces from residential areas beginning on 1 April.[5] However, immediately afterwards, and with negotiations ongoing, new government attacks on civilian centres were reported.[6] In response, the UN Security

---

[1] On the conflict in Mali see chapter 1, section I, in this volume.

[2] United Nations, Secretary-General, 'Kofi Annan appointed Joint Special Envoy of United Nations, League of Arab States on Syrian crisis', Joint statement, SG/SM 14124, 23 Feb. 2012.

[3] United Nations, Security Council, Statement by the President of the Security Council, S/PRST/2012/6, 21 Mar. 2012.

[4] 'Briefing by Special Envoy for Syria', What's in Blue blog, Security Council Report, 30 Mar 2012, <http://whatsinblue.org/2012/03/briefing-by-the-joint-special-envoy-on-syria.php>.

[5] United Nations, Security Council, Letter from Kofi Annan to the UN Secretary-General, Annex to S/2012/206, 10 Apr. 2012.

[6] Human Rights Watch (HRW), *'They Burned My Heart': War Crimes in Northern Idlib during Peace Plan Negotiations* (HRW: New York, May 2012).

Council called on the Syrian Government to immediately implement the terms of the agreement.[7]

On 14 April, when it appeared that the government was beginning to implement its commitments, the Security Council authorized an advance team of 30 unarmed military observers to report on the implementation of the ceasefire pending the deployment of a UN mission.[8] One week later, Security Council Resolution 2043 established UNSMIS to monitor the cessation of hostilities and support and monitor the implementation of Annan's six-point plan.[9] Amid growing concerns over the continuation of violence in Syria, Annan called for UNSMIS to be deployed urgently. Although it was initially planned that the mission would be deployed in three phases over a three-month period, the Arab League also emphasized the need for the urgent deployment and called for support to be provided from other UN missions in the region.[10] Subsequently, inter-mission cooperation played a vital role in the rapid deployment and operationalization of UNSMIS. Staff were redeployed from UN Interim Force in Lebanon (UNIFIL) and UN Disengagement Observer Force (UNDOF), which also provided logistical support.[11]

UNSMIS had an authorized strength of 300 unarmed military personnel and an appropriate civilian component.[12] The mission achieved full operational capacity within a month and, by the end of May, 271 military observers had been deployed to Syria. By June, 121 international civilian staff were deployed at the mission's Damascus headquarters to work on civil and political affairs, human rights, administration and support. Observers were based at the headquarters and eight sites around the country.[13]

Despite the rapid deployment of the UNSMIS observers, the security situation in Syria continued to deteriorate. On 20 July, as the ceasefire broke down, the Security Council decided that UNSMIS's mandate would be renewed for a final 30 days during which it must be reconfigured.[14] The renewal took several rounds of negotiations and demonstrated the stark divisions in the Security Council over whether or not to issue a resolution under Chapter VII of the UN Charter, which would permit action 'necessary to maintain or restore international peace and security'. Furthermore,

[7] United Nations, Security Council, Statement by the President of the Security Council, S/PRST/2012/10, 5 Apr. 2012.

[8] UN Security Council Resolution 2042, 14 Apr. 2012.

[9] UN Security Council Resolution 2043, 21 Apr. 2012.

[10] 'UNSMIS (Syria)', *Security Council Report: Monthly Forecast*, May 2012.

[11] Haq, A., Under-Secretary-General for Field Support, Statement at UN Security Council Open Meeting on Inter-Mission Cooperation, 12 Dec. 2012, <http://www.un.org/en/peacekeeping/articles/usg_ameerahhaq_12122012.pdf>.

[12] UN Security Council Resolution 2043 (note 9).

[13] United Nations, Security Council, Report of the Secretary-General on the implementation of Security Council Resolution 2043, S/2012/523, 6 July 2012.

[14] UN Security Council Resolution 2059, 20 July 2012.

in July China and Russia blocked an attempt to threaten the Syrian Government with economic sanctions for its continued use of violence, limiting the capacity and leverage of UNSMIS.[15]

From 2011, with memories of the intervention in Libya still fresh, there was much discussion, both inside and outside the Security Council, about the applicability of the responsibility to protect (R2P) to the Syrian crisis.[16] While R2P action up to and including armed intervention was vocally supported by several member states, including France, there was significant opposition from China and Russia. Also India and South Africa, among others, advocated a Syrian-led process.[17] With the failure to reach consensus, R2P was never invoked. According to many analysts, Western powers, unwilling to become embroiled in another complex, drawn out and costly conflict and fearful of the possible destabilization of the wider region, were not unhappy to use Chinese and Russian opposition as an excuse for inaction.[18]

Due to escalating violence and the mission's consequent inability to implement its mandate adequately, UNSMIS was terminated on 19 August 2012. It was to be replaced with a special liaison office mandated to support efforts to find a political solution to the crisis; however, that office had not been established by early 2013.[19]

The Sahel: the EU Capacity Building Mission in Niger and developments in Mali

Following the 2011 conflict in Libya, the Sahel region was increasingly afflicted by a combination of transnational organized crime, such as arms and drug trafficking, and groups designated by the EU and UN as terrorist organizations.[20] This exacerbated the proliferation of weapons in the region. As a result, regional stability, governance, and social and economic development, as well as the provision of humanitarian aid, came under threat, which in turn created more space for armed groups to operate.[21] Three issues received particular attention from the UN Security Council: a

[15] United Nations, Security Council, 6810th meeting, S/PV.6810, 19 July 2012; and United Nations, Security Council, Draft resolution, S/2012/538, 19 July 2012. See also chapter 10, section II, in this volume.

[16] Evans, G., 'Responding to atrocities: the new geopolitics of intervention', *SIPRI Yearbook 2012*.

[17] See International Coalition for the Responsibility to Protect, 'Crisis in Syria', <http://www.responsibilitytoprotect.org/index.php/crises/crisis-in-syria>.

[18] See e.g. Etzioni, A., 'Now is the time for U.S. to act on Syria', CNN, 16 Aug. 2012, <http://edition.cnn.com/2012/08/07/opinion/etzioni-syria>.

[19] 'Syria: UN observer mission to end, to be replaced by liaison office, official says', UN News Service, 16 Aug. 2012, <http://www.un.org/apps/news/story.asp?NewsID=42694>.

[20] On the conflict in Libya see Allansson, M. et al., 'The first year of the Arab Spring', *SIPRI Yearbook 2012*; and Fanchini, C., 'New peace operations in 2011', *SIPRI Yearbook 2012*, pp. 99–103.

[21] United Nations, Security Council, Statement by the President of the Security Council, S/PRST/2012/2, 21 Feb. 2012.

developing humanitarian crisis in the Sahel; instability in northern Mali; and the presence of extremist elements and terrorist groups, particularly al-Qaida in the Islamic Maghreb (AQIM) and the Mouvement pour le Tawhîd et du Jihad en Afrique de l'Ouest (MUJAO, Movement for Unity and Jihad in West Africa), both accused of human rights violations. The Security Council stated several times that it considered these challenges to be threats to international peace and security, that it welcomed initiatives to counter them, and that it recognized the efforts of, among others, the EU, the African Union (AU) and ECOWAS in this field. Combatting AQIM and affiliated groups was identified as a top priority and for this purpose capacity building for states in the Sahel in areas such as security sector reform (SSR) was encouraged.[22]

The EU Strategy for Security and Development in the Sahel, adopted by the Council of the EU in March 2011, argues that because the region is located in the EU's backyard, its stability and security are key concerns to the EU.[23] Instability would threaten EU interests in a number of spheres, including energy supplies, commerce and security, for example as a result of terrorism. The strategy focuses on Mali, Mauretania and Niger and advocates a 'regional, integrated and holistic strategy' to tackle the problems in the region, through fighting extremism, SSR, and strengthening governance and the rule of law. The strategy has been criticized for not including Algeria and Nigeria, two pivotal states in the region.[24] As part of the strategy's implementation, in 2012 the EU launched its first Common Security and Defence Policy (CSDP) mission in the Sahel, in Niger.[25]

The EU Capacity Building Mission in Niger

On 21 March 2012 the Council of the EU approved the crisis-management concept for a potential CSDP civilian mission in the Sahel. Two months later, the Prime Minister of Niger, Brigi Rafini, requested such a mission in his country with the aim of reinforcing the capacity of the Nigerien security forces, particularly in the field of counterterrorism and the fight against organized crime. EUCAP Sahel Niger was established on 16 July. It has its headquarters in Niamey and is supported by two liaison offices in Bamako, Mali, and Nouakchott, Mauritania. Its main tasks are to (*a*) advise and assist in the implementation of the Nigerien security strategy; (*b*) support a regional approach in the fight against terrorism and organized crime;

---

[22] United Nations, Security Council, Statement by the President of the Security Council, S/PRST/2012/26, 10 Dec. 2012.

[23] European External Action Service, Strategy for Security and Development in the Sahel, adopted 23 Mar. 2011, <http://eeas.europa.eu/africa/docs/sahel_strategy_en.pdf>. Publication of the strategy was delayed until September.

[24] Bello, O. W., *Quick Fix or Quicksand? Implementing the EU Sahel Strategy*, FRIDE Working Paper no. 114 (FRIDE: Madrid, Nov. 2012), pp. 11–15.

[25] The EU Training Mission in Mali was launched on 18 Feb. 2013.

(c) strengthen the rule of law; and (d) support the sustainability of the Nigerien security forces.[26] While the mission's mandate focuses primarily on assisting Nigerien authorities, it also has regional dimensions. In addition, in late 2012, following the increase in terrorist activities in northern Mali, it was decided that the mission should focus on preventing the spill-over of the conflict into Niger.[27]

EUCAP Sahel Niger was mandated for an initial two-year period.[28] Deployment began in August 2012. The mission has a total authorized capacity of 78 staff, comprising police and military experts. By the end of 2012 it had reached half of its capacity. The mission will run alongside EU development programmes in the country.

Developments in Mali

In addition to the instability in Niger, the Libya conflict was also directly linked to the intensification of the conflict in Mali.[29] In March elements of the armed forces, dissatisfied with the level of the support they received from the Malian Government in their fight against the Tuareg rebels in the north of the country, seized power from the democratically elected government. The rebels exploited the chaos following the coup and started an offensive in the following days.[30] Within a short time, with the help of AQIM, they seized control of the major cities of northern Mali.[31]

On 6 April, under the auspices of ECOWAS, a framework agreement was signed containing a road map for the restoration of constitutional order, a national dialogue and the organization of presidential elections. The Malian armed forces were, however, still unable to recover the territories in northern Mali, and in September the transitional authorities asked ECOWAS to assist through the deployment of an international stabilization force mandated under Chapter VII of the UN Charter. On 12 October the UN Security Council adopted Resolution 2071 calling on member states and international organizations to assist the Malian armed forces, where required, to restore the authority of the government over its territory and reduce the threat posed by AQIM.[32]

Despite the framework agreement, relations between the transitional government and the armed forces deteriorated again. The prime minister,

[26] Council Decision 2012/392/CFSP of 16 July 2012 on the European Union CSDP mission in Niger (EUCAP Sahel Niger), *Official Journal of the European Union*, L187, 17 July 2012.

[27] Mouawad, E., 'CSDP and EU mission update, Nov. 2012', CSDP Note no. 5, *European Security Review*, Nov. 2012.

[28] Council Decision 2012/392/CFSP (note 26).

[29] See chapter 2, section I, in this volume.

[30] United Nations, Security Council, Statement by the President of the Security Council, S/PRST/2012/7, 26 Mar. 2012.

[31] United Nations, Security Council, Statement by the President of the Security Council, S/PRST/2012/9, 4 Apr. 2012.

[32] UN Security Council Resolution 2071, 12 Oct. 2012.

Cheick Modibo Diarra, was arrested on 10 December and a day later he resigned and the government was dismissed. In the meantime, however, a joint strategic concept of operations for the international military force and the Malian armed forces was developed and endorsed by the ECOWAS heads of state and the AU Peace and Security Council. On 20 December the UN Security Council authorized the deployment of the African-led International Support Mission in Mali (AFISMA) for an initial period of one year. Its main tasks would be to (a) rebuild the capacity of the Malian defence and security forces; (b) support recovery of the rebel-controlled areas in the north of the country and reduce the threat of terrorist organizations; (c) transition its activities to stabilization; (d) support the protection of Malian citizens; and (e) support the creation of a secure environment for the provision of humanitarian assistance.[33]

The Security Council stressed that the military planning needed to be refined before the start of offensive operations. It called on member states and international organizations to provide financial support, troops and equipment to AFISMA to enable deployment. The EU provided such support through the mobilization of the African Peace Facility and the Security Council considered providing UN-funded logistical support packages.[34]

The UN did not expect the deployment of AFISMA to happen before September 2013. However, on 10 January 2013 Islamist forces captured the strategic town of Konna, putting the nearby Sévaré military airport, which was vital to any future intervention, at risk. Pushed by France, the Security Council reiterated the call for assistance to the Malian Government in its struggle against the Tuareg and Islamist forces.[35] In order to accelerate international involvement, France deployed a military force, Opération Serval.[36] ECOWAS then stated it would speed up its deployments to AFISMA.[37] On 17 January 2013 EU foreign ministers, in a meeting attended by the Malian foreign minister, Tièmen Hubert Coulibaly, decided to deploy the EU Training Mission Mali (EUTM Mali). This mission was designed to respond to the operational needs of the Malian armed forces.[38]

---

[33] UN Security Council Resolution 2085, 20 Dec. 2012.

[34] UN Security Council Resolution 2085 (note 33).

[35] United Nations, Security Council, 'Security Council press statement on Mali', SC/10878, 10 Jan. 2013.

[36] Irish, J. and Felix, B., 'Malian army beats back Islamist rebels with French help', Reuters, 11 Jan. 2013.

[37] 'Statement of the President of the ECOWAS Commission on the Situation in Mali', Press Release no. 006/2013, 12 Jan. 2013, <http://news.ecowas.int/presseshow.php?nb=006&lang=en&annee=2013>.

[38] Council Decision 2013/34/CFSP of 17 Jan. 2013 on a European Union military mission to contribute to the training of the Malian Armed Forces (EUTM Mali), *Official Journal of the European Union*, L14/19, 18 Jan. 2013.

Guinea-Bissau: the ECOWAS Mission in Guinea-Bissau

Guinea-Bissau, one of the smallest and poorest countries in Africa, has been prone to political instability since it gained independence in 1974. In the past 10 years, it has experienced five military coups and no president has completed his mandate.[39] In late 2010 ECOWAS and the Community of Portuguese Language Countries (Comunidade dos Países de Língua Portuguesa, CPLP) drew up a 'road map' to contribute to the peacebuilding process in Guinea-Bissau, with a focus on SSR.[40] In addition, the Angolan Technical and Military Assistance Mission in Guinea-Bissau (MISSANG)—a technical assistance mission on security and defence reform—replaced an EU mission with a similar mandate in February 2011.[41]

Relations between the government and the military remained tense in 2012 while those between the military and MISSANG deteriorated. The prime minister, Carlos Gomes Júnior, resigned in February in order to run in the 2012 presidential elections. He indicated his intention to curtail the power of the military and combat the drug cartels in the country, which reportedly have a close relationship with some military figures.[42] On 12 April, with Gomes looking likely to win, preparations for the elections were halted by a military coup. The coup leaders established the Transitional National Council and detained both Gomes and the interim president, Raimundo Pereira. Peaceful demonstrations were suppressed and civilians arbitrarily arrested.[43]

In response, the AU suspended Guinea-Bissau's membership.[44] ECOWAS immediately condemned the coup and demanded a return to constitutional order allowing the completion of the electoral process.[45] Further, it requested the immediate release of Gomes and Pereira, called on Guinea-Bissau to accept the immediate deployment of a contingent of the ECOWAS Standby Force, and established a regional contact and follow-up group on Guinea-Bissau to be chaired by Nigeria.[46] After negotiations with the

[39] Ramet, V., 'Civil–military relations in Guinea-Bissau: an unresolved issue', Policy Briefing, EU Parliament, Directorate-General for External Policies, Policy Department, DG EXPO/B/PolDep/Note/2012_149, Aug. 2012.
[40] UN Integrated Peace-building Office in Guinea-Bissau, 'SRSG calls on Bissau-Guinean authorities to endorse ECOWAS-CPLP road map', Press release, 10 Dec. 2010.
[41] 'Guinea-Bissau', *Security Council Report: Update Report*, 4 May 2012. The EU mission was the EU Advisory Mission for Security Sector Reform in Guinea-Bissau (EU SSR Guinea-Bissau).
[42] Ramet (note 39).
[43] United Nations, Security Council, Statement by the President of the Security Council, S/PRST/2012/15, 21 Apr. 2012.
[44] African Union, Peace and Security Council, 319th Ministerial Meeting, Communiqué PSC/MIN/COMM/1.(CCCXIX), 24 Apr. 2012.
[45] Ouedraogo, D. K., President of the ECOWAS Commission, 'ECOWAS reaction to on-going coup attempt in Guinea-Bissau', 12 Apr. 2012, <http://www.ecowas.int/publications/en/statement/guinebissau13042012.pdf>.
[46] ECOWAS, Extraordinary summit of ECOWAS heads of state and government, Final communiqué, 26 Apr. 2012.

Transitional National Council broke down at the end of April, ECOWAS imposed sanctions on Guinea-Bissau.[47] Eventually, a deal was reached between ECOWAS and the military command that secured the preservation of the parliament and the release of political detainees. Power was passed to a new civilian transitional government on 23 May and a period of one year was agreed to organize new elections.[48]

ECOMIB was established on 26 April for an initial period of six months. It was mandated to facilitate the withdrawal of MISSANG, to secure the transitional process, and to ensure the implementation of the Defence and Security Sector Reform Programme (DSSRP).[49] The deployment of approximately 630 troops began just over a month after the coup. The ECOMIB force was deployed to the port, the airport and most ministries in the capital, Bissau, to ensure the security of state institutions.[50] In June MISSANG withdrew without incident.[51]

In October, in the aftermath of an alleged counter-coup, a memorandum of understanding on the DSSRP was signed between the ECOWAS Commission and the Guinea-Bissau authorities. The extension of ECOMIB's mandate in November for a further six months should allow the mission to assist in securing the transition process and ensuring peaceful and fair elections in April 2013.[52]

While the UN Security Council supported the involvement of ECOWAS in the restoration of the constitutional order in Guinea-Bissau, neither the AU, the EU or the UN has recognized the new civilian transitional government.[53] The agreement negotiated by ECOWAS has divided international opinion, with some criticizing it for not being inclusive of all political parties and for creating a transitional government principally composed of opponents of Gomes.[54]

In December 2012 an AU-led joint assessment mission to Guinea-Bissau was conducted in cooperation with ECOWAS, the EU and the UN in order to improve the coordination of international efforts on SSR and political and economic reforms, on combating drug trafficking, and on fighting

[47] ECOWAS, 'ECOWAS sanctions Guinea Bissau after failed talks', Press release no. 124/2012, 1 May 2012.

[48] United Nations, Security Council, Report of the Secretary-General on developments in Guinea-Bissau and on the activities of the United Nations Integrated Peacebuilding Office in that country, S/2012/554 17 July 2012.

[49] ECOWAS (note 46), p. 8

[50] United Nations, Security Council, 'Security Council urged to call for unified strategy that would restore legitimate order to Guinea-Bissau', Press release, SC/10732, 26 July 2012.

[51] ECOWAS, Forty-first ordinary session of the ECOWAS Authority of Heads of State and Government, Final communiqué, 29 June 2012.

[52] ECOWAS, Extraordinary Summit of Heads of State and Government, Final communiqué, 11 Nov. 2012.

[53] United Nations, Security Council, Statement by the President of the Security Council, S/PRST/2012/15, 21 Apr. 2012.

[54] United Nations, Security Council (note 53).

impunity.[55] The mission in part reflected an effort to enhance international, regional and subregional engagement, despite the disagreements over the course of action following the April 2012 coup. It was later agreed that a second assessment mission would be carried out once the transitional government had accepted a 'transition road map'.[56]

Conclusions

The launch of the 2011 military intervention in Libya, with the backing of the Security Council, raised hopes that R2P was moving from idealistic words to a genuine commitment to intervene—militarily, if needed—to protect a state's civilians from state-based violence. The launch of the Arab League Observer Mission to Syria in December 2011 and UNSMIS in 2012 gave supporters of R2P further grounds for optimism. However, the rapid disintegration of these missions and the failure to agree on any international response to the mounting violence highlighted the limits of the concept and of the international commitment to R2P. The case of Syria in 2012 shows that if the Security Council is divided and permanent members have significant interests in the country at stake, R2P offers no solution.

The Syria crisis also highlighted increasing international disagreement about how to manage conflicts. Such divisions were visible, too, in relation to the military coup in Guinea-Bissau, where the AU, the EU and UN preferred to take a hard line against the coup leaders, while ECOWAS preferred mediation and less direct steps.

Finally, it is noteworthy that the budget constraints and pressure to demonstrate efficiency and effectiveness applied to existing missions were not applied to new missions with the same rigour.

---

[55] UN Security Council Resolution 2048, 18 May 2012.
[56] African Union, 'Convening of a consultative meeting on the situation in Guinea-Bissau', Press release, 27 Jan. 2013, <http://www.peaceau.org/en/article/convening-of-a-consultative-meeting-on-the-situation-in-guinea-bissau>.

III. Regional developments in peace operations

JAÏR VAN DER LIJN

Africa

In 2012, as in previous years, the largest concentration of peace operations was in Africa. Two of the three new operations during the year—the Economic Community of West African States (ECOWAS) Mission in Guinea-Bissau (ECOMIB) and the European Union (EU) Capacity Building Mission in Niger (EUCAP Sahel Niger)—were located in Africa. There were 17 operations deployed in the region, 9 of them under United Nations command—a smaller proportion than in recent years (see table 2.1). Nonetheless, UN operations accounted for about 75 000 of the 94 000 personnel deployed in Africa. About 90 000 of the personnel deployed in the region were troops. Although the African Union (AU)/United Nations Hybrid Operation in Darfur (UNAMID) decreased its personnel size by more than 2000, overall personnel deployments in the region increased due to the expansion of the AU Mission in Somalia (AMISOM) and further deployments to the UN Interim Security Force for Abyei (UNISFA) and the UN Mission in South Sudan (UNMISS), both of which opened in 2011 and continued to expand in 2012.[1]

Somalia

In 2012 the international community took a renewed interest in Somalia. The UN Political Office for Somalia and the office of the Special Representative of the Secretary-General, Augustine P. Mahiga, relocated to Mogadishu, after being based in Nairobi, Kenya, since 1995. Furthermore, the AU Peace and Security Council and the UN Security Council agreed in January on a new strategic concept for AMISOM that would both increase its force size and give it a more robust mandate. Following this concept, the Security Council mandated AMISOM to expand in four sectors in south-central Somalia, replacing Ethiopian forces and re-hatting Kenyan forces that had been fighting the Islamist group Harakat al-Shabab al-Mujahideen (Mujahedin Youth Movement, or al-Shabab) in the area.[2]

Under the new concept, AMISOM is to use all necessary means to establish conditions for effective and legitimate governance, and to reduce the threat posed by armed groups, especially al-Shabab. For this purpose the UN Security Council requested the AU to increase the force strength from 12 000 to a maximum of 17 731 troops and decided that the UN would also

---

[1] On the deployment of UNISFA and UNMISS see Fanchini, C., 'New peace operations in 2011', *SIPRI Yearbook 2012*, pp. 95–99.
[2] UN Security Council Resolution 2036, 22 Feb. 2012.

Table 2.1. Number of peace operations and personnel deployed, by region and type of organization, 2012

Conducting organization	Africa	Americas	Asia and Oceania	Europe	Middle East	World
United Nations[a]	9	1	3	2	5	20
Regional organization or alliance	7	1	2	13	4	27
Ad hoc coalition	1	–	3	–	2	6
Total operations	**17**	**2**	**8**	**15**	**11**	**53**
Total personnel	**94 351**	**9 938**	**103 892**[b]	**9 784**	**15 552**	**233 642**[b]

[a] United Nations figures include peace operations led by the UN Department of Peacekeeping Operations, the UN Department of Political Affairs and UNAMID.

[b] These figures include ISAF in Afghanistan, which had 102 052 troops in 2012.

Source: SIPRI Multilateral Peace Operations Database, <http://www.sipri.org/databases/pko/>.

increase its logistical support packages. The Security Council welcomed the support provided by the EU Training Mission Somalia (EUTM Somalia) for the purpose of strengthening training and support to the Somali security forces.[3] Military advances were made in the fight against al-Shabab and a new federal government was established following the end of the Transitional Federal Government's mandate on 20 August. However, by this time al-Shabab was no longer the only concern: inter-clan competition and warlordism were increasing, and none of the groups involved wanted a strong central government.[4] The next renewal of the AMISOM mandate was only for a four-month period, because the Security Council wanted to review the progress made before the next renewal.[5]

South Sudan and Sudan

In 2012 the UN continued to deploy three missions in South Sudan and Sudan: UNAMID in the Darfur region of Sudan, UNMISS in South Sudan and UNISFA at the border between the two countries. By the end of 2012, almost one-third of all UN peace operation troops worldwide were deployed with these three missions.

Negotiations between South Sudan and Sudan made slow progress in 2012. Even when agreements were reached, implementation was often

---

[3] UN Security Council Resolution 2036 (note 2).

[4] International Crisis Group (ICG), *Somalia: An Opportunity That Should Not Be Missed*, Africa Briefing no. 87 (ICG: Brussels, 22 Feb. 2012); and Marchal, R., 'The mercy of neighbours: security and governance in a new Somalia', NOREF Report, Norwegian Peacebuilding Resource Centre, June 2012.

[5] UN Security Council Resolution 2072, 31 Oct. 2012; and UN Security Council Resolution 2073, 7 Nov. 2012.

bogged down in discussions over their operationalization. Also, the charges Sudan imposes on South Sudan for transporting the latter's oil to the terminal at Port Sudan remained contentious, leading South Sudan to stop oil production in January at enormous economic cost and causing domestic instability. Moreover, in 2012, incidents of cross-border violence continued, such as aerial bombardments, support to proxies and troop movements.[6]

After weeks of fighting on the border, in early April the Sudanese People's Liberation Army (SPLA), the national army of South Sudan, captured the Sudanese-controlled town of Heglig and the surrounding oilfields, which are in a contested border region. Retaliatory Sudanese air raids hit Bentiu in South Sudan. The fighting escalated to the brink of all-out war. However, on 20 April the SPLA left Heglig—although whether it withdrew voluntarily or was repulsed is disputed.[7] During this period, the UN Security Council only reiterated that UNISFA was ready to support the implementation of any agreements reached.[8] Pending the creation of two joint mechanisms agreed in 2011—the Joint Border Verification and Monitoring Mechanism and the Ad Hoc Committee of the Joint Political and Security Mechanism between Sudan and South Sudan—UNMISS was mandated to monitor the flow of weapons and personnel across the border.[9]

Eventually, although belatedly, South Sudan and Sudan lived up to the Security Council's demands and largely withdrew their forces from the contested Abyei region in line with the 2011 Temporary Arrangements for the Administration and Security of the Abyei Area. On 27 September, in Addis Ababa, South Sudan and Sudan signed an agreement on security arrangements, which defined the 'safe demilitarized border zone' UNISFA has to monitor. Although neither country had provided full support to the mission by the end of 2012, in October Sudan and in November South Sudan signed a revised status-of-forces agreement.[10] At the same time the situation in Abyei remained tense, with occasional demonstrations and riots. In one incident a UNISFA peacekeeper accidently killed a local UN staff member participating in a demonstration.[11]

---

[6] United Nations, Security Council, Statement by the President of the Security Council, S/PRST/2012/5, 6 Mar. 2012.

[7] 'Sudan and South Sudan', *Security Council Report: Monthly Forecast*, Apr. 2012; and Edris Ali, A. A., 'In Sudan's Heglig: stench of death and leaking oil', Agence France-Presse, 23 Apr. 2012.

[8] United Nations, Security Council, Statement by the President of the Security Council, S/PRST/2012/12, 12 Apr. 2012; and UN Security Council Resolution 2046, 2 May 2012.

[9] UN Security Council Resolution 2057, 5 July 2012; Agreement on the Border Monitoring Support Mission between the Government of Sudan and the Government of South Sudan, signed 30 July 2011; and Agreement between the Government of the Sudan and the Government of Southern Sudan on Border Security and the Joint Political and Security Mechanism, signed 29 June 2011.

[10] UN Security Council Resolution 2075, 16 Nov. 2012.

[11] Timberlake, I., 'UN troops "shoot dead" protester in disputed Abyei', Agence France-Presse, 14 Nov. 2012.

In South Sudan the security situation deteriorated due to spillover effects of the internal conflicts in Sudan's South Kordofan and Blue Nile states, and to intercommunal violence, especially in Jonglei state. The violence in Jonglei in 2011 and January 2012, and fierce criticism of UNMISS for its failure to protect civilians under imminent threat, prompted the mission to make protection of civilians (POC) the centrepiece of its operations and to develop an ambitious POC strategy, announced in June 2012.[12] The strategy was criticized by some for raising already unrealistic expectations among the civilian population of the protection they could expect from UNMISS. To moderate these expectations, UNMISS started an outreach programme to improve understanding of its role among the South Sudanese population.[13]

UNMISS also struggled with restrictions placed on its movements in certain areas and had difficulty reaching full deployment, with shortfalls of, in particular, 'key enablers', military helicopters and civilian specialists.[14] Exacerbating the situation, several military helicopters were shot down. In January Russia threatened to withdraw all of its eight helicopters after losing one in the autumn of 2011. It then agreed to leave four with the mission until South Sudanese forces shot down another of its helicopters in December. In response, Russia stated that it would withdraw all of its helicopters in March 2013.[15]

The intensity of the conflict in Darfur decreased after the deployment of UNAMID in 2007. However, in 2012 violence and insecurity started to rise again in the area, and clashes between the government and rebel groups—including aerial bombardments, inter-tribal violence, banditry and criminality—continued. In addition, the Darfur Peace Process facilitated by the AU and the UN remained unproductive. The Doha Document for Peace in Darfur, signed by the Sudanese Government and the rebel Liberation and Justice Movement in 2011, was not implemented.[16] Moreover, UNAMID patrols came under attack several times during the year, resulting in the injury or death of several peacekeepers.[17] The Sudanese Government continued to hinder the mission by not respecting the status-of-forces agree-

[12] See e.g. Gettleman, J., 'Born in Unity, South Sudan is torn again', *New York Times*, 12 Jan. 2012.

[13] Hemmer, J., '"We are laying the groundwork for our own failure': the UN Mission in South Sudan and its civilian protection strategy—an early assessment', Conflict Research Unit (CRU) Policy Brief no. 25, Netherlands Institute of International Relations and Norwegian Peacebuilding Resource Centre, Jan. 2013.

[14] UN Security Council Resolution 2057 (note 9).

[15] 'South Sudan's army down UN helicopter in Jonglei, 4 Russians killed', *Sudan Tribune*, 21 Dec. 2012.

[16] UN Security Council Resolution 2063, 31 July 2012.

[17] 'Gunmen kill UNAMID peacekeeper in East Darfur', *Sudan Tribune*, 21 Jan. 2012; 'UN–AU peacekeepers attacked in Darfur, 4 wounded', *Sudan Tribune*, 23 Apr. 2012; 'Four Nigerian peacekeepers killed in West Darfur', *Sudan Tribune*, 3 Oct. 2012; and 'Sudanese army say rebels behind UNAMID reports on Hashaba clashes', *Sudan Tribune*, 21 Nov. 2012.

ment, delaying the provision of the necessary visas, and obstructing the use of UNAMID's aerial assets and its radio transmitter. Other parties to the conflict denied access to humanitarian workers.[18]

During the annual review of UNAMID's mandate in July, the Security Council decided to reconfigure the deployment over 12–18 months, to focus more on the areas in Darfur where the security threats are highest. For that purpose the mission's authorized strength was increased to 16 200 military personnel, 2310 police and 17 formed police units of up to 140 personnel each. The Security Council noted, however, that the contingents deployed needed to be properly trained and equipped.[19]

Democratic Republic of the Congo (DRC)

UN Organization Stabilization Mission in the Democratic Republic of the Congo (MONUSCO) continued to struggle with issues of impartiality and with POC in 2012. In April a rebellion had been started by a group of former National Congress for People's Defence (Congrès National pour la Défense du Peuple, CNDP) rebels who had been integrated into the national armed forces. The group, calling itself the 23 March Movement (M23, named for the date in 2009 when the CNDP and the government signed a peace agreement), received direct military support from the Rwandan and Ugandan governments.[20]

In June UN Security Council Resolution 2053 extended MONUSCO's mandate for another year and encouraged the mission to continue its partnership with the Congolese Government—something that has made it difficult to appear impartial in dealings with rebels in eastern DRC. Struggling with the lack of progress and increasing pressure to cut costs among a number of its members, the Security Council told MONUSCO to review its approach and establish a new strategy and timetable. Although POC was to remain MONUSCO's priority, MONUSCO should make security sector reform its primary focus.[21]

The M23 rebellion continued in the following months, as did M23's attempts to establish a parallel administration and its attacks on the civilian population, peacekeepers and humanitarian actors. Consequently, by October 320 000 people had fled their homes in Nord-Kivu.[22]

At a summit of the International Conference on the Great Lakes Region (ICGLR) in July it was announced that the ICGLR and the AU were plan-

[18] UN Security Council Resolution 2063 (note 16).

[19] UN Security Council Resolution 2063 (note 16).

[20] United Nations, Security Council, Final report of the Group of Experts on the DRC submitted in accordance with paragraph 4 of Security Council resolution 2021 (2011), annex to S/2012/843, 15 Nov. 2012.

[21] UN Security Council Resolution 2053, 27 June 2012.

[22] United Nations, Security Council, Statement by the President of the Security Council, S/PRST/2012/22, 19 Oct. 2012.

ning to deploy a 'neutral international force' in eastern DRC to 'eradicate M23' and other 'negative forces' and patrol and secure border zones.[23] There were concerns in the UN Security Council about the aims and modalities of this force and its relationship with MONUSCO.[24] Of particular concern was whether the force would involve troops from Rwanda and Uganda.[25] The Security Council also requested the UN Secretary-General to report on options to enhance implementation of MONUSCO's mandate, including POC.[26]

On 20 November M23 forces entered the city of Goma. The Security Council demanded that they withdraw, disband and restore the authority of the government in Nord-Kivu.[27] MONUSCO was widely accused of paying too little attention to its POC mandate during the episode despite outnumbering the rebels and being far better equipped. Troop-contributing countries were said to have been unwilling to put the lives of their forces at risk. The French foreign minister, Laurent Fabius, called MONUSCO's conduct 'absurd', and throughout eastern DRC angry mobs threw stones at MONUSCO personnel and facilities and burned down UN compounds.[28]

North and West Africa

During a review of the UN Support Mission in Libya (UNSMIL) in early 2012 it was decided to keep a 'light footprint' in the country because it was believed that a more intrusive mission would not be well received locally.[29] The mandate of UNSMIL was modified to assist the Libyan Government in (a) managing the democratization process; (b) promoting the rule of law; (c) restoring public security; (d) countering illicit proliferation of arms; and (e) coordinating international assistance and building the capacity of the government.[30]

With the inauguration on 25 April of the Ivoirian National Assembly, the situation in Côte d'Ivoire seemed to settle down after the electoral crisis of 2011. However, the already fragile situation, particularly in the border region with Liberia, deteriorated sharply when on 8 June a UN Operation in Côte d'Ivoire (UNOCI) patrol was attacked by armed elements and seven

[23] International Conference on the Great Lakes Region (ICGLR), 'ICGLR heads of state to discuss DRC crisis in Kampala', Press release, 5 Aug. 2012, <https://icglr.org/spip.php?article235>.
[24] United Nations, S/PRST/2012/22 (note 22).
[25] Kibangula, T., 'A neutral force in eastern DR Congo is a false solution', France 24, 19 Aug. 2012.
[26] United Nations, S/PRST/2012/22 (note 22).
[27] UN Security Council Resolution 2076, 20 Nov. 2012.
[28] Hatcher, J. and Perry, J., 'Defining peacekeeping downward: the UN debacle in eastern Congo', *Time*, 26 Nov. 2012.
[29] Mancini, F., 'Interview with Ian Martin, SRSG and Head of the UN Support Mission in Libya', Global Observatory, 11 May 2012, <http://www.theglobalobservatory.org/interviews/283-interview-with-ian-martin-srsg-and-head-of-the-un-support-mission-in-libya.html>. On the establishment of UNSMIL in 2011 see Fanchini (note 1), pp. 102–103.
[30] UN Security Council Resolution 2040, 12 Mar. 2012.

peacekeepers and a number of others were killed. In addition, numerous attacks on civilians, including internally displaced persons and returned refugees, forced UNOCI to revise its POC strategy.

Despite this, the UN Security Council deemed that the situation allowed for a reduction of the military component of UNOCI by one battalion, bringing the authorized strength down to 8837 personnel. However, cooperation between UNOCI and the UN Mission in Liberia (UNMIL) was increased.[31] From August to October the situation in the country deteriorated further. In particular, attacks on the Ivorian national security forces in and around Abidjan and in the border regions, reportedly executed by supporters of former president Laurent Gbagbo, were worrying. Intercommunal violence also remained a concern. In the light of these developments the planned troop reduction was deferred until 2013.[32]

With regard to Liberia, the Security Council decided on a phased reduction of UNMIL's authorized strength from seven to four infantry battalions, to eventually leave UNMIL with an authorized force of 3750 troops in July 2015. The first reduction, which is to take place between October 2012 and September 2013, consists of 1990 personnel. At the same time the number of UNMIL formed police units is to increase by three, totalling 420 personnel. The first new unit is to be deployed before February 2013.[33]

In Sierra Leone, the successful completion of the electoral process allowed the Security Council to request a timeline for transition and a drawdown and exit strategy for the UN Integrated Peacebuilding Office in Sierra Leone (UNIPSIL).[34]

The Americas

Two operations were active in the Americas in 2012: the Mission to Support the Peace Process in Colombia (MAPP/OEA), led by the Organization of American States, and the UN Stabilization Mission in Haiti (MINUSTAH). After a surge following the devastating January 2010 earthquake in Haiti, MINUSTAH—by far the bigger of the two operations—almost returned to its previous personnel levels. Given the relatively calm security situation, during its annual discussion on MINUSTAH's mandate extension the UN Security Council reduced the total number of authorized military and police personnel to 6270.[35]

---

[31] UN Security Council Resolution 2062, 26 July 2012.

[32] United Nations, Security Council, Thirty-first progress report of the Secretary-General on the United Nations Operation in Côte d'Ivoire, S/2012/964, 31 Dec. 2012.

[33] UN Security Council Resolution 2066, 17 Sep. 2012.

[34] United Nations, Security Council, Statement by the President of the Security Council, S/PRST/2012/25, 30 Nov. 2012.

[35] UN Security Council Resolution 2070, 12 Oct. 2012.

Under Haitian President Michel Martelly, who was elected in 2011, the debate over the withdrawal of MINUSTAH continued. The opposition stressed national pride and abuses committed by peacekeepers, as well as expressing anger over a cholera epidemic believed to have originated with MINUSTAH personnel. However, even the fiercest critics agreed that the Haitian police force could not guarantee security and therefore only called for MINUSTAH's phased withdrawal.[36] In 2012 it was proposed that MINUSTAH's military component would gradually hand over responsibility for security to formed police units, and ultimately to the national police. The mission and the UN country team, in close consultation with the Haitian Government, finalized a new 'integrated strategic framework' for the period 2013–16, which identified UN priorities. Work started on developing a 'reconfiguration and conditions-based consolidation plan' for MINUSTAH, under which its tasks would be narrowed to a core set of tasks achievable within a 'reasonable time frame' (tentatively four to five years). Benchmarks and indicators were also to be developed collaboratively with the government and other stakeholders to measure progress made in the transition process.[37]

Asia and Oceania

Eight peace operations were active in Asia and Oceania in 2012, with a total of about 103 892 personnel deployed (see table 2.1). The number of operations in 2012 remained the same as in 2011, but the total number of personnel decreased by 30 835. The International Security Assistance Force (ISAF) in Afghanistan continued to account for the overwhelming majority of personnel deployed in the region. In 2012, transition-related developments and planned withdrawals continued for two operations: ISAF focused on withdrawing by the end of 2014 and the UN Integrated Mission in Timor-Leste (UNMIT) closed at the end of 2012.

In May ISAF handed over security responsibilities to the Afghan national security forces in several districts, the third tranche of handovers in the transition process. By the end of 2012 the Afghan national security forces were in complete charge of security in 11 of Afghanistan's 34 provinces. In December Afghan President Hamid Karzai announced the next 12 provinces for transition. Once this is complete, 87 per cent of the Afghan population will be living in transitioned areas. It is expected that the fifth and last phase will commence in mid-2013. The North Atlantic Treaty Organization (NATO) has repeatedly stated that after 2014 it will continue to

[36] International Crisis Group (ICG), *Towards a Post-MINUSTAH Haiti: Making an Effective Transition*, Latin America/Caribbean Report no. 44 (ICG: Brussels, 2 Aug. 2012).
[37] United Nations, Security Council, Report of the Secretary-General on the United Nations Stabilization Mission in Haiti, S/2012/678, 31 Aug. 2012.

commit to Afghanistan through the deployment of a training, advisory and assistance mission.[38]

Europe

There were 15 peace operations active in Europe in 2012, the same number as in 2011, while the total number of personnel deployed to missions in the region fell from 11 932 in 2011 to 9784 in 2012 (see table 2.1). The decrease was largely due to the phased drawdown strategy of the NATO-led Kosovo Force (KFOR), which decreased its numbers by over 800, and the EU Military Operation in Bosnia and Herzegovina (EUFOR ALTHEA), which reduced its force by almost 700. This shows a continuation of a downward trend of peacekeeping personnel deployed in Europe: deployments have roughly halved since 2009 and have declined more or less steadily for over a decade. At the height of the deployments in the former Yugoslavia, around 85 000 peacekeepers were deployed in Europe.

The EU Police Mission in Bosnia and Herzegovina (EUPM), which provided capacity building and other support to strengthen the rule of law, closed on 30 June, and after the troop reduction EUFOR ALTHEA retained a residual force of only 600. The mission now focuses on training and capacity building of the Bosnian armed forces but maintains an out-of-country Intermediate Reserve Force that can be called on at short notice to reinforce Bosnian law enforcement agencies.[39]

The Middle East

In addition to the deployment of the United Nations Supervision Mission in Syria (UNSMIS; see section II), the Syrian conflict also had a destabilizing effect on the operations of UNDOF on the Israeli–Syrian border. Armed members of the Syrian opposition hid in the Israeli–Syrian area of separation defined by the 1973 Agreement on Disengagement, provoking military operations by the Syrian armed forces. A number of incidents across the ceasefire line showed the potential for escalating tensions between Israel and Syria.[40]

[38] International Security Assistance Force (ISAF), 'ISAF congratulates Afghan government on transition of security', Press release, 31 Dec. 2012.
[39] UN Security Council Resolution 2074, 14 Nov. 2012.
[40] UN Security Council Resolution 2084, 19 Dec. 2012.

Conclusions

Budget considerations were important in many countries' decisions to draw down their personnel contributions to ISAF, and in the speed of the drawdowns. Pressure to reduce spending on peace operations also meant that UN missions were subject to increased scrutiny; most notably, more benchmarks and indicators were established to evaluate and monitor operations in the DRC, Haiti and Sudan, among others. In addition, existing missions were increasingly told to focus on core sets of tasks achievable in a defined time frame. Inter-mission cooperation, such as that between UNMIL and UNOCI, was another strategy used to increase efficiency.

Despite the budgetary and other rigours, many politicians and civil society groups continued to place high demands on peace operations. Pressure continues to get even more value for money for peace operations. However, the UN struggled with POC in Côte d'Ivoire, the DRC and South Sudan. Unable to prevent inter-communal violence in Jonglei state in South Sudan and M23's capturing of Goma in the DRC, the UN was once again criticized by advocacy groups and politicians for its 'weakness' and inability to act. Such criticisms often overlook the fact that the ability of UN missions to respond in cases like these is dependent on the UN member states being willing to contribute the essential capacities and to agree on sufficiently robust measures.

There were markedly fewer signs of division within the international community regarding existing operations than there were regarding new operations.

IV. Table of multilateral peace operations, 2012

JANE DUNDON*

Table 2.2 provides data on the 53 multilateral peace operations that were conducted during 2012, including operations that were launched or terminated during the year. By definition, a peace operation must have the stated intention of (*a*) serving as an instrument to facilitate the implementation of peace agreements already in place, (*b*) supporting a peace process or (*c*) assisting conflict-prevention or peacebuilding efforts.

SIPRI follows the United Nations Department of Peacekeeping Operations (DPKO) description of peacekeeping as a mechanism to assist conflict-afflicted countries to create conditions for sustainable peace. Peacekeeping tasks may include monitoring and observing ceasefire agreements; serving as confidence-building measures; protecting the delivery of humanitarian assistance; assisting with the demobilization and reintegration processes; strengthening institutional capacities in the areas of the judiciary and the rule of law (including penal institutions), policing, and human rights; electoral support; and economic and social development. Table 2.2 thus covers a broad range of peace operations, reflecting the growing complexity of operation mandates and the potential for operations to change over time. The table does not include good offices, fact-finding or electoral assistance missions, nor does it include peace operations comprising non-resident individuals or teams of negotiators, or operations not sanctioned by the UN.

The table lists operations that were conducted under the authority of the UN, operations conducted by regional organizations and alliances, and operations conducted by ad hoc (non-standing) coalitions of states that were sanctioned by the UN or authorized by a UN Security Council resolution. UN operations are divided into three subgroups: (*a*) observer and multidimensional peace operations run by the DPKO, (*b*) special political and peacebuilding missions, and (*c*) the joint African Union/UN Hybrid Operation in Darfur (UNAMID).

The table draws on the SIPRI Multilateral Peace Operations Database, <http://www.sipri.org/databases/pko>, which provides information on all UN and non-UN peace operations conducted since 2000, including location, dates of deployment and operation, mandate, participating countries, number of personnel, costs and fatalities.

---

* Xenia Avezov, SIPRI Research Assistant, assisted in the compilation of table 2.2.

Table 2.2. Multilateral peace operations, 2012

New states joining an existing operation in 2012 are shown in bold type. Individual state participation that ended in 2012 is shown in italic type. Where operations were launched in 2012 the legal instrument is shown in bold type. Where operations closed in 2012 the legal instrument is shown in italic type. Designated lead states (i.e. those that either have operational control or contribute the most personnel) are underlined for operations that have a police or military component.

Legal instrument/ Deployment date/ Location	Countries contributing troops, observers (Obs.), civilian police (Civ. pol.) and civilian staff (Civ. staff) in 2012	Troops/Obs./ Civ. pol./Civ. staff		Deaths: to date/ 2012/ (by cause[a])	Cost ($ m.): 2012/ 2012/ unpaid
		Approved	Actual		
United Nations (UN) Total: 15 operations	**115 contributing countries***	**66 587**	**63 912**	**1 342**	**5 202.9**
		1 895	**1 793**	**68**	**1 020.6**
		10 064	**7 539**		
		3 392	**4 367****		

* Due to the unavailability of data on the nationalities of civilian staff for UN missions, this figure only includes countries deploying uniformed personnel to UN Department of Peacekeeping Operations (DPKO) operations during 2012.
** UN peace operations (including political and peacebuilding operations) are supported by 11 808 locally recruited (civilian) staff and 2242 UN volunteers.

UN Truce Supervision Organization (UNTSO)

UNTSO was established by SCR 50 (29 May 1948) and mandated to assist the Mediator and the Truce Commission in supervising the truce in Palestine after the 1948 Arab–Israeli War. In subsequent years it also assisted in observing the General Armistice Agreement of 1949 and the ceasefires in the aftermath of the 1967 Six-Day War. UNTSO cooperates with UNDOF and UNIFIL. A positive decision by the UN Security Council is required to terminate the operation.

SCR 50	Obs.: Argentina, Australia, Austria, Belgium, Canada, Chile, China, Denmark,	–	–	50	35.1
June 1948	Estonia, Finland, France, Ireland, Italy, **Malawi**, Nepal, Netherlands, New	150	153	–	–
Egypt, Israel,	Zealand, Norway, Russia, **Serbia**, Slovakia, Slovenia, Sweden, Switzerland,	–	–		
Lebanon, Syria	USA	120	94*		

* The operation is supported by 139 locally recruited staff.

Legal instrument/ Deployment date/ Location	Countries contributing troops, observers (Obs.), civilian police (Civ. pol.) and civilian staff (Civ. staff) in 2012	Troops/Obs./ Civ. pol./Civ. staff		Deaths: to date/ 2012/ (by cause^a)	Cost ($ m.): 2012/ unpaid
		Approved	Actual		

UN Military Observer Group in India and Pakistan (UNMOGIP)

UNMOGIP was established by SCR 91 (30 Mar. 1951) and mandated to observe the ceasefire in Kashmir under the Karachi Agreement (July 1949). A positive decision by the UN Security Council is required to terminate the operation.

Legal instrument/ Deployment date/ Location	Countries contributing	Approved	Actual	Deaths	Cost
SCR 91	Obs.: Chile, Croatia, Finland, Italy, Korea (South), Philippines, Sweden,	–	–	11	10.5
Mar. 1951	Thailand, Uruguay	48	39	–	–
India, Pakistan		–	–		
(Jammu, Kashmir)		26	25*		

* The operation is supported by 48 locally recruited staff.

UN Peacekeeping Force in Cyprus (UNFICYP)

UNFICYP was established by SCR 186 (4 Mar. 1964) and mandated to prevent hostilities between the Greek Cypriot and Turkish Cypriot communities and to contribute to the maintenance and restoration of law and order. Since the end of hostilities in 1974, the mandate has included supervising the de facto ceasefire (Aug. 1974) and maintaining a buffer zone between the two sides. SCR 2058 (19 July 2012) extended the mandate until 31 Jan. 2013.

SCR 186	Troops: Argentina, Austria, Brazil, Canada, Chile, China, Croatia, Hungary,	860	864	181	55.5
Mar. 1964	Paraguay, Serbia, Slovakia, UK	–	–	–	15.8
Cyprus	Civ. pol.: Australia, Bosnia and Herzegovina, Croatia, El Salvador, India,	69	66		
	Ireland, Italy, Montenegro, Serbia, Ukraine	39	38*		

* The operation is supported by 106 locally recruited staff.

UN Disengagement Observer Force (UNDOF)

UNDOF was established by SCR 350 (31 May 1974) and mandated to observe the ceasefire and the disengagement of Israeli and Syrian forces as well as to maintain an area of limitation and separation in accordance with the 1973 Agreement on Disengagement. SCR 2084 (19 Dec. 2012) extended the mandate until 30 June 2013.

SCR 350
June 1974
Syria

Troops: Austria, *Canada*, Croatia, India, Japan, **Philippines**

1 047	1 013	44	48.2
–	–	1	16
		(-,-,-,1)	
49	40*		

* The operation is supported by 99 locally recruited staff.

UN Interim Force in Lebanon (UNIFIL)

UNIFIL was established by SCRs 425 and 426 (19 Mar. 1978) and mandated to confirm the withdrawal of Israeli forces from southern Lebanon and to assist the Lebanese Government in re-establishing authority in the area. In 2006, following the conflict between Israel and Hezbollah, the operation's mandate was altered by SCR 1701 (11 Aug. 2006) to encompass tasks related to establishing and monitoring a permanent ceasefire. SCR 2064 (30 Aug. 2012) extended the mandate until 31 Aug. 2013.

SCRs 425 and 426
Mar. 1978
Lebanon

Troops: **Armenia, Austria**, Bangladesh, **Belarus**, Belgium, Brazil, Brunei Darussalam, Cambodia, China, Croatia, Cyprus, El Salvador, **Finland,** France, Germany, Ghana, Greece, Guatemala, Hungary, India, Indonesia, Ireland, Italy, **Kenya**, Korea (South), **Luxembourg**, Macedonia (FYR), Malaysia, Nepal, **Nigeria**, *Portugal,* Qatar, Serbia, Sierra Leone, Slovenia, Spain, Sri Lanka, Tanzania, Turkey

15 000	11 003	296	534.7
–	–	2	100.4
		(-,1,1,-)	
407	338*		

* The operation is supported by 656 locally recruited staff.

UN Mission for the Referendum in Western Sahara (MINURSO)

MINURSO was established by SCR 690 (29 Apr. 1991) and mandated to monitor the ceasefire between the Polisario Front and the Moroccan Government; to observe the reduction of troops; and to prepare for an eventual referendum on the integration of Western Sahara into Morocco. SCR 2044 (24 Apr. 2012) extended the mandate until 30 Apr. 2013.

SCR 690
Sep. 1991
Western Sahara

Troops: Bangladesh, Ghana

Obs.: Argentina, Austria, Bangladesh, Brazil, China, Croatia, Djibouti, <u>Egypt</u>, El Salvador, France, Ghana, Guinea, Honduras, Hungary, Ireland, Italy, Korea (South), **Malawi**, Malaysia, Mongolia, Nepal, Nigeria, Pakistan, Paraguay, **Peru**, *Poland,* Russia, Sri Lanka, **Togo**, Uruguay, Yemen

Civ. pol.: **Chad**, Egypt, Jordan, Yemen

–	27	15	59.8
237*	186	–	46.8
6	6		
–	95**		

* This figure refers to military observers and troops.
** The operation is supported by 165 locally recruited staff and 13 UN volunteers.

Legal instrument/ Deployment date/ Location	Countries contributing troops, observers (Obs.), civilian police (Civ. pol.) and civilian staff (Civ. staff) in 2012	Troops/Obs./ Civ. pol./Civ. staff		Deaths: to date/ 2012/ (by cause[a])	Cost ($ m.): 2012/ unpaid
		Approved	Actual		

UN Interim Administration Mission in Kosovo (UNMIK)

UNMIK was established by SCR 1244 (10 June 1999) and mandated to promote the establishment of substantial autonomy and self-government in Kosovo; to perform civilian administrative functions; to maintain law and order; to promote human rights; and to ensure the safe return of refugees and displaced persons. Following Kosovo's declaration of independence and the deployment of EULEX Kosovo, UNMIK's mandate altered to monitoring and supporting local institutions and focused on supporting security, stability and human rights. A positive decision by the UN Security Council is required to terminate the operation.

| SCR 1244 June 1999 Kosovo | Obs.: Czech Republic, **Moldova**, Norway, Poland, **Portugal**, Romania, *Spain*, **Turkey**, Ukraine   Civ. pol.: **Belgium**, **Croatia**, Germany, *Ghana*, **Hungary**, Italy, *Pakistan*, Romania, Turkey, Ukraine | – 8 8 173 | – 9 7 134* | 55 1 (–,1,–,–) | 45.9 – |

* The operation is supported by 210 locally recruited staff and 28 UN volunteers.

UN Organization Stabilization Mission in the Democratic Republic of the Congo (MONUSCO)

The UN Organization Mission in the DRC (MONUC) was established by SCR 1279 (30 Nov. 1999) and mandated by SCR 1291 (24 Feb. 2000) to monitor the implementation of the ceasefire agreement between the Democratic Republic of the Congo (DRC), Angola, Namibia, Rwanda, Uganda and Zimbabwe; to supervise and verify the disengagement of forces; to monitor human rights violations; and to facilitate the provision of humanitarian assistance. The operation was given UN Charter Chapter VII powers by SCR 1493 (28 July 2003). SCR 1856 (22 Dec. 2008) mandated the operation to protect civilians, humanitarian personnel and UN personnel and facilities; to assist the disarmament, demobilization and reintegration (DDR) of foreign and Congolese armed groups; to assist security sector reform (SSR) and train and mentor Congolese armed forces; to contribute to the territorial security of the DRC; and to support the strengthening of democratic institutions and the rule of law. SCR 1925 (28 May 2010) transformed the mission into a stabilization operation and renamed it MONUSCO. MONUSCO cooperates with EUPOL RD Congo and EUSEC RD Congo. SCR 2053 (27 June 2012) extended the mandate until 30 June 2013.

SCR 1279	Troops: Bangladesh, Belgium, Benin, China, Egypt, Ghana, Guatemala, India, Indonesia, Jordan, Morocco, Nepal, Pakistan, Serbia, South Africa, **Ukraine**,	19 815	17 090	213**	1 453.2
Nov. 1999		760	675	18	251.6
Democratic Republic	Uruguay	1 441	1 401	(1,5,8,4)	
of the Congo	Obs.: **Algeria**, Bangladesh, Belgium, Benin, Bolivia, Bosnia and Herzegovina,	1 180	977*		
	Burkina Faso, Cameroon, Canada, China, Czech Republic, Egypt, France,				
	Ghana, Guatemala, India, Indonesia, Ireland, Jordan, Kenya, Malawi,				
	Malaysia, Mali, Mongolia, Morocco, *Mozambique*, Nepal, Niger, Nigeria,				
	Norway, Pakistan, Paraguay, Peru, Poland, Romania, Russia, Senegal, Serbia,				
	South Africa, *Spain*, Sri Lanka, Sweden, Switzerland, Tanzania, Tunisia, UK,				
	Ukraine, Uruguay, USA, Yemen, Zambia				
	Civ. pol.: Bangladesh, **Belgium**, Benin, Burkina Faso, Cameroon, **Canada**,				
	Central African Republic, Chad, Côte d'Ivoire, **Djibouti**, Egypt, France,				
	Guinea, India, Jordan, Madagascar, Mali, Niger, Nigeria, Romania, Senegal,				
	Sweden, **Switzerland**, Togo, Turkey, Ukraine, *Uruguay*, Yemen				

* The operation is supported by 2895 locally recruited staff and 584 UN volunteers.
** The fatality figure for 2011 has been reduced from 33 to 24, based on new information.

UN Mission in Liberia (UNMIL)

UNMIL was established by SCR 1509 (19 Sep. 2003) under UN Charter Chapter VII and mandated to support the implementation of the 2003 Comprehensive Peace Agreement; to assist in matters of humanitarian and human rights; to support SSR; and to protect civilians. SCR 1938 (15 Sep. 2010) authorized the operation to assist the Liberian Government with the 2011 presidential and legislative elections. Its primary task now is to secure peace and stability in Liberia; to ensure the protection of civilians within the country; and to assist the successful transition of security responsibilities to the Liberian National Police (LNP) through capacity building of the LNP. UNMIL cooperates with UNOCI and UNIPSIL. SCR 2066 (17 Sep. 2012) extended the mandate until 30 Sep. 2013.

Legal instrument/ Deployment date/ Location	Countries contributing troops, observers (Obs.), civilian police (Civ. pol.) and civilian staff (Civ. staff) in 2012	Troops/Obs./ Civ. pol./Civ. staff		Deaths: to date/ 2012/ (by cause^a)	Cost ($ m.): 2012/ unpaid
		Approved	Actual		
SCR 1509 Oct. 2003 Liberia	**Troops:** Bangladesh, Benin, Bolivia, Brazil, China, Croatia, Denmark, *Ecuador*, Ethiopia, Finland, France, Ghana, Jordan, Korea (South), Namibia, Nepal, Nigeria, Pakistan, Paraguay, Peru, Philippines, Senegal, Togo, Ukraine, USA, Yemen	3 750* – 1 821 –	7 430 126 1 306 470**	172 8 (–,17, –)	510 142.6

Obs.: Bangladesh, Benin, Bolivia, Brazil, Bulgaria, China, Denmark, Ecuador, Egypt, El Salvador, Ethiopia, Gambia, Ghana, Indonesia, Jordan, Korea (South), Kyrgyzstan, Malaysia, **Mali**, Moldova, Montenegro, **Namibia**, Nepal, Niger, Nigeria, Pakistan, Paraguay, Peru, Philippines, Poland, Romania, Russia, *Senegal*, Serbia, Togo, Ukraine, USA, Zambia, Zimbabwe

Civ. pol.: Argentina, Bangladesh, Bosnia and Herzegovina, China, *Czech Republic*, Egypt, El Salvador, Fiji, Gambia, Germany, Ghana, India, ***Jamaica***, Jordan, Kenya, Kyrgyzstan, Namibia, Nepal, Nigeria, Norway, Pakistan, Philippines, Poland, Russia, Rwanda, Serbia, Sri Lanka, Sweden, Switzerland, Turkey, Uganda, Ukraine, **Uruguay**, USA, Yemen, Zambia, Zimbabwe

* SCR 2066 called for a 3-phrase reduction in troop numbers by 4200 between Aug. 2012 and July 2015. The mission's total strength is expected to be approximately 3750 by July 2015. Police deployments are to be increased by 420 personnel, reaching a new authorized level of 1795.

** The operation is supported by 989 locally recruited staff and 230 UN volunteers.

UN Operation in Côte d'Ivoire (UNOCI)

UNOCI was established by SCR 1528 (27 Feb. 2004) under UN Charter Chapter VII and mandated to monitor the cessation of hostilities, movement of armed groups and the arms embargo; to support DDR and SSR; to assist with the creation of law and order, human rights and public information; to facilitate humanitarian assistance and rebuild state institutions; and to assist in the holding of free elections. In 2007 the mandate was expanded to support the full implementation of the Ouagadougou Political Agreement (4 Mar. 2007) and of the Supplementary Agreements (28 Nov. 2007). SCR 1933 (30 June 2010) added protection of civilians to the operation's mandate. UNOCI cooperates with UNMIL and Operation Licorne. Following the political crisis after the presidential elections in Nov. 2010, SCR 1951 (24 Nov. 2010) authorized the temporary transfer of units from UNMIL to reinforce UNOCI and SCR 1967 (19 Jan. 2011) authorized the deployment of an additional 2000 troops for UNOCI. The mission's principal task at present is the protection of civilians. SCR 2062 (26 July 2012) extended the mandate until 31 July 2013.

SCR 1528		8 645	9 360	106	530.8
Apr. 2004		192	181	17	78.2
Côte d'Ivoire		1 563	1 492	(7,2,7,1)
		–	418*

Troops: <u>Bangladesh</u>, Benin, Brazil, Chad, Egypt, France, Ghana, Jordan, **Malawi**, Morocco, Nepal, Niger, **Nigeria**, Pakistan, Paraguay, Philippines, Senegal, Tanzania, Togo, Tunisia, Uganda, *Yemen*

Obs.: Bangladesh, Benin, Bolivia, Brazil, Chad, China, Ecuador, El Salvador, Ethiopia, Gambia, Ghana, Guatemala, Guinea, India, Ireland, Jordan, Korea (South), **Malawi**, Moldova, Namibia, Nepal, Niger, Nigeria, Pakistan, Paraguay, Peru, Philippines, Poland, Romania, Russia, Senegal, Serbia, Tanzania, Togo, Tunisia, Uganda, Uruguay, Yemen, Zambia, Zimbabwe

Civ. pol.: *Argentina*, Bangladesh, Benin, **Burkina Faso**, Burundi, Cameroon, Canada, Central African Republic, Chad, Congo (Dem. Rep. of), Djibouti, Egypt, France, Ghana, **Guinea**, Jordan, **Madagascar**, Niger, **Nigeria**, Pakistan, **Rwanda**, Senegal, Togo, **Tunisia**, Turkey, Ukraine, **Uruguay**, Yemen

* The operation is supported by 767 locally recruited staff and 190 UN volunteers.

UN Stabilization Mission in Haiti (MINUSTAH)

MINUSTAH was established by SCR 1542 (30 Apr. 2004) under UN Charter Chapter VII and mandated to maintain a secure and stable environment to ensure that the peace process is carried forward; to support SSR, including a comprehensive DDR programme, building the capacity of the national police and re-establishing the rule of law; to assist in the holding of free elections; to support humanitarian and human rights activities; and to protect civilians. SCR 1927 (4 June 2010) requested the operation to support the Haitian Government's preparation for municipal and presidential elections scheduled for 2010. SCR 2070 (12 Oct. 2012) extended the mandate until 15 Oct. 2013.

Legal instrument/ Deployment date/ Location	Countries contributing troops, observers (Obs.), civilian police (Civ. pol.) and civilian staff (Civ. staff) in 2012	Troops/Obs./ Civ. pol./Civ. staff		Deaths: to date/ 2012/ (by cause^a)	Cost ($ m.): 2012/ unpaid
		Approved	Actual		
MINUSTAH continued					
SCR 1542	Troops: Argentina, Bolivia, Brazil, Canada, Chile, Ecuador, France,	6 270*	6 809	169	720.9
June 2004	Guatemala, **Indonesia**, Japan, Jordan, Korea (South), Nepal, Paraguay, Peru,	–	–	4	162.5
Haiti	Philippines, Sri Lanka, Uruguay, USA	2 601	2 655	(–,1,2,1)	
	Civ. pol.: Argentina, Bangladesh, Benin, Brazil, Burkina Faso, Burundi,	–	451**		
	Cameroon, Canada, Central African Republic, Chad, Chile, *China*, Colombia,				
	Côte d'Ivoire, Croatia, Egypt, El Salvador, France, *Grenada*, Guinea, India,				
	Indonesia, *Jamaica*, Jordan, *Kyrgyzstan, Lithuania*, Madagascar, Mali, Nepal,				
	Niger, Nigeria, Norway, Pakistan, Philippines, Romania, Russia, Rwanda,				
	Senegal, Serbia, **Sierra Leone**, Spain, Sri Lanka, Sweden, Thailand, Togo,				
	Turkey, Uruguay, USA, Yemen				

* SCR 2070 (12 Oct. 2012) adjusted the operation's overall force level, to be gradually reached through a reduction of infantry and engineering personnel.
** The operation is supported by 1317 locally recruited staff and 202 UN volunteers.

UN Integrated Mission in Timor-Leste (UNMIT)

UNMIT was established by SCR 1704 (25 Aug. 2006) and mandated to support the Government of Timor-Leste in post-conflict peacebuilding, capacity building and training of the East Timorese National Police. SCR 1912 (26 Feb. 2010) endorsed the UN Secretary-General's proposal to reconfigure UNMIT's police component after national and municipal elections in 2012. SCR 2037 (23 Feb. 2012) extended the mandate until 31 Dec. 2012. The operation closed on 31 Dec. 2012.

SCR 1704				
Aug. 2006				
Timor-Leste	34	–	12	176
	1 605	3	5	50.9
	441	57	(–,–,3,2)	
		302*		

Obs.: *Australia, Bangladesh, Brazil, China, Fiji, India, Japan, Malaysia, Nepal, New Zealand, Pakistan, Philippines, Portugal, Sierra Leone, Singapore*

Civ. pol.: *Australia, Bangladesh, Brazil, China, Croatia, Egypt, El Salvador, Gambia, India, Jamaica, Jordan, Korea (South), Kyrgyzstan, Malaysia, Namibia, Nepal, New Zealand, Nigeria, Pakistan, Philippines, Portugal, Romania, Russia, Samoa, Senegal, Singapore, Spain, Sri Lanka, Thailand, Turkey, Uganda, Ukraine, Uruguay, Yemen, Zambia, Zimbabwe*

* The operation is supported by 827 locally recruited staff and 72 UN volunteers.

UN Interim Security Force for Abyei (UNISFA)

UNISFA was established by SCR 1990 (27 June 2011) and mandated to monitor and verify the redeployment of any Sudanese and South Sudanese armed forces from the Abyei Area; to provide demining assistance; to facilitate the delivery of humanitarian aid; to strengthen the capacity of the Abyei Police Service; and to provide security for oil infrastructure in the Abyei Area. SCR 2024 (14 Dec. 2011) broadened its mandate to include assistance in the South Sudan–Sudan border normalization process. SCR 2075 (16 Nov. 2012) extended the mandate until 31 May 2013.

SCR 1990	4 200	3 843	8	216.7
June 2011	–	131	3	93.3
Abyei	50	5	(–,1,1,1)	
	–	84*		

Troops: **Benin, Bolivia, Brazil,** *Egypt,* **Ethiopia,** Ghana, **Guatemala, India, Indonesia, Nepal, Nigeria, Peru, Philippines, Russia, Rwanda, Sri Lanka, Tanzania, Ukraine, Uruguay, Zimbabwe**

Obs.: **Benin, Bolivia, Brazil, Burundi, Cambodia, Ecuador, El Salvador,** Ethiopia, **Ghana, India, Indonesia,** *Japan,* **Kyrgyzstan, Malaysia, Mongolia,** *Morocco, Mozambique,* **Namibia, Nepal, Nigeria, Paraguay, Peru, Philippines, Russia, Rwanda, Sierra Leone, Sri Lanka, Tanzania, Ukraine, Uruguay, Zambia, Zimbabwe**

* The operation is supported by 47 locally recruited staff and 7 UN volunteers.

Legal instrument/ Deployment date/ Location	Countries contributing troops, observers (Obs.), civilian police (Civ. pol.) and civilian staff (Civ. staff) in 2012	Troops/Obs./ Civ. pol./Civ. staff		Deaths: to date/ 2012/ (by cause^a)	Cost ($ m.): 2012/ unpaid
		Approved	Actual		

UN Mission in South Sudan (UNMISS)

UNMISS was established by SCR 1996 (8 July 2011) for an initial period of one year, mandated to support peace consolidation in order to foster longer-term state building and economic development. It is also mandated to support the South Sudanese Government in conflict prevention, mitigation and resolution; in the protection of civilians; and in providing security, establishing the rule of law and strengthening the security and justice sectors. SCR 2057 (5 July 2012) extended the mandate until 15 July 2013.

Legal instrument/ Deployment date/ Location	Countries contributing troops, observers (Obs.), civilian police (Civ. pol.) and civilian staff (Civ. staff) in 2012	Approved	Actual	Deaths: to date/ 2012/ (by cause^a)	Cost ($ m.): 2012/ unpaid
SCR 1996 July 2011 South Sudan	Troops: Australia, Bangladesh, Brazil, Cambodia, Canada, China, **Denmark,** *Egypt,* Germany, **Ghana, Guatemala,** India, Japan, Jordan, Kenya, Korea (South), **Moldova, Mongolia, Nepal, Netherlands,** New Zealand, Nigeria, Norway, *Pakistan,* **Romania,** Russia, Rwanda, **Senegal,** Sweden, Switzerland, **Uganda,** UK, **Ukraine, USA,** Yemen, Zambia	7 000 166 900 957	6 473 140 544 831*	9 8 (–,5,3,1)	788.8 62.5
	Obs.: Australia, Bangladesh, Benin, Bolivia, Brazil, *Burkina Faso,* Cambodia, Canada, China, Denmark, Ecuador, Egypt, El Salvador, Fiji, Germany, Guatemala, Guinea, India, Indonesia, **Italy,** Jordan, Kenya, Korea (South), Kyrgyzstan, Mali, Moldova, Mongolia, Namibia, Nepal, **Netherlands,** New Zealand, Nigeria, Norway, Papua New Guinea, Paraguay, Peru, Philippines, Poland, Romania, Russia, Rwanda, **Senegal,** *Sierra Leone,* Sri Lanka, Sweden, Switzerland, Tanzania, Timor-Leste, **Uganda,** Ukraine, Yemen, Zambia, **Zimbabwe**				
	Civ. pol.: Argentina, Australia, Bangladesh, Bosnia and Herzegovina, Canada, China, El Salvador, Ethiopia, Fiji, Gambia, Germany, Ghana, India, Indonesia, *Jamaica,* Kenya, Kyrgyzstan, Malaysia, Namibia, Nepal, Nigeria, Norway, Philippines, **Russia,** Rwanda, Samoa, **South Africa,** Sri Lanka, Sweden, **Switzerland,** Turkey, Uganda, Ukraine, **UK,** USA, Zambia, Zimbabwe				

* The operation is supported by 1375 locally recruited staff and 391 UN volunteers.

UN Supervision Mission in Syria (UNSMIS)

UNSMIS was established by SCR 2043 (21 Apr. 2012) and was mandated for an initial period of 90 days to monitor a cessation of armed violence in all forms by all parties and to monitor and support the implementation of the Joint Arab League–UN Special Envoy's six-point plan to end the conflict in Syria. The mission was suspended on 15 June 2012 due to an escalation of violence. SCR 2059 (30 July 2012) renewed the mandate for another 30 days, and made any further renewal conditional on a sufficient reduction in violence to allow UNSMIS monitors to fulfil their mandate. However, the mission was terminated on 19 Aug. 2012 due to continued violence. It was to be replaced with a special liaison office mandated to support efforts towards a political solution to the Syrian crisis (S/2012/618), but such an office had not opened by the end of 2012.

SCR 2043 **Apr. 2012** *Syria*	*Obs:* *Armenia, Bangladesh, Benin, Brazil, Burkina Faso, Burundi, Fiji, Finland, France, Ghana, Indonesia, Ireland, Italy, Jordan, Kenya, Kyrgyzstan, Mauritania, Morocco, Nepal, Netherlands, New Zealand, Niger, Nigeria, Norway, Paraguay, Philippines, Romania, Russia, Senegal, Slovenia, Switzerland, Togo, Yemen, Zimbabwe*	300 – –	– 150 70*	1 1 (1, –, –)	16.8 – –

* The operation is supported by 35 locally recruited staff.

United Nations political and peacebuilding operations

Total: 4 operations **.:***		– – – 636	242 23 18 940	35 2	468 –

* UN political missions do not receive contributions of personnel from member states, unlike regular UN peace operations. Staff are recruited according to mission requirements

UN Assistance Mission in Afghanistan (UNAMA)

UNAMA was established by SCR 1401 (28 Mar. 2002) and mandated to assist with the protection of human rights, the rule of law and gender issues; to support national reconciliation and rapprochement; and to manage humanitarian relief, recovery and reconstruction activities. Its mandate was expanded by SCR 1806 (20 Mar. 2008) to coordinate international assistance; to strengthen cooperation with ISAF; to manage all UN humanitarian relief, recovery and reconstruction activities in Afghanistan; to support efforts to improve governance and the rule of law and to combat corruption; and to promote human rights and provide technical assistance to the electoral process. UNAMA will actively support Afghanistan's assumption of leadership and ownership of security, governance and development within the country. The mission has 18 regional offices as well as a support office in Kuwait. SRC 2041 (22 Mar. 2012) extended the mandate until 23 Mar. 2013.

Legal instrument/ Deployment date/ Location	Countries contributing troops, observers (Obs.), civilian police (Civ. pol.) and civilian staff (Civ. staff) in 2012	Troops/Obs./ Civ. pol./Civ. staff		Deaths: to date/ 2012/ (by cause[a])	Cost ($ m.): 2012/ unpaid
		Approved	Actual		
UNAMA continued					
SCR 1401	Obs.: Australia, **Czech Republic**, Denmark, Germany, **Italy, Mongolia,**	–	–	21	241.5
Mar. 2002	**Netherlands**, New Zealand, Norway, Poland, Portugal, **Romania**, Sweden,	–	18	1	–
Afghanistan	Turkey, *Uruguay*	–	5	(–, –, 1, –)	
	Civ. pol.: **Burkina Faso, Netherlands**, *Norway*, **Sweden, USA**	–	387*		

* The operation is supported by 1614 locally recruited staff and 71 UN volunteers.

UN Assistance Mission in Iraq (UNAMI)

UNAMI was established by SCR 1500 (14 Aug. 2003) and mandated to support dialogue and national reconciliation; to facilitate humanitarian assistance and the safe return of refugees and displaced persons; to coordinate reconstruction and assistance programmes; to assist in capacity building and sustainable development; and to promote the protection of human rights, judicial and legal reform and strengthen the rule of law. UNAMI cooperates with EUJUST LEX. SCR 2061 (25 July 2012) extended the mandate for 12 months.

SCR 1500	Troops: Fiji, **Nepal**	–	242*	13	172.8
Aug. 2003	Obs.: Australia, *Denmark*, Jordan, *Nepal*, New Zealand,	–	5	1	–
Iraq	Civ. pol.: **Jordan, Nepal, Niger**	–	4	(–, –, 1, –)	
		459	380**		

* Troops with UNAMI are classified as guard unit troops.
** The operation is supported by 463 locally recruited staff.

UN Integrated Peacebuilding Office in Sierra Leone (UNIPSIL)

UNIPSIL was established by SCR 1829 (4 Aug. 2008) and mandated to monitor and promote human rights, democratic institutions and the rule of law; to support efforts to identify and resolve potential conflict threats. SCR 1941 (29 Sep. 2010) expanded the mandate to include promoting good governance and supporting the government in preparation for presidential elections in 2012. SCR 2065 (12 Sep. 2012) extended the mandate until 15 Mar. 2013.

SCR 1829	Civ. pol: ..	–	1	17.7
Oct. 2008	Civ. staff: ..	–	–	–
Sierra Leone		7		
		36*		

* The operation is supported by 33 locally recruited staff and 8 volunteers.

UN Support Mission in Libya (UNSMIL)

UNSMIL was established by SCR 2009 (16 Sep. 2011) and is mandated to assist the Libyan Government in managing the democratization process; promoting the rule of law; restoring public security; countering illicit proliferation of arms; and coordinating international assistance and building capacity of the government. SCR 2040 (12 Mar. 2012) extended the mandate until 16 Mar.2013, subject to review after 6 months.

SCR 2009	Civ. pol: ..	–	–	36
Sep. 2011	Civ. staff: ..	–	–	–
Libya		2		
	177	137*		

* The operation was supported by 23 locally recruited staff.

African Union–United Nations

Total: 1 operation	45 contributing countries	16 200	15 596	144	1 568.9
		–	307	40	120.8
		4 690	4 877		
		–	1 087		

AU/UN Hybrid Operation in Darfur (UNAMID)

UNAMID was established by the AU PSC's 79th Communiqué on the Situation in Darfur (22 June 2007) and by SCR 1769 (31 July 2007) under UN Charter Chapter VII. The operation is mandated to contribute to the restoration of a secure environment, protect the civilian population, facilitate humanitarian assistance, monitor the implementation of related ceasefire agreements, and promote the rule of law and human rights. SCR 2063 (31 July 2012) extended the mandate until 31 July 2013.

Legal instrument/ Deployment date/ Location	Countries contributing troops, observers (Obs.), civilian police (Civ. pol.) and civilian staff (Civ. staff) in 2012	Troops/Obs./ Civ. pol./Civ. staff		Deaths: to date/ 2012/ (by cause^a)	Cost ($ m.): 2012/ unpaid
		Approved	Actual		
UNAMID continued					
SCR 1769	Troops: Bangladesh, Burkina Faso, **Burundi**, *Canada*, China, Egypt, Ethiopia,	16 200	15 596	144	1568.9
Oct. 2007	Gambia, Germany, Ghana, **Indonesia**, *Italy*, Jordan, Kenya, Korea (South),	–	307	40	120.8
Sudan	**Lesotho**, *Malawi*, Malaysia, Mongolia, Namibia, Nepal, *Netherlands*, <u>Nigeria</u>,	4 690*	4 877	(12,8,15,5)	
	Pakistan, **Palau**, <u>Rwanda</u>, Senegal, Sierra Leone, South Africa, Tanzania,	–	1 087**		
	Thailand, Yemen, Zambia, Zimbabwe				
	Obs.: **Australia**, Bangladesh, Burkina Faso, Burundi, Cameroon, *Ecuador*,				
	Egypt, Ethiopia, Ghana, *Guatemala*, Indonesia, **Iran**, Jordan, Kenya, **Lesotho**,				
	Malawi, Malaysia, Mali, Namibia, Nepal, Nigeria, Pakistan, **Palau**, **Peru**,				
	Rwanda, Senegal, Sierra Leone, South Africa, Tanzania, Thailand, Togo,				
	Uganda, <u>Yemen</u>, Zambia, Zimbabwe				
	Civ. pol.: Bangladesh, **Benin**, Burkina Faso, Burundi, *Cameroon*, Côte d'Ivoire,				
	Djibouti, Egypt, **Ethiopia**, *Fiji*, Gambia, **Germany**, Ghana, Indonesia,				
	Jamaica, <u>Jordan</u>, **Kazakhstan**, **Kyrgyzstan**, Madagascar, Malawi, Malaysia,				
	Namibia, Nepal, Niger, Nigeria, Pakistan, **Palau**, *Philippines*, Rwanda, Senegal,				
	Sierra Leone, South Africa, Tajikistan, Tanzania, Togo, **Tunisia**, Turkey,				
	Yemen, Zambia				

* SCR 2063 (31 July 2012) called for the reconfiguration of the mission over 12–18 months to comprise 16 200 military personnel, 17 formed police units of up to 140 personnel each, and a further 2310 police personnel.

** The operation is supported by 2935 locally recruited staff and 446 UN volunteers.

African Union (AU)				
Total: 1 operation	28 contributing countries	17 731	16 970	394	218.5
		–	–	..	–
		540	369		
		–	53		

AU Mission in Somalia (AMISOM)

AMISOM was established by the AU PSC's 69th Communiqué (19 Jan. 2007) and endorsed by SCR 1744 (21 Feb. 2007) under UN Charter Chapter VII. It was mandated to support the peace process, humanitarian assistance and overall security in Somalia. In 2008 the mandate was expanded by SCR 1838 (Oct. 2008) to assist implementation of the Djibouti Agreement (19 Aug. 2008), including training of Somali security forces in order to promote security in Mogadishu. UN SCR 1964 (22 Dec. 2010) endorsed an AU proposal to increase the authorized troop level to 12 000. At its 306th meeting (6 Jan. 2012) the AU PSC, supported by SCR 2036 (22 Feb. 2012), decided to increase AMISOM's authorized strength to 17 731, including 5700 Djiboutian and 're-hatted' Kenyan troops and AMISOM's police component. At the same meeting, the PSC extended AMISOM's mandate until 16 Jan. 2013. SCR 2073 (7 Nov. 2012) renewed the UN's endorsement of AMISOM's mandate until 7 Mar. 2013.

PSC 69th	Troops: Burundi, *Cameroon, Comoros,* Djibouti, *Ethiopia,* Kenya, *Senegal,*	17 731	16 970	394	218.5***
Communiqué and	*Sierra Leone,* Uganda, *Zambia*		–	..	–
SCR 1744	Civ. pol.: **Burundi,** Gambia, Ghana, Kenya, Nigeria, Sierra Leone, Uganda,	540	369		
Mar. 2007	Zimbabwe	–	53**		
Somalia*	**Civ. Staff.:** *Algeria,* Benin, Burundi, Burkina Faso, Cameroon, Chad, Côte d'Ivoire, Djibouti, Ethiopia, Gambia, Ghana, Kenya, Liberia, Libya, Malawi, *Mali,* Nigeria, Rwanda, Sierra Leone, South Africa, *Sudan,* Swaziland, Tanzania, Uganda, Zimbabwe				

* The operation's headquarters are in Nairobi, Kenya.

** The operation is supported by 49 locally recruited staff. Figures are as of 31 Jan. 2013.

*** The UN has established a trust fund to assist AMISOM's planning and deployment process. Logistical, technical, financial and personnel support are provided by the EU, the Intergovernmental Authority on Development (IGAD), the Arab League and a number of individual countries.

Legal instrument/ Deployment date/ Location	Countries contributing troops, observers (Obs.), civilian police (Civ. pol.) and civilian staff (Civ. staff) in 2012	Troops/Obs./ Civ. pol./Civ. staff		Deaths: to date/ 2012/ (by cause[a])	Cost ($ m.): 2012/ unpaid
		Approved	Actual		
Communauté Économique des États de l'Afrique Centrale (CEEAC)					
Total: 1 operation	**6 contributing countries**	387	334	..	45.3
		–	–	2	–
		104	57		
		–	–		

Mission for the Consolidation of Peace in the Central African Republic (MICOPAX)

MICOPAX was established by a decision of the 2002 Economic and Monetary Community of Central Africa (CEMAC) Libreville Summit (2 Oct. 2002) in order to secure the border between Chad and the Central African Republic (CAR). The mandate was expanded at the 2003 Libreville Summit (3 June 2003) to include contributing to the overall security environment, assisting in the restructuring of the CAR's armed forces and supporting the transition process. Coinciding with the transfer of authority on 12 July 2008 from CEMAC to CEEAC, the mission's mandate was expanded again to include promotion of political dialogue and human rights. The Final Communiqué of the Extraordinary Council of CEEAC Foreign Ministers (28 Dec. 2012) increased the authorized troop strength to 680 in response to renewed violence. The operation is mandated for 6-month periods, renewable until 2013.

Legal instrument/ Deployment date/ Location	Countries contributing troops...	Approved	Actual	Deaths	Cost
Libreville Summit, 2 Oct. 2002	Troops: Cameroon, Chad, Congo, Congo (Dem. Rep. of), Gabon	387	334*	..	45.3
Dec. 2002	Civ. pol.: **Chad**, *Equatorial Guinea*, **Congo (Dem. Rep. of)**	–	–	2	–
Central African Republic		104	57	(1,–,1,–)	
		–	–**		

* The authorized and actual personnel figures given are as of 15 Dec. 2012. The operation is supported by and co-located with a detachment of c. 250 French soldiers (Opération Boali).

** The operation is supported by 1 locally recruited staff member.

Commonwealth of Independent States (CIS)

Total: 1 operation   3 contributing countries

1 353	1 140	..	..
40	40	1	
–	–		
–	–		

Joint Control Commission Peacekeeping Force (JCC)

The JCC Peacekeeping Force was established pursuant to the Agreement on the Principles Governing the Peaceful Settlement of the Armed Conflict in the Trans-Dniester region, signed in Moscow by the presidents of Moldova and Russia (21 July 1992). The Joint Control Commission—a monitoring commission comprising representatives of Moldova, Russia, Ukraine and Trans-Dniester—was established to coordinate the activities of the joint force.

Bilateral agreement, 21 July 1992   Troops: Moldova, Russia, (Trans-Dniester)
Obs.: Moldova, Russia, (Trans-Dniester), Ukraine

July 1992
Moldova (Trans-Dniester)

1 353	1 140	..	..
40	40	1	
–	–	(1,–,–)	
–	–		

Economic Community of West African States (ECOWAS)

Total: 1 operation   4 contributing countries

665	385	..	..
–	–	..	..
–	280		
–	–		

ECOWAS Mission in Guinea-Bissau (ECOMIB)

ECOMIB was established by the Extraordinary Session of the Authority of ECOWAS Heads of State and Government, Abidjan, 27 Apr. 2012, in response to a military coup in Guinea-Bissau on 12 Apr. 2012. The mission comprises a contingent of the ECOWAS Standby Force. It was mandated to facilitate the withdrawal of the Angolan Technical and Military Assistance Mission (MISSANG); to assist in securing the political transition process, including supporting free and fair elections to be held in 2013; and to support the ECOWAS–Community of Portuguese-speaking Countries (CPLP) road map for defence and security sector reform (DSSR). The ECOWAS Commission and the Guinea-Bissau authorities signed an MOU on the DSSR Programme on 11 Nov. 2012. MISSANG completed its withdrawal in June 2012. The Final Communiqué of the Extraordinary Session of the Authority of ECOWAS Heads of State and Government (11 Nov. 2012) extended the mission's mandate for a second 6-month period until 17 May 2013.

Legal instrument/ Deployment date/ Location	Countries contributing troops, observers (Obs.), civilian police (Civ. pol.) and civilian staff (Civ. staff) in 2012	Troops/Obs./ Civ. pol./Civ. staff		Deaths: to date/ 2012/ (by cause[a])	Cost ($ m.): 2012/ unpaid
		Approved	Actual		
ECOMIB continued					
ECOWAS Summit, 26 Apr. 2012	**Troops: Nigeria, Senegal**	665*	385	..	..
3 May 2012	**Obs.: Burkina Faso, Nigeria**	–	–	..	..
		–	280		

* This figure includes both troops and civilian police

Legal instrument/ Deployment date/ Location	Countries contributing troops, observers (Obs.), civilian police (Civ. pol.) and civilian staff (Civ. staff) in 2012	Approved	Actual	Deaths	Cost
European Union (EU)					
Total: 12 operations	**39 contributing countries**	725	723	30	378.4
		283*	155	2	–
		29	798		
		710	1 045		

* The figure for total approved observers applies to EUMM only and includes both observers and international civilian staff.

EU Police Mission in Bosnia and Herzegovina (EUPM)

EUPM was established by CJA 2002/210/CFSP (11 Mar. 2002) and tasked with the establishment—through monitoring, mentoring and inspection—of a sustainable, professional and multi-ethnic police service in Bosnia and Herzegovina under Bosnian ownership. At the request of the Bosnian authorities, the mandate was modified to focus on the police reform process, strengthening of police accountability and efforts to fight organized crime. Council Decision 2009/906/CFSP (8 Dec. 2009) further strengthened the operation's mandate to include assisting the fight against organized crime and corruption within a broader rule-of-law approach in Bosnia and Herzegovina. EUPM's mandate terminated on 30 June 2012.

Legal instrument/ Deployment date/ Location	Countries contributing	Approved	Actual	Deaths	Cost
CJA 2002/210/CFSP	*Civ. staff: Bulgaria, France, Germany, Ireland, Italy, Portugal, UK*	–	–	3	6.7
Jan. 2003		–	–	..	–
Bosnia and Herzegovina		–	–		
		34	34*		

* The operation was supported by 47 locally recruited staff.

EU Military Operation in Bosnia and Herzegovina (EUFOR ALTHEA)

EUFOR ALTHEA was established by CJA 2004/570/CFSP (12 July 2004) and was endorsed and given UN Charter Chapter VII powers by SCR 1575 (22 Nov. 2004). The mission operates under the Berlin Plus agreements (2003), a set of cooperative agreements between NATO and the EU on issues of security and defence. It is mandated to maintain a secure environment for the implementation of the 1995 Dayton Agreement; to provide capacity building and training support to the Ministry of Defence and Armed Forces; and to support Bosnia and Herzegovina's progress towards EU integration. The operation was reconfigured in Sep. 2012, when troop numbers were halved to 600, to be backed by over-the-horizon reserves. SCR 2074 (14 Nov. 2012) extended the mandate until 15 Nov. 2013.

CJA 2004/570/CFSP and SCR 1575 Dec. 2004 Bosnia and Herzegovina*	Troops: Albania, Austria, Bulgaria, Chile, Czech Republic, *Estonia*, Finland, France, Germany, Greece, Hungary, Ireland, Italy, Luxembourg, Macedonia (FYR), Netherlands, Poland, *Portugal*, Romania, Slovakia, Slovenia, Spain, Sweden, Switzerland, <u>Turkey</u>, UK	600	600	21	16
		–	–	–	..
		–	–	..	

* A multinational manoeuvre battalion (made up of troops from Austria and Turkey) is stationed in Sarajevo. The operation also includes an integrated police unit (IPU) and the liaison and observer teams (LOTs), deployed to regional coordination centres.

EU Advisory and Assistance Mission for Security Reform in the Democratic Republic of the Congo (EUSEC RD Congo)

EUSEC RD Congo was established by CJA 2005/355/CFSP (2 May 2005). The operation's initial mandate was to advise and assist the DRC authorities, specifically the MOD, on security matters, ensuring that their policies are congruent with international humanitarian law, principles of democratic governance and the rule of law. In 2009 the operation's mandate was broadened to include advising and assisting in SSR by facilitating the implementation of the guidelines adopted by the Congolese authorities in the revised plan for reform of the Congolese armed forces. In carrying out its activities, EUSEC operates in close coordination with MONUSCO and EUPOL RD Congo. Council Decision 2012/515/CFSP (24 Sep. 2012) extended the mandate until 30 Sep. 2013.

CJA 2005/355/CFSP June 2005 Democratic Republic of the Congo	Civ. staff: Austria, Belgium, Finland, France, Germany, Hungary, Italy, Luxembourg, *Netherlands*, Portugal, **Romania**, *Spain*, UK, **USA**	–	–	3	16.6
		–	–	1	–
		–	45*	(–,–,1,–)	
		51			

* The majority of the deployed personnel are military advisers. The operation is supported by 34 locally recruited staff.

Legal instrument/ Deployment date/ Location	Countries contributing troops, observers (Obs.), civilian police (Civ. pol.) and civilian staff (Civ. staff) in 2012	Troops/Obs./ Civ. pol./Civ. staff		Deaths: to date/ 2012/ (by cause[a])	Cost ($ m.): 2012/ unpaid
		Approved	Actual		

EU Integrated Rule of Law Mission for Iraq (EUJUST LEX-Iraq)

EUJUST LEX was established by CJA 2005/190/CFSP (7 Mar. 2005), in accordance with SCR 1546 (8 June 2004), to strengthen Iraq's criminal justice system through the training of magistrates, senior police officers and senior penitentiary staff. The operation cooperates with UNAMI. Council Decision 2012/372/CFSP (10 July 2012) extended the mandate until 31 Dec. 2013.

Legal instrument/ Deployment date/ Location	Countries contributing troops, observers (Obs.), civilian police (Civ. pol.) and civilian staff (Civ. staff) in 2012	Approved	Actual	Deaths	Cost
CJA 2005/190/CFSP and SCR 1546	Civ. staff: **Austria**, *Belgium*, **Bulgaria**, *Czech Republic*, Denmark, **Estonia**, Finland, **France**, Germany, Hungary, Ireland, Italy, Netherlands, **Norway**,	–	–	–	29.1
July 2005	Portugal, Romania, *Spain*, Sweden, <u>UK</u>	–	–	–	–
Iraq		52	44*		

* The operation is supported by 11 locally recruited staff.

EU Border Assistance Mission for the Rafah Crossing Point (EU BAM Rafah)

EU BAM Rafah was established by CJA 2005/889/CFSP (12 Dec. 2005) on the basis of the Agreement on Movement and Access between Israel and the Palestinian Authority (15 Nov. 2005). It is mandated to monitor, verify and evaluate the performance of Palestinian Authority border control, security and customs officials at the Rafah Crossing Point with regard to the 2005 Agreed Principles for Rafah Crossing; and to support the Palestinian Authority's capacity building in the field of border control. Following riots in 2007, the Rafah Crossing Point was closed and only to be opened under exceptional circumstances. However, EU BAM Rafah retained full operational capabilities and resumed activity when the crossing was reopened on 28 May 2011. Council Decision 2012/332/CFSP (25 June 2012) extended the mandate until 30 June 2013.

Legal instrument/ Deployment date/ Location	Countries contributing troops, observers (Obs.), civilian police (Civ. pol.) and civilian staff (Civ. staff) in 2012	Approved	Actual	Deaths	Cost
CJA 2005/889/CFSP	Civ. pol.: *France*, Germany, <u>Italy</u>	–	–	–	1.87
Nov. 2005	Civ. staff: *Finland*, France, *Hungary, Italy, Romania, Spain, UK*	–	–	–	–
Egypt, Palestine (Rafah Crossing Point)		3	3		
		1	1*		

* The operation is supported by 4 locally recruited staff.

EU Police Mission for the Palestinian Territories (EUPOL COPPS)*

EUPOL COPPS was established by CJA 2005/797/CFSP (14 Nov. 2005). It is mandated to provide a framework for and advice to Palestinian criminal justice and police officials and coordinate EU aid to the Palestinian Authority. CJA 2010/784/CFSP (17 Dec. 2010) decided the operation should be referred to as the EU Coordinating Office for Palestinian Police Support. Council Decision 2012/324/CFSP (25 June 2012) extended the mandate until 30 June 2013.

CJA 2005/797/CFSP	Civ. pol.: Belgium, Canada, **Cyprus**, **Denmark**, Finland, France, Germany,	–	–	12.5
Jan. 2006	Italy, *Netherlands*, **Slovakia**, *Slovenia*, Spain, Sweden, UK	–	–	–
Palestinian territories	Civ. staff: Bulgaria, **Czech Republic**, **Denmark**, Estonia, Finland, **France**,	26	29	–
	Germany, Ireland, Italy, Lithuania, <u>Netherlands</u>, Romania, Spain, Sweden, *UK*	44	27**	

* The mission is also officially referred as the EU Coordinating Office for Palestinian Police Support.
** The operation is supported by 42 locally recruited staff.

EU Police Mission in Afghanistan (EUPOL Afghanistan)

EUPOL Afghanistan was established by CJA 2007/369/CFSP (30 May 2007) at the invitation of the Afghan Government. The operation is tasked with strengthening the rule of law by contributing to the establishment of civil policing arrangements and law enforcement under Afghan ownership. Council Decision 2010/279/CFSP (18 May 2010) extended the mandate until 31 May 2013.

CJA 2007/369/CFSP	Civ. staff: **Austria**, **Belgium**, *Bulgaria*, Canada, *Croatia*, **Czech Republic**,	–	–	81.8
June 2007	Denmark, Estonia, Finland, France, Germany, **Greece**, **Hungary**, **Ireland**,	–	–	–
Afghanistan	Italy, Latvia, Lithuania, Netherlands, *New Zealand*, Norway, **Poland**,	–		
	Romania, Slovakia, **Spain**, Sweden, UK	400*	347**	–

* Figure includes both civilian staff and civilian police
** The operation is supported by 200 locally recruited staff.

EU Police Mission in the Democratic Republic of the Congo (EUPOL RD Congo)

EUPOL RD Congo was established by CJA 2007/405/CFSP (12 June 2007). CJA 2009/769/CFSP (19 Oct. 2009) mandated the operation to assist the Congolese authorities in reforming and restructuring the Congolese Police; improving interaction between police and the criminal justice system; supporting efforts against sexual violence; and promoting gender, human rights and children aspects of the peace process. The operation cooperates with EUSEC RD Congo and MONUSCO. Council Decision 2012/514/CFSP (24 Sep. 2012) extended the mandate until 30 Sep. 2013.

Legal instrument/ Deployment date/ Location	Countries contributing troops, observers (Obs.), civilian police (Civ. pol.) and civilian staff (Civ. staff) in 2012	Troops/Obs./ Civ. pol./Civ. staff Approved	Actual	Deaths: to date/ 2012 (by cause^a)	Cost ($ m.): 2012/ unpaid
EUPOL RD Congo continued					
CJA 2007/405/CFSP	Civ. pol.: Belgium, Finland, France, *Italy, Sweden*	–	–	–	8.8
July 2007	Civ. staff: **Belgium**, France, Germany, Poland, Portugal, Sweden	–	15	–	–
Democratic Republic of the Congo*		50	19**		

* With headquarters in Kinshasa, EUPOL also operates in eastern DRC, specifically Goma and Bukavu.
** The operation is supported by 17 locally recruited staff.

EU Rule of Law Mission in Kosovo (EULEX Kosovo)

EULEX Kosovo was established by CJA 2008/124/CFSP (4 Feb. 2008). With executive responsibilities, the operation is tasked to monitor, mentor and advise Kosovan institutions in the wider field of the rule of law, with a specific focus on the judiciary. The operation is structured into two divisions: the Executive Division and the Strengthening Division. The executive division focuses on the legal aspect, investigating, prosecuting and adjudicating cases while the strengthening division focus on supporting institutions, judicial authorities and law enforcement agencies. EULEX Kosovo provides support for the 2 newly opened border checkpoints at Jarinje and Merdare, which are jointly managed by the Kosovan and Serbian authorities. It cooperates with UNMIK and OMIK. Council Decision 2012/291/CFSP (5 June. 2012) extended the mandate until 14 June 2014.

Legal instrument/ Deployment date/ Location	Countries contributing troops, observers (Obs.), civilian police (Civ. pol.) and civilian staff (Civ. staff) in 2012	Troops/Obs./ Civ. pol./Civ. staff Approved	Actual	Deaths: to date/ 2012 (by cause^a)	Cost ($ m.): 2012/ unpaid
CJA 2008/124/CFSP	Civ. pol.: Austria, Belgium, Bulgaria, Croatia, Czech Republic, Denmark,	–	–	3	164.9
Feb. 2008	Estonia, Finland, France, Germany, Greece, Hungary, Ireland, Italy, Latvia,	–	–	1	–
Kosovo	Lithuania, *Luxembourg*, Malta, Netherlands, Norway, Poland, **Portugal**,	–	751	(–,–,1, –)	
	Romania, Slovakia, Slovenia, **Spain**, Sweden, Switzerland, Turkey, UK, USA	–	391*		
	Civ. staff: Austria, Belgium, Bulgaria, Croatia, Czech Republic, Denmark,				
	Estonia, Finland, France, Germany, Greece, Hungary, Ireland, Italy, Latvia,				
	Lithuania, **Malta**, Netherlands, Norway, Poland, Portugal, Romania, *Slovakia*,				
	Slovenia, Spain, Sweden, Switzerland, Turkey, UK, USA				

* The mission is supported by 962 national staff.

EU Monitoring Mission (EUMM)

EUMM was established by CJA 2008/736/CFSP (15 Sep. 2008) in accordance with an EU–Russia agreement of 8 Sep. 2008, following the conflict in South Ossetia in Aug. 2008. The operation is tasked with monitoring and analysing progress in the stabilization process, focusing on compliance with the six-point peace plan of 12 Aug. 2008, and in the normalization of civil governance; monitoring infrastructure security and the political and security aspects of the return of internally displaced persons and refugees; and supporting confidence-building measures. Council Decision 2012/503/CFSP (13 Sep. 2012) extended the mandate until 14 Sep. 2013.

CJA 2008/736/CFSP	Obs.: Austria, Belgium, **Bulgaria**, **Cyprus**, Czech Republic, Denmark, Estonia,	–	–	30
Oct. 2008	Finland, **France**, Germany, Greece, Hungary, **Ireland**, **Italy**, Latvia, Lithuania,	283	155*	–
Georgia	Luxembourg, Malta, **Netherlands**, Poland, *Portugal*, Romania, Slovakia,	–	–	101**
	Slovenia, Spain, Sweden, UK			
	Civ. staff: Austria, Belgium, **Bulgaria**, Czech Republic, Denmark, *Estonia*,			
	Finland, **France**, Germany, *Greece*, *Ireland*, Italy, Lithuania, Netherlands,			
	Poland, Romania, **Slovakia**, Spain, Sweden, UK			

* These figures include both civilian police and staff.
** The operation is supported by 116 locally recruited staff.

EU Training Mission (EUTM) Somalia

EUTM Somalia was established by Council Decision 2010/197/CFSP (31 Mar. 2010) and is mandated to strengthen the Federal Government of Somalia and Somali institutions by training and providing support to Somali security forces. Council Decision 2012/835/CFSP (21 Dec. 2012) extended the mandate until 31 Jan. 2013.

Council Decision	Troops: *Belgium*, Finland, France, Germany, Hungary, Ireland, Italy, Malta,	125	–	4.5
2010/197/CFSP	Portugal, **Serbia**, Spain, Sweden, UK	–	–	–
Mar. 2010	Civ. staff: Belgium, *France*, **Kenya**, *Uganda*, *UK*	–	123	1**
Uganda*				

* The training mainly takes place in Uganda.
**The operation is supported by 21 locally recruited staff.

Legal instrument/ Deployment date/ Location	Countries contributing troops, observers (Obs.), civilian police (Civ. pol.) and civilian staff (Civ. staff) in 2012	Troops/Obs./ Civ. pol./Civ. staff		Deaths: to date/ 2012/ (by cause[a])	Cost ($ m.): 2012/ unpaid
		Approved	Actual		

EU Capacity Building Mission in Niger (EUCAP Sahel Niger)

EUCAP Sahel Niger was established by Council Decision 2012/392/CFSP (16 July 2012) and mandated to support capacity building of Nigerien security actors to fight organized crime and terrorism. The mission's tasks include advising and assisting in the implementation of the security dimension of the Nigerien Strategy for Security and Development; supporting the development of regional and international coordination in the fight against terrorism and organized crime; and training on criminal investigation. Its initial focus is on helping to improve control of Nigerien territory, including in coordination with the Nigerien Armed Forces. It provides training, mentoring, assistance, advice and military expertise to the Nigerien Armed Forces. The mandate runs until Aug. 2014.

Legal instrument/ Deployment date/ Location	Countries contributing	Approved	Actual	Deaths	Cost
Council Decision 2012/392/CFSP	Civ. Staff: Belgium, Denmark, France, Italy, Luxembourg, Spain, Sweden	–	–	–	5.59
July 2012		–	–	–	–
Niger		78	35*		

* The mission had not yet recruited any national staff. The authorized figure for locally recruited staff is 28.

League of Arab States

		Approved	Actual	Deaths	Cost
Total: 1 operation	**14 contributing countries**	166	166	–	1
		–	–	–	–

Arab League Observer Mission to Syria

The Arab League Observer Mission to Syria was established by Arab League Observer Mission to Syria was established by Arab League Council Resolution 7439 (16 Nov. 2011). It was mandated to verify implementation of the provisions of the Arab plan of action to resolve the Syrian crisis and protect Syrian civilians, adopted by the Arab League Council on 2 Nov. 2011. Its tasks included observing the ceasefire and monitoring violence between all parties to the Syrian crisis; verifying the release of protesters and other detainees; and confirming free media presence in the country. The mission suspended operations on 28 Jan. 2012 due to an escalation of violence towards civilians and observers.

Arab League Council Resolution 7439 Nov. 2011 Syria*	Obs.: Algeria, Bahrain, Egypt, Iraq, Jordan, Kuwait, Mauritania, Morocco, Qatar, Saudi Arabia, Sudan, Tunisia, UAE, Yemen	166 – –	166 – –	– – –	1** – –

* The observers were divided into 15 zones covering 20 cities and districts across Syria.

** At the 22 Jan. 2012 Continued Extraordinary Arab League Council Ministerial Meeting, the Council agreed to increase the budget for the mission to $5 million.

North Atlantic Treaty Organization (NATO) and NATO-led

Total: 2 operations	50 contributing countries	– – – –	107 186 – – –	– – – –	3 162 289	609.3 –

NATO Kosovo Force (KFOR)

KFOR was established by SCR 1244 (10 June 1999). Its mandated tasks include deterring renewed hostilities, establishing a secure environment, supporting UNMIK and monitoring borders. In 2008 NATO expanded the operation's tasks to include efforts to develop a professional, democratic and multi-ethnic security structure in Kosovo, through the establishment of the Kosovo Security Force (KSF) and a civilian structure to oversee the KSF. In 2009, due to an improved security situation, KFOR began its gradual drawdown. In Aug. 2011 a NATO Operational Reserve Force battalion was deployed in response to clashes in northern Kosovo. As result of these tensions, further drawdown of troops was postponed in July 2012. A second Operational Reserve Force battalion was deployed between Aug. and Dec. 2012 to provide extra security in the run-up to the 2012 Serbian elections A positive decision of the UN Security Council is required to terminate the operation.

SCR 1244 June 1999 Kosovo*	Troops: Albania, Armenia, Austria, Bulgaria, Canada, Croatia, Czech Republic, Denmark, Estonia, Finland, France, Germany, Greece, Hungary, Ireland, Italy, **Lithuania**, Luxembourg, Morocco, Netherlands, Norway, Poland, Portugal, Romania, Slovenia, Sweden, Switzerland, Turkey, Ukraine, UK, USA	– – – –	5 134** – – –	– – –	129	8.52 –

* The Headquarters of Kosovo Force (HQ) are located in Pristina and support a NATO-led operation of 2 Multinational Battle Groups (MNBGs) and 5 Joint Regional Detachments. A Multinational Specialized Unit (MSU) and a Tactical Reserve Manoeuvre Battalion (KTM) are also stationed in Pristina.

** Figure includes KFOR Operational Reserve Forces of approximately 700

Legal instrument/ Deployment date/ Location	Countries contributing troops, observers (Obs.), civilian police (Civ. pol.) and civilian staff (Civ. staff) in 2012	Troops/Obs./ Civ. pol./Civ. staff		Deaths: to date/ 2012/ (by cause[a])	Cost ($ m.): 2012/ unpaid
		Approved	Actual		

International Security Assistance Force (ISAF)

ISAF was established by SCR 1386 (20 Dec. 2001) under UN Charter Chapter VII as a multinational force mandated to assist the Afghan Government to maintain security, as envisaged in Annex I of the 2001 Bonn Agreement. NATO took over command and control of ISAF in Aug. 2003. ISAF completed the third tranche of the transition process, transferring security responsibilities to the Afghan National Security Forces (ANSF), which began in July 2011. Consequently the ANSF were leading in security at the end of 2012 in 11 of Afghanistan's 34 provinces. SCR 2069 (9 Oct. 2012) extended ISAF's mandate until 13 Oct. 2013.

Legal instrument/ Deployment date/ Location	Countries contributing troops, observers (Obs.), civilian police (Civ. pol.) and civilian staff (Civ. staff) in 2012	Approved	Actual	Deaths: to date/ 2012/ (by cause[a])	Cost ($ m.): 2012/ unpaid
SCR 1386 Dec. 2001 Afghanistan*	Troops: Albania, Armenia, Australia, Austria, Azerbaijan, **Bahrain**, Belgium, Bosnia and Herzegovina, Bulgaria, Canada, Croatia, Czech Republic, Denmark, **El Salvador**, Estonia, Finland, France, Georgia, Germany, Greece, Hungary, Iceland, Ireland, Italy, **Jordan**, Korea (South), Latvia, Lithuania, Luxembourg, Macedonia (FYR), Malaysia, Mongolia, Montenegro, Netherlands, New Zealand, Norway, Poland, Portugal, Romania, Singapore, Slovakia, Slovenia, Spain, Sweden, **Tonga**, Turkey, Ukraine, **UAE**, UK, USA	– – – –	102 052** – – –	3 033 289 (289,–,–)	600.8 –

* The territory of Afghanistan is divided into 6 areas of responsibility: Regional Command (RC) Centre (Kabul), currently led by Turkey; RC North (Mazar i Sharif), led by Germany; RC West (Herat), led by Italy; RC South (Kandahar), RC South-West (Lashkar Gah) and RC East (Bagram), all led by the USA.
** The NATO Training Mission in Afghanistan (NTM-A) is included in ISAF personnel figures as it is under ISAF command. It is tasked to mentor and train Afghan police and military personnel. NTM-A has an authorized strength of 2774 troops and police. In Dec. 2012 approximately 4000 personnel were deployed, from Albania, Australia, Belgium, Canada, Croatia, Czech Republic, Denmark, Estonia, Finland, France, Germany, Greece, Hungary, Italy, Jordan, Korea (South), Mongolia, Netherlands, Norway, Poland, Portugal, Romania, Singapore, Slovenia, Spain, Sweden, Turkey, UK and USA.

Organization of American States (OAS)

Total: 1 operation	15 contributing countries				
		–	–	–	7.4
		–	–	–	–
		–	–	2	–
		–	23	–	–

Mission to Support the Peace Process in Colombia (MAPP/OEA)

MAPP/OEA was established by OAS Permanent Council Resolution CP/RES 859 (1397/04) of 6 Feb. 2004 to support the peace process in Colombia, in particular the efforts of the Colombian Government to engage in a political dialogue with the Ejército de Liberación Nacional (ELN, National Liberation Army). It is also mandated to facilitate the DDR process, by providing verification and advisory support.

CP/RES. 859	Civ. staff: Argentina, Bolivia, Brazil, Bulgaria, Chile, Ecuador, Guatemala,	2	7.4
Feb. 2004	Italy, *Mexico, Netherlands*, Nicaragua, Peru, Spain, Sweden, *USA*	–	–
Colombia		–	–
		23*	

* The operation is supported by 69 locally recruited staff.

Organization for Security and Co-operation in Europe (OSCE)

Total: 7 operations	**43 contributing countries**	**10**	**73**
		–	–
		–	
		320	

OSCE Spillover Monitor Mission to Skopje

The OSCE Spillover Monitor Mission to Skopje was established at the 16th Committee of Senior Officials (CSO) meeting (18 Sep. 1992). It was authorized by the Macedonian Government through articles of understanding agreed by an exchange of letters on 7 Nov. 1992. Its tasks include monitoring, police training, development and other activities related to the 2001 Ohrid Framework Agreement. PC.DEC/1058 (29 Nov. 2012) extended the mandate until 31 Dec. 2013.

CSO 18 Sep. 1992	Civ. staff: Austria, *Bosnia and Herzegovina*, Croatia, Czech Republic, **Estonia,**	1	8.8
Sep. 1992	**Finland,** France, Germany, Greece, **Hungary,** *Iceland*, Ireland, Italy, **Moldova,**	–	–
Former Yugoslav	Netherlands, Romania, **Russia, Serbia,** Spain, **Tajikistan, Turkey,** UK, USA	–	
Republic of		37*	
Macedonia			

* The operation is supported by 112 locally recruited staff.

Legal instrument/ Deployment date/ Location	Countries contributing troops, observers (Obs.), civilian police (Civ. pol.) and civilian staff (Civ. staff) in 2012	Troops/Obs./ Civ. pol./Civ. staff		Deaths: to date/ 2012/ (by cause[a])	Cost ($ m.): 2012/ unpaid
		Approved	Actual		

OSCE Mission to Moldova

The OSCE Mission to Moldova was established at the 19th CSO meeting (4 Feb. 1993) and authorized by the Moldovan Government through an MOU (7 May 1993). Its tasks include assisting the conflicting parties in pursuing negotiations on a lasting political settlement, and gathering and providing information on the situation. PC.DEC/1054 (29 Nov. 2012) extended the mandate until 31 Dec. 2013.

CSO 4 Feb. 1993	Civ. staff: Bulgaria, **Czech Republic**, Estonia, France, **Germany**, Italy, *Latvia*,	–	–	–	2.7
Apr. 1993	*Poland, Russia*, Sweden, UK, <u>USA</u>	–	–	–	–
Moldova		–	–	–	
		–	13*		

* The operation is supported by 40 locally recruited staff.

Personal Representative of the Chairman-in-Office on the Conflict Dealt with by the OSCE Minsk Conference

A Personal Representative on the Conflict Dealt with by the OSCE Minsk Conference was appointed by the OSCE Chairman-in-Office (CIO) on 10 Aug. 1995. The Personal Representative's mandate consists of assisting the CIO in planning a possible peacekeeping operation, assisting the parties in confidence-building measures and humanitarian matters, and monitoring the ceasefire between the parties. The mandate is extended annually as part of the OSCE Unified Budget Approval; in 2012 this decision was PC.DEC/1068 (13 Dec. 2012).

CIO 10 Aug. 1995	Civ. staff: Bulgaria, **Czech Republic**, *Hungary, Lithuania*, **Poland, Ukraine**,	–	–	–	1.5
Aug. 1995	<u>UK</u>	–	–	–	–
Azerbaijan (Nagorno-Karabakh)		–	6*		

* The operation is supported by 11 locally recruited staff.

OSCE Mission to Bosnia and Herzegovina

The OSCE Mission to Bosnia and Herzegovina was established by decision MC(5).DEC/1 of the 5th meeting of the OSCE Ministerial Council (8 Dec. 1995), in accordance with Annex 6 of the 1995 Dayton Agreement. The operation is mandated to assist the parties in regional stabilization measures and democracy building. PC.DEC/1061 (29 Nov. 2012) extended the mandate until 31 Dec. 2013.

		18.6	–	–

MC(5).DEC/1
Dec. 1995
Bosnia and Herzegovina

Civ. staff: Armenia, Austria, Belarus, Belgium, Canada, **Croatia**, Czech Republic, Finland, France, Germany, Greece, Hungary, Ireland, Italy, Kyrgyzstan, **Moldova**, *Netherlands*, Norway, **Poland**, Portugal, Russia, Slovakia, Spain, Sweden, *Tajikistan*, Turkey, UK, <u>USA</u>

63*

* The operation is supported by 427 locally recruited staff.

OSCE Presence in Albania

The OSCE Presence in Albania was established by PC.DEC/160 (27 Mar. 1997). In 2003 the operation's mandate was revised to include assisting in legislative, judicial and electoral reform; capacity building; anti-trafficking and anti-corruption activities; police assistance; and good governance. PC.DEC/1056 (29 Nov. 2012) extended the mandate until 31 Dec. 2013.

		4	–	–

PC.DEC/160
Apr. 1997
Albania

Civ. staff: *Albania*, Austria, Bulgaria, **Canada**, Czech Republic, **France**, Germany, **Italy**, Lithuania, Montenegro, Norway, **Slovenia**, <u>Spain</u>, UK, <u>USA</u>

21*

* The operation is supported by 68 locally recruited staff.

OSCE Mission in Kosovo (OMIK)

OMIK was established by PC.DEC/305 (1 July 1999). Its mandate includes training police, judicial personnel and civil administrators and monitoring and promoting human rights. The operation is a component of UNMIK. PC.DEC/835 (21 Dec. 2007) extended the mandate until 31 Jan. 2008, after which the mandate is renewed on a monthly basis unless 1 of the participating states objects.

		28.1	–	9	–

PC.DEC/305
July 1999
Kosovo

Civ. staff: Armenia, Austria, Azerbaijan, Belarus, Belgium, Bosnia and Herzegovina, **Bulgaria**, Canada, Croatia, **Czech Republic**, **Finland**, France, Georgia, Germany, Greece, Hungary, **Iceland**, Ireland, Italy, Macedonia (FYR), Malta, **Moldova**, Montenegro, *Netherlands*, Poland, Portugal, *Romania*, Russia, Slovakia, Spain, Sweden, Turkey, Ukraine, UK, <u>USA</u>, *Uzbekistan*

148*

* The operation is supported by 478 locally recruited staff.

Legal instrument/ Deployment date/ Location	Countries contributing troops, observers (Obs.), civilian police (Civ. pol.) and civilian staff (Civ. staff) in 2012	Troops/Obs./ Civ. pol./Civ. staff		Deaths: to date/ 2012/ (by cause[a])	Cost ($ m.): 2012/ unpaid
		Approved	Actual		
OSCE Mission to Serbia	The OSCE Mission to Serbia was established by PC.DEC/401 (11 Jan. 2001). It is mandated to advise on the implementation of laws and to monitor the proper functioning and development of democratic institutions and processes in Serbia. It assists in the training and restructuring of law enforcement bodies and the judiciary. PC.DEC/1054 (29 Nov. 2012) extended the mandate until 31 Dec. 2013.				
PC.DEC/401	Civ. staff: Austria, Bosnia and Herzegovina, Bulgaria, Canada, *Croatia*, France,	–	–	–	9.3
Mar. 2001	*Georgia*, Germany, *Greece*, Hungary, Ireland, Italy, *Moldova*, Netherlands,	–	–	–	–
Serbia	Norway, Russia, Slovenia, Spain, Sweden, **Switzerland**, *Ukraine*, UK, USA	–	32*		
	* The operation is supported by 134 locally recruited staff.				
Ad-hoc coalitions					
Total: 6 operations	**32 contributing countries**	611	810	106	511.8
		1 698	1 697	1	–
		154	146		
		36	244		
Neutral Nations Supervisory Commission (NNSC)	The NNSC was established by the agreement concerning a military armistice in Korea signed at Panmunjom (27 July 1953). It is mandated with the functions of supervision, observation, inspection and investigation of implementation of the armistice agreement.				
Armistice Agreement	Obs.: Sweden, Switzerland	–	–	–	2.96
July 1953		10	10	–	–
North Korea, South		–	–		
Korea		–	–		

Multinational Force and Observers (MFO)

The MFO was established on 3 Aug. 1981 by the Protocol to the Treaty of Peace between Egypt and Israel, signed on 26 Mar. 1979. Deployment began on 20 Mar. 1982, following the withdrawal of Israeli forces from the Sinai peninsula, but the mission did not become operational until 25 Apr. 1982, the day that Israel returned the Sinai peninsula to Egyptian sovereignty. The operation is mandated to observe the implementation of the peace treaty and to contribute to a secure environment.

Protocol to Treaty of Peace	Obs.: Australia, Canada, Colombia, Czech Republic, Fiji, France, Hungary, Italy, New Zealand, Norway, Uruguay, USA	1 656	–	71	81.7
Apr. 1982	Civ. staff: Australia, Canada, France, New Zealand, **Romania**, UK, USA	–	1 656	1	–
Egypt (Sinai)		–	67*	(–,–,1,–)	–

* The operation is supported by 535 locally recruited staff.

Temporary International Presence in Hebron (TIPH 2)

TIPH 2 was established by the Protocol Concerning the Redeployment in Hebron (17 Jan. 1997) and the Agreement on the Temporary International Presence in Hebron (21 Jan. 1997). It is mandated to contribute to a secure and stable environment and to monitor and report breaches of international humanitarian law. The mandate is renewed every 6 months subject to approval from both the Israeli and Palestinian parties.

Hebron Protocol	Civ. Pol.: Denmark, Italy, Norway, Turkey	–	–	2	::
Feb. 1997	Civ. staff: Denmark, Norway, Sweden, Switzerland	32	31	–	–
Palestine (Hebron)		36	36*		

* The operation is supported by 12 locally recruited staff. All figures are as of 30 Sep. 2012.

Legal instrument/ Deployment date/ Location	Countries contributing troops, observers (Obs.), civilian police (Civ. pol.) and civilian staff (Civ. staff) in 2012	Troops/Obs./ Civ. pol./Civ. staff		Deaths: to date/ 2012/ (by cause[a])	Cost ($ m.): 2012/ unpaid
		Approved	Actual		

Operation Licorne

Operation Licorne was deployed under the authority of SCR 1464 (4 Feb. 2003) and given UN Charter Chapter VII powers to support the ECOWAS mission (2003–2004)—in accordance with UN Charter Chapter VIII—in contributing to a secure environment and, in particular, to facilitate implementation of the 2003 Linas-Marcoussis Agreement. SCR 1528 (27 Feb. 2004) revised the mandate to working in support of UNOCI. SCR 1795 (15 Jan. 2008) expanded the mandate to support implementing the Ouagadougou Political Agreement (4 Mar. 2007) and the Supplementary Agreements (28 Nov. 2007), in particular to assist in the holding of elections. The mission is also mandate to secure the protection of French nationals living in the country. SCR 2062 (26 July 2012) extended the mandate until 31 July 2013.

SCR 1464	Troops: France	–	450*	24	74.5
Feb. 2003		–	–	–	–
Côte d'Ivoire		–	–		

* The operation is supported by a naval attachment in the Gulf of Guinea (Mission Corymbe).

Regional Assistance Mission to Solomon Islands (RAMSI)

RAMSI was established under the framework of the 2000 Biketawa Declaration (28 Oct. 2000). It is mandated to assist the Solomon Islands Government in restoring law and order, strengthening democratic governance and in building up the capacity of the police force.

Biketawa Declaration	Troops: <u>Australia</u>, New Zealand, Papua New Guinea, Tonga	160	160	7	257.1**
July 2003	Civ. pol.: <u>Australia</u>, Fiji, Kiribati, **Marshall Islands**, Micronesia, Nauru, New	–	–	–	–
Solomon Islands	Zealand, **Niue**, Palau, Papua New Guinea, Samoa, Tonga, Tuvalu, Vanuatu	154	146		
	Civ. staff: <u>Australia</u>, *Canada*, Fiji, New Zealand, **Nigeria**, Papua New Guinea,	–	141*		
	South Africa, **Tanzania**, Tonga, **UK**, **USA**				

* The operation is supported by a staff of 130 locally recruited professionals.
** This figure covers the period 1 July 2011–30 June 2012.

International Stabilization Forces (ISF)

The ISF was deployed at the request of the Government of Timor-Leste to assist in stabilizing the security environment in the county and endorsed by SCR 1690 (20 June 2006). Its status is defined by a status-of-forces agreement (26 May 2006) between Australia and Timor-Leste and an MOU between Australia, Timor-Leste and the UN (26 Jan. 2007). The operation has cooperated with UNMIT. The mission ceased all security operations on 22 Nov. 2012 and began withdrawal from the country, which is expected to be completed by Apr. 2013.

Bilateral agreement, 25 May 2006, and SCR 1690	Troops: Australia, New Zealand	451	200	2	95.5*
May 2006		–	–	–	–
Timor-Leste		–	–	–	–
		–	–	–	–

* This figure represents Australia's contribution to the operation.

– = not applicable; . . = information not available; CJA = EU Council Joint Action; CP/RES = OAS Permanent Council Resolution; CSO = OSCE Senior Council (previously the Committee of Senior Officials); DDR = disarmament, demobilization and reintegration; ECOWAS = Economic Community of West African States; MC = OSCE Ministerial Council; MOU = Memorandum of Understanding; PC.DEC = OSCE Permanent Council Decision; PSC = AU Peace and Security Council; SCR = UN Security Council Resolution; SSR = security sector reform.

[a] Where cause of death can be attributed, the 4 figures in parentheses are, respectively, deaths due to hostilities, accident, illness and other causes in 2011. As causes of death were not reported for all deaths in the year, these figures do not always add up to the total annual fatality figure.

Source: SIPRI Multilateral Peace Operations Database, <http://www.sipri.org/databases/pko/>.

Sources and methods

Methods

The figures for approved personnel numbers listed are those most recently authorized for 2012. Numbers of locally recruited support staff and volunteers are not included in the table but, where available, are given in the notes. For European Union (EU) operations, the approved total civilian personnel number is given in the civilian police row. The category 'observers' includes both military and civilian observers.

Personnel fatalities are recorded since the beginning of an operation and in 2012. Known causes of death—whether hostile acts, accidents, illness or other causes—are recorded for fatalities in 2012. As causes of death were not reported for all deaths in the year, these figures do not always add up to the total annual fatality figure. While the UN provides data on fatalities of locally recruited staff, other organizations and alliances do not.

Costs are reported in millions of US dollars at 2012 prices. The budget figures are given for the calendar year rather than for financial years. Costs for the calendar year are calculated on the assumption of an even rate of spending throughout the financial year. Budgets set in currencies other than the US dollar are converted based on the International Monetary Fund's aggregated market exchange rates for 2012. The costs recorded for UN and Organization for Security and Co-operation in Europe (OSCE) operations are the amounts budgeted. The figures provided for other operations represent actual spending.

The costs recorded for UN operations are core operational costs, which include the cost of deploying personnel, per diem payments for deployed personnel and direct non-field support costs (e.g. requirements for the support account for peace operations and the UN logistics base in Brindisi, Italy). The cost of UN peace operations is shared by all UN member states through a specially derived scale of assessed contributions that takes no account of their participation in the operations. Political and peacebuilding operations are funded through regular budget contributions. UN peacekeeping budgets do not cover programmatic costs, such as those for disarmament, demobilization and reintegration, which are financed by voluntary contributions.

The costs recorded for operations conducted by the North Atlantic Treaty Organization (NATO) only represent common costs. These include mainly the running costs of the NATO headquarters (i.e. costs for civilian personnel and costs for operation and maintenance) and investments in the infrastructure necessary to support the operation. The costs of deploying personnel are borne by individual contributing states and are not reflected in the figures given here.

Most EU operations are financed in one of two ways: civilian missions are funded through the Common Foreign and Security Policy (CFSP) budget, while military operations or operations with a military component are funded by contributions by the participating member states through the Athena mechanism.

No figures for cost are provided for Commonwealth of Independent States (CIS) operations as there is no designated common budget and countries participating in the missions bear the cost of troop deployments.

In operations conducted or led by other organizations, such as by the Organization of American States (OAS) or ad hoc coalitions, budget figures may include resources for programme implementation.

For all these reasons, the budget figures presented in table 2.2 are estimates and the budgets for different operations should not be compared.

Unless otherwise stated, all figures are as of 31 December 2012 or, in the case of operations that were terminated in 2012, the date of closure.

Sources

Data on multilateral peace operations is obtained from the following categories of open source: (*a*) official information provided by the secretariat of the organization concerned;

(*b*) information provided by operations themselves, either in official publications or in written responses to annual SIPRI questionnaires; and (*c*) information from national governments contributing to the operation under consideration. In some instances, SIPRI researchers may gather additional information on an operation from the conducting organizations or governments of participating states by means of telephone interviews and email correspondence. These primary sources are supplemented with a wide selection of publicly available secondary sources consisting of specialist journals, research reports, news agencies, and international, regional and local newspapers.

Part II. Military spending and armaments, 2012

Chapter 3. Military expenditure

Chapter 4. Arms production and military services

Chapter 5. International arms transfers

Chapter 6. World nuclear forces

3. Military expenditure

Overview

World military expenditure in 2012 is estimated to have been $1756 billion, representing 2.5 per cent of global gross domestic product or $249 for each person (see section I and the tables in section VII of this chapter). The total is about 0.4 per cent lower in real terms than in 2011, the first fall since 1998. Nonetheless, the total is higher than in any year between the end of World War II and 2010. The distribution of global spending in 2012 shows what may be the beginnings of a shift from the West—the United States, Western and Central Europe, and other developed countries—to other parts of the world, in particular Eastern Europe and the developing world.

US spending is falling from its peaks from the Afghanistan and Iraq wars and the build-up during the presidency of George W. Bush, as the wars wind down and budget cuts—and disruption from disputes over budget cuts—take effect (see section II). In Western and Central Europe, austerity measures continued to reduce military spending. In Asia and Oceania, while military spending still increased in 2012, it did so at a slower pace, partly as a result of weaker economic growth in the wake of the 2008 global financial crisis.

The rapid growth in Russia's military spending continued, indeed accelerated, in 2012 (see section III). The government is reforming, modernizing and re-equipping its armed forces, after two decades with largely unreformed Soviet-era structures and unmodernized Soviet-era armaments. However, these efforts face major industrial, demographic and economic challenges, and most experts believe that the modernization goals will only be partially met.

In most other regions, military spending continued to grow, but unevenly (see section I). In Asia, increases in China, Indonesia and Viet Nam continued, but formerly rapid increases in India reversed. There were substantial increases in the Middle East and North Africa, but military spending in sub-Saharan Africa appears to have fallen.

In Central America, where military spending has traditionally been very low, there have been rapid increases in both military and non-military security expenditure as governments from Mexico to Panama struggle to combat extreme levels of violent crime from drug cartels and criminal gangs (see section IV). However, these efforts have not reduced levels of violence, while the blurring of military and internal security roles has created human rights problems and may threaten democratic civilian control of the armed forces.

Military expenditure is an area in which, even in democratic countries, there is frequently a severe gap in transparency and accountability, owing to the sensitivity and confidentiality surrounding the military sector and the special status of the military in many countries (see section V). Lack of transparency and accountability means that the public lacks a voice in the choice of whether to allocate resources to the military or other priorities, and lacks a means of assessing how its money is being spent. Moreover, poor transparency can frequently lead to waste and corruption, especially in the case of off-budget spending that often falls outside the remit of governmental monitoring and control. The examples of Colombia and Indonesia illustrate many of the challenges for transparency that states face.

Indonesia, having emerged from a long period of dictatorship, has undergone extensive security sector reform, including in the financial management of the military; however, civilian control of the military remains ambiguous. Efforts to disengage the military from its widespread business interests—a major source of corruption and human rights abuses—have fallen short of a complete withdrawal from such activities, and corruption remains a major problem, especially in arms procurement. However, significant progress has been made in some areas, and the issues remain a subject of fervent debate in Indonesia.

Colombia presents a contrasting case. It has no recent history of military rule and its military is more clearly subordinate to civilian authority. However, the parliament plays little role in monitoring military activities, including financial matters, due to a tradition of the military and civilian sectors avoiding involvement in what is seen as each other's domain. However, improving transparency in military spending and arms procurement has been the subject of considerable efforts in recent years, including the introduction of 'defence integrity pacts' to oversee arms procurement, and the establishment of democratic mechanisms to oversee the expenditure of extraordinary funds from a special 'wealth tax' to support the military's war against insurgents. A problematic area, however, is the presence of off-budget spending, some of which is a consequence of the internal conflict, funding from local authorities to support military operations in their areas, and direct payments by oil companies to the military for protection. The use of these funds lacks proper monitoring, and it is not clear if they are included in overall budget and expenditure reporting.

As a mechanism for interstate transparency at the global level, each year the United Nations requests that its member states report their levels of military spending. There were signs in 2012 that reporting levels had fallen substantially, to approximately a quarter of states (see section VI). While this is discouraging, it may in part reflect the fact that more countries increasingly make their data available through other means.

SAM PERLO-FREEMAN

I. Global developments in military expenditure

SAM PERLO-FREEMAN, CARINA SOLMIRANO AND HELÉN WILANDH

World military expenditure fell in 2012, for the first time since 1998. The world total is estimated to have been $1756 billion, which is 0.4 per cent lower in real terms than in 2011. Military expenditure as a share of global gross domestic product (GDP)—the global 'military burden'—also remained stable, at around 2.5 per cent (see table 3.1). The 2008 global financial crisis and subsequent economic turmoil, combined with the winding down of wars in Afghanistan and Iraq, has clearly led to an end to the overall trend of rising military spending that started in 1999.

At the regional level, there was a definite shift in the balance of spending. Significant falls in North America and Western and Central Europe (part of ongoing austerity measures) were offset by increases in Eastern Europe and most of the developing world, excepting sub-Saharan Africa (see figure 3.1 and table 3.2). Military spending in the West has been falling since 2009, and while it has been increasing elsewhere, the rate of growth since 2009 has been considerably slower in most regions than in the preceding years (see figure 3.2). In Central and South Asia, North America, Oceania, and Western and Central Europe, increases in the period 2003–2009 were followed by decreases in 2009–12; in sub-Saharan Africa, East Asia, and Latin America, there was a major slowdown in the growth rate, with smaller slowdowns in Eastern Europe and South East Asia. In contrast, the rate of growth accelerated in the Middle East and North Africa. The overall effect on the world total was a lowering in growth in 2010–11, now followed by the fall in 2012.[1]

Regional trends

In Western and Central Europe, the trends from 2011 continued in 2012.[2] Overall spending declined by 1.6 per cent in real terms, with the largest decreases generally coming in Central Europe and the most debt-blighted countries of Southern Europe, with the possible exception of Greece.[3]

---

[1] The totals for certain regions or subregions are dominated by particular countries (e.g. Algeria in North Africa, Brazil in South America, Russia in Eastern Europe, India in Central and South Asia, and Saudi Arabia in the Middle East). However, general trends in these regions or subregions in 2012 were broadly similar to those in the dominant country: with the exception of Central and South Asia, the relative growth rates in each region or subregion before and after 2009 are similar when the dominant country is omitted. In the case of Central and South Asia, the rates of growth are broadly similar in each subperiod, implying that the slowdown in that subregion is particular to India.

[2] Perlo-Freeman, S., 'Europe and the impact of austerity on military expenditure', *SIPRI Yearbook 2012*.

[3] Greece's defence budget increased by 4% in real terms in 2012, but its implementation is uncertain. In recent years, actual expenditure has been significantly below the budget amount.

Table 3.1. Military expenditure by region, by international organization and by income group, 2003–12

Figures for 2003–12 are in US$ b. at constant (2011) prices and exchange rates. Figures for 2012 in the right-most column, marked *, are in current US$ b. for 2012. Figures do not always add up to totals because of the conventions of rounding.

	2003	2004	2005	2006	2007	2008	2009	2010	2011	2012	2012*
World total	1 291	1 364	1 423	1 470	1 528	1 609	1 715	1 744	1 749	1 742	1 756
Geographical regions											
Africa	20.7	23.2	24.2	25.9	(26.7)	(30.4)	(31.8)	(33.8)	(37.8)	(38.3)	(39.2)
North Africa	7.0	7.6	7.9	7.9	8.5	10.1	(11.1)	(12.0)	(15.1)	16.2	16.4
Sub-Saharan Africa	13.7	15.6	16.3	(18.0)	(18.1)	(20.4)	(20.7)	(21.8)	(22.8)	(22.0)	(22.7)
Americas	571	620	651	665	685	737	793	817	808	770	782
Central America and the Caribbean	5.1	4.7	5.1	5.6	6.2	6.3	7.1	7.7	8.0	8.6	8.5
North America	524	571	598	607	625	671	724	743	735	694	708
South America	41.8	44.8	48.7	52.0	54.6	59.5	62.2	66.3	65.2	67.6	65.9
Asia and Oceania	234	247	260	275	296	313	349	356	369	382	390
Central and South Asia	38.2	43.4	46.0	46.6	47.9	52.8	60.6	61.7	62.9	61.9	59.8
East Asia	151	157	167	180	194	204	229	235	247	259	268
Oceania	21.4	22.3	23.0	24.3	25.7	26.6	28.6	29.0	28.5	27.5	28.2
South East Asia	24.2	23.8	24.3	24.9	28.3	28.9	30.3	30.0	31.3	33.2	33.7
Europe	380	383	387	397	408	419	428	419	411	419	407
Eastern Europe	46.2	48.3	55.5	63.0	70.0	76.6	78.9	80.2	87.0	100	100
Western and Central Europe	333	334	331	334	338	343	349	338	324	318	307
Middle East	85.4	91.3	100	107	113	110	112	(118)	(123)	(134)	(138)
Organizations											
African Union	23.4	25.8	26.7	28.4	(29.0)	(32.1)	(33.1)	(34.7)	(38.0)	(38.9)	(40.1)
Arab League	66.5	72.9	79.1	83.7	93.4	96.6	101	108	115	(127)	(131)
CIS	47.2	49.5	56.9	64.5	72.1	77.5	80.2	81.9	88.9	103	103
CSTO	44.0	45.9	52.4	58.7	64.8	71.0	74.5	76.1	81.7	94.6	94.8
ECOWAS	2.2	2.2	2.1	2.2	2.6	3.1	3.3	3.6	3.8	3.6	3.8

European Union	280	299	298	300	307	312	317	307	291	285	274
NATO	827	881	906	918	938	990	1 051	1 059	1 036	990	994
NATO Europe	302	311	308	311	314	319	327	316	302	296	286
OSCE	905	954	986	1 006	1 035	1 092	1 154	1 164	1 148	1 116	1 118
SADC	7.6	7.6	8.9	9.4	8.9	10.0	10.0	10.3	10.2	10.7	10.7
SCO	101	109	123	142	161	177	202	211	227	251	260
Income group											
Low	4.8	(5.1)	(5.2)	(5.5)	(5.7)	(6.1)	(6.3)	(7.2)	(7.6)	(7.3)	(7.7)
Lower middle	65.2	71.5	74.4	76.1	81.6	87.4	94.7	97.2	101	103	101
Upper middle	203	215	237	263	284	306	336	349	370	399	407
High	1 019	1 073	1 106	1 125	1 156	1 209	1 277	1 290	1 270	1 234	1 240

World military spending per capita (current US$)

144	160	172	181	199	222	228	238	251	249

World military burden (i.e. world military spending as a % of world gross domestic product, both measured in current US$)

2.4	2.4	2.4	2.4	2.4	2.7	2.6	2.5	2.5

( ) = total based on country data accounting for less than 90% of the regional total; . . = available data accounting for less than 60% of the regional total.

Notes: The totals for the world, regions, organizations and income groups are estimates, based on data in table 3.11 for the countries covered by the SIPRI Military Expenditure Database. When military expenditure data for a country is missing for a few years, estimates are made, most often on the assumption that the rate of change in that country's military expenditure is the same as that for the region to which it belongs (see also 'Sources and methods' below). When no estimates can be made, countries are excluded from the totals. The countries excluded from all totals here are Cuba, North Korea, Myanmar, Somalia and Zimbabwe. Totals for regions and income groups cover the same groups of countries for all years. Totals for organizations cover only the member countries in the year given. The coverage of the geographical regions and subregions is based on the grouping of countries in tables 3.10–3.12. Income groups are based on the World Bank World Development Indicators 2012, with a gross national income per capita in 2011 of $1005 or less for low-income countries; $1006–$3975 for lower-middle-income countries; $3976–$12 275 for upper-middle-income countries; and more than $12 275 for high-income countries.

Sources: SIPRI Military Expenditure Database, <http://www.sipri.org/databases/milex/>; International Monetary Fund (IMF), *World Economic Outlook: Coping with High Debt and Sluggish Growth* (IMF: Washington, DC, Oct. 2012); and United Nations Population Fund (UNFPA), *State of World Population, 2003–12* (UNFPA: New York, 2003–12).

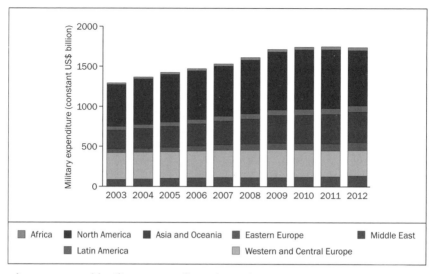

Figure 3.1. World military expenditure by region, 2003–12

Between 2008 and 2012, 20 of the 37 countries in Western and Central Europe reduced military spending by more than 10 per cent in real terms, including all countries in Central Europe apart from Bosnia and Herzegovina, Montenegro, and Poland. The countries that increased military spending between 2008 and 2012 include Poland and Turkey (including increases in 2012) and, at a more modest rate, the Nordic countries. Among the major spenders in Western and Central Europe, between 2008 and 2012 the United Kingdom cut spending by 5.2 per cent and France by 3.8 per cent, while Germany increased its spending by 2.6 per cent, although this follows several years of falling spending prior to 2008. The UK's spending is expected to fall further in the period up to financial year 2014/15, by perhaps as much as 10 per cent in real terms, including an expected reduction on spending in Afghanistan.[4] Germany plans for spending to be constant in nominal terms up to 2016, implying a moderate fall in real terms.[5] Overall, military spending in Western and Central Europe was 6.9 per cent lower in 2012 than when the financial crisis struck in 2008, while that of the 26 European members of the North Atlantic Treaty Organization (NATO) was 7.5 per cent lower.

Military expenditure has continued to increase in Asia and Oceania in recent years, although unevenly. The rate of increase has been slower since 2009, following the global financial crisis. Despite tensions on the India–

---

[4] Chalmers, M., 'Mid-term blues? Defence and the 2013 spending review', RUSI Briefing Paper, Feb. 2013, <http://www.rusi.org/publications/other/ref:N512B80F201A9B/>.

[5] German Parliament (Bundestag), 'Finanzplan des Bundes 2012 bis 2016' [The federal budget 2012 to 2016], Briefing by the Federal Government, Drucksache 17/10201, 10 Aug. 2012, p. 13.

Table 3.2. Key military expenditure statistics by region, 2012

Region/ Subregion	Military expenditure, 2012 (US$ b.)	Change (%)[a] 2011–12	2003–12	Major changes, 2012 (%)[b] Increases		Decreases	
Africa	(39.2)	1.2	85	Zimbabwe	53	Uganda	−57
North Africa	16.4	7.8	133	Côte d'Ivoire	22	South Sudan	−42
Sub-Saharan Africa	(22.7)	−3.2	61	Ghana	20	Nigeria	−12
				Tunisia	20	Botswana	−7.0
Americas	782	−4.7	35	Paraguay	42	El Salvador	−9.0
Central America and Caribbean	8.6	8.1	70	Venezuela	39	Jamaica	−8.2
				Peru	16	Ecuador	−7.8
North America	708	−5.5	32	Colombia	11	USA	−5.6
South America	65.9	3.8	62				
Asia and Oceania	390	3.3	63	Kazakhstan	[30]	Afghanistan	−12
Central and South Asia	59.8	−1.6	62	Viet Nam	26	Sri Lanka	−9.6
				Mongolia	24	Australia	−4.0
East Asia	268	5.0	72	Indonesia	24	Thailand	−3.4
Oceania	28.2	−3.7	28				
South East Asia	33.7	6.0	37				
Europe	407	2.0	10	Ukraine	24	Hungary	−20
Eastern Europe	100	15	117	Estonia	17	Portugal	−18
Western and Central Europe	307	−1.6	−4.5	Bosnia	17	Slovenia	−15
				Russia	[16]	Spain	−13
Middle East	(138)	8.3	57	Oman	51	Iraq	−3.6
				Saudi Arabia	12	Egypt	−2.6
				Kuwait	10		

( ) = uncertain estimate; [ ] = SIPRI estimate.

[a] Changes are in real terms.

[b] The list shows the largest increases or decreases for each region as a whole, rather than by subregion. Countries with a military expenditure in 2012 of less than $100 m., or $50 m. in Africa, are excluded.

China border, in the South China Sea and on the Korean Peninsula, China and South Korea increased military spending at a significantly slower rate between 2009 and 2012, while India actually cut spending (see figure 3.3). Nonetheless, in 2012 China's military spending increased at a substantial rate—7.8 per cent in real terms—and it passed some significant milestones in its military technological development, including the commissioning of its first aircraft carrier and the successful landing of an aircraft on it, and the test flight of a second prototype stealth combat aircraft.[6] China has

[6] Erickson, A. and Collins, G., 'China aircraft carrier style! Assessing the first take-off and landing', China Real Time Report, *Wall Street Journal*, 27 Nov. 2012, <http://blogs.wsj.com/chinarealtime/ 2012/11/27/china-aircraft-carrier-style-what-first-takeoff-and-landing-means/>; and Foster, R., 'China's latest stealth fighter takes to the air', *Jane's Defence Weekly*, 7 Nov. 2012, p. 4. See also chapter 5, section I, in this volume.

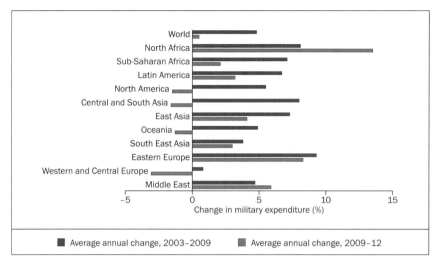

Figure 3.2. Average annual changes in military expenditure, by region or subregion, 2003–2009 and 2009–12

announced a further increase of 10.7 per cent for 2013, which in real terms is likely to be roughly in line with targeted GDP growth of 7.5 per cent.[7]

Thailand and Cambodia reduced spending in 2012, as their border dispute, which led to violent border skirmishes in 2010 and 2011, eased.[8] Similarly, Sri Lanka has cut spending since the end of its civil war in 2009. In contrast, Indonesia and Viet Nam maintained high rates of military spending growth, with respective increases of 130 per cent and 73 per cent between 2003 and 2012. Viet Nam is investing heavily in major naval and aircraft acquisitions, motivated by the need to counter China's growing military power and ambitions in the South China Sea, in what could now be regarded as a naval arms race.[9] Indonesia is undertaking a major military modernization, especially in the naval sphere, as it seeks to build up a 'minimum essential force' to control its vast archipelago and territorial waters by 2024.[10] In the absence of any obvious threat, this can perhaps be seen as a way of reorienting the Indonesian armed forces towards external defence as it withdraws from politics and business (see also section V below).

[7] 'China's defense budget to grow 10.7 pct in 2013', *Global Times*, 5 Mar. 2013.

[8] Jamaluddin, J. M., 'ASEAN meeting cools Thai–Cambodia border tensions', *Asian Defence Journal*, Mar. 2011, pp. 4–6. See also chapter 1, section II, in this volume.

[9] Wezeman, S. T., 'The maritime dimension of arms transfers to South East Asia, 2007–11', *SIPRI Yearbook 2012*.

[10] Grevatt, J., 'Island ambition', *Jane's Defence Weekly*, 11 July 2012, pp. 22–27; and Supriyanto, R. A., 'Indonesia's naval modernisation: a sea change?', S. Rajaratnam School of International Studies (RSIS) Commentaries no. 020/2012, 27 Jan. 2012, <http://www.rsis.edu.sg/publications/commentaries.asp?selYear=2012>.

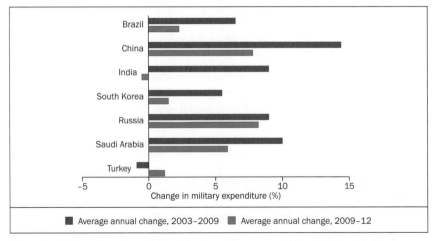

Figure 3.3. Average annual changes in military expenditure of emerging powers with the highest military spending, 2003–2009 and 2009–12

The largest military spenders in 2012

The list of the top 15 military spenders worldwide in 2012 includes the same countries as in 2011, with some changes in order (see table 3.3). The shift in spending from the West to other parts of the world is reflected in this list: the spending of the established powers in the list—Australia, Canada, France, Germany, Italy, Japan, the UK and the United States—either fell significantly or changed only slightly (by less than 1 per cent), while the spending of most of the emerging powers in the list—China, South Korea, Russia, Saudi Arabia and Turkey—increased. India was the only emerging power in the list whose spending decreased in 2012, while Brazil's changed by less than 1 per cent. While the USA remained by far the world's largest military spender, its share of the total decreased to 39 per cent, the first time it has fallen below 40 per cent since the collapse of the Soviet Union in 1991. Nonetheless, US military spending in 2012 was still roughly equal to the spending of the next 11 countries combined.

Turkey was the only one of the emerging powers in the top 15 whose rate of increase of military spending rose in 2009–12 compared with 2003–2008. In most other cases, the rate of increase fell; in the case of India, spending fell (see figure 3.3). This further illustrates how the global financial crisis has affected military spending even in regions not directly affected by its consequences: by reducing export demand in the developed world, it has slowed economic growth also in emerging regions, with a knock-on effect on military expenditure.

Table 3.3. The 15 countries with the highest military expenditure in 2012

Spending figures are in US$, at current prices and exchange rates. Countries are ranked according to military spending calculated using market exchange rates (MER).

Rank			Spending, 2012	Change, 2003–12	Share of GDP (%)[a]		World share,	Spending, 2012
2012	2011	Country	($ b., MER)	(%)	2012	2003	2012 (%)	($ b., PPP)[b]
1	1	USA	685	32	4.4	3.7	39	685
2	2	China	[166]	175	[2.0]	[2.1]	[9.5]	[249]
3	3	Russia	[90.7]	113	[4.4]	[4.3]	[5.2]	[116]
4	5	UK	60.8	4.9	2.5	2.5	3.5	57.5
5	6	Japan	59.3	–3.6	1.0	1.0	3.4	46.0
Subtotal top 5			**1 062**	..	..	..	**60**	..
6	5	France	58.9	–3.3	2.3	2.6	3.4	50.7
7	8	Saudi Arabia	56.7	111	8.9	8.7	3.2	63.9
8	7	India	46.1	65	2.5	2.8	2.6	119
9	9	Germany	[45.8]	–1.5	[1.4]	1.4	[2.6]	[42.8]
10	11	Italy	[34.0]	–19	1.7	2.0	1.9	31.0
Subtotal top 10			**1 304**	..	..	..	**74**	..
11	10	Brazil	33.1	56	[1.5]	1.5	[1.9]	[34.4]
12	12	South Korea	31.7	44	2.7	2.5	1.8	44.2
13	13	Australia	26.2	29	1.7	1.9	1.5	16.3
14	14	Canada	[22.5]	36	[1.3]	1.1	[1.3]	[18.3]
15	15	Turkey[c]	[18.2]	–2.1	2.3	3.4	[1.0]	[25.9]
Subtotal top 15			**1 436**	..	..	..	**82**	..
World			**1 756**	**35**	**2.5**	**2.4**	**100**	..

[ ] = estimated figure; GDP = gross domestic product; PPP = purchasing power parity.

[a] The figures for national military expenditure as a share of GDP are based on estimates for 2012 GDP from the International Monetary Fund's (IMF) World Economic Outlook database, Oct. 2012.

[b] The figures for military expenditure at PPP exchange rates are estimates based on the projected implied PPP conversion rates for each country from the IMF World Economic Outlook database, Oct. 2012.

[c] It is possible that the United Arab Emirates (UAE) would be in 15th position in place of Turkey, but data is not available for the UAE in 2012. In 2011, the UAE's military spending (in current prices) was estimated by SIPRI to have been $19.2 billion.

Sources: SIPRI Military Expenditure Database, <http://www.sipri.org/databases/milex/>; and IMF, World Economic Outlook database, Oct. 2012, <http://www.imf.org/external/pubs/ft/weo/2011/02/weodata/index.aspx>.

II. US military expenditure

ELISABETH SKÖNS

Military spending by the United States declined by 5.6 per cent in real terms in 2012. Together with the 1 per cent fall in 2011, this is the first clear manifestation of an adjustment of US military spending to a post-war situation. However, spending in 2012—$685.3 billion—was still 69 per cent higher in real terms than in 2001, which marked the beginning of the wars on 'terrorism', in Afghanistan and, from 2003, in Iraq.

The future level and trend in US military expenditure was a prominent topic in the political debate in the USA during 2012. However, much of the decision-making process on future military spending was linked to, and subordinated to, the political process of addressing high and rising government debt, which in turn was linked to the government borrowing limit and the size of the budget deficit. These debt-related issues to some extent overshadowed the security-related issues, such as the degree and nature of adjustment of US military spending to the post-war security environment and assessments of future security threats and challenges.

The debt deal, sequestration and the impact on military spending

There was much confusion in the budget debate and process during 2012 due to the results of the 2011 bipartisan debt deal and the resulting 2011 Budget Control Act (BCA).[1] The BCA contained measures intended to reduce the projected budget deficit by at least $2.1 trillion over the 10-year period covering financial years (FYs) 2012–21.[2] These measures included caps (limits) on discretionary spending and a process for automatic and largely indiscriminate across-the-board reductions, known as seques-tration.[3] The statutory caps were intended to result in total reductions of $917 billion in projected spending over the 10 years, implemented from FY 2012 onwards.[4] If the Joint Select Committee on Deficit Reduction—a bipartisan committee established by the BCA—could not reach agreement on a deficit-reduction solution by November 2011, the process for add-

---

[1] Budget Control Act of 2011, US Public Law no. 112-25, signed into law 2 Aug. 2011, <http://thomas.loc.gov/cgi-bin/bdquery/z?d112:SN00365:>. See also Sköns, E. and Perlo-Freeman, S., 'The United States' military spending and the 2011 budget crisis', *SIPRI Yearbook 2012*.

[2] US financial (or fiscal) years run from 1 Oct. of the previous year until 30. Sep. of the nominal year.

[3] Discretionary spending is budget authority that is provided and controlled by appropriation acts and the outlays that result from that budget authority. In contrast, mandatory (or direct) spending is the budget authority provided by laws other than appropriation acts and the outlays that result from that budget authority, such as the more long-term rules for pension and health care spending.

[4] Cuts in FY 2012 expenditure were to take place in the congressional process, since the FY 2012 budget proposal had already been submitted.

Table 3.4. US outlays for 'National defense', financial years 2001 and 2012–17

Figures are in current US$ b. unless otherwise stated. Years are financial years (starting 1 Oct. of the previous year).

	2001	2012	2013[a]	2014[a]	2015[a]	2016[a]	2017[a]
Outlays at current prices							
DOD, military programmes	290.2	650.9	633.3	597.6	584.0	561.9	562.1
Atomic energy, defence	12.9	19.2	19.1	20.7	19.9	19.0	19.1
Other, defence-related	1.6	7.8	7.7	8.5	8.4	8.4	8.5
Total 'National defense' outlays	**304.7**	**677.9**	**660.0**	**626.8**	**612.3**	**589.2**	**589.7**
At constant (FY 2005) prices	363.0	580.6	553.6	518.8	497.4	469.8	461.4
As a share (%) of GDP	*3.0*	*4.4*	*4.1*	*3.7*	*3.4*	*3.1*	*3.0*
As a share (%) of total government outlays	*16.4*	*19.2*	*17.9*	*16.6*	*15.7*	*14.4*	*13.9*

DOD = Department of Defense; FY = financial year; GDP = gross domestic product.

Note: In accordance with SIPRI's definition of military expenditure, SIPRI's figures for total US military expenditure include foreign military aid provided by the US Department of State, in addition to the figures shown here.

[a] Figures for FYs 2013–17 are estimates.

Source: US Office of Management and Budget, *Budget of the United States Government, Fiscal Year 2014: Historical Tables* (Government Printing Office: Washington, DC, 2013), tables 3.2 and 6.1.

itional, automatic, cuts of $1.2 trillion over the period FYs 2013–21 was to be triggered from January 2013 onwards, unless the Congress and President Barack Obama had enacted legislation to eliminate or change the process before then.[5]

The impact of BCA on military spending is difficult to assess because of the variety of definitions (e.g. 'defense' versus 'non-defense'; 'security' versus 'non-security') and the various exemptions from cuts for certain measures and time periods. However, by and large, roughly half of the cuts required by the BCA, or $1 trillion, were to apply to military spending. Since the level of spending on Overseas Contingency Operations (OCO)—that is, foreign military operations—is not limited by the BCA, these cuts were to apply to base defence spending.[6]

The caps on discretionary military expenditure were incorporated in the defence budget proposal for FY 2013, presented in February 2012, which proposed reducing the base defence budget (i.e. excluding OCO) by $259 billion over 2013–17 and by a total of $487 billion over the 10 years,

---

[5] Labonte, M. and Levit, M. R., *The Budget Control Act of 2011: Effects on Spending Levels and the Budget Deficit*, Congressional Research Service (CRS) Report for Congress R42013 (US Congress, CRS: Washington DC, 29 Nov. 2011), p. 1.

[6] Labonte and Levit (note 5), p. 2.

compared with previous plans.[7] The impact of this first round of cuts was a reduction of 21 per cent in real terms in projected outlays on the 'National defense' budget item over the period FYs 2012–17.[8] However, the resultant spending in FY 2017 would still be 27 per cent higher in real terms than in FY 2001, the financial year before the 'global war on terrorism' began (see table 3.4), and the same level as in FY 1990, the last year of the cold war.[9]

The sequestration measure contained in the BCA originally required additional total cuts of $109.3 billion, of which $54.7 billion were for defence, from projected spending levels in each FY from 2013 to 2021. In FY 2017 this would still result in base defence spending 15 per cent higher in real terms than in FY 2001.

Following the failure of the Joint Select Committee on Deficit Reduction to reach an agreement, the defence budget debate during 2012 was dominated by the prospect and potential implications of sequestration, to begin in January 2013 if the Congress and President Obama also failed to reach agreement. A further complication was that sequestration would coincide with the expiry (at the end of 2012) of tax reductions initiated during the administration of President George W. Bush. It was widely feared that this combination of major spending cuts and tax increases, referred to as the 'fiscal cliff', would lead to an economic recession. A partial agreement was reached at the last hour of 2012 that preserved most of the tax cuts but only postponed the automatic spending cuts due to sequestration until 1 March 2013.[10] It also reduced the required cuts for 2013, from $109.3 billion to $85.3 billion in overall spending and thus from $54.7 billion to $42.7 billion for defence.[11] By 1 March, no further agreement had been reached and so the sequestration—including military expenditure cuts—was expected to take effect, at least until any new deal was reached.

The debate on the consequences of sequestration

Many of the alarmist assessments of the defence cuts—including by the Secretary of Defense, Leon Panetta—were actually more about the seques-

---

[7] US Department of Defense, 'DOD releases fiscal 2013 budget proposal', Press Release no. 098-12, 13 Feb. 2012, <http://www.defense.gov/releases/release.aspx?releaseid=15056>.

[8] SIPRI's estimate for US military spending includes expenditure on foreign military aid by the Department of State, in addition to 'National defense' expenditure.

[9] US Office of Management and Budget, *Budget of the United States Government, Fiscal Year 2014: Historical Tables* (Government Printing Office: Washington, DC, 2013), table 6.1.

[10] The American Taxpayer Relief Act of 2012, US Public Law no. 112-240, signed into law 2 Jan. 2013, <http://thomas.loc.gov/cgi-bin/query/D?c112:5:./temp/~c112Ln9b2h::>. See also Spar, K., *Budget 'Sequestration' and Selected Program Exemptions and Special Rules*, Congressional Research Service (CRS) Report for Congress R42050 (US Congress, CRS: Washington DC, 22 Mar. 2013), p. 3.

[11] Kogan, R., 'Sequestration by the numbers', Center on Budget and Policy Priorities, 22 Mar. 2013, <http://www.cbpp.org/cms/?fa=view&id=3937>, p. 1.

tration technique than about the size of the cuts.[12] In a letter to two senators, Panetta argued that sequestration would leave the USA with 'the smallest ground force since 1940, the smallest number of ships since 1915, and the smallest Air Force in its history', and the smallest ever Department of Defense (DOD) workforce.[13] The sequestration mechanism leaves almost no scope to choose how to implement the cuts, which are dictated by a detailed statutory scheme.[14] Thus, there is no way to make choices based on strategic security considerations. Indeed, the sequestration technique was never meant to be applied: rather, the threat of sequestration was meant to drive the two sides to a compromise.[15]

An important source of confusion was that the cuts required by the BCA were not in relation to actual current spending levels but rather in relation to planned, or projected, spending levels for the coming 10 years. This makes it difficult to assess the likely level of future military spending as a result of the measures contained in the BCA, with different analysts using different numbers. However, given that US outlays on 'National defense' increased by 68 per cent in real terms during the war period of FYs 2001–12 (see table 3.4), and considering the remaining differences in position among the various stakeholders, it is unlikely that this process will result in a return to pre-war levels of military spending.[16]

Throughout 2012, a number of efforts were made to put pressure on the Congress to block the sequestration. For example, the chief executive officers (CEOs) of the major arms-producing companies—such as Robert J. Stevens of Lockheed Martin—argued before congressional committee hearings that the cuts would lead to closures of defence plants, massive personnel reductions, erosion of engineering expertise, and loss of skills and knowledge in the US arms industry.[17] In July, the Aerospace Industries Association (AIA) released a report estimating that, if the automatic budget cuts went ahead, 2.14 million jobs would be lost in 2013, including 1 million due to DOD budget cuts.[18] This is a rather high estimate, considering that

---

[12] For a series of such assessments see US House of Representatives, Armed Services Committee, '"Shooting ourselves in the head": what they're saying on sequestration', 28 Feb. 2012, <http://armedservices.house.gov/index.cfm/defense-cuts-resources>.

[13] Panetta, L., Letter to Senator John McCain, 14 Nov. 2011, <http://www.mccain.senate.gov/public/index.cfm?FuseAction=PressOffice.PressReleases&ContentRecord_id=a4074315-fd3e-2e65-2330-62b95da3b0e9>.

[14] US Office of Management and Budget (OMB), 'OMB report pursuant to the Sequestration Transparency Act of 2012 (P.L. 112-155)', 14 Sep. 2012, <http://www.whitehouse.gov/omb/legislative_reports/>, p. 1.

[15] US Office of Management and Budget (note 14), p. 1.

[16] Note that the 69% increase over this period referred to above is in terms of SIPRI's wider definition of US military expenditure. See also note 8.

[17] Pianin, E., 'Congress plays war games with defense budget', *Fiscal Times*, 19 July 2012.

[18] Fuller, S. S. and Chumura Economics & Analytics, *The Economic Impact of the Budget Control Act of 2011 on DOD and non-DOD Agencies* (Aerospace Industry Association: Arlington, VA, 17 July 2012).

total employment in the entire US (military and civil) aerospace industry is only 625 000, and the uncertainty of such estimates was subsequently pointed out by the Congressional Research Service.[19]

Despite the arms industry spending significant amounts on campaigns against defence cuts ($1.7 million by the AIA alone), industry representatives complained about their lack of impact, which they found unusual and blamed on congressional paralysis.[20] However, another explanation might be the difficulty of arguing that, for the sake of employment, military spending should continue at wartime levels after wars had ended. Indeed, these arms industry concerns illustrate the problems associated with permanent arms-producing companies that are highly dependent on military contracts and lack strategies to adjust to variations in military spending.[21]

In contrast, a number of security analysts and researchers argued that the size of the requested defence cuts was reasonable and that the resulting level of military spending would be sufficient to provide security to the USA and keep a sufficient lead in military capability over any other military power. One line of argument that has been pointed out by several observers is based on historical experience: after previous wars the US Government has been able to reduce military spending by more than required by the BCA (see figure 3.4), and the US military was able to accommodate the cuts.[22]

Balancing the US defence budget

Panetta and others argued that the requested cuts would result in 'hollow forces' that lack the people, training and equipment to fulfil their tasks. This was questioned in a report by the Congressional Research Service.[23] An analysis by the Center for Strategic and International Studies, a US think tank, argued that the DOD has major problems even without the BCA, due to failures to control costs, develop realistic budgets, and close

[19] Aerospace Industry Association, 'Aerospace statistics', Group 2, Series 12, <http://www.aia-aerospace.org/economics/aerospace_statistics/>; and Levine, L., *Sequestration: A Review of Estimates of Potential Job Losses*, Congressional Research Service (CRS) Report for Congress R42763 (US Congress, CRS: Washington, DC, 1 Oct. 2012).

[20] Shalal-Esa, A. and Stern, M., 'A comedown for America's defense lobby', Reuters, 19 Sep. 2012.

[21] On the efforts of arms-producing companies to adjust to government spending cuts see chapter 4, section I, in this volume.

[22] On how previous US presidents managed the shift from wartime to peacetime budgets see Korb, L. J., Conley, L. and Rothman, A., *A Return to Responsibility: What President Obama and Congress can Learn about Defense Budgets from Past Presidents* (Center for American Progress: Washington, DC, July 2011).

[23] Feickert, A. and Daggett, S., *A Historical Perspective on 'Hollow Forces'*, Congressional Research Service (CRS) Report for Congress R42334 (US Congress, CRS: Washington, 31 Jan. 2012).

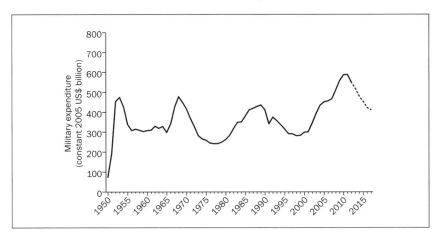

Figure 3.4. US military spending, 1950–2017

Figures are for 'National defense' outlays. Figures for financial years 2013–17 are estimates.

Source: US Office of Management and Budget, *Budget of the United States Government, Fiscal Year 2014: Historical Tables* (Government Printing Office: Washington, DC, 2013).

the gap between its strategy and budgets.[24] Reports by the Stimson Center, the Brookings Institution and the Council on Foreign Relations, three other US think tanks, concluded that the consequences of the defence budget cuts required by the BCA would not be dramatic, but rather would leave the US force structure basically unchanged, with the USA still able to dominate any other military in the world.[25]

Going beyond the issues of military defence, to analyse the overall balance of US security spending, the Task Force on a Unified Security Budget for the United States—formed in 2004 by a group of independent experts on US budgetary and defence issues—presented its annual report in October 2012. The report analyses three types of security tool—offensive, defensive and preventative—managed by three types of institution—the DOD, the Department for Homeland Security, and the non-military foreign engagements by the Department of State and the US Agency for International Development (USAID), respectively. It recommends a shift of resources from offensive security measures towards preventive and defensive measures, which are far less expensive.

[24] Cordesman, A. H., *The New US Strategy, the FY2013 Defense Budget, Sequestration, and the Growing Strategy-Reality Gap* (Center for Strategic and International Studies: Washington, DC, 3 Oct. 2012).
[25] Rumbaugh, R., 'Budgeting for foreign affairs and defense: the reality of the defense builddown', Stimson Center, 13 Feb. 2012, <http://www.stimson.org/summaries/the-reality-of-the-defense-build down/>; Singer, P. W., 'Sequestration and what it would do for American military power, Asia, and the flashpoint of Korea', *Time*, 23 Sep. 2012; and Zenko, M., 'Top twelve defense sequestration scare tactics', Council for Foreign Relation, 23 Aug. 2012, <http://blogs.cfr.org/zenko/2012/08/23/top-twelve-defense-sequestration-scare-tactics/>.

For the DOD, the recommendations include $71.8 billion in cuts for FY 2013 and a long-term plan for achieving the $1 trillion in reductions over 10 years requested by the BCA that can be achieved without sacrificing US security.[26] The proposed cuts for FY 2013 include cuts in spending on nuclear forces ($20 billion), health care ($15 billion), retirement ($13 billion), personnel ($10 billion) and in some procurement programmes, including for the F-35 (Joint Strike Fighter, JSF) combat aircraft, the V-22 Osprey aircraft and Virginia class submarines ($8.8 billion).[27] The 10-year reductions focus on savings from budget reform as well as on resetting US security along more realistic lines.[28]

Although the proposals in the Unified Security Budget for budgetary shifts are based to a great extent on President Obama's stated commitment to a security policy with a reality-based balance between military security and other security tools, including economic and social development tools, the prospects for a full rebalancing of the security budget are probably meagre in the short-to-medium term.[29]

[26] Task Force on a Unified Security Budget, *Rebalancing our National Security Budget: The Benefits of Implementing a Unified Security Budget* (Center for American Progress/Institute for Policy Studies: Washington, DC, Oct. 2012), pp. 4, 13, 17.

[27] Task Force on a Unified Security Budget (note 26), p. 13.

[28] Task Force on a Unified Security Budget (note 26), pp. 36–38.

[29] Task Force on a Unified Security Budget (note 26), p. 2.

III. Russian military expenditure, reform and restructuring

SAM PERLO-FREEMAN

The rising trend in Russia's military expenditure, which started in 1999, accelerated sharply in 2012, with a real-terms increase of 16 per cent compared with 2011. The draft budget for 2013–15 contains plans for a further rise in nominal terms of just over 40 per cent by 2015 (see table 3.5).[1] This would amount to a real-terms increase of approximately 17 per cent between 2012 and 2015, based on current inflation projections, and military spending as a share of gross domestic product (GDP) would rise to 4.8 per cent.[2] The increases come as Russia implements the ambitious 2011–20 State Armaments Programme (Gosudarstvennaya Programma Vooruzhen-iya, GPV), and undertakes a wide-ranging reform of its armed forces. This section summarizes the reforms and discusses widespread doubts as to how far they can be implemented.

The reform plans

The GPV aims to spend 20.7 trillion roubles ($705 billion) on military equipment by 2020. Of this total, 19 trillion roubles ($647 billion) is for the Ministry of Defence and the remainder is for other forces such as the Border Guards and troops of the Ministry of the Interior.[3] The programme aims to replace 70 per cent of Russia's armaments with modern weapons and is part of a broader effort to reform and modernize the Russian armed forces.[4]

The reforms also include (*a*) changes in the structure of the armed forces to promote greater mobility and combat-readiness; (*b*) the replacement of a mass-mobilization strategy, which aimed to be able to mobilize up to 4 million troops over a long period in a major war situation, with a strategy based on a more readily deployable standing force of around 1 million troops and a much smaller reserve of around 700 000; (*c*) a major increase

---

[1] Russian State Duma, Draft law 'On the federal budget for 2013 and the planning period of 2014 and 2015', Bill no. 143344-6, 28 Sep. 2012, <http://www.asozd2.duma.gov.ru/main.nsf/(Spravka)?OpenAgent&RN=143344-6>.

[2] Cooper, J., 'Military expenditure in the Russian Federation during the years 2012 to 2015', Research note, 9 Oct. 2012, <http://www.sipri.org/research/armaments/milex/publications/>. The figure for military spending as a share of GDP is based on Russian Government projections of GDP. The equivalent figure for 2012 is 4.6% (see table 3.5). SIPRI estimates that Russian military spending in 2012 was equal to 4.4% of GDP, based on the International Monetary Fund's estimate of Russia's GDP. See also table 3.12 in section VII below.

[3] The GPV is not a public document. See Westerlund, F., 'The defence industry', ed. C. Vendil Palling, *Russian Military Capability in a Ten-year Perspective—2011* (FOI: Stockholm, Aug. 2012); and Cooper, J., 'Can Russia afford to modernize its military?', Presentation, SIPRI, Stockholm, 8 Nov. 2012, <http://www.sipri.org/research/armaments/milex/publications/>.

[4] Cooper (note 3).

Table 3.5. Russian military expenditure, 2011–15

Figures are billions of Russian roubles, in current prices.

	2011[a]	2012[a]	2013[a]	2014[a]	2015[a]
Spending on 'National defence'	1 516	1 865	2 141	2 501	3 078
Other military expenditure[b]	786	933	912	888	895
Total military expenditure	**2 302**	**2 799**	**3 053**	**3 389**	**3 973**
Military expenditure as a share of total government expenditure (%)	21.07	21.83	22.80	23.86	25.44
Military expenditure as a share of GDP (%)[c]	4.22	4.57	4.59	4.58	4.79

[a] Figures for 2011 are actual spending. Figures for 2012 are from the updated budget as of 1 Aug. 2012. Figures for 2013–15 are from the draft budget for 2013.

[b] Other military expenditure includes spending on military housing, education and health, military pensions, paramilitary forces and military-related research and development.

[c] These figures are based on the Russian Ministry of Economic Development's estimates of gross domestic product (GDP). SIPRI estimates are based on the International Monetary Fund's estimate of Russia's GDP. SIPRI estimates military spending to have been 4.1% of GDP in 2011 and 4.4% in 2012.

Sources: Cooper, J., 'Military expenditure in the Russian Federation during the years 2012 to 2015', Research note, 9 Oct. 2012, <http://www.sipri.org/research/armaments/milex/pub lications/>, based on: Russian State Duma, Draft law 'On the 2011 federal budget for the year 2011', Draft law no. 106468-6, 5 July 2012, <http://www.asozd2.duma.gov.ru/main.nsf/ (Spravka)?OpenAgent&RN=106468-6>; Russian Federal Treasury, 'Information on execution of the consolidated budget of the Russian Federation and budgets of state extra-budgetary funds, as of August 1, 2012', <http://www.roskazna.ru/the-information-on-execution-of-budgets/>; and Russian State Duma, Draft law 'On the federal budget for 2013 and the planning period of 2014 and 2015', Bill no. 143344-6, 28 Sep. 2012, <http://www.asozd2.duma.gov.ru/main.nsf/(Spravka)?OpenAgent&RN=143344-6>.

in the ratio of contract soldiers and non-commissioned officers to conscripts; (*d*) a reduction in the number of senior officers in the current top-heavy structure; and (*e*) the outsourcing of a range of non-core tasks to civilian contractors.[5]

The motivation for modernization was Russia's intervention in the brief war in South Ossetia in 2008, which exposed severe weaknesses in Russian command, communication, mobility, readiness and equipment quality. The Russian armed forces had been in a state of decline since the collapse of the Soviet Union. It had procured almost no new major conventional armaments before 2008, leaving increasing proportions of its equipment obsolete or even non-functioning.[6]

[5] Carlsson, M. and Norberg, J., 'The armed forces', ed. Vendil Palling (note 3).
[6] Cooper (note 3).

Challenges to implementation

The reform and modernization plans face several challenges. First, as has been well documented, the Russian arms industry remains in a weak state, with ageing machinery, two decades of low levels of research and development, a lack of new recruitment of skilled engineers and scientists, and inefficient organizational structures.[7] The industry's relationship with government has been increasingly strained by its inability to deliver advanced weapons in many areas, leading to Russia beginning to import certain weapons as a means of obtaining modern military technology.[8] As part of the GPV, the government is investing 2.3 trillion roubles ($78 billion) in the industry to help it modernize. How quickly it will be able to overcome decades of atrophy is open to question.

Moreover, there is rampant corruption in the Russian arms industry. Dmitry Medvedev is reported to have said that it led to the loss of 20 per cent of procurement funds while he was president (in 2008–12).[9] In November 2012 allegations of corruption led President Vladimir Putin to remove Anatoly Serdyukov, the architect of the military reform process, from the post of Minister of Defence. Whether the direction of the military reform will be affected by Serdyukov's removal is as yet uncertain.[10]

Second, the spending levels planned for the GPV, which was designed on the basis of economic conditions prevailing before the 2008 global financial crisis, may be unrealistic. A simulation by Professor Julian Cooper of the University of Birmingham suggests that, unless military spending as a share of GDP were to rise even higher than is planned, the defence budget would only be sufficient to fund around 80 per cent of the GPV by 2020.[11] Moreover, some independent projections of Russian GDP growth are considerably lower than those of the Russian Government, which are the basis of this simulation.[12] Concerns over the financial sustainability of Russia's military and other spending plans led to clashes between the Minister of

---

[7] Westerlund (note 3). See also Perlo-Freeman, S. et al., 'Military expenditure', *SIPRI Yearbook 2011*, pp. 163–66; and e.g. Cooper, J., 'Developments in the Russian arms industry', *SIPRI Yearbook 2006*.

[8] E.g. Cooper (note 3); and Holtom, P. et el., 'International arms transfers', *SIPRI Yearbook 2011*, pp. 289–91.

[9] Putilov, S. and Savina, Yu., 'Neither give nor take?', *Novye Izvestiya*, 15 Nov. 2012, Translation from Russian, Open Source Center.

[10] Various commentators give opposite views on this. E.g. Felgenhauer, P., 'Serdyukov has been disgraced, but his reforms will continue', Eurasia Daily Monitor, 6 Dec. 2012, <http://www.jamestown.org/single/?tx_ttnews[tt_news]=40209>; and Mikhaylov, A., [Defeat of the Russian army], Gazeta.ru, 10 Dec. 2012, <http://www.gazeta.ru/comments/2012/12/09_a_4884697.shtml>, Translation from Russian, Open Source Center.

[11] Cooper (note 3).

[12] Cooper (note 3).

Finance, Alexei Kudrin, who opposed the plans, and President Medvedev, leading to the former's sacking in October 2011.[13]

Third, structural reforms of the armed forces are threatened by deficiencies in personnel recruitment. Russia's population is shrinking and ageing, leading to an ongoing fall in the available pool of recruits, as either conscripts or contract soldiers.[14] Moreover, there are serious problems of poor education, health and nutrition among young Russian men. Current plans involve a considerable reduction in the number of conscripts, and an increase in the number of contract soldiers; but poor terms and conditions, including issues such as violent initiation of new recruits, make the armed forces an unattractive career for many.[15]

This combination of economic, industrial, demographic and institutional problems has produced a clear consensus among observers both within and outside Russia that the ambitious goals of the GPV will not be fulfilled in their entirety.[16] Nonetheless, the major increases in military spending, involving increased investment in both new equipment and human capital, will lead to some increased capability of the Russian armed forces by 2020, whether or not the fundamental structural problems are successfully addressed.

[13] Alexandrova, L., 'Kudrin, dismissed from all posts, offers his own plan for preventing new crisis wave', Itar-Tass, 18 Oct. 2011, <http://www.itar-tass.com/en/c39/250177.html>.

[14] Oxenstierna, S. and Bergstrand, B.-G., 'Defence economics', ed. Vendil Palling (note 3), pp. 53–56.

[15] Carlsson and Norberg (note 5), pp. 103–104.

[16] E.g. ed. Vendil Palling (note 3); Cooper (note 3); McDermott, R., 'Russia's armed forces: reflections on 2012', Eurasia Daily Monitor, 8 Jan. 2013, <http://www.jamestown.org/single/?tx_ttnews[tt_news]=40274>; and 'Russian pundits assess successes, failures of military reform', Rossiya 24, 23 Nov. 2012, Transcription and translation from Russian, Open Source Center.

IV. Security spending and violent organized crime in Central America

CARINA SOLMIRANO

Central America—from Mexico to Panama—has had some of the lowest levels of military expenditure as a share of gross domestic product (GDP) in the world.[1] Following the end of the region's civil wars in the 1990s and in the absence of any external military threats, defence spending in most Central American countries was constant or falling until at least the mid-2000s. However, in more recent years this trend has reversed, as some of the region's militaries have become involved in the fight against drug cartels and organized crime groups, alongside internal security forces. This section examines the trends in both military and internal security spending in the context of these developments, which has seen the boundary between 'military' and 'internal' security increasingly blurred.[2]

Government responses to organized crime and drug-related violence

Most Central American countries have experienced high levels of violence associated with drug trafficking, organized crime and gang activities.[3] In Mexico, over 47 000 people were killed due to drug-related violence between the declaration by President Felipe Calderón of a war on organized crime in 2006 and September 2011.[4] Most of these dead were members of drug trafficking organizations or their associated youth gangs.[5] Mexico's murder rate in 2010 was 18.1 per 100 000 inhabitants, while in the 'northern triangle' of Guatemala, Honduras and El Salvador (see figure 3.5), rates were even higher: 41.4 per 100 000 in Guatemala, 66.0 per 100 000 in El Salvador and 82.1 per 100 000—the world's highest murder rate—in Honduras.[6] According to one estimate, the cost of crime and violence in Costa Rica, El Salvador, Guatemala, Honduras and Nicaragua in 2006—including

[1] Central America is defined here to include Belize, Costa Rica, El Salvador, Guatemala, Honduras, Mexico, Nicaragua and Panama. Other definitions of Central America often exclude Mexico.

[2] Central American governments often refer to internal security as 'public security'.

[3] For examples of non-state conflicts and acts of one-sided violence in Central America in 2002–11 see chapter 1, section III, in this volume.

[4] Mexican Attorney General's Office, 'Estadística' [Statistics], <http://www.pgr.gob.mx/temas relevantes/estadistica/estadisticas.asp>; and 'Mexico drug war deaths over five years now total 47,515', BBC News, 12 Jan. 2012, <http://www.bbc.co.uk/news/world-latin-america-16518267>.

[5] Felbab-Brown, V., *Peña Nieto's Piñata: The Promise and Pitfalls of Mexico's New Security Policy against Organized Crime* (Brookings: Washington, DC, Feb. 2013), p. 3.

[6] United Nations Office on Drugs and Crime (UNODC), *2011 Global Study on Homicide: Trends, Contexts, Data* (UNODC: Vienna, 2011), Methodological annex, p. 8.

Figure 3.5. Map of Central America and neighbouring states

health, institutional, private security and material costs—averaged 7.7 per cent of GDP.[7]

The response of states in the region to this violence has become increasingly militarized. This trend started in 2009, when the Government of El Salvador gave internal security tasks to the military.[8] In November 2011 the Honduran National Congress also gave its military a greater role to '"participate permanently in the fight against drug trafficking, arms trafficking and organised crime" at the request of the authorities'.[9] In January 2012 Guatemalan President Otto Pérez Molina announced his intention of giving the military a greater role in fighting organized crime; his predecessor, President Álvaro Colom, had laid the foundation for this in July 2011 when he announced the repeal of a 2004 decision to limit Guatemala's defence budget to 0.33 per cent of GDP, to allow the military to acquire new equipment.[10] After his election as Mexican President in July 2012, Enrique Peña Nieto pledged 'to continue the fight against organized crime and said

---

[7] Acevedo, C., 'Los costos económicos de la violencia en Centroamérica' [The economic costs of violence in Central America] (Consejo Nacional de Seguridad: San Salvador, 2008); and Serrano-Berthet, R. and Lopez, H., *Crime and Violence in Central America: A Development Challenge* (World Bank: Washington, DC, 2011), p. 6. This average does not include the possible loss of GDP resulting from slower growth due to the violence.

[8] López, A., 'Militarización de la seguridad publica en Centroamérica' [Militarization of public security in Central America], Infodefensa.com, 14 Dec. 2011, <http://www.infodefensa.com/?opinion=militarizacion-de-la-segur>.

[9] 'Honduras: with a new legal shield, Lobo keeps army in policing role', *Latin American Security & Strategic Review*, Dec. 2011, p. 17

[10] Contreras, G., 'Presidente Colom derogara acuerdo que limita presupuesto del Ejercito' [President Colom abolishes agreement limiting army budget], *Prensa Libre* (Guatemala City), 1 July 2011; and 'Perez Molina wastes no time', *LatinNews Daily Report*, 16 Jan. 2012.

Table 3.6. Military spending in Central America, 2006–12

Figures are in US $m. at constant (2011) prices and exchange rates.

	2006	2007	2008	2009	2010	2011	2012	Change, 2006–12 (%)
Belize	13.0	14.2	18.2	17.0	15.0	15.7	[14.6]	12
Costa Rica	–	–	–	–	–	–	–	–
El Salvador	222	229	225	229	237	256	[233]	5.0
Guatemala	172	170	182	170	187	197	205	19
Honduras	106	126	156	175	182	201	192	81
Mexico	4 440	5 013	5 019	5 689	6 203	6 472	7 103	60
Nicaragua	46.0	46.0	43.6	43.1	45.6	51.5	65.4	42
Panama	–	–	–	–	–	–	–	–
Total	**4 999**	**5 598**	**5 644**	**6 323**	**6 870**	**7 193**	**7 813**	**56**

– = nil or a negligible value; [ ] = SIPRI estimate.

Source: Table 3.11.

that maintaining some form of military involvement in antidrug operations will be necessary'.[11] He intends to increase the size of federal police forces, create a national gendarmerie (under civilian control) comprised of some of the military forces currently fighting organized crime and establish unified police forces in each of Mexico's 31 states and Mexico City. This trend could have an impact on civil–military relations in Central America, which had been moving towards stronger civilian control of the military following the end of the civil wars in El Salvador, Guatemala and Nicaragua in the 1990s.

In line with this trend, there have been rapid increases in both military and internal security spending in recent years in Central America. Total military expenditure in the region in 2012 was $8.5 billion (in current prices), a real-terms increase of 8.6 per cent since 2011 and of 56 per cent since 2006 (see table 3.6). The largest annual increases in 2012 were in Mexico (10 per cent) and Nicaragua (27 per cent). In contrast, Belize, El Salvador and Honduras cut expenditure. Mexico, the largest spender in the region, increased its spending by 60 per cent in real terms between 2006 and 2012, Honduras's military expenditure increased by 81 per cent between 2006 and 2012, while Guatemala's spending has been increasing steadily since 2009. Nonetheless, military spending in the region remains low as a share of GDP: only Honduras spent more than 1 per cent of its GDP on the military in 2012 (see table 3.13 in section VII below).

The increase in Mexico's spending occurred mostly after President Calderón made the war on organized crime a top priority of his 2006–12

---

[11] Seelke, C. R., *Mexico: Issues for Congress*, Congressional Research Service (CRS) Report for Congress RL32724 (US Congress, CRS: Washington, DC, 24 Sep. 2012), p. 6.

administration and put the military at the forefront of the efforts.[12] The increase of the past decade does indeed seem to be due to the efforts by the Mexican military to tackle drug trafficking.[13] However, these efforts have been hindered by corruption and weak police and law enforcement institutions; although these have been prevalent features of the Mexican system, drug trafficking has exacerbated them.[14]

The problem of drug trafficking is not limited to Mexico, but is a regional problem. Drugs leaving Colombia on their way to the United State via Mexico pass along the Central American corridor. In order to improve the protection of their airspace and 'better combat the air supply of drug traffickers', some governments in the region have announced their intention to modernize or upgrade some of their aircraft.[15] For example, in 2012 the Guatemalan Government sought a line of credit of $140 million to acquire six trainer/combat aircraft and to upgrade its old trainer fleet.[16]

Internal security spending

As military expenditure has increased in Central America, so has spending on internal security, but at a much higher rate. It is not a straightforward matter to define government spending on non-military 'security'; while the definition should certainly include spending on police, gendarmeries, intelligence agencies, and border and coastal security, as well as the ministries that run them, grey areas include the justice sector and the prison system. For the present purposes, limited data availability means that the only definition of internal security spending that can be applied is total spending on central government ministries (or secretariats) of internal security. However, some of the functions of these ministries (such as issuing passports) are not necessarily security related. Furthermore, in some countries, such ministries are a recent creation and so comparisons over time need to take into account past spending on security by other ministries. For example, prior to the creation of the Panamanian Ministry of Public Security in 2010, internal security functions were the responsi-

[12] Stålenheim, P., Perdomo, C. and Sköns, E., 'Military expenditure', *SIPRI Yearbook 2008*, p. 202.

[13] Sparrow, T., 'Los ejércitos de Centroamérica vuelven a salir de compras' [The armies of Central America go arms shopping again], BBC Mundo, 5 Oct. 2011, <http://www.bbc.co.uk/mundo/noticias/2011/10/111003_america_central_armamento_tsb.shtml>.

[14] See e.g. Freeman, L., *State of Siege: Drug-Related Violence and Corruption in Mexico—Unintended Consequences of the War on Drugs*, Washington Office on Latin America (WOLA) Special Report (WOLA: Washington, DC, June 2006), p. 5.

[15] Sparrow (note 13) (author's translation).

[16] López, A., 'El Gobierno de Guatemala gestiona préstamo para adquisición de aviones Super Tucano y radares españoles' [The Guatemalan Government seeks credit for acquisition of Super Tucano aircraft and Spanish radars], Infodefensa.com, 28 Aug. 2012, <http://www.infodefensa.com/?noticia=el-gobierno-de-guatemala-gestiona-prestamo-para-adquisicion-de-aviones-super-tucano-y-radares-espanoles>.

Table 3.7. Internal security spending in Central America, 2006–12

Figures are in US $m. at constant (2011) prices and exchange rates.

	2006	2007	2008	2009	2010	2011	2012	Change, 2006–12 (%)
Belize[a]	..	..	..	..	..	..	..	..
Costa Rica	148	168	170	205	234	281	331	*124*
El Salvador	265	237	337	299	345	336	328	*24*
Guatemala	346	377	372	464	447	421	490	*42*
Honduras	144	164	164	182	162	195	202	*40*
Mexico	925	1 311	1 799	2 854	2 700	2 859	3 133	*239*
Nicaragua	74.2	80.5	81.6	75.4	78.5	79.6	80.5	*8.5*
Panama	301	315	335	419	550	490	518	*72*
Total[a]	**2 203**	**2 653**	**3 259**	**4 498**	**4 517**	**4 662**	**5 083**	*131*

[a] No consistent data is available for Belize. The total excludes Belize.

Sources: Costa Rican Ministry of Finance, 'Leyes de Presupuestos' [Budget laws], <https://www.hacienda.go.cr/Msib21/Espanol/Direccion+General+de+Presupuesto+Nacional/leypres upuesto.htm>; Salvadorean Ministry of Finance, 'Informe de Gestión Financiera del Estado' [State financial report], <http://www.transparenciafiscal.gob.sv/portal/page/portal/PTF/Pre supuestos_Publicos/Presupuestos_ejecutados>; Guatemalan Ministry of Public Finance, 'Pre supuestos Aprobados' [Approved budgets], <http://www.minfin.gob.gt/presupaprobado/pre supaprobados.html>; Honduran Secretariat of Finances, 'Informes de Ejecución Pre supuestaria de la Administración Central', [Budget execution reports for the central adminis tration], <http://www.sefin.gob.hn/?page_id=8246>; Mexican Secretariat of Finance and Public Credit, 'Presupuesto de Egresos de la Federación' [Federal expenditure budget], <http://www.shcp.gob.mx/EGRESOS/PEF/Paginas/PresupuestodeEgresos.aspx>; Nicaraguan Ministry of Finance and Public Credit, 'Informes de Ejecución Presupuestaria' [Budget execu tion reports], <http://www.hacienda.gob.ni/documentos/presupuesto/informes>; and Pana manian Ministry of Economy and Finance, 'Presupuesto General del Estado' [State budget], <http://www.mef.gob.pa/es/direcciones/presupuestoNacion/Paginas/presupuestos.aspx>.

bility of the Ministry of Government and Justice. The data presented here takes into consideration such changes.

Between 2006 and 2012, internal security spending in Central America increased by 131 per cent in real terms (see table 3.7). The largest increase was in Mexico, where expenditure by the Ministry of Security more than tripled. There are indications that the Mexican administration of President Peña Nieto will continue to increase internal security spending, although with a shift of approach from punishment to prevention. 'Pacto por Mexico' (Pact for Mexico), the security plan announced early in his presidency, emphasizes crime prevention and seeks to reorganize Mexico's security and law enforcement agencies.[17] It is not clear what this shift of focus

[17] 'México: Peña Nieto propone "auténtica política" contra crimen tras sexenio violento' [Mexico: Peña Nieto proposes 'proper policy' against violent crime after six years], Infolatam, 17 Dec. 2012, <http://www.infolatam.com/2012/12/17/mexico-pena-nieto-anuncia-politica-de-seguridad-con-enfoque-regional-y-gendarmeria/>

would mean in practice. As a report by the Brookings Institution, a US think tank, highlights, Peña Nieto 'has been rather vague about how he actually plans to reduce violence, particularly homicides, kidnappings, and extortion'.[18]

After Mexico, the countries that increased their internal security spending the most are Costa Rica, Panama, Guatemala and Honduras. The high increases in Costa Rica and Panama can be partially explained by the fact that these two countries have no regular armed forces, so that internal security forces are their only means of response to violent crime.

The largest portion of internal security spending goes to current expenses, with a minor portion allocated to capital investment.[19] In most Central American countries, increased internal security spending has been used to expand police forces and improve the salary of police officers. For example, in an effort to reduce dependence on the military to combat drug trafficking, Mexico is reported to have raised the number of federal police from 6500 agents in 2006 to 35 500 in 2010.[20] However, even after this increase it still lacked 'the technical capability, infrastructure, and numbers to provide a permanent nation-wide presence'.[21]

To support the costs of the current military and internal security efforts, some governments have created special 'security taxes'. For example, in December 2011 the Costa Rican Legislative Assembly approved a tax of $300 on each company. The tax is expected to raise $70 million a year to help purchase new equipment for the security forces.[22] In June 2011 the Honduran National Congress also established a new tax on mining, telephone and other industries that should collect about $79 million per year over a five-year period for equipment and other improvements for the police and the military.[23] As a consequence of resistance to the new tax from some businesses, which argued that it would discourage investment, the government cut the tax on mining export from 5 to 2 per cent and

[18] Felbab-Brown (note 5), p. 4.

[19] Red de Seguridad y Defensa de America Latina (RESDAL, Latin America Security and Defence Network), *Indice de Seguridad Publica y Ciudadana en America Latina: El Salvador, Guatemala y Honduras* [Index of public and citizen security in Latin America: El Salvador, Guatemala, and Honduras] (RESDAL: Buenos Aires, 2011), p. 87.

[20] Guevara Moyano, I., *Adapting, Transforming, and Modernizing Under Fire: The Mexican Military 2006–11* (US Army War College, Strategic Studies Institute: Carlisle, PA, Sep. 2011), p. 15. See also Roig-Franzia, M., 'Mexico plan adds police to take on drug cartels', *Washington Post*, 11 July 2008.

[21] Guevara Moyano (note 20), p. 15.

[22] Williams, A., 'Costa Rica hopes security tax, new prison construction will aid in anti-crime fight', Diálogo, 13 Feb. 2012, <http://www.dialogo-americas.com/en_GB/articles/rmisa/features/regional_news/2012/02/13/aa-costa-rica-security>; and López, A., 'Costa Rica aprueba un impuesto para financiar la seguridad del país' [Costa Rica approves tax to finance security], Infodefensa.com, 4 Jan. 2012, <http://www.infodefensa.com/?noticia=costa-rica-aprueba-un-impuesto-para-financiar-la-seguridad-del-pais>.

[23] 'Aprueban impuesto temporal para la seguridad de Honduras' [New temporary tax for the security of Honduras is approved], *La Prensa* (Managua), 23 June 2011.

eliminated a 3 per cent tax on bank withdrawals.[24] Proposals to create similar taxes in El Salvador and Guatemala have not succeeded.[25] Salvadorean President Mauricio Funes sought to apply a tax aimed at collecting $120 million a year but could not find support among business leaders.[26]

The role of the United States

The USA is the main destination for Central America's drug trade. According to the US Department of State, 'Approximately 95 percent of the estimated cocaine flow toward the United States transits the Mexico–Central America corridor from its origins in South America'.[27] The USA thus makes substantial security-related aid available to the governments in the region to supplement the domestic financial resources available to combat drug-related violence and organized crime.

In 2007 Mexico and the USA agreed a security assistance package—the Mérida Initiative (Iniciativa Mérida)—aimed at tackling criminal violence in Central America.[28] The initiative has provided (*a*) non-intrusive inspection equipment, ion scanners and canine units for use in Central America to intercept trafficked drugs, arms, cash and persons, (*b*) technology to improve and secure communication systems that collect criminal information in Mexico, (*c*) technical advice and training for prosecutors, defenders and investigators to strengthen justice sector institutions, (*d*) helicopters and surveillance aircraft to support interdiction activities and rapid response by law-enforcement agencies in Mexico, and (*e*) equipment, training, and community action programmes in Central American countries to implement anti-gang measures.[29] The Mérida Initiative has

[24] 'Honduras cuts security tax after angering businesses', Reuters, 14 Sep. 2011.
[25] Bailey, J., '¿Un impuesto de seguridad?' [A security tax?], *El Universal* (Mexico City), 6 Oct. 2012.
[26] López, A., 'El Salvador aplicará un impuesto a los grandes capitales para financiar la Seguridad' [El Salvador applies a tax on big businesses to fund security], Infodefensa.com, 24 May 2011, <http://www.infodefensa.com/?noticia=el-salvador-aplicara-un-impuesto-a-los-grandes-capitales-para-financiar-la-seguridad>; and 'Continua El Salvador sin acuerdo sobre impuesto de seguridad [El Salvador continues without agreement about security tax], Notimex, 31 Aug. 2011, <http://es-us.noticias.yahoo.com/continúa-salvador-acuerdo-impuesto-seguridad-185200295.html>.
[27] US Department of State, Bureau for International Narcotics and Law Enforcement Affairs, *International Narcotics Control Strategy Report*, vol. 1, *Drug and Chemical Control* (US Department of State: Washington, DC, Mar. 2011), p. 383.
[28] Seelke, C. R., *Mérida Initiative for Mexico and Central America: Funding and Policy Issues*, Congressional Research Service (CRS) Report for Congress R40135 (US Congress, CRS: Washington, DC, 21 Aug. 2009), p. 2.
[29] US Department of State, Bureau of International Narcotics and Law Enforcement Affairs, 'The Merida Initiative', Fact Sheet, 23 June 2009, <http://www.state.gov/j/inl/rls/fs/122397.htm>; and US Department of State, Bureau of Western Hemisphere Affairs, 'The Merida Initiative: expanding the U.S./Mexico partnership', 29 Mar. 2012, <http://www.state.gov/p/wha/rls/fs/2012/187119.htm>.

been criticized for focusing on hardware and not on the root causes of drug trafficking, violence and corruption in Central America.[30]

The majority of the money for the Mérida Initiative has gone to Mexico. Between financial years (FYs) 2008 and 2012 the US Congress appropriated more than $1.9 billion for counternarcotics and anti-crime assistance for Mexico as part of this initiative.[31] In 2010 the US Government 'relaunched' the non-Mexican portion of the initiative as the Central America Regional Security Initiative (CARSI). Between FYs 2008 and 2012, the US Congress appropriated $466.5 million for Central America (excluding Mexico) through the Mérida Initiative and CARSI.[32] While Mérida mostly focuses on infrastructure, 'CARSI not only provides equipment, training, and technical assistance to support immediate law enforcement and interdiction operations, but also seeks to strengthen the capacities of governmental institutions to address security challenges and the underlying conditions that contribute to them.'[33]

The impact of security expenditure

These increases in financial resources—domestic and from the USA—for Central America's military and internal security forces have not been followed by noticeable decreases in levels of armed violence. There have been some notable achievements: 25 of Mexico's 37 most wanted drug lords were captured or killed between 2009 and 2012, and many drug routes have been blocked.[34] Yet in 2008 and 2009 some analyses suggested that Mexico was on the verge of becoming a failed state, as violence escalated to unprecedented levels.[35] The militarized response to drug trafficking has

[30] E.g. Pérez Rocha, M., 'The failed war on drugs in Mexico', Transnational Institute, 1 Apr. 2009, <http://www.tni.org/article/failed-war-drugs-mexico>; and Abbot, P., 'The Merida Initiative: a flawed counterdrug policy?', Small Wars Journal, 6 Jan. 2011, p. 8.

[31] Seelke (note 11), p. 13. Although SIPRI includes foreign military aid in the total military expenditure of the recipient state, most of the US aid under the Mérida Initiative comes under the State Department's account for International Narcotics Control and Law Enforcement, rather than the military aid categories of Foreign Military Finance and International Military Equipment and Training, and so is not counted as military spending by SIPRI.

[32] Meyer, P. J. and Seelke, C. R., Central America Regional Security Initiative: Background and Policy Issues for Congress, Congressional Research Service (CRS) Report for Congress R41731 (US Congress, CRS: Washington, DC, 21 Feb. 2012), p. 1.

[33] Meyer and Seelke (note 32), p. 2.

[34] Castillo, E. E. and Weissenstein, M., 'Mexico's security policy failing, says incoming official Miguel Angel Osorio Chong', Huffington Post, 17 Dec. 2012, <http://www.huffingtonpost.com/2012/12/17/mexicos-security-policy-failing-miguel-angel-osorio-chong_n_2319102.html>; and 'Kingpin bowling', The Economist, 20 Oct. 2012.

[35] E.g. Friedman, G., 'Mexico: on the road to a failed state?', Stratfor Global Intelligence, 13 May 2008, <http://www.stratfor.com/weekly/mexico_road_failed_state>; and Debusmann, B., 'Among top U.S. fears: a failed Mexican state', New York Times, 9 Jan. 2009.

also caused the 7 large cartels to transform into approximately 80 smaller and more violent ones.[36]

Meanwhile, the involvement of the military in internal security functions has brought accusations of human rights abuses, while failing to bring down levels of violence. For example, Human Rights Watch has reported cases of torture, rape and murder committed by the Mexican military, and that in the first half of 2010 the Mexican National Human Rights Commission received more than 1100 complaints of human rights violations.[37] Increased participation of the armed forces in internal security in El Salvador and Guatemala also raises concerns, given the history of human rights abuses during the civil wars in both countries. This has led to calls 'for an end to military involvement in the fight against drug cartels and an end to the drug war that has brought repression, militarization, violation of human rights by security forces, and a huge increase in bloodshed'.[38]

The paradox of increased violence and increased security spending is certainly worrisome and requires novel ways to address the challenges that drug trafficking and other organized crime activities pose to the governments of Central America. More efforts on prevention and more commitments to eliminate corruption and abuses in the security forces should be on their security agendas in the coming years.

[36] Jones, N. P., 'Mexico drug policy and security review 2012', *Small Wars Journal*, 11 Jan. 2013.

[37] Human Rights Watch (HRW), *World Report 2011* (HRW: New York, 2011), pp. 256–62.

[38] Carlsen, L., 'Phase 2 of the drug war', Americas Program, 30 Apr. 2010, <http://www.cip americas.org/archives/2068>.

V. Two case studies in the governance of military budgeting and expenditure: Colombia and Indonesia

SAM PERLO-FREEMAN AND CARINA SOLMIRANO

The importance of sound governance of government expenditure in promoting development is widely recognized. Where transparency and accountability are lacking, spending may be inefficient and wasteful, fail to match the needs and priorities of a country's population, or be squandered in corruption. Due to the sensitivity and secrecy associated with the military sector, military spending is often the least transparent area of the government budget. Opaque military budgeting practices are a near global problem, affecting regions more or less intensely around the world.[1]

However, there are signs that transparency is improving in many regions, as the various 'waves of democratization' that have taken place in Eastern Europe, Latin America and parts of Asia over the past 30 years have in turn led to greater transparency in the military sector, although the military budget can be one of the last areas to see such change.[2]

This section looks at progress in improving transparency in Colombia and Indonesia. Indonesia is a recent democracy with a history of military influence in politics and the economy, which has been undergoing a process of security sector reform since 1999; while Colombia has a much longer tradition of civilian control of the military, but its long-running civil war, accompanied by a culture of impunity in relation to human rights abuses, creates a different set of challenges for transparency.

The terms transparency and accountability can be used in varying ways. In particular, there is an important distinction between transparency in the context of interstate relations, referring to the voluntary disclosure of information (especially relating to defence and security), which may be part of confidence-building measures, and transparency as an aspect of internal governance, referring to the ability of citizens to access relevant information on government activities.[3] The two clearly overlap, as information available to citizens is also available to other states; but the two

---

[1] A SIPRI study analysed the sources of deficiencies in military budgeting practices in its 8 case study countries in Africa. Omitoogun, W. and Hutchful, E. (eds), SIPRI, *Budgeting for the Military Sector in Africa: The Processes and Mechanisms of Control* (Oxford University Press: Oxford, 2006). Similar problems affect other regions.

[2] See e.g. Solmirano, C. and Bromley, M., *Transparency in Military Spending and Arms Acquisitions in Latin America and the Caribbean*, SIPRI Policy Paper no. 31 (SIPRI: Stockholm, Jan. 2012). SIPRI researchers have also noted an increase in the quality of information available for many countries in Central Europe and in parts of Asia over the past 10–20 years.

[3] On confidence-building measures in Asia and the Americas see chapter 9, sections IV and V, respectively, in this volume.

senses of transparency serve different purposes and are measured in different ways.[4]

'Transparency' is taken here to include both transparency of information and transparency of process. Transparency of information is determined by whether information on the military budget and actual spending is readily available to the public, and the level of reliability, detail and comprehensiveness of this information. Transparency of process is determined by whether budgetary decision making is open and visible, with the reasons for spending clearly outlined. 'Accountability' includes (*a*) accountability of the budget decision process, to parliament and to citizens; (*b*) the implementation of expenditure, that is if spending—and especially procurement—is controlled by rigorous procedures and subject to civilian control; and (*c*) auditing and parliamentary scrutiny of military spending, with improper practices investigated and prosecuted. There are thus many ways in which transparency and accountability can be lacking.[5] Some of these are enumerated below.

1. *Lack of effective defence policy and planning.* Many countries lack effective defence policy and planning. Military budgeting and procurement should be clearly linked to established defence policy goals. However, many countries lack a well-defined defence policy that spells out the country's security needs. As a result, decision making is carried out in a policy vacuum, wasting money on unnecessary systems while failing to meet genuine security needs and enhancing the risk of corruption. Even when defence policies are clearly elucidated, policy and budgeting may be disconnected from procurement practice.

2. *Weak civilian and democratic control.* Many developing countries, even those with generally democratic governments, suffer from weak civilian and democratic control of the military, especially concerning parliamentary oversight. There are several reasons for this. Lack of capacity or interest by parliamentarians can be a major obstacle to proper scrutiny, as can lack of political will.[6] This can result from an ingrained belief that the military sector is an area outside parliamentary purview. The military itself may discourage 'interference' from the parliament, or indeed from the civilian government more generally. The consequence is a deficient assessment of

---

[4] See e.g. Solmirano and Bromley (note 2).

[5] Many of these issues are discussed in e.g. Ball, N. and le Roux, L., 'A model for good practice in budgeting for the military sector', eds Omitoogun and Hutchful (note 1); Solmirano and Bromley (note 2); and Perlo-Freeman, S. and Perdomo, C., 'The developmental impact of military budgeting and procurement: implications for an arms trade treaty', Report prepared for Oxfam GB, Apr. 2008, <http://www.sipri.org/research/armaments/milex/publications/unpubl_milex/>.

[6] See e.g. Born, H., Fluri, P. and Johnson, A., *Parliamentary Oversight of the Security Sector: Principles, Mechanisms and Practices* (Geneva Center for the Democratic Control of Armed Forces: Geneva, 2003), p. 38.

military needs against other public priorities, often to the military's advantage. In some newly democratizing countries, entrenched military privileges may restrict effective civilian control of the military, by the parliament or even by the defence ministry.

3. *Insufficient transparency.* Governments and militaries often use claims of sensitivity or security concerns as an excuse for secrecy, resulting in insufficient transparency in defence budgeting and procurement. It is argued that the military requires special treatment compared to other government sectors, since it deals with national security matters. The result is insufficient disclosure of the military budget, with only figures for broad budget subcategories publicly available. This makes it difficult for the parliament and other civilian bodies to monitor and control the military budget.

4. *Extra-budgetary and off-budget military spending.* In many countries, the defence budget is supplemented by extra-budgetary and off-budget military spending, which can compromise transparency and accountability. Extra-budgetary spending occurs when the military is financed from non-military sections of the state budget. This may include, for example, science or infrastructure budgets, special presidential funds or foreign loans which are repaid by the finance ministry (rather than the defence ministry). Extra-budgetary spending is often neither clearly disaggregated nor reported, making it hard or impossible to disentangle all elements of military spending. Off-budget spending comes from sources outside the state budget altogether. This may include dedicated natural resource funds used for arms purchases, payments from the private sector for security, or income from military business activities. Off-budget finance may allow the military to procure arms without oversight from the parliament or the defence ministry, with one negative outcome being that purchases are not assessed against strategic needs. Off-budget spending means that resources are allocated to the military outside of any general budget deliberations, and in many cases automatically, without relation to an overall assessment of defence needs, and without the possibility of weighing them against other possible uses.

5. *Inadequate monitoring, control and auditing.* Inadequate monitoring, control and auditing of military spending facilitates corruption and waste. A SIPRI study of budgeting practice in Africa has found extremely weak capacity for controlling spending in many of its case study countries, and there are likely to be similar weaknesses in many other countries.[7] Public scrutiny institutions, in particular audit institutions, anti-corruption agen-

---

[7] eds Omitoogun and Hutchful (note 1).

cies and parliamentary public accounts committees may be reluctant to investigate the military, or may be actively prevented from doing so.[8]

Colombia

Colombia's five-decade war against guerrilla and drug trafficking groups has been the primary determinant of the country's level of military expenditure. Despite the long-running civil war and severe problems of human rights abuses by the security forces, Colombia has no recent history of military rule. It has had a civilian defence minister since 1991 and generally demonstrates strong civilian control of the military. Transparency in military spending is also fairly good, and has been improving in recent years. However, significant problems remain, especially in relation to off-budget sources of funding.

Transparency in military budgeting

Following a joint review in 2010 by the Colombian Ministry of National Defence (MND) and the National Planning Department (Departamento Nacional de Planeación, DNP) of the overall methodology to measure Colombia's military expenditure, there have been some improvements in military budget transparency.[9] The purpose of the revised methodology was to present a clearer picture of military and security expenditure in Colombia.

Information about the military budget is publicly available, including disaggregated information about both operational and investment expenses. The annual budget law provides a limited degree of detail regarding expenditure, in particular for arms acquisitions. In contrast, the MND publishes an annual plan of acquisitions in considerable detail. In the past, the MND has published information related to the implementation of security policies, including the execution of acquisition projects.[10]

The overall budgetary process for the MND involves both military and civilian individuals and agencies such as the DNP, the Ministry of Finance and Public Credit, the Congress and the Comptroller General's Office, among others. The National Development Plan is the core input for budget

---

[8] For reasons of space, the following case studies do not address issues relating to the decision-making processes for military spending. In particular, while the lack of a proper parliamentary role in decision making is a problem in both Colombia and Indonesia, a proper discussion of this would require a far longer piece.

[9] See Colombian Ministry of National Defence (MDN) and National Planning Department (DNP), *Metodologiá para el cálculo del gasto en defensa y seguridad* [Methodology for the calculation of spending on defense and security] (MDN/DNP: Bogota, 2010).

[10] Department of National Planning official, Author's interview, Mar. 2010.

programming, security policies, guides of strategic planning and sectorial analyses. It sets the national budgetary priorities.[11]

Transparency in arms procurement

In the past 11 years, a number of transparency-related initiatives have been introduced in Colombia. Some of the most important of these related to military spending are defence integrity pacts, anti-corruption documents and centralized procurement practices. Although transparency in the arms procurement process has improved somewhat, the results of the efforts to diminish corruption have been mixed overall.[12] In 2002 the MND requested the assistance of Transparencia por Colombia (TC)—the local chapter of Transparency International—to 'find mechanisms to reinforce transparency in defense procurement processes'.[13] TC recommended the use of defence integrity pacts (DIPs): legally binding agreements, overseen by an independent monitor, signed by competing bidders for a contract and the agencies involved in the procurement process. TC also recommended an anti-corruption commitment document, subsequently combined with the DIP policy into a single, unified document.[14] In 2004 Transparency International, through its chapters in Colombia and the United Kingdom, helped the MND to implement an integrity pact in a tender process for the acquisition of 22 aircraft worth $237 million, intended for use for drug interdiction.[15] A strong rationale for this transparency exercise was Colombia's desire 'to attract a wider range of potential contractors as many companies believed that corruption and human rights issues detracted from Colombia as an appropriate marketplace'.[16]

Six companies expressed interest in bidding, but the tender process collapsed after the withdrawal of all but one company.[17] The MND ultimately decided to continue negotiating with the remaining company, Embraer.[18] Although the exercise of the integrity pact could not be finalized, important lessons were drawn for future implementation of such

---

[11] Department of National Planning official (note 10).

[12] Ospina Robledo, R. I., 'Los pactos de integridad: una herramienta para buscar limpieza en contrataciones de interés público' [Integrity pacts: a tool for seeking probity in public-sector contracting], Conference on Transparency and Development in Latin America and the Caribbean, Inter-American Development Bank, May 2000, <http://www.iadb.org/leg/Documentos.asp>, p. 1.

[13] Transparencia por Colombia and Transparency International UK, 'Defence procurement and integrity pacts in Colombia, Report 1: smaller contracts', Mar. 2006, <http://www.ti-defence.org/publications/617-defence-procurement-and-integrity-pacts-in-colombia-report-1>, p. 3.

[14] Transparencia por Colombia and Transparency International UK (note 13), pp. 4–8.

[15] Transparency International UK, 'Defence procurement and integrity pacts in Colombia, Report 2: combat aircraft', Mar. 2006, <http://www.ti-defence.org/publications/711-defence-procurement-and-integrity-pacts-in-colombia--report-2>.

[16] Transparency International UK (note 15), p. 7.

[17] The 5 companies that withdrew identified a series of reasons for withdrawing, including insufficient time for bid preparation, perceived favouritism of turboprop over turbofan, and the high cost of shipping airframes to Colombia for evaluation. Transparency International UK (note 15), p. 12.

[18] Transparency International UK (note 15).

pacts. The most important was the determination by the Colombian Air Force and the MND to show their commitment to a transparent procurement process.

In 2011 the Minister of National Defence, Rodrigo Rivera Salazar, issued a new directive to centralize acquisitions in the MND, rather than under the three services. The goal of this new directive is to strengthen controls in order to avoid corruption, following a scandal involving the Fondo Nacional para la Defensa de la Libertad Personal (Fondelibertad, National Fund for the Defence of Personal Liberty), which coordinates the resources used in the fight against kidnapping and is controlled by the MND. More than 3000 million pesos ($1.7 million) was allegedly diverted from the fund through the signing of irregular contracts.[19]

The use of extraordinary resources and the role of civil society

Another notable area of improvement in transparency related to military spending is connected to oversight of extraordinary resources received by the Ministry of National Defence. In 2002, as the civil war intensified, the Colombian Government declared a state of siege and requested the moral and financial support of the population to preserve the security of the country.[20] The administration of President Alvaro Uribe decided to increase the military budget by implementing a one-time wealth tax, the Impuesto a la Seguridad Democrática (democratic security tax).[21] Between 2002 and 2003, the government collected more than $800 million.[22] The tax was renewed, under different names, for the periods 2004–2006, 2007–10 and 2011–14 with variations in the tax rate.[23]

In 2007, to monitor the execution of expenditure from these resources, the MND created the Committee on Ethics and Transparency, consisting of businessmen, academics, members of non-governmental organizations and former defence ministers. The committee was invited to participate in the definition of projects that the MND would execute with the extraordinary

---

[19] 'El Ministerio de Defensa de Colombia centralizará el sistema de adquisiciones de material' [The Colombian Ministry of Defence will centralize its acquisitions system], Infodefensa.com, 21 Mar. 2011, <http://www.infodefensa.com/?noticia=el-ministerio-de-defensa-de-colombia-central izara-el-sistema-de-adquisiciones-de-material>; and 'Santos ordena intervenir Fondelibertad por presunta corrupción' [Santos orders intervention of Fondelibertad for alleged corruption], *Semana* (Bogota), 12 Nov. 2010.

[20] Lozano, P., 'Uribe decreta el estado de excepción en Colombia para frenar a las FARC' [Uribe decrees a state of emergency in Colombia to stop the FARC], *El País* (Madrid), 13 Aug. 2002.

[21] The tax rate was 1.2% calculated on the value of liquid assets owned on 31 Aug. 2002 by both natural and legal persons with gross assets over 165.5 million pesos ($92 000). Colombian Ministry of Finance and Public Credit, Decreto Reglamentario Pago de Impuesto a la Seguridad Democrática [Decree regulating payment of the democratic security tax], Decree no. 1949 of 2002, 22 Aug. 2002, <http://www.presidencia.gov.co/prensa_new/decretoslinea/>.

[22] Pino, H. N., *Gasto público y justicia en Centroamérica* [Justice and public spending in Central America] (Comisión Económica para América Latina y el Caribe: Mexico City, Oct. 2011), p. 31.

[23] See Pino (note 22), p. 31.

resources. All procurement projects for the period 2007–10 were presented to the committee.[24] It also received auditing reports prepared by the MND's Office of Internal Control.[25] According to Juan Manuel Santos, who was Minister of National Defence at the time and became president in 2010— the committee 'became an open forum of discussion that allowed us to guide important decisions to strengthen the security of the country and to make the execution of resources more accountable'.[26] In 2009 the MND announced that the committee, which had not been intended to be permanent, would continue to operate, as a new pool of extraordinary resources was approved for the period 2011–14.[27] In March 2012 the committee was revived again to monitor the allocation of more than 7 billion pesos ($4 million) from the wealth tax.[28] The ongoing work of the committee is another step on the path to improving transparency and accountability of the government's policies.

Extra-budgetary resources

Two sources of extra-budgetary military spending represent a gap in Colombia's otherwise positive efforts to increase and improve transparency: the Fondo de Seguridad Territorial (Fonset, territorial security fund) and security service agreements between the MND and the national oil company, Ecopetrol.

At the provincial and municipal level, security forces receive funds from Fonset, which was created in 1997. The money for the fund is derived from contracts signed between the province or municipality and corporations, whereby corporations pay 5 per cent of the total value of the contract to the public body with which has contracted.[29] These resources are used for military purposes including acquisition of war materiel, reconstruction of barracks and other facilities, purchase of communication equipment, and

[24] Transparency International UK (TI), Defence and Security Programme, *A Review of Anti-Corruption Reform Measures in the Defence Sector in Colombia* (TI: London, May 2011), p. 7.

[25] Colombian Ministry of National Defence, Administrative Department of Security, Ministry of Finance and Public Credit, and National Planning Department (DNP), *Política de consolidación de la seguridad democrática: fortalecimiento de las capacidades del sector defensa y seguridad* [Policy for consolidation of democratic security: capacity building of the defence and security sector], Conpes Document no. 3460 (DNP: Bogota, 26 Feb. 2007), pp. 21–22.

[26] Santos, J. M., Minister of National Defence, *Consolidación de la seguridad democrática: Un esfuerzo con decisión y resultados* [Consolidation of democratic security: an effort with determination and results] (Ministry of National Defence: Bogota, 2009), p. 44 (author's translation).

[27] 'Colombianos sabrán en que se invertirá impuesto al patrimonio: Mindefensa' [Colombians know that the estate tax will be reversed: defence minister], *El Espectador* (Bogota), 30 Dec. 2009.

[28] 'MinDefensa presenta comisión de ética y transparencia' [Ministry of Defence presents ethics and transparency commission], Terra, 17 Mar. 2012, <http://noticias.terra.com.co/nacional/min defensa-presenta-comision-de-etica-y-transparencia,1e54fa11bd026310VgnVCM3000009af154d0RC RD.html>.

[29] Ley 1106 de 2006 [Colombian law no. 1106 of 2006], *Diario Oficial* (Bogota), no. 46 490 (22 Dec. 2006), Article 6.

installation of intelligence networks.[30] Each fund is managed separately by the provincial governor or town mayor administering the contract.[31] It is unclear if any monitoring mechanism has been in place since the introduction of Fonset, or if information about the execution of spending from these resources has been made available. Moreover, there is no evidence in the provincial or municipal budgets that these funds are included in reported military spending. In 2010 the Colombian Senate requested that the Ministry of Justice and Interior put a system in place to monitor the investment made with territorial funds.[32]

A second source of extra-budgetary funds for military spending comes from security service agreements between the MND and the national oil company Ecopetrol and its subsidiaries. Ecopetrol provides funding for military and security forces in exchange for protection of the infrastructure of oil companies.[33] These agreements started as a result of increasing attacks on oil pipelines and related energy infrastructure in the 1990s.[34] Some limited information on the agreements is available on Ecopetrol's website, and the MND publishes a list of the agreements, which includes the amounts that oil companies transfer to the military. However, these reports are not presented in a systematic way, making it difficult to monitor how money is spent. It is also unclear whether these funds are included in the reporting of the overall budget and expenditure of the MND. In the past five years, as oil exploration has expanded in Colombia, so have attacks on extraction infrastructure, leading to questions of whether oil companies should have their own private security forces to compensate for the lack of manpower supplied by the armed forces.[35] This has implications for future agreements, as it is uncertain if the Colombian military will be able to continue providing protection to the country's more than 130 oil exploration

[30] Colombian Ministry of the Interior and Justice, 'Asuntos territoriales y de orden público' [Land affairs and public order], <http://www.mij.gov.co/econtent/newsdetailmore.asp?id=1458andid company=>.

[31] Secure Departments and Municipalities Programme, 'Instrumentos para el manejo y la gestión local de la seguridad ciudadana y el orden público' [Instruments for handling and local management of public safety and public order], Document no. 2, 2005, <http://www.resdal.org/ultimos-docu mentos/policia-instrumentos-colombia.pdf>, p. 18.

[32] Ley 1421 de 2010 [Colombian law no. 1421 of 2010], *Diario Oficial* (Bogota), no. 47.930 (21 Dec. 2010), Article 6.

[33] Villamizar, A. et al., *Transparencia del presupuesto de defensa: El caso de Colombia* [Defence budget transparency: the case of Colombia], RESDAL Research Paper (RESDAL: Buenos Aires, July 2005), p. 65.

[34] Schemo, D. J., 'Oil companies buying an army to ward off rebels in Colombia', *New York Times*, 22 Aug. 1996.

[35] Molinsky, D., 'Oil companies in Colombia say security is government's job', Colombia Reports, 10 Aug. 2011, <http://colombiareports.com/colombia-news/economy/18216-oil-companies-in-colom bia-say-security-is-governments-job.html>.

fields. In 2011 the Minister of Defence, Juan Carlos Pinzón, announced that
6000 more troops would be assigned to protecting the oil fields.[36]

Indonesia

The extensive security sector reform that accompanied Indonesia's transition to democracy after the downfall of the dictatorial President Suharto
in 1998 has largely ended the military's dominant role in politics. Some of
the key reforms include the separation of the military from the police; the
removal of the political role of the Indonesian armed forces (Tentara
Nasional Indonesia, TNI), including its reserved seats in the parliament;
the creation of a civilian Ministry of Defence (MOD); and the publication of
defence white papers in 2003 and 2008 that establish an overarching policy
framework for military-related decisions.[37]

However, while the TNI no longer seeks to interfere in politics, democratic civilian control of the military remains weak, and serious gaps in
transparency and accountability in relation to military finance, budgeting
and procurement remain, although some progress has been made in these
areas. Some of the main ongoing problems include a fairly poor level of
general transparency of military spending; weak democratic civilian control of the military; the military's private income-generating activities; and
high levels of corruption, especially in arms procurement.

Civilian control of the military

Meaningful democratic, civilian control over the military is still limited in
Indonesia. The political accountability of the TNI to the MOD is legally
ambiguous, and the relationship between the two bodies has been described by one commentator as one 'of equals' as opposed to one of clear
subordination. Notably, the TNI commander-in-chief is also a full member
of the cabinet. A 2004 act stated that the TNI headquarters may be placed
under the full control of the MOD in future, but no timetable has been set
for this.[38] A further problem is that, while the defence minister is a civilian,
key positions in the MOD are mostly staffed by uniformed officers, meaning
that, in practice, the military itself remains largely in charge of defence
policy formation. Commentators have described TNI Headquarters as

[36] 'Gobierno aumentará protección a sectores petrolero y minero' [Government will increase
protection to oil and mining sectors], Terra, 9 Nov. 2011, <http://noticias.terra.com.co/nacional/
gobierno-aumentara-proteccion-a-sectores-petrolero-y-minero,389e647f58a83310VgnVCM3000009
af154d0RCRD.html>.
[37] On Indonesia's military reform process and its limitations see e.g. Anggoro, K., 'The Department of Defence of the Republic of Indonesia: civil supremacy without effective control', ed. B.
Sukadis, Almanac on Indonesian Security Sector Reform 2007 (Geneva Centre for the Democratic
Control of Armed Forces: Geneva, 2007); and Rüland, J., Manea, M.-G. and Born, H. (eds), The
Politics of Military Reform: Experiences from Indonesia and Nigeria (Springer: Heidelberg, 2012).
[38] Anggoro (note 37).

having 'tacit control' of the MOD bureaucracy and the development of its defence policy, with the MOD providing cover for military errors and malpractice.[39]

Budget reporting

Transparency of Indonesia's defence budget—as with other areas of the budget—is mediocre. Most budget lines are only disaggregated into broad categories.[40] The military budget in particular is typically broken down by service or by functional categories of personnel, functional expenses and procurement. Only very general information on the reasons for military spending are provided. While there has been increased disaggregation in recent years, and the 2012 budget provided a breakdown both by service and by major categories within each service, the Indonesian military budget still falls well short of providing a detailed picture of military spending. Additional funds for arms procurement provided by export credit facilities based on foreign loans are also reported within the defence budget.[41]

Military businesses and other income-generating activities

One of the most serious gaps in the economic transparency and accountability of the TNI has been its various sources of off-budget finance. Of these, the most important was the TNI's large-scale business activities, a feature of the Indonesian armed forces since their origins as a guerrilla movement in the struggle for independence. Largely through a network of 'cooperatives' and 'foundations', the TNI owned 1520 businesses in 2005; in 2008, these businesses owned assets of 3.2 trillion rupiah (about $349 million).[42] It is unclear how revenue from these businesses is used. One Indonesian military analyst suggests that the revenues from this source that are available for military operations amount to just 1.5–3 per cent of the official military budget.[43] While revenue generated by the military businesses is officially claimed to support the military as an institution for purposes such as improving the welfare of troops, it appears that the funds are directed

---

[39] Anggoro (note 37); Sebastian, L. C. and Gindarsah, I., 'Assessing 12-year military reform in Indonesia: major strategic gaps for the next stage of reform', S. Rajaratnam School of International Studies (RSIS) Working Paper no. 227, 6 Apr. 2011, <http://www.rsis.edu.sg/publications/Working_papers.html>; and Al-Ahlaq, M., 'The role of civil society organisations (CSOs) in security sector reform', ed Sukadis (note 37).

[40] See e.g. Indonesian Ministry of Finance, 'Nota keuangan dan anggaran pendapatan dan belanja negara: tahun anggaran 2013' [Financial memorandum and budget revenue and expenditure: financial year 2013], <http://www.anggaran.depkeu.go.id/dja/edef-konten-view.asp?id=945>.

[41] Al-Ahlaq (note 39); and Sebastian and Gindarsah (note 39).

[42] More recent figures do not seem to be available. Michaels, S. and Haryanto, U., 'What's the Indonesian military's business', *Jakarta Globe*, 11 May 2012.

[43] Jaleswari Pramodhawardani of the Indonesian Institute of Sciences, quoted in Michaels and Haryanto (note 42).

elsewhere. A 2006 report argued that a significant portion of the revenue is being channelled to individuals through the military hierarchy, with the lion's share going to senior officers and smaller amounts going to those lesser in command.[44]

A law passed by the Indonesian Parliament in 2004 ordered all military-run businesses to be taken over by the government by 2009. Following slow progress in implementing this law, a further presidential decree in 2009 reiterated the divestment order, and by 2011 the process was said to be complete by the government.[45] However, civil society and media sources argue that the law and its implementation have not gone far enough, bringing about only a partial withdrawal of the military from business activities, and failing to create transparency in what remains. The 2009 decree forbade direct military involvement in businesses but allowed continued indirect ownership, though the TNI's cooperatives (of which there were 13 in 2011) and foundations (of which there were 1301 in 2011).[46] While it is claimed that serving military personnel are no longer directly involved in the running of these organizations, their profits still go to the military. Moreover, there has been little transparency in the process of divestment and of restructuring of the foundations and cooperatives, and there is little monitoring of their current activities.[47]

The military also earns revenue from leasing as much as 2500 square kilometres of land to the private sector. The TNI is legally required to obtain permits for the leasing, but as of 2012 it had obtained permits for less than 1 per cent of such land. Investigations by the Audit Board (Badan Pemeriksa Keuangan, BPK) have found that the TNI has failed to return lease-related revenue to the government, as required by the 2004 divestment law and 2009 decree.[48]

A further means by which the military has secured off-budget revenue is, or has been, by acting as a 'gatekeeper'—in return for payment—for access to business licensing at the local level. Other sources of off-budget revenue include proceeds from illegal activities such as illegal logging and direct payments for providing security for domestic and international business. For example, in 2002 Freeport, a United States-based mining firm,

---

[44] Misol, L., *Too High a Price: The Human Rights Cost of the Indonesian Military's Economic Activities* (Human Rights Watch: New York, June 2006).

[45] Michaels and Haryanto (note 42); and Peraturan Presiden Republik Indonesia nomor 43 tahun 2009 tentang Pengambilalihan Aktivitas Bisnis Tentara Nasional Indonesia [Decree of the President of the Republic of Indonesia number 43 of 2009 on the Takeover of the Business Activity of the Indonesian National Army], 11 Oct. 2009, <http://www.bphn.go.id/jdih/index.php?action=reg&cat=regPeraturanPusat&cid=2009121805000003>.

[46] Misol, L., *'Unkept Promise': Failure to End Military Business Activity in Indonesia* (Human Rights Watch: New York, Jan. 2010); and Michaels and Haryanto (note 42).

[47] Michaels, S. and Haryanto, U., 'Who is minding the Indonesian military's business ties?', *Jakarta Globe*, 13 May 2012.

[48] Michaels and Haryanto (note 47).

admitted to paying the Indonesian military tens of millions of dollars to protect its operations in West Papua.[49] Although information on specific cases is difficult to obtain, it is thought that this type of transaction remains a widespread phenomenon in Indonesia.[50] The overall sums involved in this type of practice cannot be assessed.

The significance of off-budget revenue to overall Indonesian military spending is thus hard to gauge. In the past, Indonesian generals have claimed that the state budget accounted for only 25 per cent of the military's funding. However, this may well be self-serving, as a means of justifying the off-budget financing of military activity due to the inadequacies of the state budget.[51] But such activities and their related revenue are, in any event, highly problematic. Even when they are not illegal, they are almost completely non-transparent, represent a source of funding outside of civilian control or budgetary planning process, and are highly susceptible to corruption. It has also been alleged that the practices of military-run businesses—especially concerning resource exploitation and providing protection to private companies—frequently involves human rights abuses.[52] As recently as 2011 there have been reported incidents in which civilian protestors were killed by the military in protests related to land disputes between the TNI and local people.[53]

Corruption

Corruption in Indonesia was endemic under the Suharto regime, and tackling corruption has been a major theme of the post-Suharto reform process. According to Transparency International's Corruption Perceptions Index, Indonesia's position has improved steadily since 2003, rising from a score of 1.9 out of 10, in 122nd place out of 133 countries surveyed, to a score of 3.2 in 2012, in 118th place out of 180.[54]

In particular, Indonesia's military sector is highly corrupt. While much of the corruption related to the military sector is associated with the military's independent business activities, there is also evidence of corruption related to regular military expenditure. In two random surveys of military budget disbursements in 2009 (mostly relating to operational expenditure), the BPK found $15.7 million in financial deviations. However, as the BPK has no law-enforcement role, the finding did not lead to any consequences. The

---

[49] Misol (note 46).

[50] Carter, S., International Crisis Group, Conversations with author, Jakarta, Mar. 2013; and Prajuli, W., Institute for Defense, Security and Peace Studies, Conversations with author, Jakarta, Mar. 2013.

[51] Misol (note 44).

[52] Misol (note 46).

[53] Michaels, S. and Haryanto, U., 'The hazy state of the Indonesian military's land', *Jakarta Globe*, 14 May 2012.

[54] Transparency International (TI), *Corruption Perceptions Index*, 2003–12 (TI: Bonn, 2003–12).

MOD's management and control of military expenditure is worsened by its own cumbersome bureaucracy that mirrors the military hierarchy.[55]

A major problem in tackling corruption in the Indonesian military is that the 2002 law establishing Indonesia's Corruption Eradication Commission (Komisi Pemberantasan Korupsi, KPK) exempted the military from investigation by the KPK.[56]

The most severe corruption problem faced by the MOD is probably found in the area of arms procurement. Speakers at an anti-corruption seminar in January 2008—attended by members of civil society and MOD officials among others, including the head of the MOD procurement department—stated that due to corrupt pricing practices and political interference the costs of weapons were systematically increased. While numerous cases of corruption had been identified over the years few had been prosecuted.[57] In 2007 the Minister of Defence, Juwono Sudarsono, complained of persistent 'middlemanship' in arms procurement, accusing parliamentarians of involvement. Meanwhile, the head of the Parliamentary Defence Committee blamed the MOD for the same thing.[58] There have been significant efforts to try to curb corrupt arms procurement practices. For example, in 2005, a system of 'defence integrity pacts' (described above) was introduced for contracts involving export credit (i.e. foreign loan) facilities.[59] However, as of January 2013, no information on procurements made involving defence integrity pacts has been made available. In further attempt to tackle corrupt military spending, in 2011 the MOD established another commission, the Consulting Team to Address Misappropriation in the Procurement of Goods and Services, to attempt to tackle the problem.[60] However, at least one newspaper report—which quotes arms brokers themselves as well as military officers, members of civil society and parliamentarians—documents the ongoing active involvement of brokers in arms deals, and implicates legislators associated with parliamentary budget discussions in seeking commissions to approve procurement projects. The cost of arms deals was still inflated by commissions and other expenses, such as lavish travel and entertainment spending for senior officers travel-

---

[55] Sebastian and Gindarsah (note 39).

[56] Sudarsono, J., former Defence Minister, Interview with author, Jakarta, Mar. 2013; and Undang-Undang Republik Indonesia Nomor 30 Tahun 2002 tentang Komisi Pemberantasan tindak Pidana Korupsi [Law of the Republic of Indonesia no. 30 of 2002 on the Corruption Eradication Commission], enacted 27 Dec. 2002, <http://portal.mahkamahkonstitusi.go.id/eLaw/perundangan_uu_detail.php?peraturan=fc77969a>.

[57] Khalik, A., 'Arms procurement dogged by markups', Jakarta Post, 26 Jan. 2008.

[58] 'The politics of defense budgeting in Indonesia', Institute for Defense, Security and Peace Studies, Newsletter, no. 4/09, 11 June 2009, <http://idsps.org/index.php?option=com_docman&task=doc_details&gid=179&Itemid=15>.

[59] Widjajanto, A., 'Transforming Indonesia's armed forces', UNISCI Discussion Papers, no. 15 (Oct. 2007).

[60] 'Indonesia: Kemhan, TNI to form supervisory body to address corruption linked to procurement process', Jakarta detikcom, 10 Jan. 2011, Translation from Indonesian, Open Source Center.

ling to supplier countries; the reports suggested that anti-corruption procedures had merely generated extra bureaucracy, lengthening the time taken to conduct procurement, but had not adequately or directly addressed the issue of corruption.[61]

Similar to Indonesia's overall reform efforts, improving transparency and accountability in military expenditure and finance has been gradual and patchy. However, the efforts continue, and they retain the attention of the government, the parliament, civil society and the media. The experience of Indonesia suggests that, even when the military withdraws from politics and accepts subordination to civilian control, bringing military finances under such control can continue to be difficult.

---

[61] Afrida, N. and Widhiatro, H., 'Buying the right to snap up arms contracts', *Jakarta Post*, 6 Oct. 2011; and Afrida, N. and Widhiatro, H., 'Lengthy, costly arms deals put TNI firepower at risk', *Jakarta Post*, 6 Oct. 2011.

VI. The reporting of military expenditure data to the United Nations

CHRISTINA BUCHHOLD

The United Nations Report on Military Expenditures is an important source of official data on military expenditure.[1] The original purpose of the system was to provide a baseline for reductions in military spending, as proposed by some UN member states. The purpose subsequently changed to building confidence and trust among states through increased transparency.[2]

Since its inception three decades ago, rates of reporting military expenditure to the United Nations have fluctuated from a low of 12 per cent of all UN member states in its first year of operation in 1981 to a high of 42 per cent in 2002.[3] In the 1980s on average 15 per cent of all UN member states reported. Reports from newly independent states in Eastern Europe and Asia as well as increased reporting from Latin American and Caribbean states raised average reporting rates in the 1990s to 17 per cent.[4] In the period 2002–2008 average reporting rates reached 40 per cent. This increase has been attributed to 'efforts undertaken by the United Nations Office for Disarmament Affairs [UNODA], with the support of interested Member States, and to the introduction in 2002 of the simplified reporting form'.[5]

Since 2008, however, there has been a noticeable fall in the reporting rate (see table 3.8). By 2010 it had fallen to 60 states, the lowest level since 2000. Initial reporting rates in 2011 indicated a further decline, due to a large number of late reports and UNODA publication delays, but the final figures showed that the number of reports increased to 68 states.[6]

---

[1] Until 2012 the UN Report on Military Expenditures was known as the UN Standardized Instrument for Reporting Military Expenditures. UN General Assembly Resolution 66/20, 2 Dec. 2011.

[2] For details of the UN reporting instrument see e.g. Kelly, N., 'The reporting of military expenditure data to the United Nations, 2002–11', *SIPRI Yearbook 2012*.

[3] See United Nations, General Assembly, 'Group of Governmental Experts on the Operation and Further Development of the United Nations Standardized Instrument for Reporting Military Expenditures', Note by the Secretary-General, A/66/89, 14 June 2011, p. 25.

[4] United Nations, A/66/89 (note 3), p. 13.

[5] United Nations, A/66/89 (note 3), p. 14.

[6] The initial report to the General Assembly and its 1st addendum list only 51 states as reporting in 2011. A list including a further 17 states was published on the UNODA website in Jan. 2013. A 2nd addendum including the reports of these 17 states is expected to be published in 2013. United Nations, General Assembly, 'Objective information on military matters, including transparency of military expenditures', Report of the Secretary-General, A/66/117, 29 June 2011; A/66/117/Add.1, 28 Sep. 2011; and UN Office for Disarmament Affairs, 'United Nations Report on Military Expenditures: participation by member states (2011)', [n.d.], <http://www.un.org/disarmament/convarms/Milex/>.

Table 3.8. Number of countries reporting their military expenditure to the United Nations, 2002, 2007–12[a]

	2002	2007	2008	2009	2010	2011[b]	2012[c]
No. of UN member states	191	192	192	192	192	193	193
Total no. of reports[d]	**81**	**78**	**77**	**58**	**60**	**68**	**49**
Standardized reports	70	48	53	42	41	47	31
Simplified reports[e]	..	18	16	10	12	10	12
Nil reports[f]	11	12	8	6	7	10	5
Response rate (%)	42	41	40	30	31	35	25
Reports from non-UN member states[g]	1	1	–	–	–	–	–

[a] Years are the year of the Secretary-General's request (the deadline of which is 30 Apr. of the following year). The reports relate to spending in the most recently completed financial year.

[b] The figures for 2011 are higher than those presented in *SIPRI Yearbook 2012* since they include late submissions of data to the UN. Panama is included in the total although, according to the UNODA, it submitted neither a standardized, simplified or nil report in 2011 but 'provided its views on the operation of the United Nations Report on Military Expenditure'.

[c] Figures for 2012 only include submissions up to 24 Jan. 2013. Some countries may report after this date. Madagascar is included in the total, although the UNODA provides no information on the form of submission.

[d] Total figures include nil reports.

[e] Countries reporting to the UN with both standardized and simplified reports are listed as standardized reports to avoid double counting.

[f] A nil report is a questionnaire returned to the UN with no data entered, usually submitted by a country that does not maintain regular armed forces.

[g] Reports from non-UN member states are not included in other totals.

Sources: United Nations, General Assembly, 'Objective information on military matters, including transparency of military expenditures', Reports of the Secretary-General, Various dates, 2003–12; *The United Nations Disarmament Yearbook*, vol. 36 (2011), Part II, pp. 116–18; and UN Office for Disarmament Affairs (UNODA), 'Military spending', <http://www.un.org/disarmament/convarms/Milex/>.

It is too early to say whether participation in the reporting system has been affected by the report of the Group of Governmental Experts (GGE) that reviewed the military expenditure reporting system in 2010–11.[7] Provisional figures for 2012 temper hopes for a general upward trend following the GGE review. As of January 2013, the UNODA listed 49 of the 193 UN member states as having submitted reports: a drop to 25 per cent from 35 per cent in 2011, although late submissions may increase the total (see table 3.8).[8]

[7] United Nations, A/66/89 (note 3). On the GGE report see Kelly (note 2), pp. 185–86. The GGE Report was endorsed by UN General Assembly Resolution 66/20 (note 1).

[8] UN Office for Disarmament Affairs, 'United Nations Report on Military Expenditures: participation by member states (2012)', [n.d.], <http://www.un.org/disarmament/convarms/Milex/>.

This overall decrease reflects a decline in reporting in all regions (see table 3.9). Participation by European states has dropped most significantly: from 81 per cent in 2011 to 56 per cent in 2012. Participation in the Americas dropped from 40 per cent to 31 per cent; and in Asia and Oceania it dropped from 26 per cent to 21 per cent. Only two African countries reported in 2012 (down from three in 2011) and no Middle Eastern state provided information (down from one in 2011). Of the 49 countries that submitted reports to the UN, 31 submitted standardized reports, 12 submitted only simplified reports and 5 reported through a 'nil report' (i.e. a report with no data entered).

Table 3.9. Reporting of military expenditure data to the United Nations, by region and subregion, 2012

Region/ subregion	No. of countries	Countries reporting	Total	Response rate (%)
Africa	54		2	4
North Africa	4	–		
Sub-Saharan Africa	50	Burkina Faso[a], Madagascar[d]	2	
Americas	35		11	31
Central America and the Caribbean	21	Costa Rica[c], El Salvador[a], Guatemala, Honduras[a], Jamaica[a], Mexico	6	
North America	2	Canada, USA	2	
South America	12	Argentina, Colombia[b], Uruguay	3	
Asia and Oceania	42		9	21
Central and South Asia	12	Kazakhstan, Nepal	2	
East Asia	5	China[a], Japan, Mongolia	3	
Oceania	14	Australia, Samoa[c]	2	
South East Asia	11	Malaysia[a], Thailand[a]	2	
Europe	48		27	56
Eastern Europe	7	Armenia[a], Russia, Ukraine[b]	3	
Western and Central Europe	41	Albania, Austria, Bulgaria[a], Croatia[b], Czech Republic[b], Denmark[b], Finland, Germany, Hungary, Italy, Latvia, Liechtenstein[c], Luxembourg[c], FYR Macedonia[b], Netherlands[b], Poland, Portugal, Romania, San Marino[c], Serbia[a], Slovenia[a], Spain, Switzerland[a], UK	24	
Middle East	14	–	–	–
Total	**193**		**49**	**25**

[a] These countries reported with the simplified UN form. [b] These countries reported with both simplified and standardized forms. [c] These countries reported with the simplified and standardized forms. [d] No information is available on the form of submission by this country.

Sources: United Nations, General Assembly, 'Objective information on military matters, including transparency of military expenditures', Report of the Secretary-General, A/67/128, 9 July 2012; Addendum A/67/128/Add.1, 18 Sep. 2012; and United Nations Office for Disarmament Affairs, 'Participation by member states (2012)', <http://www.un.org/disarmament/convarms/Milex/>.

VII. Military expenditure data, 2003–12

SAM PERLO-FREEMAN, WAEL ABDUL-SHAFI, CHRISTINA BUCHHOLD,
CARINA SOLMIRANO AND HELÉN WILANDH

The following tables contain data on military expenditure in local currency at current prices (table 3.10), constant (2011) US dollars (table 3.11) and as a share of gross domestic product (GDP, table 3.12) for the 167 countries covered by the SIPRI Military Expenditure Database, <http://www.sipri.org/databases/milex/>.

The main purpose of the data on military expenditure is to provide an easily identifiable measure of the scale of resources absorbed by the military. Military expenditure is an 'input' measure, which is not directly related to the 'output' of military activities, such as military capability or military security. Long- and short-term changes in military spending may be signs of a change in military output, but interpretations of this type should be made with caution.

The country data on military expenditure in local currency (table 3.10) is the original data for all the other tables. This data is provided to contribute to transparency and to enable comparison with data reported in government sources and elsewhere. Data in constant dollars is provided to allow for comparison over time (table 3.11) and for calculating world, regional and other totals (see table 3.1 in section I). Data in current dollars for 2012 is provided to allow international comparison across countries (table 3.11) and across regions (table 3.1). The current dollar figures also facilitate comparison with other economic indicators, which are often expressed in current dollar terms. Data on military expenditure as a share of GDP is provided (table 3.12) as an indicator of the proportion of a country's resources used for military activities, that is, as an indicator of the economic burden of military expenditure—the 'military burden'.

Conversion to constant US dollars has been made using market exchange rates. As the base year for conversion to constant US dollars used here is 2011, the figures in table 3.11 are substantially different from those in *SIPRI Yearbook 2012*, where the base year 2010 was used.

Military expenditure data from different editions of the SIPRI Yearbook should not be combined because the data series are continuously revised and updated as new and better data becomes available. This is true in particular for the most recent years as figures for budget allocations are replaced by figures for actual expenditure. Revisions in constant dollar series can also be caused by revisions in the economic statistics used for these calculations. The SIPRI Military Expenditure Database includes consistent series dating back to 1988 for most countries.

Further notes and the sources and methods for the data follow the tables.

Table 3.10. Military expenditure by country, in local currency, 2003–12

Figures are in local currency at current prices. Years are financial years (Jan.–Dec. except where indicated). Countries are grouped by region and subregion.

State	Currency	2003	2004	2005	2006	2007	2008	2009	2010	2011	2012
Africa											
North Africa											
Algeria[1]	b. dinars	171	202	214	225	273	334	384	422	631	723
Libya[‡ ¶ 2]	m. dinars	700	894	904	807	807	1 346	. .	. .	. .	3 769
Morocco	m. dirhams	17 418	17 182	18 006	18 775	19 730	22 824	24 615	26 605	27 042	29 360
Tunisia	m. dinars	525	554	608	662	629	713	763	818	[877]	[1 108]
Sub-Saharan Africa											
Angola[∥]	b. kwanzas	50.0	68.3	119	158	156	237	263	322	342	396
Benin	b. CFA francs	20.1	22.1	23.6	24.5	. .	29.0	. .	. .	. .	39.9
Botswana[a]	m. pula	1 503	1 464	1 446	1 642	1 961	2 372	2 359	2 400	2 581	2 527
Burkina Faso[†]	b. CFA francs	25.6	30.3	33.6	37.1	45.6	55.1	51.9	61.5	65.7	74.3
Burundi	b. francs	47.0	49.4	53.6	46.0	50.1	52.0	. .	. .	. .	85.1
Cameroon[§]	b. CFA francs	110	117	118	134	142	155	162	175	164	181
Cape Verde	m. escudos	565	573	614	614	640	646	667	690	768	. .
Central African Rep.[‡ 3]	m. CFA francs	8 729	7 979	8 121	. .	9 160	14 111	16 995	25 549	. .	. .
Chad[4]	b. CFA francs	23.8	26.7	29.3	. .	187	274	206	[112]	[114]	. .
Congo, DRC[5]	b. francs	31.9	55	78.3	96	106	89.5	99.1	166	220	283
Congo, Republic of[§]	b. CFA francs	38.7	40.0	42.0	44.1	50.8	63.4	. .	66.2	. .	. .
Côte d'Ivoire[6]	b. CFA francs	124	133	132	140	155	165	198	192	169	[208]
Djibouti	m. francs	7 422	6 639	7 970	[8 800]	6 135	6 447	. .	. .	. .	. .
Equatorial Guinea	b. CFA francs	. .	. .	. .	. .	94.1	131	176	. .	. .	. .
Eritrea	m. nakfa	2 520	. .	. .	. .	. .	. .	. .	. .	. .	. .
Ethiopia[b]	m. birr	2 452	29 20	3 009	3 005	3 453	4 000	4 000	4 750	6 500	7 000
Gabon[7]	b. CFA francs	63.0	65.0	60.0	58.0	(59.0)	. .	. .	62.0	. .	128
Gambia[‡ 8]	m. dalasis	57.0	58.0	85.3	78.2	113	120	159	179	149	196
Ghana[∥ 9]	m. cedis	46.2	50.7	58.2	69.4	118					

Country	Currency										
Guinea[10]	b. francs	167	182	:	:	:	:	:	:	:	:
Guinea-Bissau||	m. CFA francs	4 362	:	6 391	:	:	:	6 490	8 484	8 267	8 465
Kenya[a]	m. shillings	19 921	21 219	26 652	27 540	39 062	41 183	48 247	50 327	64 537	70 290
Lesotho[a]	m. maloti	207	202	218	245	292	204	468	534	385	392
Liberia[b]	m. dollars	43.4	175	458	228	214	247	491	604	959	1 165
Madagascar||[11]	b. ariary	89.8	102	108	116	154	176	139	119	146	151
Malawi[a]	m. kwacha	1 309	2 753	5 116	3 933	4 959	6 678	8 841	:	[9 286]	[10 083]
Mali[¶]	b. CFA francs	[38.8]	[40.9]	45.6	50.2	52.9	64.0	68.2	72.7	76.0	76.0
Mauritania[‡]	b. ouguiyas	16.4	18.6	17.7	22.0	:	29.4	30.1	:	:	:
Mauritius[12]	m. rupees	308	293	349	337	392	495 /	242 /	458	503	666
Mozambique||	m. meticais	1 422	1 753	1 436	1 459	1 773	2 034	2 320	2 801	:	:
Namibia[a]	m. dollars	994	1 107	1 260	1 382	1 683	2 372	2 593	3 006	3 126	3 415
Niger	b. CFA francs	14.3	16.7	17.3	:	:	24	:	23.4	:	35.6
Nigeria	b. naira	75.9	85	88.5	99.9	122	192	224	299	369	365
Rwanda[13]	b. francs	24.3	23.8	25.1	30.1	30.4	37 /	64.2 /	44.1	46.4	51.7
Senegal[§]||	b. CFA francs	5.2	56.8	65.6	77.7	92.4	97.1	98.1	98.9	:	:
Seychelles	m. rupees	66.1	87.6	81	79.3	102	105	118	86.4	108	126
Sierra Leone	b. leones	66.8	62.0	68.0	[83.7]	[88.0]	[70.3]	[89.7]	[97.6]	[103]	119
Somalia	shillings	:	:	:	:	:	:	:	:	:	:
South Africa[a]	m. rand	19 473	20 201	23 511	23 819	25 180	27 801	31 324	30 442	34 349	37 493
South Sudan[14]	m. pounds	:	:	:	1 198	1 185	1 874	1 404	1 501	4 720	2 542
Sudan[‡]||[15]	m. pounds	1 039	3 200	2 838	3 338	:	:	:	:	:	:
Swaziland[‡][a][16]	m. emalangeni	255	283	410	392	451	[584]	[942]	[895]	[895]	[1 003]
Tanzania[b]	b. shillings	135	143	172	197	217	247	332	373	465	547
Togo	b. CFA francs	16.8	16.8	17.5	:	:	25.5	:	28.1	27.8	:
Uganda[b]	b. shillings	331	379	393	407	462	611	581	2 070	848	[593]
Zambia	b. kwacha	:	[490]	626	747	596	1 120	1 068	1 326	1 486	1 649
Zimbabwe||[17]	m. US dollars	195	256	131	(162)	:	:	:	98.3	198	318

State	Currency	2003	2004	2005	2006	2007	2008	2009	2010	2011	2012
Americas											
Central America and the Caribbean											
Belize[a]	m. dollars	17.6	19.4	22.1	25.4	28.2	40.5	32.5	30.1	31.8	[29.2]
Costa Rica[18]	colones	–	–	–	–	–	–	–	–	–	–
Cuba[19]	m. pesos	1 259	1 303	1 650	1 708	1 892	2 022	2 099	2 140	. .	. .
Dominican Republic	m. pesos	4 804	6 436	8 305	8 621	9 153	11 629	11 587	13 239	13 326	14 238
El Salvador[20]	m. US dollars	166	162	170	185	200	209	215	226	256	[237]
Guatemala	m. quetzales	1 420	913	798	993	1 043	1 259	1 203	1 368	1 537	1 655
Haiti[a]	gourdes	–	–	–	–	–	–	–	–	–	–
Honduras[21]	m. lempiras	[1 426]	[1 103]	[1 179]	1 428	1 813	2 503	2 963	3 216	3 790	3 808
Jamaica[a]	m. dollars	3 244	3 368	3 804	5 100	6 005	10 677	9 896	10 138	11 926	11 141
Mexico	m. pesos	[35 014]	35 314	39 467	44 496	52 235	54 977	65 615	74 517	80 396	91 907
Nicaragua[22]	m. córdobas	533	520	571	655	728	826	849	946	1 154	1 549
Panama	balboas	–	–	–	–	–	–	–	–	–	–
Trinidad and Tobago	m. dollars	136	444	581	719	760	1 588	1 598	. .	. .	. .
North America											
Canada[a]	m. dollars	14 143	14 951	16 001	17 066	19 255	21 100	21 828	21 935	23 436	[22 220]
United States[23]	m. dollars	415 223	464 676	503 353	527 660	556 961	621 138	668 604	698 281	711 402	685 334
South America											
Argentina	m. pesos	3 988	4 285	4 935	5 643	7 109	8 769	11 063	13 541	16 654	19 696
Bolivia[24]	m. bolivianos	1 331	1 343	1 368	1 441	1 740	2 371	2 431	2 300	2 438	2 738
Brazil	m. reais	25 829	28 608	33 080	35 686	39 887	44 841	51 283	59 819	61 788	64 795
Chile[§ 25]	b. pesos	1 264	1 519	1 680	1 978	2 068	2 375	2 109	2 402	2 631	2 668
Colombia[26]	b. pesos	9 434	10 664	11 405	12 577	14 082	17 810	19 496	19 787	19 048	21 820
Ecuador	m. US dollars	739	710	954	950	1 310	1 646	1 949	2 094	2 454	2 379
Guyana[‡ 27]	m. dollars	2 697	2 791	3 148	3 267	4 300	5 289	5 798	5 862	6 161	6 324
Paraguay[28]	b. guaraníes	[422]	[523]	[499]	[619]	684	776	882	1 024	1 266	1 869
Peru[29]	m. nuevos soles	3 092	3 397	3 820	4 011	3 918	4 057	5 157	5 532	5 587	6 742

Uruguay	m. pesos	7 815	8 269	8 847	9 723	10 106	12 422	14 682	15 807	17 417	19 732
Venezuela‖ 30	m. bolívares	1 588	2 740	4 292	6 436	6 377	9 286	8 631	8 683	10 229	17 200
Asia and Oceania											
Central and South Asia											
Afghanistan³¹	m. afghanis	[5 622]	[5 404]	5 544	6 358	11 506	11 471	12 783	29 571	43 273	36 565
Bangladesh^b	b. takas	38.1	41.2	44.9	54.0	59.5	62.6	87.6	109	120	127
India^a 32	b. rupees	774	965	1 035	1 102	1 190	1 518	1 993	2 146	2 373	2 495
Kazakhstan	b. tenge	47.5	58.0	78.7	100	167	185	188	221	265	[363]
Kyrgyzstan³³	m. som	2 408	2 688	3 105	3 606	4 807	6 423	7 080	9 270	10 702	..
Nepal^b ¶	m. rupees	8 255	10 996	11 745	11 136	11 389	14 712	17 811	19 491	19 101	..
Pakistan^b ¶ ‡ 34	b. rupees	220	244	281	292	327	376	448	517	[614]	641
Sri Lanka	b. rupees	[52.3]	62.7	64.7	82.2	117	164	175	173	189	184
Tajikistan	m. somoni	107	134	..	..	..	..	..	..	..	..
Turkmenistan	manat	..	..	..	..	..	..	..	..	..	..
Uzbekistan³⁵	b. sum	53.0	..	..	..	..	..	..	..	..	..
East Asia											
China³⁶	b. yuan	[288]	[331]	[379]	[452]	[547]	[638]	[764]	[836]	[944]	[1 049]
Japan^a † 37	b. yen	4 969	4 920	4 928	4 898	4 878	4 818	4 815	4 691	4 775	4 714
Korea, North³⁸	b. won	(50.8)	(54.4)	(64.5)	(67.1)	(68.5)	(71.3)	(76.3)	(82.6)	(89.8)	(98.8)
Korea, South³⁹	b. won	[18 884]	[20 421]	22 694	24 039	25 765	28 733	31 168	31 876	34 229	35 665
Mongolia	b. tugriks	27.9	32.9	35.9	46.2	66.2	77.8	54.1	74.4	110	155
Taiwan	b. dollars	257	262	258	249	268	282	302	288	295	318
Oceania											
Australia^b	m. dollars	15 873	16 748	17 921	19 899	21 179	23 249	25 372	25 250	26 320	24 217
Fiji†	m. dollars	70.7	81.1	72.9	93.6	122	85.4	100	96.8	98.3	102
New Zealand^b	m. dollars	1 518	1 528	1 645	1 807	1 875	2 083	2 201	2 254	2 284	2 383
Papua New Guinea‡ 40	m. kina	68.8	78.7	94.2	93.7	112	100	118	126	175	175

State	Currency	2003	2004	2005	2006	2007	2008	2009	2010	2011	2012
South East Asia											
Brunei Darussalam[41]	m. dollars	530 /	308	449	472	492	520	505	542	516	513
Cambodia	b. riel	270	272	296	389	383	501	977	746	780	876
Indonesia[42]	b. rupiah	[19 876]	[21 712]	208 29	23 923	30 611	31 349	34 333	42 392	50 034	64 437
Laos	b. kip	(115)	(121)	(125)	(135)	(140)	(150)	(119)	(134)	(150)	..
Malaysia	m. ringgit	10 950	10 728	11 817	11 981	13 649	14 717	13 974	12 415	14 709	14 508
Myanmar[a 43]	b. kyats	173	174	198	..	..	..	..	.. ≡	1 790	1 878
Philippines[44]	b. pesos	70.5	[69.7]	75.6	82.5	93.0	101	101	110	117	126
Singapore[a]	m. dollars	8 238	8 620	9 252	9 268	10 009	10 726	11 043	11 061	11 775	12 279
Thailand	b. baht	79.9	74.1	78.1	85.1	1 145	142	168	154	168	167
Timor-Leste[45]	m. US dollars	..	6.6	9.8	24.4 /	[11.5] /	23.7	36.5	26.4	28.4	37.7
Viet Nam	b. dong	13 058	14 409	16 278	20 577	28 735	34 848	40 981	49 739	55 100	70 000
Europe											
Eastern Europe											
Armenia[† 46]	b. drams	44.3	52.3	64.4	78.3	95.8	121	131	148	146	[156]
Azerbaijan[‖ 47]	m. manats	[173]	[224]	288	641	812	1 321	1 184	1 185	2 432	2 504
Belarus	b. roubles	475	679	975	1 355	1 603	1 887	1 887	2 287	3 762	6 354
Georgia[† 48]	m. lari	91.5	135	388	720	1 556	1 625	1 008	810	[790]	[754]
Moldova[† ¶ 49]	m. lei	115	116	151	216	276	383	277	227	245	264
Russia[50]	b. roubles	[568]	[656]	[841]	[1 030]	[1 231]	[1 544]	[1 815]	[1 976]	[2 302]	[2 799]
Ukraine[§ 51]	m. hryvnias	7 615	8 963	12 328	15 082	20 685	25 341	[26 077]	[29 445]	[31 251]	[38 976]
Western and Central Europe											
Albania[§ ¶ 52]	m. leks	9 279	10 373	11 000	13 831	17 619	21 450	23 633	19 749	19 865	19 910
Austria	m. euros	2 111	2 158	2 160	2 105	2 557	2 558	2 401	2 430	2 453	2 513
Belgium	m. euros	3 434	3 433	3 400	3 434	3 773	4 298	4 046	3 960	3 986	3 957
Bosnia–Herzegovina[† ¶ 53]	m. marka	351	315	273	278	279	311	341	325	295	351
Bulgaria[† 54]	m. leva	[986]	1 025	1 101	1 171	1 475	1 388	1 355	1 320	1 166	1 132
Croatia[55]	m. kunas	[4 757]	4 410	4 754	4 959	5 251	6 396	5 966	5 587	[5 832]	[5 612]

Country	Unit										
Cyprus†‖	m. euros	[255]	271	302	304	295	310	339	361	385	[367]
Czech Republic[56]	m. koruny	53 194	52 481	58 445	55 358	54 949	49 827	51 824	47 706	43 874	43 474
Denmark	m. kroner	21 075	21 441	20 800	23 173	22 731	24 410	23 252	25 328	24 259	25 730
Estonia‖ [57]	m. euros	152	165	214	251	325	346	314	249	[269]	[327]
Finland	m. euros	2 006	2 131	2 206	2 281	2 203	2 468	2 591	2 567	2 697	2 849
France[58]	m. euros	40 684	42 690	42 545	43 457	44 273	45 063	48 146	46 648	45 111	45 858
Germany	m. euros	31 060	30 610	30 600	30 365	31 090	32 824	34 171	34 925	34 630	[35 621]
Greece[59]	m. euros	4 462	5 048	5 652	6 064	6 235	7 219	7 612	6 171	4 824	(5 087)
Hungary	b. forint	314	311	319	297	326	321	299	281	277	234
Iceland[60]	m. krónur	..	..	–	–	–	–	2 781	2 431	2 261	2 182
Ireland	m. euros	855	887	921	949	1 003	1 081	1 019	962	935	902
Italy[61]	m. euros	26 795	27 476	26 959	26 631	[26 275]	[28 156]	[27 571]	[27 201]	[27 085]	[26 455]
Latvia	m. lats	108	124	154	206	247	280	184	138	149	143
Lithuania[62]	m. litai	967	[936]	[1 040]	[1 174]	[1 355]	[1 571]	1 251	1 068	[1 104]	[1 099]
Luxembourg	m. euros	176	189	196	197	199	[199]	[199]	[250]	[261]	[265]
Macedonia, FYR[63]	m. denars	6 292	6 683	6 259	6 149	7 272	7 229	7 000	6 044	5 859	6 346
Malta†‖	m. euros	30.0	32.5	42.3	35.3	35.8	38.3	42.6	44.3	40.2	41.3
Montenegro[64]	m. euros	..	..	..	[49.7]	46.9	58.1	55.2	56.8	63.1	[62.0]
Netherlands	m. euros	7 404	7 552	7 693	8 145	8 388	8 448	8 733	8 472	8 156	7 655
Norway	m. kroner	31 985	32 945	31 471	32 142	34 439	35 932	38 960	39 279	40 534	40 574
Poland[65]	m. złotys	16 141	17 479	19 078	20 541	23 774	[22 190]	[24 701]	[26 475]	[27 995]	[30 469]
Portugal	m. euros	2 755	2 996	3 248	3 242	3 190	3 285	3 561	3 672	3 499	[2 940]
Romania‖	m. lei	4 151	4 994	5 757	6 324	6 358	7 558	6 785	6 630	7 255	7 577
Serbia[66]	m. dinars	42 070	43 154	41 996	47 342	56 792	61 944	65 843	67 806	72 377	[72 651]
Slovakia†‖	m. euros	762	762	848	898	929	994	967	853	763	798
Slovenia‖	m. euros	360	396	413	485	506	566	575	583	478	415
Spain	m. euros	8 587	9 132	9 508	11 506	12 219	12 756	12 196	11 132	10 059	[8 974]
Sweden	m. kronor	42 903	40 527	41 240	41 150	43 163	39 710	38 751	42 423	41 070	42 072
Switzerland† ¶ [67]	m. francs	4 404	4 357	4 339	4 174	4 231	4 439	4 413	4 292	4 417	4 530
Turkey‖	m. liras	15 426	15 568	16 232	18 747	19 664	21 983	25 033	26 706	29 631	32 659
United Kingdom[a]	m. pounds	29 338	29 524	30 603	31 454	33 486	36 431	37 425	37 645	37 608	38 651

State	Currency	2003	2004	2005	2006	2007	2008	2009	2010	2011	2012
Middle East											
Bahrain[68]	m. dinars	175	180	183	203	222	248	287	292	330	358
Egypt[b]	m. pounds	14 563	14 804	15 933	17 922	19 350	21 718	22 831	25 397	25 472	27 529
Iran[a q 69]	b. rials	34 955	49 628	69 664	81 283	74 859	70 684	80 944	..	..	..
Iraq[70]	b. dinars	..	(892)	(1 649)	(1 814)	(2 437)	3 428	3 473	4 190	6 908	7 061
Israel[71]	m. shekels	[51 989]	[49 480]	[48 264]	[52 518]	[51 251]	[51 481]	[53 656]	[53 251]	[54 255]	[56 504]
Jordan	m. dinars	434	416	428	497	716	949	976	952	951	1 028
Kuwait[a]	m. dinars	950	1 039	1 020	1 052	1 209	1 185	1 220	1 250	1 568	1 725
Lebanon	b. pounds	1 392	1 439	[1 451]	[1 521]	[1 737]	1 763	2 150	[2 390]	2 452	2 616
Oman[‡ 72]	m. rials	1 010	1 144	1 404	1 550	1 663	1 775	1 726	1 882	1 650	2 585
Qatar	m. riyals	[2 856]	2 811	3 231	3 879	5 687	8 436	7 092	6 831	..	..
Saudi Arabia[§ 73]	b. riyals	70.3	78.4	95.1	111	133	143	155	170	182	213
Syria[74]	b. pounds	67.1	70.2	75.7	74.9	82.7	86.8	101	109	120	..
United Arab Emirates[75]	m. dirhams	[21 428]	[25 035]	[24 254]	[26 315]	[31 073]	[42 497]	[50 814]	[64 286]	[70 387]	..
Yemen	b. riyals	148	136	156	162	209	239	..	..	251	308

Notes: See below table 3.12.

Table 3.11. Military expenditure by country, in constant US dollars for 2003–12 and current US dollars for 2012

Figures are in US $m. at constant (2011) prices and exchange rates for 2003–12 and, in the right-most column, marked *, in current US$ m. for 2012. Years are calendar years except for the USA, where the figures are for financial years. Countries are grouped by region and subregion.

State	2003	2004	2005	2006	2007	2008	2009	2010	2011	2012	2012*
Africa											
North Africa											
Algeria[1]	3 152	3 585	3 753	3 847	4 514	5 259	5 712	6 045	8 652	9 104	9 325
Libya[‡¶2]	831	1 085	1 069	941	885	1 338	..	..	..	2 800	2 987
Morocco	2 483	2 413	2 504	2 528	2 603	2 904	3 101	3 319	3 343	3 582	3 402
Tunisia	500	510	548	571	525	567	586	602	[623]	[746]	[709]
Sub-Saharan Africa											
Angola	1 989	1 893	2 682	3 151	2 763	3 741	3 640	3 894	3 647	3 827	4 146
Benin	55.1	60	60.9	60.9	..	65.9	..	..	..	79.4	78.2
Botswana	429	396	359	354	390	417	402	381	371	345	333
Burkina Faso[†]	67.9	80.8	84.3	90.8	112	122	112	134	139	153	146
Burundi	83.9	79.7	76.1	63.6	63.9	53.4	..	..	..	57.7	59
Cameroon[§]	285	303	299	325	341	353	358	383	347	372	354
Cape Verde	8.9	9.2	9.8	9.3	9.3	8.8	9.0	9.1	9.7	..	..
Central African Republic[‡3]	23.3	21.8	21.6	22.6	31.8	37	54.8	..	..	..	..
Chad[4]	57.2	67.8	68.9	..	446	594	406	[226]	[242]	..	..
Congo, DRC[5]	142	235	275	299	282	203	154	209	239	279	308
Congo, Republic of[§]	114	115	117	115	130	151	..	142	..	..	..
Côte d'Ivoire[6]	331	349	334	346	377	377	448	427	357	[435]	[407]
Djibouti	59.6	51.7	60.2	[64.2]	42.6	40.0	..	..	..	..	..
Equatorial Guinea	..	..	..	..	256	335	429	..	..	..	..
Eritrea	591	..	..	..	..	..	..	..	..	..	..
Ethiopia	486	527	521	471	431	345	341	345	333	329	381
Gabon[7]	159	163	145	142	(138)	..	..	133	..	264	251
Gambia[‡8]	3.0	2.7	3.7	3.4	4.6	..	..	..	..	..	..

State	2003	2004	2005	2006	2007	2008	2009	2010	2011	2012	2012*
Ghana[9]	81.3	79.3	79.0	85.0	130	114	127	129	98.8	119	109
Guinea[10]	111	103	..	..	..	..	..	..	..	..	..
Guinea-Bissau	12.0	..	16.9	..	..	..	14.8	18.9	17.5	17.5	16.6
Kenya	532	525	553	547	613	585	597	633	647	694	798
Lesotho	45.8	42.7	43.5	45.8	49.9	36.3	60.2	74.8	58.2	50.6	47.5
Liberia	..	4.6	11.4	5.3	4.3	4.3	7.9	9.1	13.3	13.8	14.4
Madagascar[11]	104	104	92.9	89.5	108	114	82	64.3	72	70	68.6
Malawi	17.6	29.6	48.5	39.7	40.9	50.0	61.3	..	[44.5]	[54.1]	[39.5]
Mali	[101]	[110]	115	125	130	144	150	158	161	153	149
Mauritania‡	102	104	88.4	103	..	120	120	..	..	..	..
Mauritius[12]	17.0	16.1	16.4	16.0	15.7	17.4	18.7	17.0	17.5	22.3	22.1
Mozambique	102	112	85.7	76.9	86.4	89.9	99.3	106	..	..	..
Namibia	212	224	248	262	292	362	384	420	426	432	407
Niger	39.5	46.0	44.2	..	..	55.1	..	51.0	..	75.3	69.8
Nigeria	1 190	1 159	1 024	1 067	1 239	1 741	1 825	2 143	2 386	2 100	2 327
Rwanda[13]	81.0	70.7	68.4	75.3	69.8	73.5	77	76.5	75.4	76.8	79.8
Senegal§¶	144	145	165	191	215	213	218	217	..	..	..
Seychelles	10.6	13.5	12.4	12.2	14.8	11.2	9.5	7.2	8.7	9.7	9.2
Sierra Leone	42.1	34.2	33.5	[37.6]	[35.4]	[24.6]	[28.8]	[26.6]	[23.6]	24.2	27.4
Somalia	..	..	..	..	..	..	..	..	..	..	..
South Africa	4 122	4 179	4 580	4 581	4 475	4 384	4 590	4 434	4 596	4 785	4 470
South Sudan[14]								736	1 047	612	964
Sudan‡[15]	900	2 561	2 093	2 296	..	..	..	..	..	..	..
Swaziland‡[16]	55.1	60.8	79.6	79.2	80.6	[90.4]	[130]	[132]	[123]	[125]	[119]
Tanzania	155	158	170	186	195	198	221	253	266	278	319
Togo	45.9	45.7	44.8	..	..	58.2	..	61.8	59.0	..	..
Uganda	237	272	272	263	269	297	292	624	578	[250]	[288]
Zambia	..	[212]	229	250	180	302	254	290	306	319	320
Zimbabwe[17]	..	..	..	..	..	..	..	102	198	303	318

Americas

Central America and the Caribbean											
Belize	10.1	10.9	11.8	13.0	14.2	18.2	17.0	15.0	15.7	[14.6]	[14.9]
Costa Rica[18]	–	–	–	–	–	–	–	–	–	–	–
Cuba[19]	297	62.0	78.6	76.6	83.4	89.1	92.5	94.3	:	:	:
Dominican Republic	293	259	321	310	310	356	350	376	349	359	362
El Salvador[20]	227	212	212	222	229	225	229	237	256	[233]	[237]
Guatemala	305	182	147	172	170	182	170	187	197	205	211
Haiti	[132]	–	–	–	–	–	–	–	–	–	–
Honduras[21]	92.8	[94.2]	[92.5]	106	126	156	175	182	201	192	201
Jamaica	–	86.1	82.7	98.4	109	147	142	126	134	123	128
Mexico	[3 941]	3 797	4 081	4 440	5 013	5 019	5 689	6 203	6 472	7 103	6 978
Nicaragua[22]	48.6	43.7	43.7	46.0	46.0	43.6	43.1	45.6	51.5	65.4	65.7
Panama	–	–	–	–	–	–	–	–	–	–	–
Trinidad and Tobago	34.3	57.7	121	144	159	188	288	:	:	:	:
North America											
Canada	16 439	17 062	17 811	18 640	20 322	21 900	22 900	22 773	23 294	[22 382]	[22 547]
United States[23]	507 781	553 441	579 831	588 837	604 292	649 010	701 087	720 386	711 402	671 628	685 334
South America											
Argentina	1 876	1 931	2 028	2 091	2 421	2 750	3 264	3 607	4 052	4 356	4 340
Bolivia[24]	318	307	296	299	333	398	394	364	351	377	396
Brazil	23 573	24 493	26 502	27 441	29 595	31 488	34 334	38 127	36 932	36 751	33 143
Chile[§][25]	3 397	4 040	4 335	4 937	4 944	5 222	4 569	5 131	5 440	5 357	5 484
Colombia[26]	7 372	7 868	8 011	8 470	8 985	10 621	11 158	11 072	10 307	11 446	12 146
Ecuador	1 011	945	1 240	1 198	1 616	1 873	2 109	2 188	2 454	2 263	2 379
Guyana[‡][27]	21.1	20.9	22.0	21.4	25.1	28.6	30.5	30.2	30.2	30.1	31.1
Paraguay[†][28]	[170]	[202]	[181]	[204]	209	215	238	264	302	430	421
Peru[29]	1 403	1 487	1 646	1 694	1 626	1 591	1 965	2 076	2 029	2 363	2 557
Uruguay	709	687	702	725	697	794	877	885	902	944	971
Venezuela[30]	1 955	2 772	3 745	4 940	4 124	4 569	3 302	2 574	2 385	3 316	4 010

State	2003	2004	2005	2006	2007	2008	2009	2010	2011	2012	2012*
Asia and Oceania											
Central and South Asia											
Afghanistan[31]	[205]	[210]	189	199	313	259	309	652	877	770	741
Bangladesh	899	916	928	999	1 052	1 039	1 212	1 469	1 548	1 514	1 510
India[32]	29 165	33 879	36 054	36 225	36 664	41 585	48 963	49 159	49 634	48 255	46 125
Kazakhstan	654	747	942	1 102	1 658	1 574	1 485	1 635	1 804	[2 355]	[2 434]
Kyrgyzstan[33]	110	118	131	144	174	187	193	234	232	. .	. .
Nepal¶	198	236	261	245	227	237	265	276	261	. .	. .
Pakistan¶‡ 34	5 686	5 924	6 153	6 224	6 250	5 899	6 078	6 251	[6 547]	6 630	6 719
Sri Lanka	[1 040]	1 159	1 073	1 239	1 517	1 737	1 794	1 672	1 706	1 543	1 443
Tajikistan	50.8	59.6	. .	. .	. .	. .	. .	. .	. .	. .	. .
Turkmenistan	. .	. .	. .	. .	. .	. .	. .	. .	. .	. .	. .
Uzbekistan[35]	73.8	. .	. .	. .	. .	. .	. .	. .	. .	. .	. .
East Asia											
China[36]	[57 400]	[63 600]	[71 500]	[84 000]	[96 900]	[106 800]	[128 900]	[136 500]	[146 200]	[157 600]	[166 100]
Japan† 37	61 460	61 201	61 288	60 892	60 574	59 140	59 735	59 003	59 572	59 242	59 271
Korea, North[38]	. .	. .	. .	. .	. .	. .	. .	. .	. .	. .	. .
Korea, South[39]	[21 898]	[22 859]	24 722	25 613	26 773	28 525	30 110	29 912	30 884	31 484	31 660
Mongolia	49.4	53.8	52.1	63.9	83.8	78.8	51.6	64.4	87.2	108	115
Taiwan	9 765	9 782	9 412	9 030	9 555	9 729	10 479	9 903	9 998	10 513	10 721
Oceania											
Australia	19 868	20 687	21 414	22 562	23 947	24 820	26 676	27 006	26 610	25 555	26 158
Fiji†	57.0	63.6	55.9	70.0	86.8	56.6	64.1	58.6	54.8	54.4	57.1
New Zealand	1 467	1 488	1 504	1 583	1 649	1 705	1 808	1 838	1 792	1 809	1 891
Papua New Guinea‡ 40	42.4	47.5	55.9	54.3	64.4	51.9	57.3	57.6	73.9	68.9	83.9
South East Asia											
Brunei Darussalam[41]	367	290	351	395	409	422	414	432	415	402	411
Cambodia	114	111	114	140	128	135	264	194	192	210	217

Indonesia[42]	[4 079]	[4 194]	3 643	3 699	4 448	4 150	4 336	5 092	5 705	7 048	6 866
Laos	(23.2)	(22.1)	(21.3)	(21.6)	(21.4)	(21.3)	(16.9)	(18.0)	(18.7)	..	..
Malaysia	4 400	4 247	4 543	4 446	4 964	5 077	4 792	4 186	4 807	4 662	4 697
Myanmar[43]	..	..	..	..	..	..	..	..	..	..	..
Philippines[44]	2 419	[2 279]	2 322	2 401	2 630	2 630	2 532	2 657	2 701	2 815	2 977
Singapore	7 987	8 138	8 645	8 718	9 055	9 126	9 430	9 250	9 218	9 249	9 722
Thailand	3 377	3 047	3 070	3 199	4 216	4 962	5 917	5 227	5 520	5 334	5 387
Timor-Leste[45]	..	..	12.6	25.1	[31.6]	28.9	44.2	30.0	28.4	33.7	37.7
Viet Nam	1 471	1 507	1 572	1 850	2 386	2 350	2 581	2 878	2 686	3 397	3 363
Europe											
Eastern Europe											
Armenia†[46]	181	199	244	288	337	392	408	427	391	[408]	[387]
Azerbaijan[47]	[454]	[550]	644	1 322	1 438	1 936	1 708	1 618	3 079	3 078	3 186
Belarus	309	374	487	632	690	707	626	704	756	797	762
Georgia†[48]	96.3	134	357	607	1 201	1 140	695	521	[469]	[451]	[457]
Moldova†¶[49]	20.4	18.2	21.2	26.9	30.6	37.7	27.2	20.8	20.8	21.5	21.8
Russia[50]	[42 658]	[44 379]	[50 505]	[56 417]	[61 824]	[67 986]	[71 566]	[72 918]	[78 330]	[90 646]	[90 749]
Ukraine§[51]	2 496	2 694	3 263	3 661	4 449	4 352	[3 865]	[3 990]	[3 922]	[4 865]	[4 879]
Western and Central Europe											
Albania§¶[52]	115	126	130	160	198	233	251	202	197	194	184
Austria	3 465	3 471	3 396	3 262	3 879	3 759	3 510	3 490	3 411	3 411	3 230
Belgium	5 739	5 620	5 415	5 373	5 798	6 321	5 953	5 702	5 544	5 352	5 086
Bosnia and Herzegovina†¶[53]	316	283	237	227	225	234	257	239	210	245	231
Bulgaria†[54]	[1 123]	1 097	1 122	1 113	1 293	1 083	1 029	978	829	782	744
Croatia[55]	[1 118]	1 016	1 060	1 071	1 102	1 266	1 153	1 069	[1 091]	[1 015]	[959]
Cyprus†	[434]	451	490	481	456	457	499	518	536	[499]	[472]
Czech Republic[56]	3 691	3 541	3 872	3 576	3 449	2 941	3 027	2 748	2 479	2 379	2 221
Denmark	4 418	4 287	4 311	4 108	4 492	4 332	4 499	4 230	4 504	4 515	4 859
Estonia[57]	301	317	395	444	538	519	473	363	[374]	[438]	[420]
Finland	3 197	3 390	3 480	3 542	3 338	3 593	3 772	3 692	3 751	3 856	3 662

State	2003	2004	2005	2006	2007	2008	2009	2010	2011	2012	2012*
France[58]	64 749	66 526	65 123	65 470	65 691	65 037	69 426	66 251	62 741	62 582	58 943
Germany	49 366	47 851	47 102	46 015	46 060	47 382	49 174	49 692	48 164	[48 617]	[45 785]
Greece[59]	8 008	8 804	9 520	9 898	9 891	10 995	11 455	8 869	6 709	(6 972)	(6 539)
Hungary	2 336	2 162	2 141	1 919	1 955	1 817	1 619	1 452	1 378	1 100	1 038
Iceland[60]	–	–	–	–	–	..	26.3	21.8	19.5	17.9	17.4
Ireland	1 371	1 392	1 410	1 398	1 408	1 459	1 440	1 373	1 301	1 235	1 160
Italy[61]	43 867	44 011	42 342	40 976	[39 736]	[41 160]	[40 002]	[38 869]	[37 670]	[35 719]	[34 004]
Latvia	354	382	444	559	609	597	379	287	297	279	261
Lithuania[62]	543	[520]	[562]	[611]	[668]	[698]	532	448	[445]	[430]	[409]
Luxembourg	296	311	314	308	319	[294]	[293]	[360]	[363]	[359]	[341]
Macedonia, FYR[63]	172	181	169	161	187	171	167	142	132	139	132
Malta[†]	51.0	53.8	67.9	55.1	55.2	56.6	61.7	63.4	55.9	56.0	53.1
Montenegro[64]	..	..	..	[84.3]	76.2	86.8	79.7	81.5	87.8	[83.4]	[79.7]
Netherlands	11 712	11 802	11 821	12 375	12 541	12 325	12 590	12 061	11 344	10 395	9 839
Norway	6 598	6 764	6 365	6 352	6 757	6 794	7 210	7 099	7 232	7 189	6 973
Poland[65]	6 917	7 232	7 731	8 232	9 306	[8 324]	[8 924]	[9 316]	[9 448]	[9 912]	[9 355]
Portugal	4 532	4 813	5 102	4 957	4 744	4 762	5 205	5 294	4 866	[3 980]	[3 779]
Romania	2 371	2 549	2 697	2 779	2 665	2 937	2 498	2 300	2 380	2 406	2 185
Serbia[66]	1 260	1 165	976	985	1 110	1 077	1 059	1 028	987	[923]	[826]
Slovakia[†]	1 402	1 303	1 412	1 432	1 440	1 474	1 410	1 233	1 061	1 072	1 026
Slovenia	624	662	675	773	778	823	829	825	665	562	533
Spain	14 755	15 230	15 339	17 932	18 527	18 584	17 820	15 977	13 990	[12 185]	[11 535]
Sweden	7 398	6 962	7 053	6 943	7 125	6 337	6 215	6 726	6 324	6 424	6 209
Switzerland[†¶67]	5 297	5 199	5 117	4 871	4 902	5 021	5 016	4 844	4 974	5 136	4 829
Turkey	18 287	16 689	15 799	16 511	15 924	16 119	17 275	16 976	17 690	17 906	18 184
United Kingdom	57 009	57 669	58 154	58 531	60 379	63 074	64 301	62 946	60 284	59 795	60 840
Middle East											
Bahrain[68]	555	559	553	602	637	688	774	774	878	924	953
Egypt	5 227	4 945	4 936	5 050	5 086	4 737	4 597	4 473	4 287	4 175	4 376

Iran⁹ [69]	9 635	12 199	15 128	16 384	13 636	10 188	9 809	.	.	.	.
Iraq[70]	.	(1 882)	(2 541)	(1 824)	(2 724)	3 401	3 225	3 782	5 905	5 693	6 054
Israel[71]	[17 279]	[16 514]	[15 898]	[16 940]	[16 447]	[15 796]	[15 933]	[15 398]	[15 163]	[15 536]	[14 638]
Jordan	916	850	845	924	1 262	1 456	1 507	1 400	1 340	1 382	1 448
Kuwait	4 854	5 225	5 056	4 999	5 309	4 888	4 782	4 716	5 393	5 945	6 021
Lebanon	1 259	1 280	[1 300]	[1 291]	[1 417]	1 298	1 564	[1 665]	1 627	1 622	1 735
Oman‡ [72]	3 687	4 145	4 997	5 343	5 413	5 154	4 822	5 094	4 291	6 489	6 714
Qatar	[1 263]	1 164	1 229	1 320	1 700	2 193	1 938	1 913	.	.	.
Saudi Arabia§ [73]	25 751	28 628	34 495	39 294	45 264	44 425	45 655	47 511	48 531	54 218	56 724
Syria[74]	2 322	2 326	2 339	2 104	2 236	2 027	2 301	2 366	2 495	.	.
United Arab Emirates[75]	[9 170]	[10 200]	[9 305]	[9 238]	[9 816]	[11 960]	[14 081]	[17 658]	[19 166]	.	.
Yemen	1 663	1 357	1 419	1 328	1 588	1 526	.	.	1 164	1 243	1 439

Notes: See below table 3.12.

Table 3.12. Military expenditure by country as percentage of gross domestic product, 2003–2012

Countries are grouped by region and subregion. Figures for 2012 are based on projections for GDP from the IMF World Economic Outlook database, October 2012, and are thus subject to a higher margin for error than figures for other years.

State	2003	2004	2005	2006	2007	2008	2009	2010	2011	2012
Africa										
North Africa										
Algeria[1]	3.3	3.3	2.8	2.6	2.9	3.0	3.8	3.5	4.4	4.5
Libya[‡][¶][2]	1.9	1.9	1.4	1.0	0.9	1.2	..	..	..	3.2
Morocco	3.7	3.4	3.4	3.3	3.2	3.3	3.4	3.5	3.4	3.5
Tunisia	1.7	1.6	1.5	1.4	1.3	1.3	1.3	1.3	[1.4]	[1.6]
Sub-Saharan Africa										
Angola	4.8	4.1	4.5	4.4	3.4	3.7	4.3	4.2	3.5	3.5
Benin	1.0	1.0	1.0	1.0	..	1.0	..	..	..	1.1
Botswana	3.7	3.1	2.8	2.4	2.5	2.5	2.9	2.4	2.1	1.9
Burkina Faso[†]	1.0	1.1	1.2	1.4	1.6	1.9	1.3	1.4	1.4	1.5
Burundi	7.3	6.6	4.4	3.5	3.4	2.7	..	..	..	2.4
Cameroon[§]	1.4	1.4	1.3	1.4	1.5	1.4	1.4	1.5	1.3	1.3
Cape Verde	0.7	0.7	0.7	0.6	0.6	0.5	0.5	0.5	0.5	..
Central African Rep.[‡][3]	1.3	1.2	1.1	..	1.1	1.5	1.7	2.5	..	..
Chad[4]	1.5	1.1	0.9	..	5.5	7.1	6.2	[2.7]	[2.6]	..
Congo, DRC[5]	1.4	2.1	2.3	2.4	2.1	1.4	1.1	1.4	1.5	1.7
Congo, Republic of[§]	1.9	1.7	1.3	1.1	1.4	1.4	..	1.2	..	..
Côte d'Ivoire[6]	1.4	1.5	1.5	1.5	1.6	1.6	1.8	1.7	1.6	[1.8]
Djibouti	7.2	5.6	6.3	[6.4]	4.1	3.7	..	..	..	..
Equatorial Guinea	..	..	..	..	1.8	1.9	3.7	..	..	..
Eritrea	20.9	..	..	..	..	..	..	..	..	..
Ethiopia	2.8	2.5	2.3	1.7	1.3	1.1	1.0	0.9	0.8	0.8
Gabon[7]	1.8	1.7	1.3	1.1	(1.1)	..	..	0.9	..	1.4
Gambia[‡][8]	1.1	0.4	0.5	0.4	0.6	..	..	..	..	..

Ghana[9]	0.3	0.3	0.4	0.4	0.4	0.5	0.4	0.4	0.4	0.5
Guinea[10]	:	:	:	:	:	:	:	:	2.2	2.4
Guinea-Bissau	2.0	1.9	2.1	1.7	:	:	1.7	2.1	:	1.6
Kenya	1.9	1.9	1.9	1.9	1.9	1.8	2.5	1.7	1.6	1.7
Lesotho	1.9	2.3	3.2	2.8	1.7	2.5	0.5	2.5	2.5	2.8
Liberia	0.8	0.9	0.7	0.6	0.4	0.4	1.0	1.2	0.6	:
Madagascar[11]	0.7	0.7	0.7	0.8	1.1	1.1	1.0	1.1	1.2	1.3
Malawi	[0.9]	[0.8]	:	1.2	1.0	0.9	1.6	1.4	0.8	0.5
Mali	1.6	1.6	1.6	1.6	1.6	1.5	3.0	1.6	[1.6]	[1.6]
Mauritania[‡]	:	:	:	3.8	3.4	:	0.2	3.7	4.9	4.9
Mauritius[12]	0.2	0.2	0.2	0.2	0.2	0.1	0.8	0.2	0.2	0.2
Mozambique	:	:	0.9	0.9	0.8	0.9	2.9	0.9	1.4	1.3
Namibia	3.9	4.0	4.1	3.9	3.5	3.0	:	3.1	2.9	2.9
Niger	1.0	:	0.8	:	1.0	:	0.5	1.0	0.6	0.9
Nigeria	1.0	1.1	1.0	0.9	0.8	0.6	1.8	0.6	0.7	0.9
Rwanda[13]	1.1	1.2	1.3	1.4	1.4	1.5	1.6	1.7	2.0	2.4
Senegal[§][¶]	:	:	1.6	1.6	1.6	1.7	1.4	1.4	1.3	1.4
Seychelles	1.0	0.9	0.8	1.1	1.2	1.5	1.6	1.6	1.8	1.7
Sierra Leone	0.8	[0.9]	[1.1]	[1.3]	[1.1]	[1.5]	[1.7]	1.6	1.6	2.0
Somalia	:	:	:	:	:	:	:	:	:	:
South Africa	1.1	1.1	1.2	1.3	1.2	1.2	1.3	1.4	1.4	1.5
South Sudan[14]	8.4	6.0	4.5	:	:	:	:	:	:	:
Sudan[‡][15]	:	:	:	:	:	:	3.4	3.3	:	1.9
Swaziland[‡][16]	[3.1]	[2.8]	[3.0]	[3.0]	[2.1]	1.8	1.9	2.0	4.7	1.6
Tanzania	1.1	1.1	1.1	1.0	0.9	1.0	1.0	1.0	1.0	1.1
Togo	:	1.7	1.8	:	1.8	:	:	1.6	1.6	1.7
Uganda	[1.3]	3.2	3.4	1.8	1.9	1.9	2.0	2.2	2.3	2.3
Zambia	1.6	1.6	1.7	1.7	2.0	1.3	1.9	2.0	[1.9]	:
Zimbabwe[17]	3.1	2.2	1.4	:	:	:	(3.0)	2.3	5.5	2.5

State	2003	2004	2005	2006	2007	2008	2009	2010	2011	2012
Americas										
Central America and the Caribbean										
Belize	0.9	0.9	1.0	1.0	1.1	1.4	1.3	1.1	1.1	[1.0]
Costa Rica[18]	–	–	–	–	–	–	–	–	–	–
Cuba[19]	..	..	..	..	..	..	..	..	..	..
Dominican Republic	0.8	0.7	0.8	0.7	0.7	0.7	0.7	0.7	0.6	0.6
El Salvador[20]	1.1	1.0	1.0	1.0	1.0	1.0	1.0	1.1	1.1	[1.0]
Guatemala	0.8	0.5	0.4	0.4	0.4	0.4	0.4	0.4	0.4	0.4
Haiti	–	–	–	–	–	–	–	–	–	–
Honduras[21]	[1.0]	[0.7]	[0.6]	0.7	0.8	1.0	1.1	1.1	1.1	1.1
Jamaica	0.6	0.5	0.5	0.6	0.7	0.9	0.9	0.9	0.9	0.8
Mexico	[0.5]	0.4	0.4	0.4	0.5	0.5	0.6	0.6	0.6	0.6
Nicaragua[22]	0.9	0.7	0.7	0.7	0.7	0.7	0.7	0.7	0.7	0.8
Panama	–	–	–	–	–	–	–	–	–	–
Trinidad and Tobago	0.2	0.3	0.5	0.5	0.5	0.6	1.3	..	..	..
North America										
Canada	1.1	1.1	1.1	1.2	1.2	1.3	1.4	1.4	1.3	[1.3]
United States[23]	3.7	3.9	4.0	3.9	4.0	4.3	4.8	4.8	4.7	4.4
South America										
Argentina	1.1	1.0	0.9	0.9	0.9	0.8	1.0	0.9	0.9	0.9
Bolivia[24]	2.2	1.9	1.8	1.6	1.7	2.0	2.0	1.7	1.5	1.5
Brazil	1.5	1.5	1.5	1.5	1.5	1.5	1.6	1.6	1.5	1.5
Chile[§ 25]	2.4	2.5	2.4	2.4	2.3	2.5	2.2	2.2	2.2	2.1
Colombia[26]	3.5	3.5	3.4	3.3	3.3	3.7	3.9	3.6	3.1	3.3
Ecuador	2.6	2.2	2.6	2.3	2.9	3.0	3.7	3.6	3.7	3.4
Guyana[‡ 27]	1.9	1.8	1.9	1.8	2.0	2.2	2.3	2.1	1.9	1.8
Paraguay[† 28]	[1.2]	[1.3]	[1.1]	[1.2]	1.1	1.1	1.2	1.2	1.3	1.8
Peru[29]	1.5	1.4	1.5	1.3	1.2	1.1	1.4	1.3	1.1	1.3

Country										
Uruguay	2.3	2.1	2.1	2.1	1.8	2.0	2.1	2.0	1.9	1.9
Venezuela30	1.2	1.3	1.4	1.6	1.3	1.4	1.2	0.9	0.8	1.0
Asia and Oceania										
Central and South Asia										
Afghanistan31	[2.1]	[2.2]	1.8	1.8	2.4	2.2	2.0	3.7	4.7	3.8
Bangladesh	1.1	1.1	1.0	1.0	1.0	1.0	1.1	1.2	1.3	1.1
India32	2.8	2.8	2.8	2.5	2.3	2.6	2.9	2.7	2.6	2.5
Kazakhstan	1.1	1.0	1.0	1.0	1.3	1.1	1.1	1.1	1.0	[1.2]
Kyrgyzstan33	2.9	2.8	3.1	3.2	3.4	3.4	3.5	4.2	3.9	..
Nepal¶	1.5	1.6	1.7	1.6	1.4	1.3	1.4	1.4	1.2	..
Pakistan¶‡34	3.7	3.6	3.4	3.3	3.0	2.8	2.8	2.6	[2.7]	2.7
Sri Lanka	[2.9]	3.0	2.6	2.8	3.3	3.7	3.6	3.1	2.9	2.4
Tajikistan	..	..	..	..	..	..	..	..	..	..
Turkmenistan	..	..	..	..	..	..	..	..	..	..
Uzbekistan35	0.5	2.2	..	..	..	..	..	..	..	..
East Asia										
China36	[2.1]	[2.1]	[2.1]	[2.1]	[2.1]	[2.0]	[2.2]	[2.1]	[2.0]	[2.0]
Japan†37	1.0	1.0	1.0	1.0	1.0	1.0	1.0	1.0	1.0	1.0
Korea, North38	..	..	..	..	..	..	..	..	..	..
Korea, South39	[2.5]	[2.5]	2.6	2.6	2.6	2.8	2.9	2.7	2.8	2.7
Mongolia	1.5	1.4	1.2	1.1	1.3	1.2	0.8	0.9	1.0	1.1
Taiwan	2.4	2.3	2.2	2.0	2.1	2.2	2.4	2.1	2.1	2.3
Oceania										
Australia	1.9	1.8	1.8	1.8	1.8	1.8	1.9	1.9	1.8	1.7
Fiji†	1.6	1.7	1.4	1.7	2.2	1.5	1.8	1.6	1.4	1.4
New Zealand	1.1	1.0	1.0	1.0	1.1	1.0	1.2	1.2	1.1	1.1
Papua New Guinea‡40	0.5	0.6	0.6	0.5	0.6	0.5	0.5	0.5	0.6	0.5

State	2003	2004	2005	2006	2007	2008	2009	2010	2011	2012
South East Asia										
Brunei Darussalam[41]	3.7	2.5	2.6	2.6	2.6	2.5	3.3	3.2	2.5	2.4
Cambodia	1.5	1.3	1.2	1.3	1.1	1.2	2.3	1.6	1.5	1.6
Indonesia[42]	[1.0]	[0.9]	0.8	0.7	0.8	0.6	0.6	0.7	0.7	0.8
Laos	(0.6)	(0.5)	(0.4)	(0.4)	(0.4)	(0.3)	(0.3)	(0.3)	(0.2)	..
Malaysia	2.6	2.3	2.2	2.0	2.1	1.9	2.0	1.6	1.7	1.5
Myanmar[43]	1.9	1.9	1.6	..	..	..	..	..	3.4	4.2
Philippines[44]	1.6	[1.4]	1.3	1.3	1.3	1.3	1.3	1.2	1.2	1.2
Singapore	4.9	4.5	4.4	4.0	3.7	3.9	4.1	3.6	3.5	3.6
Thailand	1.3	1.1	1.1	1.1	1.3	1.6	1.9	1.5	1.6	1.5
Timor-Leste[45]	..	0.3	0.5	0.6	[0.8]	0.5	1.1	0.6	0.5	0.7
Viet Nam	2.1	2.0	1.9	2.1	2.5	2.3	2.5	2.5	2.2	2.4
Europe										
Eastern Europe										
Armenia[†][46]	2.7	2.7	2.9	2.9	3.0	3.4	4.2	4.3	3.9	[3.8]
Azerbaijan[47]	[2.4]	[2.6]	2.3	3.4	2.9	3.3	3.3	2.8	4.9	4.6
Belarus	1.3	1.4	1.5	1.7	1.6	1.5	1.4	1.4	1.4	1.3
Georgia[†][48]	1.1	1.4	3.3	5.2	9.2	8.5	5.6	3.9	[3.3]	[2.9]
Moldova[†][¶][49]	0.4	0.4	0.4	0.5	0.5	0.6	0.5	0.3	0.3	0.3
Russia[50]	[4.3]	[3.8]	[3.9]	[3.8]	[3.7]	[3.7]	[4.6]	[4.3]	[4.1]	[4.4]
Ukraine[§][51]	2.8	2.6	2.8	2.8	2.9	2.7	[2.9]	[2.7]	[2.4]	[2.7]
Western and Central Europe										
Albania[§][¶][52]	1.3	1.4	1.4	1.6	1.8	2.0	2.1	1.6	1.5	1.5
Austria	0.9	0.9	0.9	0.8	0.9	0.9	0.9	0.8	0.8	0.8
Belgium	1.2	1.2	1.1	1.1	1.1	1.2	1.2	1.1	1.1	1.1
Bosnia and Herzegovina[†][¶][53]	2.4	1.9	1.5	1.3	1.1	1.1	1.2	1.2	1.0	1.2
Bulgaria[†][54]	[2.8]	2.6	2.4	2.3	2.5	2.0	2.0	1.9	1.5	1.5
Croatia[55]	[2.1]	1.8	1.8	1.7	1.6	1.9	1.8	1.7	1.5	[1.7]

Cyprus†	[2.2]	2.1	2.2	2.1	1.9	1.8	2.0	2.1	2.2	[2.1]
Czech Republic[56]	2.1	1.9	2.0	1.7	1.6	1.3	1.4	1.3	1.2	1.1
Denmark	1.5	1.5	1.3	1.4	1.3	1.4	1.4	1.4	1.4	1.4
Estonia[57]	1.7	1.7	1.9	1.9	2.1	2.1	2.3	1.7	1.7	[1.9]
Finland	1.4	1.4	1.4	1.4	1.2	1.3	1.5	1.4	1.4	1.5
France[58]	2.6	2.6	2.5	2.4	2.3	2.3	2.6	2.4	2.3	2.3
Germany	1.4	1.4	1.4	1.3	1.3	1.3	1.4	1.4	1.3	[1.4]
Greece[59]	2.6	2.7	2.9	2.9	2.8	3.1	3.3	2.7	2.2	(2.5)
Hungary	1.7	1.5	1.4	1.3	1.3	1.2	1.2	1.1	1.0	0.8
Iceland[60]	–	–	–	–	–	:	0.2	0.2	0.1	0.1
Ireland	0.6	0.6	0.6	0.5	0.5	0.6	0.6	0.6	0.6	0.6
Italy[61]	2.0	2.0	1.9	1.8	[1.7]	[1.8]	[1.8]	[1.8]	[1.7]	[1.7]
Latvia	1.7	1.7	1.7	1.9	1.7	1.7	1.4	1.1	1.0	0.9
Lithuania[62]	1.7	[1.5]	[1.4]	[1.4]	[1.4]	[1.4]	1.4	1.1	[1.0]	[1.0]
Luxembourg	0.7	0.7	0.6	0.6	0.6	[0.5]	[0.5]	[0.6]	[0.6]	[0.6]
Macedonia, FYR[63]	2.4	2.5	2.1	1.9	2.0	1.8	1.7	1.4	1.3	1.3
Malta†	0.7	0.7	0.9	0.7	0.7	0.7	0.7	0.7	0.6	0.6
Montenegro[64]	:	:	:	[2.3]	1.7	1.9	1.9	1.8	1.9	[1.8]
Netherlands	1.6	1.5	1.5	1.5	1.5	1.4	1.5	1.4	1.4	1.3
Norway	2.0	1.9	1.6	1.5	1.5	1.4	1.7	1.6	1.5	1.4
Poland[65]	1.9	1.9	1.9	1.9	2.0	[1.7]	[1.8]	[1.9]	[1.8]	[1.9]
Portugal	1.9	2.0	2.1	2.0	1.9	1.9	2.1	2.1	2.0	[1.8]
Romania	2.1	2.0	2.0	1.8	1.5	1.5	1.4	1.3	1.3	1.2
Serbia[66]	3.7	3.1	2.5	2.4	2.5	2.3	2.4	2.4	2.3	[2.2]
Slovakia†	1.9	1.7	1.7	1.6	1.5	1.5	1.5	1.3	1.1	1.1
Slovenia	1.4	1.5	1.4	1.6	1.5	1.5	1.6	1.6	1.3	1.2
Spain	1.1	1.1	1.0	1.2	1.2	1.2	1.2	1.1	0.9	[0.8]
Sweden	1.7	1.5	1.5	1.4	1.4	1.2	1.2	1.3	1.2	1.2
Switzerland†[67]	1.0	0.9	0.9	0.8	0.8	0.8	0.8	0.7	0.7	0.8
Turkey	3.4	2.8	2.5	2.5	2.3	2.3	2.6	2.4	2.3	2.3
United Kingdom	2.5	2.5	2.4	2.3	2.3	2.5	2.7	2.6	2.5	2.5

State	2003	2004	2005	2006	2007	2008	2009	2010	2011	2012
Middle East										
Bahrain[68]	4.8	4.3	3.6	3.4	3.2	3.0	3.9	3.5	3.3	3.5
Egypt	3.3	3.0	2.9	2.7	2.5	2.3	2.1	2.0	1.9	1.7
Iran[q][69]	2.8	3.1	3.5	3.5	2.7	2.1	2.2	..	..	..
Iraq[70]	..	(1.7)	(2.2)	(1.9)	(2.2)	2.2	2.5	2.5	3.0	2.7
Israel[71]	[9.6]	[8.7]	[8.0]	[8.1]	[7.5]	[7.1]	[7.0]	[6.5]	[6.2]	[6.2]
Jordan	6.0	5.1	4.8	4.7	5.9	6.1	5.8	4.9	4.6	4.6
Kuwait	6.5	5.8	4.3	3.5	3.6	3.0	4.0	3.5	3.2	3.3
Lebanon	4.6	4.4	[4.4]	[4.5]	[4.6]	3.9	4.1	[4.2]	4.1	4.1
Oman[‡][72]	12.2	12.1	11.8	11.0	10.3	7.6	9.3	8.3	5.9	8.4
Qatar	[3.3]	2.4	2.0	1.8	2.0	2.0	2.0	1.5	..	..
Saudi Arabia[§][73]	8.7	8.4	8.0	8.3	9.2	8.0	11.0	10.0	8.4	8.9
Syria[74]	6.2	5.5	5.0	4.4	4.1	3.6	4.0	4.1	..	..
United Arab Emirates[75]	[4.7]	[4.6]	[3.7]	[3.2]	[3.3]	[3.7]	[5.1]	[5.9]	[5.4]	..
Yemen	6.9	5.3	4.9	4.3	4.9	4.4	..	..	3.5	4.0

.. = not available or not applicable; – = nil or a negligible value; [ ] = SIPRI estimate; / = change of financial year (FY).

[a] The FY runs from Apr. of the year indicated to Mar. of the following year.

[b] The FY runs from July of the year indicated to June of the following year.

[†] All figures exclude military pensions.

[‡] All figures are for current spending only (i.e. exclude capital spending).

[§] All figures are for the adopted budget, rather than actual expenditure.

[q] All figures exclude spending on paramilitary forces.

[||] This country changed or redenominated its currency during the period; all figures have been converted to the latest currency.

[1] The figures for Algeria for 2004–12 are budget figures. In July 2006 the Algerian Government issued supplementary budgets increasing total government expenditure by 35%. It is not clear if any of these extra funds were allocated to the military.

[2] The figures for Libya do not include development expenditure, which in 2008 was 1000 million dinars. The figures for 2012 are not necessarily comparable to those from earlier years.

[3] The figures for the Central African Republic do not include investment expenditure, which in 2005 totalled 775 000 CFA francs.

[4] Chad's military expenditure increased sharply after 2005 due to conflict in the east of the country, with exceptional military expenditure financed by oil revenues. Figures for 2006 are not available, but available information suggests a large increase over 2005 followed by a smaller increase between 2006 and 2007.

[5] The figures for the Democratic Republic of the Congo do not include profits from extensive military-run mining operations.

[6] The figures for Côte d'Ivoire for 2003 are for budgeted spending rather than actual expenditure.

[7] The figures for Gabon exclude off-budget spending financed by the Provisions pour Investissements Hydrocarbures (PIH), an investment fund based on tax revenues from foreign oil companies active in Gabon.

[8] The 2009 budget speech by the Gambian Minister of Finance gave figures for the Ministry of Defence (MOD) budget of 381 million dalasis for 2008 and 189 million dalasis for 2009. However, these figures represent a different definition of military expenditure than earlier figures and would imply a much higher increase in spending in 2008 than is likely to be the case, so they cannot be used to form a consistent series.

[9] Estimates of Ghana's GDP from the IMF were revised substantially upwards in 2012. As a result, the figures for Ghana for military expenditure as a share of GDP shown in table 3.12 are substantially lower than those shown in previous editions of the SIPRI Yearbook. The figures for Ghana for 2006–12 are for the adopted budget rather than actual spending.

[10] The figures for Guinea might be an underestimate as the IMF reports large extra-budgetary spending for the military.

[11] The figures for Madagascar include expenditure for the gendarmerie and the National Police.

[12] Mauritius changed its FY in 2010 from July–June to Jan.–Dec. Local currency figures for 2009 are for a transitional 6-month FY from July–Dec. 2009.

[13] Rwanda changed its FY in 2009 from Jan.–Dec. to July–June. The local currency figure for Rwanda for 2009 is the sum of a special 6-month budget for Jan.–June 2009 (20.6 billion Rwandan francs) and the first full July–June FY of 2009–2010 (43.6 billion Rwandan francs). The figures for 2005 and 2006 include allocations for African Union (AU) peace operations.

[14] South Sudan became independent from Sudan on 9 July 2011. Under the terms of the Comprehensive Peace Agreement of 2005, Southern Sudan was governed by the autonomous Government of Southern Sudan (GOSS) within the Sudanese state pending a referendum on final status in 2011. Figures for South Sudan for 2006–10 refer to the military spending of the GOSS on the Sudan People's Liberation Army (SPLA). On independence, South Sudan replaced the Sudanese pound with a new currency, the South Sudanese pound, at a rate of 1 for 1. Conversion to the new currency therefore does not affect the figures.

[15] The figures for Sudan are for defence and security. The figures for 2006–10 exclude spending by the Government of Southern Sudan. See also note 14.

[16] The figures for Swaziland for 2008–12 are based on an estimated share of the Defence, Public Order and Safety budget and are highly uncertain.

[17] Zimbabwe abandoned the Zimbabwean dollar in April 2009 and now mainly uses the US dollar. All figures for Zimbabwe have been converted into US dollars at the market exchange rate for the year in question. Due to lack of meaningful price data in 2008 due to hyperinflation, it is not possible to provide a constant price series for Zimbabwe before 2009.

[18] Costa Rica has no armed forces. Expenditure on paramilitary forces, border guards, and maritime and air surveillance is less than 0.05% of GDP.

[19] Figures for Cuba are for defence and internal order. The figures shown in table 3.11 are for current US dollars, converted at the official exchange rate for each year, instead of constant (2011) US dollars, due to the lack of reliable inflation data for Cuba. Data for military expenditure as a share of GDP is not given due to the lack of reliable GDP data for Cuba.

20 The figures for El Salvador for 2003–11 include military pensions from the Armed Forces Pensions Fund. The figure for 2012 includes an estimate of $90.7 million for pensions, the same as the actual figure for 2011. The pensions figures may be slightly overestimated as they include financial investments by the Pensions Fund, which amounted to $17 million in 2010.

21 The figures for Honduras do not include expenditure on arms imports.

22 The figures for Nicaragua include military aid from Taiwan and the USA for the years 2002–2009 of 12.5, 16.9, 13.6, 11.1, 7.3, 28.8, 12.2 and 11.6 million cordobas, respectively.

23 All figures for the USA are for FY (1 Oct. of the previous year to 30 Sep. of the stated year), rather than calendar year.

24 The figures for Bolivia include some expenditure for civil defence.

25 The figures for Chile presented here are considerably lower than reported in previous editions of the SIPRI Yearbook. This is due to new, more complete data being received from the Chilean authorities and a decision by SIPRI that the Carabineros should not be considered a paramilitary force from 1990 onwards (and so should be excluded from the SIPRI figures). The figures for Chile include direct transfers from the state-owned copper company Corporacion Nacional del Cobre (CODELCO) for military purchases. Since 2004 the Ministry of National Defence has built up a surplus from unspent portions of these transferred funds, which in 2011 were placed in a Strategic Contingency Fund for future equipment spending. The SIPRI figures continue to count the transfers from CODELCO rather than actual spending.

26 The figures for Colombia for 2002–2007 include special allocations totalling 2.5 billion pesos from a war tax decree of 12 Aug. 2002. Most of these allocations were spent between 2002 and 2004.

27 The figures for Guyana do not include capital expenditure, which for 2003–2006 was 147, 154, 155 and 172 million Guyanese dollars, respectively.

28 The figures for Paraguay in 2003 are for the modified budget, rather than actual expenditure. The figures for Paraguay have been revised to include spending or estimated spending on military pensions, and are therefore substantially higher than reported in previous editions of the SIPRI Yearbook.

29 The figures for Peru from 2005 do not include the transfer of 20% of gas production revenues from the state-owned company CAMISEA for the armed forces and national police.

30 The figures for Venezuela exclude an unknown amount of additional funding from the National Development Fund (FONDEN), created in 2005 and funded by contributions from the Central Bank and the state oil company, PDVSA.

31 Afghanistan's FY runs from Mar. to Feb. The figures are for core budget expenditure on the Afghan National Army. Military aid from foreign donors—which in 2009 included $4 billion from the USA, 16 times Afghanistan's domestic military expenditure—is not included.

32 The figures for India include expenditure on the paramilitary forces of the Border Security Force, the Central Reserve Police Force, the Assam Rifles, the Indo-Tibetan Border Police and, from 2007, the Sashastra Seema Bal, but do not include spending on military nuclear activities.

33 The figures for Kyrgyzstan include spending on internal security, which accounts for a substantial part of total military spending.

34 The figures for Pakistan do not include spending on paramilitary forces—the Frontier Corps (Civil Armed Forces) and Pakistan Rangers. For 2008, 2009, 2010 and 2012, these totalled 16.7, 20.8, 31.4 and 43.1 billion rupees, respectively. Defence spending in the Public Sector Development Plan amounted to 2.3, 5, 3.9, 1.4 and 2.0 billion rupees in 2008, 2009, 2010 and 2012, respectively.

35 The figures for Uzbekistan expressed in constant US dollars should be seen in the light of considerable difference between the official and the unofficial exchange rates.

36 The figures for China are for estimated total military expenditure, including estimates for items not included in the official defence budget. They are based on (a) publicly available figures for official military expenditure and for certain other items; (b) estimates based on official data and the methodology of Wang, S., 'The military expenditure of China, 1989–98', *SIPRI Yearbook 1999*; and (c) for the most recent years, where no official data is available for certain items, either the percentage change in official military expenditure, recent trends in spending in the same category, or, in the case of the commercial earnings of the People's Liberation Army (PLA), on the assumption of a gradual decrease. See 'Sources and methods' below.

37 The figures for Japan are for adopted budget for 2003–2004 and 2010–11. The figures include the budgeted amount for the Special Action Committee on Okinawa (SACO) and exclude military pensions.

38 The figures for North Korea are as reported by North Korean authorities. They do not include investment in the arms industry and R&D in dual-use technology, or various social welfare services provided through the military sector. Due to lack of a credible exchange rate between the North Korean won and the US dollar, no dollar estimates can be provided.

39 The figures for South Korea do not include spending on 3 'special funds' for relocation of military installations, relocations of US bases, and welfare for troops. These amounted to 449.3, 1048.8, 1285.2 and 916.7 billion won in 2009, 2010, 2011 and 2012, respectively.

40 Figures for Papua New Guinea are for the recurrent part of the budget. For the years 2008–11, development expenditure was 6, 25.2, 0 and 47 million kina, respectively.

41 The local currency figure for Brunei Darussalam for 2003 is for a special 15-month FY from Jan. 2003 to Mar. 2004. FYs from 2004 onwards are Apr.–Mar.

42 The figures for Indonesia exclude substantial off-budget funds received by the armed forces from a variety of sources including revenues from military-owned foundations and cooperatives, and the leasing of land from the private sector. The size of these revenues is not known but is thought to be small as a percentage of overall military spending.

43 The figures for Myanmar are not presented in US dollar terms owing to the extreme variation in the exchange rate between the kyat and the US dollar. Stated exchange rates vary from 6.076 to 960 kyat per dollar (2003). The figures for 2011 and 2012 are from the official state budget and may not be directly comparable with earlier figures, which are from secondary sources. The new 2011 constitution also allows the chief of staff of the armed forces to draw unlimited additional funds from a special fund without the consent of parliament. It is not known if this facility was used in 2011 or 2012.

44 The figures for the Philippines are slightly overstated as they include spending on Veterans Affairs. Up to 2010 these amounted to around 1 billion pesos or less, but in 2011 and 2012 this increased to 13.9 and 8.3 billion pesos, respectively.

45 The local currency figure for Timor-Leste for 2007 is for a special 6-month FY July–Dec. 2007. Previous FYs are July–June; FYs from 2008 are Jan.–Dec. Estimates of Timor-Leste's GDP from the IMF were revised substantially upwards in 2012 due to the inclusion of oil revenues that were previously excluded. As a result, the figures in table 3.12 for Timor-Leste's military spending as a share of GDP are much lower than those in previous editions of the SIPRI Yearbook.

46 If the figures for Armenia were to include military pensions they would be 15–20% higher.

[47] The figures for Azerbaijan for 2011 and 2012 include allocations of 1087 and 1123 million manats, respectively, for 'Special defence projects' in addition to the main defence budget.

[48] The figure for Georgia for 2003 is believed to be an underestimation of actual spending because of the political turmoil during the year.

[49] Adding all military items in Moldova's budget, including expenditure on military pensions and paramilitary forces, would give total military expenditure for 2005, 2006 and 2007 of 343, 457 and 530 million lei, respectively.

[50] For the sources and methods of the military expenditure figures for Russia see Cooper, J., 'The military expenditure of the USSR and the Russian Federation, 1987–97', *SIPRI Yearbook 1998*.

[51] The figures for Ukraine are for the adopted budget except in 2011.

[52] The figures for Albania prior to 2006 do not fully include pensions. The figures in 2007, 2008 and 2011 are for the modified budget.

[53] The figures for Bosnia and Herzegovina from 2005 onwards are for the armed forces of Bosnia and Herzegovina, which was formed in 2005 from the Croat–Bosniak Army of the Federation of Bosnia and Herzegovina and the Bosnian Serb Army of Republika Srpska. The figures prior to 2005 include expenditure for the Army of the Federation of Bosnia and Herzegovina and the Army of Republika Srpska. The figures do not include spending on arms imports.

[54] According to NATO figures, Bulgaria's total spending, including pensions, was 1393, 1712 and 1749 million leva in 2006, 2007 and 2008, respectively.

[55] The figures for Croatia for 2004–10 include sums allocated from central government expenditure for repayments on a loan for a military radar system. The sums allocated were 160, 431.1, 147.8, 91.4, 53.2, 54.6 and 55.2 million kunas in 2004–10, respectively. Payments continued in 2011, but figures are not available, so 55.2 million kunas has been included in the figures for 2011 as an estimate. Information is not available on whether repayments continued in 2012 and no estimate has been included.

[56] The figures for the Czech Republic do not include military aid to Afghanistan or Iraq. Aid to Afghanistan was 18.7 million koruny in 2004 and 612.6 million koruny in 2007. Aid to Iraq was 1.1 million koruny in 2005.

[57] The Estonian Border Guard Service merged with the National Police in 2010, and it is no longer classed as a paramilitary force by SIPRI. This accounts for much of the decrease in Estonian military spending in 2010.

[58] The figures for France from 2006 are calculated with a new methodology due to a change in the French budgetary system and financial law.

[59] The figures for Greece for 2012 should be treated with caution, as the economic and financial crisis may lead to actual expenditure being significantly lower than the revised budget that has been used as a basis for the current estimate.

[60] Iceland does not have an army. The figures for Iceland relate to spending on maintaining the Icelandic Air Defence System, intelligence gathering and military exercises, for which Iceland has been responsible since 2008, NATO membership fees, and spending on the *Víkingasveitin* paramilitary special forces.

[61] The figures for Italy include spending on civil defence, which typically amounts to about 4.5% of the total.

[62] Due to a change in the way Lithuania reports spending on paramilitary forces, it is possible that the figure for 2003 includes spending on some forces not included from 2004.

[63] The definition of military expenditure for the Former Yugoslav Republic of Macedonia changed from 2006. Border troops were transferred from the Ministry of Defence to the Ministry of Interior Affairs and part of the military pensions, previously entirely excluded, are now included.

[64] Montenegro became independent of the State Union of Serbia and Montenegro on 3 June 2006. See also note 66.

[65] The figures for Poland exclude some defence spending in other ministries, and additional domestic defence spending such as the Armed Forces Modernization Fund and some additional defence R&D. Between 2004 and 2011 these additional sums varied between 240 million and 640 million zlotys.

[66] Montenegro seceded from the State Union of Serbia and Montenegro on 3 June 2006. The figures for Serbia up to 2005 are for Serbia and Montenegro (known as the Federal Republic of Yugoslavia until Feb. 2003) and for 2006 onwards for Serbia alone.

[67] Figures for Switzerland do not include spending by cantons and local government. In 1990–2006 military spending by cantons and local government typically amounted to 5–8% of the central government spending figures.

[68] The figures for Bahrain do not include extra-budgetary spending on defence procurement.

[69] The figures for Iran do not include spending on paramilitary forces such as the Islamic Revolutionary Guards Corps (IRGC).

[70] The figures for Iraq do not include spending on the National Defence Council, the Office of the Chief of the Armed Forces or the Directorate of Disarmament and Integration of Militias, which totalled 308 and 314 billion dinars in 2011 and 2012, respectively.

[71] The figures for Israel include supplemental budgets for operations in occupied Palestinian territories and elsewhere, and an estimate for the paramilitary Border Police.

[72] The figures for Oman are for expenditure on defence and national security. In 2011 the government enacted a supplemental budget of 1000 million rials, equal to 12% of the original total budget, but it is not known if any of this additional allocation went to military spending.

[73] The figures for Saudi Arabia are for expenditure on defence and security.

[74] The figures for Syria in US dollars have been converted from local currency using the market exchange rate for the base year of 2011 of 1 dollar = 48.215 Syrian pounds. Previously, Syria operated an official exchange rate of 1 dollar = 11.225 Syrian pounds, which was used in editions of the SIPRI Yearbook up to 2009. Syria abolished the official rate in 2007, moving to the parallel market rate that had previously operated unofficially.

[75] The military expenditure of the United Arab Emirates is uncertain and lacking in transparency. Official documents and IMF reports sometimes give figures for defence spending, but only covering 'goods and services' (i.e. not salaries or military equipment). However, IMF reports give figures for spending on 'Abu Dhabi Federal Services', said to be mostly for military spending. Total UAE military spending has been estimated by taking 80% of the Federal Services figure, plus the MOD goods and services figure, or estimates of this where figures are not available.

Sources and methods

The definition of military expenditure

The guideline definition of military expenditure used by SIPRI includes expenditure on the following actors and activities: (*a*) the armed forces, including peacekeeping forces; (*b*) defence ministries and other government agencies engaged in defence projects; (*c*) paramilitary forces, when judged to be trained and equipped for military operations; and (*d*) military space activities. It includes all current and capital expenditure on (*a*) military and civil personnel, including retirement pensions of military personnel and social services for personnel; (*b*) operations and maintenance; (*c*) procurement; (*d*) military research and development; and (*e*) military aid (in the military expenditure of the donor country). It does not include civil defence and current expenditure for past military activities, such as for veterans' benefits, demobilization, conversion and weapon destruction. While this definition serves as a guideline, in practice it is often difficult to adhere to due to data limitations.

Limitations of the data

There are three main types of limitation of the data: reliability, validity and comparability.

The main problems of reliability are due to the less than comprehensive coverage of official military expenditure data, the lack of detailed information on military expenditure and the lack of data on actual, rather than budgeted, military expenditure. In many countries the official data covers only a part of total military expenditure. Important items can be hidden under non-military budget headings or can even be financed entirely outside the government budget. Many such extra-budgetary and off-budget mechanisms are employed in practice.

The validity of expenditure data depends on the purpose for which it is used. Since expenditure data is a measure of monetary input, its most valid use is as an indicator of the economic resources consumed for military purposes. For the same reason, its utility as an indicator of military strength or capability is limited. While military expenditure does have an impact on military capability, so do many other factors such as the balance between personnel and equipment, the technological level of military equipment, and the state of maintenance and repair, as well as the overall security environment in which the armed forces are to be employed.

The comparability of the data is limited by two different types of factor: the varying coverage (or definition) of the data and the method of currency conversion. The coverage of official data on military expenditure varies significantly between countries and over time for the same country. For the conversion into a common currency, the choice of exchange rate makes a great difference in cross-country comparisons (see below). This is a general problem in international comparisons of economic data and is not specific to military expenditure. However, since international comparison of military expenditure is often a sensitive issue, it is important to bear in mind that the interpretation of cross-country comparisons of military expenditure is greatly influenced by the choice of exchange rate.

Methods

SIPRI data is based on open sources and reflects the official data reported by governments. However, the official data does not always conform to the SIPRI definition of military expenditure. Nor is it always possible to recalculate data according to the definition, since this would require detailed information about what is included in the official defence budgets and about extra-budgetary and off-budget military expenditure items. In many cases SIPRI is confined to using the data provided by governments, regardless of definition. If several data series are available, which is often the case, SIPRI chooses the data series that corresponds most closely to the SIPRI definition of military expenditure. Nevertheless, priority is given to choosing a uniform time series for each country, in order to achieve consistency over time, rather than to adjusting the figures for individual years according to a common definition. In addition, estimates have to be made in specific cases.

Estimation. Estimates of military expenditure are predominantly made (*a*) when the coverage of official data diverges significantly from the SIPRI definition or (*b*) when no complete consistent time series is available. In the first case, estimates are made on the basis of an analysis of primarily official government budget and expenditure accounts. The most comprehensive estimates of this type are for China (as presented in *SIPRI Yearbook 1998* and updated in *SIPRI Yearbook 2011*) and Russia (as presented in *SIPRI Yearbook 1999*). In the second case, when only incomplete times series are available, the figures from the data series which corresponds most closely to the SIPRI definition are used for the years covered by that series. Figures for the missing years are then estimated by applying the percentage change between years in an alternative series to the data in the first series, in order to achieve consistency over time.

All estimates are based on official government data or other empirical evidence from open sources. Thus, no estimates are made for countries that do not release any official data, and no figures are displayed for these countries.

SIPRI estimates are presented in square brackets in the tables. Round brackets are used when data is uncertain for reasons beyond SIPRI's control, for example, when the data is based on a source of uncertain reliability and in cases when data expressed in constant dollars or as shares of GDP is uncertain due to uncertain economic data.

The data for the most recent years includes two types of estimate, which apply to all countries. First, figures for the most recent years are for adopted budget, budget estimates or revised estimates, the majority of which will be revised in subsequent years. Second, in table 3.11 the deflator used for the final year in the series is an estimate based on part of a year or as provided by the International Monetary Fund (IMF). Unless exceptional uncertainty is involved, these estimates are not bracketed.

The totals for the world, regions, organizations and income groups in table 3.1 are estimates because data is not available for all countries in all years. In cases where data for a country is missing at the beginning or end of the series, these estimates are made on the assumption that the rate of change for that country is the same as the average for the region to which it belongs. In cases where data is missing in the middle of the series, the estimates are made on the assumption of an even trend between the end values. When no estimate can be made, countries are excluded from all totals.

Calculations. The original country data is provided in local currency at current prices (table 3.10) for financial years. Those countries with financial years that do not coincide with calendar years are indicated in table 3.10. In all but one such case, the figure shown for a given year is for the financial year *beginning* in that calendar year. The exception is the USA, where each figure is for the financial year beginning on 1 October of the year previous to that indicated. A few countries changed their financial year during the period 2003–12. These cases are indicated in footnotes.

Figures in constant US dollars and as a share of GDP (tables 3.9 and 3.10) are displayed on a calendar year basis, which makes it necessary to convert financial year figures to calendar year figures for some countries. These calculations are made on the assumption of an even rate of expenditure throughout the financial year. Local currency data is then converted to US dollars at constant prices and exchange rates (table 3.11) using the national consumer prices index (CPI) for the respective country and the annual average market exchange rate (MER).

The use of CPIs as deflators means that the trend in the SIPRI military expenditure for each country (in constant dollars) reflects the real change in its purchasing power for country-typical baskets of civilian consumer goods. A military-specific deflator would be a more appropriate choice, but these are unavailable for most countries.

GDP-based purchasing power parity (PPP) exchange rates would be an alternative to MERs. PPP rates better represent the volume of goods and services that can be purchased with a given sum of money in each country than do MERs. However, they are not necessarily a better measure than MERs of the volume of *military* goods and services that may be obtained (as discussed in detail in *SIPRI Yearbook 2006*). In particular, PPP rates are unlikely to reflect the relative costs of advanced weapons technology and systems in each country. In fact, military spending figures, whatever exchange rate is used, do not directly measure military capability. PPP rates thus do not give a 'better' indication of what a country is 'really' spending; rather, they measure what alternative volume of goods and services could be bought within the country in question if the money was used for other purposes. MERs on the other hand measure what the military spending could purchase on international markets. In addition to these issues, as PPP rates are estimates, they are less reliable than MERs. Thus, SIPRI uses market exchange rates to convert military expenditure data into US dollars, despite their limitations, as the simplest and most objective measure for comparing international spending levels.

Sources

The sources for military expenditure data are, in order of priority, (*a*) primary sources, that is, official data provided by national governments, either in their official publications or in response to questionnaires; (*b*) secondary sources that quote primary data; and (*c*) other secondary sources.

The first category consists of national budget documents, defence white papers and public finance statistics as well as responses to a SIPRI questionnaire that is sent out annually to the finance and defence ministries, central banks, and national statistical offices of the countries in the SIPRI Military Expenditure Database. It also includes government responses to questionnaires about military expenditure sent out by the United Nations and, if made available by the countries themselves, the Organization for Security and Co-operation in Europe (OSCE).

The second category includes international statistics, such as those of the North Atlantic Treaty Organization (NATO) and the IMF. The data for the 16 pre-1999 NATO member states has traditionally been taken from military expenditure statistics published in a number of NATO sources. The introduction by NATO of a new definition of military expenditure in 2005 has made it necessary to rely on other sources for some NATO countries for the most recent years. The data for many developing countries is taken from the IMF's *Government Finance Statistics Yearbook*, which provides a defence heading for most IMF member countries, and from country reports by IMF staff. This category also includes publications of other organizations that provide references to the primary sources used, such as the Country Reports of the Economist Intelligence Unit.

The third category of sources consists of specialist journals and newspapers.

The main sources for economic data are the publications of the IMF: *International Financial Statistics*, *World Economic Outlook* and country reports by IMF staff.

The SIPRI Military Expenditure Network

Contribution of military expenditure data, estimates and advice are gratefully acknowledged from Julian Cooper (University of Birmingham, Centre for Russian and East European Studies), Dimitar Dimitrov (University of National and World Economy, Sofia), Iñigo Guevara y Moyano (Colectivo de Análisis de la Seguridad con Democracia, Querétaro), Gülay Günlük-Şenesen (Istanbul University), Iduvina Hernández (Asociación para el estudio y la promoción de la seguridad en democracia, Guatemala City), Shir Hever (Alternative Information Center, Jerusalem), Pavan Nair (Jagruti Seva Sanstha, Pune), Tamara Pataraia (Caucasus Institute for Peace, Democracy and Development, Tbilisi), Thomas Scheetz (Lincoln University College, Buenos Aires), Nerhan Yentürk (Istanbul Bilgi Universty), Tasheen Zayouna (International IDEA, Stockholm) and Ozren Zunec (University of Zagreb).

4. Arms production and military services

Overview

Austerity measures in North America and Western Europe as a result of the 2008 global financial crisis had a varied impact on sales of arms and military services by companies in the SIPRI Top 100 arms-producing and military services companies for 2011. Ongoing spending discussions have generated uncertainty in the largest arms and military services market—the United States—and are a key reason companies based there and in Western Europe are seeking increased market shares in other regions, including Asia, Latin America and the Middle East. In efforts to shield their industries from potential sales decreases due to decreased military spending in austerity packages, governments have stepped up efforts to increase arms exports and support cost reductions. Lowered military spending due to austerity measures in North America and Western Europe has already led to decreases in sales of arms and military services, although in some cases company subsidiaries have maintained or increased arms and military services sales outside of the countries in which the parent companies are headquartered (see section I in this chapter).

Public and private entities and individuals are becoming increasingly reliant on the Internet and networked technologies. As a result, each year, public and private entities around the globe increase spending on cybersecurity. Coupled with decreases in spending on traditional arms and military services, growing cybersecurity spending is a key explanation for why many of the companies in the SIPRI Top 100 for 2011 are increasingly interested in the cybersecurity market. A wide range of companies, including leading systems integrators, information technology companies and military services companies, operate across the various segments of cybersecurity services. These services can be categorized as network and data protection software and services; testing and simulation services; training and consulting services; and operational support (see section II).

Sales of arms and services by companies in the SIPRI Top 100 totalled $410 billion in 2011, a 5 per cent decrease in real terms (see section III). At the same time, while overall arms and military services sales have decreased, the cut-off for inclusion in the Top 100—that is, the arms sales of the company ranked 100—more than doubled, from $280 billion in 2002 to $660 billion in 2011, reflecting an increase in the number of medium-sized companies in the Top 100. Major subsidiaries play a significant role in the arms sales and company strategies of many of the parent companies in the SIPRI Top 100. The

20 major subsidiaries listed (but not ranked) in the SIPRI Top 100 accounted for 14 per cent of the parent companies' arms and military services sales in 2011.

Several factors contributed to changes in the Top 100 for 2011, including company restructuring and significant new contracts, the impact of armed conflict, and changes in government spending on arms and military services. For example, Northrop Grumman's arms sales decrease is largely attributable to spinning off Huntington Ingalls Industries. In particular, the withdrawal of US troops from Iraq and the imposition of United Nations sanctions against Libya had varying impacts on arms and military services sales. Some companies' sales decreased due to decreases in contracts (e.g. US-based AM General, KBR and L-3 Communications and Russia-based TRV Corporation), while others had increases (e.g. US-based Navistar, Fluor and DynCorp). Sales from force modernization also contributed to some increases.

SUSAN T. JACKSON

I. Key developments in the main arms-producing countries, 2011–12

SUSAN T. JACKSON*

The economic downturn following the 2008 global financial crisis and the subsequent austerity measures imposed in North America and Western Europe began to have an impact on sales in the world's arms industry in 2011–12. However, the impact on the industry was not uniform, with varied results for individual company.[1] For example, the withdrawal of United States forces from Iraq has had different impacts on sales in different sectors of the arms and military services industry; the largest impact has been in the armoured vehicles and logistics sectors. While the USA remains the largest market for arms and military services, ongoing debates about budget cuts continue to generate uncertainty in that market as well as elsewhere as many of the top arms-producing and military services companies rely on and look to the US market for sales.[2] In the context of decreasing military spending—despite the continuing high levels of US military spending on weapons—governments and arms-producing and military services companies in North America and Western Europe are pushing for export markets in Asia, Latin America and the Middle East.

Between 2002 and 2011, global arms sales by the 100 largest arms-producing and military services companies—the SIPRI Top 100—increased by 51 per cent in real terms (see table 4.1). This increase was partly due to high levels of military spending over the decade, especially in the USA as it militarized its response to the terrorist attacks of 11 September 2001 and followed up with wars in Afghanistan and Iraq. However, in 2010 the increase in arms sales by the SIPRI Top 100 slowed and in 2011 they decreased by 5 per cent in real terms (see also section III below). It is important to note, however, that while the overall total sales figure for the SIPRI Top 100 accounts for currency exchange rates, the weak US dollar has had a varied impact on individual companies.

Many countries in North America and Western Europe have begun to impose austerity measures in order to lower deficits, including both tax increases and cuts to government spending. In most cases, these measures have included cuts to military expenditure, or proposals for such cuts. At

---

[1] On the austerity measures and their impact on military expenditure more generally see chapter 3, sections I and II, in this volume. On industry reactions to these cuts see Jackson, S. T., 'Key developments in the main arms-producing countries', *SIPRI Yearbook 2012*, p. 219.

[2] On the US budget debate see chapter 3, section II, in this volume.

* Mikael Grinbaum, SIPRI Research Assistant, assisted in the data collection for this section.

Table 4.1. Arms sales of companies in the SIPRI Top 100 arms-producing and military services companies, 2002–11

	2002	2003	2004	2005	2006	2007	2008	2009	2010	2011	2002–11
Arms sales at current prices and exchange rates											
Total ($ b.)	196	235	274	289	312	347	385	398	412	410	
Change (%)		20	17	5	8	11	11	3	4	0	*110*
Arms sales at constant (2011) prices and exchange rates											
Total ($ b.)	271	305	334	341	358	375	398	426	434	410	
Change (%)		13	9	2	5	5	6	7	2	–5	*51*

Note: The figures in this table refer to the companies in the SIPRI Top 100 in each year, which means that they refer to a different set of companies each year, as ranked from a consistent set of data. In particular, the figures shown above for 2010 differ from those in table 4.5.

Source: Table 4.5; and the SIPRI Arms Industry Database.

the same time, such measures have been debated widely in terms of their effectiveness in achieving the stated goals, as well as what other costs they might create. Indeed, countries are taking steps—including arms export promotion and support for cost reductions—to protect their domestic arms and military services industries from potential decreases in sales of arms and services caused by proposed and enacted austerity measures.

Individual companies in the arms and military services industry in North America and Western Europe are also taking steps to insulate themselves against austerity measures through military specialization, downsizing, diversification, and exports and other forms of internationalization. In addition, changes in countries' perceptions of the threat environment since September 2001 have contributed to corresponding changes in security policies. These, in turn, have led to changes in customer requirements in terms of the products and services of the global arms and military services industry. This section examines the strategies adopted by both countries and companies in reaction to austerity measures and changing customer requirements.

Country strategies and austerity

Governments spend time, energy and money to build and maintain their country's domestic arms industry for a variety of reasons, including security of supply; perceived economic gain; prestige and power relationships; and the identification of national security as military security.[3] In general,

---

[3] On motivations for supporting a domestic arms and military services industry see Jackson, S. T., 'Arms production', *SIPRI Yearbook 2011*, pp. 233–34; and Jackson, S. T., 'The national security exception, the global political economy and militarization', eds K. Gouliamos and C. Kassimeris, *The Marketing of War in the Age of Neo-Militarism* (Routledge: London, 2011).

they are hesitant to enact policies and measures that lead to decreased sales by their domestic arms and military services industries. This generalization is especially relevant to austerity discussions about supporting or cutting programmes and interests. While many countries in North America and Western Europe, including the United Kingdom and the USA, have opted for austerity measures that include cuts to military expenditure, these same countries are also seeking to maintain their arms industries and are therefore faced with the challenge of cutting spending without decreasing arms sales (and so, as emphasized in many cases, preserving arms industry jobs). Governments use a number of strategies to assist their industries outside of their home markets. These include direct government arms export promotion; support for cost reductions; and the use of rhetoric about arms industry employment. Conversely, countries that have not cut military expenditure see this dilemma as an opportunity to either obtain more favourable terms on arms imports or to develop their own industries, as can be seen in the cases of the United Arab Emirates (UAE) and Brunei Darussalam.

Arms export promotion

Regardless of the economic climate, most governments promote arms exports by engaging in direct government-to-government lobbying. While this type of assistance to domestic arms industries is common and longstanding, it has taken on a new sense of urgency in the context of proposed and actual austerity measures in terms of what buyer countries can expect from arms purchases and cooperation deals. For example, arms sales promotions in 2012 by the US Secretary of Defense, Leon Panetta (in Brazil), and by the British Prime Minister, David Cameron (in Japan and the Middle East), were carried out with the specific goal of maintaining arms sales of companies based in the USA and Western Europe.[4]

Many governments approach arms export promotion through designated arms export promotion programmes or offices.[5] These government-run offices, which are part of the military structure, specifically market domestic arms industries and undertake promotion that for other industries is carried out only by commerce or trade ministries. The British Government's 2010 Strategic Defence and Security Review specifically mentioned its active arms export promotion as a primary means for maintaining

---

[4] Garamone, J., 'Panetta calls for closer military relations with Brazil', American Forces Press Service, 25 Apr. 2012, <http://www.defense.gov/news/newsarticle.aspx?id=116089>; Watt, N., 'David Cameron seeks slice of Japanese defence contracts on Tokyo trip', *The Guardian*, 10 Apr. 2012; British Prime Minister's Office, 'Prime Minister visits Oman', 21 Dec. 2012, <http://www.number10.gov.uk/news/prime-minister-visits-oman/>; and British Prime Minister's Office, 'Prime Minister's Gulf and Middle-East visit', 5 Nov. 2012, <http://www.number10.gov.uk/news/prime-ministers-gulf-visit>.

[5] See Holtom, P. et al, 'International arms transfers', *SIPRI Yearbook 2010*, pp. 295–96.

domestic British industry during military expenditure cuts.[6] In July 2012 Australia established an arms export promotion office.[7] In addition to facilitating government-to-government contracts, this office will promote and market Australian-produced weapons and services more broadly. In October 2012 Spain announced it would open an arms export promotion office to assist its industry in seeking new markets.[8] Sweden established a Defence and Security Export Agency in 2010.[9]

Support for cost reductions

In the 1990s, following the cold war, countries generally decreased their military expenditure, which led to a large-scale consolidation in the arms and military services industry, especially in North America and Western Europe. While the administration of US President Barack Obama has been hesitant to change its position on discouraging large-scale consolidation in the US arms and military services industry, its Western European counterparts have continued to raise concerns regarding the lack of consolidation in and between their national arms industries.[10] However, these concerns are not necessarily leading to large-scale consolidation in Western Europe, in part because, while companies are increasingly internationalized, they still operate within national political borders. The most prominent case in 2012 illustrating this tension was the proposed merger of Europe's two leading arms and military services companies—EADS (a trans-European company) and BAE Systems (of the UK)—which stalled due to the dissatisfaction of two of the governments that own shares (Germany and the UK, respectively) in these two companies.[11]

At the same time, however, the financial crisis and its aftermath have heightened existing concerns over duplication and a general need for consolidation in Western Europe. The European Commission's Defence Industry and Markets Task Force issued a 'non-paper' identifying the current decreases in military spending, coupled with new threats, as catalysts for

[6] British Government, *Securing Britain in an Age of Uncertainty: The Strategic Defence and Security Review*, Cm 7948 (Stationery Office: London, Oct. 2010).

[7] Clare, J., Australian Minister for Defence Materiel, 'Australian military sales office established', 2 July 2012, <http://www.minister.defence.gov.au/2012/07/02/australian-military-sales-office-established>.

[8] Spanish Government, 'Services of España Expansión Exterior and CECO to become part of ICEX', 23 Oct. 2012, <http://www.lamoncloa.gob.es/idiomas/9/gobierno/news/2012/20121023_icex.htm>.

[9] Swedish Defence and Security Export Agency (FXM), 'About FXM: exports and international cooperation for our future defence', [n.d.], <http://fxm.se/en/om-fxm/>.

[10] On consolidation in the USA and Western Europe see Jackson (note 1), p. 223.

[11] 'BAE–EADS merger cancelled amid political impasse', BBC News, 10 Oct. 2012, <http://www.bbc.co.uk/news/business-19897699>; Pickard, J., Jones, C. and Wiesmann, G., 'Germans blamed for BAE–EADS failure', *Financial Times*, 12 Oct. 2012; and Hawley, C., 'EADS–BAE failure a wasted chance for Europe', Spiegel Online, 11 Oct. 2012, <http://www.spiegel.de/international/business/eads-bae-merger-failure-is-bad-politics-say-german-papers-a-860741.html>.

restructuring the European arms industry. According to the task force, such restructuring should include the creation of consolidated naval, land and aviation centres of excellence, and should be supported by European Union (EU) member states.[12] In June 2012 the European Commission issued a report on how the EU member states were implementing a 2009 directive on defence and sensitive security procurement, highlighting that while many member states have implemented the directive, others have not yet done so, therefore impeding wider EU arms industry integration.[13] In May 2012, at the North Atlantic Treaty Organization (NATO) summit in Chicago, participants did not go as far as offering cross-border consolidation but agreed to 20 multinational projects, claiming this agreement as a step towards lowering costs.[14]

At the national level, France has stepped up its efforts to consolidate its state-owned arms producers in some areas, with Renault Trucks Défense acquiring Panhard, and Thales and Safran creating an optronics joint venture.[15] However, privatization of Nexter has not moved forward, further hindering the French Government's efforts to lessen its participation in domestic industry.[16] Meanwhile, consolidation has continued in Russia. In 2012 Rostekhnologii brought 16 more companies under its umbrella and TRV Corporation and MIC merged into a super-holding, in part to increase the pace of development of hypersonic devices.[17] Overall, these mixed results in Western Europe and elsewhere demonstrate the difficulties countries face when their domestic industries and so-called national champions become cross-border merged entities and private sector actors.

Government rhetoric about arms industry employment

Consistent, comprehensive data on employment in the global arms industry is difficult to obtain because the majority of companies do not break down employment figures by sector. Therefore, the direct impact of the financial crisis and austerity on arms production employment is difficult to measure. However, it is possible to examine government rhetoric concerning

[12] European Commission, Defence Industry and Markets Task Force, 'Non-paper', June 2012, <http://ec.europa.eu/enterprise/sectors/defence/files/defence_tf_non_paper_final_en.pdf>.
[13] European Commission, 'On transposition of Directive 2009/43/EC simplifying terms and conditions for transfer of defence-related products within the EU', Report from the Commissions to the European Parliament and the Council, COM(2012) 359 final, Brussels, 29 June 2012. See also chapter 10, section V, in this volume.
[14] North Atlantic Treaty Organization (NATO), 'NATO delivers at Chicago Summit', 20 May 2012, <http://www.nato.int/cps/en/natolive/news_87600.htm>.
[15] Volvo AB, 'Renault Truck Defense finalizes acquisition of French Panhard', Press release, 25 Oct. 2012, <http://www.volvogroup.com/group/global/en-gb/_layouts/CWP.Internet.VolvoCom/NewsItem.aspx?News.ItemId=132735&News.Language=en-gb>; and Thales Group, 'Thales and Safran sign optronics partnership agreement', Press release, 20 Dec. 2011, <http://www.thalesgroup.com/Press_Releases/Group/2011/Safran_and_Thales_sign_optronics_partnership_agreement/>.
[16] Tran, P., 'Little movement seen on Nexter privatization', *Defense News*, 21 Nov. 2012.
[17] Dunai, P., 'Russian missile companies in merger', *Jane's Defence Industry*, 25 Sep. 2012.

employment.[18] For example, on his trip to Japan in 2012, Cameron emphasized the importance of industry jobs to the British economy as a key
reason for supporting British arms exports and international partnerships
in arms production.[19] Canada had touted jobs creation as a key reason for
participating in the F-35 (Joint Strike Fighter, JSF) programme, even as the
expense of the programme continues to climb.[20] The Swedish Government
has argued that support for the arms industry amounts to support for jobs.[21]

Other countries are looking to promote employment by developing
indigenous arms industries in the hope that this will spill over into other
sectors. For example, Brunei Darussalam seeks to integrate the skill sets
acquired through technology transfers via arms purchases into the civilian
labour market as a means for socio-economic development more broadly.[22]
Brazil is another case in point, where the arms industry receives government benefits in part to promote industry employment.[23]

Company strategies and austerity

Proposed and actual cuts to military expenditure, particularly in North
America and Western Europe, have created uncertainty in terms of how
and where companies operate. The implications for the arms and military
services industry are broad. Threat perceptions since September 2001 have
influenced both customer requirements and the ways in which standard
business practices are implemented. These practices include strategies to
build access to international markets, and strategic acquisitions and divestitures to handle changes in spending and customer requirements. In contrast to the 1990s, however, large-scale industry consolidation has so far not
been a feature of company strategies. In general, depending on the economic climate, companies use a set of strategic tools including diversification through acquisitions, joint ventures, efforts to increase exports, and
coordination with government marketing promotion efforts.

[18] Pollin, R. and Garrett-Peltier, H., *The U.S. Employment Effects of Military and Domestic Spending Priorities: An Updated Analysis* (University of Massachusetts, Political Economy Research
Institute: Amherst, MA, 2009). See also Wulf, H., 'Arms industry limited: the turning point in the
1990s', ed. H. Wulf, SIPRI, *Arms Industry Limited* (Oxford University Press: Oxford, 1993), p. 12.

[19] Watt (note 4).

[20] Canadian Department of National Defence, 'Industrial Participation—Joint Strike Fighter Program', <http://www.forces.gc.ca/site/mobil/news-nouvelles-eng.asp?id=4066>.

[21] The Swedish Government has argued that technology and job opportunities are a key reason
for continued support of the development of SAAB's Gripen. Reinfeldt, F. et al., 'Sverige köper 40–60
Jas Gripen' [Sweden buys 40–60 Jas Gripens], *Svenska Dagbladet*, 25 Aug. 2012.

[22] Bruneian Ministry of Defence, 'Shaping the force today: defence white paper update 2007',
[n.d.], <http://www.mindef.gov.bn/MOD2/index.php?option=com_docman&task=doc_download&
gid=40&Itemid=328>.

[23] Rocha, A., 'Arms industry to double in size', Brazil Arab News Agency, 4 Oct. 2011, <http://
www2.anba.com.br/noticia_especiais.kmf?cod=12494151&indice=20>.

Accessing international markets: exports and joint ventures

Due to contracting domestic markets in North America and Western Europe—the two regions where the majority of the SIPRI Top 100 companies are headquartered—arms producers and military services companies have become more vocal in recent years about the role international market access plays in their financial results. Companies are particularly interested in those markets that are expected to maintain or increase their respective military spending levels. While this strategy is not new, it has taken on increasing importance, particularly in countries where austerity measures have either been proposed or enacted.[24]

Companies seeking to build international market share often pursue export and cooperative production arrangements, for example by forming joint ventures.[25] Specifically, over the past few years, companies have reiterated their interest in accessing key markets in Asia, Latin America and the Middle East. These interests are exemplified in export strategies as well as in the locations in which these companies now operate, either through home offices or joint ventures. This has implications for smaller arms markets, especially in those countries that do not possess (but wish to develop) indigenous arms and military services industries. Foreign ownership as a strategy for maintaining domestic arms industries in small markets in Western Europe is discussed further in section III.

German company Rheinmetall is restructuring in preparation for international expansion and has included Australia among the other potential markets listed above.[26] UK-based QinetiQ's provision of services to overseas firing ranges is an example of an emerging niche market for companies seeking to capitalize on military spending cutbacks made by governments.[27] SEPI, owner of Navantia in Spain, is relying on exports to keep Navantia afloat and is looking for contracts in Australia, Mexico, Saudi Arabia and Venezuela.[28] Israel Aerospace Industries (IAI) sees Brazil and Chile as key

[24] At the same time, many companies in the SIPRI Top 100 that emphasize increasing foreign arms sales are not headquartered in countries subject to austerity measures. E.g. Rosoboronexport of Russia is targeting exports to Asia, an area of long interest to Russia. Grevatt, J., 'Rosoboronexport targets Asian growth despite tougher competition', *Jane's Defence Industry*, 24 Apr. 2012. Aselsan of Turkey also is looking to increase arms exports. İş Investment, 'Aselsan', 30 May 2012, <http://www.isyatirim.com.tr/WebMailer/.../2_20120530152732784_1.pdf>, p. 14.

[25] Jackson, S. T., 'Arms production', *SIPRI Yearbook 2010*, p. 267.

[26] Rheinmetall, 'Rheinmetall maintains two-pillar strategy.' Press release, 20 Mar. 2013, <http://www.rheinmetall.com/en/rheinmetall_ag/press/news/aktuell_1/news_details_2304.php>.

[27] QinetiQ, 'QinetiQ expands services provision to new international markets', Press release, [n.d.], <http://www.qinetiq.com/news/PressReleases/Pages/QinetiQ-expands-services-provision-to-new-international-markets.aspx>; and Bell, M., 'QinetiQ targets rapid overseas growth in firing range outsourcing', *Jane's Defense Industry*, 21 Mar. 2012.

[28] Navantia, 'Navantia signs two contracts in Australia', Press release, 16 Dec. 2011, <http://www.navantia.es/noticia.php?id_noti=164>; and Navantia, 'South Australian Minister for Defence Industries visits Cartagena shipyard', Press release, 18 Sep. 2012, <http://www.navantia.es/noticia.php?id_noti=219>.

markets in the near future.[29] US-based Oshkosh also emphasizes export potential to Latin America (especially Brazil, Colombia and Mexico), as well as the Middle East and the Nordic countries. It also views India as a long-term prospect in terms of converting its existing commercial presence there into a lead into the military market.[30] These examples demonstrate that companies are seeking a share of international markets.

In the Middle East, the UAE has become a destination for both exports and joint ventures.[31] For example, Italy's Fincantieri has a joint venture with the UAE's Etihad Ship Building LLC and is also working on vessels for the UAE's Navy.[32] US-based Raytheon is using acquisitions to push exports and is looking at the UAE as a new market in which to expand.[33] French Nexter exports to the UAE but has some concerns regarding the increasing level of competition to complete export contracts.[34]

Implementing strategies through mergers and acquisitions

The desirability of international market share beyond North America and Western Europe is also evident in foreign acquisitions, for example, in Australia and Brazil. Further, companies continue to diversify into markets adjacent to the arms and military services industry (e.g. the cybersecurity and health care information technology sectors) and increase their military sector products and services, both through acquisitions to cover gaps in their capabilities and acquisitions relating to existing competencies. Companies are also divesting non-core businesses as a means to streamline their portfolios to be better able to handle military spending cuts and changing customer requirements.

As the push for international market share intensifies due to spending cuts in North America and Western Europe, companies are using foreign direct investment as a means to increase market access. For example, Israel's Rafael acquired a Brazilian company in part to improve local capabilities but also to increase export opportunities for Israel.[35] One of the reasons Italy's Fincantieri acquired Norway's STX was to broaden its market base (especially in Brazil) and diversify by offering a mix of military

[29] 'IAI targets Brazil, Chile for special aircraft mission aircraft deals', Flightglobal, 15 May 2012, <http://www.flightglobal.com/news/articles/iai-targets-brazil-chile-for-special-mission-aircraft-deals-371918/>.

[30] Oshkosh, 2012 Oshkosh Corporation Annual Report (Oshkosh: Oshkosh, WI, 2012).

[31] As with arms exports, companies headquartered outside of austerity countries seek access to markets through joint ventures. See e.g. the Turkish company Aselsan's joint venture in the UAE. Aselsan, Annual Report 2011 (Aselsan: Ankara, 2011), p. 7.

[32] Fincantieri, Fincantieri Annual Report 2011 (Fincantieri: Trieste, 2011), pp. 15, 65.

[33] Felstead, P., 'Raytheon continues Mid-East push to offset US downturn', Jane's Defence Industry, 1 Nov. 2012.

[34] Tran, P., 'Gulf states squeeze suppliers', Defense News, 23 Feb 2013.

[35] 'Rafael buys 40% stake in Brazilian aerospace co', Globes, 11 Apr. 2012, <http://www.globes.co.il/serveen/globes/docview.asp?did=1000740680&fid=1725>.

and civilian applications.[36] Other companies have bought into the Australian market, including the Swiss company RUAG (which is seeking to increase its presence in the Pacific region's ammunition market) and the UK's Serco (which is seeking to increase its presence in Australia's military and civil markets).[37] In addition to smaller arms markets such as Australia and Brazil, the USA remains a key market for many companies seeking acquisitions. In an effort to diversify beyond its reliance on Airbus, EADS has committed to making acquisitions in the US market.[38] BAE Systems is seeking to expand its US maritime market share.[39] Saab's new Americas office will focus on Brazil and the USA.[40] Turkey's Aselsan is also seeking to acquire companies in the US market.[41]

A number of companies in the arms industry have continued diversifying into adjacent markets, in part to accommodate changing customer requirements. This strategy maintains the shift some companies began earlier in the 2000s and highlights a related trend in certain sectors, in particular in cybersecurity (see section II below) and in adjacent civilian sectors such as health care IT. In some cases, these acquisitions overlap with companies' intentions to move into international markets. For example, in 2012 US-based companies Raytheon, ManTech and General Dynamics made acquisitions with the intention of bolstering their respective cybersecurity capabilities for both military and civilian applications.[42] Raytheon's acquisition is for wireless applications, ManTech's for threat and malware detection and diagnosis, and General Dynamics' for network security tools. General Dynamics' purchase, together with the cyber and intelligence solutions centre it initiated in 2012, reflects its increased focus on cyber-

---

[36] While the STX Group is headquartered in South Korea, its European offices are based in Norway. Fincantieri, 'Fincantieri acquires STX OSV and becomes the world number one player in high value-added segments', Press release, 21 Dec. 2012, <http://www.fincantieri.it/cms/data/browse/news/000484.aspx>; and Fincantieri (note 32), p. 33.

[37] RUAG, 'RUAG acquires Rosebank Engineering Pty Ltd—introducing new lifecycle support capabilities to the market', Media release, 17 Dec. 2012, <http://www.ruag.com/en/Group/Media/Media/Media_releases/Mediadetail?id=473>; and Serco, 'Serco purchases remaining stake in Australian defence and marine services joint venture', Press release, 7 Nov. 2012, <http://www.serco.com/media/internationalnews/DMSmaritimestakepurchase.asp>.

[38] Shalal-Esa, A., 'EADS keeps sights firmly on expansion in US', Reuters, 10 Oct. 2012, <http://www.reuters.com/article/2012/10/10/us-eads-bae-usa-idUSBRE8990W620121010>.

[39] Anderson, G., 'BAE Systems boosts US maritime capability through acquisition', Jane's Defence Industry, 15 Nov. 2012.

[40] Saab, 'Market focus drives changes in Saab's management group', Press release, 20 June 2012, <http://www.saabgroup.com/en/about-saab/newsroom/press-releases--news/2012---6/market-focus-drives-changes-in-saabs-management-group/>.

[41] İş Investment (note 24).

[42] Raytheon, 'Raytheon acquires government business of data protection firm SafeNet', Press release, 12 Dec. 2012, <http://raytheon.mediaroom.com/index.php?s=43&item=2238>; ManTech, 'ManTech completes acquisition of business of HBGary', Press release, 2 Apr. 2012, <http://www.mantech.com/news/Pages/04022012_hbgary.aspx>; and General Dynamics, 'General Dynamics completes acquisition of IPWireless', Press release, 11 June 2012, <http://www.generaldynamics.com/news/press-releases/detail.cfm?customeL_dataPageID_1811=17775>.

security. Ultra Electronics (UK) also acquired two UK-based companies, one with expertise in cryptographic management services and the other in the financial services sector.[43]

Elsewhere, companies are using cybersecurity acquisitions as a means to gain access to foreign markets. For example, Northrop Grumman's purchase of the Australian company M5 Network Security demonstrates increased interest in the Australian market, as well as the growing emphasis on cybersecurity in Australia's overall security approach.[44] Other foreign-based arms producers and military services companies have made similar acquisitions in recent years, including BAE System's purchase (through an Australian subsidiary) of Stratsec in 2011 and Raytheon's Australian subsidiary's purchase of Compucat in 2010.[45] BAE Systems has begun realigning its business in the Asia–Pacific region to reflect a growing customer demand for cybersecurity products and services.[46] The acquisition by Cassidian Cybersecurity, a subsidiary of EADS, of Netasq gives both Netasq and EADS a combined international market access, and EADS aims to establish itself as a leader in cybersecurity.[47]

Companies have also been moving into other adjacent markets in order to extend their market reach. For instance, Rheinmetall moved into adjacent sectors beyond its land systems when it acquired an Australian simulation and training specialist immediately after setting up its Australian simulation subsidiary.[48] Another area of continuing interest for acquisition is in the health care IT sector. ManTech's threat and malware detection and diagnosis purchase marks its entrance into a growing adjacent market and can be seen as a means to counter austerity measures in traditional sectors. SAIC followed suit with an acquisition that makes it one of the largest handlers of electronic health records in the USA.[49]

[43] Ultra, 'Ultra acquires specialist cyber security companies', 27 June 2012, <http://www.ultra-electronics.com/press_releases/287_Barron_McCann_acquisition_final.pdf>; and 'Ultra targets "lucrative" financial cyber sector with Barron McCann acquisitions', *Jane's Defence Industry*, 27 June 2012.

[44] Northrop Grumman, 'Northrop Grumman agrees to acquire Australian cybersecurity company M5 Network Security', News release, 7 June 2012, <http://www.irconnect.com/noc/press/pages/news_releases.html?d=258507>; and Australian Government, *Cyber Security Strategy* (Australian Government: Canberra, 2009).

[45] Raytheon, 'Raytheon Australia boosts cybersecurity capabilities with key acquisition', Press release, 22 Feb. 2010, <http://raytheon.au.mediaroom.com/index.php?s=43&item=10>; and Jackson (note 1), p. 228.

[46] Grevatt, J., 'BAE Systems to merge Stratsec in Detica to strengthen cybersecurity capabilities', *Jane's Defence Industry*, 3 Dec. 2012.

[47] EADS, 'Cassidian CyberSecurity strengthens its business with acquisition of Netasq', Press release, 2 Oct. 2012, <http://www.eads.com/eads/int/en/news/press.20121002_cassidian_netasq.html>.

[48] Rheinmetall Defence, 'Rheinmetall Simulation Australia acquires defence operations of Sydac Pty Ltd', Press release, 31 Oct. 2012, <http://www.rheinmetall-defence.com/en/rheinmetall_defence/public_relations/news/archive_2012/aktuellesdetailansicht_4_2241.php>.

[49] SAIC, 'SAIC completes acquisition of maxIT Healthcare', Press release, 13 Aug. 2012, <http://investors.saic.com/phoenix.zhtml?c=193857&p=irol-newsArticle&ID=1724995&highlight=>.

Companies also use acquisitions to improve the products and services they already deliver. In 2012 this type of acquisition spanned a variety of sectors including radio monitoring and intelligence fusions systems (e.g. Sweden's Saab); emerging submarine requirements (e.g. US-based General Dynamics); satellites and related systems (e.g. the UK's Ultra Electronics and Cobham); UAV systems (e.g. US-based Lockheed Martin); aircraft electrical systems (e.g. France's Safran); training systems (e.g. US-based Cubic and L-3 Communications); aerospace engine solutions (e.g. UK-based GKN); and services added to existing platforms (e.g. US-based General Electric).

While much attention is paid to acquisitions, a number of divestitures also indicate the ways in which the industry is restructuring to accommodate the austerity environment and changing customer requirements (see table 4.2). For example, in order to focus on its core aerospace and commercial businesses, US-based United Technologies Corporation (UTC) is selling Pratt and Whitney Power Systems and Rocketdyne in the first half of 2013.[50] Other divestitures of non-core businesses include BAE Systems' sale of the Safariland, Tensylon and O'Gara companies, and UK-based Babcock's sale of VT Services.[51]

Despite increases in overall arms and military services sales over the past decade, sales decreased in 2011. Governments in North America and Western Europe are proposing and implementing austerity measures while trying to minimize the impact on their respective arms and military services industries. As a result of these proposed and actual austerity measures, companies headquartered in these regions are seeking to maintain and expand their market shares in smaller markets in Asia, Latin America and the Middle East.

---

[50] United Technologies Corporation, 'United Technologies to sell Pratt & Whitney Power Systems unit to Mitsubishi Heavy Industries', Press release, 12 Dec. 2012, <http://www.utc.com/News/Press+Releases/United+Technologies+to+sell+Pratt+and+Whitney+Power+Systems+unit+to+Mitsubishi+Heavy+Industries>; and United Technologies Corporation, 'United Technologies to sell Rocketdyne unit to GenCorp Inc', Press release, 23 July 2012, <http://www.utc.com/News/United+Technologies+to+sell+Rocketdyne+unit+to+GenCorp+Inc>.

[51] BAE Systems, 'BAE Systems announces agreement to sell Safariland business', 2 May 2012, <http://www.baesystems.com/article/BAES_046568/bae-systems-announces-agreement-to-sell-safariland-business>; 'DuPont buys BAE unit, takes stake in start up', Reuters, 8 June 2012; 'BAE Systems completes sale of vehicle armouring business to O'Gara Group', *Jane's Defence Industry*, 6 Feb. 2013; and Babcock, 'Disposal of VT Services Inc', 14 May 2012, <http://www.babcockinternational.com/media-centre/disposal-of-vt-services-inc/>.

Table 4.2. Selected acquisitions and divestitures in the OECD arms industries, 2012, by motivation

Figures for deal value and revenue are in US $m., at current prices. The table lists major acquisitions in the arms industries of member states of the Organisation for Economic Co-operation and Development (OECD) that were announced or completed between 1 Jan. and 31 Dec. 2012. It is not an exhaustive list of all acquisition activity but gives a general overview of strategically significant and financially noteworthy transactions.

Buyer company (country)/ Subsidiary (country)[a]	Acquired company (country)	Seller company (country)[b]	Deal value ($ m.)[c]	Revenue or employees[d]
Footholds				
Fincantieri (Italy)	STX Osv (Norway)	Publicly listed	602	c. 9200 employees
Rafael (Israel)	Gespi Aeronautics (Brazil)	Privately owned	..	..
RUAG (Switzerland)	Rosebank Engineering (Australia)	Privately owned	..	154 employees
Serco	DMS Maritime (Australia)	P&O Maritime Services	110	c. 450 employees
Cybersecurity				
Raytheon (USA)	Telligy (USA)	Privately owned	..	..
ManTech (USA)	HBGary (USA)	Privately owned	..	c. 40 employees
General Dynamics (USA)	Fidelis Security Systems (USA)	Privately owned	..	70 employees
Northrop Grumman (USA)	M5 Network Security (Australia)	Privately owned	..	..
Cassidian Cybersecurity/ EADS	Netasq (France)	Privately owned	70	c. 120 employees
Rheinmetall Simulation Australia (Australia)	Sydac Pty Ltd (Australia)	Privately owned	..	c. 20 employees
Ultra Electronics (USA)	Barron McCann Technology and Barron McCann Payments (UK)	Privately owned	18.7	$52 m.
Health care IT				
SAIC (USA)	maxIT Healthcare (USA)	Privately owned	473	$1.3 b.
ManTech (USA)	Evolvent	Privately owned	..	189 employees
Expansion or infill				
Saab (Sweden)	Medav (Germany)	Privately owned	35	c. 27.5 m.
General Dynamics (USA)	Applied Physical Sciences Corp. (USA)	Privately owned	..	c. 90 employees

Ultra Electronics (UK)	Giga Communications (UK)	Privately owned	..	$58 m.
Cobham (UK)	Thrane and Thrane (Denmark)	Publicly listed	..	$446 m.
Lockheed Martin (USA)	Procerus Technologies (USA)	Privately owned	..	..
Lockheed Martin (USA)	CDL Systems (Canada)	Privately owned	..	60 employees
Safran (France)	Goodrich Electric Power Systems (USA)	Goodrich (USA)	401	$560 m.
GKN (UK)	Volvo Aero (Sweden)	Volvo AB (Sweden)	933	$3 b.
General Electric (USA)	Avio (Italy)	Cinven/Finmeccanica	344	..
L-3 Communications (USA)	Thales Training & Simulation (UK)	Privately owned	131.9	$400 m.
NEK Services/ Cubic Corp. (USA)	NEK Special Programs Group (USA)	NEK Advanced Securities Group (USA)	52	$200 m.
Divestitures				
Mitsubishi Heavy Industries (Japan)	Pratt & Whitney Power Systems (USA)	United Technologies (USA)	..	$430 m.
GenCorp (USA)	Pratt & Whitney rocket propulsion unit (USA)	United Technologies (USA)	..	$550 m.
Kanders & Co (USA)	Safariland (USA)	BAE Systems (UK)	..	$124 m.
EI DuPont de Nemours (USA)	Tensylon High Performance Materials (USA)	BAE Systems (UK)	18	..
O'Gara Group (USA)	Commercial armoured vehicle division	BAE Systems Inc. (USA)	10	..
The Resolute Fund II (USA)	VT Services (USA)	Babcock International (UK)	98.75	..

[a] In cases where the acquisition was completed by a subsidiary, rather than directly by the parent company, the name of the subsidiary is given.

[b] 'Publicly listed' means that the company's shares were publicly traded on a stock exchange of its home country, with no single majority shareholder. 'Privately owned' means the company was owned by one or more private shareholders, with its shares not traded on any stock exchange.

[c] In cases where the deal value is not available in US dollars, currency conversion has been made using the International Monetary Fund average exchange rate for the calendar month in which the transaction was made. Companies do not always disclose the values of transactions.

[d] The acquired company's annual revenue is listed where known (either actual revenue for 2011 or expected revenue for 2012). Where revenue is not available in US dollars, currency conversion has been made using the International Monetary Fund average exchange rate for the appropriate year. Where information is not available for the acquired company's revenue, the acquired company's number of employees is shown, where known.

II. Cybersecurity and the arms industry

VINCENT BOULANIN

The growing importance of cybersecurity in the military and civil realms has led to noteworthy diversification by arms production and military services companies into the cybersecurity market. This section presents a brief overview of cybersecurity, provides provisional information on the size of the cybersecurity market and reviews the involvement of arms-producing and military services companies in this market.

The rise of cybersecurity as a national security issue

Cybersecurity is defined and understood in different ways.[1] In a narrow and technical sense, cybersecurity has been defined as 'the ability to control access to network systems and the information they contain'—thus, strictly referring to the protection of cyberspace itself.[2] Security objectives are then traditionally framed in terms of preserving the confidentiality, integrity and availability of cyberspace.[3] The cybersecurity concept has also gained a national security dimension as the public, businesses and the military have become increasingly dependent on computer and networked technologies—in fact, it has been 'securitized'.[4] Hence, within the political realm, cybersecurity deals with the challenges produced by cyberspace as a new medium for threatening activities (e.g. criminality, terrorism, espionage or warfare) and the belief that a lack of cybersecurity might affect the security of the economy, the state and society in general.[5] From an industry perspective, cybersecurity has been defined as 'an emerging field of protecting computer systems and data from interference through the Internet'.[6]

---

[1] The adjective 'cyber-' and the concept 'security' are themselves objects of definitional controversy. On the definition of cybersecurity see e.g. Dunn Cavelty, M., 'Cybersecurity', ed. P. Burgess, *The Routledge Handbook of New Security Studies* (Routledge: New York, 2010), pp. 154–55.

[2] Bayuk, J. L. et al., *Cyber Security Policy Guidebook* (John Wiley: Hoboken, NJ, 2012), p. 1. 'Cyberspace' has been defined as 'the combination of the virtual structure, the physical components that support it, the information it contains, and the flow of that information within it'. Fischer, E. A., *Creating a National Framework for Cybersecurity: An Analysis of Issues and Options*, Congressional Research Service (CRS) Report for Congress RL32777 (US Congress, CRS: Washington, DC, 22 Feb. 2005), p. 5.

[3] Nissenbaum, H., 'Where computer security meets national security', *Ethics and Information Technology*, vol. 7, no. 2 (June 2005), p. 63.

[4] On securitization see Buzan, B., Wæver, O. and de Wilde, J., *Security: A New Framework for Analysis* (Lynne Rienner: Boulder, CO, 1998), p. 25; and Hansen, L. and Nissenbaum, H., 'Digital disaster, cybersecurity and the Copenhagen School', *International Studies Quarterly*, vol. 53, no. 4 (2009), pp. 1155–75.

[5] Hansen, L. and Nissenbaum, H., 'Digital disaster, cyber security, and the Copenhagen School', *International Studies Quarterly*, vol. 53, no. 4 (Dec. 2009), pp. 1155–75.

[6] EADS, *EADS Annual Review 2011: Progressing, Innovating, Transforming* (EADS: Leiden, 2012), p. 64.

The 'securitization' of cyberspace—that is, the process that transformed the security of cyberspace into a national security concern—began in the late 1980s, focusing first on issues of military relevance. As individual states began to rely increasingly on network systems for the management of weapon platforms and critical infrastructure, military institutions also began to identify the threat of cyberattacks that could paralyse arsenals or lead to leakages of strategic information. Subsequently, these institutions began developing both defensive and offensive capacities to take action within cyberspace. For some analysts, cyberspace has since become a fourth 'battle space'—after air, land and sea.[7]

In the 1990s, as economic activities and social infrastructures became increasingly reliant on Internet and networked technologies, the securitization process accelerated and gained a civil dimension (i.e. it became a national security issue beyond the traditional military sense).[8] Information technology (IT) experts and security analysts observed vulnerabilities arising from the interconnectivity of computer systems, warning of the cascading effects of cyberattacks on the economy and society—and, therefore, on national security.[9] An accumulation of small and relatively simple attacks targeting companies, governments and private persons (e.g. phishing, fraud or espionage) may cause major losses for national economies, while major targeted cyberattacks have the potential to significantly disrupt society's smooth functioning. For instance, cybersabotage leading to the disruption of national or local electric power systems would 'involve at least opportunity costs—interruption of business, forgoing of various activities and associated benefits'.[10]

While no major cyberdisaster—or 'electronic Pearl Harbor'—has yet occurred, several events in recent years have reinforced the credibility of such scenarios, leading to political and institutional responses from international and national security communities.[11] Notably, the Estonian

---

[7] Rid, T., 'Cyber war will not take place', *Journal of Strategic Studies*, vol. 35, no. 1 (Feb. 2012), pp. 5–32.

[8] Dunn Cavelty, M., *Cyber-security and Threat Politics: US Efforts to Secure the Information Age* (Routledge: London, 2008), p. 2.

[9] From a technical perspective, cyberattacks can be classified according to their ability to (*a*) destabilize, e.g. through a denial of service (DoS) attack; (*b*) spy and control, e.g. through use of a trojan horse; or (*c*) destroy, as in the case of the Stuxnet virus. On the political dimensions of cyberattacks see Deibert, R. J. and Rohozinski, R., 'Risking security: policies and paradoxes of cyberspace security', *International Political Sociology*, vol. 4, no. 1 (Mar. 2010), pp. 15–32; and Dunn Cavelty, M., 'Cyberwar: concept, status quo and limitations', Centre for Strategic Studies (CSS) Analysis in Security Policy no. 71, Apr. 2010, <http://www.css.ethz.ch/publications/CSS_Analysis_EN>, pp. 1–2.

[10] US National Research Council, Computer Science and Telecommunications Board, *Cyber-security Today and Tomorrow: Pay Now or Pay Later* (National Academy Press: Washington, DC, 2002) p. 6; and Andersson, R. H. and Hearn, A. C., *An Exploration of Cyberspace Security R&D Investment strategies for Darpa: "The Days After . . . Cyberspace II"* (RAND: Santa Monica, CA, 1996).

[11] The term 'electronic Pearl Harbor' was allegedly coined in 1991 by Winn Schwartau during testimony before the US Congress. See Schwartau, W., *Information Warfare: Cyberterrorism: Pro-*

Government and its agencies were victims of a large-scale cyberattack in 2007.[12] Portrayed as the 'first war in cyberspace', this incident eventually led Estonia and nine other EU member states to adopt national cyber-security strategies.[13] It also prompted the North Atlantic Treaty Organization (NATO) to adopt a policy on cyberdefence, under which it created a cyberdefence management authority and supported the creation of a cooperative cyberdefence centre of excellence in Tallin, Estonia, in 2008.[14] In the United States, President Barack Obama has made cybersecurity a priority of his presidency.[15] In 2010 the US Army established the US Cyber Command (USCYBERCOM) and in 2011 the US Department of Defense published a new cybersecurity strategy, colloquially known as Cyber 3.0.[16]

In 2012 cybersecurity continued to rise on the agendas of the international political and security communities. Revelations about Flames and Stuxnet—two viruses described as Western cyberweapons targeting Iran—made headlines and inspired fresh discussions about the growing use of cyberweapons and cyberwarfare.[17] While there is no reliable evidence, a growing number of countries—including China, Iran, Israel, Russia and the USA—were suspected of using cyberweapons and making offensive interventions across cyberspace.[18] In that context, at the 2012 Security Jam, officials from NATO and the EU and researchers from top European think tanks discussed the need for global governance in cyberspace.[19] At the

tecting Your Personal Security in the Electronic Age (Thunder's Mouth Press: New York, 1994), p. 43; and Bendrath, R., 'The American cyber-angst and the real world: any link?', ed. R. Latham, Bombs and Bandwidth: The Emerging Relationship Between Information Technology and Security (New Press: New York, 2003), p. 50.

[12] A list of major cyber incidents since 2006 has been compiled by the Center for Strategic and International Studies (CSIS). Lewis, J. A., 'Significant cyber events', <http://csis.org/publication/cyber-events-2006/>.

[13] Landler, M. and Markoff, J., 'In Estonia, what may be the first war in cyberspace', New York Times, 28 May 2007. The 9 other EU member states that have adopted cybersecurity strategies are Finland (in 2008), Slovakia (2008), the Czech Republic (2011), France (2011), the UK (2011), Germany (2011), Lithuania (2011), Luxembourg (2011) and the Netherlands (2011). European Network and Information Security Agency, 'National cyber security strategies: setting the course for national efforts to strengthen security in cyberspace', May 2008, <http://www.enisa.europa.eu/activities/Resilience-and-CIIP/national-cyber-security-strategies-ncsss/cyber-security-strategies-paper>.

[14] North Atlantic Treaty Organization (NATO), Cooperative Cyber Defence Centre of Excellence (CCDCOE), 'About', [n.d.], <https://www.ccdcoe.org/3.html>.

[15] White House, 'Remarks by the President on securing our nation's cyber infrastructure', 29 May 2009, <http://www.whitehouse.gov/the_press_office/Remarks-by-the-President-on-Securing-Our-Nations-Cyber-Infrastructure>.

[16] US Department of Defense (DOD), Department of Defense Strategy for Operating in Cyberspace, (DOD: Washington, DC, July 2011).

[17] Kaspersky Lab, 'Kaspersky Lab and ITU research reveals new advanced cyber threat', 28 May 2007, <http://www.kaspersky.com/about/news/virus/2012/Kaspersky_Lab_and_ITU_Research_Reveals_New_Advanced_Cyber_Threat>.

[18] Perlroth, N., 'Hackers in China attacked The Times for last 4 months', New York Times, 30 Jan. 2013; and Sanger, D. E., 'Obama order sped up waves of cyber attacks against Iran', New York Times, 1 June 2012.

[19] Of the 2012 Security Jam's 10 recommendations, 2 concerned cybersecurity: recommendation 6 proposed 'confidence-building measures for cyber global governance', while recommendation 7 con-

national level, the US Senate discussed the adoption of a comprehensive cybersecurity act, while the French Senate published a report calling for cyberdefence and information network protection to be made national priorities, as well as a public doctrine for offensive capacity within cyberspace.[20]

Two notable developments in cybersecurity occurred in early 2013. First, in February 2013 the European Union published its cyberspace strategy.[21] Second, in March 2013 US officials stated that cyberattacks have now replaced al-Qaeda as the greatest threat to US national security.[22]

The cybersecurity market and the arms and military services industry

The rise of cybersecurity on the political and military agenda has evident economic implications. Globally, public and private cybersecurity spending was estimated to be approximately $60 billion in 2011.[23] If accurate, this would be equal to 3.5 per cent of world military expenditure in 2011.[24] The USA was the number one spender on cybersecurity, accounting for half of the total, and was the only country where the levels of public and private spending on cybersecurity were almost equal.[25] In the rest of the world, the private sector accounted for the majority of national spending on cybersecurity.[26] With cybersecurity becoming a top national security concern, public demand is expected to experience sustained growth in the next

cerned the need to introduce hacker recruitment into public cybersecurity policy. See Dowdall, J., *The New Global Security Landscape: 10 Recommendations from the 2012 Security Jam* (Security and Defence Agenda: Brussels, 2012), pp. 17–19.

[20] US Senate, Homeland Security Committee, 'Cosponsors discuss revised Cybersecurity Act, S.3414, and the concessions made to win support for the legislation to address a threat that is well upon us', 24 July 2012, <http://www.hsgac.senate.gov/hearings/cosponsors-to-discuss-revised-cyber security-act-concessions-made-to-obtain-support-for-threat-thats-already-here->; and Bockel, J. M., *Rapport d'information fait au nom de la commission des affaires étrangères, de la défense et des forces armées sur la cyber défense* [Report on behalf of the Committee on Foreign Affairs, Defence and Armed Forces on cyberdefence], Senate Report no. 681 (Sénat: Paris, 2012), pp. 96, 113–19.

[21] European Commission, *Cybersecurity Strategy of the European Union: An Open, Safe and Secure Cyberspace* (European Commission: Brussels, 2013).

[22] Dilanian, K., 'Cyber-attacks a bigger threat than Al-Qaeda, officials say', *Los Angeles Times*, 12 Mar. 2013.

[23] PriceWaterhouseCoopers, 'Cybersecurity M&A: decoding deals in the global cybersecurity industry', Nov. 2011, <http://www.pwc.com/gx/en/aerospace-defence/publications/cyber-security-mergers-and-acquisitions.jhtml>, p. 5. These figures should be treated with caution, as they are rough estimates made by market research companies. Such companies tend to overestimate the size of the market and do not make public the methodology for their calculation.

[24] According to SIPRI estimates, world military expenditure in 2011 totalled $1738 billion. Freeman, S. and Solmirano, C., 'Global developments in military expenditure', *SIPRI Yearbook 2012*.

[25] PriceWaterhouseCoopers (note 23).

[26] PriceWaterhouseCoopers (note 23), p. 5; and Wagley, J., 'Report: cybersecurity market to almost double in five years', 7 Nov. 2012, <http://securitymanagement.com/news/report-cyber security-market-almost-double-five-years-0010070>.

decade.[27] According to some forecasts, the cybersecurity market should double in size by 2017, to about $120 billion.[28]

This strong growth—coupled with the actual and potential cuts in military spending in some key weapon markets—helps explain why many arms-producing and military services companies show increasing interest in the cybersecurity market. In 2012 major arms-producing companies continued to acquire cybersecurity providers (see table 4.2 in section I above).[29] Diversifying into cybersecurity enables these companies to widen their customer base into the civilian sector, while also developing technical competences for electronic warfare and cyberdefence for the military market.

Cybersecurity companies in the SIPRI Top 100

Leading system integrators (LSIs), IT companies and military services companies are the primary providers of cybersecurity products and services in the SIPRI Top 100 for 2011.[30] Almost all the major LSIs—including BAE Systems, the European Aeronautic Defence and Space Company (EADS), Finmeccanica, Lockheed Martin, Northrop Grumman, Raytheon, Saab and Thales—operate in the cybersecurity market, in some cases via specific divisions. However, these companies differ in terms of the strategies they have followed when establishing their respective cybersecurity businesses. For example, BAE has pursued an acquisition strategy in order to build its cyber and intelligence segment. It acquired Detica in 2008, Norkom Group and the Danish company ETI in 2010 and three divisions of L-1 Identity Solutions in 2011. In 2013 BAE also collaborated with Vodafone to develop security solutions for mobile communications.[31] In contrast, in 2012 EADS regrouped all of its existing cyber-related capacities in order to develop a specific cybersecurity business, while Lockheed Martin made strategic alliances with key IT and cybersecurity companies, such as Microsoft, Hewlett Packard (HP), McAfee and Cisco.[32]

---

[27] Wagley (note 26).

[28] PR Newswire, 'Cybersecurity market worth $ 120.1 billion by 2017', Wallstreet Online, 28 June 2012, <http://www.wallstreet-online.de/nachricht/4952697-marketsandmarkets-global-cyber-security-market-worth-120-1-billion-by-2017>.

[29] Acquisitions of cybersecurity providers by arms-producing companies are also discussed in e.g. Jackson, S. T., 'Key developments in the main arms-producing countries', *SIPRI Yearbook 2012*, pp. 228–29; and Boulanin, V., 'Major arms industry acquisitions, 2010', *SIPRI Yearbook 2011*, p. 264.

[30] Leading systems integrators are generally prime contractors in charge of leading major weapon programmes. They design and build major military systems by combining components, subsystems and software from multiples sources. Such companies constitute the upper end of the arms industry. See Gholz, E., 'System integration in the US defence industry: who does it and why is it important ?', eds A. Prencipe, A. Davies and M. Hobbey, *The Business of System Integration* (Oxford University Press: Oxford, 2005), pp. 281–82.

[31] BAE Systems, *Annual Report 2011* (BAE Systems: London, 2011); and Gribben, R., 'BAE and Vodafone partner for cyber-security market push', *Daily Telegraph*, 17 Feb. 2013.

[32] Trévidic, B., 'EADS Cassidian veut devenir un grand de la cybersécurité' [EADS Cassidian wants to become a giant of cybersecurity], *Les Echos*, 27 Apr. 2012; and Lockheed Martin, 'The

In addition, 10 of the 20 military services companies in the SIPRI Top 100 in 2011 provide cybersecurity solutions. Some of these companies—including HP, Computer Sciences Corporation (CSC) and CACI International—already specialized in IT-related services.[33] Others, such as L3 Communication, SAIC, QinetiQ and ManTech, specialize in the provision of national security-related services.

The lack of satisfactory data makes it difficult to evaluate and compare companies' cybersecurity-related revenues. In addition, arms-producing and military services companies tend not to report cybersecurity sales data unless it relates to specific cybersecurity divisions. When they do report such figures, companies usually do not differentiate between military and civil cybersecurity revenues. Available data suggests that cybersecurity remains a relatively minor source of revenue for LSIs. However, given the size of their total arms sales, this small proportion can still represent substantial revenue. For example, while only 7 per cent of BAE Systems' total revenue in 2011 was generated by its Cyber and Intelligence segment, this nevertheless represented £1.4 billion ($2.2 billion) in earnings.[34] Northrop Grumman reported that 30 per cent of its total revenues in 2011 came from its Information Systems division, while Lockheed Martin's Information Systems and Global Solutions division generated 20 per cent of the group's total sales.[35] In both cases, however, cybersecurity was just one activity among others for these divisions and neither company provided a further breakdown of revenues.

Cybersecurity provision and cybersecurity customers

Arms industry cybersecurity offerings consist primarily of services that can be divided into four main categories: network and data protection software and services; testing and simulation services; training and consulting services; and operational support (see table 4.3). While subcategories of services can also be identified, all of the LSIs and military services companies mentioned above provide 'solutions' (i.e. a combination of products and services) within these four categories. In most cases, companies set up a cybersecurity operations centre to provide these solutions in an integrated fashion.

Companies providing cybersecurity services target a wide range of customers. Public sector customers include the military, the intelligence com-

Lockheed Martin cyber security alliance', [n.d.], <http://www.lockheedmartin.com/content/dam/lockheed/data/corporate/documents/LM-Cyber-Security-Alliance-Brochure.pdf>.

[33] HP first appeared in the SIPRI Top 100 after it acquired EDS in 2008. Jackson, S. T., 'Arms production', *SIPRI Yearbook 2010*, p. 280.

[34] BAE Systems (note 31), p. iii.

[35] Northrop Grumman, *Annual Report 2011* (Northrop Grumman: Falls Church, VA, 2011), p. 42; and Lockheed Martin, *Annual Report 2011* (Lockheed Martin: Bethesda, MD, 2011), p. 5.

Table 4.3. Main types of cybersecurity product and service by arms-producing and military services companies

Type of activity/ subcategories	Examples of companies
Network and data protection software and services	
Encryption solutions	BAE Systems, CACI, CSC, EADS,
Identity management authentication solutions	ManTech, Raytheon, SAIC
System configuration	
Data-loss prevention	
Malware defection and mitigation	
Testing and simulation services	
Penetration testing and vulnerability assessment	BAE Systems, CSC, EADS,
Business/economic impact analysis	Lockheed Martin, ManTech, SAIC
Accreditation/technology compliance assessment	
Training and consulting services	
Personnel training	BAE Systems, CACI, CSC, EADS,
Consulting, including:	Lockheed Martin, ManTech, SAIC
infrastructure design,	
planning and implementation,	
cybersecurity policy definition	
Operational support	
Network monitoring software and services	BAE Systems, CSC, EADS,
Incident management, digital forensics and	L-3 Communications,
recovery solutions	Northrop Grumman
Incident response/counter-intrusion support	
Offensive cyberspace operations	

Source: SIPRI Arms Industry Database and company annual reports and websites.

munity and other government agencies, while private customers include operators of critical infrastructure (e.g. energy suppliers, telecommunication companies, banks and hospitals) and other major companies. A number of LSIs (e.g. Lockheed Martin, BAE Systems and EADS) and major military services providers (e.g. CACI and ManTech) deal primarily with military and government agencies and, to some extent, major operators of critical infrastructure. These companies rarely provide standard cybersolutions for companies whose activities have no direct national security relevance. For instance, in 2011 BAE's Cyber and Intelligence segment classed 91 per cent of its sales as government sales, and only 9 per cent as private commercial sales.[36] There are two possible explanations for this. First, while traditional arms producers have less experience in competing under commercial market conditions, they are more accustomed to dealing with large government contracts (both military and non-military). Their extensive contact with government customers also gives them an advantage

[36] BAE Systems (note 31).

in this sector of the market. Second, states have clearly indicated that cybersecurity will remain exempt from security-related budgets cuts. In contrast to LSIs and major military services providers, IT cybersecurity specialists such, as CSC and SAIC, have a wider customer base in the private sector.

Prospects and challenges

The expansion of arms-producing companies into the cybersecurity market is a clear trend in the first tier of the SIPRI Top 100.[37] These companies expect to benefit from long-term and increasing demand for cybersecurity services. The sustainability of this demand will depend on continued increases in the political, economic and strategic importance attached to cybersecurity, as well as the levels of public technical expertise and governments' political room to manoeuvre in this domain. While many Western states are actively recruiting cybersecurity experts the scarcity of this expertise, as well as the fast pace and technical complexity of cyberaffairs, means that these states may need to continue to rely on the private sector. Cybersecurity service providers commonly argue that they are better positioned to face cyber-related challenges. As national cyberinfrastructures—including fibre cable networks and relay antennas, as well as other critical infrastructure that might be targeted by cyberattacks, such as power plants—are generally not state-owned, but rather the responsibility of private actors, governments must also consider these actors as essential interlocutors in the implementation of their national cybersecurity policies. Some cybersecurity providers have even called for cybersecurity policy to be governed via public–private partnership (PPP) frameworks.[38]

However, in terms of the use of private security companies in warfare and other public security contexts, states' reliance on private cybersecurity providers could become a matter of political concern, particularly with regard to democratic transparency, oversight, accountability and cost.[39] Indeed, such outsourcing could be seen as a case of what Anna Leander has

---

[37]'First tier' refers to the top of the arms production pyramid, which primarily includes prime contractors specializing in systems integration, major producers of sub-systems and major military services companies.

[38] Intelligence and National Security Alliance (INSA), *Addressing Cyber Security through Public-Private Partnership: An Analysis of Existing Models* (INSA: Arlington, VA, 2009); Grauman, B., *Cyber-Security: The Vexed Question of Global Rules* (Security and Defence Agenda: Brussels, 2012), pp. 32–34; and Dowdall, J., 'Public–private cooperation in cyber-security', Security and Defence Agenda (SDA) Policymakers' Dinner Report, Brussels, 30 Jan. 2012, <http://www.securitydefenceagenda. org/Contentnavigation/Activities/Activitiesoverview/tabid/1292/EventType/EventView/EventId/1 097/EventDateID/1109/PageID/5428/Publicprivatecooperationincybersecurity.aspx>.

[39] On these issues see Buckland, B. S., Schreier, F. and Winkler, T. H., 'Democratic governance challenges of cyber security', Geneva Centre for the Democratic Control of Armed Forces (DCAF) Horizon 2015 Working Paper no. 1, 2010.

described as the 'privatization of the politics of protection'.[40] The provision of services by arms-producing companies—as well as traditional cyber-security providers—may change the way in which states define and manage their cybersecurity and cyberdefence policies. Indeed, the services of cybersecurity companies help to shape the understanding and political reactions of public officials as they define threats and vulnerabilities (through the companies' testing and simulation and consulting services), interpret security situations (through the companies' consulting services) and suggest means to deal with them (through the companies' operational support services). More research remains to be done on the governance of the cybersecurity sector to understand and reflect on the actual involvement and responsibility of private companies in the design and implementation of states' cybersecurity and cyberdefence policies.

[40] In other words, the 'privatization of politics surrounding the definition of threats and the protection needed to secure them'. Leander, A., 'Privatizing the politics of protection: military companies and the definition of security concerns', eds J. Huysmans, A. Dobson and R. Prokohvnik, *The Politics of Protection: Site of Insecurity and Policy* (Routledge: New York, 2006), p. 19.

III. The SIPRI Top 100 arms-producing and military services companies, 2011

SUSAN T. JACKSON

The SIPRI Top 100 lists the world's 100 largest arms-producing and military services companies (excluding Chinese companies), ranked by their arms sales in 2011. Sales of arms and services by companies in the SIPRI Top 100 totalled $410 billion in 2011. In comparison with the Top 100 companies in 2010 (which is a slightly different set of companies), the 2011 arms sales represent a 5 per cent decrease in real terms (see table 4.4). The decrease in arms sales by the SIPRI Top 100 companies in 2011 is due to several factors, including the drawdown in Iraq and the United Nations embargo on arms transfers to Libya; programme delays due to austerity-related military spending cuts and related postponements in weapon programme commitments (see section I above); and the weak US dollar in many countries in 2011.[1]

Many of the companies ranked at the lower end of the Top 100 increased arms sales but, because of their size, this had less impact on the total than if the larger companies had had similarly steep increases. In addition, in parallel with an increase of 51 per cent in the total sales of the Top 100 between 2002 and 2011 (see table 4.1 above), the cut-off for inclusion in the Top 100 (i.e. the arms sales of the company ranked 100) more than doubled from $280 billion in 2002 to $660 billion in 2011, reflecting an increase in the number of medium-sized companies in the Top 100 list. This is also reflected in the decrease of the shares of the top 10 and top 15 companies of the total for the Top 100 over the past decade; the top 10 were responsible for 54 per cent of the total arms sales in 2011 (down from 60 per cent in 2002) and the top 15 for 61 per cent (down from 68 per cent), marking a notable decrease in concentration. Overall, this difference shows that the largest companies account for a smaller, albeit still quite large, part of the world's arms sales. In part, this change is a reflection of how services are becoming a larger part of the sales of the largest companies.[2] It also reflects the way in which lower barriers to entry into the military services market allow more small companies to be involved in related areas.

The SIPRI Top 100 for 2011 appears in table 4.5. The companies in the SIPRI Top 100 account for the majority of the global financial value of sales of military goods and services—in particular, high-technology systems and services. Because of the lack of comparable financial data, the SIPRI

[1] Jackson, S. T., 'Arms production', *SIPRI Yearbook 2011*, p. 254.
[2] On military services see Jackson, S. T., 'The military services industry', *SIPRI Yearbook 2012*.

Table 4.4. Regional and national shares of arms sales for the SIPRI Top 100 arms-producing and military services companies, 2011 compared to 2010[a]

Arms sales figures are in US$ b., at current prices and exchange rates. Figures do not always add up to totals because of the conventions of rounding.

Number of companies	Region/ country[b]	Arms sales ($ b.)		Change in arms sales, 2010–11 (%)		Share of total Top 100 arms sales, 2011 (%)
		2011	2010[c]	Nominal[d]	Real[e]	
45	**North America**	**245.7**	**248.9**	**−1**	**−4**	**59.9**
44	United States	244.8	248.1	−1	−4	59.6
1	Canada	0.9	0.8	7	–	0.2
30	**Western Europe**	**119.2**	**120.6**	**−1**	**−9**	**29.1**
10	United Kingdom	46.4	49.9	−7	−14	11.3
6	France	23.0	23.0	–	−7	5.6
1	Trans-European[f]	16.4	16.4	–	−7	4.0
3	Italy	16.5	16.0	3	−4	4.0
4	Germany	8.2	6.8	20	12	2.0
2	Spain	2.4	2.8	−15	−22	0.6
1	Sweden	3.1	2.8	11	−3	0.8
1	Norway	1.4	1.5	−4	−12	0.4
1	Switzerland	1.0	0.8	25	7	0.3
1	Finland	0.8	0.7	17	8	0.2
6	**Eastern Europe**	**14.3**	**11.3**	**26**	**13**	**3.5**
6	Russia[g]	14.3	11.3	26	13	3.5
14	**Other OECD**	**22.8**	**18.3**	**25**	**15**	**5.6**
5	Japan[h]	9.8	6.6	48	35	2.4
3	Israel	7.1	6.7	7	−1	1.7
4	South Korea	4.4	3.8	17	8	1.1
1	Turkey	0.9	0.8	12	17	0.2
1	Australia	0.7	0.5	40	21	0.2
5	**Other non-OECD**	**8.5**	**7.9**	**7**	**−2**	**2.1**
3	India[i]	5.8	5.5	4	−3	1.4
1	Singapore	1.9	1.8	9	−5	0.5
1	Brazil	0.9	0.7	28	15	0.2
100	**Total**	**410.4**	**406.9**	**1**	**−4**	**100.0**

OECD = Organisation for Economic Co-operation and Development

[a] Although it is known that several Chinese arms-producing enterprises are large enough to rank among the SIPRI Top 100, a lack of comparable and sufficiently accurate data makes it impossible to include them. There are also companies in other countries, such as Kazakhstan and Ukraine, that could be large enough to appear in the SIPRI Top 100 list were data available, but this is less certain.

[b] Figures for a country or region refer to the arms sales of the Top 100 companies headquartered in that country or region, including those in its foreign subsidiaries. They do not reflect the sales of arms actually produced in that country or region.

[c] Arms sales figures from 2010 refer to companies in the SIPRI Top 100 for 2011 and not to the companies in the Top 100 from 2010.

[d] This column gives the change in arms sales in 2010–11 in current US dollars.

[e] This column gives the change in arms sales in 2010–11 in constant (2011) US dollars.

f The company classified as trans-European is EADS.

g Russian arms sales for 2011 include the reported arms sales of UAC and UEC subsidiaries.

h Figures for Japanese companies are based on contracts with the Japanese Ministry of Defence.

i Figures for India include a rough estimate for Ordnance Factories.

Source: Table 4.5.

Top 100 does not cover all arms-producing countries. However, with a few exceptions, the volume of arms production in omitted countries is believed to be relatively small. Several Chinese companies would appear in the Top 100 (and probably in the top 50) if data on their arms sales was available. Apart from the omission of China, analysis of the companies in the Top 100 is sufficient to capture the major trends in the global arms industry.

The role of subsidiaries in the Top 100

Major subsidiaries play a significant role in the company strategies of many of the parent companies in the SIPRI Top 100, and also account for a significant percentage of arms sales by these companies. Indeed, the activities of subsidiaries often explain more about individual domestic arms industries and company strategies than the financial reports of parent companies. Twenty major subsidiaries are listed (but not ranked) in table 4.5.[3] These subsidiaries accounted for 14 per cent, or \$55 billion, of total arms sales in the Top 100 for 2011. While the number of major subsidiaries has remained consistent since 2002, their total arms sales has increased: the arms sales of major subsidiaries in the SIPRI Top 100 for 2002 totalled \$19 billion, or 10 per cent of total Top 100 arms sales.

While these figures do not capture all major subsidiaries, they are indicative of the major trends in subsidiaries in these major arms producers and represent company strategies more broadly. For instance, Sweden has significant foreign presence in its arms industry and, in particular in terms of foreign-ownership of former Swedish companies such as Hägglunds, Bofors and Kockums. However, data is not always available and these subsidiaries might be excluded from the table simply due to lack of data. The major subsidiary figures also do not reflect the level of international collaboration between countries. This information is based on SIPRI Top 100 lists for each year and include a different list of companies depending on the year.

---

[3] While subsidiaries are not ranked in the Top 100 and their arms sales are not included in the country, regional and global totals (in order to avoid double counting), they are placed in table 4.5 to show where these subsidiaries would rank if they were independent companies. Not all companies report separately on the financial results of their subsidiaries, so the data presented here is incomplete.

Many of these subsidiaries operate outside the market in which the parent company is headquartered. There are a number of countries in which predominantly foreign-owned arms companies form a large part of the domestic arms industry but report their arms sales in the parent company's headquarter country. For example, while ASC's $660 million in arms sales in 2011—due primarily to its participation in the Air Warfare Destroyer project—led to Australia re-entering the Top 100, three foreign-owned subsidiaries in Australia (BAE Systems Australia, Raytheon Australia and Thales Australia) recorded combined arms sales in 2011 of five times this amount ($3320 million).[4] Australia had left the SIPRI Top 100 in 2008 following BAE Systems' acquisition of Tenix in 2007.

Changes in the Top 100 for 2011

Factors that contributed to changes in the Top 100 for 2011 include company restructuring and significant new contracts, the impact of armed conflicts, and changes in government spending. The weak US dollar in many countries in 2011 is unlikely to have had a large overall impact on the total arms sales figure for the Top 100 for 2011, although there is quite a marked difference on a company-by-company basis depending on the position of the dollar for the markets in which those companies sell and according to the currency in which they report sales. For example, arms sales by Swiss-based RUAG increased by 25 per cent in nominal dollar terms but only by 7 per cent in Swiss francs; similarly, Sweden's Saab arms sales were unchanged in Swedish kronor but in nominal dollar terms increased by 11 per cent; in contrast, sales by Aselsan of Turkey increased by 23 per cent in Turkish lira and by only 12 per cent in nominal dollar terms.

Among changes attributable to acquisitions and divestitures is the entry of the US company Huntington Ingalls Industries as a new independent company following its spin-off from Northrop Grumman in early 2011.[5] Mission Essential, a US military services company, also entered the list because of an increase in contracts with the US Government. The impact of armed conflict on arms and military services sales in 2011 was also notable. US-based companies such as AM General, KBR and L-3 Communications all attribute at least part of their sales decreases to the withdrawal of US troops from Iraq.[6] In addition, the Russian company TRV Corporation left

---

[4] ASC, *ASC Pty Ltd Annual Report 2011* (ASC: Adelaide, 2011), p. 7.

[5] Bell, J. and Anderson, G., 'Northrop Grumman completes shipbuilding spin-off', *Jane's Defence Industry*, 31 Mar. 2011; and Northrop Grumman, 'Northrop Grumman completes spin-off of Huntington Ingalls Industries, Inc', News release, 31 Mar. 2011, <http://investor.northropgrumman.com/phoenix.zhtml?c=112386&p=irol-newsArticle&id=1544584>.

[6] Coyne, T., 'AM General to lay off 350, cut Humvee production', Yahoo Finance, 29 Sep. 2011, <http://news.yahoo.com/am-general-lay-off-350-cut-humvee-production-221612926.html>; KBR, *KBR Annual Report 2011* (KBR: Houston, 2012), p. 33; and L-3 Communications, *Form 10-K Annual*

the SIPRI Top 100 in 2011 due to a decrease of $790 million in arms sales following the imposition of UN sanctions against Libya.[7] Conversely, several companies—including US-based Navistar, Fluor and DynCorp—increased arms sales because of continuing orders for vehicles, as well as logistics provision in those two countries.[8]

The impact of lowered military spending as part of austerity programmes began to be seen in weapon procurement cuts and delays in 2011. For example, the decrease in Nexter's arms sales in 2011 was due in large part to declining orders from the French armed forces.[9] Navantia's decrease was due to programme delays caused by reduced military spending resulting from Spain's austerity measures; this was also the case for the British company QinetiQ.[10] At the same time, however, even with decreasing orders from their home governments, some companies increased arms sales in 2011. Fincantieri increased its arms sales by securing contracts in markets without domestic suppliers and by participating in the Littoral Combat Ships programme with the Lockheed Martin–Austal USA consortium.[11] Meggitt had organic growth in training as well as increases due to the acquisition of PacSec.[12] Chemring's increase in arms sales in 2011 can be attributed to organic growth in munitions and counter-improvised explosive devices.[13] Arms sales by all of the Japanese companies in the Top 100 in 2011 increased. Because Japanese arms sales are calculated on contracts rather than actual sales, this increase could be a sign that the Japanese Government is spending on domestic arms. If so, this increase could signal

Report under Section 13 or 15(d) of the Securities and Exchange Act of 1934 for the Fiscal Year Ended December 31, 2011 (US Securities and Exchange Commission: Washington, DC, 2012), pp. 51–52.

[7] 'Russian missile maker lost $790 mln over Libya war', RIA Novosti, 31 Jan. 2012, <http://en.rian.ru/business/20120131/171042832.html>.

[8] Navistar International Corporation, *Form 10-K Annual Report under Section 13 or 15(d) of the Securities and Exchange Act of 1934 for the Fiscal Year Ended October 31, 2011* (US Securities and Exchange Commission: Washington, DC, 20 Dec. 2011), p. 24; Fluor Corporation, *Form 10-K Annual Report under Section 13 or 15(d) of the Securities and Exchange Act of 1934 for the Fiscal Year Ended December 31, 2011* (US Securities and Exchange Commission: Washington, DC, 22 Feb. 2012), p. 37; and DynCorp, *Form 10-K Annual Report under Section 13 or 15(d) of the Securities and Exchange Act of 1934 for the Fiscal Year Ended December 31, 2011* (US Securities and Exchange Commission: Washington, DC, 2012).

[9] Belan, G., 'Nexter: objective exports', European Security and Defence Press Association, 2 Mar. 2012, <http://www.esdpa.org/2012/03/nexter-objective-exports>.

[10] Spanish Ministry of Finance and Public Administrations, Sociedad Estatal de Participaciones Industriales (SEPI), 'Navantia', [n.d.], <http://www.sepi.es/default.aspx?cmd=0004&IdContent=15022&idLanguage=_EN>; and QinetiQ, *People Who Know: Annual Report 2011* (QinetiQ: Farnborough, 2011).

[11] Fincantieri, *Fincantieri Annual Report 2011* (Fincantieri: Trieste, 2011), pp. 6, 34.

[12] Meggit, *Annual Report and Accounts 2011* (Meggit: Fareham, 2011), p. 18.

[13] Bell, M., 'Chemring reports interim FY11 results below expectations', *Jane's Defence Industry*, 21 Nov. 2011; and Chemring Group PLC, 'Pre-close trading update', 18 Nov. 2011, <http://www.chemring.co.uk/media/press-releases/2011/2011-11-18.aspx>.

its support as Japan moves into the international arms market following the lifting of its 44-year ban on arms exports in 2011.[14]

As in previous years, increases in arms sales in 2011 by several companies can be partly explained by purchases for the purpose of force modernization. For example, part of the 29 per cent increase in Embraer's arms sales is attributed to deliveries of the Super Tucano to the Brazilian Air Force and to others in the region.[15] Aselsan's increase is in large part because of the Turkish armed forces' modernization programme.[16]

[14] See Jackson, S. T., 'Key developments in the main arms-producing countries', *SIPRI Yearbook 2012*, p. 220.

[15] Embraer, *Embraer Annual Report 2011* (Embraer: São Paulo, 2011).

[16] İş Investment, 'Aselsan', 30 May 2012, <http://www.isyatirim.com.tr/WebMailer/.../2_2012053 0152732784_1.pdf>.

Table 4.5. The SIPRI Top 100 arms-producing and military services companies in the world excluding China, 2011[a]

Figures for arms sales, total sales and profit are in US$ million. Dots (.) indicate that data is not available. Sector abbreviations are explained below.

Rank[b] 2011	2010	Company[c]	Country	Sector	Arms sales 2011	Arms sales 2010	Total sales, 2011	Arms sales as % of total sales, 2011	Profit, 2011	Total employment, 2011
1	1	Lockheed Martin	USA	Ac El Mi Sp	36 270	35 730	46 499	78	2 655	123 000
2	3	Boeing	USA	Ac El Mi Sp	31 830	31 360	68 735	46	4 018	171 700
3	2	BAE Systems	UK	Ac A El MV Mi SA/A Sh	29 150	32 880	30 689	95	2 349	93 500
4	5	General Dynamics	USA	A El MV SA/A Sh	23 760	23 940	32 677	73	2 526	95 100
5	6	Raytheon	USA	El Mi	22 470	22 980	24 857	90	1 896	71 000
6	4	Northrop Grumman	USA	Ac El Mi Sh Sp	21 390	28 150	26 412	81	2 118	72 500
7	7	EADS	Trans-Eur.	Ac El Mi Sp	16 390	16 360	68 295	24	1 442	133 120
8	8	Finmeccanica	Italy	Ac A El MV Mi SA/A	14 560	14 410	24 074	60	-3 206	70 470
S	S	BAE Systems Inc. (BAE Systems, UK)	USA	A El MV SA/A	13 560	17 900	14 417	94	5 178	37 300
9	9	L-3 Communications	USA	El	12 520	13 070	15 169	83	956	61 000
10	10	United Technologies	USA	Ac El Eng	11 640	11 410	58 190	20	5 347	199 900
11	11	Thales	France	El MV Mi SA/A	9 480	9 950	18 111	52	787	68 330
12	12	SAIC	USA	Comp(MV) Ser	7 940	8 230	10 587	75	56	41 100
13	–	Huntington Ingalls Industries	USA	Sh	6 380	–	6 575	97	-94	38 000
14	15	Honeywell	USA	El	5 280	5 400	36 529	14	2 067	132 000
15	16	Safran	France	El	5 240	4 800	16 315	32	895	59 800
S	S	Sikorsky (United Technologies)	USA	Ac	4 970	4 530	7 655	65	840	17 780
16	14	Computer Sciences Corp.	USA	Ser	4 860	5 940	15 877	31	-4 225	98 000
17	17	Rolls-Royce	UK	Eng	4 670	4 330	18 068	26	1 854	40 400
18	21	United Aircraft Corp.	Russia[d]	Ac	4 400	3 440	5 502	80	404	97 500
19	13	Oshkosh Truck	USA	MV	4 370	7 080	7 585	58	273	13 100
S	S	MBDA (BAE Systems, UK/EADS, trans-European/Finmeccanica, Italy)	Trans-Eur.	Mi	4 170	3 710	4 170	100	227	9 850
20	18	General Electric	USA	Eng	4 100	4 300	147 300	3	14 151	301 000
21	19	ITT Exelis[e]	USA	El	4 020	4 000	5 839	69	326	20 500

Rank[b]		Company[c]	Country	Sector	Arms sales		Total sales, 2011	Arms sales as % of total sales, 2011	Profit, 2011	Total employment, 2011
2011	2010				2011	2010				
S	S	CASA (EADS, trans-Eur.)	Spain	Ac	3 940	..	4 332	*91*	132	6 980
S	S	Pratt & Whitney (United Technologies)	USA	Eng	3 700	4 080	13 430	*28*	1 999	35 870
22	20	Almaz-Antei	Russia[d]	Mi	3 690	3 950	4 337	*85*	32	93 280
23	25	Mitsubishi Heavy Industries	Japan[g]	Ac MV Mi Sh	3 620	2 960	35 347	*10*	307	68 890
24	22	DCNS	France	Sh	3 610	3 320	3 614	*100*	249	12 830
S	S	Eurocopter Group (EADS, trans-Eur.)	France	Ac	3 540	2 940	7 528	*47*	359	20 800
S	S	AgustaWestland (Finmeccanica)	Italy	Ac	3 440	2 920	5 443	*63*	320	13 300
25	29	Saab	Sweden	Ac El Mi	3 080	2 780	3 619	*85*	341	13 070
26	32	Rheinmetall	Germany	A El MV SA/A	2 980	2 660	6 192	*48*	313	21 520
27	31	Textron	USA	Ac El Eng MV	2 930	2 740	11 275	*26*	242	32 000
28	26	HewlettPackard	USA	Ser	2 930	2 890	127 245	*2*	7 074	349 600
29	36	CACI International	USA	Ser	2 860	2 450	3 578	*80*	144	13 700
30	30	Babcock International Group	UK	Sh	2 850	2 770	4 919	*58*	277	25 140
31	28	Rockwell Collins	USA	El	2 810	2 860	4 806	*59*	634	20 500
32	34	ManTech International	USA	Ser	2 770	2 500	2 870	*97*	133	9 300
33	33	Hindustan Aeronautics	India	Ac Mi	2 740	2 590	3 043	*90*	713	32 660
34	35	Elbit Systems	Israel	El	2 680	2 480	2 818	*95*	25	12 550
35	24	URS Corp.	USA	El	2 670	3 030	9 545	*28*	–466	46 000
36	42	Harris	USA	El	2 670	2 130	5 925	*45*	597	16 900
37	27	Alliant Techsystems	USA	SA/A	2 670	2 870	4 613	*58*	263	17 000
38	68	Kawasaki Heavy Industries	Japan[g]	Ac Eng Mi Sh	2 630	1 020	16 337	*16*	292	33 270
S	S	Sukhoi (United Aircraft Corp.)	Russia[d]	Ac	2 630	1 360	2 825	*93*	..	26 000
39	40	DynCorp International (Cerberus Capital)	USA	Ser	2 600	2 210	3 721	*70*	–58	29 000
40	47	Vertolety Rossii (OPK Oboronprom)	Russia[d]	Ac	2 560	1 910	3 537	*72*	238	40 000
41	37	Israel Aerospace Industries	Israel	Ac El Mi	2 500	2 400	3 440	*73*	83	17 000
42	39	Goodrich	USA	Comp(Ac)	2 420	2 230	8 075	*30*	810	28 000
S	S	EADS Astrium (EADS, trans-Eur.)	France	Sp	2 350	2 450	6 901	*34*	366	16 600

		Company	Country	Sector						
43	41	CEA	France	Oth	2 300	2 200	5 800	40	46	15 770
S	S	MBDA France (MBDA, trans-Eur.)	France	Mi	2 300	2 190	2 295	100	229	4 300
44	60	Fluor[j]	USA	Comp(Oth)	2 260	1 300	2 381	95	594	43 090
45	43	Serco	UK	Oth	2 230	2 130	7 444	30	381	100 000
46	23	KBR[f]	USA	Ser	2 180	3 310	9 261	24	480	27 000
47	38	Cobham	UK	Comp(Ac El)	2 160	2 260	2 970	73	376	9 330
48	45	Indian Ordnance Factories	India	A SA/A	2 120	1 960	2 655	80	..	98 910
49	57	ThyssenKrupp	Germany	Sh	2 080	1 340	68 244	3	−2 479	180 050
S	S	Alenia Aeronautica (Finmeccanica)	Italy	Ac	2 050	1 920	3 712	55	−1 256	11 990
50	49	Navistar	USA	MV	2 000	1 800	13 958	14	1 778	20 800
51	50	Rafael	Israel	Ac Mi SA/A Oth	1 940	1 780	1 979	98	111	6 500
52	51	ST Engineering (Temasek)	Singapore	Ac El MV SA/A Sh	1 900	1 750	4 762	40	419	22 380
S	S	BAE Systems Australia (BAE Systems, UK)	Australia	Ac Sh	1 860	1 380	1 857	100	..	6 000
53	53	Samsung Techwin	South Korea	A El Eng MV	1 860	1 590	2 809	66	209	6 770
54	54	Krauss-Maffei Wegmann[i]	Germany	MV	1 740	1 590	1 807	96	..	..
55	44	Navantia	Spain	Sh	1 650	2 010	1 737	95	−60	5 530
56	46	QinetiQ	UK	Ser	1 580	1 920	2 355	67	413	10 180
57	64	Mitsubishi Electric	Japan[g]	El Mi	1 440	1 160	45 603	3	1 404	117 310
58	70	NEC	Japan[g]	El	1 440	980	38 052	4	−1 382	109 100
59	55	Kongsberg Gruppen	Norway	El Mi SA/A	1 440	1 500	2 699	53	255	6 680
60	63	Diehl	Germany	Mi SA/A	1 380	1 210	4 072	34	71	13 970
61	62	United Engine Corp.	Russia[d]	Eng	1 330	1 250	2 221	60	4	..
62	61	Groupe Dassault	France	Ac	1 240	1 270	4 594	27	392	11 470
63	73	Fincantieri	Italy	Sh	1 220	940	3 311	37	14	9 990
64	91	Uralvagonzavod	Russia[d]	MV	1 200	730	3 000	40	454	..
65	48	AM General[h]	USA	MV	1 130	1 900	..	..	..	2 000
66	56	Nexter	France	A MV SA/A	1 120	1 430	1 183	95	158	2 700
S	S	Thales Air Defence (Thales, France)	UK	Mi	1 120	..	1 117	100	37	..
67	65	Triumph Group	USA	Ac	1 090	1 080	3 408	32	281	12 600
68	75	Chemring Group	UK	SA/A	1 080	890	1 194	90	201	4 680
S	S	Irkut Corp. (United Aircraft Corp.)	Russia[d]	Ac	1 070	1 330	1 248	86	..	12 000

Rank[b]		Company[c]	Country	Sector	Arms sales		Total sales, 2011	Arms sales as % of total sales, 2011	Profit, 2011	Total employment, 2011
2011	2010				2011	2010				
69	–	Radiotechnicheskie i Informatsionnie Sistemi	Russia[d]	El	1 050	..	2 093	50	–18	..
70	78	RUAG	Switzerland	Ac A Eng SA/A	1 040	830	2 001	52	109	7 740
71	72	Moog	USA	Comp(El Mi)	1 000	960	2 331	43	136	10 320
72	66	GKN	UK	Comp(Ac)	970	1 050	9 206	11	562	44 000
73	99	AAR Corp	USA	Oth	940	650	1 776	53	70	6 100
74	83	Meggitt	UK	Oth	940	780	2 331	40	518	19 540
75	77	CAE	Canada	El	900	840	1 840	49	184	8 000
S	S	Selex Elsag (Finmeccanica)	Italy	Comp(El Oth)	900	750	1 674	54	–281	7 170
76	90	Korea Aerospace Industries	South Korea	Ac	890	740	1 160	77	68	3 000
77	71	Bharat Electronics	India	El	890	970	1 222	73	178	10 790
78	82	Cubic Corp.	USA	Comp(El) Ser	870	810	1 285	68	85	7 800
79	74	SRA International	USA	El	870	890	1 705	51	66	6 100
80	81	Precision Castparts Corp.	USA	Comp(Ac)	870	810	7 215	12	1 226	21 500
81	95	Embraer	Brazil	Ac	860	670	5 893	15	93	17 270
82	88	Aselsan	Turkey	El	850	760	897	94	96	4 390
S	S	Selex Galileo (Finmeccanica)	Italy	El	840	820	972	87	12	2 690
83	–	Doosan Group	South Korea	Comp(Oth)	830	610	23 723	4	271	38 000
84	86	Curtiss-Wright Corp.	USA	Comp(Ac Sh)	820	780	2 054	40	130	8 900
85	79	LIG Nex1	South Korea	El	820	810	817	100	23	26 480
86	67	Jacobs Engineering Group[k]	USA	Ser	800	1 020	10 382	8	331	45 700
87	97	Patria	Finland	Ac MV SA/A	770	660	859	90	56	3 430
S	S	Raytheon Australia (Raytheon, USA)	Australia	Comp(Ac) Ser	770	640	785	99	..	1 450
88	84	Hawker Beechcraft	USA	Ac	770	780	2 435	32	–633	6 000
89	89	Mitre[l]	USA	Oth	770	740	1 389	55	..	7 890
90	76	Ultra Electronics	UK	El	760	880	1 172	65	184	4 470
S	S	MBDA Italia (MBDA, trans-Eur.)	Italy	Mi	750	640	746	100	–8	1 250
91	100	GenCorp	USA	El Eng	740	650	918	81	3	3 270

			Company	Country	Sector						
92	87		Alion Science and Technology	USA	Oth	730	770	92	787	−44	2 990
93	–		Avio (Cinven)	Italy	Eng	730	640	26	2 818	16	5 120
S	S		Thales Nederland (Thales, France)	trans-Eur.	El	720	1 060	100	723	42	..
94	85		Indra	Spain	El	710	780	19	3 737	252	21 080
95	–		Mission Essential Personnel	USA	Ser	700	540	96	726	..	8 000
96	–		Aerospace Corp.	USA	Ser	700	640	74	939	..	4 600
S	S		Thales Australia (Thales, France)	Australia	A El MV Mi SA/A Sh	690	680	91	759	..	3 000
97	92		Esterline Technologies	USA	Comp(Ac Sh)	690	690	40	1 718	133	12 000
98	–		Fujitsu	Japan[g]	El	660	490	1	55 980	535	173 160
99	–		ASC	Australia	Sh	660	470	92	718	11	2 000
100	–		Flir Systems	USA	El	660	440	43	1 544	222	3 080

A = artillery; Ac = aircraft; El = electronics; Eng = engines; Mi = missiles; MV = military vehicles; SA/A = small arms/ammunition; Ser = services; Sh = ships; Sp = space; Oth = other; Comp( ) = components, services or anything else less than final systems in the sectors within the parentheses—used only for companies that do not produce final systems.

[a] Although several Chinese arms-producing enterprises are large enough to rank among the SIPRI Top 100, it has not been possible to include them because of lack of comparable and sufficiently accurate data. In addition, there are companies in other countries such as Kazakhstan and Ukraine, that also could be large enough to appear in the SIPRI Top 100 list if data were available, but this is less certain.

[b] Companies are ranked according to the value of their arms sales in 2011. An S denotes a subsidiary company. A dash (−) indicates that the company did not rank among the SIPRI Top 100 for 2010. Company names and structures are listed as they were on 31 Dec. 2011. Information about subsequent changes is provided in these notes. The 2010 ranks may differ from those published in SIPRI Yearbook 2012 owing to continual revision of data, most often because of changes reported by the company itself and sometimes because of improved estimations. Major revisions are explained in these notes.

[c] For subsidiaries and operational companies owned by a holding or investment company, the name of the parent company is given in parentheses along with its country, where it differs.

[d] This is the 10th year in which Russian companies have been covered by the SIPRI Top 100. There may be other Russian companies that should be in the list but for which insufficient data is available. Vertolety Rossii has operated as a subsidiary of OPK Oboronprom since 2005. However, since comparable financial data for Oboronprom for 2011 is not currently available, Vertolety Rossii is reported here as an independent company. For more detail on Russian arms industry consolidation see Jackson, S. T., 'Arms production', SIPRI Yearbook 2011; Jackson, S. T., 'Arms production', SIPRI Yearbook 2010; and Perlo-Freeman, S. et al., 'The SIPRI Top 100 arms-producing companies, 2007', SIPRI Yearbook 2009, pp. 286–87.

[e] In 2011 ITT Corporation split into 3 stand-alone companies. ITT Exelis now accounts for all of the former corporation's arms sales.

[f] The arms sales figures for KBR are an estimate based on payments from the US Department of Defense (DOD) for LOGCAP III and IV contracts and payments by the British Ministry of Defence (MOD).

g Arms sales figures for Japanese companies represent new military contracts rather than arms sales.

h Limited financial data is available for AM General. The SIPRI estimate of arms sales is based on a 2-year average of US DOD prime contract awards.

i The arms sales figures for Krauss-Maffei Wegmann are based on a small estimate of the company's non-military sales.

j The arms sales figures for Fluor are based on US DOD LOGCAP IV contracts.

k The arms sales figures for Jacobs Engineering Group are based on a 3-year average of US DOD prime contract awards.

l The arms sales figures for Mitre are based on a 5-year average of US DOD prime contract awards.

Sources and methods

Selection criteria and sources of data

The SIPRI Arms Industry Database includes public and private companies but excludes manufacturing or maintenance units of the armed services. Only companies with operational activities in the field of military goods and services are included; holding or investment companies are not.

The sources of data on the companies include company annual reports and websites, and news published in the business sections of newspapers, in military journals and by Internet news services specializing in military matters. Press releases, marketing reports, government publications of contract awards and country surveys are also consulted. Publicly available financial and employment data on the arms industry worldwide is limited. The scope of the data and the geographical coverage are largely determined by the availability of information.

SIPRI data on arms-producing and military services companies is revised on an ongoing basis as improved data becomes available. For this reason, it is not possible to make a strict comparison between editions of the SIPRI Yearbook. In addition, coverage may differ because of problems with obtaining data to make satisfactory estimates for all companies every year.

Definitions

Arms and military services sales ('arms sales') are defined by SIPRI as sales of military goods and services to military customers, including sales for both domestic procurement and export. Military goods and services are those that are designed specifically for military purposes and include the technologies related to these goods and services. Military goods are military-specific equipment and do not include general-purpose goods, such as oil, electricity, office computers, uniforms and boots. Military services are also military-specific. They include technical services, such as information technology, maintenance, repair and overhaul, and operational support; services related to the operation of the armed forces, such as intelligence, training, logistics and facilities management; and armed security in conflict zones. They do not include the peacetime provision of purely civilian services—such as health care, cleaning, catering and transport—but supply services to operationally deployed forces are included.

The SIPRI definition of arms sales serves as a guideline; in practice it is difficult to apply. Nor is there any good alternative, since no generally agreed standard definition exists. In some cases, the data on arms sales reflects only what a company considers to be the defence share of its total sales. In other cases, SIPRI uses the figure for the total sales of a 'defence' division, although the division may also have some civil sales.

When the company does not report a sales figure for a defence division or similar entity, arms sales are sometimes estimated by SIPRI. Such estimates are based on data on contract awards, information on the company's current arms production and military services programmes, and figures provided by company officials in media or other reports. For all these reasons, the comparability of the company arms sales figures given in table 4.5 is limited.

Data on total sales, profit and employment is for entire companies, not for arms-producing and military services activities alone. All data is for consolidated sales, that is, including those of domestic as well as foreign subsidiaries. The data on profit represents profit after taxes. Employment data represents year-end figures except for those companies that publish only a yearly average. All data is presented on the financial year basis reported by the company in its annual report.

Calculations

All data is collected in local currency and at current prices. For conversion from local currencies to US dollars, SIPRI uses the International Monetary Fund (IMF) annual average of market exchange rates provided in *International Financial Statistics*. The data in table 4.5 is provided in current dollars. Changes between years in this data are difficult to interpret because the change in dollar values is made up of several components: the change in arms and military services sales; the rate of inflation; and, for sales conducted in local currency, fluctuations in the exchange rate. Sales on the international arms market are often conducted in dollars. Fluctuations in exchange rates thus do not have an impact on the dollar values but affect instead the value in local currency. Calculations in constant dollar terms are difficult to interpret for the same reasons. Without knowing the relative shares of arms and military services sales derived from domestic procurement and from arms exports, it is impossible to interpret the exact meaning and implications of the arms sales data. This data should therefore be used with caution. This is particularly true for countries with strongly fluctuating exchange rates.

The SIPRI Arms Industry Network

Arms industry data was supplied by Laxman K. Behera (Institute for Defence Studies and Analyses, New Delhi), Vincent Boulanin (École des hautes études en sciences sociales, Paris), Gülay Günlük-Şenesen (Istanbul University), Jang Won Joon (Korea Institute for Industrial Economics and Trade, Seoul), Shinichi Kohno (Mitsubishi Research Institute, Tokyo), Valerie Miranda (Istituto Affari Internazionali, Rome) and Pere Ortega (Centre d'Estudis per la Pau J. M. Delàs, Barcelona).

5. International arms transfers

Overview

The volume of international transfers of major conventional weapons grew by 17 per cent between 2003–2007 and 2008–12. The five largest suppliers in 2008–12—the United States, Russia, Germany, France and China—accounted for 75 per cent of the volume of exports. This is the first time since the end of the cold war that China has ranked among the five largest arms exporters, which had consisted solely of the USA and European states. China may represent the vanguard of an increase in the significance of Asian suppliers in the international arms trade, as South Korea is an emerging arms supplier and Japan and Singapore have potential to become major suppliers. Other significant changes in 2008–12 include the absence from the top five suppliers of the United Kingdom for the first five-year period since 1950; the departure of the Netherlands from the 10 largest suppliers; and the ranking of Ukraine as the ninth largest supplier (see section I in this chapter).

One of the consequences of the impact of the financial crisis in the USA and Europe has been the additional pressure to seek new export markets. This has led the USA and European states to streamline bureaucratic procedures and to be more willing to engage in licensed production, technology transfer and cooperative production arrangements.

The flow of arms to Asia, Africa and the Americas increased between 2003–2007 and 2008–12, with notable decreases for Europe and the Middle East. States in Asia and Oceania received 43 per cent of all imports of major conventional weapons in 2008–12. The five largest recipients of major conventional weapons—India, China, Pakistan, South Korea and Singapore—were all located in Asia and Oceania. Combined, they accounted for 32 per cent of all arms imports. A notable trend among the major recipients was the acquisition of systems that make them capable of military power projection. Among the noteworthy deliveries in 2012 were China's commissioning of its first aircraft carrier and India's receipt of a nuclear-powered submarine from Russia.

There has been a dramatic decline in arms imports by states in Western and Central Europe in recent years, as a result of declining military spending and rising economic uncertainty (see section II). These factors have also resulted in delays and cancellations in acquisitions from abroad as well as attempts to favour domestic arms producers when making procurement decisions. The most notable declines in the volume of arms imports between 2003–2007 and 2008–12 occurred in Greece, where imports fell by 61 per cent, and Italy, where imports fell by 55 per cent. Procurement budget cuts may hamper

SIPRI Yearbook 2013: Armaments, Disarmament and International Security
www.sipriyearbook.org

efforts to increase the competitiveness of the European arms market and promote the joint development and acquisitions of weapon systems.

As the conflict in Syria intensified in 2012, the issue of supplying arms to the parties to the conflict—the Syrian Government and anti-government forces—remained a critical issue (see section III). In the five-year period prior to the outbreak of the conflict (2006–10), the Syrian Government received arms from Russia (48 per cent of imports), Iran (21 per cent), Belarus (20 per cent), North Korea (9 per cent) and China (2 per cent). It appears that the anti-government forces relied primarily on equipment captured from Syrian Government forces; they also reportedly received small arms, light weapons and ammunition supplied via black markets in Iraq and Lebanon. Despite repeated requests for arms and military equipment, European and US governments are reported to have supplied only 'non-lethal equipment' to anti-government forces. However, arms shipments have been seized that indicate that the Arab states of the Gulf might have been the origin for some of the anti-government forces' arsenal.

Overall, 2012 was a particularly disappointing year for transparency in international arms transfers (section IV). The number of states reporting their arms imports and exports to the United Nations Register of Conventional Arms (UNROCA) decreased to an all time low of 52 in 2012, down from 86 in 2011. In recent years the 10 largest suppliers of conventional arms, as recorded by SIPRI, have reported to UNROCA, but in 2012 only 7 of the largest exporters for 2008–12 reported: Israel, Italy and Spain did not report. Four of the 10 largest importers did not report during 2012, most notably India and Pakistan, which have been regular reporters. No reports were submitted by states in the Middle East, with no report for the first time since 2002 for Lebanon.

While SIPRI data on international arms transfers does not represent their financial value, a number of states also publish figures on the financial value of their arms exports (see section V). Based on national data, SIPRI estimates that the total value of the global arms trade in 2011 was at least $43 billion.

PAUL HOLTOM

I. Developments in arms transfers, 2012[1]

PAUL HOLTOM, MARK BROMLEY, PIETER D. WEZEMAN AND
SIEMON T. WEZEMAN

The volume of international arms transfers in the period 2008–12 was
17 per cent higher than in 2003–2007 (see figure 5.1).[2] The composition of
the five largest suppliers of arms changed between these two periods, with
China replacing the United Kingdom as the fifth largest supplier. This
represents the first change in the composition of the top five suppliers since
the end of the cold war. India was the largest recipient of arms during
2008–12, with China in second place.

Major supplier developments

The five largest suppliers in 2008–12—the United States, Russia, Germany,
France and China—accounted for 75 per cent of the volume of exports of
major conventional weapons, down from 78 per cent in 2003–2007 (see
tables 5.1 and 5.2).

The United States

The USA was the largest exporter of major conventional weapons in the
period 2008–12, accounting for 30 per cent of all transfers. The volume of
US arms exports increased by almost 16 per cent between 2003–2007 and
2008–12. Existing orders combined with those agreed or planned in 2012
indicate that the USA will maintain its position as the largest exporter in
the coming years. However, the preeminent position of the USA will be
strongly influenced by orders and delivery schedules for the troubled F-35
combat aircraft.

---

[1] Except where indicated, the information on arms deliveries and orders referred to here is taken
from the SIPRI Arms Transfers Database, <http://www.sipri.org/databases/armstransfers>. The
database contains data on transfers of major conventional weapons between 1950 and 2012. The data
for 2008–12 and for 2012, on which most of this section is based, is given in the 'Register of major
conventional weapon transfers, 2008–12' and the 'Register of major conventional weapon transfers,
2012', which are available at <http://www.sipri.org/databases/armstransfers/recent_trends>. The
data on which this section is based is valid as of 18 Feb. 2013. The figures here may differ from those
in previous editions of the SIPRI Yearbook because the SIPRI Arms Transfers Database is updated
annually.

[2] SIPRI data on arms transfers refers to actual deliveries of major conventional weapons,
including sales, licences, aid, gifts and leases. SIPRI uses a trend-indicator value (TIV) to compare
the data on deliveries of different weapons and to identify general trends. TIVs give an indication
only of the volume of international arms transfers—based on an assessment of the arms' capabilities—and not of their financial values. Since year-on-year deliveries can fluctuate, a 5-year moving
average is employed to provide a more stable measure for trends in international transfers of major
conventional weapons. For a description of the TIV and its calculation, see 'Sources and methods'
below.

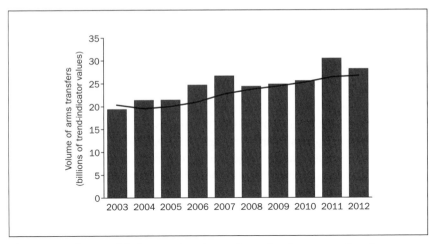

Figure 5.1. The trend in international transfers of major conventional weapons, 2003–12

Note: The bar graph shows annual totals and the line graph shows the five-year moving average (plotted at the last year of each five-year period). See 'Sources and methods' below for an explanation of the SIPRI trend-indicator value.

Source: SIPRI Arms Transfers Database, <http://www.sipri.org/databases/armstransfers/>.

Asia and Oceania received 45 per cent of US deliveries of major conventional weapons in 2008–12, followed by the Middle East and Europe (see table 5.1). Deliveries to Asia and Oceania increased by 51 per cent between 2003–2007 and 2008–12. Moreover, of the five largest recipients of US arms in the period 2008–12—South Korea (12 per cent of US deliveries), Australia (10 per cent), the United Arab Emirates (UAE, 7 per cent), Pakistan (5 per cent) and Singapore (6 per cent)—four were in Asia and Oceania.

While the Middle East was the main recipient region of US major conventional weapons in 2003–2007, deliveries to the region were 14 per cent lower in 2008–12. The perceived threat of Iran to the Arab states of the Gulf, in particular the threat of Iranian ballistic missiles, is driving new acquisitions of air defence and missile defence systems. In 2012 Kuwait requested a possible sale of 4 Patriot surface-to-air missile (SAM) systems with 60 PAC-3 missiles for anti-ballistic missile (ABM) use.[3] The UAE requested 48 additional missiles for 2 THAAD ABM systems ordered in 2011, and Qatar requested 2 THAAD systems with 150 missiles and 11 Patriot SAM systems with approximately 770 PAC-3 missiles.[4]

[3] US Defense Security Cooperation Agency, 'Kuwait—PATRIOT advanced capability (PAC-3) missiles', News release, Transmittal no. 12-29, 20 July 2012, <http://www.dsca.mil/PressReleases/ 36-b/2012/Kuwait_12-29.pdf>.

[4] US Defense Security Cooperation Agency, 'United Arab Emirates—terminal high altitude area defense system missiles (THAAD)', News release, Transmittal no. 12-40, 5 Nov. 2012, <http://www. dsca.mil/PressReleases/36-b/2012/UAE_12-40.pdf>; US Defense Security Cooperation Agency,

Afghanistan and Iraq have become significant recipients of US major weapons in connection with the drawdown and withdrawal of US combat forces and the handover of operations to local forces. They each received 4 per cent of US exports during 2008–12. Exports to Afghanistan primarily consisted of over 12 000 second-hand and new light armoured vehicles. While air power is deemed essential for Afghan counterinsurgency operations, the USA has only delivered or funded the delivery from third countries of a limited number of light aircraft and helicopters.[5] This could potentially leave US forces with a significant role following the withdrawal of most ground forces by the end of 2014. Iraq received large numbers of second-hand and newly produced tanks, armoured vehicles and artillery, with deliveries ongoing. Deliveries of at least 36 F-16 combat aircraft are scheduled for the period 2014–18.

Aircraft accounted for 62 per cent of the volume of US exports in 2008–12, and combat aircraft made up the bulk of aircraft deliveries. Sales of the F-35 (Joint Strike Fighter, JSF) combat aircraft will probably continue that trend. The first 2 F-35s were delivered to an export customer (the UK) in 2012 as part of the final testing phase. However, the programme encountered serious problems in 2012 due to cost increases and delays, and several potential customers cancelled or began a review of their F-35 procurement plans: Canada cancelled its order of 65 F-35s due to steeply increased costs; Italy announced a decrease in its planned purchase of F-35s from 131 to 90 aircraft; Turkey announced a review of an order for up to 100 F-35s due to increasing costs; and the Dutch Parliament urged its government to cancel a plan to acquire up to 85 F-35s for cost reasons.[6] At the same time, older designs continued to be in demand; roughly 220 F-16 and F-15 aircraft were on order, with potential for more orders to follow.

Following reductions in the US military budget, the US Government and arms industry are looking more towards export markets to offset decreasing domestic demand.[7] However, processes to facilitate US arms

'Qatar—terminal high altitude area defense system missiles (THAAD)', News release, Transmittal no. 12-49, 5 Nov. 2012, <http://www.dsca.mil/PressReleases/36-b/2012/Qatar_12-49.pdf>; and US Defense Security Cooperation Agency, 'Qatar—PATRIOT missile system and related support and equipment', News release, Transmittal no. 12-58, 7 Nov. 2012, <http://www.dsca.mil/PressReleases/ 36-b/2012/Qatar_12-58.pdf>.

[5] US Department of Defense (DOD), *Report on Progress toward Security and Stability in Afghanistan: United States Plan for Sustaining Afghanistan National Security Forces* (DOD: Washington, DC, Apr. 2012), pp. 26–28; and 'Afghan Air Force may not be ready to fly solo', Wall Street Journal Live, 24 July 2012, <http://live.wsj.com/video/afghan-air-force-may-not-be-ready-to-fly-solo/E8B84ED 0-1AC1-4C00-88F6-AA3231067927.html>.

[6] Hoffman, M., 'Canada halts planned F-35 purchase', *DOD Buzz*, 13 Dec. 2012; Peruzzi, L., 'Italian force cuts hit JSF numbers', *Jane's Defence Weekly*, 22 Feb. 2012, p. 14; 'Annual defence report 2012', *Jane's Defence Weekly*, 12 Dec. 2012, p. 26; and Bekdil, B. E., 'Turkey says cost, problems prompted JSF purchase delay', *Defense News*, 7 Feb. 2013.

[7] Felstead, P., 'Raytheon continues Mid-East push to offset US downturn', *Jane's Defence Weekly*, 7 Nov. 2012, p. 23.

Table 5.1. The 10 largest suppliers of major conventional weapons and their destinations, by region, 2008–12

Figures are the percentage shares of the supplier's total volume of exports delivered to each recipient region. Figures may not add up because of the conventions of rounding. For the states in each region and subregion see page xxi.

Recipient region	Supplier									
	USA	Russia	Germany	France	China	UK	Spain	Italy	Ukraine	Israel
Africa	3	17	4	13	13	4	2	6	31	4
North Africa	2	14	–	12	4	2	–	4	2	–
Sub-Saharan Africa	0	3	4	1	10	2	2	2	29	4
Americas	6	6	17	8	6	28	25	20	1	22
South America	3	6	11	4	6	5	14	6	1	18
Asia and Oceania	45	65	31	54	74	27	20	32	48	36
Central Asia	0	2	0	–	–	–	–	1	1	1
East Asia	19	15	12	17	–	7	–	1	25	1
Oceania	10	–	1	5	–	2	12	0	–	1
South Asia	10	36	2	6	63	18	–	21	12	23
South East Asia	7	12	15	27	11	0	8	9	10	9
Europe	18	4	35	14	–	10	41	25	9	18
European Union	17	0	34	11	–	8	10	23	–	17
Middle East	27	9	14	11	7	31	11	17	10	19
Other	1	–	–	–	–	–	–	–	–	1

– = nil; 0 = <0.5.

Source: SIPRI Arms Transfers Database, <http://www.sipri.org/databases/armstransfers/>.

exports have been under way for some time. First, US export control regulations have been under review since 2010 with the aim of simplifying the process of export licensing to all countries. Second, defence trade cooperation treaties with Australia and the UK—intended to remove administrative barriers for cooperative programmes—came into force in 2012.[8] At present there are no plans for similar treaties to be concluded with other countries.

Despite its efforts to increase its arms exports, the USA is more reluctant than other suppliers to include technology transfers in export deals. This issue has come to be regarded as one of the obstacles to securing large export orders with India.[9] Nevertheless, in 2012 India selected 22 AH-64E combat helicopters, 15 CH-47F heavy transport helicopters, and a US engine for both its indigenous Tejas combat aircraft and the modernization of 125 Jaguar combat aircraft. India also ordered 145 M-777 155-mm guns and 6 C-130J transport aircraft from the USA. In late 2012 India received the first of 12 P-8I anti-submarine warfare (ASW) aircraft on order—an advanced design so new that the USA has only just received the first few for its own forces. The fact that the US Department of Defense is planning to include technology protection features, such as 'anti-tampering characteristics', in the weapon design from the outset could make equipment developed for the USA export-ready without additional costs and time.[10]

Russia

Russia accounted for 26 per cent of the volume of global arms exports in the period 2008–12. The volume of Russia's major conventional weapons exports increased by 28 per cent between 2003–2007 and 2008–12. Asia and Oceania received 65 per cent of Russian exports, followed by Africa and the Middle East (see table 5.1). The largest individual recipients were India (35 per cent), China (14 per cent), Algeria (14 per cent), Viet Nam (6 per cent) and Venezuela (5 per cent).

During 2012 Russian President Vladimir Putin used meetings of the Russian Commission for Military Technology Cooperation (which discusses policies for Russian arms trade) with foreign states to consider the ways in which Russia should use arms exports as 'an effective instrument for

[8] Bell, M., 'US–UK defence trade treaty takes effect', *Jane's Defence Weekly*, 18 Apr. 2012, p. 5; and Grevatt, J., 'Canberra finally ratifies trade treaty with US', *Jane's Defence Weekly*, 7 Nov. 2012, p. 5. For details of how the treaty affects US export licensing procedures see US Department of State, Directorate of Defense Trade Controls, 'Frequently asked questions (FAQs): defense trade cooperation treaties & resources', <http://www.pmddtc.state.gov/faqs/treaties.html#1>.

[9] Pandit, R., 'Israel pips US in anti-tank guided missile supply to India', *Times of India*, 29 Nov. 2012.

[10] Malenic, M., 'US targets exportability as part of acquisition overhaul', *Jane's Defence Weekly*, 21 Nov. 2012, p. 10.

Table 5.2. The 50 largest suppliers of major conventional weapons, 2008–12

The table lists the 50 largest exporters (both states and non-state actors) of major conventional weapons in 2008–12. Ranking is according to total volume of exports in 2008–12. Figures may not add up because of the conventions of rounding.

Rank 2008–12	Rank 2003–2007[a]	Supplier	Volume of exports (TIV, millions) 2012	Volume of exports (TIV, millions) 2008–12	Share, 2008–12 (%)	Change since 2003–2007 (%)
1	1	United States	8 760	40 495	30	16
2	2	Russia	8 003	35 184	26	28
3	3	Germany	1 193	9 919	7	−8
4	4	France	1 139	8 042	6	−18
5	8	China	1 783	6 462	5	162
6	5	United Kingdom	863	4 997	4	1
7	12	Spain	720	4 036	3	136
8	7	Italy	847	3 159	2	20
9	10	Ukraine	1 344	3 087	2	49
10	9	Israel	533	2 694	2	17
11	6	Netherlands	760	2 673	2	−24
12	11	Sweden	496	2 600	2	25
13	14	Switzerland	210	1 432	1	14
14	13	Canada	276	1 240	1	−7
15	24	Norway	169	746	1	211
16	16	South Korea	183	733	1	50
17	17	South Africa	145	692	1	49
18	18	Uzbekistan	–	627	0	64
19	19	Belgium	21	599	0	109
20	27	Belarus	–	488	0	165
21	31	Brazil	32	383	0	167
22	34	Australia	75	363	0	255
23	15	Poland	140	324	0	−45
24	26	Turkey	53	236	0	21
25	21	Finland	62	220	0	−16
26	33	Iran	0	217	0	109
27	39	Jordan	12	163	0	117
28	..	Portugal	0	145	0	..
29	41	Singapore	76	143	0	107
30	29	Austria	9	117	0	−32
31	42	Romania	108	112	0	67
32	38	Ireland	25	104	0	39
33	..	Chile	–	100	0	..
34	22	Denmark	23	83	0	−66
35	55	Serbia	1	81	0	913
36	25	Czech Republic	8	79	0	−63
37	20	Libya	–	78	0	−71
38	62	New Zealand	75	75	0	7 400
39	43	Moldova	–	60	0	20
40	49	Saudi Arabia	–	59	0	228
41	35	India	2	46	0	−55
42	56	Venezuela	–	43	0	438
43	47	United Arab Emirates	–	43	0	26

Rank			Volume of exports (TIV, millions)		Share, 2008–12	Change since 2003–2007
2008–12	2003–2007[a]	Supplier	2012	2008–12	(%)	(%)
44	60	Syria	–	40	0	1 233
45	23	North Korea	–	40	0	–83
46	48	Bulgaria	3	29	0	–80
47	51	Brunei Darussalam	–	24	0	..
48	30	Montenegro	–	18	0	–90
49	49	Kyrgyzstan	–	14	0	–89
50	52	Bosnia and Herzegovina	–	14	0	..
..	..	Others (9 suppliers)	6	22	0	..
..	..	Unknown supplier(s)	16	87	0	..
Total			**28 172**	**133 468**	**100**	**17**

0 = <0.5.

Note: The SIPRI data on arms transfers relates to actual deliveries of major conventional weapons. To permit comparison between the data on such deliveries of different weapons and to identify general trends, SIPRI uses a trend-indicator value (TIV). This value is only an indicator of the volume of international arms transfers and not of the financial values of such transfers. Thus, it is not comparable to economic statistics such as gross domestic product or export/import figures. The method for calculating the trend-indicator value is described in 'Sources and methods' below.

[a] The rank order for suppliers in 2003–2007 differs from that published in *SIPRI Yearbook 2008* because of subsequent revision of figures for these years.

Source: SIPRI Arms Transfers Database, <http://www.sipri.org/databases/armstransfers/>.

advancing national interests, both political and economic'.[11] He noted that Russia enjoys closer cooperation with partners on joint research and development and production, and is seeking more opportunities for modernizing and repairing Soviet-supplied arms.[12] However, to remain a major exporter on the world market, Putin stressed that there should be 'a clear and effective coordination and decision-making mechanism [for arms exports]'.[13]

India remains Russia's most important recipient. In 2012 and early 2013 Russian Government officials and arms companies stressed the importance of developing joint projects with India.[14] Deliveries of naval vessels remain a problem, as the scheduled delivery of the Gorshkov aircraft carrier has

[11] President of Russia, 'Meeting of the Commission for Military Technology Cooperation with foreign states', 2 July 2012, <http://eng.kremlin.ru/news/4121>.

[12] President of Russia, 'Meeting of the Commission for Military Technology Cooperation with foreign states', 17 Dec. 2012, <http://eng.news.kremlin.ru/news/4760>.

[13] President of Russia (note 11).

[14] President of Russia, 'Meeting of the Commission for Military Technology Cooperation with foreign states', 17 Oct. 2012, <http://eng.kremlin.ru/news/4531>; and 'Russia remains key arms supplier for India—Rosoboronexport', RIA Novosti, 5 Feb. 2013, <http://en.rian.ru/military_news/20130205/179229598.html>.

been delayed yet again, from December 2012 to November 2013.[15] Delivery has also slipped on 3 Talwar frigates, although two were delivered in 2012. Despite continuing delays and competition from Israel, the USA and major European suppliers, India continues to place significant orders with Russia, ensuring that it remains India's largest supplier. In December 2012 India confirmed an order for 71 Mi-17-V5 helicopters (worth $1.3 billion) and 42 Su-30MKI combat aircraft kits (worth $1.6 billion) to be assembled in India with delivery in 2017–18, which brought the value for Russian agreements concluded with India in 2012 to over $3 billion.[16]

Russia's arms transfer relationship with China seems more positive from the Russian perspective for the first time in many years. Russia appears to have acquiesced to the Chinese proposal for a deal to acquire 24 Su-35 combat aircraft, although a contract is not expected to be signed before 2014.[17] China is reportedly interested in cooperation to develop a submarine based on the Russian Project-1650 design.[18]

Russia has contributed to the arms build-up in South East Asia.[19] South East Asia accounted for 12 per cent of Russian exports during 2008–12, with Russia delivering an estimated 37 Su-30MK and Su-27S combat aircraft, along with a variety of missiles, to Indonesia, Malaysia and Viet Nam. In 2012 Indonesia ordered 6 Su-30MK2s and 37 BMP-3F armoured vehicles. Russia will supply the Vietnamese Navy with two more Gepard-3 frigates that were ordered in 2012, and the first of 6 Project-636 submarines is due to be delivered in 2013, with delivery of all 6 to be completed by 2016. Deliveries of Su-30MK2s continued in 2012 and negotiations for more Su-30MK2s and also S-300PMU-1 SAM systems are ongoing.[20]

Anatoly Isaikin, the general director of the Russian state arms trading corporation, Rosoboronexport, drew attention in mid-2012 to the fact that Russia only recently began to use long-term export credits to support arms exports.[21] According to Isaikin, in the previous three years decisions had been taken to grant long-term export credits for arms worth approximately $7 billion. The recipient of the largest export credit arrangements in recent years is Venezuela, which was granted a $4 billion credit line for arms

[15] [Deputy director of the FSMTC of Russia Vyacheslav Dzirkali: 'Military-technical cooperation with India, China and Viet Nam has very good prospects for further development'], Interfax, 24 Dec. 2012, <http://www.militarynews.ru/excl.asp?ex=151> (in Russian).

[16] 'Russia remains key arms supplier for India—Rosoboronexport' (note 14).

[17] Nikolskiy, A., [Big batch of originals], Vedomosti, 21 Nov. 2012 (in Russian).

[18] Kiseleva, E., [Amur on the Chinese coast], Kommersant, 20 Dec. 2012 (in Russian).

[19] Wezeman, S. T., 'The maritime dimension of arms transfers to South East Asia, 2007–11', SIPRI Yearbook 2012. See also chapter 9, section IV, in this volume.

[20] [Deputy director of the FSMTC of Russia Vyacheslav Dzirkali: 'Military-technical cooperation with India, China and Viet Nam has very good prospects for further development'] (note 15).

[21] Nikolskiy, A., [We must not purchase weapons without understanding for what purpose], Vedomosti Online, 9 June 2012, Translation from Russian, Open Source Center.

purchases.[22] In late December 2012, the Russian state corporation Vnesh-econombank (Bank for Foreign Economic Activity) agreed to provide almost $400 million in credit to finance Indonesia's acquisitions (see above).[23] At the beginning of 2013 President Putin confirmed that Russia would grant $1 billion worth of credit to Bangladesh for arms purchases, which could include Yak-130 trainer/combat aircraft, armoured vehicles and Mi-17 helicopters.[24]

In addition to increasing the use of export credits, in 2012 Russia pledged to provide a significant quantity of military aid to Kyrgyzstan and Tajikistan. Kyrgyzstan is due to receive $1.1 billion worth of military aid for small arms and light weapons, armoured vehicles and helicopters and training.[25] For Tajikistan, Russia is to provide $200 million for upgrading air defence systems. At the same time, Tajikistan agreed to extend Russia's lease for the 201st military base for 30 years without new payments.

European suppliers

The three largest exporters in Europe (excluding Russia) were Germany, France and the UK. Debates have occurred, to a greater or lesser degree, in all three countries about the extent to which recent arms exports to states in the Middle East are in line with European Union (EU) and national guidelines.[26] Despite these concerns, the Middle East remains one of the most attractive markets for each states' arms exports.

Germany

Between 2003–2007 and 2008–12 Germany's major conventional weapons exports decreased by 8 per cent, although it retained its position as the third largest exporter. Other states in Europe received 35 per cent of German exports in 2008–12, followed by states in Asia and Oceania and the Americas (see table 5.1). The fall in German exports coincides with the completion of deliveries under several significant deals for naval and land

---

[22] 'Russia to lend Venezuela $4 bln to pay for arms deals', RIA Novosti, 7 Oct. 2011, <http://en.rian.ru/world/20111007/167461572.html>.

[23] Bonar, J., 'Russia to finance Indonesian purchase of six Flanker fighter aircraft', BSR Russia, 21 Dec. 2012, <http://www.bsr-russia.com/en/defence/item/2592-russia-to-finance-indonesian-purchase-of-six-flanker-fighter-aircraft.html>; and [Military leadership of Indonesia pleased with MTC development with Russia], RIA Novosti, 9 Nov. 2012 (in Russian).

[24] President of Russia, 'Press statements following talks with Prime Minister of Bangladesh Sheikh Hasina', 15 Jan. 2013, <http://eng.kremlin.ru/transcripts/4868>; and Kravchenko, S. and Devnath, A., 'Russia, Bangladesh to discuss $1 billion loan to fund arms sales', Bloomberg, 14 Jan. 2013, <http://www.bloomberg.com/news/2013-01-14/russia-bangladesh-to-discuss-1-billion-loan-to-fund-arms-sales.html>.

[25] Karabekov, K. et al., [Kyrgyzstan and Tajikistan to be armed with Russian money], *Kommersant*, 6 Nov. 2012 (in Russian).

[26] Bromley, M. and Wezeman, P. D., 'Policies on exports of arms to states affected by the Arab Spring', *SIPRI Yearbook 2012*.

systems in the mid- to late 2000s. German companies are pursuing deals that may serve to reverse this trend, particularly with states in the Middle East. These include the possible sale of 600–800 Leopard-2A7+ tanks and several hundred Boxer armoured vehicles to Saudi Arabia and the possible sale of up to 200 Leopard-2A7+ tanks to Qatar.[27]

During 2012 the prospective sales to Saudi Arabia and Qatar—together with the confirmed sales to Algeria of around 1200 Tpz-1 armoured vehicles and 2 MEKO-A200 frigates—were at the centre of a long-running political debate about the level of restrictiveness of German arms export controls.[28] During 2012 several media reports indicated that German Chancellor Angela Merkel was seeking to use arms exports as a means of strengthening and supporting allied states in crisis-affected regions.[29] Merkel's statements—combined with the deals signed or under discussion with states in the Middle East and North Africa—led to calls from opposition parties and parliamentarians from the governing Christian Democratic and Free Democratic parties for greater transparency in arms export policies and improved parliamentary oversight over how these policies are formulated and implemented.[30]

France

France retained its position as the fourth largest exporter in 2008–12 despite its major conventional weapons exports decreasing by 18 per cent since 2003–2007. States in Asia and Oceania received 54 per cent of French exports in 2008–12, followed by other states in Europe and Africa (see table 5.1). Like Germany, the fall in French exports coincides with the completion of deliveries under several major deals for naval, air and land systems in the mid- to late 2000s. The fall in deliveries is likely to be temporary, with several exports on order but undelivered at the close of 2012. In January 2012 India had selected the French Rafale as the winner of its $10.4 billion purchase of 126 combat aircraft, the first sale to an export

[27] Von Hammerstein, K. et al., 'German weapons for the world: how the Merkel Doctrine is changing Berlin policy', Spiegel Online, 3 Dec. 2012, <http://www.spiegel.de/international/germany/german-weapons-exports-on-the-rise-as-merkel-doctrine-takes-hold-a-870596.html>.

[28] Holtom, P. et al., 'Developments in arms transfers in 2011', *SIPRI Yearbook 2012*, pp. 267–68.

[29] 'Berlin wants to arm Gulf states: government is planning relaxation of the German arms export rules—joint NATO policy sought', *Financial Times Deutschland*, 30 July 2012, Translation from German, Open Source Center; and Demmer, U., Neukirch, R. and Holger, S., 'Arming the world for peace, Merkel's risky weapons exports', Spiegel Online, 30 July 2012, <http://www.spiegel.de/international/germany/merkel-s-risky-weapons-sales-signal-change-in-german-foreign-policy-a-847137.html>.

[30] German Parliament (Bundestag), Social Democratic Party Group, 'Frühzeitige Veröffentlichung der Rüstungsexportberichte sicherstellen' [Ensuring timely publication of arms export reports], Motion, 28 Mar. 2012, Drucksache 17/179188; German Parliament (Bundestag), Green Party Group, 'Rüstungsexporte kontrolliere' [Controlling arms exports], Motion, 25 Apr. 2012, Drucksache 17/9412; German Parliament (Bundestag), Minutes of the plenary debate, 31 Jan. 2013, Plenary Protocol 17/219, item 4; and 'Abgeordnete fordern: Bundestag soll Rüstungsexporte stoppen können' [Parliamentarians demand: Bundestag should be able to stop arms exports], *Der Tagesspiegel*, 4 Jan. 2013.

customer. However, the process of reaching final agreement on the deal has been delayed, and no contract had been signed by the end of 2012.

Transfers to the Middle East accounted for 11 per cent of French exports during 2008–12, and France has a number of major conventional weapons on order with states in the region. These include orders by Saudi Arabia for 164 Aravis armoured vehicles, 1000 BONUS-2 guided shells and 32 CAESAR 155-mm self-propelled guns. The issue of arms transfers to the Middle East is less politically controversial in France than in Germany, and there are indications that national decision making on approving and denying transfers to the region differs in certain key respects between the two countries. In particular, there are indications that France is willing to grant approval for export licences that Germany would deny. For example, it was reported in 2012 that Germany had blocked the export of chassis and engines for the Aravis armoured vehicles that France sold to Saudi Arabia.[31]

United Kingdom

Between 2003–2007 and 2008–12 British major conventional weapons exports increased by 1 per cent. However, between these periods the UK fell from being the fifth largest supplier to the sixth largest. States in the Middle East received 31 per cent of British exports in 2008–12, followed by states in the Americas and Asia and Oceania (see table 5.1). The period 2008–12 is the first five-year period since 1950 that the UK has not been among the top five suppliers. There are indications that the volume of British exports may increase in the near future. In particular, the volume of major conventional weapons on order from the UK but undelivered at the close of 2012 was the highest since 1994.

Saudi Arabia was the UK's largest recipient, accounting for 30 per cent of deliveries. British policies on arms export to the Middle East have been sharply criticized in recent years, particularly in the reports of the Arms Export Controls Committees of the House of Commons (the lower house of the British Parliament).[32] Nonetheless, in November 2012 the British Prime Minister, David Cameron, visited Oman, Saudi Arabia and the UAE in an effort to boost arms sales to states in the Gulf region.[33] In May 2012 Saudi Arabia ordered 22 Hawk-100 trainer/combat aircraft as part of a larger

[31] Ruello, A. and Lienhardt, C., 'Berlin bloque deux gros contrats français en Arabie Saoudite' [Berlin blocks two large French contracts in Saudi Arabia], *Les Echoes*, 21 Dec. 2012.

[32] See British House of Commons, Business, Innovation and Skills, Defence, Foreign Affairs and International Development Committees, *Scrutiny of Arms Exports (2012): UK Strategic Export Controls Annual Report 2010, Quarterly Reports for July to December 2010 and January to September 2011, the Government's Review of arms exports to the Middle East and North Africa, and wider arms control issues*, First Joint Report of Session 2012–13, vol. 1 (Stationery Office: London, July 2012).

[33] Black, I., 'David Cameron: UK arms sales to Gulf countries "legitimate"', *The Guardian*, 6 Nov. 2012.

£1.6 billion ($2.2 billion) deal.[34] In December 2012 Oman agreed a £2.5 billion ($4 billion) deal for 12 Typhoon combat aircraft and 8 Hawk-100 trainer/combat aircraft.

Asian suppliers

Of the 20 largest arms exporting countries for 2008–12, 15 were located in North America and Europe (including Russia), 3 in Asia, 1 in the Middle East and 1 in Africa. However, developments in several Asian countries illustrate how countries can grow into larger arms suppliers, changing the ranking and the variety of arms exporting states.

China

The volume of Chinese exports of major conventional weapons rose by 162 per cent between 2003–2007 and 2008–12, and China's share of the volume of global arms exports increased from 2 to 5 per cent. As a result, for the first time since 1986–90, China ranked as the fifth largest supplier in 2008–12. Asia and Oceania received 74 per cent of the volume of Chinese exports and Africa received 13 per cent in 2008–12 (see table 5.1).

Pakistan accounted for 55 per cent of the volume of Chinese exports, receiving, among other items, an estimated 61 JF-17 combat aircraft. Pakistan is likely to remain China's largest recipient of arms in the coming years due to large outstanding and planned orders for JF-17 combat aircraft, submarines and F-22P frigates. Myanmar was the second largest importer during 2008–12, accounting for 8 per cent of exports. The third largest recipient was Bangladesh, accounting for 7 per cent of exports.

In recent years a steady stream of new Chinese major conventional weapons has been revealed, such as a prototype of the J-31 combat aircraft first presented in 2012 and offered for export.[35] However, China's deliveries during 2008–12 still involved many older or low-end technologies for low-income countries. For example, China has not yet exported its most capable combat aircraft (J-10 and J-11) but continued to deliver F-7s (the least advanced of its newly produced combat aircraft available globally) to Bangladesh, Namibia, Nigeria, Sri Lanka and Tanzania, and JF-17s to Pakistan. Like many other arms-producing countries, China uses imported components and technology for many of the weapons it produces for its own use and for export. For example, the JF-17 and J-10 combat aircraft have engines supplied by Russia.

---

[34] The deal also includes 55 PC-21 trainer aircraft from Switzerland and 25 primary training aircraft.

[35] Perett, B. et al., 'Avic promotes J-31 as an export fighter', *Aviation Week & Space Technology*, 19 Nov. 2012.

A number of recent deals indicate that China can compete with more established suppliers in securing orders from major recipients. In 2012 it emerged that 54 Type 90-2 tanks had been supplied in 2010 to Morocco, its first major arms deal with China. Algeria reportedly ordered 3 F-22A frigates in 2012. Deliveries of 8 Y-8 transport aircraft to Venezuela started in 2012, and it was reported in 2012 that Venezuela planned to order armoured vehicles from China for $500 million.[36] An important limitation on Chinese exports is that, for political reasons, several of the largest arms importers—including India, Japan, South Korea, major European countries and the USA—do not consider China a suitable supplier.

South Korea

Based on technology imports and its own indigenous technological capacity, South Korea has built up a significant and advanced arms industry.[37] However, it ranked as only the 16th largest supplier, accounting for 0.5 per cent of the volume of global arms transfers in the period 2008–12. Turkey accounted for 59 per cent and Indonesia for 30 per cent of South Korean exports. According to official figures, South Korean arms export agreements grew from $144 million in 2002 to $2.4 billion in 2011, with a marginal decrease to $2.35 billion in 2012.[38]

South Korea has ambitions to increase its arms exports and has designated the arms industry as one of the country's new growth engines.[39] In early 2012 the head of the South Korean Defense Acquisition Program Administration (DAPA) claimed that South Korean arms exports could be boosted to $10 billion.[40] Less ambitious and more realistic was the goal stated in 2011 by the South Korean Government to increase arms exports to $4 billion by 2020.[41] South Korea also intends to become a leading country in cooperative arms development programmes. For example, in 2010 it took the lead in a programme to develop a new combat aircraft, the KF-X, with Indonesia.[42]

Several export developments in 2011 and 2012 show that South Korea is using its technical potential to become an exporter of a broad range of arms, challenging established arms suppliers. The first export orders for South Korean trainer/combat aircraft and submarines were secured when Indonesia ordered 16 T-50 trainer/combat aircraft in 2011 and 3 Type-209

---

[36] 'Chavez: Venezuela to buy tanks from China', Associated Press, 3 July 2012.

[37] Jackson, S. T., 'Arms production', *SIPRI Yearbook 2011*, pp. 240–44.

[38] [Recent trends in defence industry exports and future challenges], Korea Institute for Industrial Economics and Trade (KIET), no. 544, 19 Nov. 2012 (in Korean), p. 2; and Grevatt, J., 'Seoul reports USD2.35bn military exports for 2012', *Jane's Defence Weekly*, 6 Feb. 2013, p. 25.

[39] [Recent trends in defence industry exports and future challenges] (note 38), p. 5.

[40] Tae-hoon, L., 'Korea eyes tenfold growth in defense exports', *Korea Times*, 16 Jan. 2012.

[41] Tae-hoon, L., 'Arms exports reach record $1.19 bil.', *Korea Times*, 4 Jan. 2011.

[42] 'Indonesia agrees to join S. Korea's fighter development', Agence France-Presse, 15 July 2010.

submarines in 2012. Although Israel chose the Italian M-346 trainer/combat aircraft over the T-50 in 2012, the Philippines decided to procure 12 T-50s, and the aircraft remains a strong candidate in the competition to supply at least 350 advanced trainer aircraft to the USA.[43] South Korea signed significant contracts with South American countries in 2012: Colombia ordered 16 anti-ship missiles and Peru ordered 18 KP-SAM portable SAM systems (the first known South Korean exports of guided missiles), 2 large landing ships and 20 KT-1 trainer aircraft. Notably, for the first time, South Korean ships were procured for a European navy when the UK ordered 4 MARS oilers in 2012.

Japan and Singapore

Developments in Japan and Singapore indicate that their arms exports could grow.

Japan has a highly developed and diversified arms industry but, due to its restrictive arms export policy, its exports of major arms have been very low.[44] However, in 2011 the Japanese Government took steps to relax its arms export policy to facilitate (a) development and production of military equipment together with other countries and (b) exports that it deems in support of peacebuilding or humanitarian objectives.[45] Tangible results of the shift in Japanese policy in 2012 included discussions about the export of Japanese submarine technology to Australia; marketing of maritime patrol aircraft, patrol vessels and electronic warfare equipment in India; and the first ever participation of Japanese arms producers in India's largest international defence exhibition.[46]

While Singapore ranked as only the 29th largest arms exporter in the period 2008–12, several recent deals suggest that its arms industry is increasingly competitive on the international arms market. In 2011 it finished delivery of 115 Bronco armoured vehicles to the UK. In 2012 it delivered an Endurance amphibious assault ship to Thailand and won a $700 million contract for the supply of four patrol vessels to Oman.

[43] 'Time for T-X', *Air Forces Monthly*, no. 298 (Jan. 2013), pp. 60–64.
[44] On Japan's arms export policy see Japanese Ministry of Foreign Affairs, <http://www.mofa.go.jp/policy/un/disarmament/policy/index.html>.
[45] Defense Production Committee, KEIDANREN Aerospace and Defense Committee, American Chamber of Commerce in Japan, 'Joint statement on defense industry cooperation between Japan and the United States', 17 July 2012, <http://www.keidanren.or.jp/en/policy/2012/059.html>; and 'Govt decides to ease arms export ban', Yomiuri Shimbun, 28 Dec. 2011, <http://www.yomiuri.co.jp/dy/national/T111227003855.htm>.
[46] 'Japan tech deal could help power our subs', *The Australian*, 27 Sep. 2012; and 'Our focus is to first introduce the US-2 in the Indian Navy', SP's Navalforce.net, Apr.–May 2012, <http://www.sps navalforces.net/story.asp?mid=24&id=12>.

Major recipient developments

In the period 2008–12, Asia was the largest recipient region of major conventional weapons, accounting for 43 per cent of global imports. The next largest recipient region was the Middle East (17 per cent), followed by Europe (15 per cent), the Americas (11 per cent), Africa (9 per cent) and Oceania (4 per cent). Compared to 2003–2007, there was a notable increase for Asia (up from 38 per cent in 2003–2007) and for Africa (up from 5 per cent), and a clear decrease for Europe and the Middle East (both down from 22 per cent).

The five largest recipients of major conventional weapons—India, China, Pakistan, South Korea and Singapore—were all in Asia (see tables 5.3 and 5.4). The high levels of deliveries to South and South East Asia reported in *SIPRI Yearbook 2012* continued, as did China's dependence on Russia for certain key components and the simultaneous development of indigenous Chinese weapons.[47]

The increase in African imports was the result of deliveries to North Africa. Deliveries to sub-Saharan Africa were slightly higher in 2008–12 than in 2003–2007, but deliveries to North Africa increased by 350 per cent. Deliveries to Algeria increased by 277 per cent, and Algeria rose from being 22nd largest recipient to 6th place. Morocco rose from 69th place to 12th, with an increase of 1460 per cent in deliveries, most of which were in 2011–12. Both countries will continue to be major importers as they continue the modernization of their armed forces.

The decrease of 20 per cent in deliveries to European states between 2003–2007 and 2008–12 seems largely related to the financial crisis and the resulting budget constraints (see section II below). The smaller decrease of 7 per cent for the Middle East is expected to be temporary. Many of the countries in the Middle East have placed significant orders in recent years and additional orders are planned.

Importing military power projection capabilities

Military power projection is the ability of a state to 'rapidly and effectively deploy and sustain forces in and from multiple dispersed locations to respond to crises, to contribute to deterrence and to enhance regional stability'.[48] A notable trend among the major importers in recent years has been the acquisition of long-range strike and support systems with ranges that make them capable of military power projection substantially beyond their national territories. Deliveries and orders of major weapons in 2012 umder-

---

[47] Holtom et al. (note 28), pp. 269–71; and Wezeman (note 19).
[48] US Joint Chiefs of Staff, 'Power projection', US Department of Defense (DOD), *Dictionary of Military and Associated Terms* (DOD: Washington, DC, 15 Dec. 2012), p. 231.

Table 5.3. The 10 largest recipients of major conventional weapons and their suppliers, 2008–12

Figures are the shares of the recipient's total volume of imports received from each supplier. Only suppliers with a share of 1 per cent or more of total imports by any of the 10 largest recipients are identified.

Supplier	Recipient									
	India	China	Pakistan	S. Korea	Singapore	Algeria	Australia	USA	UAE	Saudi Arabia
Australia	–	–	–	–	1	–	..	3	–	–
Belgium	–	–	–	–	–	–	–	–	–	1
Canada	–	–	–	–	0	–	–	16	1	2
China	–	..	50	–	–	0	–	–	–	2
France	1	13	5	5	30	3	7	5	9	6
Germany	1	0	1	15	11	–	2	12	1	4
Ireland	–	–	–	–	–	–	2	–	–	–
Israel	4	–	–	1	5	–	1	1	11	–
Italy	2	–	2	0	3	0	1	6	1	1
Libya	–	–	1	1	–	–	–	1	–	–
Netherlands	0	–	–	–	–	–	–	1	–	1
New Zealand	–	–	–	1	–	–	–	1	–	–
Norway	–	–	–	–	–	–	0	10	–	–
Poland	–	–	–	–	–	–	–	3	–	–
Russia	79	69	2	–	–	93	–	0	14	–
South Africa	0	–	–	–	–	0	–	5	0	0
Spain	–	–	–	–	–	–	9	0	–	7
Sweden	–	–	5	1	4	–	0	0	2	0
Switzerland	–	4	2	–	2	–	–	8	3	1
Turkey	–	–	1	–	–	–	–	–	0	–
Ukraine	1	10	4	–	–	1	–	–	–	–
United Kingdom	6	3	0	–	–	2	2	–	–	36
United States	2	–	27	77	44	0	77	22	68	39
Uzbekistan	4	–	–	–	–	–	–	..	–	–
Other suppliers	–	–	0	–	0	–	–	0	0	0

– = nil; 0 = <0.5.

Source: SIPRI Arms Transfers Database, <http://www.sipri.org/databases/armstransfers/>.

score this trend. Several importers have doctrines or ideas for out-of-area operations.[49]

Among the deliveries in 2012 that stand out in this regard is the delivery of an Akula nuclear-powered submarine from Russia to India. It is only the second time that a nuclear-powered submarine has been exported by Russia. The acquisition provides India with a sea-interdiction and land-attack weapon of nearly unlimited range. It will also be used for training crews for nuclear submarines currently being produced in India that are to be armed with ballistic missiles.[50]

China's commissioning of the former Soviet Kuznetsov class aircraft carrier *Varyag* was another exceptional event in 2012. A civilian Chinese company bought the ship in 1998 in an unfinished state from Ukraine, which had inherited the shipyard and the ship during the break-up of the Soviet Union. The ship was said to be for use as an entertainment centre, but on arrival in China, it was moved to a Chinese naval shipyard and completed as an aircraft carrier for the Chinese Navy. It remains uncertain to what extent Ukraine was aware of the real purpose of the acquisition, but there have been reports that Ukraine also sold blueprints of the carrier, which would have made it possible (or at least easier) for China to finish the ship. Once operational, the ship will be a limited military power projection tool, but it is probably more important for training crews for aircraft carriers being produced in China and developing doctrines for their use.[51]

Both India and China are also acquiring long-range transport and tanker aircraft. In alignment with India's stated ambition of being a regional power and its capability for long-range operations are its acquisition of 10 C-17 transport aircraft and plans for at least 6 more along with an order for 12 C-130J transport aircraft from the USA and its planned order for up to 9 A-330 tanker/transport aircraft from Spain.[52] In 2010 China ordered 10 second-hand Il-76 transport aircraft from Russia and Belarus after a planned order for 34 newly produced Il-76 and 4 Il-78 tanker aircraft from Russia fell through. The Il-76 can be seen as an interim solution, since China has also developed the Y-20 transport aircraft, reportedly with help from Ukraine. The aircraft was first flown in early 2013 and fitted with Russian engines. Such transport and tanker aircraft would be useful to support Chinese operations in the South China Sea.

The ongoing operations in Afghanistan and the interventions in Libya in 2011 and in Mali in early 2013 have shown the importance of transport and

[49] E.g. Holton, P. et al., 'International arms transfers', *SIPRI Yearbook 2011*, pp. 280–83.
[50] See chapter 6, section IV, in this volume.
[51] Friedman, N., 'A long wait', *Proceedings* (US Naval Institute), Oct. 2011, pp. 88–89.
[52] Holtom et al. (note 49); and Bedi, R., Subramaniam, P. and Hardy, J., 'Critical mix', *Jane's Defence Weekly*, 23 Jan. 2013, p. 26.

Table 5.4. The 50 largest recipients of major conventional weapons, 2008–12

The table lists the 50 largest importers (both states and non-state actors) of major conventional weapons in 2008–12. Ranking is according to total volume of imports in 2008–12. Figures may not add up because of the conventions of rounding.

Rank			Volume of imports (TIV, millions)		Share,	Change since
2008–12	2003–2007[a]	Recipient	2012	2008–12	2008–12 (%)	2003–2007 (%)
1	2	India	4 764	15 609	12	59
2	1	China	1 689	7 483	6	–47
3	12	Pakistan	1 244	7 079	5	194
4	5	South Korea	1 078	6 527	5	8
5	21	Singapore	627	5 496	4	279
6	22	Algeria	650	5 247	4	277
7	8	Australia	889	5 207	4	62
8	9	USA	1 297	5 011	4	63
9	3	UAE	1 094	4 310	3	–40
10	17	Saudi Arabia	923	4 145	3	118
11	10	Turkey	1 269	3 866	3	45
12	69	Morocco	790	2 574	2	1 460
13	25	Venezuela	643	2 552	2	110
14	14	United Kingdom	598	2 530	2	18
15	4	Greece	35	2 520	2	–61
16	26	Malaysia	53	2 511	2	112
17	33	Iraq	455	2 359	2	183
18	27	Norway	163	2 120	2	91
19	79	Afghanistan	576	2 111	2	2 244
20	38	Viet Nam	364	2 077	2	194
21	7	Egypt	226	1 984	1	–43
22	13	Japan	239	1 972	1	–11
23	44	Portugal	35	1 666	1	211
24	11	Chile	56	1 592	1	–37
25	61	Syria	376	1 521	1	511
26	30	Germany	183	1 439	1	44
27	34	Brazil	410	1 425	1	78
28	58	Myanmar	619	1 387	1	425
29	20	Spain	256	1 371	1	–10
30	6	Israel	387	1 352	1	–68
31	28	Indonesia	188	1 339	1	21
32	24	Canada	188	1 256	1	3
33	15	Poland	182	1 117	1	–47
34	18	South Africa	148	1 116	1	–40
35	48	Azerbaijan	158	1 088	1	155
36	46	Colombia	279	1 045	1	121
37	16	Italy	215	912	1	–55
38	29	Netherlands	260	897	1	–13
39	39	Jordan	158	857	1	23
40	19	Taiwan	412	841	1	–52
41	120	Qatar	316	808	1	7 245
42	47	Mexico	267	684	1	48
43	89	Uganda	342	680	1	1 185

Rank			Volume of imports (TIV, millions)		Share, 2008–12 (%)	Change since 2003–2007 (%)
2008–12	2003–2007[a]	Recipient	2012	2008–12		
44	52	Thailand	297	650	0	76
45	53	Sweden	228	568	0	61
46	54	Bangladesh	325	539	0	55
47	37	Sudan	64	531	0	–29
48	50	Austria	9	526	0	29
49	81	Ecuador	108	462	0	463
50	74	NATO	22	442	0	281
..	..	Others (105 recipients)	2 017	10 048	8	..
..	..	Unknown recipient(s)		26	0	..
Total			**28 172**	**133 468**	**100**	**17**

0 = <0.5; NATO = North Atlantic Treaty Organization.

Note: The SIPRI data on arms transfers relates to actual deliveries of major conventional weapons. To permit comparison between the data on such deliveries of different weapons and to identify general trends, SIPRI uses a trend-indicator value (TIV). This value is only an indicator of the volume of international arms transfers and not of the financial values of such transfers. Thus, it is not comparable to economic statistics such as gross domestic product or export/import figures. The method for calculating the trend-indicator value is described in 'Sources and methods' below.

[a] The rank order for suppliers in 2003–2007 differs from that published in *SIPRI Yearbook 2008* because of subsequent revision of figures for these years.

Source: SIPRI Arms Transfers Database, <http://www.sipri.org/databases/armstransfers/>.

tanker aircraft.[53] European countries have invested and are continuing to invest in large transport aircraft and tanker aircraft for military and humanitarian interventions outside Europe. The USA delivered 7 C-17 transport aircraft to the UK between 2001 and 2013, and 3 C-17s to the North Atlantic Treaty Organization (NATO) in 2009 for a pool for use by NATO members. While NATO countries have plans for additional aircraft, most of them will come from European cooperative production arrangements, such as the A-400M transport aircraft and the A-330 MRTT tanker aircraft.

[53] Hoyle, C., 'UK extends support role in Mali, but rules out UAVs', *Flightglobal*, 31 Jan. 2013; and Svitak, A. and Osborne, T., 'Stretched thin', *Aviation Week & Space Technology*, 21 Jan. 2013, p. 29.

Sources and methods

The SIPRI Arms Transfers Programme maintains the SIPRI Arms Transfers Database, <http://www.sipri.org/databases/armstransfers/>, which contains information on deliveries of major conventional weapons to states, international organizations and non-state armed groups from 1950 to 2012. Data collection and analysis are continuous processes: the database is updated as new data becomes available and a new set of data is published annually. Thus, data from several editions of the SIPRI Yearbook or other SIPRI publications cannot be combined or compared. Revisions of coverage are applied retroactively for the whole period covered by the database.

Sources and estimates

Data on arms transfers is collected from a wide variety of sources. The common criterion for all these sources is that they are open; that is, published and available to the public. Such open information cannot, however, provide a complete picture of world arms transfers. Sources often provide only partial information, and substantial disagreement between them is common. Since publicly available information is inadequate for the tracking of all weapons and other military equipment, SIPRI covers only what it terms major conventional weapons. Order and delivery dates and the exact numbers (or even types) of weapon ordered and delivered, or the identity of suppliers or recipients, may not always be clear. Exercising judgement and making informed cautious estimates are therefore important elements in compiling the SIPRI Arms Transfers Database.

Types of transfer

SIPRI's definition of an arms transfer includes sales of weapons, including manufacturing licences, as well as aid, gifts and most loans or leases. The recipient of the arms must be the armed forces, paramilitary forces or intelligence agencies of another country, a non-state armed group, or an international organization. In cases where deliveries are identified but it is not possible to identify either the supplier or the recipient with an acceptable degree of certainty, transfers are registered as coming from an 'unknown supplier' or going to an 'unknown recipient'.

Types of weapon: major conventional weapons

The SIPRI Arms Transfers Database only includes 'major conventional weapons', which are defined as (*a*) most aircraft (including unmanned), (*b*) most armoured vehicles, (*c*) artillery over 100 millimetres in calibre, (*d*) sensors (radars, sonars and many passive electronic sensors), (*e*) air defence missile systems and larger air defence guns, (*f*) guided missiles, torpedoes, bombs and shells, (*g*) most ships, (*h*) engines for combat-capable aircraft and other larger aircraft, for combat ships and larger support ships, and for armoured vehicles, (*i*) most gun or missile-armed turrets for armoured vehicles and ships, (*j*) reconnaissance satellites, and (*k*) air refuelling systems.

The transferred item must have a military purpose. In cases where a sensor, turret or refuelling system (items *d*, *i* and *k*) is fitted on a platform (vehicle, aircraft or ship), the transfer only appears as a separate entry in the database if the item comes from a different supplier than that of the platform.

The SIPRI trend indicator

SIPRI has developed a unique system to measure the volume of transfers of major conventional weapons using a common unit, the trend-indicator value (TIV). The TIV is based on the known unit production costs of a core set of weapons and is intended to represent the transfer of military resources rather than the financial value of the transfer. Weapons for which a production cost is not known are compared with core weapons based on: a comparison with core weapons using size and performance characteristics (weight, speed, range and payload);

type of electronics, loading or unloading arrangements, engine, tracks or wheels, armament and materials; and, finally, the year in which the weapon was produced. A weapon that has been in service in another armed force is given a value 40 per cent of that of a new weapon; a used weapon that has been significantly modernized or modified by the supplier before delivery is given a value of 66 per cent of the value when new.

SIPRI calculates the volume of transfers to, from and between all parties using the TIV and the number of weapon systems or subsystems delivered in a given year. This quantitative data is intended to provide a common unit to allow the measurement of trends in the flow of arms to particular countries and regions over time. Therefore, the main priority is to ensure that the measurement system remains consistent over time, and that any changes introduced are backdated.

SIPRI TIV figures do not represent sales prices for arms transfers. They should therefore not be compared with gross domestic product (GDP), military expenditure, sales values or the financial value of export licences in an attempt to measure the economic burden of arms imports or the economic benefits of exports. They are best used as the raw data for calculating trends in international arms transfers over periods of time, global percentages for suppliers and recipients, and percentages for the volume of transfers to or from particular states.

II. Arms transfers to Western and Central Europe

MARK BROMLEY

There is no necessary, direct relationship between trends in military spending and trends in arms transfers. For example, the majority of most states' military budget is spent on personnel costs, rather than arms acquisitions. Also, a number of states acquire the majority of their arms domestically. Nonetheless, falling military spending can lead to reductions in the funds available for arms procurement. Moreover, reduced military budgets combined with overall declines in government spending and rising economic uncertainty can lead states to favour arms procurement from domestic producers over imports. This section looks at the effect of declining military spending on the volume of international arms transfers to states in Western and Central Europe in the light of rising economic uncertainty.[1] In particular, it examines delays and cancellations of imports as well as attempts to favour domestic arms producers when making procurement decisions. It also examines how these processes have interacted with, and affected, efforts to consolidate and strengthen the European arms industry and national efforts to boost arms exports.[2]

The 2008 global financial crisis and consequent economic crisis has led to declining military spending in Europe. In Western Europe military spending started to decline in 2010, while in Central Europe it began to fall in 2009 and at a sharper rate. Between 2008 and 2012 military spending decreased in Western Europe by 8 per cent and in Central Europe by 10 per cent. However, there have been steeper decreases in spending in some states than others, while states that have been less affected by the financial crisis have increased spending. Between 2008 and 2012, military spending fell in Greece (by 37 per cent), Romania (18 per cent), Portugal (16 per cent) and Italy (13 per cent), while it rose in Poland (by 19 per cent) and Norway (6 per cent).[3] These falls in military spending came at a time when both Western and Central Europe were more exclusively reliant on commercial arms acquisitions for their procurement needs than at any point since the end of the cold war. Aid, which was still an important component of

---

[1] Western Europe is taken here to consist of Austria, Belgium, Cyprus, Denmark, Finland, France, Germany, Greece, Iceland, Ireland, Italy, Luxembourg, Malta, the Netherlands, Norway, Portugal, Spain, Sweden, Switzerland and the United Kingdom. Central Europe consists of Albania, Bosnia and Herzegovina, Bulgaria, Croatia, Czech Republic, Estonia, Hungary, Latvia, Lithuania, FYR Macedonia, Montenegro, Poland, Romania, Serbia, Slovakia and Slovenia.

[2] For a more in-depth discussion on these issues see chapter 4, section I, in this volume.

[3] In certain cases, the proportion of military spending devoted to equipment expenditure has also fallen sharply. Between 2008 and 2011 it fell from 16% to 7% in Greece and from 21% to 7% in Spain. NATO, 'Financial and economic data relating to NATO defence', Press Release (2012) 047 13, 13 Apr. 2012, <http://www.nato.int/cps/en/natolive/news_85966.htm?mode=pressrelease>.

transfers to states in Central and Western Europe in the early-1990s, has been essentially non-existent since 2008.

The trend in the volume of major conventional weapons imported by states in Western and Central Europe broadly matches recent trends in military spending in the region. Between 2003–2007 and 2008–12, imports in Western Europe fell by 16 per cent and in Central Europe by 49 per cent. In Western Europe the overall fall in imports was largely driven by declines in imports by Greece and Italy, which fell by 61 per cent and 55 per cent between 2003–2007 and 2008–12, respectively. During this period, Greece fell from being fourth largest arms importer in the world to 15th largest, while Italy fell from being 16th largest to 37th largest. In Central Europe the overall decrease in arms imports was largely driven by declines in imports by Hungary, the Czech Republic and Romania, which fell by 93 per cent, 83 per cent and 63 per cent, respectively. At the same time, some states whose military spending rose also increased imports. For example, Norwegian arms imports increased by 91 per cent between 2003–2007 and 2008–12.

In certain cases, trends in military spending and major conventional weapon imports do not correlate, particularly when weapons have been delivered long after they were paid for or if there have been gaps between the completion of one round of acquisitions and the start of another. For example, despite its military spending falling, imports by Portugal increased by 211 per cent between 2003–2007 and 2008–12. Portugal has not placed an order for the import of major conventional weapons since 2009 and had only a limited number of items on order but undelivered at the close of 2012.[4] Conversely, despite seeing an increase in military spending, Poland's arms imports decreased by 47 per cent between 2003–2007 and 2008–12. Poland's fall in imports followed a series of large-scale deliveries in the early-to-mid-2000s. The country had a number of items on order but undelivered at the close of 2012 and has plans for a series of additional arms acquisitions in the near future (see below).

Delayed or cancelled arms acquisitions

As part of their cuts in military spending, several states in Western and Central Europe have taken steps to delay or cancel planned arms acquisitions from abroad since 2008 and these processes continued in 2012. Italy and the Netherlands have reduced or delayed planned acquisitions of F-35 combat aircraft from the USA (see section I above). Elsewhere, states' plans

---

[4] The Type-214 submarines imported from Germany are reportedly being kept in port for months at a time in order to save money on fuel costs. 'Portuguese military equipment getting less use due to fuel costs, budget cuts', Publico Online, 15 May 2012, Published by Forecast International, 16 May 2012.

for the acquisition of combat aircraft have been put on hold, cancelled or downgraded. Croatia expressed interest in purchasing 12 combat aircraft in 2007.[5] However, in October 2012 the government reportedly concluded that funds were insufficient for the acquisition of either new or second-hand aircraft and would instead focus on overhauling its inventory of MiG-21s.[6] Greece has delayed or cancelled a range of import plans, including the acquisition of 6 FREMM frigates from France and over 400 armoured vehicles from Russia, while Portugal is seeking to offload part of its F-16 combat aircraft fleet. Both Bulgaria and Romania have abandoned previous plans to purchase new combat aircraft: Bulgaria is investigating plans to purchase 9 second-hand F-16Cs; and Romania has decided to purchase 12 second-hand F-16Cs for $600 million—both from Portugal.[7]

In the context of seeking to reduce the financial burdens imposed by past acquisitions, states in Western and Central Europe have also sought to renegotiate and, in some cases, abrogate existing deals. In October 2012, citing 'repeated delays' in the delivery of the equipment, Portugal announced that it was cancelling a 2004 contract with Austria for 260 Pandur-2 armoured vehicles. It stated that it would keep the 166 vehicles that had been paid for and delivered and was hoping to receive €55 million in compensation from the supplier.[8] In September 2012 it was announced that the Slovenian Government had cancelled its 2006 deal for 135 AMV armoured vehicles via a settlement agreement with the Finnish supplier.[9] Slovenia has been pushing for the deal to be abandoned since 2010 as part of wider cost-cutting measures, arguing that the manner in which the contract was awarded breached both fair play and competition laws.[10] Greece's acquisition of Type-214 submarines from Germany has also been the subject of repeated delays due to a lack of funding, although no official statement has been issued about cancelling the contract.[11]

---

[5] 'Croatian Air Force mulling MiG-29M2 for new fighter program', Interfax, 13 Dec. 2007.

[6] Radaljac, D., 'Swedes and Gripens: order arrived, decision coming—there is no money, so MiG-21s will be overhauled?', Novi List Online, 12 Oct 2012, Translation from Croatian, Open Source Center.

[7] 'Bulgarian Govt to buy third-hand fighter jets from Portugal—Report', Novinite.com, 3 Jan. 2013, <http://www.novinite.com/view_news.php?id=146529>.

[8] Portuguese Ministry of Defence, 'Comunicado do Conselho de Ministros de 18 de Octubro de 2012' [Communication of the Council of Ministers of 18 October 2012], 18 Oct. 2012, <http://www.portugal.gov.pt/pt/os-ministerios/primeiro-ministro/secretario-de-estado-da-presidencia-do-conselho-de-ministros/documentos-oficiais/20121018-cm-comunicado.aspx>.

[9] Patria, 'The Ministry of Defense of Slovenia, Rotis Plus and Patria sign a settlement agreement', Press release, 4 Sep. 2012, <http://www.patria.fi/en/news+and+events/news/the+ministry+of+defense+of+slovenia,+rotis+plus+and+patria+sign+a+settlement+agreement.html>.

[10] O'Dwyer, G., 'Lawsuit clouds Patria AMV deal with Slovenia', Defense News, 31 Mar. 2011.

[11] 'Greek police clash with protesting shipyard workers', Reuters, 4 Oct. 2012.

The wider implications of declining arms imports

Decisions to delay and cancel import contracts appear to be affecting European states' efforts to boost their own arms exports, which have been stepped up in recent years in order to help offset losses in revenues caused by reduced domestic procurement spending.[12] For example, during the period 2006–10 Greece was the largest recipient of German exports and the third largest recipient of French exports. In addition, prior to their shift in focus from new to second-hand aircraft, Bulgaria, Croatia and Romania had all been named as potential customers for Sweden's JAS-39C combat aircraft.[13] European states' efforts to boost exports via supplies to other states in Europe are also challenged by the presence of international suppliers that sometimes prove more able to deliver equipment on time and under budget. In 2011 Sweden ordered 15 UH-60M helicopters from the USA following prolonged delays in the delivery of European-manufactured NH-90 helicopters. In 2012 Norway indicated that it was also investigating the acquisition of helicopters from the USA, due to delays in the delivery of its own order of NH-90 helicopters.[14] There are also increasing signs that European states are looking beyond the traditional arms suppliers for their procurement needs (see Asia suppliers section).

The budget cuts of European states may also affect efforts to promote the consolidation of arms production in Europe and the joint development and acquisition of weapon systems. In recent years the European Union (EU) has taken a series of steps to deregulate the market for defence goods in Europe by relaxing controls on the internal movement of military goods, limiting the situations in which states can award acquisition contracts without issuing international tenders and curtailing the use of offsets.[15] In addition, the EU and the North Atlantic Treaty Organization (NATO) have sought to encourage the common development and procurement of weapon systems, as part of their broader efforts in the field of 'pooling and

[12] For more on national efforts to boost arms exports, see chapter 4, section I, in this volume.

[13] Saab, 'Sweden offers Gripen to Croatia', Press release, 14 Oct. 2011, <http://www.saabgroup.com/en/About-Saab/Newsroom/Press-releases--News/2011--10/Sweden-offers-Gripen-to-Croatia/>; 'Sweden offers price cuts to Romania for Gripen', Agence France-Presse, 15 Apr. 2010; and 'Bulgarian defense chief gets Saab offer on Gripen fighter jets', Novinite.com, 4 Feb. 2011, <http://www.novinite.com/view_news.php?id=124921>.

[14] 'Norway may buy Seahawks instead of European helicopters', Reuters, 16 Aug. 2012.

[15] Directive 2009/43/EC of the European Parliament and of the Council of 6 May 2009 simplifying terms and conditions of transfers of defence-related products within the Community, *Official Journal of the European Union*, L146, 10 June 2009; Directive 2009/81/EC of the European Parliament and of the Council of 13 July 2009 on the coordination of procedures for the award of certain works contracts, supply contracts and service contracts by contracting authorities or entities in the fields of defence and security, and amending Directives 2004/17/EC and 2004/18/EC, *Official Journal of the European Union*, L216, 20 Aug. 2009; and European Defence Agency, Code of Conduct on Offsets, <http://www.eda.europa.eu/offsets/>. On the Directive on Intra-Community Transfer see chapter 10, section V, in this volume.

sharing' (by the EU) and 'smart defence' (by NATO).[16] However, the wider adoption of these practices may prove more challenging in a period when governments have less money to spend on procurement and may be more eager than ever to ensure that procurement funds are spent domestically. For example, Poland plans to spend 100 billion złotys ($30 billion) on a series of large-scale arms acquisitions, including armoured vehicles, helicopters, tanks, unmanned aerial vehicles and surface-to-air missile systems.[17] The Polish Government has made clear that a large proportion of this money will be spent domestically.[18]

[16] Hale, J., 'EDA countries agree on pooling and sharing code of conduct', *Defense News*, 19 Nov. 2012; and NATO, 'Smart defence', <http://www.nato.int/cps/en/natolive/78125.htm>. Similar efforts are also taking place at the subregional level, such as among the Nordic states, between the UK and France, and between states in Central Europe. See Möckli, D., 'Smart pooling: state of play in European defence and armament cooperation', Centre for Security Studies (CSS) Analysis in Security Policy no. 126, Dec. 2012, <http://www.css.ethz.ch/policy_consultancy/products_INT/CSS_Analysis/index_EN>.

[17] Lentowicz, Z., 'Defense Ministry: domestic leaders', *Rzeczpospolita*, 12 Nov. 2012, p. B7, Translation from Polish, Open Source Center.

[18] Adamowski, J., 'Poland's spending up as most of E. Europe cuts back', *Defence News*, 24 Oct. 2012.

III. Arms transfers to Syria

PIETER D. WEZEMAN

As the conflict in Syria intensified in 2012, the international community remained at an impasse on how to respond.[1] It could not agree on how to deal with the conflict in general or with supplying arms to the parties in the conflict in particular. Whereas the European Union (EU), Turkey, the League of Arab States and the United States maintained arms embargoes against the Syrian Government, Iran and Russia continued to supply it with arms. Rebel forces called for foreign military aid and neighbouring countries seemed to supply arms or provide funds for arms acquisitions.

Arms supplies to Syrian Government forces

Before the start of the conflict in 2011, Syria's imports of major conventional weapons had increased by 330 per cent between 2001–2005 and 2006–10. After many years of economic difficulties, Syria had failed to keep its armed forces abreast of modern military technology, and the increase indicates a subsequent effort to upgrade the armed forces. During 2006–10, Russia provided 48 per cent of Syria's imports, with air defence systems and anti-ship missiles making up the bulk of the deliveries. Other suppliers of major conventional weapons were Iran (21 per cent), Belarus (20 per cent), North Korea (9 per cent) and China (2 per cent). More countries are likely to have been involved in the supply of other military equipment, including items used widely during the conflict. For example Russian and Italian companies were involved in upgrading Syrian T-72 tanks.[2]

Since the start of the conflict in 2011 there has been a sharp division between states that oppose the imposition of United Nations sanctions on Syria and that continue to supply arms to the Syrian Government, and states that have imposed arms embargoes on Syria and called for a UN embargo.[3] Russian officials have been most vocal with regard to the former position and made clear statements that arms supplies were continuing in 2011–12. However, there have been some indications of a growing Russian reluctance to supply weapons to the Syrian Government. Vyacheslav

---

[1] On the conflict in Syria see Allansson, M. et al., 'The first year of the Arab Spring', *SIPRI Yearbook 2012*; and chapter 1, section I, in this volume.

[2] Beretta, G., 'Siria: ministro Frattini, quei carro armati sparano italiano sui civili di Hama' [Syria: Minister Frattini, those tanks fire 'made in Italy' on civilians in Hama], Unimondo.org, 1 Aug. 2011, <http://www.unimondo.org/Notizie/Siria-ministro-Frattini-quei-carro-armati-sparano-italiano-sui-civili-di-Hama-131207>; and Barabanov, M., 'Russian interests in Syria: myths and reality', Moscow Defence Brief no. 4, 2012, <http://mdb.cast.ru/mdb/4-2012/>.

[3] On the debate on multilateral arms embargoes on Syria see chapter 10, section II, in this volume. For background on Russian motives for supplying arms to Syria see Barabanov (note 2).

Dzirkaln, deputy head of the Russian Federal Service for Military-Technical Cooperation, announced in July 2012 that although existing contracts would be fulfilled, 'Until the situation stabilizes we will not deliver any new weapons [to Syria]' and that the Russian Government had not given permission for a planned sale of 36 Yak-130 trainer/combat aircraft to Syria.[4] In early 2013 Anatoly Isaikin, the general director of the Russian state arms trading corporation, Rosoboronexport, stated that Russia continued to supply air defence systems and 'maintenance and servicing equipment' but not combat aircraft.[5] However, although it is unclear if Russia was still prepared to supply 12 MiG-29M2 combat aircraft that Syria had ordered around 2007, several reports of actual deliveries in 2012 indicate that the weapons supplied by Russia included more than air defence systems. In January 2012 a Russian ship reportedly delivered 60 tonnes of ammunition and explosives to Syria.[6] A Russian company reported it would continue the supply of KAB-500 guided aircraft bombs to Syria in 2012.[7] Furthermore, Russia has continued to return Syrian Mi-24 combat helicopters that had been overhauled in Russia.[8]

Iran and Ukraine are also known to have continued to supply arms to the Syrian Government in 2011–12. Two shipments from Iran to Syria including small arms, mortar ammunition and rocket propellant were intercepted in 2011 in Turkey as part of the enforcement of the UN embargo on Iranian arms exports.[9] It was also reported that 'Western intelligence' concluded that Iran continued to supply large quantities of weapons to Syria via air in 2012.[10] The Ukrainian Government reported the export of 4000 rifles to Syria in 2011.[11]

The EU, Turkey and the USA imposed arms embargoes on Syria and tried to prevent the delivery of weapons by other states when legally possible. In October 2012 Turkey ordered a Syrian aircraft passing through Turkish airspace on a flight from Russia to Syria to land in Turkey, where it was searched before being allowed to fly on. While both Russia and Syria pro-

[4] 'Russia suspends new arms shipments to Syria', CNN, 9 July 2012, <http://edition.cnn.com/2012/07/09/world/meast/syria-unrest>.
[5] '"No warplanes" for Syria says Russian arms sales boss', RIA Novosti, 13 Feb. 2013, <http://en.rian.ru/world/20130213/179443688.html>.
[6] 'Arms-laden ship docks in Syrian port: official', Hurriyet Daily News, 12 Jan. 2012.
[7] [Portfolio of export orders KTRV], 15 July 2012, <bmpd.livejournal.com/290141.html> (in Russian).
[8] 'Russia will deliver first Mi-25 gunships to Syria on time—arms official', RIA Novosti, 28 June 2012, <http://en.rian.ru/military_news/20120628/174282882.html>.
[9] United Nations, Security Council, Final report of the Panel of Experts established pursuant to resolution 1929 (2010), S/2012/395, 12 June 2012, pp. 28, 64–65.
[10] Charbonneau, L., 'Exclusive: Western report—Iran ships arms, personnel to Syria via Iraq', Reuters, 19 Sep. 2012.
[11] Ukrainian State Export Control Service, [Information on the international transfer of certain categories of weapon made by Ukraine in 2011], Aug. 2012 <http://www.dsecu.gov.ua/control/uk/publish/article?art_id=46460&cat_id=46454> (in Ukrainian).

tested against the action, the Turkish Government claimed to have found 'illegal cargo' on board, reportedly spare parts for radar systems, and argued that it had acted in accordance with the 1944 Convention on International Civil Aviation (Chicago Convention).[12] In June 2012 a British company withdrew its insurance for a ship transporting several overhauled Mi-24 combat helicopters from Russia to Syria, forcing the ship to return to Russia, from where an alternative delivery route for the helicopters had to be found.[13] The USA pressured Iraq to prevent Iran from flying weapons to Syria through Iraqi air space, even though its formal concern was that such deliveries were in violation of the UN embargo on arms exports from Iran.[14]

Arms supplies to Syrian rebel groups

The main source of weapons for Syrian rebel groups appears to have been the capture of arms from government troops and arsenals. Small arms and light weapons were also bought on the black market in Iraq and Lebanon.[15] Nevertheless, rebel forces repeatedly called in 2012 for governments supporting their cause to supply them with weapons and other military equipment.[16] As of January 2013 the actual volume of foreign military aid to the rebels is hard to measure.

The rebels' requests for arms prompted mixed reactions. During 2012 the Friends of the Syrian People—a group of over 70 countries that supported the Syrian opposition—could not agree a common policy of supplying arms.[17] Instead, individual countries pursued their own policies. Several states supplied Syrian opposition groups with non-lethal equipment. Within the US Government several high-level decision makers were in favour of providing arms to rebel groups. However, others—including US President Barack Obama—were against the idea because of fears that this might draw the USA into a proxy war and that supplied weapons might end

[12] Omanovic, E., 'Effective embargo enforcement: overflight denial and control', Non-proliferation Papers no. 26, EU Non-proliferation Consortium, Feb. 2013, <http://www.nonproliferation.eu/activities/activities.php>, p. 10.

[13] Saul, J. and Grove, T., 'Syria faces ire over fresh Russia arms shipments', Reuters, 19 June 2012.

[14] Omanovic (note 12), p. 11.

[15] Constantine, Z., 'Guns from Beirut: Syria uprising good for business for Lebanese arms dealers', The National (Abu Dhabi), 29 Feb. 2012; Stephan, L., 'Un trafic d'armes au profit des insurgés syriens se développe dans le nord du Liban' [Weapons trafficking from Northern Lebanon helps Syrian insurgents], Le Monde, 10 Mar. 2012; and Nichols, M., 'Weapons being smuggled between Lebanon, Syria: U.N.', Reuters, 8 May 2012.

[16] Myers, S. L., 'U.S. joins effort to equip and pay rebels in Syria', New York Times, 1 Apr. 2012; Weaver, M., 'Friends of Syria grant Assad's opponents recognition but not weapons', The Guardian, 12 Dec. 2012; and Karouny, M., 'Syria rebels hope arms will flow to new fighter command', Reuters, 10 Dec. 2012.

[17] Barnard, A., 'U.S. and Turkey to step up "nonlethal" aid to rebels in Syria', New York Times, 25 Mar. 2012.

up in the wrong hands, within or outside Syria.[18] Instead, the USA sent equipment, including communication equipment, which according to the US Secretary of State, Hillary Rodham Clinton, would 'help activists organize, evade attacks by the regime, and connect to the outside world'.[19] In late 2012 the United Kingdom provided non-lethal aid, including communication equipment and body armour.[20] Both France and the UK argued in favour of amendments to the EU arms embargo on Syria to allow the supply of additional types of non-lethal military equipment to opposition groups.[21]

Government representatives of Libya, Qatar and Saudi Arabia proposed in early 2012 providing weapons to the rebels.[22] In mid-April the Prime Minister of Qatar, Hamad bin Jasim bin Jabir Al Thani, stated that his country was not arming the Syrian rebels.[23] Despite the fact that no government openly admitted to supplying arms to the Syrian rebels, there were reports that several states supplied arms directly or provided the funds to acquire arms on the black market.[24] The chairman of the Syrian National Council claimed in March 2012 that the council had received funding from 'Arab and foreign countries' to procure weapons.[25]

In June 2012 it was rumoured that Syrian rebels received arms paid for by Qatar, Saudi Arabia and Turkey.[26] In July 2012 it was claimed that Qatar and Saudi Arabia were advocating the supply of man-portable air defence systems (MANPADS) to the Syrian rebels.[27] However, reportedly they had been holding back on supplying advanced weapons, such as MANPADS, because of US objections.[28] Nevertheless, in early 2013 it was reported that MANPADS had been supplied via Turkey and that this was a relaxation of

[18] Landler, M. and Gordon, M. R., 'Obama could revisit arming Syria Rebels as Assad holds firm', *New York Times*, 18 Feb. 2013.

[19] Gaouette, N., 'Clinton says Assad is ignoring UN's plan to end Syria violence', Bloomberg, 1 Apr. 2012; and Barnard (note 17).

[20] British Foreign and Commonwealth Office, 'Foreign Secretary remarks at Friends of the Syrian People meeting', 12 Dec. 2012, <https://www.gov.uk/government/speeches/foreign-secretary-remarks-at-the-friends-of-syria-meeting>; and Loveluck, L., 'What's non-lethal about aid to the Syrian opposition', *Foreign Policy*, 20 Sep. 2012.

[21] See chapter 10, section I, in this volume.

[22] 'Gulf states propose funding Syrian opposition army', France 24, 2 Apr. 2012, <http://www.france24.com/en/20120401-friends-syria-talks-get-underway-istanbul-six-point-annan-peace-plan-assad>; and Kennedy, E. A., 'With smuggling choked, Syria rebels feel arms curb', Associated Press, 25 May 2012.

[23] 'Qatar PM: no arms to Syrian rebels from Gulf state', Associated Press, 17 Apr. 2012.

[24] Worth, R. F., 'Citing U.S. fears, Arab allies limit Syrian rebel aid', *New York Times*, 6 Oct. 2012.

[25] Astih, P., 'The National Council reveals that it is obtaining financial resources to secure qualitative weapons for the dissidents', Al-Sharq al-Awsat Online, 10 Mar. 2012, Translation from Arabic, Open Source Center.

[26] Schmitt, E., 'C.I.A. said to aid in steering arms to Syrian opposition', *New York Times*, 21 June 2012.

[27] 'Syrian rebels acquire surface-to-air missiles: report', Reuters, 31 July 2012.

[28] Dettmer, J., 'Syrian rebels step up efforts to get anti-aircraft missiles', Voice of America, 16 Aug. 2012, <http://www.voanews.com/content/syrian-rebels-step-up-efforts-to-get-anti-aircraft-missiles/1489899.html>; Worth (note 24); and Hosenball, M., 'As militants join Syria revolt, fears grow over arms flow', Reuters, 22 June 2012.

the restrictions that Turkey and the USA had imposed on arms flows to the rebels.[29]

Reports of interceptions of arms shipments and the analysis of images of weapons used by Syrian rebels provide further indications that foreign governments were supplying arms to the rebel forces. While it is possible to ascertain the ultimate origins of these weapons, there is uncertainty regarding the immediate suppliers and the volume of arms flows to the rebels. For example, in April 2012 Lebanese authorities seized a consignment of rocket-propelled grenades and other ammunition on a ship from Libya that was believed to be destined for Syrian rebels.[30] However, it was not established with certainty who in Libya was behind the shipment. A Swiss Government investigation established that hand grenades photographed in the possession of Syrian rebels had originally been delivered from Switzerland to the United Arab Emirates in 2003–2004 and had then been given to Jordan in 2004.[31] However, it was not established how the hand grenades reached the Syrian rebels. The large number of videos and photographs of the Syrian conflict made available on the Internet have provided analysts opportunities to assess arming trends. For example, in late 2012, videos posted on the Internet showed rebels using weapons originating from the former Yugoslavia.[32] Investigations by journalists resulted in reports that the weapons had been supplied from Croatia, via Jordan, to rebels in Syria in a deal financed by Saudi Arabia.[33]

[29] Borger, J., 'Syria crisis: European countries expected to start arming rebels', *The Guardian*, 1 Mar. 2013.

[30] Nichols (note 15).

[31] Swiss State Secretariat for Economic Affairs, 'Swiss hand grenades in Syria: conclusion of investigation and measures', 21 Sep. 2012, <http://www.seco.admin.ch/aktuell/00277/01164/01980/index.html?lang=en&msg-id=46075>.

[32] Higgins, E., 'Weapons from the former Yugoslavia spread through Syria's war', At War Blog, *New York Times*, 25 Feb. 2013, <http://atwar.blogs.nytimes.com/2013/02/25/weapons-from-the-former-yugoslavia-spread-through-syrias-war/>.

[33] Chivers, C. J. and Schmitt, E., 'Saudis step up help for rebels in Syria with Croatian arms', *New York Times*, 25 Feb. 2013.

IV. Transparency in arms transfers

PAUL HOLTOM AND MARK BROMLEY

Official and publicly accessible data on arms transfers is important for assessing states' arms export and arms procurement policies. However, publishing data on arms sales and acquisitions is a sensitive issue for nearly all states. This section analyses recent developments in official international, regional and national reporting mechanisms that aim, in whole or in part, to increase the quality and quantity of publicly available information on international arms transfers. This includes the United Nations Register of Conventional Arms (UNROCA) as well as national and regional reports on arms exports.[1]

The United Nations Register of Conventional Arms

UNROCA, which was established in 1992, is the key international mechanism for official transparency on arms transfers. Each year all UN member states are requested to report information to UNROCA on the export and import of seven categories of conventional weapons in the previous calendar year.[2] States are also invited to provide information on their international transfers of small arms and light weapons (SALW) and their holdings and procurement from domestic production of major conventional weapons.

The level of reporting decreased from 86 states in 2011 to an all-time low in 2012 (see figure 5.2).[3] As of December 2012, 52 states had submitted reports on their arms transfers for 2011 (including 15 nil reports, i.e. reports indicating no imports or exports of major conventional weapons).[4] All but one region recorded a significant decline in reporting (see table 5.5). The exception was Africa, where reporting increased from 1 state in 2011 to 2 in 2012, with Mozambique providing a nil report for the seven categories of

---

[1] This section does not address confidential intergovernmental exchanges of information on arms transfers, such as those that occur within the Organization for Security and Co-operation in Europe, the Organization of American States and the Wassenaar Arrangement. Another source of information on the international arms trade is the customs data of the UN Commodity Trade Statistics Database (Comtrade). Comtrade data is not discussed here because it is neither intended nor designed to be a tool for increasing the amount of publicly available information on international arms transfers. Comtrade data is included in the Norwegian Initiative on Small Arms Transfers (NISAT) Small Arms Trade Database, <http://www.prio.no/NISAT/Small-Arms-Trade-Database/>.

[2] These categories are battle tanks, armoured combat vehicles, large-calibre artillery systems, combat aircraft, attack helicopters, warships, and missiles or missile launchers.

[3] 2013 Group of Governmental Experts on the United Nations Register of Conventional Arms, *Background* (United Nations Office of Disarmament Affairs: New York, Mar. 2013), p. 3.

[4] Information on 36 submissions was made publicly available before 31 Dec. 2012. Information submitted by a further 11 states was made publicly available on 30 Jan. 2013. As of 27 Mar. 2013, information provided by 5 states, including the USA, has not been made publicly available.

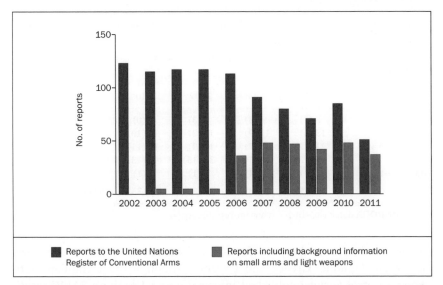

Figure 5.2. Reports submitted to the United Nations Register of Conventional Arms, 2002–11

Years refer to the year covered by the report, not the year of its submission.

Source: UNROCA database, <http://www.un-register.org/>.

the register for the first time since 2007. For the first time, no reports were submitted by states in the Middle East.

Previous analyses have highlighted the strong correlation between the decline in the number of states submitting nil reports and the overall level of reporting.[5] However, only 7 of the 10 largest suppliers of major conventional weapons in 2008–12 (as recorded by SIPRI) reported for 2011; for the first time, Israel, Italy and Spain did not report. Four of the 10 largest importers did not report for 2011, including India and Pakistan—both regular reporters. This dramatic decline in reporting is likely to be a priority issue for consideration by the Group of Governmental Experts (GGE) on UNROCA that will meet in 2013.[6] It should also be an issue to be explored for those hoping that an arms trade treaty (ATT) will lead to an increase in transparency in the international arms trade.[7]

Of the 52 states that provided information to UNROCA for 2011, 32 provided background information on international transfers of SALW (63 per cent), including 5 nil reports. For the first time, Malaysia provided background information on international transfers of SALW. However, three states that had previously included background information on SALW

---

[5] Holtom, P. and Bromley, M., 'Transparency in arms transfers', *SIPRI Yearbook 2010*, p. 323.

[6] The GGE was supposed to meet in 2012, but it was postponed until after the final UN conference on an arms trade treaty.

[7] On the arms trade treaty negotiations in 2012 see chapter 10, section I, in this volume.

Table 5.5. Reports submitted to the United Nations Register of Conventional Arms (UNROCA), by region, 2007–11

Years refer to the year covered by the report, not the year of its submission. Figures in brackets are numbers of nil reports.

	2007	2008	2009	2010	2011
Africa	8 (7)	4 (3)	4 (3)	1 (0)	2 (1)
Americas	13 (6)	15 (9)	10 (2)	19 (10)	7 (3)
Asia and Oceania	21 (12)	19 (7)	17 (9)	19 (11)	11 (3)
Europe	46 (13)	40 (10)	39 (15)	45 (13)	32 (8)
Middle East	3 (1)	2 (1)	2 (1)	2 (1)	0 (0)
Total	**91 (39)**	**80 (30)**	**72 (30)**	**86 (35)**	**52 (15)**

Source: UNROCA database, <http://www.un-register.org/>.

transfers and submitted reports for 2011 did not report on SALW transfers: the Czech Republic, Greece and Ukraine. Although the Ukrainian State Export Control Service published information on Ukraine's SALW transfers in UNROCA format on its website, it does not appear to have provided this information to UNROCA.[8] Australia provided information on international transfers of SALW, but the information related to export licences issued and did not contain information on the actual number of small arms authorized for export.

Eleven states have submitted views on the inclusion of SALW in UNROCA since being invited to do so by the UN General Assembly at the end of 2009.[9] In 2012 Germany and the United States expressed support for the expansion of UNROCA to include SALW. Germany called for the GGE to conduct a 'fundamental debate on the nature of the categories'.[10]

National and regional reports on arms exports

Since the early 1990s an increasing number of governments have published national reports on arms exports.[11] As of January 2013, 35 states had published at least one national report on arms exports since 1990, including

[8] Ukrainian State Export Control Service, [Information on the international transfer of certain categories of weapon made by Ukraine in 2011], Aug. 2012 <http://www.dsecu.gov.ua/control/uk/publish/article?art_id=46460&cat_id=46454> (in Ukrainian).

[9] These states were Burkina Faso, Colombia, Germany, Israel, Japan, Mauritius, Mexico, the Netherlands, Singapore, Switzerland and the USA.

[10] United Nations, General Assembly, United Nations Register of Conventional Arms, 'German policy and practice on exports of conventional weapons and related technology, Berlin, May 2012', Annex to A/67/212/add.2, 30 Jan. 2013, p. 37.

[11] A database of the published reports is maintained by SIPRI at <http://www.sipri.org/research/armaments/transfers/transparency/national_reports>. See also Weber, H. and Bromley, M., 'National reports on arms exports', SIPRI Fact Sheet, Mar. 2011, <http://books.sipri.org/product_info?c_product_id=423>.

32 that had done so since 2009.[12] Of the 32 states, 28 included information in their reports on arms export licences granted and 23 included information on actual arms exports. During 2012 no state produced a national report on arms exports that had not done so previously.

In several states, governments make information available about decision making in the field of arms export controls to the parliament as a whole or to a specific parliamentary committee. In certain cases, this information is made available on a confidential basis and therefore does not contribute to the overall transparency in the states' arms exports. For example, the Swedish Export Control Council (ECC), which is appointed by the Swedish Parliament, meets regularly to discuss certain export licence applications that have yet to be approved or denied.[13] These consultations are confidential. In other cases, this information is also made available to the public at large and thus contributes to the overall transparency of the states' arms exports. For example, the 1976 US Arms Export Control Act requires the US Department of Defense and the US Department of State to formally notify the US Congress of potential arms sales that exceed a certain value.[14] These notifications are made public.

During 2012 there were improvements in the amount of publicly accessible information made available to certain European parliaments on arms exports. In April 2012 the Netherlands began issuing publicly accessible notifications to the parliament about any export licence granted worth more than €2 million ($2.6 million).[15] The system applies to transfers to all destinations apart from member states of the European Union (EU) or the North Atlantic Treaty Organization as well as Australia, Japan, New Zealand and Switzerland. Notifications are provided within two weeks of a licence being issued and include information on the government's assessment of the deal in the light of its own export licensing criteria. In July 2012 the British Committee on Arms Export Controls published its annual report on British strategic export controls.[16] During the compilation of the report, the committee requested and received information on the

---

[12] The 3 states that have produced a report since 1990 but not since 2009 are Australia, Belarus and the Former Yugoslav Republic of Macedonia.

[13] Swedish Ministry for Foreign Affairs, Strategic export control in 2011—military equipment and dual-use products, Government communication, Skr. 2011/12:114, presented to the Swedish Parliament 15 Mar. 2012, pp. 19–20.

[14] See Schroeder, M. and Stohl, R., 'US export controls', SIPRI Yearbook 2005, pp. 732–33.

[15] Dutch Estates General, Second Chamber, 'Brief van de staatssecretaris van economische zaken, landbouw en innovatie' [Letter from the secretary of state for economic affairs, agriculture and innovation], Arms Export Control Policy no. 192, The Hague, 12 Apr. 2012, <https://zoek.officiele bekendmakingen.nl/kst-22054-192.html>.

[16] British House of Commons, Business, Innovation and Skills, Defence, Foreign Affairs and International Development Committees, Scrutiny of Arms Exports (2012): UK Strategic Export Controls Annual Report 2010, Quarterly Reports for July to December 2010 and January to September 2011, the Government's Review of arms exports to the Middle East and North Africa, and wider arms control issues, First Joint Report of Session 2012–13, vol. 1 (Stationery Office: London, July 2012).

Table 5.6. Submissions of information to the European Union annual report on arms exports, 2003–2011

Annual report	Year covered	No. of states making submissions	No. of states making full submission[a]	Proportion of states making full submission (%)
14th	2011	27	18	67
13th	2010	27	17	63
12th	2009	27	17	63
11th	2008	27	19	70
10th	2007	27	16	59
9th	2006	25	16	64
8th	2005	25	17	68
7th	2004	25	13	52
6th	2003	22[b]	6	27

[a] A 'full submission' is taken to be data on the financial value of both arms export licences issued and actual exports, broken down by both destination and EU Common Military List category.

[b] Because the 6th annual report covers export licences issued and actual exports in 2003, the 10 member states that joined the EU in May 2004 were not obliged to submit data. Instead, they were invited to submit figures for 2003 if they were available, which 7 of them did.

Source: Council of the European Union, EU annual reports, <http://www.eeas.europa.eu/non-proliferation-and-disarmament/arms-export-control/index_en.htm>.

reasons certain export licences were granted or refused during 2011. The committee also requested and received details on the equipment covered by arms export licences for transfers to China during 2011 and the reasons the licences were issued. This information, which is more detailed than the information in the British Government's annual report, was reproduced in full in the committee's final report.

The EU Common Position defining common rules governing the control of exports of military technology and equipment requires EU member states to exchange data on the financial values of their export licence approvals and actual exports along with information on their denials of arms export licences.[17] The Council of the EU compiles and publishes this data in an annual report. For the 14th annual report, published in December 2012 and covering transfers during 2011, 18 of the 27 EU member states provided full submissions; that is, they provided data on the number of licences issued and the financial value of both arms export licences and actual arms exports, broken down by both destination and EU Military List category. This figure is up from 17 for the 12th and 13th annual reports (see

[17] Council Common Position 2008/944/CFSP of 8 Dec. 2008 defining common rules governing control of exports of military technology and equipment, *Official Journal of the European Union*, L335, 13 Dec. 2008. On developments related to the EU Common Position see chapter 10, section V, in this volume.

table 5.6).[18] Sweden was able to provide a full submission for the first time. Sweden had previously been unable to submit disaggregated data on the financial values of arms export licences and actual arms exports because of differences between its national control list and the EU Common Military List.[19] However, several states—including France, Germany and the United Kingdom, the EU's three largest arms exporters—continue to have difficulties collecting and submitting data on actual arms exports disaggregated by EU Common Military List categories.[20]

Reflecting the ongoing problems many states have in this area, the 14th annual report, for the first time, does not present aggregated data on actual arms exports for all destinations listed in the report. Instead, aggregated data for a particular destination is only provided when all the EU member states that exported arms to that destination have provided disaggregated data on actual arms exports.[21] The 11th EU annual report listed 'earlier adoption and harmonisation of national reports' as the first 'priority guideline' for EU member states.[22] In subsequent reports, EU member states have highlighted the need for 'early finalisation and publishing' of the EU annual report, but have made no mention of harmonizing national reports. This change in language—combined with the omission of aggregated data on actual arms exports for all destinations—implies that it may be a long time before all EU member states make full submissions to the EU annual report.

[18] Council of the European Union, Fourteenth Annual Report according to Article 8(2) of Council Common Position 2008/944/CFSP defining common rules governing control of exports of military technology and equipment, *Official Journal of the European Union*, C386, 14 Dec. 2012; Council of the European Union, Thirteenth Annual Report according to Article 8(2) of Council Common Position 2008/944/CFSP defining common rules governing control of exports of military technology and equipment, *Official Journal of the European Union*, C382, 30 Dec. 2011; and Council of the European Union, Twelfth Annual Report according to Article 8(2) of Council Common Position 2008/944/CFSP defining common rules governing control of exports of military technology and equipment, *Official Journal of the European Union*, C9, 13 Jan. 2011.

[19] Bauer, S. and Bromley, B., *The European Union Code of Conduct on Arms Exports: Improving the Annual Report*, SIPRI Policy Paper no. 8 (SIPRI: Stockholm, 2004), p. 24.

[20] Holtom, P. and Bromley, M., 'Transparency in arms transfers', *SIPRI Yearbook 2012*, p. 298.

[21] Council of the European Union, Fourteenth Annual Report (note 18), p. 8.

[22] Council of the European Union, Eleventh Annual Report according to Article 8(2) of Council Common Position 2008/944/CFSP defining common rules governing control of exports of military technology and equipment, *Official Journal of the European Union*, C265, 6 Nov. 2009, p. 4.

V. The financial value of states' arms exports

MARK BROMLEY

Table 5.7 presents official data on the financial value of states' arms exports in the years 2002–11. The countries included in the table are those that provide official data on the financial value of 'arms exports', 'arms export licences' or 'arms export agreements' for at least 6 of the 10 years covered and for which the average of the values given exceeds $10 million. The data is taken from reports by, direct quotes from or direct communication with governments or official industry bodies. In all cases, the stated data coverage reflects the language used by the original source. National practices in this area vary, but 'arms exports' generally refers to the financial value of arms actually delivered; 'arms export licences' generally refers to the financial value of licences for arms exports issued by the national export licensing authority; and 'arms export agreements' refers to the financial value of agreements signed for arms exports. Conversion to constant (2011) US dollars has been made using the market exchange rates of the reporting year and the US consumer price index (CPI).

There is no internationally agreed definition of what constitutes 'arms' and governments use different lists when collecting and reporting data on the financial value of their 'arms exports', 'arms export licences' or 'arms export agreements'. Moreover, there is no standardized methodology for how to collect and report such data on 'arms exports'; some states report on export licences issued or used, and other states use data collected from customs agencies. The arms export data for the different states in table 5.7 is thus not necessarily comparable.

According to the SIPRI Arms Transfers Database, the countries that produce official data on the financial value of their arms exports account for over 90 per cent of the total volume of deliveries of major conventional weapons. By adding together the data in table 5.7 it should therefore be possible to arrive at a rough estimate of the financial value of the global arms trade. However, there are significant limitations in using this data in this way. First, as noted above, the data sets used based on different definitions and methodologies and may not be directly comparable. Second, several states—including the United Kingdom—do not release data on 'arms exports', while others—including China—do not release any data on 'arms exports', 'arms export licenses' or 'arms export agreements'. By adding together the data that states have made available on the financial value of their 'arms exports' it is possible to say that that the total value of the global arms trade in 2011 was at least $43 billion. However, the true figure is likely to be higher.

Table 5.7. The financial value of states' arms exports according to national government and industry sources, 2002–11

Figures are in constant (2011) US$ m.. Years are calendar years, unless otherwise stated.

State	2002	2003	2004	2005	2006	2007	2008	2009	2010	2011	Stated data coverage
Austria	52	160	6	162	203	184	321	507	510	598	Arms exports
	275	339	24	367	428	2 048	1 448	3 277	2 416	2 269	Arms export licences
Belgium	1 349	919	804	367	1 230	1 336	2 043	1 605	1 370	1 161	Arms export licences
Bosnia and Herzegovina	..	..	52	92	70	56	89	67	38	..	Arms export licences
Brazil	209	60	339	328	393	174	40	104	..	..	Arms exports
Bulgaria	..	..	..	203	157	220	230	211	352	321	Arms exports
	..	..	..	457	615	561	727	460	404	310	Arms export licences
Canada	540	632	589	306	354	329	546	497	..	..	Arms exports[a]
Czech Republic	91	115	133	126	130	258	291	255	296	254	Arms exports
	..	146	183	173	255	708	324	568	616	481	Arms export licences
Denmark	133	110	149	127	182	291	249	367	514	329	Arms export licences
Estonia	..	..	–	1	–	4	9	12	3	487	Arms export licences
Finland	64	68	62	148	74	111	142	127	81	135	Arms exports
	69	141	485	63	120	85	516	272	83	256	Arms export licences
France	5 214	5 927	10 280	5 317	5 568	6 708	4 807	5 376	5 061	5 070	Arms exports
	4 419	5 822	4 999	5 893	8 054	8 404	10 076	11 891	6 992	7 669	Arms export licences[b]
Germany	374	1 840	1 669	2 335	1 923	2 242	2 184	1 950	2 895	1 786	Arms export licences
	3 834	6 713	5 629	6 039	5 864	5 446	8 858	7 345	6 495	7 526	Arms export licences
Greece	61	155	22	42	123	49	73	331	403	314	Arms exports
Hungary	..	15	13	17	22	25	23	25	26	25	Arms export licences
India	..	68	59	46	87	143	182	185	189	217	Arms exports[c]
Ireland	29	115	84	67	106	90	206	72	33	..	Arms export licences
	42	48	40	43	64	49	47	66	..	38	Arms exports
Israel	2 501	2 874	3 096	2 995	3 347	..	..	7 235	7 427	7 000	Arms export agreements
Italy	5 032	3 668	4 406	4 031	5 467	6 075	6 609	7 759	7 530	6 000	Arms exports
	573	869	710	1 190	1 358	1 881	2 720	3 212	842	1 422	Arms export licences
Korea, South	1 083	1 769	2 203	1 949	3 068	7 044	8 664	9 749	4 442	7 316	Arms export agreements
	180	295	498	302	282	917	1 077	1 223	1 226	2 382	Arms exports
Lithuania	..	..	..	..	6	65	47	64	20	67	Arms exports
	16	..	4	7	11	94	72	115	31	71	Arms export licences

State	2002	2003	2004	2005	2006	2007	2008	2009	2010	2011	Stated data coverage
Netherlands	..	..	..	977	1 131	1 298	765	826	924	1 073	Arms exports
	530	1 588	923	1 683	1 575	1 065	1 925	1 915	1 247	578	Arms export licences
Norway	360	522	356	439	508	592	721	751	626	638	Arms exports
	..	253	389	415	385	426	563	2 026	624	1 180	Arms export licences
Poland	..	35	18	10	1	..	109	23	27	35	Arms exports
	7	43	25	17	1	40	116	41	29	43	Arms export licences
Portugal	..	84	50	53	112	91	127	143	168	182	Arms exports
Romania	55	..	..	114	123	183	182	240	208	256	Arms exports
Russia	6 028	6 848	6 883	7 056	7 253	8 028	8 724	8 912	10 316	13 700	Arms exports
Slovakia	..	..	30	30	45	55	58	64	20	14	Arms exports
South Africa	..	52	96	72	90	110	109	156	79	42	Arms exports
Spain	304	501	504	..	478	616	746	967	1 174	1 265	Arms exports
	324	529	600	600	1 183	1 385	1 429	1 962	1 541	3 379	Arms export licences
Sweden	666	368	651	1 762	1 814	2 913	3 866	4 651	3 058	3 991	Arms exports
	442	980	1 182	1 330	1 569	1 542	2 013	1 858	1 967	2 143	Arms export licences
Switzerland	755	1 364	1 052	2 335	2 274	1 097	1 522	1 521	1 893	1 678	Arms exports
	223	344	385	239	354	420	696	701	634	983	Arms export licences
Turkey	310	405	233	388	393	456	602	702	654	817	Arms exports
Ukraine	625	611	..	..	..	759	836	839	987	1 004	Arms exports
United Kingdom	7 722	9 074	11 255	9 480	9 643	11 883	..	..	..	..	Arms exports[d]
	9 448	9 747	9 912	8 354	11 347	20 950	8 368	11 844	9 291	8 652	Arms export agreements[d]
	3 763	6 195	4 399	4 320	3 337	1 948	3 774	5 043	3 876	9 735	Arms export licences
United States	12 185	13 261	13 826	13 551	13 727	13 341	12 450	14 909	12 351	16 160	Arms exports
	16 149	17 469	15 920	13 936	17 223	25 702	37 949	23 069	21 769	66 274	Arms export agreements

[a] These figures exclude exports to the USA.

[b] These figures cover only exports of 'war weapons' as defined by German national legislation.

[c] Figures for India for 2002–2008 are for the period 1 Apr.–31 Mar. The figure for 2009 covers the period 1 Apr.–31 Dec. 2009.

[d] These figures cover exports of defence equipment and additional aerospace equipment and services.

Sources: Published information or direct communication with governments or official industry bodies. For a full list of sources and all available financial data on arms exports see <http://www.sipri.org/research/armaments/transfers/measuring/financial_values>.

6. World nuclear forces

Overview

At the start of 2013 eight states possessed approximately 4400 operational nuclear weapons. Nearly 2000 of these are kept in a state of high operational alert. If all nuclear warheads are counted—operational warheads, spares, those in both active and inactive storage, and intact warheads scheduled for dismantlement—the United States, Russia, the United Kingdom, France, China, India, Pakistan and Israel together possess a total of approximately 17 270 nuclear weapons (see table 6.1).

All five legally recognized nuclear weapon states, as defined by the 1968 Treaty on the Non-Proliferation of Nuclear Weapons (Non-Proliferation Treaty, NPT)—China, France, Russia, the UK and the USA—appear determined to remain nuclear powers for the indefinite future. Russia and the USA have major modernization programmes under way for nuclear delivery systems, warheads and production facilities (see sections I and II in this chapter). At the same time, they continue to reduce their nuclear forces through the implementation of the bilateral 2010 Treaty on Measures for the Further Reduction and Limitation of Strategic Offensive Arms (New START) and through unilateral force reductions. Since the nuclear weapon arsenals of Russia and the USA are by far the largest, one result has been that the total number of nuclear weapons in the world has been declining. The nuclear arsenals of the other three legally recognized nuclear weapon states are considerably smaller, but all three states are either deploying new weapon systems or have announced their intention to do so (see sections III–IV). Of the five legally recognized nuclear weapon states, China is the only one that appears to be expanding the size of its nuclear arsenal.

The availability of reliable information about the nuclear weapon states' arsenals varies considerably. France, the UK and the USA have recently disclosed important information about their nuclear capabilities. In contrast, transparency in Russia has decreased as a result of its decision not to publicly release detailed data about its strategic nuclear forces under New START, even though it shares the information with the USA. China remains highly non-transparent as part of its long-standing deterrence strategy, and little information is publicly available about its nuclear forces and weapon production complex.

Reliable information on the operational status of the nuclear arsenals and capabilities of the three states that have never been party to the NPT—India, Israel and Pakistan—is especially difficult to find. In the absence of official

Table 6.1. World nuclear forces, January 2013

All figures are approximate. The estimates presented here on nuclear forces are based on public information and contain some uncertainties, as reflected in the notes to tables 6.1–6.9.

Country	Year of first nuclear test	Deployed warheads[a]	Other warheads[b]	Total inventory
United States	1945	2 150[c]	5 550	~7 700[d]
Russia	1949	~1 800	6 700[e]	~8 500[f]
United Kingdom	1952	160	65	225
France	1960	~290	~10	~300
China	1964	–	~250	~250
India	1974	–	90–110	90–110
Pakistan	1998	–	100–120	100–120
Israel	. .	–	~80	~80
North Korea	2006	. .	. .	6–8
Total		**~4 400**	**~12 865**	**~17 270**

[a] 'Deployed' means warheads placed on missiles or located on bases with operational forces.

[b] These are warheads in reserve, awaiting dismantlement or that require some preparation (e.g. assembly or loading on launchers) before they become fully operationally available.

[c] In addition to strategic warheads, this figure includes nearly 200 non-strategic (tactical) nuclear weapons deployed in Europe.

[d] This figure includes the US Department of Defense nuclear stockpile of c. 4650 warheads and another c. 3000 retired warheads that are awaiting dismantlement.

[e] This figure includes c. 700 warheads for nuclear-powered ballistic missile submarines (SSBNs) in overhaul and bombers, 2000 non-strategic nuclear weapons for use by short-range naval, air force and air defence forces, and c. 4000 retired warheads awaiting dismantlement.

[f] This includes a military stockpile of c. 4500 nuclear warheads and another 4000 retired warheads await dismantlement.

declarations, the available information is often contradictory, incorrect or exaggerated. India and Pakistan are both expanding their nuclear weapon stockpiles as well as their missile delivery capabilities, while Israel appears to be waiting to see how the situation in Iran develops (see sections VI–VIII). A ninth state—the Democratic People's Republic of Korea (DPRK, North Korea)—has demonstrated a military nuclear capability. However, there is no public information to verify that it possesses operational nuclear weapons (see section IX).

The raw material for nuclear weapons is fissile material, either highly enriched uranium (HEU) or separated plutonium. The five nuclear weapon states have produced both HEU and plutonium. India, Israel and North Korea have produced mainly plutonium, and Pakistan mainly HEU for weapons. All states with a civilian nuclear industry are capable of producing fissile materials (see section X).

SHANNON N. KILE AND HANS M. KRISTENSEN

I. US nuclear forces

HANS M. KRISTENSEN

As of January 2013, the United States maintained an estimated arsenal of approximately 2150 deployed nuclear warheads, consisting of roughly 1950 strategic and 200 non-strategic warheads (see table 6.2). In addition to this operational arsenal, about 2500 warheads are held in reserve, for a total stockpile of approximately 4650 warheads. Another 3000 retired warheads are awaiting dismantlement for a total inventory of roughly 7700 warheads.

The operational force level is comparable to the estimate presented in *SIPRI Yearbook 2012*.[1] The reduction in the total stockpile reflects the retirement of the nuclear-tipped Tomahawk sea-launched cruise missile (SLCM).

As of 1 September 2012, the USA was counted under the 2010 Russian–US Treaty on Measures for the Further Reduction and Limitation of Strategic Offensive Arms (New START) as having 1722 strategic warheads attributed to 806 deployed missiles and bombers, a modest reduction of 15 warheads and 6 launchers compared with the count six months earlier, in March 2012.[2] The total reduction since the treaty entered into force in February 2011 was 78 strategic warheads and 76 launchers.[3]

The reductions have involved, first and foremost, the elimination of so-called 'phantom' launchers (i.e. bombers that are no longer assigned a nuclear delivery mission but are still counted under New START as nuclear launchers), as well as fluctuations in the number of launchers in overhaul at any given time. The elimination of actual nuclear launchers will not occur until 2015, when the US Navy will begin reducing the number of missile tubes on each nuclear-powered ballistic missile submarine (SSBN) from 24 to 20. The US Air Force (USAF) will probably reduce the intercontinental ballistic missile (ICBM) force from 450 to 400 missiles later in the decade.

Nuclear modernizations

Over the next decade, the US Government intends to spend as much as $214 billion to modernize nuclear delivery vehicles, warheads and

---

[1] Kile, S. N., Schell, P. and Kristensen, H. M., 'US nuclear forces', *SIPRI Yearbook 2012*.

[2] For a summary and other details of New START see annex A in this volume.

[3] For analysis of the 2012 New START aggregate numbers see Kristensen, H. M., 'New detailed data for US nuclear forces counted under New START Treaty', Strategic Security Blog, Federation of American Scientists, 30 Nov. 2012, <http://blogs.fas.org/security/2012/11/newstart2012-2/>.

Table 6.2. US nuclear forces, January 2013

Type	Designation	No. deployed[a]	Year first deployed	Range (km)[b]	Warheads x yield	No. of warheads
Strategic forces						~1 950
Bombers		*111/60*				*300*
B-52H	Stratofortress	91/44	1961	16 000	ALCM 5–150 kt	200[c]
B-2A	Spirit	20/16	1994	11 000	B61-7, -11, B83-1 bombs	100[d]
ICBMs		*449/500*				*500*
LGM-30G	Minuteman III					
	Mk-12A	200	1979	13 000	1–3 x 335 kt	250
	Mk-21 SERV	250	2006	13 000	1 x 300 kt	250
SSBNs/SLBMs[e]		*239/288*				*1 152*
UGM-133A	Trident II (D5)[f]					
	Mk-4	..	1992	>7 400	4 x 100 kt	368
	Mk-4A	..	2008	>7 400	4 x 100 kt	400
	Mk-5	..	1990	>7 400	4 x 475 kt	384
Non-strategic forces						**200**
B61-3, -4 bombs		..	1979	..	0.3–170 kt	200[g]
Total deployed warheads						**~2 150**
Reserve warheads						~2 500
Total military stockpile						**~4 650**
Retired awaiting dismantlement						~3 000
Total inventory						**~7 700**[h]

.. = not available or not applicable; ALCM = air-launched cruise missile; ICBM = intercontinental ballistic missile; kt = kiloton; SERV = security-enhanced re-entry vehicle; SLBM = submarine-launched ballistic missile; SLCM = sea-launched cruise missile; SSBN = nuclear-powered ballistic missile submarine.

[a] The first figure in the 'No. deployed' column is the number counted as 'deployed' under New START. The second figure is the number assigned for nuclear missions.

[b] Aircraft range is for illustrative purposes only; actual mission range will vary according to flight profile and weapon loading.

[c] The B-52H can also carry B61-7 and B83-1 gravity bombs but is currently only planned for the delivery of ALCMs. The total ALCM inventory has been reduced to 528, of which an estimated 200 are deployed. New START only attributes one weapon to each aircraft and does not count weapons stored at bomber bases.

[d] Only the B-2A bomber is assigned to deliver nuclear gravity bombs for strategic missions.

[e] Of 14 SSBNs, 2 or more are normally undergoing overhaul at any given time. Their missiles and warheads are not included in the deployed total.

[f] Although D5 missiles were counted under New START as carrying 8 warheads each, the US Navy is estimated to have downloaded each missile to an average of 4–5 warheads.

[g] Since 2001 the number of B61 bombs deployed in Europe has been unilaterally reduced by almost two-thirds, from 480 to nearly 200. An additional 300 non-strategic bombs are in reserve. The nuclear Tomahawk land-attack missile (TLAM/N) has been retired.

[h] In addition to these 7700 intact warheads, c. 15 000 plutonium pits are stored at the Pantex Plant, Texas, and c. 5000 uranium secondaries are stored at the Y-12 facility at Oak Ridge, Tennessee.

Sources: US Department of Defense, various budget reports and press releases; US Department of Energy, various budget reports and plans; US Department of Defense, various documents obtained under the Freedom of Information Act; US Air Force, US Navy and US Department of Energy, personal communications; 'Nuclear notebook', *Bulletin of the Atomic Scientists*, various issues; and authors' estimates.

warhead-production facilities. This includes designing a new class of ballistic missile submarines, a new long-range bomber with nuclear capability and a new air-launched cruise missile; studying options for the next-generation land-based ICBM; deploying a new nuclear-capable combat aircraft; producing or modernizing three types of nuclear warhead; and building new nuclear weapon-production facilities.

All existing US warhead types are scheduled to undergo extensive life-extension and modernization programmes over the next several decades. Full-scale production of approximately 1200 W76-1 warheads for the Trident II (designated D5) submarine-launched ballistic missile (SLBM) is well under way, scheduled for completion in 2018. Production of the B61-12 precision-guided nuclear bomb—a consolidation of the B61-3, -4, -7 and -10 bombs—is scheduled to follow in 2019–21. The programme is estimated to cost in excess of $10 billion. Design work has begun on a new 'common or adaptable warhead', using components from excess W87 warheads, for possible deployment on both ICBMs and SLBMs. Many of these programmes were described in the financial year (FY) 2012 Stockpile Stewardship and Management Plan.[4]

The 2010 Nuclear Posture Review (NPR) pledged that the USA 'will not develop new nuclear warheads' but consider the 'full range' of life-extension programme options, including 'refurbishment of existing warheads, reuse of nuclear components from different warheads, and replacement of nuclear components'.[5] This is intended to obviate the need to resume nuclear explosive testing, which the USA halted in 1992. The NPR also decided that any life-extension programme 'will use only nuclear components based on previously tested designs, and will not support new military missions or provide for new military capabilities'.[6] However, this will depend on how such capabilities are defined, since the installation of a new

---

[4] US Department of Energy (DOE), National Nuclear Security Administration (NNSA), *FY 2012 Stockpile Stewardship and Management Plan*, Report to Congress (DOE: Washington, DC, 15 Apr. 2011). See also Roth, N., Kristensen, H. M. and Young, S., 'Nuclear plan conflicts with new budget realities', 'Ambitious warhead life extension programs', 'Hydrodynamic tests: not to scale', and 'Produce to reduce: the hedge gamble', Strategic Security Blog, Federation of American Scientists, 12–19 Sep. 2011, <http://blogs.fas.org/security/2011/09/stockpileplan2011/>.

[5] US Department of Defense (DOD), *Nuclear Posture Review Report* (DOD: Washington, DC, Apr. 2010), p. xiv.

[6] US Department of Defense (note 5), p. xiv.

arming, fusing and firing (AF&F) unit or a guided tail kit, for example, can significantly enhance a warhead's ability to destroy certain types of target.[7]

Nuclear strategy and planning

The completion of the long-awaited review of nuclear weapon targeting by the US administration (sometimes referred to as the post-NPR review or NPR implementation study) was delayed by the November 2012 presidential election. The review is intended to identify options for further reductions in the US nuclear stockpile, including potential changes in targeting requirements and alert postures.

A presidential decision directive (PDD) will be issued to form the basis of a Nuclear Weapons Employment Policy (NUWEP) prepared by the Secretary of Defense and a nuclear supplement to the Joint Strategic Capabilities Plan (JSCP-N) prepared by the chairman of the Joint Chiefs of Staff. These documents will then guide the revision by the US Strategic Command (STRATCOM) of the strategic nuclear war plan, now known as Strategic Deterrence and Global Strike (or OPLAN 8010). The changes could take several years to implement.

The post-NPR review has reportedly determined that the USA can meet its national security and allied commitments with 1000–1100 deployed strategic warheads, about 500 fewer than permitted by New START.[8]

Bombers

The US Air Force currently operates a fleet of 20 B-2 and 91 B-52H bombers at three Air Force bases (AFBs). Of these aircraft, 18 B-2s and 76 B-52Hs are nuclear-capable, but only 60 bombers (16 B-2s and 44 B-52Hs) are thought to have nuclear missions at any given time.[9] Under New START, individual bombers are counted as carrying only one weapon, even though each dedicated B-2 can carry up to 16 nuclear bombs (B61-7, B61-11 and B83-1) and each dedicated B-52 can carry up to 20 air-launched cruise missiles (ALCMs).

The USAF is designing a new bomber intended to begin replacing existing bombers from the mid-2020s. Procurement of 80–100 aircraft is envisioned, some of which are planned to be nuclear-capable, at a cost of

[7] Kristensen, H. M., 'Small fuze—big effect', Strategic Security Blog, Federation of American Scientists, 14 Mar. 2007, <http://blogs.fas.org/security/2007/03/small_fuze_-_big_effect/>.

[8] Smith, R. J., 'Obama administration embraces major new nuclear weapons cut', Center for Public Integrity, 8 Feb. 2013, <http://www.publicintegrity.org/2013/02/08/12156/obama-administration-embraces-major-new-nuclear-weapons-cut>.

[9] New START counted 141 nuclear bombers as of 1 Sep. 2012, an anomaly caused by counting so-called phantom bombers that no longer have a nuclear task but still carry some equipment that makes them accountable under the treaty.

perhaps $55 billion. The new bomber might be equipped to deliver the B83-1 gravity bomb (if it is retained in the stockpile) or the planned B61-12 precision-guided bomb. The USAF is also planning a nuclear ALCM, currently known as the Long-Range Stand-Off (LRSO) missile. The current ALCM is scheduled to remain operational until the 2020s.

Land-based ballistic missiles

The US Air Force operates a force of 450 silo-based Minuteman III ICBMs split evenly across three wings: the 90th Missile Wing at Francis E. Warren AFB, Wyoming; the 91st Missile Wing at Minot AFB, North Dakota; and the 341st Missile Wing at Malmstrom AFB, Montana. New START data shows that 449 Minuteman III missiles were operational on 1 September 2012, and another 263 ICBMs (including 58 MX Peacekeeper ICBMs retired in 2003–2005) were in storage.[10] To comply with New START's limit on deployed nuclear delivery vehicles, the USA is expected to reduce the ICBM force to no more than 400 missiles.

Each Minuteman III carries either the 335-kiloton W78 warhead or the 300-kt W87 warhead. Nearly all missiles carry a singled warhead; downloading of the remaining missiles with a multiple independently targetable re-entry vehicle (MIRV) began in 2012, but no announcement has yet been made that the download has been completed. The Minuteman force will retain a MIRV capability as an option, with hundreds of warheads kept in storage.

The USAF is carrying out a multibillion dollar, decade-long Minuteman modernization programme. Although the USA is officially not deploying a new ICBM, the upgraded Minuteman IIIs 'are basically new missiles except for the shell'.[11] The programme is scheduled to be completed in 2015 and will extend the service life of the Minuteman III until 2030.

The USAF budget request for 2013 includes $9.4 million to study a replacement for the Minuteman III missiles, and on 17 May 2012 the Air Force Requirements Oversight Council signed off on an 'initial capabilities document' for a next-generation ICBM.[12] One potential option is a mobile ICBM that would increase survivability and reduce the requirement to keep missiles on high alert.

In 2012 the US Air Force conducted two successful Minuteman flight tests from Vandenberg AFB, California, the same number as in 2011. The first test occurred on 25 February and the second on 12 November and

[10] Kristensen (note 3).

[11] Pampe, C., 'Life extension programs send missiles into the future', Air Force Global Strike Command, 24 Oct. 2012, <http://www.afgsc.af.mil/news/story.asp?id=123323606>.

[12] Grossman, E. M., 'U.S. Air Force approves concept for future ICBM, eyes Navy collaboration', Global Security Newswire, 1 June 2012, <http://www.nti.org/gsn/article/us-air-force-approves-con cept-future-icbm-eyes-navy-collaboration/>.

involved missiles taken from silos at Warren AFB and Malmstrom AFB, respectively. In addition to the flight tests, two simulated launches—known as Simulated Electronic Launch–Minuteman (SELM)—were carried out in 2012 and were intended to test personnel and equipment 'from the initial "on alert" transmission all the way to simulated first stage ignition'.[13]

Ballistic missile submarines

All of the US Navy's 14 Ohio class SSBNs carry Trident II SLBMs. Eight of the SSBNs are based in the Pacific and six in the Atlantic. Normally, 12 are considered operational with the 13th and 14th boat in overhaul at any given time, but New START data shows that fewer than 12 SSBNs are fully equipped with missiles. As of 1 September 2012, for example, only 239 missiles were counted as deployed, 49 fewer than the capacity of 12 boats, so three SSBNs were not deployed at the time of the count. Starting in 2015, the number of missile tubes on each Ohio class SSBN will be reduced from 24 to 20. The reduction is intended to reduce the number of deployed SLBMs to no more than 240 SLBMs at any given time to meet the limit on deployed strategic delivery vehicles set by New START for 2018.

US SSBN operations are being modified, with each SSBN now conducting an average of 2.5 patrols per year, compared with 3.5 patrols a decade ago. More than 60 per cent of the patrols take place in the Pacific Ocean. At any given time, approximately 8 of the 12 operational SSBNs are at sea, with about half of these on 'hard alert' (i.e. in patrol areas within range of designated targets in accordance with the strategic war plan). The remaining boats are in port, probably in dry dock with their missiles removed.

The US Navy has ambitious modernization plans to replace the Ohio class SSBNs with a new design. The Navy has chosen a submarine that is 2000 tonnes larger than the Ohio class submarine but equipped with 16 missile tubes instead of 24.[14] Twelve replacement SSBNs (tentatively known as SSBNX) are planned, a reduction of two boats compared with the current fleet of 14, at an estimated cost of $90.4 billion. Procurement of the first boat is scheduled for 2021, with deployment starting in 2031.[15]

At least during the first decade of its service life, the SSBNX will be armed with a life-extended version of the current Trident II SLBM, desig-

[13] Tyson, M., 'Another year, another SELM test complete for the Mighty Nine', Air Force Print News Today, 12 Oct. 2012, <http://www.afgsc.af.mil/news/story_print.asp?id=123322003>; and Balken, S., '91st MW successfully completes simulated launch', Air Force Print News Today, 9 May 2012, <http://www.minot.af.mil/news/story_print.asp?id=123299257>.

[14] For an unclassified overview of the SSBNX programme see Brougham, W. J., 'Ohio replacement program', Presentation to the 2012 Navy Submarine League, 18 Oct. 2012, <http://news.usni.org/news-analysis/documents/ohio-replacement-program>.

[15] See O'Rourke, R., Navy Ohio Replacement (SSBN[X]) Ballistic Missile Submarine Program: Background and Issues for Congress, Congressional Research Service (CRS) Report for Congress R41129 (US Congress, CRS: Washington, DC, 10 Dec. 2012).

nated the D5LE. The D5LE, which has a new guidance system designed to 'provide flexibility to support new missions' and make the missile 'more accurate', will also be back-fitted onto existing Ohio class SSBNs, starting in 2017.[16]

The US Navy conducted one Trident II (D5) SLBM flight test in 2012. On 22 February the USS *Tennessee* launched a missile equipped with the new D5 life-extension guidance system. The launch took place off of the coast of Florida and marked 136 consecutive successful flight tests of the D5 missile.[17]

Non-strategic nuclear weapons

As of January 2013, the USA retained an inventory of approximately 500 non-strategic (tactical) nuclear weapons, all B61 gravity bombs. All remaining nuclear Tomahawk land-attack cruise missiles (TLAM/Ns) and their W80-0 warheads have now been retired.[18] This completes a decades-long unilateral elimination of all US non-strategic naval nuclear weapons.

Nearly 200 of the US B-61 bombs are deployed at six airbases in five European member states of the North Atlantic Treaty Organization (NATO): Belgium, Germany, Italy, the Netherlands and Turkey. Approximately half of the bombs are earmarked for delivery by US F-15E and F-16 combat aircraft. The Belgian, Dutch, and Turkish air forces (with F-16 combat aircraft) and German and Italian air forces (with PA-200 Tornado aircraft) are assigned nuclear strike missions with the US nuclear weapons.

The NATO Summit meeting in Chicago in May 2012 approved the conclusion of the Deterrence and Defence Posture Review (DDPR) that the existing 'nuclear force posture currently meets the criteria for an effective deterrence and defence posture'.[19] However, NATO plans to modernize its nuclear posture in Europe. This will involve the deployment of the new B61-12 nuclear bomb and the stealthy F-35A (Joint Strike Fighter) combat aircraft. The B61-12 will also be deliverable by F-15E, F-16 and PA-200 Tornado fighter–bombers as well as the US Air Force's B-2 long-range bomber.

---

[16] Draper Laboratory, 'Keeping Trident ever ready', *Explorations*, Spring 2006, p. 8; and Naval Surface Warfare Center Crane Division, 'Underwater wonder, submarines: a powerful deterrent', *Warfighter Solutions*, fall 2008, p. 14.

[17] Benedict, T. (Rear Admiral), US Navy, Strategic Systems Program, 'FY2013 Strategic Systems', Statement before the US Senate, Armed Services Committee, Subcommittee on Strategic Forces, 28 Mar. 2012, <http://www.armed-services.senate.gov/hearings/event.cfm?eventid=be752ef61c2a40 52a676d149c98615b9>, p. 5.

[18] Kristensen, H. M., 'US Navy instruction confirms retirement of nuclear Tomahawk cruise missile', Strategic Security Blog, Federation of American Scientists, 18 Mar. 2012, <http://blogs.fas. org/security/2013/03/tomahawk/>.

[19] North Atlantic Treaty Organization, 'Deterrence and defence posture review', 20 May 2012, <http://www.nato.int/cps/en/natolive/official_texts_87597.htm>, para. 8. On the DDPR see also chapter 7, section III, in this volume.

Compared with the B61-3 and -4 bombs currently deployed in Europe, the B61-12 will bring significant new military capabilities when deployment begins in 2018. The new bomb will use the nuclear explosive package of the B61-4, which has a maximum yield of approximately 50 kilotons. However, since the B61-12 also has to meet the mission requirements of the more powerful strategic B61-7 (360-kt maximum), the bomb will be equipped with a $1 billion guided tail kit to increase its accuracy. This will improve the B61-12's capability to destroy underground targets and enable strike planners to select lower yields for existing targets to reduce collateral damage.[20]

[20] For a description of the B61-12 and its implications see Kristensen, H. M., 'B61 LEP: increasing NATO nuclear capability and precision low-yield strikes', Strategic Security Blog, Federation of American Scientists, 15 June 2011, <http://www.fas.org/blog/ssp/2011/06/b61-12.php>.

II. Russian nuclear forces

VITALY FEDCHENKO, HANS M. KRISTENSEN AND PHILIP SCHELL

As of January 2013 Russia maintained an arsenal of approximately 4500 nuclear warheads assigned to operational forces. About 2500 of these are strategic warheads, including 1800 that are deployed on ballistic missiles and at bomber bases, and 700 that are kept in storage. Russia also possessed approximately 2000 non-strategic (tactical) nuclear warheads. A further 4000 warheads were retired or awaiting dismantlement, for a total inventory of roughly 8500 warheads (see table 6.3).

In 2012 Russia and the United States completed two biannual exchanges of data on numbers, locations and technical characteristics of their strategic nuclear forces subject to New START. As of 1 September 2012, Russia was counted as deploying a total of 1499 warheads attributed to 491 treaty-accountable strategic launchers, including intercontinental ballistic missiles (ICBMs), submarine-launched ballistic missile (SLBMs) and heavy bombers.[1] This represented a decrease of 67 deployed warheads and 25 accountable launchers since 1 September 2011.[2] Russia thus met the New START ceiling of 1550 deployed warheads in 2012, six years earlier than envisaged by the treaty.

The arms reductions mandated by New START codified existing trends in Russian strategic forces. Russia has continued to retire Soviet-era missiles (RS-20V, RS-18 and RS-12M) that have reached the end of their service lives. At the same time, Russia has been introducing new mobile ICBMs and SLBMs, albeit at a slower rate than it has been retiring the older systems.

The Russian National Security Strategy, approved in 2009, states that Russia will maintain parity with the USA's offensive strategic weapons in the most cost-effective way.[3] According to senior military experts, Russia's strategic nuclear forces can guarantee minimum deterrence under the existing arms control limitations, but in order to assure a future second-strike capability, Russia needs to improve both survivability of its missiles

---

[1] US State Department, Bureau of Arms Control, Verification and Compliance, 'New START Treaty aggregate numbers of strategic offensive arms', Fact Sheet, 30 Nov. 2012, <http://www.state.gov/t/avc/rls/201216.htm>. Under New START, each heavy bomber is counted as carrying only 1 warhead, even though the aircraft can carry larger payloads of nuclear-armed cruise missiles or nuclear gravity bombs.

[2] Russia continued to abstain from publicly releasing the full unclassified data exchanged under New START, including a breakdown of deployed and non-deployed missiles and bombers at individual bases as well as the warheads attributed to them.

[3] [National security strategy of the Russian Federation for the period until 2020], Russian Presidential Decree no. 537, 12 May 2009, <http://www.scrf.gov.ru/documents/99.html>.

Table 6.3. Russian nuclear forces, January 2013

Type/ Russian designation (NATO designation)	No. deployed	Year first deployed	Range (km)[a]	Warhead loading	No. of warheads (deployed/ assigned)[b]
Strategic offensive forces					~1 800/~2 500[c]
Bombers	72				60/810[d]
Tu-95MS6 (Bear-H6)	29	1981	6 500–10 500	6 x AS-15A ALCMs, bombs	24/174
Tu-95MS16 (Bear-H16)	30	1981	6 500–10 500	16 x AS-15A ALCMs, bombs	25/480
Tu-160 (Blackjack)	13	1987	10 500–13 200	12 x AS-15B ALCMs or AS-16 SRAMs, bombs	11/156
ICBMs	326				1 050/1 050
RS-20V (SS-18 Satan)	55	1992	11 000–15 000	10 x 500–800 kt	550/550
RS-18 (SS-19 Stiletto)	35	1980	10 000	6 x 400 kt	210/210
RS-12M Topol (SS-25 Sickle)	140	1985	10 500	1 x 800 kt	140/140
RS-12M2 Topol-M (SS-27, silo)	60	1997	10 500	1 x 800 kt	60/60
RS-12M1 Topol-M (SS-27)	18	2006	10 500	1 x (800 kt)	18/18
RS-24 Yars, mobile (SS-27 Mod 2)	18	2010	10 500	(4) x (100 kt)	72/72
RS-24 Yars, silo (SS-27 Mod 2)	–	2013	10 500	(4) x (100 kt)	–/–
SLBMs	160				448/624[e]
RSM-50 Volna (SS-N-18 M1 Stingray)	48	1978	6 500	3 x 50 kt	96/144
RSM-54 Sineva (SS-N-23 Skiff)	96	1986/2007	9 000	4 x 100 kt	256/384
RSM-56 Bulava (SS-NX-32)	16	2013	>8 050	6 x (100 kt)	96/96
Non-strategic forces					–/(~2 000)[f]
ABM, air/coastal defence[g]	~1 100				–/(~425)
53T6 (SH-08, Gazelle)	68	1986	30	1 x 10 kt	–/(68)
S-300 (SA-10/12/20)	1 000	1980	..	1 x low kt	–/(~340)
SSC-1B (Sepal)	34	1973	500	1 x 350	–/(~17)
Air force weapons[h]	430				–/(~730)
Tu-22M3 (Backfire-C)	150	1974	..	3 x ASM, bombs	–/(~450)
Su-24M/M2 (Fencer-D)	260	1974	..	2 x bombs	–/(~260)
Su-34 (Fullback)	20	2006	..	2 x bombs	–/(~20)
Army weapons[i]	170				–/(~170)
OTR-21 Tochka (SS-21 Scarab)	140	1981	120	(1 x 10 kt)	–/(~140)
Iskander (SS-26 Stone)	30	2005	500	(1 x 10 kt)	–/(~30)
Navy weapons					–/(~700)
Submarines/surface ships/air		SLCM, ASW, SAM, depth bombs, torpedoes[j]			
Total deployed/assigned warheads					~1 800/4 500
Retired awaiting dismantlement					~4 000
Total inventory					~8 500

.. = not available or not applicable; ( ) = uncertain figure; ABM = anti-ballistic missiles; ALCM = air-launched cruise missile; ASM = air-to-surface missile; ASW = anti-submarine warfare; ICBM = intercontinental ballistic missile; kt = kiloton; SAM = surface-to-air missile; SLBM = submarine-launched ballistic missile; SLCM = sea-launched cruise missile; SRAM = short-range attack missile.

[a] Aircraft range is for illustrative purposes only; actual mission range will vary according to flight profile and weapon loading.

[b] In this column, the first number is the estimated number of warheads deployed to each delivery system, and the second number is the estimated number of warheads assigned to the delivery system.

[c] This first total includes warheads estimated to be counted by New START plus approximately 300 bomber weapons that are thought to be present at bomber bases. Unlike the New START Treaty, it also includes full SSBN loads. A further 700 strategic warheads are estimated to be in reserve for SSBNs and bombers.

[d] Of the 810 weapons that are estimated to be assigned to long-range bombers, only 300 are estimated to be present at the bomber bases. The remaining weapons are thought to be stored at central storage facilities.

[e] Two or three of the SSBNs are in overhaul at any given time and do not carry their assigned nuclear missiles and warheads.

[f] According to the Russian Government, all non-strategic nuclear warheads are in storage, and so they are not counted in the total deployed warheads. In addition to the 2000 warheads available for non-strategic nuclear-capable forces listed here, another 2000–3000 warheads are estimated to have been retired and awaiting dismantlement.

[g] The 51T6 (SH-11 Gorgon) is no longer operational. The S-300 system is thought to have some nuclear capability, but there is uncertainty about which and how many of the different interceptors (SA-10 Grumble, SA-12 Gargoyle, SA-12A Gladiator, SA-12B Giant, SA-21 Growler) have nuclear capability. Some air-defence missiles may have a limited capability against some ballistic missiles. Only c. one-third of the 1000 deployed air-defence launchers are counted as having nuclear capability.

[h] These figures assume that only half of Russia's land-based strike aircraft have nuclear missions.

[i] According to the North Atlantic Treaty Organization (NATO) International Military Staff, Russia's Zapad and Ladoga exercises held in Aug.–Sep. 2009 included 'missile launches, some of which may have simulated the use of tactical nuclear weapons'. Daalder, I., US Ambassador to NATO, 'NATO–Russia: NAC discusses Russian military exercises', Cable to US State Department no. USNATO546, 23 Nov. 2009, <http://wikileaks.org/cable/2009/11/09USNATO546.html>.

[j] Surface ships are not thought to be assigned nuclear torpedoes.

Sources: Russian Ministry of Defence press releases; US Department of State, START Treaty Memoranda of Understanding, 1990–July 2009, and New START aggregate data releases, 2012; US Air Force, National Air and Space Intelligence Center (NASIC), *Ballistic and Cruise Missile Threat* (NASIC: Wright-Patterson Air Force Base, OH, June 2009); World News Connection, National Technical Information Service (NTIS), US Department of Commerce, various issues; Russian news media; Russian Strategic Nuclear Forces, <http://www.russian forces.org/>; International Institute for Strategic Studies, *The Military Balance 2010* (Routledge: London, 2010); Cochran, T. B. et al., *Nuclear Weapons Databook*, vol. 4, *Soviet Nuclear Weapons* (Harper & Row: New York, 1989); *Jane's Strategic Weapon Systems*, various issues; *Proceedings*, US Naval Institute, various issues; 'Nuclear notebook', *Bulletin of the Atomic Scientists*, various issues; and authors' estimates.

and their ability to evade missile defences.[4] Russia is working towards the former goal by introducing more survivable systems such as road-mobile ICBMs and new-generation nuclear-powered ballistic missile submarines (SSBNs) and SLBMs. To reach the latter goal, it is testing ICBM payloads designed to penetrate missile defences and developing a new heavy ICBM. The Russian Government pledged firm financial and organizational support to these programmes on a number of occasions in 2012. It reportedly spent 27.4 billion roubles ($933 million) on nuclear armaments in 2012 and plans to spend 29.3 billion roubles ($998 million) in 2013, 33.3 billion roubles ($1134 million) in 2014 and 38.6 billion roubles ($1314 million) in 2015.[5]

Strategic bombers

Russia's Long-range Aviation Command includes 13 Tu-160, 30 Tu-95MS16 and 29 Tu-95MS6 bombers. The maximum loading on these bombers is about 810 nuclear weapons, of which 200–300 may be stored at the bomber bases.[6] In 2012 the command conducted 'over 35' strategic bomber sorties, continuing the routine practice that was resumed in 2007 after having been suspended in 1992.[7] On 19 October 2012, the bombers successfully launched four cruise missiles as part of what appears to have been a larger military exercise. All missiles reached Pemboi testing ground, Komi Republic, and one was shot down by a Pantsyr'-S mobile air defence system.[8]

Russia continues its efforts to upgrade and extend the service life of its ageing Tu-95MS bombers. The Russian Ministry of Defence announced in September 2012 that the modernization of the bombers' electronic equipment would begin in 2013. This would allow the Tu-95MS to remain in service until the new strategic bomber, known as the PAK DA (from the Russian abbreviation of advanced aviation complex for long-range aviation), enters service, which is not expected before 2025. Only 'a few tens' of the 59 remaining Tu-95MS aircraft will be modernized, and the rest will

[4] Umnov, S., [Russia's SNF: building up ballistic missile defence penetration capacities], *Voenno-Promyshlennyi Kur'er*, 8–14 Mar. 2006; and Esin, V., [The United States: in pursuit of a global missile defence], *Voenno-Promyshlennyi Kur'er*, 25–31 Aug. 2010.

[5] [Russia plans to spend more than 100 billion roubles on nuclear weapons by 2015], RIA Novosti, 17 Oct. 2012, <http://ria.ru/atomtec_news/20121017/903330028.html>; Putin, V., 'Being strong', *Foreign Policy*, 21 Feb. 2012; and President of Russia, [Meeting concerning implementation of the state arms procurement programme in the area of nuclear deterrence], 26 July 2012, <http://kremlin.ru/news/16058>. On total Russian military expenditure see chapter 3, section III, in this volume.

[6] Kristensen, H.M., *Trimming Nuclear Excess: Options for Further Reductions of U.S. and Russian Nuclear Forces*, Federation of Atomic Scientists (FAS) Special Report no. 5 (FAS: Washington, DC, Dec. 2012).

[7] Russian Ministry of Defence, [Long-range aviation patrols became routine], 2 Jan. 2012, <http://function.mil.ru/news_page/world/more.htm?id=11569911@egNews>.

[8] 'Bombers launch cruise missiles in a strategic forces exercise', Russian Strategic Nuclear Forces, 19 Oct. 2012, <http://russianforces.org/blog/2012/10/bombers_launch_cruise_missiles.shtml>.

be retired.[9] Russia is also modernizing its Tu-160 bombers and Il-78 refuelling aircraft.[10]

Land-based ballistic missiles

As of January 2013 Russia's Strategic Rocket Forces (SRF)—the branch of the armed forces that controls Russia's ICBMs—consisted of 12 missile divisions grouped into three armies and deploying a total of 326 ICBMs of different types. The RS-20V (designated SS-18 by NATO) and RS-18 (SS-19) liquid-fuelled, silo-based ICBMs, which date from the Soviet era, are expected to be gradually phased-out by 2020 and the RS-18 replaced by a new liquid-propellant missile currently under development.[11] The Commander of the SRF, Colonel-General Sergei Karakaev, stated in December 2012 that the service life of the RS-18 would be extended to 2019 and the RS-20V to 2022.[12] The solid-fuelled road-mobile RS-12M Topol (SS-25) is also planned to be retired by 2019; meanwhile it is undergoing a life-extension programme. During 2012, the programme included test-launches on 7 June (which also tested missile defence countermeasures) and 19 October.[13]

The solid-fuel RS-12 Topol-M (SS-27 Mod 1) has been developed in both road-mobile (RS-12M1) and silo-based (RS-12M2) versions.[14] In 2010 the SRF abandoned further procurement of the RS-12M1 in favour of the mobile version of the RS-24 Yars (SS-27 Mod 2), which is a variant of the RS-12M1 with multiple independently targetable re-entry vehicles (MIRV); deployment began in 2011. By the end of 2012 the SRF had 18 operational RS-24 missiles, all of which were deployed with the 54th Guards Missile Division (GMD), based in Teykovo District, Ivanovo Oblast.[15] Preparations began to replace the RS-12Ms of the 29th GMD at Irkutsk and the 39th GMD at Novosibirsk with the mobile version of the RS-24.[16] In 2012 the decision was taken to also stop procurement of the RS-12M2; the last

[9] Mikhailov, A., [Strategic bomber 'Bear' is left in service], *Izvestiya*, 20 Sep. 2012.

[10] [First flying prototype of the PAK DA is planned for 2017], *Vzglyad*, 23 Dec. 2012, <http://vz.ru/news/2012/12/23/613368.html>.

[11] Isby, D. C., 'Russian exercise highlights SRF modernization plans', *Jane's Missiles and Rockets*, vol. 16, no. 12 (Dec. 2012), p. 4.

[12] 'Russia's Voyevoda ICBM to remain in service for another decade—commander', Interfax-AVN, 15 Dec. 2012, Translation from Russian, BBC Monitoring International Reports.

[13] 'Test of Topol from Kapustin Yar', 7 June 2012, Russian Strategic Nuclear Forces, <http://russianforces.org/blog/2012/06/test_of_topol_from_kapustin_ya.shtml>; and Isby (note 11).

[14] Lennox, D. (ed.), *Jane's Strategic Weapon Systems*, no. 54 (IHS Global Limited: Coulsdon, 2011), p. 175.

[15] 'Topol-M and RS-24 Yars deployment plans', 14 Dec. 2012, Russian Strategic Nuclear Forces, <http://russianforces.org/blog/2012/12/topol-m_and_rs-24_yars_deploym.shtml>.

[16] Russian Ministry of Defence, [Two more missile divisions will be re-equipped with the new missile system 'Yars'], 19 Dec. 2011, <http://function.mil.ru/news_page/country/more.htm?id=10854015@egNews>.

four missiles of this kind were put into service with the 60th Missile Division at Tatischevo Airbase, Saratov Oblast. Preparations began in 2012 to equip the 28th GMD, based at Kozelsk, Kaluga Oblast, with the silo version of the RS-24, which will replace the RS-18.[17] From 2013, all new silo-based ICBMs will be RS-24s.[18]

On 23 May and 24 October 2012 the SRF was reported to have launched two new mobile ICBMs of an unspecified type, although they were probably RS-24s with modified payloads.[19]

Ballistic missile submarines and sea-launched ballistic missiles

As of January 2013 the Russian Navy operated a total of 10 SSBNs: 7 with the Northern Fleet and 3 with the Pacific Fleet.

Three Project 667BDR Kalmar (designated Delta III class by NATO) submarines, each carrying 16 RSM-50 Volna (SS-N-18 M1) SLBMs, were assigned to the Pacific Fleet. One of them, the K-433 *Svyatoy Georgiy Pobedonosets*, successfully test-launched an RSM-50 SLBM on 19 October 2012.[20] Six Project 667BDRM Delfin (Delta IV class) submarines, each carrying 16 RSM-54 Sineva (SS-N-23) SLBMs, were assigned to the Northern Fleet. One of them, the K-84 *Ekaterinburg*, was damaged in December 2011 and is not expected to be back in service until 2014.[21]

On 10 January 2013 Russia's first Project 955 Borei SSBN, the K-535 *Yuri Dolgoruky*, entered service with the Northern Fleet. The second submarine of this class, the K-550 *Alexander Nevsky*, is still undergoing sea trials, while the third, *Vladimir Monomakh*, was launched on 30 December 2012.[22] The construction of the *Knyaz Vladimir*, the first SSBN of an upgraded Project 955A Borei class, began in July 2012.[23] Russia plans to build a total of eight Borei SSBNs, equipped with RSM-56 Bulava (SS-NX-32) SLBMs, to replace the existing Kalmar and Delfin SSBNs.

[17] [Fifth generation missile complex is being deployed in Kaluga region], TV Zvezda, 12 July 2012, <http://tvzvezda.ru/news/forces/content/201207122252-8xqt.htm>.

[18] Isby, D. C., 'Silo-based Yars ICBMs to enter service', *Jane's Missiles and Rockets*, vol. 17, no. 1 (Jan. 2013), p. 6.

[19] Safronov, I., ['Bulava' surfaced in Plesetsk], *Kommersant*, 24 May 2012; and 'New ICBM tested in Kapustin Yar', Russian Strategic Nuclear Forces, 24 Oct. 2012, <http://russianforces.org/blog/2012/10/new_icbm_tested_in_kapustin_ya.shtml>.

[20] 'Russia successfully tests ballistic missiles', Russia Today, 30 Oct. 2012, <http://rt.com/news/bulava-sineva-topol-launch/>.

[21] Kile, S. N. et al., 'Russian nuclear forces', *SIPRI Yearbook 2012*, p. 320.

[22] 'Russia to lay down two improved Borey class subs in 2013', RIA Novosti, 14 Jan. 2013, <http://en.ria.ru/military_news/20130114/178766923/Russia_to_Lay_Down_Two_Improved_Borey_Class_Subs_in_2013.html>.

[23] 'Putin attends nuclear sub ceremony', RIA Novosti, 30 July 2012, <http://en.rian.ru/military_news/20120730/174865317.html>.

In addition, one Project 941 Akula (Typhoon class) submarine has been converted for use as a test platform. It is not considered part of the armed SSBN force.[24]

Non-strategic nuclear weapons

There is considerable uncertainty about the size and location of Russia's non-strategic nuclear inventory. The estimate made here is that there are approximately 2000 warheads available to Russian forces with another 2000 retired and awaiting dismantlement (see table 6.3). This estimate is based on previous estimates of the Soviet non-strategic warheads arsenal, information released in connection with the 1991–92 Presidential Nuclear Initiatives (PNIs) and statements by Russian officials on the progress in non-strategic weapon reductions under the PNIs, as well as analysis of the Russian order of battle and of a nominal delivery platform warhead loading.[25] The estimate is consistent with a statement made in November 2011 by the US Department of Defense that unclassified estimates set the Russian inventory at approximately 2000–4000 non-strategic nuclear weapons.[26]

Another study published in 2012 suggests that the number of Russian 'operationally assigned' non-strategic nuclear warheads may be as low as approximately 1000, with the total stockpile being about 1900.[27] This study assumes that non-strategic nuclear warheads are assigned not to individual delivery vehicles but to nuclear-capable military units, which have a fixed number of nuclear warheads assigned to them.

[24] 'Russia set to keep Typhoon class nuclear subs until 2019—Navy', RIA Novosti, 7 May 2010, <http://en.rian.ru/mlitary_news/20100507/158917310.html>.

[25] For more information see Kristensen, H. M., *Non-Strategic Nuclear Weapons*, Federation of American Scientists (FAS) Special Report no. 3 (FAS: Washington, DC, May 2012), pp. 51–65. See also Kristensen (note 6), pp. 26–27.

[26] Miller, J., Principal Deputy Under Secretary of Defense for Policy, Statement before the US House of Representatives, Armed Services Committee, 2 Nov. 2011, <http://armedservices.house.gov/index.cfm/2011/11/the-current-status-and-future-direction-for-u-s-nuclear-weapons-policy-and-posture>, p. 2; and Kile (note 21), p. 321.

[27] Sutyagin, I., *Atomic Accounting: A New Estimate of Russia's Non-Strategic Nuclear Forces*, Occasional Paper (Royal United Services Institute: London, Nov. 2012), pp. 2–3.

III. British nuclear forces

SHANNON N. KILE AND HANS M. KRISTENSEN

The United Kingdom's nuclear deterrent consists exclusively of a sea-based component: Vanguard class Trident nuclear-powered ballistic missile submarines (SSBNs) armed with Trident II (designated D5) submarine-launched ballistic missiles (SLBMs) and associated warheads, and their support infrastructure. The UK possesses an arsenal of about 160 operational nuclear warheads that are available for use by a fleet of four Trident SSBNs based at Faslane, Scotland (see table 6.4). The UK leases 58 Trident II (D5) SLBMs from the United States Navy under a system of 'mingled asset ownership'.

Each Vanguard class SSBN is equipped with 16 Trident II missiles carrying up to 48 warheads. The warhead is similar to the US W76 warhead; it has been upgraded with the US-produced arming, fusing and firing system for the Trident II's Mk-4A re-entry vehicle, which improves the accuracy of the missile and increases its ability to destroy hardened targets.[1] While each Trident II missile can carry three warheads, it is believed that a number of them are deployed with only one warhead, possibly with a reduced explosive yield. This reflects a decision by the British Ministry of Defence (MOD) in 1998 to give a 'sub-strategic', or limited-strike, role to the Trident fleet, with the intention of enhancing the flexibility of nuclear targeting options—specifically, 'an option for a limited strike that would not automatically lead to a full scale nuclear exchange'.[2] An addendum in 2002 extended the role of nuclear weapons to include deterring 'leaders of states of concern and terrorist organisations'.[3]

In a posture known as Continuous At-Sea Deterrence (CASD), one British SSBN is on patrol at all times.[4] While the second and third SSBNs can be put to sea rapidly, the fourth would take longer because of its cycle of extensive overhaul and maintenance. Since the end of the cold war, the SSBN on patrol has been kept at a level of reduced readiness with its missiles de-targeted and a 'notice to fire' measured in days.[5]

---

[1] According to some reports, the UK is procuring the US-produced W76-1 warhead for its Trident missiles. Kristensen, H. M., 'British submarines to receive upgraded US nuclear warhead', Strategic Security Blog, Federation of American Scientists, 1 Apr. 2011, <http://blogs.fas.org/security/2011/04/britishw76-1/>.

[2] British Ministry of Defence, The Strategic Defence Review: Modern Forces for the Modern World, Cm 3999 (The Stationery Office: London, July 1998), para. 63.

[3] British Ministry of Defence, The Strategic Defence Review: A New Chapter, Cm 5566, vol. 1 (Stationery Office: London, July 2002), para. 21.

[4] British Ministry of Defence and British Foreign and Commonwealth Office, The Future of the United Kingdom's Nuclear Deterrent, Cm 6994 (Stationery Office: London, Dec. 2006), p. 27.

[5] British Ministry of Defence and British Foreign and Commonwealth Office (note 4), p. 13.

Table 6.4. British nuclear forces, January 2013

Type	Designation	No. deployed	Year first deployed	Range (km)^a	Warheads x yield	Warheads in stockpile
Submarine-launched ballistic missiles						
D5	Trident II	48	1994	>7 400	1–3 x 100 kilotons	225^b

^{a} Range is for illustrative purposes only; actual mission range will vary according to flight profile and weapon loading.

^{b} Fewer than 160 warheads are operationally available, *c.* 144 to arm 48 missiles on 3 of 4 nuclear-powered ballistic missile submarines (SSBNs). Only 1 SSBN is on patrol at any time, with up to 48 warheads.

Sources: British Ministry of Defence, white papers, press releases and website, <https://www.gov.uk/government/organisations/ministry-of-defence>; British House of Commons, *Hansard*, various issues; Norris, R. S. et al., *Nuclear Weapons Databook*, vol. 5, *British, French, and Chinese Nuclear Weapons* (Westview: Boulder, CO, 1994), p. 9; 'Nuclear notebook', *Bulletin of the Atomic Scientists*, various issues; and authors' estimates.

On 23 October 2012 the submarine HMS *Vigilant* successfully test-fired a Trident II SLBM in the Atlantic Ocean off the coast of Florida. The test was part of a demonstration and shakedown operation (DASO) for HMS *Vigilant*'s return to service following a three-year mid-life overhaul and reactor refuelling period. It was the British Royal Navy's first flight test of a Trident missile since 2009 and its 10th overall.[6]

In the 2010 Strategic Defence and Security Review (SDSR) the British Government made a commitment to retain a continuous submarine-based nuclear deterrent force for the indefinite future.[7] The MOD currently plans to replace the four Vanguard class SSBNs, which will reach the end of their service lives from 2024, with new submarines equipped with modified Trident II (D5) SLBMs at an estimated initial cost of £20 billion ($37 billion) at 2006 prices.[8] As a cost-saving measure they will have a smaller missile compartment equipped with 8 launch tubes carrying no more than 40 warheads.[9] The SDSR deferred the 'main gate' decision—on when the detailed acquisition plans, design and number of the successor submarines are to be finalized—until 2016. In 2011 the MOD announced the completion of the 'initial gate' phase setting out the broad design parameters for the new SSBN class.[10] In June 2012 it awarded a £1 billion ($1.6 billion) contract for

[6] British House of Commons, Written Answers to Questions, *Hansard*, 19 Nov. 2012, Column 238W; and 'Royal Navy conducts test firing of Trident missile', Nuclear Information Service, 3 Nov. 2012, <http://www.nuclearinfo.org/article/uk-trident/royal-navy-conducts-test-firing-trident-missile>.

[7] British Ministry of Defence, *Securing Britain in an Age of Uncertainty: The Strategic Defence and Security Review*, Cm 7948 (Stationery Office: London, Oct. 2010), paras 3.8–3.9.

[8] British Ministry of Defence (note 7), para. 3.10.

[9] British Ministry of Defence (note 7), paras 3.11–3.12, 3.14.

[10] British Ministry of Defence (MOD), *The United Kingdom's Future Nuclear Deterrent: The Submarine Initial Gate Parliamentary Report* (MOD: London, May 2011), p. 4.

refurbishing the plant that will build nuclear reactors for the next generation of attack and ballistic missile submarines.[11]

The cost of the proposed plan to replace the existing Trident fleet with a 'like for like' system has drawn criticism from the Liberal Democrat party, the smaller of the two parties in the current governing coalition. As part of its coalition deal with the Conservative party in 2010, it demanded a formal review of 'credible and compelling' nuclear deterrence alternatives.[12] Potential alternatives under consideration include acquiring nuclear cruise missiles or a multi-role submarine, or abandoning the CASD posture.[13] While the report of the Trident Alternatives Review is due in June 2013, critics have pointed out that it will be difficult to halt the successor submarine replacement programme given the amount of investment already made.[14] If the programme is given final approval, the new submarine is expected to enter service beginning in 2028.

The 2010 SDR revealed plans for cutting the size of the British nuclear arsenal. The stockpile of operational nuclear warheads will be reduced from fewer than 160 at present to no more than 120, of which 40 will be on patrol at any given time. Likewise, the overall size of the nuclear stockpile, including non-deployed weapons, will decrease from the current 225 warheads to 'not more than 180 by the mid 2020s'.[15]

[11] Watts, N., 'Coalition faces split over Trident nuclear replacement', *The Guardian*, 17 June 2012.

[12] Hopkins, N., 'Trident: no need for like-for-like replacement, says Danny Alexander', *The Guardian*, 23 Jan. 2013.

[13] Lehrke, D. L., 'Deterrent dilemma: UK examines its nuclear options', *Jane's Intelligence Review*, Aug. 2012, pp. 49–53.

[14] 'Minister Danny Alexander dismisses Trident replacement', BBC News, 23 Jan. 2013, <http://www.bbc.co.uk/news/uk-politics-21155000>; and Hopkins, N. and Norton-Taylor, R., 'New Trident nukes seem certain despite Lib Dem concerns', Guardian Defence and Security Blog, 22 June 2012, <http://www.guardian.co.uk/uk/defence-and-security-blog/2012/jun/22/trident-nuclear-weapons>.

[15] British Ministry of Defence (note 7), para. 3.11.

IV. French nuclear forces

PHILLIP SCHELL AND HANS M. KRISTENSEN

France's nuclear arsenal consists of approximately 300 warheads for delivery by submarine-launched ballistic missiles (SLBMs) and air-launched cruise missiles (see table 6.5).[1]

Four Triomphant class nuclear-powered ballistic missile submarines (SSBNs) form the backbone of France's nuclear deterrent. France is currently upgrading its SSBNs to the new M51.1 SLBM, replacing the ageing M45 missile. As of early 2013 two submarines, *Le Terrible* and *Le Vigilant*, are equipped to be armed with up to 16 M51.1 SLBMs. *Le Vigilant* completed its overhaul in October 2012 and is expected to be fully operational again in the summer of 2013.[2] The third SSBN, *Le Triomphant*, is preparing to begin this process. The overhaul of all four submarines is expected to be completed by 2018.[3] An improved version of the M51.1 SLBM, the M51.2, is designed to carry the new Tête Nucléaire Océanique (TNO, Oceanic Nuclear Warhead) with a yield of up to 150 kilotons and will replace the M51.1 after 2015.[4]

The air-based component of the French nuclear forces consists of two types of land-based (Mirage 2000N and Rafale F3) and one type of sea-based (Rafale M F3) nuclear-capable combat aircraft. The Mirage 2000Ns are scheduled to be replaced by Rafales in 2018. The aircraft are equipped with the Air–Sol Moyenne Portée–Améliorée (ASMP-A, Medium-Range Air-to-Surface–Improved) missile. The missiles are armed with the Tête Nucléaire Aeroportée (TNA, Airborne Nuclear Warhead), a new thermonuclear warhead that is reported to have a selectable yield of 20, 90 or 300 kilotons.[5]

---

[1] For an in-depth review of French nuclear forces see Kristensen, H. M., 'France', ed. R. Acheson, *Assuring Destruction Forever: Nuclear Weapon Modernization around the World* (Reaching Critical Will: New York, 2012), pp. 27–33.

[2] 'Le SNLE Le Vigilant retrouve l'Île Longue' [The SSBN Le Vigilant returns to Île Longue], Mer et Marine, 22 Oct. 2012, <http://www.meretmarine.com/fr/content/le-snle-le-vigilant-retrouve-lile-longue>.

[3] Lennox, D. (ed.), *Jane's Strategic Weapon Systems*, no. 54 (IHS Global Limited: Coulsdon, 2011), p. 51; and French Senate, *Avis présenté au nom de la commission des affaires étrangères, de la défense et des forces armées (1) sur le projet de loi de finances pour 2013* [Opinions submitted on behalf of the Committee on Foreign Affairs, Defence and Armed Forces (1) on the finance bill for 2013], vol. 8, *Défense: Equipement des forces* [Defence: equipping the forces], no. 150 (French Senate: Paris, 22 Nov. 2012), pp. 46–47.

[4] ed. Lennox (note 3), p. 50.

[5] 'Les derniers ASMPA ont été livrés fin 2011' [The last ASMPAs were delivered in late 2011], Mere et Marine, 26 Feb. 2012, <http://www.meretmarine.com/fr/content/les-derniers-asmpa-ont-ete-livres-fin-2011>; and ed. Lennox (note 3), p. 48.

Table 6.5. French nuclear forces, January 2013

Type	No. deployed	Year first deployed	Range (km)[a]	Warheads x yield	No. of warheads
Land-based aircraft					
Mirage 2000N	~20	1988	2 750	1 x up to 300 kt TNA	~20
Rafale F3	~20	2010–11	2 000	1 x up to 300 kt TNA	~20
Carrier-based aircraft					
Rafale M F3	~10	2010–11	2 000	1 x up to 300 kt TNA	~10
Submarine-launched ballistic missiles[b]					
M45	32	1996	6 000[c]	4–6 x 100 kt TN-75	160[d]
M51.1	16	2010–11	6 000	4–6 x 100 kt TN-75	80
M51.2	–	(2015)	6 000	4–6 x TNO	–
Total					~290[e]

( ) = uncertain figure; kt = kiloton; TNA = Tête Nucléaire Aéroportée; TNO = Tête Nucléaire Océanique.

[a] Aircraft range is for illustrative purposes only; actual mission range will vary according to flight profile and weapon loading.

[b] France transitioned to a posture of 4 SSBNs in the mid-1990s, which meant having enough SLBMs to equip 3 operational SSBNs, with the 4th SSBN being overhauled.

[c] The range of the M45 is listed as only 4000 km in a 2001 report from the French National Assembly's National Defence Commission.

[d] The missile upgrade started with the *Le Vigilant* submarine does not affect its warheads, which will be fitted back to the new M51.1 missiles.

[e] France does not have a reserve but may have a small inventory of spare warheads for a total stockpile of *c.* 300 warheads.

Sources: Sarkozy, N., French President, Speech on defence and national security, Porte de Versailles, 17 June 2008, <http://archives.livreblancdefenseetsecurite.gouv.fr/information/les_dossiers_actualites_19/livre_blanc_sur_defense_875/livre_blanc_1337/discours_president_republique_1338/>; Sarkozy, N., French President, 'Presentation of SSBM "Le Terrible"', Speech, Cherbourg, 21 Mar. 2008, <https://pastel.diplomatie.gouv.fr/editorial/actual/ael2/bulletin.gb.asp?liste=20080331.gb.html>; French Ministry of Defence, various publications, <http://www.defense.gouv.fr/>; French National Assembly, various defence bills; Norris, R. S. et al., *Nuclear Weapons Databook*, vol. 5, *British, French, and Chinese Nuclear Weapons* (Westview: Boulder, CO, 1994), p. 10; *Air Actualités*, various issues; *Aviation Week & Space Technology*, various issues; 'Nuclear notebook', *Bulletin of the Atomic Scientists*, various issues; and authors' estimates.

V. Chinese nuclear forces

PHILLIP SCHELL AND HANS M. KRISTENSEN

Among the five legally recognized nuclear weapon states, China has long been the least transparent about its nuclear forces. The Chinese Government provides no official information about the size and composition of its nuclear forces. It is estimated that China maintains a total stockpile of about 250 nuclear warheads, indicating a gradual expansion of its nuclear arsenal. It is widely believed that in peacetime China stores its nuclear warheads in storage facilities separate from their delivery vehicles and that they are not ready for immediate launch.[1] Of its planned triad of land, air and maritime nuclear forces, only the land-based ballistic missiles and nuclear-configured aircraft are currently considered operational: about 185 of the total stockpile of 250 warheads are assigned to these forces. None are deployed on delivery systems but are thought to be in central storage. The remaining warheads are assigned to non-operational forces, including new systems that are under development, operational systems that will increase in number in the future and spares (see table 6.6).

The Second Artillery of the Chinese People's Liberation Army (PLA) maintains strict control over China's nuclear arsenal and land-based missiles through a centralized management system, in which missile units appear to be organized into six geographically dispersed basing areas and one central storage facility.[2] The Second Artillery reports directly to the Chinese Government's Central Military Commission (CMC), chaired by President Xi Jinping.[3] The year 2012 was an active period of missile testing: the Second Artillery reportedly test launched all types of its nuclear-capable missile arsenal.

The modernization and moderate expansion of China's nuclear arsenal is part of a long-term programme that can be linked to improvements being made by other countries in advanced offensive and defensive non-nuclear weapon systems that might threaten China's nuclear forces. The modernization of China's nuclear forces is aimed at developing a more survivable force and strengthening its nuclear retaliatory capabilities. To achieve these goals, China is focusing on qualitative modernization, rather than a

---

[1] See e.g. Zhang, H., 'China', ed. R. Acheson, *Assuring Destruction Forever: Nuclear Weapon Modernization around the World* (Reaching Critical Will: New York, 2012), p. 17; and Li Bin, 'Tracking Chinese strategic mobile missiles', *Science and Global Security*, vol. 15, no. 1 (2007), p. 11.

[2] Stokes, M. A., *China's Nuclear Warhead Storage and Handling System* (Project 2049 Institute: Arlington, VA, 12 Mar. 2010), p. 7.

[3] Gill, B. and Medeiros, E. S., 'China', eds H. Born, B. Gill and H. Hänggi, SIPRI, *Governing the Bomb: Civilian Control and Democratic Accountability of Nuclear Weapons* (Oxford University Press: Oxford, 2010), p. 147.

Table 6.6. Chinese nuclear forces, January 2013

Type/Chinese designation (US designation)	No. deployed	Year first deployed	Range (km)[a]	Warhead loading	No. of warheads[b]
Land-based missiles[c]	~144				~144
DF-3A (CSS-2)	~12	1971	3 100[d]	1 x 3.3 Mt	~12
DF-4 (CSS-3)	~12	1980	5 500	1 x 3.3 Mt	~12
DF-5A (CSS-4)	20	1981	13 000	1 x 4–5 Mt	20
DF-15 (CSS-6)	~350	1990	600	1 x ..	..
DF-21 (CSS-5)	~60	1991	2 100[e]	1 x 200–300 kt	~60
DF-31 (CSS-10 Mod 1)	~20	2006	>7 200	1 x 200–300 kt?	~20
DF-31A (CSS-10 Mod 2)	~20	2007	>11 200	1 x 200–300 kt?	~20
SLBMs	(48)				(48)
JL-1 (CSS-N-3)	(12)	1986	>1 770	1 x 200–300 kt	(12)
JL-2 (CSS-NX-14)	(36)	(2013)	>7 400	1 x 200–300 kt?	(36)
Aircraft[f]	>20				(40)
H-6 (B-6)	~20	1965	3 100	1 x bomb	(~20)
Attack	..	1972–..	..	1 x bomb	(~20)
Cruise missiles	150–350				..
DH-10	150–350	2007	>1 500	1 x ..	..[g]
Total					**(~250)**[h]

.. = not available or not applicable; ( ) = uncertain figure; kt = kiloton; Mt = Megaton; SLBM = submarine-launched ballistic missile.

[a] Aircraft range is for illustrative purposes only; actual mission range will vary.

[b] A distinction can be made between warheads assigned to operational forces and warheads assigned to non-operational forces. Only China's land-based ballistic missiles and nuclear-configured aircraft are considered operational, comprising a total of *c*. 185 nuclear warheads assigned to operational forces. The second category includes warheads produced for systems that are not yet operational (SLBMs), warheads produced for operational systems that will increase in number (DF-31/A), and spares.

[c] China defines missile ranges as short-range, <1000 km; medium-range, 1000–3000 km; long-range, 3000–8000 km; and intercontinental range, >8000 km.

[d] The range of the DF-3A may be greater than is normally reported.

[e] The DF-21A (CSS-5 Mod 2) variant is believed to have a range of up to 2500 km.

[f] Figures for aircraft are for nuclear-configured versions only.

[g] It is unclear if the DH-10 has nuclear capability, but US Air Force intelligence lists the weapon as 'conventional or nuclear', the same as for the Russian nuclear-capable AS-4. The US Department of Defense, however, does not list the DH-10 as nuclear-capable.

[h] Additional warheads are thought to be in storage to arm future DF-31, DF-31A and JL-2 missiles. The total stockpile is believed to comprise *c*. 250 warheads.

Sources: US Department of Defense, *Military Power of the People's Republic of China*, various years; US Air Force, National Air and Space Intelligence Center (NASIC), various documents; US Central Intelligence Agency, various documents; Kristensen, H. M., Norris, R. S. and McKinzie, M. G., *Chinese Nuclear Forces and U.S. Nuclear War Planning* (Federation of American Scientists/Natural Resources Defense Council: Washington, DC, Nov. 2006); Norris, R. S. et al., *Nuclear Weapons Databook*, vol. 5, *British, French, and Chinese Nuclear Weapons* (Westview: Boulder, CO, 1994); 'Nuclear notebook', *Bulletin of the Atomic Scientists*, various issues; Google Earth; and authors' estimates.

simple increase in the number of nuclear weapons.[4] This perspective on the modernization of China's nuclear forces was reiterated by the latest Chinese Government biennial defence white paper, released in March 2011.[5] The document repeated China's commitment to the policy of no-first-use of nuclear weapons and its intention to limit its nuclear capabilities to the minimum level required for national security. However, it provided no information about the size or structure of China's nuclear forces.

China is estimated to possess the smallest inventories of military highly enriched uranium (HEU) and plutonium of the legally recognized nuclear weapon states (see section X below). Although China has never officially declared a formal moratorium on fissile material production for military purposes, it is believed to have ceased military HEU production at some time between 1987 and 1989 and military plutonium production in 1991. The current inventories mean that China could not significantly expand its nuclear warhead stockpile without restarting production of military fissile material.

In 2011 and 2012 some US and Russian academics and former officials speculated that China's nuclear arsenal could be much larger than previously estimated—as many as 1600–3000 warheads—because it may have hidden warheads and missiles in underground facilities.[6] These claims were rejected by General Robert Kehler, the commander of US Strategic Command.[7]

Land-based ballistic missiles

China is modernizing its land-based ballistic missiles and replacing ageing silo-based, liquid-fuelled missiles with newer road-mobile and solid-fuelled models. By being more mobile and able to launch their missiles more quickly, the new models will increase the survivability of the deterrent. This has become an increasingly important consideration for Chinese planners in assuring the credibility of the country's nuclear retaliatory capabilities.

The Second Artillery conducted a series of missile tests in the second half of 2012. According to an unconfirmed Western media report, it test fired all Chinese types of nuclear-capable intercontinental ballistic missile (ICBM).[8]

[4] Hu S., [The road towards China's nuclear weapons], *Huánqiú kēxué*, no. 12 (2007).
[5] Chinese State Council, *China's National Defense in 2010* (Information Office of the Chinese State Council: Beijing, Mar. 2011).
[6] Esin, V., [Third after the USA and Russia], *Voenno-Promyshlennyi Kurier*, 2 May 2012; and Stephens, B., 'How many nukes does China have?', *Wall Street Journal*, 24 Oct. 2011.
[7] Kristensen, H. M., 'STRATCOM commander rejects high estimates for Chinese nuclear arsenal', Strategic Security Blog, Federation of American Scientists, 22 Aug. 2012, <http://blogs.fas.org/security/2012/08/china-nukes/>.
[8] Gertz, B., 'Chinese missile tests continue', Washington Free Beacon, 4 Sep. 2012, <http://freebeacon.com/chinese-missile-tests-continue-2/>.

While the Chinese Ministry of National Defence acknowledged the tests, it did not specify what types of missile were launched.[9]

China's nuclear-capable ballistic missile arsenal consists of approximately 144 missiles of six different types. One of China's oldest ballistic missiles, the liquid-fuelled, single-stage Dong Feng-3A (DF-3A), is being replaced by the newer road-mobile, solid-fuelled, two-stage DF-21 medium-range ballistic missile (MRBM), which acts as a regional nuclear deterrent. Additionally, China fields the road-mobile, solid-fuelled, three-stage DF-31 ICBM, capable of reaching the western United States (Alaska), Russia and Europe. The DF-31 ICBM is replacing the ageing liquid-fuelled, two-stage DF-4 ballistic missile.

The liquid-fuelled, two-stage DF-5A and the road-mobile, solid-fuelled, three-stage DF-31A, both with an estimated range of over 10 000 kilometres, are China's furthest reaching ICBMs. It remains unclear whether the Second Artillery will replace the ageing DF-5A, which has recently been upgraded, with the DF-31A or will maintain both missile systems.

Unconfirmed Western media reports in 2012 suggesting an apparent test of a next-generation ICBM, referred to as the DF-41, revived speculation about possible Chinese follow-on ICBM systems.[10] The US Department of Defense (DOD) had previously reported that 'China may also be developing a new road-mobile ICBM, possibly capable of carrying a multiple independently targetable re-entry vehicle (MIRV)'.[11] No reliable information about the missile's status and technical characteristics is available.[12]

Following the PLA's missile trials, the Chinese state media reported that the Second Artillery had fully transitioned from 'troops in the mountains' to 'troops on wheels', referring to the evolution of China's land-based nuclear forces to road-mobile delivery vehicles from previous silo and cave-based systems.[13] The increasing number of deployed road-mobile, nuclear-capable missiles reflects the Second Artillery's emphasis on increasing the survivability and mobility of its nuclear forces. However, according to the US DOD, the Second Artillery has relatively limited experience in man-

[9] 'Defense spokesman says missile tests targeted at no specific country', Xinhua, 30 Aug. 2012, <http://news.xinhuanet.com/english/china/2012-08/30/c_131818392.htm>.

[10] Kulaki, G. 'New York Times: distorting Chinese press report on missile capabilities?', All Things Nuclear, Union of Concerned Scientists, 27 Aug. 2012, <http://allthingsnuclear.org/new-york-times-distorting-chinese-press-report-on-missile-capabilities/>; Gertz, B., 'Ready to launch', Washington Free Beacon, 21 Aug. 2012, <http://freebeacon.com/ready-to-launch/>; and Gertz, B., 'Manchu missile launch', Washington Free Beacon, 15 Aug. 2012, <http://freebeacon.com/manchu-missile-launch/>.

[11] US Department of Defense (DOD), Military and Security Developments Involving the People's Republic of China 2011, Annual Report to Congress (DOD: Washington, DC, May 2011), p. 3. The 2012 version of the report did not reiterate this statement.

[12] For a comprehensive account on the DF-41 see Lewis, J. W. and Hua D., 'China's ballistic missiles programs: technologies, strategies, goals', International Security, vol. 17, no. 2 (fall 1992), pp. 29–31.

[13] 'China's strategic missiles realize mobile launch', Global Times, 2 Sep. 2012.

aging mobile missile patrols, which could pose serious challenges for China's current command and control structures.[14]

China is also expanding its conventional DF-21 MRBM programme and has deployed the dual-capable (i.e. both conventional and nuclear-capable) DF-21C and DF-15 short-range ballistic missile (SRBM). Mixing conventional and nuclear missiles poses a critical risk of mistaken escalation of a conflict, as an adversary would not be able to determine whether the missile fired is armed with a conventional or nuclear warhead.[15]

Ballistic missile submarines

China has encountered considerable difficulties in developing a sea-based nuclear deterrent. The PLA Navy (PLAN) has built a single Type 092 (designated Xia class by NATO) nuclear-powered ballistic missile submarine (SSBN) equipped to carry 12 solid-fuelled, two-stage Ju Lang-1 (JL-1) submarine-launched ballistic missiles (SLBMs). The JL-1 is the sea-based derivative of the DF-21. The submarine has never conducted a deterrent patrol and is not thought to be fully operational, despite several refits.

The PLAN has developed a successor SSBN, the Type 094 (designated Jin class by NATO) submarine. According to the US DOD, two Type 094 SSBNs are in operational service.[16] One is believed to be associated with the PLAN's North Sea Fleet, with its home port at Jianggezhuang near Qingdao, and one with the South Sea Fleet, with its home port at Yulin on Hainan.[17] The status of a third boat under construction remains unclear. How many Type 094 SSBNs China intends to build and the future roles and missions of its current and future SSBN fleet also remain uncertain.

The Type 094 SSBN can be armed with up to 12 three-stage, solid-fuelled JL-2 SLBMs, the sea-based derivative of the DF-31. The JL-2 programme has encountered several delays due to technical difficulties. According to unconfirmed reports, what could be a series of final JL-2 flight tests conducted from a Type 094 SSBN occurred in January and August 2012.[18] In its annual report to the US Congress, in 2012 the US–China Economic and Security Review Commission projected that the Type 094–JL-2 com-

---

[14] US Department of Defense (DOD), *Military and Security Developments Involving the People's Republic of China 2012*, Annual Report to Congress (DOD: Washington, DC, May 2012), p. 25.

[15] Some analysts also believe nuclear and conventional DF-21 missiles are mixed at the same bases. See Lewis, J. W. and Xue L., 'Making China's nuclear war plan', *Bulletin of the Atomic Scientists*, vol. 68, no. 5 (Sep./Oct. 2012). Other analysts believe nuclear and conventional missiles are deployed at separate bases.

[16] US Department of Defense (note 14), p. 24.

[17] Wu R., 'Survivability of China's sea-based nuclear forces,' *Science & Global Security*, vol. 19, no. 2 (2011), pp. 94–96.

[18] Richardson, D., 'Chinese navy conducts series of Julang-2 SLBM firings', *Jane's Missiles and Rockets*, vol. 16, no. 3 (Mar. 2012), p. 10; and Gertz, 'Ready to launch' (note 10).

bination could become operational within two years.[19] The US DOD reiterated this assessment and further expressed concerns that the progress in China's sea-based nuclear forces will also pose challenges to the Second Artillery's existing command and control structures, as it has only limited experience in managing submarines on patrol.[20] So far, Chinese SSBNs have never conducted a deterrent patrol.

Aircraft and cruise missiles

The PLA Air Force (PLAAF) is believed to maintain a small number of gravity bombs to be delivered by the H-6 medium-range bomber and potentially also a shorter-range fighter-bomber. Nevertheless, the PLAAF is not believed to have units whose primary mission is to deliver nuclear bombs.[21]

The PLA operates several types of cruise missile. However, only the ground-launched Donghai-10 (DH-10, also designated Changjian-10, CJ-10), has been reported as being possibly nuclear capable.[22] Relatively little is known about the DH-10's technical characteristics, and claims about the missile's derivation and classification are inconsistent.[23] China is also developing an air-launched version of the DH-10, possibly for delivery by an upgraded version of the H-6 aircraft. According to unconfirmed media reports in 2012, a sea-launched version of the DH-10 also appears to be under development.[24]

---

[19] United States–China Economic and Security Review Commission, *2012 Report to Congress* (US Government Printing Office: Washington, DC, Nov. 2012), p. 7.

[20] US Department of Defense (note 14), p. 24.

[21] US National Security Council, 'Report to Congress on the status of China, India and Pakistan nuclear and ballistic missile programs', 28 July 1993, obtained under the US Freedom of Information Act by the Federation of American Scientists, <http://fas.org/irp/threat/930728-wmd.htm>.

[22] The US Air Force refers to the DH-10 as 'conventional or nuclear', the same designation as the Russian AS-4, which is known to be dual-capable. US Air Force, National Air and Space Intelligence Center (NASIC), *Ballistic and Cruise Missile Threat* (NASIC: Wright-Patterson Air Force Base, OH, June 2009), p. 29. In its 2012 report to the US Congress, the US–China Economic and Security Review Commission referred to the air-launched version of the DH-10 as possibly being nuclear capable. United States–China Economic and Security Review Commission (note 19), p. 181.

[23] Easton, I., 'The assassin under the radar: China's DH-10 cruise missile program', Futuregram no. 09-005, Project 2049 Institute, 1 Oct. 2009, <http://project2049.net/publications.html>.

[24] Minnick, W., 'Glimpse of China's new fighter fuels rumors', *Defense News*, 5 Aug. 2012.

VI. Indian nuclear forces

SHANNON N. KILE AND HANS M. KRISTENSEN

India is estimated to have an arsenal of 90–110 nuclear weapons for delivery by aircraft and land-based missiles. This figure is based on calculations of India's inventory of weapon-grade plutonium as well as the number of operational nuclear-capable delivery systems.

India's nuclear weapons are believed to be plutonium-based. India's stockpile of weapon-grade plutonium is estimated to have been 400–680 kilograms in 2012 (see section X below). The plutonium was produced by the 40-megawatt-thermal (MW(t)) heavy water CIRUS reactor, which was shut down at the end of 2010, and the 100-MW(t) Dhruva heavy water reactor. Both are located at the Bhabha Atomic Research Centre (BARC) near Mumbai, Maharashtra. A new high-flux plutonium-production reactor is under construction at the new BARC complex near the port city of Visakhapatnam (also know as Vizag), Andhra Pradesh. India plans to build six fast-breeder reactors, which will significantly increase its capacity to produce plutonium for weapons. A 1250-MW(t) prototype fast breeder reactor (PFBR) is nearing completion at the Indira Gandhi Centre for Atomic Research (IGCAR) complex at Kalpakkam, Tamil Nadu, and is scheduled to be commissioned in early 2013.[1] At 75 per cent operating capacity the reactor, which is liquid sodium-cooled, could potentially produce around 140 kg of weapon-grade plutonium per year, or enough for 28–35 weapons depending on bomb design and fabrication skills.[2] The IGCAR also houses a reprocessing facility that is not subject to International Atomic Energy Agency (IAEA) safeguards.

India continues to enrich uranium at the centrifuge facility at Rattehalli Rare Materials Plant near Mysore, Karnataka, to produce highly enriched uranium (HEU) for use as naval reactor fuel. In 2010 the Indian Atomic Energy Commission announced plans to build a Special Material Enrichment Facility, at a site in Chitradurga district, Karnataka, which could potentially be used to produce HEU for weapons, among other purposes.[3]

India's nuclear doctrine is based on the principle of a minimum credible deterrent and no-first-use of nuclear weapons.[4] There has been no official

---

[1] Press Trust of India, 'India's breeder reactor to be commissioned in 2013', *Hindustan Times*, 20 Feb. 2012.

[2] Cochran, T. B. et al., *Fast Breeder Reactor Programs: History and Status*, International Panel on Fissile Materials (IPFM) Research Report no. 8 (IPFM: Princeton, NJ, Feb. 2010), pp. 41, 45.

[3] Jha, S., '"Enrichment capacity enough to fuel nuke subs"', IBNLive, 26 Nov. 2011, <http://ibnlive.in.com/news/enrichment-capacity-enough-to-fuel-nuke-subs/206066-61.html>.

[4] Indian Ministry of External Affairs, 'Draft report of National Security Advisory Board on Indian nuclear doctrine', 17 Aug. 1999, <http://www.mea.gov.in/in-focus-article.htm?18916>.

Table 6.7. Indian nuclear forces, January 2013

Type	Range (km)[a]	Payload (kg)	Status
Aircraft[b]			
Mirage 2000H Vajra	1 850	6 300	Reportedly certified for delivery of nuclear gravity bombs
Land-based ballistic missiles[c]			
Prithvi I/II	150/350	800/500	Prithvi I entered service in 1994; Prithvi I reportedly had nuclear capability; Prithvi II also widely rumoured to have nuclear capability; nuclear role likely diminished with introduction of Agni; fewer than 50 launchers deployed; most recent flight tests 12 Dec. 2012 (Prithvi I) and 20 Dec. 2012 (Prithvi II)
Agni I[d]	~700	1 000	Most recent Indian Army operational test on 12 Dec. 2012; deployed with the Indian Army's 334 Missile Group
Agni II	2 000	1 000	In service with the Indian Army's 555 Missile Group; test-launched on 9 Aug. 2012
Agni III	~3 000	1 500	Inducted into service but not fully operational; test launched on 21 Sep. 2012
Agni IV[e]	~4 000	1 000	Under development; test launched on 19 Sep. 2012.
Agni V	>5 000	1 000?	Under development; test launched on 19 Apr. 2012
Sea-based missiles			
Dhanush	350	500	Induction underway but probably not operational; test launched on 5 Oct. 2012
K-15[f]	700	500–600	Under development; final test-launch from a submerged pontoon conducted on 27 Jan. 2013; to be integrated with the submarine INS *Arihant* beginning in 2013

[a] Aircraft range is for illustrative purposes only; actual mission range will vary according to flight profile and weapon loading. Missile payloads may have to be reduced in order to achieve maximum range.

[b] The Jaguar IS Shamsher and Sukhoi Su-30MKI combat aircraft have also been mentioned as having a possible nuclear delivery role.

[c] India has also begun developing a subsonic cruise missile with a range of 1000 km, known as the Nirbhay, which may have a nuclear capability.

[d] The original Agni I, now known as the Agni, was a technology demonstrator programme that ended in 1996. The Indian Ministry of Defence refers to the current Agni I as A1.

[e] An earlier version was known as the Agni II Prime.

[f] The DRDO is developing a land-based variant of the K-15, called the Shourya. It was test launched in Nov. 2008 and Sep. 2011.

Sources: Indian Ministry of Defence, annual reports and press releases; International Institute for Strategic Studies, *The Military Balance 2010* (Routledge: London, 2010); US Air Force, National Air and Space Intelligence Center (NASIC), *Ballistic and Cruise Missile Threat* (NASIC: Wright-Patterson Air Force Base, OH, June 2009); Indian news media reports; 'Nuclear notebook', *Bulletin of the Atomic Scientists*, various issues; and authors' estimates.

statement specifying the size of the arsenal required for a 'minimum credible deterrent' but, according to the Indian Ministry of Defence (MOD), it involves 'a mix of land-based, maritime and air capabilities' (a 'triad').[5] In June 2012 the Indian Prime Minister, Manmohan Singh, convened a meeting of India's Nuclear Command Authority, which reportedly stressed the need for the 'faster consolidation' of India's nuclear deterrence posture based on an operational triad of nuclear forces.[6] However, it is not clear if the maritime element of the triad is operational.

Strike aircraft

Aircraft constitute the most mature component of India's nuclear strike capabilities (see table 6.7). The Indian Air Force (IAF) has reportedly certified the Mirage 2000H multi-role combat aircraft for delivery of nuclear gravity bombs. The IAF's Jaguar IS Shamsher and Sukhoi Su-30MKI combat aircraft have also been mentioned as having a possible nuclear role.

The Indian Strategic Forces Command (SFC), the body responsible for the operational management of the country's nuclear force and for their command and control, depends on the IAF for delivering nuclear weapons under its command. However, it has reportedly sought to acquire two squadrons of combat aircraft with a dedicated nuclear delivery role.[7]

Land-based missiles

The Prithvi short-range ballistic missile was India's sole operational ballistic missile for many years. The 150 kilometre-range Prithvi I is a single-stage, road-mobile, liquid-fuelled missile that was inducted into Indian Army service in 1994. A number of Prithvi I missiles are widely believed to have been modified for a nuclear delivery role, although this has never been officially confirmed. The Prithvi II is a longer-range variant that is rumoured to also have a nuclear role. In 2012 the SFC conducted three successful test flights of Prithvi II missiles—on 25 August, 4 October and 20 December—as part of its regular user-readiness trials.[8]

---

[5] Indian Ministry of Defence (MOD), *Annual Report 2004–05* (MOD: New Delhi, 2005), p. 14.

[6] Pandit, R., 'PM takes stock of country's nuclear arsenal', *Times of India*, 14 June 2012. The NCA comprises the Political Council, chaired by the prime minister, and the Executive Council, chaired by the national security adviser to the prime minister. The NCA's directives are operationalized by a Strategic Forces Command under the control of a commander-in-chief. The Political Council is the sole body that can authorize the use of nuclear weapons by India. Sidhu, W. P. S., 'India', eds H. Born, B. Gill and H. Hänggi, SIPRI, *Governing the Bomb: Civilian Control and Democratic Accountability of Nuclear Weapons* (Oxford University Press: Oxford, 2010), pp. 180–81.

[7] PTI, 'Strategic Command to acquire 40 nuclear capable fighters', *Hindustan Times*, 12 Sep. 2010.

[8] Indian Ministry of Defence, 'Prithvi-II missile successfully test- fired', 20 Dec. 2012, <http://pib.nic.in/newsite/erelease.aspx?relid=91027>; Indian Ministry of Defence, 'Prithvi-II missile test- fired

The family of longer-range Agni ballistic missiles, which are designed to provide a quick-reaction nuclear capability, has largely taken over the Prithvi's nuclear delivery role. Like the Prithvi, the Agni was developed by India's Defence Research and Development Organisation (DRDO) as part of its problem-plagued Integrated Guided Missile Development Programme, which ended in 2008.[9] The 700 km-range Agni I (designated the A1 by the Indian MOD) is a single-stage, solid-fuelled missile. The SFC carried out successful test-launches of Agni I missiles during routine training exercises on 13 July and 12 December 2012.[10] The Agni II is a two-stage solid-fuelled missile, based on the Agni I, that can deliver a 1000-kg payload to a maximum range of 2000 km. On 9 August 2012 the SFC successfully launched an Agni II from a rail-mobile launcher at the Integrated Test Range on Wheeler Island off the coast of Orissa. The test was intended to validate the SFC's operational readiness to fire the missile.[11]

The DRDO has been developing a variant of the Agni II, known previously as the Agni II Prime but redesignated as the Agni IV. According to DRDO officials, the two-stage Agni IV incorporates several technological advances, including composite rocket engines, improved stage separation and a state-of-the-art navigational system.[12] On 19 September 2012 an Agni IV was successfully launched from the Wheeler Island complex and travelled 4000 km to a target zone in the Bay of Bengal.[13] This marked the second successful test of the missile since an initial failure in 2010.

The DRDO has developed the Agni III, a two-stage, solid-fuelled missile capable of delivering a 1500-kg payload to a range of 3000–3500 km. On 21 September 2012, the SFC launched from Wheeler Island a rail-mobile Agni III missile that had been randomly chosen from a production lot. The launch was the SFC's first user trial of the missile following three consecutive successful flight tests.[14]

The DRDO has prioritized the development of the long-range, three-stage Agni V missile. The new missile incorporates a number of the new indigenously developed propulsion and navigation system technologies

successfully: hits target area, across 350 km', 4 Oct. 2012, <http://pib.nic.in/newsite/erelease.aspx?relid=88130>; and Subramanian, T. S., 'Prithvi-II missile test, a success', The Hindu, 25 Aug. 2012.

[9] E.g. Verma, B., 'How DRDO failed India's military', Rediff, 15 Jan. 2008, <http://www.rediff.com/news/2008/jan/15guest.htm>.

[10] Indian Ministry of Defence, 'Successful flight test of Agni-1', 12 Dec. 2012, <http://pib.nic.in/newsite/erelease.aspx?relid=90425>; and PTI, 'India tests nuclear-capable Agni-I missile', Times of India, 13 July 2012.

[11] Mallikarjun, Y. and Subramanian, T. S., 'Agni-II launch, a flawless mission', The Hindu, 9 Aug. 2012.

[12] Pandit, R., 'With China in mind, India tests new-generation Agni missile with high "kill efficiency"', Times of India, 16 Nov. 2011.

[13] Indian Ministry of Defence, 'Successful flight testing of Agni-IV', 19 Sep. 2012, <http://pib.nic.in/newsite/erelease.aspx?relid=87855>.

[14] Mallikarjun, Y., 'Agni-III test-fired successfully', The Hindu, 21 Sep. 2012; and Rout, H. K., 'Agni-III user trial today', New Indian Express, 21 Sep. 2012.

used in the Agni IV. On 19 April 2012 the DRDO test-launched an Agni V for the first time. The missile flew 5000 km from Wheeler Island before impacting in a pre-designated target zone in the Indian Ocean.[15] India media reports hailed the successful test as evidence that India had joined China, France, Russia, the United Kingdom and the United States as the only countries possessing intercontinental ballistic missiles (ICBMs).[16] Some Indian analysts emphasized that the Agni V had sufficient range to strike targets throughout China and thereby strengthened India's nuclear deterrence capabilities.[17] The Agni V is expected to become operational in 2014–15 after 'four to five repeatable tests' and user trials.[18]

Sea-based missiles

India continues to encounter delays in developing the naval element of its triad of nuclear forces. Its first indigenously built nuclear-powered submarine, INS *Arihant*, was launched in 2009, under the Advanced Technology Vessel (ATV) project. The Indian Navy's plan to commence sea trials in 2012 had to be postponed because of problems with the vessel's propulsion system.[19]

The DRDO has tested components of an underwater missile-launch system and is developing a two-stage missile that can be launched from a submerged submarine using a gas-charged booster. Indian MOD statements have designated the missile as the K-15 or B-05, although other sources have referred to it as Sagarika, which is the name of the DRDO development project.[20] The K-15 has been described as a 'hybrid' missile that combines aspects of both cruise and ballistic missiles; unlike the latter, its flight trajectory can be controlled after launch.[21] The nuclear-capable missile will be able to deliver a 500–600-kg payload to a distance of up to 700 km. On 27 January 2013 the DRDO successfully launched a K-15 missile from a submerged pontoon in the Bay of Bengal. The launch marked the final development test of the missile prior to its integration with the INS *Arihant*; DRDO officials stated that the missile was already in pro-

---

[15] Indian Ministry of Defence, 'India launches new generation strategic missile Agni-V', 19 Apr. 2012, <http://pib.nic.in/newsite/erelease.aspx?relid=82371>.

[16] Dixit, R., 'India successfully test-fires Agni-V, joins ICBM club', *Mail Today* (Delhi), 19 Apr. 2012.

[17] PTI, 'Agni-V, capable of reaching China, test-fired successfully', *Times of India*, 19 Apr. 2012.

[18] Pandit, R., 'India test-fires nuclear-capable Prithvi-II missile', *Times of India*, 25 Aug. 2012.

[19] Ray, K., 'INS Arihant will miss December deadline', *Deccan Herald*, 10 Nov. 2012.

[20] Unnithan, S., 'The secret "K" missile family', *India Today*, 20 Nov. 2010; and Subramanian, T. S., 'DRDO plans another K-15 missile launch', *The Hindu*, 28 Jan. 2011.

[21] Rout, H. K., 'K-15 test off Andhra coast next month', *New Indian Express*, 27 Nov. 2012; and Sharma, S., 'DRDO headline mistake makes Pak go ballistic', *Sunday Guardian* (Delhi), 16 Feb. 2013.

duction.[22] The K-15 was also test-launched on 11 March, 16 March and 26 December 2012.

The DRDO is developing a submarine-launched ballistic missile, known as the K-4, which may have a range of up to 3500 km.[23] The K-4 will eventually replace the K-15 missile in arming the *Arihant*, although this will probably require the rebuilding of the submarine's hull.

India also continues to work on the Dhanush missile, a naval version of the Prithvi II, which is launched from a stabilization platform mounted on a surface ship. It can reportedly carry a 500-kg warhead to a maximum range of 350 km and is designed to be able to hit both sea- and shore-based targets. A Dhanush was successfully test launched from an Indian Navy ship off the coast of Orissa on 5 October 2012.[24]

[22] Fiddian, P., 'Indian Navy K-15 SLBM launched', Armed Forces International News, 28 Jan 2013, <http://www.armedforces-int.com/news/indian-navy-k-15-slbm-launched.html>; and Mallikarjun, Y., 'India to integrate K-15 missiles into nuclear submarine soon', *The Hindu*, 20 Nov. 2012.

[23] Unnithan (note 20).

[24] PTI, 'India successfully test-fires nuclear-capable Dhanush missile', *Times of India*, 5 Oct. 2012.

VII. Pakistani nuclear forces

PHILLIP SCHELL AND HANS M. KRISTENSEN

Pakistan is estimated to possess about 100–120 nuclear weapons for delivery by aircraft and land-based missiles (see table 6.8). It is widely believed that, in peacetime, Pakistan stores its nuclear warheads separate from their delivery vehicles. According to some accounts it is also possible that the warheads are kept in disassembled form.[1] However, the Strategic Plans Division (SPD), which operates Pakistan's nuclear forces, has never confirmed such arrangements. In 2012 Pakistan conducted a series of missile trials testing most of its nuclear-capable missile types that are currently in operational service or still under development.

Pakistan's current warhead designs are believed to use highly enriched uranium (HEU). However, the expansion of Pakistan's plutonium-production capabilities and the development of smaller nuclear-capable ballistic and cruise missiles could indicate a trend towards an arsenal based partly on plutonium. Warheads using plutonium could be lighter and more compact than those using HEU to achieve similar yields. Nevertheless, there is no confirmation of a successful test of a plutonium-based warhead design so far.

Pakistan is expanding its main plutonium production complex at Khushab, Punjab. The complex currently consists of three heavy water nuclear reactors and a heavy water production plant. Work on a fourth heavy water reactor appears to have started in late 2010 and is reportedly halfway to completion.[2] It remains unclear whether Pakistan intends to construct a fifth reactor at the Khushab site. It is widely believed that each of the four reactors has a capacity of 40–50 megawatts-thermal. The first reactor at the site, Khushab-I, has been operational since 1998 and is estimated to produce 6–12 kilograms of plutonium annually (depending on operational efficiency), or enough for one to three nuclear warheads, depending on warhead design and fabrication skills.[3] The second reactor, Khushab-II, may have commenced operation in late 2009 or 2010. Construction of the third reactor at Khushab began in 2006 and appears to have

---

[1] See Tertrais, B., 'Pakistan's nuclear and WMD programmes: status, evolution and risks', Non-Proliferation Papers no. 19, EU Non-Proliferation Consortium, July 2012, <http://www.nonproliferation.eu/activities/activities.php>, p. 5.

[2] Albright, D. and Avagyan, R., 'Construction progressing rapidly on the fourth heavy water reactor at the Khushab nuclear site', Institute for Science and International Security (ISIS) Imagery Brief, 21 May 2012, <http://isis-online.org/isis-reports/>.

[3] International Panel on Fissile Materials, 'Countries: Pakistan', 3 Feb. 2013, <http://fissilematerials.org/countries/pakistan.html>.

Table 6.8. Pakistani nuclear forces, January 2013

Type	Range (km)[a]	Payload (kg)	Status
Aircraft			
F-16A/B	1 600	4 500	Undergoing mid-life upgrades, to be completed in 2014
Mirage V	2 100	4 000	Used to test launch the Ra'ad; possibly nuclear-capable
Land-based ballistic missiles			
Abdali (Hatf-2)	~180	200–400	Under development; test launched on 5 and 11 Mar. 2012
Ghaznavi (Hatf-3)	290[b]	500	Entered service with the Pakistani Army in 2004; fewer than 50 launchers deployed; most recent test-launch on 10 May 2012
Shaheen I (Hatf-4)[c]	650[d]	750–1 000	Entered service with the Pakistani Army in 2003; fewer than 50 launchers deployed
Ghauri (Hatf-5)	>1 200	700–1 000	Entered service with the Pakistani Army in 2003; fewer than 50 launchers deployed; last test-launched on 28 Nov. 2012
Shaheen II (Hatf-6)	2 500	(~1 000)	Under development; last known test-launch on 21 Apr. 2008; expected to become operational soon
Nasr (Hatf-9)	~60	..	Under development; test launched on 29 May 2012
Cruise missiles			
Babur (Hatf-7)	600[e]	400–500	Under development; test launched on 17 Sep. 2012; initially ground-launched, but sea- and air-launched versions reportedly also under development
Ra'ad (Hatf-8)	350	..	Under development; air-launched; most recent test-launch on 31 May 2012

.. = not available or not applicable; ( ) = uncertain figure.

[a] Aircraft range is for illustrative purposes only; actual mission range will vary according to flight profile and weapon loading. Missile payloads may have to be reduced in order to achieve maximum range.

[b] The US Government estimates the range of the Ghaznavi to be 400 km.

[c] An extended-range version of the Shaheen I, the Shaheen 1A (also designated Hatf-4), is under development. The Shaheen 1A was test launched on 25 Apr. 2012.

[d] The US Government estimates the range of the Shaheen I to be 450 km or more.

[e] Since 2006 the range of flight-tests has increased from 500 km and the goal is rumoured to be 1000 km.

Sources: Pakistani Ministry of Defence; US Air Force, National Air and Space Intelligence Center (NASIC), *Ballistic and Cruise Missile Threat* (NASIC: Wright-Patterson Air Force Base, OH, June 2009); US Central Intelligence Agency, 'Unclassified report to Congress on the acquisition of technology relating to weapons of mass destruction and advanced conventional munitions, 1 January through 30 June 2002', Apr. 2003, <https://www.cia.gov/library/reports/archived-reports-1/>; US National Intelligence Council (NIC), *Foreign Missile Developments and the Ballistic Missile Threat through 2015*, Unclassified summary of a National Intelligence Estimate (NIC: Washington, DC, Dec. 2001); International Institute for Strategic Studies, *The Military Balance 2006–2007* (Routledge: London, 2007); 'Nuclear notebook', *Bulletin of the Atomic Scientists*, various issues; and authors' estimates.

been completed in late 2011.[4] Analysis of commercial satellite imagery suggests an increase in the Khushab reactors' cooling capacity. This could allow the reactors to operate at an increased capacity and produce slightly more plutonium than previously estimated.[5]

Pakistan also continues to produce HEU for military purposes. The enrichment is believed to be taking place at the uranium centrifuge facilities at Kahuta and Gadwal. Pakistan's stockpile of HEU is estimated to have been 3 tonnes in 2012 (see section X below).

The Khushab nuclear complex, combined with Pakistan's continuing HEU production, could increase Pakistan's annual nuclear warhead production capacity several-fold. This will depend, however, on the country having sufficient capacity to reprocess spent fuel as well as an adequate supply of uranium to fuel the reactors at Khushab.

Land-based missiles

Pakistan is expanding its nuclear-capable missile arsenal. The SPD currently deploys the Ghaznavi (also designated Hatf-3) and Shaheen I (Hatf-4) solid-fuelled, road-mobile short-range ballistic missiles (SRBMs). An extended-range version of the Shaheen I, the Shaheen IA, is under development. Pakistan's only operational medium-range ballistic missile (MRBM), the liquid-fuelled, road-mobile Ghauri I (Hatf-5), is believed to be based on the North Korean Nodong missile.

Additional types of nuclear-capable ballistic missile are currently under development. The Shaheen II (Hatf-6) is a two-stage, solid-fuelled, road-mobile MRBM that may eventually replace the Ghauri I MRBM.

Unlike India, Pakistan is developing several nuclear-capable SRBMs that appear to be intended for battlefield missions. According to the Pakistani military, the short-range Abdali (Hatf-2), which was test-fired on 5 and 11 March 2012, provides 'an operational level capability, additional to the strategic level capability'.[6] This could suggest that the Abdali will become operational soon. Similarly, the Pakistani military has described the 60 kilometre-range, road-mobile Nasr (Hatf-9) SRBM as a 'quick response

---

[4] International Panel on Fissile Materials, *Global Fissile Material Report 2011: Nuclear Weapon and Fissile Material Stockpiles and Production* (IPFM: Princeton, NJ, 2011), p. 19; and Albright, D. and Brannan, P., 'Pakistan appears to be building a fourth military reactor at the Khushab nuclear site', Institute for Science and International Security (ISIS) Imagery Brief, 9 Feb. 2011, <http://isis-online.org/isis-reports/>.

[5] Patton, T., 'Combining satellite imagery and 3D drawing tools for nonproliferation analysis: a case study of Pakistan's Khushab plutonium production reactors', *Science & Global Security*, vol. 20, nos 2–3 (2012).

[6] Pakistani Inter Services Public Relations, Press Release no. PR34/2012-ISPR, 5 Mar. 2012, <http://ispr.gov.pk/front/main.asp?o=t-press_release&id=1979>; and Pakistani Inter Services Public Relations, Press Release no. PR62/2011-ISPR, 11 Mar. 2011, <http://www.ispr.gov.pk/front/main.asp?o=t-press_release&id=1689>.

system', which 'add[s] deterrence value' to the posture 'at shorter ranges' in order 'to deter evolving threats'.[7] The missile is launched from a mobile multi-tube launcher that can 'fire a four missile salvo' in 'evolving scenarios'.[8]

Pakistan's missile development organization, the National Engineering and Scientific Commission (NESCOM), is also developing two types of nuclear-capable cruise missile: the ground-launched Babur and the air-launched Ra'ad.

The development of new types of nuclear-capable SRBM and cruise missile may be an indication of Pakistan's growing concern about being able to counter India's superior conventional forces and nascent ballistic missile defences. It further suggests that Pakistan's strategic planning has evolved to include a wider range of contingencies for the use of nuclear weapons, possibly in response to the Indian Army's Cold Start doctrine, under which India could carry out rapid but limited conventional attacks on Pakistani territory using forward-deployed forces.

Strike aircraft

It is widely believed that the Pakistani Air Force (PAF) has previously given a nuclear delivery role to its 32 F-16A/B combat aircraft, but it is unclear whether they are currently assigned a nuclear mission. The F-16 aircraft, which are organized in three squadrons, were supplied by the United States in the 1980s. They are currently undergoing a mid-life upgrade (MLU), which is expected to be completed in 2014. Turkish Aerospace Industries, which was contracted to upgrade the aircraft, handed over the first batch of F-16 Block 15 MLU aircraft to the PAF in February 2012.

The PAF's Mirage V combat aircraft could also have a nuclear-delivery role. The range of the Mirage aircraft has been extended by the PAF's development of an aerial refuelling capability using Il-78 aircraft.

---

[7] Pakistani Inter Services Public Relations, Press Release no. PR94/2011-ISPR, 19 Apr. 2011, <http://www.ispr.gov.pk/front/main.asp?o=t-press_release&id=1721>.

[8] Pakistani Inter Services Public Relations, Press Release no. PR17/2013-ISPR, 11 Feb. 2013, <http://www.ispr.gov.pk/front/main.asp?o=t-press_release&id=2240>.

VIII. Israeli nuclear forces

PHILLIP SCHELL AND HANS M. KRISTENSEN

Israel continues to maintain its long-standing policy of nuclear opacity. It neither officially confirms nor denies that it possesses nuclear weapons.[1] It is estimated here that Israel has approximately 80 intact nuclear weapons, of which 50 are for delivery by Jericho II medium-range ballistic missiles and 30 are gravity bombs for delivery by aircraft (see table 6.9). The operational status of the longer-range Jericho III ballistic missile is unknown. Israel may also have produced non-strategic nuclear weapons, including artillery shells and atomic demolition munitions.

Israel is widely believed to have produced plutonium for its undeclared nuclear weapon programme at the Negev Nuclear Research Center, near Dimona. It is estimated that Israel had 710–970 kilograms of weapon-grade plutonium as of 2012 (see section X below). However, only part of this plutonium could have been used for nuclear weapons.

In 2012, there was intensified speculation that Israel may be equipping its current fleet of four Type 800 Dolphin class diesel-electric submarines, which were purchased from Germany, with indigenously produced nuclear-armed sea-launched cruise missiles (SLCMs). Israel has consistently denied these reports. The missile is believed to be based on the Israeli-made Popeye Turbo, but no reliable open-source information on the missile's technical characteristics is available. Two additional boats of the same class are expected to be delivered to the Israeli Navy in 2013 and 2017, respectively. The submarines are under construction at the Howaldtswerke-Deutsche Werft AG shipyard, near Kiel, Germany. The fourth, fifth and sixth submarines are advanced Dolphin class vessels equipped with air-independent propulsion (AIP), which makes the submarines extremely quiet and allows them to remain submerged for an extended period of time.[2]

According to one media report, German Government officials had long assumed that Israel had an undeclared nuclear weapon capability and might use its submarines in a nuclear delivery role.[3] Officially, the German Government has not explicitly denied these reports, but in 2006 and 2012 it replied to parliamentary inquiries stating that the non-proliferation of nuclear weapons was a principal norm of the German Government's policies and the provision of nuclear-capable delivery vehicles would never

---

[1] On the role of this policy in Israel's national security decision making see Cohen, A., 'Israel', eds H. Born, B. Gill and H. Hänggi, SIPRI, *Governing the Bomb: Civilian Control and Democratic Accountability of Nuclear Weapons* (Oxford University Press: Oxford, 2010).

[2] Von Bergman, R. et al., 'Made in Germany', *Der Spiegel*, 4 June 2012 (in German).

[3] Von Bergman (note 2).

Table 6.9. Israeli nuclear forces, January 2013

Type	Range (km)^a	Payload (kg)	Status
Aircraft^b			
F-16A/B/C/D/I Falcon	1 600	5 400	205 aircraft in the inventory; some are believed to be certified for nuclear weapon delivery
Ballistic missiles^c			
Jericho II	1 500–1 800	750–1 000	c. 50 missiles; first deployed in 1990; test-launched on 27 June 2001
Jericho III	>4 000	1 000–1 300	Test-launched on 17 Jan. 2008 and 2 Nov 2011; status unknown

^{a} Aircraft range is for illustrative purposes only; actual mission range will vary. Missile payloads may have to be reduced in order to achieve maximum range.

^{b} Some of Israel's 25 F-15I aircraft may also have a long-range nuclear delivery role.

^{c} There is speculation that Israel might also have developed a nuclear-capable cruise missile for use on its attack submarines.

Sources: Cohen, A., *The Worst-kept Secret: Israel's Bargain with the Bomb* (Columbia University Press: New York, 2010); Cohen, A. and Burr, W., 'Israel crosses the threshold', *Bulletin of the Atomic Scientists*, vol. 62, no. 3 (May/June 2006); Cohen, A., *Israel and the Bomb* (Columbia University Press: New York, 1998); Albright, D., Berkhout, F. and Walker, W., SIPRI, *Plutonium and Highly Enriched Uranium 1996: World Inventories, Capabilities and Policies* (Oxford University Press: Oxford, 1997); *Jane's Strategic Weapon Systems*, various issues; Fetter, S., 'Israeli ballistic missile capabilities', *Physics and Society*, vol. 19, no. 3 (July 1990)—for an updated analysis, see unpublished 'A ballistic missile primer', <http://faculty.publicpolicy.umd.edu/fetter/pages/publications>; 'Nuclear notebook', *Bulletin of the Atomic Scientists*, various issues; and authors' estimates.

be approved.[4] German Government officials stated that the vessels were handed over to Israel without any weapons and referred to the Israeli Government as being solely responsible for the decision about how the submarines were equipped.[5]

[4] German Parliament (Bundestag), 'Deutsche Rüstungsexporte nach Israel' [German arms exports to Israel], Response of the Federal Government, Drucksache 16/3430, 16 Nov. 2006; and German Parliament (Bundestag), Written questions that received responses from the Federal Government in the week of 7 May 2012, Drucksache 17/9615, 11 May 2012, p. 50.

[5] Weiland, S., 'Deutsche Waffenlieferungen: Heikler U-Boot-Deal mit Israel' [German arms supplies: tricky submarine deal with Israel], *Der Spiegel*, 3 June 2012, <http://www.spiegel.de/politik/deutschland/lieferung-deutscher-u-boote-an-israel-provoziert-kritik-a-836715.html>; and 'Israels Regierungschef würdigt deutsche U-Boote' [Israeli Prime Minister praises German submarines], *Die Welt*, 5 June 2012.

IX. North Korea's military nuclear capabilities

SHANNON N. KILE

The Democratic People's Republic of Korea (DPRK, North Korea) maintains a secretive and highly opaque military nuclear programme. There is no public information to verify that it possesses operational nuclear weapons. However, in January 2012, James R. Clapper, the US Director of National Intelligence, assessed that North Korea had produced nuclear weapons, although he gave no estimate of the size of the country's weapon inventory.[6] In 2011 he had stated that North Korea possessed the capability to build nuclear weapons but that the US intelligence community did not know whether it had done so.[7]

As of January 2013, North Korea had carried out two underground tests of nuclear explosive devices: the first in October 2006, which had an estimated yield of less than 1 kiloton and was widely considered to be a failure; and the second in May 2009, which had an estimated yield of 2–6 kt.[8] During 2012 several non-governmental reports concluded, based on the analysis of satellite imagery and other evidence, that North Korea was making technical preparations for carrying out a third underground nuclear test in tunnels at its nuclear test site, Punggye-ri, in the north-east of the country.[9]

There has been considerable speculation that North Korea is seeking to build nuclear weapons using highly enriched uranium (HEU), rather than plutonium as the fissile material, as the tests in 2006 and 2009 are believed to have used.[10] While it is not known whether North Korea has produced

[6] Clapper, J. R., US Director of National Intelligence, 'Worldwide threat assessment of the US intelligence community for the Senate Select Committee on Intelligence', Unclassified statement for the record, 31 Jan. 2012, <http://www.dni.gov/index.php/newsroom/testimonies/>, p. 6.

[7] Clapper, J. R., US Director of National Intelligence, 'Worldwide threat assessment of the U.S. Intelligence Community for the House Permanent Select Committee on Intelligence', Statement for the record, 10 Feb. 2011, <http://www.dni.gov/index.php/newsroom/testimonies/>, p. 6.

[8] Fedchenko, V. and Ferm Hellgren, R., 'Nuclear explosions, 1945–2006', *SIPRI Yearbook 2007*; and Fedchenko, V., 'Nuclear explosions, 1945–2009', *SIPRI Yearbook 2010*. For a description of the methods used to estimate the explosive yields of the tests and attendant uncertainties see Pabian, F. V. and Hecker, S. S., 'Contemplating a third nuclear test in North Korea', *Bulletin of the Atomic Scientists*, 6 Aug. 2012, <http://www.thebulletin.org/web-edition/features/contemplating-third-nuclear-test-north-korea>.

[9] 'North Korean nuclear test preparations: an update', 38North, 27 Apr. 2012, <http://38north.org/2012/04/punggyeri042712/>; and Pabian and Hecker (note 8). North Korea carried out a 3rd nuclear test explosion at Punggye-ri on 12 Feb. 2013, which will be discussed in *SIPRI Yearbook 2014*.

[10] North Korea reportedly obtained clandestine design assistance for an HEU-based weapon from Pakistani nuclear engineer Abdul Qadeer Khan. United Nations, Security Council, Report of the Panel of Experts established pursuant to Resolution 1874 (2009), 11 May 2012, annex to S/2012/422, 14 June 2012, p. 15.

HEU for use in nuclear weapons, it is believed to have an active uranium-enrichment programme. In 2010 a delegation of US scientists visiting the nuclear complex at Yongbyon, North Pyongan, was shown a previously undisclosed centrifuge enrichment facility, located in a former metal fuel rod fabrication building.[11] A leaked 2011 report by the United Nations Security Council's Panel of Experts on North Korea assessed that it was 'highly likely that one or more parallel covert facilities capable of [low-enriched uranium] or HEU production exist elsewhere [in the country]'.[12] In addition, the IAEA has reported circumstantial evidence that North Korea acquired the capability to produce uranium hexafluoride (UF_6) feed gas for enrichment centrifuges prior to 2001.[13]

By using HEU for nuclear weapons, North Korea could potentially overcome the constraints posed by its limited stock of weapon-grade plutonium. In 2008 North Korea declared that it had separated 31 kilograms of plutonium from the spent fuel produced by its 5-megawatt-electric graphite-moderated research reactor at Yongbyon prior to the reactor being shut down; it subsequently produced an estimated 8–10 kg of separated plutonium (see section X). Following the 2006 and 2009 tests, and depending on the amount of plutonium used in those tests, North Korea had sufficient plutonium to construct six to eight rudimentary nuclear weapons, assuming that each weapon used 5 kg of plutonium. North Korea is currently building a new indigenously designed pressurized light water reactor at the Yongbyong site; while this is ostensibly a step toward a nuclear power generation capacity, it could be used to produce plutonium for its nuclear weapon programme.[14]

There is circumstantial evidence that North Korea may be interested in testing both plutonium and HEU explosive devices, either simultaneously or in quick succession.[15] The plutonium test could provide information on the yield-to-weight ratio needed for building a warhead that is compact and light enough to fit on a long-range ballistic missile, while a test using HEU could pave the way for an expanded future arsenal.[16] However, if an

---

[11] Hecker, S. S., 'A return trip to North Korea's Yongbyon nuclear complex', Stanford University, Center for International Security and Cooperation, 20 Nov. 2010, <http://cisac.stanford.edu/ publications/north_koreas_yongbyon_nuclear_complex_a_report_by_siegfried_s_hecker/>.

[12] Panel of experts established pursuant to Resolution 1874 (2009), Report, para. 53. The leaked report is available at <http://www.scribd.com/doc/55808872/UN-Panel-of-Experts-NORK-Report-May-2011>.

[13] North Korea is suspected of having transferred UF_6 to Libya's clandestine uranium-enrichment programme in 2000 and 2001. International Atomic Energy Agency, Board of Governors and General Conference, 'Application of Safeguards in the Democratic People's Republic of Korea', Report by the Director General, GOV/2011/53–GC(55)24, 2 Sep. 2011, para. 50.

[14] Puccioni, A., 'Pyongyang takes a major step in new reactor project', *Jane's Defence Weekly*, 22 Aug. 2012, p. 8.

[15] Pabian and Hecker (note 8).

[16] Hecker, S. S., 'What to expect from a North Korean nuclear test?', *Foreign Policy*, 4 Feb. 2013.

underground test were well contained, it would be difficult for airborne sampling techniques outside the country to determine whether HEU or plutonium had been used.[17] There has also been speculation that North Korea may attempt to test a fusion-boosted fission device or possibly even a thermonuclear weapon.[18]

[17] Choe, S., 'North Korea: a third nuclear test may not answer basic questions', *New York Times*, 6 Feb. 2013.

[18] Lewis, J., 'Setting expectations for a DPRK test', Arms Control Wonk, 29 Jan. 2013, <http://lewis.armscontrolwonk.com/archive/6200/setting-expectations-for-a-dprk-test>; and Makino, Y., 'N. Korea likely to test fusion-boosted fission bomb able to reach U.S.', Asahi Shimbun Asia and Japan Watch, 25 Jan. 2013, <http://ajw.asahi.com/article/asia/korean_peninsula/AJ201301250058>.

X. Global stocks and production of fissile materials, 2012

ALEXANDER GLASER AND ZIA MIAN

INTERNATIONAL PANEL ON FISSILE MATERIALS

Materials that can sustain an explosive fission chain reaction are essential for all types of nuclear explosives, from first-generation fission weapons to advanced thermonuclear weapons. The most common of these fissile materials are highly enriched uranium (HEU) and plutonium of almost any isotopic composition. This section gives details of current stocks of HEU (table 6.10) and separated plutonium (table 6.11), including in weapons, and details of the current capacity to produce these materials (tables 6.12 and 6.13, respectively). The information in the tables is based on new estimates prepared for the *Global Fissile Material Report 2012–2013*.[1]

The production of both HEU and plutonium starts with natural uranium. Natural uranium consists almost entirely of the non-chain-reacting isotope U-238, with about 0.7 per cent U-235, but the concentration of U-235 can be increased through enrichment—typically using gas centrifuges. Uranium that has been enriched to less than 20 per cent U-235 (typically, 3–5 per cent)—known as low-enriched uranium—is suitable for use in power reactors. Uranium that has been enriched to contain at least 20 per cent U-235—known as HEU—is generally taken to be the lowest concentration practicable for use in weapons. However, in order to minimize the mass of the nuclear explosive, weapon-grade uranium is usually enriched to over 90 per cent U-235. Plutonium is produced in nuclear reactors through the exposure of U-238 to neutrons and is subsequently chemically separated from spent fuel in a reprocessing operation. Plutonium comes in a variety of isotopic mixtures, most of which are weapon-usable. Weapon designers prefer to work with a mixture that predominantly consists of Pu-239 because of its relatively low rate of spontaneous emission of neutrons and gamma rays and the low generation of heat through this radioactive decay. Weapon-grade plutonium typically contains more than 90 per cent of the isotope Pu-239. The plutonium in typical spent fuel from power reactors (reactor-grade plutonium) contains 50–60 per cent Pu-239 but is weapon-usable, even in a first-generation weapon design.

The five nuclear weapon states party to the 1968 Non-Proliferation Treaty—China, France, Russia, the UK and the USA—have produced both HEU and plutonium. India, Israel and North Korea have produced mainly plutonium, and Pakistan mainly HEU for weapons. All states with a civilian nuclear industry have some capability to produce fissile materials.

---

[1] International Panel on Fissile Materials (IPFM), *Global Fissile Material Report 2012–2013: Increasing Transparency of Nuclear-warhead and Fissile-material Stocks as a Step toward Disarmament* (IPFM: Princeton, NJ, forthcoming 2013).

Table 6.10. Global stocks of highly enriched uranium (HEU), 2012

State	National stockpile (tonnes)[a]	Production status	Comments
China	16 ± 4	Stopped 1987–89	
France[b]	30 ± 6	Stopped 1996	Includes 4.6 tonnes declared civilian
India[c]	2.4 ± 0.3	Continuing	
Israel[d]	0.3	–	
Pakistan	3.0 ± 0.4	Continuing	
Russia[e]	666 ± 120	Stopped 1987–88	Includes 50 tonnes assumed to be reserved for naval and research reactor fuel; does not include 29 tonnes to be blended down
UK[f]	21.2	Stopped 1962	Includes 1.4 tonnes declared civilian
USA[g]	532	Stopped 1992	Includes 152 tonnes reserved for naval reactor fuel and 20 tonnes for other HEU reactor fuel; does not include 63 tonnes to be blended down or for disposal as waste
Other states[h]	~15		
Total	**~1285**		Rounded to the nearest 5 tonnes; does not include 92 tonnes to be blended down

[a] Most of this material is 90–93% enriched uranium-235, which is typically considered as weapon-grade. Important exceptions are noted. Blending down (i.e. reducing the concentration of U-235) of excess Russian and US weapon-grade HEU up to the end of 2012 has been taken into account.

[b] France declared 4.64 tonnes of civilian HEU to the International Atomic Energy Agency (IAEA) as of the end of 2011; it is assumed here to be weapon-grade, 93% enriched HEU, even though some of the material is in irradiated form. The uncertainty in the estimate applies only to the military stockpile of 26 tonnes and does not apply to the declared stock of 4.64 tonnes.

[c] It is believed that India is producing HEU (enriched to 30–45%) for use as naval reactor fuel. The estimate is for HEU enriched to 30%.

[d] Israel may have acquired c. 300 kg of weapon-grade HEU from the USA in or before 1965.

[e] As of 31 Dec. 2012, 488 tonnes of Russia's weapon-grade HEU had been blended down. The estimate given for the Russian reserve for naval reactors is the authors' estimate based on the size of the Russian fleet.

[f] The UK declared a stockpile of 21.9 tonnes of HEU as of 31 Mar. 2002, the average enrichment of which was not given. An estimated 0.7 tonnes may have been consumed since then in naval reactor fuel. The UK declared a stock of 1.4 tonnes of civilian HEU to the IAEA as of the end of 2011.

[g] The amount of US HEU is given in actual tonnes, not 93% enriched equivalent. The USA has declared that as of 30 Sep. 1996 it had an inventory of 741 tonnes of HEU containing 620 tonnes of U-235. As of the end of 2012 it had blended down 141 tonnes excess; however, little if any of this HEU was weapon-grade. In 2012 the USA withdrew 24 tonnes of HEU from its stockpile of material declared excess for military purposes and earmarked for blend-down; this material is now reserved for naval fuel, bringing the total amount of HEU in this category to 152 tonnes of (fresh) weapon-grade HEU. In addition, at least 100 tonnes is in the form of irradiated naval fuel.

[h] The 2011 IAEA Annual Report lists 213 significant quantities of HEU under comprehensive safeguards in non-nuclear weapon states. In order to reflect the uncertainty in the enrichment levels of this material, mostly in research reactor fuel, a total of 15 tonnes of HEU is assumed. About 10 tonnes of this is in Kazakhstan and has been irradiated; it was initially slightly higher than 20%-enriched fuel.

Table 6.11. Global stocks of separated plutonium, 2012

State	Military stocks as of 2012 (tonnes)	Military production status	Civilian stocks as of 2012, unless indicated (tonnes)[a]
China	1.8 ± 0.8	Stopped in 1991	0.01
France	6 ± 1.0	Stopped in 1992	57.5 (not including 22.8 foreign owned)
Germany	–	–	5.8 (in France, Germany and UK)
India[b]	0.54 ± 0.14	Continuing	4.94 (including 4.7 outside safeguards)
Israel[c]	0.84 ± 0.13	Continuing	–
Japan	–	–	44.3 (including 35 in France and UK)
Korea, North[d]	0.03	Stopped	–
Pakistan[e]	0.15 ± 0.02	Continuing	–
Russia[f]	128 ± 8 (34 declared excess)	Stopped	49.5
UK[g]	3.2	Stopped in 1995	91.2 (including 0.9 abroad but not 27.9 foreign owned)
USA[h]	83.2 (49.3 declared excess)	Stopped in 1988	–
Other states[i]	–	–	11 (foreign owned in France and UK)
Totals	**~224 (83 declared excess)**		**~264**

[a] Some countries own civilian plutonium that is stored overseas, mostly in France and the UK, but do not submit an IAEA INFCIRC/549 declaration.

[b] As part of the 2005 Indian–US Civil Nuclear Cooperation Initiative, India has included in the military sector much of the plutonium separated from its spent power-reactor fuel. While it is labelled civilian here since it is intended for breeder reactor fuel, this plutonium was not placed under safeguards in the 'India-specific' safeguards agreement signed by the Indian Government and the IAEA on 2 Feb. 2009.

[c] Israel is believed to still be operating the Dimona plutonium production reactor but may be using it primarily for tritium production.

[d] North Korea reportedly declared plutonium production of 31 kg in June 2008; carried out nuclear tests in 2006 and 2009; and resumed production in 2009, adding 8–10 kg. In Feb. 2013, North Korea carried out another test and declared in Apr. 2013 that it intended to resume plutonium production.

[e] Pakistan is operating the Khushab-1 and -2 plutonium reactors. Two additional plutonium production reactors are under construction at the same site.

[f] Russia does not include its plutonium declared as excess in its INFCIRC/549 statement. The military stockpile includes 6 tonnes of weapon-grade plutonium that is not part of the material declared excess nor declared as civilian and was produced between 1994 and 2010.

[g] The UK declared 91.2 tonnes of civilian plutonium (not including 27.9 tonnes of foreign-owned plutonium in the UK). This includes 4.4 tonnes of military plutonium declared excess and placed under Euratom safeguards and designated for IAEA safeguarding.

[h] In its IAEA INFCIRC/549 statement, the USA declared 49.3 tonnes of unirradiated plutonium (both separated and in MOX) as excess for military purposes as of the end of 2011. An additional 4.4 tonnes have been sent for disposal at the Waste Isolation Pilot Plant, New Mexico.

[i] This includes Italy, which has 4.5 tonnes of plutonium at La Hague, France.

Sources for table 6.10: International Panel on Fissile Materials (IPFM), *Global Fissile Material Report 2012–2013: Increasing Transparency of Nuclear-warhead and Fissile-material Stocks as a Step toward Disarmament* (IPFM: Princeton, NJ, forthcoming 2013).; *Israel*: Myers, H., 'The real source of Israel's first fissile material', *Arms Control Today*, vol. 37, no. 8 (Oct. 2007), p. 56; see also Gilinsky, V. and Mattson, R. J., 'Revisiting the NUMEC affair', *Bulletin of the Atomic Scientists*, vol. 66, no. 2 (Mar./Apr. 2010); *Russia*: United States Enrichment Corporation, 'Megaton to megawatts', <http://www.usec.com/russian-contracts/megatons-megawatts>; *UK*: British Ministry of Defence, 'Historical accounting for UK defence highly enriched uranium', Mar. 2006, <http://webarchive.nationalarchives.gov.uk/+/http:/www.mod.uk:80/defenceinternet/aboutdefence/corporatepublications/healthandsafetypublications/uranium/>; International Atomic Energy Agency (IAEA), Communication received from the United Kingdom of Great Britain and Northern Ireland concerning its policies regarding the management of plutonium, INFCIRC/549/Add.8/15, 3 Aug. 2012; *USA*: US Department of Energy (DOE), *Highly Enriched Uranium, Striking a Balance: A Historical Report on the United States Highly Enriched Uranium Production, Acquisition, and Utilization Activities from 1945 through September 30, 1996* (DOE: Washington, DC, 2001); Person, G., Davis, D. and Schmidt, R., 'Progress down-blending surplus highly enriched uranium', Paper presented at the 53rd Annual Meeting Institute for Nuclear Materials Management, Orlando, FLA, July 2012; *Non-nuclear weapon states*: IAEA, *IAEA Annual Report 2011* (IAEA: Vienna, 2012), Annex, Table A.4, p. 109.

Sources for table 6.11: International Panel on Fissile Materials (IPFM), *Global Fissile Material Report 2012–2013: Increasing Transparency of Nuclear-warhead and Fissile-material Stocks as a Step toward Disarmament* (IPFM: Princeton, NJ, forthcoming 2013); *United States*: National Nuclear Security Administration (NNSA), *The United States Plutonium Balance, 1944–2009* (NNSA: Washington, DC, June 2012); International Atomic Energy Agency (IAEA), Communication received from the United States of America concerning its policies regarding the management of plutonium, INFCIRC/549/Add.6/15, 29 Oct. 2012; *Civilian stocks (except for India)*: declarations by countries to the IAEA under INFCIRC/549, <http://www.iaea.org/Publications/Documents/>; *North Korea*: Kessler, G., 'Message to U.S. preceded nuclear declaration by North Korea', *Washington Post*, 2 July 2008; *Russia*: Russian–US Agreement concerning the Management and Disposition of Plutonium Designated as No Longer Required for Defense Purposes and Related Cooperation (Russian–US Plutonium Management and Disposition Agreement), signed 29 Aug. and 1 Sep. 2000, amended Apr. 2010, and entered into force July 2011, <http://www.state.gov/t/isn/trty/>; *Non-nuclear weapon states*: Areva, *Traitement des combustibles usés provenant de l'étranger dans les installations d'AREVA NC La Hague: Rapport 2011* [Reprocessing of foreign spent fuel at the facilities of AREVA NC La Hague] (Areva: Beaumont-Hague, 2012).

Table 6.12. Significant uranium enrichment facilities and capacity worldwide, as of December 2012

State	Facility name or location	Type	Status	Enrichment process[a]	Capacity (thousands SWU/yr)[b]
Argentina	Pilcaniyeu	Civilian	Resuming operation	GD	..
Brazil	Resende Enrichment	Civilian	Under construction	GC	115–200
China	Lanzhou 2	Civilian	Operational	GC	500
	Lanzhou (new)	Civilian	Operational	GC	1 000
	Shaanxi	Civilian	Operational	GC	1 000
France[c]	Georges Besse II	Civilian	Operational	GC	7 500–11 000
Germany	Urenco Gronau	Civilian	Operational	GC	2 200–4 500
India	Rattehalli	Military	Operational	GC	15–30
Iran	Natanz	Civilian	Under construction	GC	120
	Qom	Civilian	Under construction	GC	5–10
Japan	Rokkasho[d]	Civilian	Resuming operation	GC	50–1 500
Korea, North	Yongbyon[e]	..	..	GC	8
Netherlands	Urenco Almelo	Civilian	Operational	GC	5 000–6 000
Pakistan	Gadwal	Military	Operational	GC	..
	Kahuta	Military	Operational	GC	15–45
Russia[f]	Angarsk	Civilian	Operational	GC	2 200–5 000
	Novouralsk	Civilian	Operational	GC	13 300
	Seversk	Civilian	Operational	GC	3 800
	Zelenogorsk	Civilian	Operational	GC	7 900
UK	Capenhurst	Civilian	Operational	GC	5 000
USA	Areva Eagle Rock	Civilian	Planned	GC	3 300–6 600
	Paducah	Civilian	To be shut down	GD	11 300
	Piketon, Ohio	Civilian	Planned	GC	3 800
	Urenco Eunice	Civilian	Operating	GC	2 000–5 900

[a] The gas centrifuge (GC) is the main isotope-separation technology used to increase the percentage of U-235 in uranium, but a few facilities continue to use gaseous diffusion (GD).

[b] SWU/yr = Separative work units per year: a SWU is a measure of the effort required in an enrichment facility to separate uranium of a given content of uranium-235 into 2 components, 1 with a higher and 1 with a lower percentage of uranium-235. Where a range of capacities is shown, the facility is expanding its capacity.

[c] In June 2012 France permanently ended production at the George Besse 1 GD uranium enrichment plant, after 33 years of operation.

[d] The Rokkasho centrifuge plant is being refitted with new centrifuge technology and is operating at very low capacity.

[e] North Korea revealed its Yongbyon enrichment facility in 2010. Its operating status is unknown.

[f] Angarsk was formerly known as Angarsk-10. Novouralsk was formerly known as Sverdlovsk-44. Seversk was formerly known as Tomsk-7. Zelenogorsk was formerly known as Krasnoyarsk-45; it is to begin operating a cascade for HEU production for fast reactor and research reactor fuel.

Sources: Enrichment capacity data is based on International Atomic Energy Agency (IAEA), Integrated Nuclear Fuel Cycle Information Systems (INFCIS), <http://www-nfcis.iaea.org/>; International Panel on Fissile Materials (IPFM), *Global Fissile Material Report 2012–2013: Increasing Transparency of Nuclear-warhead and Fissile-material Stocks as a Step toward Disarmament* (IPFM: Princeton, NJ, forthcoming 2013).

Table 6.13. Significant reprocessing facilities worldwide, as of December 2012

All facilities process light water reactor (LWR) fuel, except where indicated.

State	Facility name or location	Type	Status	Design capacity (tHM/yr)[a]
China	Lanzhou pilot plant	Civilian	Operational	50–100
France	La Hague UP2	Civilian	Operational	1 000
	La Hague UP3	Civilian	Operational	1 000
India[b]	Kalpakkam (HWR fuel)	Dual-use	Operational	100
	Tarapur-I (HWR fuel)	Dual-use	Operational	100
	Tarapur-II (HWR fuel)	Dual-use	Operational	100
	Trombay (HWR fuel)	Military	Operational	50
Israel	Dimona (HWR fuel)	Military	Operational	40–100
Japan	JNC Tokai	Civilian	Temporarily shut down	200
	Rokkasho	Civilian	Starting up	800
Korea, North	Yongbyon	Military	On standby	100–150
Pakistan	Chashma (HWR fuel?)	Military	Under construction	50–100
	Nilore (HWR fuel)	Military	Operational	20–40
Russia[d]	Mayak RT-1, Ozersk	Civilian	Operational	200–400
	Seversk	Military	Shut down	6 000
	Zheleznogorsk	Military	Shut down	3 500
UK	BNFL B205 Magnox	Civilian	To be shut down	1 500
	BNFL Thorp, Sellafield	Civilian	To be shut down[c]	1 200
USA	H-canyon, Savannah River Site	Civilian	Operational	15

HWR = Heavy water reactor.

[a] Design capacity refers to the highest amount of spent fuel the plant is designed to process and is measured in tonnes of heavy metal per year (tHM/yr), tHM being a measure of the amount of heavy metal—uranium in these cases—that is in the spent fuel. Actual throughput is often a small fraction of the design capacity. E.g. Russia's RT-1 plant has never reprocessed more than 130 tHM/yr and France, because of the non-renewal of its foreign contracts, will soon only reprocess 850 tHM/yr. LWR spent fuel contains about 1% plutonium, and heavy-water- and graphite-moderated reactor fuel about 0.4%.

[b] As part of the 2005 Indian–US Civil Nuclear Cooperation Initiative, India has decided that none of its reprocessing plants will be opened for IAEA safeguards inspections.

[c] In July 2012 the British Nuclear Decommissioning Authority (NDA) announced the planned closure by 2018 of its Thorp reprocessing plant at Sellafield, when it is expected to complete its current reprocessing contracts.

[d] Mayak RT-1 was formerly known as Chelyabinsk-65. Seversk was formerly known as Tomsk 7. Zheleznogorsk was formerly known as Krasnoyarsk-26.

Sources: Data on design capacity is based on International Atomic Energy Agency (IAEA), Integrated Nuclear Fuel Cycle Information Systems (INFCIS), <http://www-nfcis.iaea.org/>; and International Panel on Fissile Materials (IPFM), *Global Fissile Material Report 2012–2013: Increasing Transparency of Nuclear-warhead and Fissile-material Stocks as a Step toward Disarmament* (IPFM: Princeton, NJ, forthcoming 2013).

Part III. Non-proliferation, arms control and disarmament, 2012

7. Nuclear arms control and non-proliferation

Overview

In 2012 the nuclear programme of Iran remained at the centre of inter-national concerns about the spread of nuclear weapons (see section I in this chapter). Little progress was made towards resolving the long-running con-troversy over the scope and nature of the programme. The resumption of talks between Iran and the five permanent members of the United Nations Security Council plus Germany (the 'P5+1' states) failed to break the deadlock over Iran's non-compliance with the Security Council's demands that Iran suspend all uranium enrichment and other sensitive nuclear fuel cycle activities. Iran and the International Atomic Energy Agency (IAEA) were also unable to agree on a framework plan for addressing the IAEA's concerns that Iran had pursued nuclear activities with possible military dimensions, in contravention of its commitments under the 1968 Non-Proliferation Treaty (NPT). The impasse led to renewed calls to expand the IAEA's legal powers to investigate NPT parties suspected of violating their treaty-mandated safeguards agree-ments, even beyond those set out in the Model Additional Protocol.

The lack of progress in these two separate but closely related sets of talks fuelled speculation that some states—specifically, Israel or the United States—might prioritize extra-legal measures, or even resort to the preventive use of military force, to deal with Iran's suspected nuclear weapon programme. The renewed attention to military options raised further doubts about the efficacy of international legal approaches, in particular the use of punitive economic sanctions, in dealing with suspected or known cases of states violating important arms control treaty obligations and norms.

The Six-Party Talks on the denuclearization of North Korea remained sus-pended in 2012, while North Korea reaffirmed its status as a nuclear weapon-possessing state (see section II). In an apparent breakthrough, North Korea agreed to suspend its nuclear and ballistic missile programmes in exchange for humanitarian assistance from the USA. However, the deal soon broke down when North Korea launched a satellite-carrying rocket that the USA and its allies in the region described as a disguised ballistic missile test.

There was a bright spot for the nuclear non-proliferation regime when, in November 2012, Myanmar announced that it would sign an additional protocol to its safeguards agreement with the IAEA giving the agency expanded rights of access to nuclear-related sites and information in the country. Myanmar also pledged full transparency and cooperation with the agency in answering questions about alleged undeclared nuclear activities in the past, including the procurement of sensitive equipment from North Korea. This unexpected decision boosted international efforts to increase nuclear transparency and universalize the Model Additional Protocol.

The issue of the future of non-strategic (tactical) nuclear weapons in Europe came to the fore with the completion by the North Atlantic Treaty Organization (NATO) of its Defence and Deterrence Posture Review (DDPR) in 2012 (see section III). The DDPR reaffirmed that nuclear weapons remained a core component of NATO's overall capabilities for deterrence and defence, as outlined in NATO's 2010 Strategic Concept, and did not recommend any force posture changes regarding US nuclear weapons stationed in Europe. At the same time, by saying that NATO would consider options to further reduce non-strategic nuclear weapons if Russia undertook reciprocal measures, the DDPR left open the possibility for extending nuclear arms control measures beyond the 2010 Russian–US New START treaty.

In 2012 the risks of nuclear terrorism and the illicit diversion of nuclear and radioactive materials continued to be discussed at the highest political level. In March, 53 heads of state and government gathered at the Nuclear Security Summit in Seoul, South Korea, for a meeting aimed at strengthening legal and regulatory arrangements for securing nuclear materials and facilities worldwide (see section IV). The leaders reviewed implementation of the voluntary commitments made at the 2010 Washington Nuclear Security Summit and issued a communiqué identifying priority areas for increasing the security of nuclear and radiological materials. They also considered the relationship between nuclear safety and security in the light of the accident in 2011 at the nuclear power plant in Fukushima, Japan. The leaders agreed to convene a third summit meeting, in the Netherlands in 2014, amid discussions about how to sustain nuclear security cooperation.

The nearly 40-year-old proposal for establishing a zone free of nuclear and other weapons of mass destruction (WMD) in the Middle East raised new controversy in 2012. Finland, acting in the role of a special facilitator, was scheduled to host an international conference on the issue in December, in line with a decision taken at the 2010 NPT Review Conference and pursuant to a resolution adopted at the 1995 NPT Review and Extension Conference. However, in November the conference co-sponsors—Russia, the United Kingdom and the USA—announced that the meeting would not be held in 2012 because some states in the region had not yet agreed to participate. A key question dividing the states was whether the zone should be seen as a means towards a more stable and secure Middle East, or whether it would come as a result of an improved security environment in the region. The decision to postpone the conference was met with little surprise but considerable disappointment. One effect of the postponement was to call into question the credibility of the NPT action plan for the 2010–15 review cycle.

SHANNON N. KILE

I. Iran and nuclear proliferation concerns

SHANNON N. KILE

During 2012 there was a renewal of international diplomatic efforts aimed at resolving the controversy over the scope and nature of Iran's nuclear programme. The controversy had arisen in 2002, when evidence of undeclared Iranian nuclear facilities was first made public.[1] The discussions during 2012 made some procedural progress in outlining an approach to further negotiations but failed to achieve a breakthrough on any of the substantive issues of concern. At the same, Iran and the International Atomic Energy Agency (IAEA) remained unable to agree on a work plan for resolving the agency's questions about Iranian nuclear activities with possible military dimensions.

Renewed international negotiations on Iran's nuclear programme

In 2012 Iran and the P5+1 states (the five permanent members of the UN Security Council—China, France, Russia, the United Kingdom, and the United States—plus Germany) resumed negotiations on a long-term agreement to ensure that Iran's nuclear programme remained solely for peaceful purposes.[2] On 14 April the parties met in Istanbul, Turkey, to hold talks for the first time since January 2011. The talks, which were headed by the High Representative for Foreign Affairs and Security Policy of the European Union (EU), Catherine Ashton, and the Secretary of Iran's Supreme National Security Council, Saeed Jalili, were described by both sides as positive and constructive.[3] US officials attributed the improved atmosphere to an apparent change in Iran's approach to the talks, in which it no longer insisted on the lifting of international sanctions as a precondition for discussing its nuclear programme.[4] In a statement issued at the end of the meeting, Ashton said that the parties agreed to establish a 'sustained process' of negotiations, based on the 1968 Treaty on the Non-proliferation of Nuclear Weapons (Non-Proliferation Treaty, NPT), 'to ensure all the obligations under the NPT are met by Iran while fully respecting Iran's right to the peaceful use of nuclear energy'.[5] According to one Iranian

---

[1] On developments in earlier years see Kile, S. N., 'Iran and nuclear proliferation concerns', *SIPRI Yearbook 2012*; and other relevant editions of the SIPRI Yearbook.

[2] See Davenport, K., 'History of official proposals on the Iranian nuclear issue', Fact Sheet, Arms Control Association, Aug. 2012, <http://www.armscontrol.org/factsheets/Iran_Nuclear_Proposals>.

[3] 'Iran talks in Istanbul "constructive"', BBC News, 15 Apr. 2012, <http://www.bbc.co.uk/news/world-middle-east-17716241>.

[4] Peterson, S., 'Iran nuclear talks: why all sides kept positive', *Christian Science Monitor*, 15 Apr. 2012.

[5] European Union, 'Statement by High Representative Catherine Ashton on behalf of the E3+3 following the talks with Iran, Istanbul, 14 April 2012', Press release A 173/12, 14 Apr. 2012, <http://

negotiator, the acceptance of the NPT framework for future talks reflected the P5+1 states' new-found 'respect' for Iran's nuclear technology capabilities and rights under the NPT.[6]

The optimism following the Istanbul meeting soon dissipated in the follow-on round of talks between Iran and the P5+1 states held in Baghdad, Iraq, on 23–24 May 2012. The discussion revealed fundamental incompatibilities between the two sides' goals and expectations and failed to produce an agreement on even a modest set of confidence-building steps.[7]

The main goal of the P5+1 states in the talks was to halt Iran's production of uranium enriched to nearly 20 per cent in the isotope uranium-235 (U-235) and sharply limiting its stockpile of the material. Iran announced in 2010 that it had commenced production of the uranium in order to make fuel for the ageing Tehran Research Reactor, which is used to produce medical isotopes. Iran's growing stockpile of the 19.75 per cent-enriched uranium has raised international concern because the material, if diverted for weapon purposes, could be enriched to weapon-grade highly enriched uranium (HEU) more rapidly than the 3.5 per cent-enriched uranium typically used for nuclear power plant fuel.[8]

During the Baghdad meeting, the P5+1 states put forward what was described as a 'stop, shut and ship' proposal.[9] It called on Iran to immediately stop the enrichment of uranium to the near-20 per cent level; shut down all enrichment activities at a fortified underground enrichment facility located at Fordow, near the city of Qom; and ship out of the country most of its stockpile of near-20 per cent-enriched uranium. In return, Iran would receive fuel plates for the Tehran Research Reactor, assistance with nuclear safety and US spare parts for the country's civilian aircraft fleet.

Iran promptly rejected the P5+1 states' proposal, primarily because it contained no provision for easing the sanctions that were increasingly damaging the Iranian economy.[10] A former Iranian nuclear negotiator, Hossein Mousavian, later dismissed the proposal as calling for Iran to trade 'diamonds for peanuts'.[11] Some Western analysts argued that Iran's expectations for a deal in Baghdad exceeded what was politically possible for the

www.consilium.europa.eu/press/press-releases/latest-press-releases/newsroomrelated?bid=78&grp =20909>. For a summary and other details of the NPT see annex A in this volume.

[6] 'P5+1 group takes new approach toward Iran', Iran Press TV, 15 Apr. 2012, <http://www.presstv. ir/detail/236297.html>.

[7] Barry, E. and Gladstone, R., 'Setback in talks on Iran's nuclear program in a "gulf of mistrust"', *New York Times*, 20 June 1012.

[8] Heinonen, O., 'The 20 percent solution', *Foreign Policy*, 11 Jan. 2012. Enrichment from natural uranium to 20% U-235 is significantly more time-consuming and resource-intensive than subsequent enrichment to the weapon-grade uranium (typically enriched above 90%) required for a nuclear weapon.

[9] Barry and Gladstone (note 7).

[10] Peterson, S., 'Iran nuclear talks a "complete failure", says Iranian diplomat', *Christian Science Monitor*, 25 May 2012.

[11] Dahl, F., 'Powers want "diamonds for peanuts:" Iran ex-official', Reuters, 15 June 2012.

P5+1 states to offer.[12] However, others pointed out that the one measure—meaningful relief from sanctions—that would allow Iranian leaders to present a suspension of its enrichment programme as a victory to the public, and hence form the basis for a deal, was also the measure that the West was unwilling to concede.[13]

Despite the deadlock at Baghdad, the parties held a further round of talks in Moscow, on 18–19 June 2012, during which Iran provided details about the proposal it had presented to the P5+1 states.[14] The Iranian proposal set out a five-step plan consisting of reciprocal measures to be taken by the two sides within the framework of the NPT.[15] As a first step, the P5+1 states would acknowledge Iran's claim that it had a right under the NPT to carry out uranium enrichment. In conjunction with this acknowledgment, Iran would make legally binding a fatwa (religious decree) that the Supreme Leader, Ayatollah Ali Khamenei, is said to have issued in 2004 condemning the production, possession and use of nuclear weapons as forbidden in Islam.[16] The second step would involve the ending of unilateral sanctions imposed against Iran by some of the P5+1 states in return for Iran's full cooperation with the investigation by the IAEA of 'possible military dimensions' to its nuclear activities. The third step envisioned cooperation on nuclear energy and safety. The fourth step was contingent on the completion of the first two and involved Iran limiting or halting the production of 20 per cent-enriched uranium as a confidence-building measure. The fifth and final step called for cooperation between Iran and the P5+1 states on regional security issues.

The talks in Moscow ended with the two sides increasingly committed to competing strategies for addressing the standoff over Iran's nuclear programme. Iranian officials complained that the P5+1 states, in particular the Western powers, had shown little interest in discussing Iran's proposal and were interested only in Iran's response to the proposal they had put forward in Baghdad.[17] They also complained that the P5+1 states were reneging on their promise made at the Istanbul meeting to recognize Iran's right under the NPT as the basis of the talks.[18] In response, an EU spokes-

---

[12] Fitzpatrick, M., 'Tehran's expectations exceed the possible in Baghdad talks', *The National* (Abu Dhabi), 24 May 2012.

[13] Moran, M., 'Back to the future for Iranian nuclear diplomacy?', WMD Junction, 15 June 2012, <http://wmdjunction.com/120615_iran_diplomacy.htm>.

[14] Borger, J., ' "Progress" in Moscow: Iran says no with PowerPoint', The Guardian Global Security Blog, 18 June 2012, <http://www.guardian.co.uk/world/julian-borger-global-security-blog/2012/jun/18/iran-russia>.

[15] Sadri, M., 'Iran–P5+1: what happened from Moscow to Almaty?', Iran Review, 23 Feb. 2013, <http://www.iranreview.org/content/Documents/Iran-P5-1-What-Happened-from-Moscow-to-Almaty-.htm>.

[16] For a description of the fatwa see Mehr News Agency, 'Iran's statement at IAEA emergency meeting', 10 Aug. 2005, <http://www.fas.org/nuke/guide/iran/nuke/mehr080905.html>.

[17] Sahimi (note 15).

[18] 'Iran, major powers start nuclear talks in Moscow', *Tehran Times*, 19 June 2012.

man stated that the NPT did not explicitly mention that every state party had the right to enrich uranium.[19] US diplomats emphasized that the stop, shut and ship proposal had to remain the focus of negotiations, since it addressed the core issue of bringing Iran into compliance with its international obligations.[20]

With the diplomatic deadlock spurring calls in Israel and the USA for military action against Iran's nuclear facilities, the two sides attempted to avert the collapse of negotiations. On 3 July 2012 they convened a meeting of experts in Istanbul to discuss technical aspects of the proposals made during the earlier talks, followed by a deputy-level meeting on 24 July.[21] On 18 September, Ashton and Jalili met informally in Istanbul to discuss 'common points' reached by the technical experts for creating a framework for future talks.[22] The discussions took place against the background of moves by the USA and the EU to significantly increase their commercial and economic sanctions against Iran over its nuclear programme, including the EU's adoption of a boycott on Iranian oil imports as of 1 July 2012.[23]

During the autumn of 2012 representatives from Iran and the P5+1 states reaffirmed the importance of restarting formal negotiations. This included an agreement within the P5+1 group to 'update' the proposal that it had presented to Iran during the meeting in Baghdad.[24] As the year ended, however, the two sides had not set a date for a new round of talks.

Impasse between Iran and the IAEA

In 2012 Iran and the IAEA failed to reach agreement on a framework for resolving the agency's concerns about past Iranian nuclear activities with possible military dimensions. The concerns had been summarized in a report submitted by the IAEA Director General, Yukiya Amano, to the IAEA Board of Governors in November 2011.[25] The weapon-related activities that Iran allegedly pursued involved high-explosives tests with nuclear weapon applications; neutron initiation and detonator experiments; research and development work to fit a nuclear warhead on a missile, along with arming, firing and fusing mechanisms; and procurement

---

[19] Borger, J., 'Oil embargo on Iran will not be postponed, says EU', *The Guardian*, 18 June 2012.

[20] Barry, E., 'No one budges in tense Iran nuclear talks in Moscow', *New York Times*, 19 June 2012.

[21] Davenport, K., 'Future of Iran talks in question', *Arms Control Today*, vol. 42, no. 7 (Sep. 2012).

[22] 'EU's Catherine Ashton meets Iran nuclear negotiator', BBC News, 19 Sep. 2012, <http://www.bbc.co.uk/news/world-middle-east-19634052>.

[23] See chapter 10, section III, in this volume.

[24] Lakshmanan, I. A. R., 'U.S. and partners agree on revised nuclear offer for Iran', Bloomberg, 13 Dec. 2012, <http://www.bloomberg.com/news/2012-12-13/u-s-and-partners-agree-on-revised-nuclear-offer-for-iran.html>.

[25] IAEA, Board of Governors, 'Implementation of the NPT safeguards agreement and relevant provisions of the Security Council resolutions in the Islamic Republic of Iran', Report by the Director General, GOV/2011/65, 8 Nov. 2011.

activities related to the alleged warhead work.[26] Most of this alleged weapon-related work took place prior to 2003.

During 2012 senior IAEA and Iranian officials met intermittently to discuss a 'structured approach' document setting the terms and conditions for the agency's investigation of specific activities of concern. The discussions were hindered by two procedural disputes. The first had to do with the sequencing of the questions the IAEA wanted to address. Iran insisted that this had to be done in a pre-determined order; after agreed steps were taken on each issue, it would be considered closed.[27] In contrast, IAEA officials expressed a preference for addressing multiple issues at the same time, since many of the activities under investigation appeared to be linked. They also emphasized the possible need for follow-up questions either to clarify specific issues or to deal with any new evidence that might emerge.[28]

The second dispute had to do with Iran's demand for access to the largely Western intelligence documents that formed the basis of the IAEA's report about Iran's alleged nuclear weapon-related activities. Iran has rejected the allegations, and the documents on which they were based, as the fabrications of hostile foreign intelligence services. While promising to accede to Iran's request 'when appropriate', Amano noted that it was difficult for the IAEA to do so when it had been given the material in confidence by member states whose sources might be exposed if Iran saw the original files.[29]

On 13 September 2012 the 35-member IAEA Board of Governors approved a resolution stating, among other things, that it was 'essential' for Iran to conclude with the IAEA an agreement on a 'structured approach' for addressing the agency's questions about possible Iranian nuclear weapon-related activities.[30] As a 'first step', the Board called on Iran to provide IAEA inspectors with access to sites that the agency had asked to visit.

The Board's call for Iran to grant inspectors access to sites inside the country reflected the dispute during 2012 between the IAEA and Iran over the former's request to visit a large Iranian military production complex

---

[26] For a summary of the IAEA's findings see Kile (note 1), pp. 366–68.

[27] Hibbs, M., 'Iran and the IAEA talk again', Carnegie Endowment for International Peace, 12 May 2012, <http://carnegieendowment.org/2012/05/12/iran-and-iaea-talk-again/apy9>.

[28] 'IAEA Board calls on Iran to cooperate with IAEA, but Tehran continues to balk', Arms Control Association, *Issues Briefs*, vol. 3, no. 13 (18 Sep. 2012), <http://www.armscontrol.org/issuebriefs/IAEA-Board-of-Governors-Call-on-Iran-to-Cooperate-with-IAEA-But-Tehran-Continues-to-Balk>.

[29] Slavin, B., 'IAEA chief willing to share data with Iran on weapons claims', Al-Monitor, 6 Dec. 2012, <http://www.al-monitor.com/pulse/originals/2012/al-monitor/amano-iran-weapons-claims.html>.

[30] IAEA, Board of Governors, 'Implementation of the NPT safeguards agreement and relevant provisions of United Nations Security Council resolutions in the Islamic Republic of Iran', Resolution, GOV/2012/50, 13 Sep. 2012, p. 2.

located at Parchin, near Tehran.[31] The agency repeatedly sought permission to make a 'transparency visit' to a building there, based on information provided by a member state that Iran had constructed a large steel chamber in the building that was used for conducting high-explosives experiments—some of which may have involved uranium—and which could be associated with a programme to develop a nuclear explosive device. Iran maintained that the Parchin complex was used solely for conventional military purposes, with no connection to nuclear material, and had already been adequately inspected by the agency.[32]

On 13 December an IAEA team led by Herman Nackaerts, Head of the IAEA Department of Safeguards, held talks with Iranian officials in Tehran about a framework agreement for resolving the agency's outstanding questions. Both sides reported that the talks made progress towards an agreement and that a new round would be held in mid-January 2013.[33] At the same time, however, Iran did not grant the IAEA team access to the Parchin site. The refusal came amid mounting concern among some experts, based on satellite imagery analysis, that Iran might be 'sanitizing' the site to hinder an investigation into alleged nuclear weapon-related explosives tests conducted there in the past.[34]

The IAEA Director General's assessment of Iran's nuclear programme

On 16 November 2012 the IAEA Director General issued the latest in a series of regular reports to the IAEA Board of Governors on safeguards implementation in Iran.[35] Amano's report stated that Iran continued to make progress with its uranium enrichment programme and the construction of a heavy-water research reactor, in defiance of the UN Security Council's demands, set out in five resolutions, that it suspend all enrich-

[31] Esfandiari, G., 'Explainer: why do UN inspectors want access to Iran's Parchin military complex?', Radio Free Europe/Radio Liberty, 7 June 2012, <http://www.rferl.org/content/explainer-why-do-un-inspectors-want-access-to-iran-parchin-military-complex/24606630.html>.

[32] IAEA inspectors visited the Parchin complex in 2005 but did not ask to see the building where the chamber was allegedly built. 'Iran to allow IAEA visit Parchin military site: ISNA', Reuters, 6 Mar. 2012.

[33] 'IAEA says "progress" in nuclear talks', Al Jazeera, 14 Dec. 2012, <http://www.aljazeera.com/news/middleeast/2012/12/20121214143742829541.html>.

[34] See 'Significant changes made to Parchin high explosives test site, further activity likely', Institute for Science and International Security (ISIS) Imagery Brief, 29 Nov. 2012, <http://isis-online.org/isis-reports/>. For a contrary view of Iran's activities at the site see Kelley, R. E., 'The IAEA and Parchin: questions and concerns', SIPRI Expert Comment, 18 Jan. 2013, <http://www.sipri.org/media/expert-comments/18jan2013_IAEA_Kelley>.

[35] IAEA, Board of Governors, 'Implementation of the NPT Safeguards Agreement and relevant provisions of the Security Council resolutions in the Islamic Republic of Iran', Report by the Director General, GOV/2012/55, 16 Nov. 2012.

ment and other sensitive nuclear fuel cycle activities.[36] The report described technical advances made by Iran in the following areas.

Increased centrifuge numbers and capabilities

During the second half of 2012 Iran continued to increase its uranium-enrichment capabilities by installing additional first-generation IR-1 centrifuges at two declared facilities: the Fuel Enrichment Plant (FEP) at Natanz; and the smaller Fordow Fuel Enrichment Plant (FFEP). However, none of the newly installed centrifuges were in operation as of November 2012.[37]

The Director General's report stated that Iran continued to develop advanced centrifuge models. It was testing second-generation IR-2m and IR-4 centrifuges at the Pilot Fuel Enrichment Plant (PFEP) at Natanz; the new centrifuges remained in a research and development area of the plant and were not ready for production-scale use.[38] The report noted that Iran had yet to begin testing the more advanced centrifuge models (IR-5, IR-6 and IR-6s) that it had announced in 2010.[39] Iran's ability to produce these advanced centrifuges remains uncertain, due in part to international sanctions that prevent it from acquiring the necessary materials and components.[40]

Increased stockpiles of low-enriched uranium

The report stated that Iran continued to produce low-enriched uranium (LEU), in the form of uranium hexafluoride gas, at Natanz and Fordow. In addition, Iran had increased its stockpile of near-20 per cent-enriched uranium to a total of 233 kilograms. Approximately 135 kg of this material was in storage at the Fordow and Natanz plants; the remaining 96 kg was being converted into uranium oxide (U_3O_8), a solid powder from which nuclear fuel is made, at the Fuel Plate Fabrication Plant near Esfahan.[41] Some observers pointed out that at its monthly production rate, by mid-2013 Iran would have accumulated 200–220 kilograms of near-20 per cent-enriched uranium—enough to give it a capability to produce one 'significant quantity' of weapon-grade uranium.[42]

---

[36] UN Security Council resolutions 1737, 23 Dec. 2006; 1747, 24 Mar. 2007; 1803, 3 Mar. 2008; 1835, 27 Sep. 2008; and 1935, 9 June 2010.

[37] IAEA, GOV/2012/55 (note 35), pp. 4–5.

[38] According to one estimate, the IR-2m and IR-4 centrifuges could achieve 3–4 times the enrichment output of the current IR-1 centrifuge. Witt, W. C. et al., 'Iran's evolving breakout potential', Institute for Science and International Security (ISIS) Report, 8 Oct. 2012, <http://www.isis-online.org/isis-reports/>, p. 21.

[39] IAEA, GOV/2012/55 (note 35), p. 5.

[40] Dahl, F., 'Iran makes little headway on key nuclear equipment', Reuters, 31 Aug. 2012.

[41] IAEA, GOV/2012/55 (note 35), p. 4.

[42] Witt et al. (note 38). A significant quantity, defined by the IAEA as 25 kg of uranium enriched to 90% U-235, is the amount required for one nuclear weapon.

This milestone took on special significance when the Israeli Prime Minister, Benyamin Netanyahu, warned in a speech to the UN General Assembly on 27 September 2012 that Israel might strike Iran's nuclear facilities before Iran could reach the milestone of 'one bomb's worth' of uranium enriched to 20 per cent.[43] However, others cautioned that the importance of the milestone should not be overstated, since all nuclear material and installed cascades were subject to IAEA containment and surveillance measures and any Iranian attempt to 'break out' of the NPT and produce weapon-grade HEU would alert the international community.[44]

Continued work on Arak research reactor

The Director General's report stated that Iran continued to build the IR-40 heavy-water research reactor located near Arak. The date for the reactor's planned initiation of operations had been pushed back from mid-2013 to the early part of 2014, but the report did not offer a cause for the delay.[45] Similar reactors ostensibly built for research have been used to produce plutonium for nuclear weapons in India, Israel, North Korea and Pakistan.[46]

The report stated that the IAEA continued to verify the non-diversion of nuclear material at the nuclear facilities declared by Iran under its comprehensive safeguards agreement with the agency. However, it warned that Iran was not providing the necessary cooperation, including by not implementing its additional safeguards protocol, for the IAEA to be able to provide credible assurance about the absence of undeclared nuclear material and activities in Iran.[47]

During 2012 the optimism accompanying the resumption of negotiations between Iran and P5+1 states after a tense one-year hiatus dissipated as it become clear that the two sides remained committed to incompatible goals and strategies for the talks that precluded any near-term breakthroughs. The year ended with scepticism growing among the P5+1 states, in particular China and Russia, about the relevance of the 'carrot-and-stick' approach of the USA and EU to the negotiations, amid signs that Iran remained determined not halt its enrichment programme as a precondition for a negotiated deal.

---

[43] Heller, J., 'Netanyahu draws "red line" on Iran's nuclear program', Reuters, 27 Sep. 2012.

[44] Witt et al. (note 38).

[45] IAEA, GOV/2012/55 (note 35), p. 7.

[46] 'Iran Arak plant set to begin operations in 2014: IAEA', Global Security Newswire, 19 Nov. 2012, <http://www.nti.org/gsn/article/iran-arak-plant-begin-operations-2014-iaea/>.

[47] IAEA, GOV/2012/55 (note 35), p. 12. Iran never ratified the additional protocol agreement signed with the IAEA in Dec. 2003, and in Feb. 2007 informed the IAEA that it would no longer act in accordance with the protocol's provisions.

II. North Korea's nuclear programme

SHANNON N. KILE

The Six-Party Talks on the nuclear programme of the Democratic People's Republic of Korea (DPRK, North Korea) were launched following the country's announcement of its withdrawal from the 1968 Treaty on the Non-proliferation of Nuclear Weapons (Non-Proliferation Treaty, NPT) in 2003.[1] Five rounds of negotiations were held until North Korea walked out in April 2009 in protest against a new round of United Nations sanctions imposed in response to its nuclear weapon and missile tests. Disagreement over the terms for restarting negotiations have subsequently blocked the talks.[2]

In early 2012 a potential break in this diplomatic impasse was made. On 29 February, following three rounds of bilateral talks held since July 2011, North Korea and the United States announced in separate statements that the former had agreed to halt its uranium-enrichment programme and observe a voluntary moratorium on further long-range missile and nuclear weapon tests.[3] North Korea had also agreed to invite International Atomic Energy Agency (IAEA) inspectors to return to its Yongbyon nuclear complex, for the first time since their expulsion in 2009, to verify the cessation of uranium-enrichment activities and the shutdown of the partially dismantled nuclear research reactor that had been used to produce plutonium for North Korea's two nuclear explosive tests. In return, the USA announced that it would provide North Korea with 240 000 tonnes of food aid, contingent on the latter's acceptance of intrusive external monitoring of its distribution.[4] The announcement of the so-called Leap Day deal was welcomed by other states in the region as a step towards resuming the Six-Party Talks and as an important initial test of the intentions of the new North Korean leader, Kim Jong Un, following the death of his father in December 2011.[5]

---

[1] The Six-Party Talks began in Aug. 2003 as a Chinese diplomatic initiative to reach a deal under which international aid would be provided to North Korea in return for North Korea verifiably giving up its nuclear weapon capabilities. The 6 parties to the talks are China, Japan, North Korea, South Korea, Russia and the USA. For a summary and other details of the NPT see annex A in this volume.

[2] On developments in 2011 see Kile, S. N., 'North Korea's nuclear programme', *SIPRI Yearbook 2012*. On developments in earlier years see relevant editions of the SIPRI Yearbook.

[3] Korean Central News Agency (KCNA), 'DPRK Foreign Ministry spokesman on result of DPRK–U.S. talks', 29 Feb. 2012, <http://www.kcna.co.jp/item/2012/201202/news29/20120229-37ee.html>.

[4] US Department of State, 'U.S.–D.P.R.K. bilateral discussions', Press statement, 29 Feb. 2012, <http://www.state.gov/r/pa/prs/ps/2012/02/184869.htm>.

[5] Choe, S., 'In North Korea deal, son inherits father's framework', *New York Times*, 2 Mar. 2012.

Breakdown of the North Korean–US nuclear suspension agreement

Hopes for a diplomatic breakthrough proved to be short-lived. On 16 March North Korea's news agency announced plans for the launch of a rocket that would place in orbit a civilian earth observation satellite as part of the celebration of the 100th anniversary of the birth of the state's founder, Kim Il Sung.[6] The USA, the Republic of Korea (South Korea) and Japan promptly denounced the planned launch as a disguised attempt by North Korea to continue the flight testing of its Taepodong-2 long-range ballistic missile that had been under development for more than a decade.[7] Declaring that the launch would violate North Korea's moratorium on missile launches under the Leap Day deal, the USA announced that it had suspended the food assistance package.[8]

The subsequent launch, conducted on 13 April 2012 in the presence of international observers, was a widely publicized failure. The three-stage Unha-3 rocket exploded shortly after lift-off from the new Sohae Launching Station at Tongchang-ri, North Pyongan province, near North Korea's western border with China.[9]

North Korea's decision to proceed with the launch elicited a wave of international criticism. On 16 April the UN Security Council unanimously adopted a presidential statement condemning the launch as a 'serious violation' of resolutions 1718 (of 2006) and 1874 (of 2009), which prohibited North Korea from conducting any type of launch using ballistic missile technology.[10] The Security Council ordered its Sanctions Committee on North Korea to designate additional 'individuals, entities and items' to be subjected to the arms and technology embargoes imposed in 2006 and strengthened in 2009. The order came amid reports that a Chinese firm had supplied North Korea with the chassis for a new type of mobile launch vehicle, in contravention of the UN arms embargo on North Korea.[11]

North Korea responded with a strongly worded statement dismissing the UN Security Council's 'unreasonable behaviour' in violating its 'legitimate

---

[6] Korean Central News Agency (KCNA), 'DPRK to launch application satellite', 16 Mar. 2012, <http://www.kcna.co.jp/item/2012/201203/news16/20120316-20ee.html>.

[7] 'China "concerned" over North Korea rocket launch plan', BBC News, 17 Mar. 2012, <http://www.bbc.co.uk/news/world-asia-17413054>.

[8] Parrish, K., American Forces Press Service, 'Officials suspend North Korea nutrition aid over planned launch', US Department of Defense, 28 Mar. 2012, <http://www.defense.gov/News/News Article.aspx?ID=67738>; and Ide, W., 'US suspends food assistance to North Korea', Voice of America, 27 Mar. 2012, <http://www.voanews.com/content/us-suspends-north-korea-food-aid-144680 865/181146.html>.

[9] Choe, S. and Gladstone, R., 'North Korean rocket fails moments after liftoff', New York Times, 13 Apr. 2012.

[10] United Nations, Security Council, Statement by the President of the Security Council, S/PRST/ 2012/13, 16 Apr. 2012.

[11] On this and other reported breaches of the embargo see chapter 10, section II, in this volume.

right to launch satellites' for peaceful space research.[12] It described the US-drafted presidential statement as another example of the USA reneging on 'its promise [in the Leap Day deal] that "it respects the sovereignty of [North Korea] and has no hostile intent toward it"'. The statement declared that since the USA had repeatedly violated the agreement through its 'undisguised hostile acts', North Korea would no longer be bound by it. It also warned that North Korea would take unspecified 'necessary retaliatory measures'—a formulation that raised international concern that the country would conduct another nuclear test explosion, as it had done following the failure of a rocket launch in 2009.[13]

Renewed concern about North Korea's nuclear and missile programmes

North Korea's announcement that it had cancelled the Leap Day deal with the USA also led to renewed speculation about its long-term nuclear intentions and the sincerity of its professed willingness to 'abandon' its nuclear programme. In revisions to the country's constitution approved in April 2012, North Korea was formally identified as a 'nuclear power'.[14] While North Korea had called itself a nuclear power for the past several years, the inclusion of its capability in the constitution highlighted the importance the regime attached to possessing nuclear weapons.[15]

During the second half of 2012 North Korea's ballistic missile capabilities remained a focus of concern for the USA and its allies in North East Asia. In October 2012 the USA consented to South Korea revising its missile guidelines—required by the USA in 1979 because of its concern over a regional arms race—to allow it to deploy ballistic missiles with a range of up to 800 kilometres. This would enable the missile to reach any target in North Korea. The amendment to the guidelines also allowed South Korea to increase its previous missile payload limit of 500 kilograms, depending on the range of the missile.[16]

---

[12] Korean Central News Agency (KCNA), 'DPRK rejects UNSC's act to violate DPRK's legitimate right to launch satellite', 17 Apr. 2012, <http://www.kcna.co.jp/item/2012/201204/news17/20120417-25ee.html>.

[13] Lim, B. K., 'China pushes North Korea to drop nuclear test plan: sources', Reuters, 16 May 2012. On North Korea's nuclear test preparations see chapter 6, section IX, in this volume.

[14] 'N. Korea puts nuclear arms in constitution', Chosun Ilbo, 31 May 2012, <http://english.chosun.com/site/data/html_dir/2012/05/31/2012053100646.html>; and Constitution of the Democratic People's Republic of Korea, <http://naenara.com.kp/ko/great/constitution.php>, Preamble (in Korean).

[15] E.g. Hayes, P., 'The DPRK's nuclear constitution', Nautilus Peace and Security Weekly, 14 June 2012, <http://nautilus.org/napsnet/napsnet-weekly/the-dprks-nuclear-constitution/>.

[16] Choe, S., 'U.S. allows South Korea to extend range of missiles', New York Times, 8 Oct. 2012. The previous guidelines, as amended in 2001, had prevented South Korea from deploying ballistic missiles with a range of more than 300 km.

On 12 December North Korea announced with considerable fanfare that it had launched a Unha-3 rocket that successfully put into orbit an earth-observation satellite named Kwangmyongsong-3.[17] The Canadian–US North American Aerospace Defense Command (NORAD) confirmed that the rocket had apparently placed a satellite into polar orbit, although subsequent reports indicated that it was tumbling out of control and presumably non-functional.[18] However, the event confirmed that North Korea was mastering the technology for multistage rockets—one of several steps required for developing an intercontinental ballistic missile (ICBM) capable of delivering a nuclear warhead.[19]

The UN Security Council promptly condemned the North Korean rocket launch as a clear violation of its resolutions banning the country from conducting ballistic missile tests.[20] Several member states urged the Council to expand existing UN sanctions against North Korea.[21] However, the year ended with no decision by the Council to impose new punitive measures or take other steps in response to the North Korean rocket launch.

Developments in North Korea's nuclear and ballistic missile programmes in 2012 suggested that the new North Korean leadership under Kim Jong-un would prioritize the country's so-called 'military-first' policy underpinned by advances in its nuclear and ballistic missile capabilities. The year ended with deepening pessimism in North East Asia about the prospects for restarting multilateral negotiations aimed at inducing North Korea to give up its nascent nuclear arsenal in exchange for international assistance.

---

[17] Korean Central News Agency (KCNA), 'KCNA releases report on satellite launch', 12 Dec. 2012, <http://www.kcna.co.jp/item/2012/201212/news12/20121212-09ee.html>.

[18] Broad, W. J., and Choe, S., 'Astronomers say North Korean satellite is most likely dead', *New York Times*, 18 Dec. 2012.

[19] Richardson, D., 'Unha-3 was largely of North Korean manufacture', *Jane's Missiles and Rockets*, Mar. 2013, pp. 4–6.

[20] United Nations, Security Council, Press Statement on Democratic People's Republic of Korea, 12 Dec. 2012, <http://www.new-york-un.diplo.de/Vertretung/newyorkvn/en/__pr/press-releases/2012/20121212-sc-on-dprk.html>; and Penn, D., 'Security Council condemns North Korea rocket launch', United Nations Radio, 12 Dec. 2012, <http://www.unmultimedia.org/radio/english/2012/12/security-council-condemns-north-korea-rocket-launch/>.

[21] 'UN Security Council condemns North Korea rocket launch', BBC News, 13 Dec. 2012, <http://www.bbc.co.uk/news/world-asia-20697922>.

III. NATO and non-strategic nuclear weapons

IAN ANTHONY

At their summit in Chicago, USA, in May 2012, the member states of the North Atlantic Treaty Organization (NATO) endorsed the outcome of a Deterrence and Defence Posture Review (DDPR).[1] Ostensibly mandated by the NATO Summit in Lisbon, Portugal, in November 2010 to examine NATO's overall posture in deterring and defending against the full range of threats to the alliance, in reality the DDPR continued a still unresolved discussion of the role of nuclear weapons in NATO strategy—and in particular the future approach to US non-strategic nuclear weapons stored in Europe.[2]

The NATO Strategic Concept adopted in Lisbon tried to reconcile two different perspectives within the alliance. One is the view that, given its conventional armed strength and the benign security environment in Europe, NATO should make significant changes to its nuclear force posture to strengthen the international momentum behind nuclear arms reductions. This is a view often associated with Germany and Norway, for example.[3] The second view is that NATO should maintain its nuclear posture without significant changes in order to avoid giving any impression that it is losing its primary focus on effective collective defence, both now and in an uncertain future. This view is often associated with France and with some of the countries in Central Europe, including the Baltic states.[4]

The DDPR elaborated some mechanisms to prepare for future nuclear arms reduction, such as a new consultative forum for NATO members to discuss the possible elements of a future dialogue with Russia on non-strategic nuclear weapons.[5] However, by finding that 'the Alliance's nuclear force posture currently meets the criteria for an effective deterrence and defence posture', NATO signalled that no immediate changes to current policy can be expected.[6]

---

[1] NATO, 'Deterrence and defence posture review', 20 May 2012, <http://www.nato.int/cps/en/natolive/official_texts_87597.htm>.

[2] In this context, non-strategic nuclear weapons can be defined as those nuclear weapons not limited by the 2010 Russian–US Treaty on Measures for the Further Reduction and Limitation of Strategic Offensive Arms (New START). New START applies to intercontinental ballistic missiles, submarine-launched ballistic missiles and heavy bombers and the warheads for use on these delivery vehicles. For a summary and other details of New START see annex A in this volume.

[3] See e.g. Westerwelle, G., German Foreign Minister, Speech at the conference 'From a nuclear test ban to a nuclear weapons-free world', Astana, 29 Aug. 2012, <http://www.auswaertiges-amt.de/EN/Infoservice/Presse/Reden/2012/120829-BM_Astana.html>.

[4] Kulesa, Ł. (ed.), *The Future of NATO's Deterrence and Defence Posture: Views from Central Europe* (Polish Institute of International Affairs: Warsaw, Dec. 2012).

[5] NATO (note 1), para. 30.

[6] NATO (note 1), para. 8.

This section first describes the history of reductions in NATO non-strategic nuclear forces prior to the DDPR. It then identifies three key issues raised during the review: harmonizing NATO's nuclear declaratory policy with the positions of its nuclear-armed member states; the modernization of non-strategic nuclear capabilities; and the relationship between missile defence and nuclear forces. Finally, it considers NATO's role in a future arms control agenda.

Background: from the cold war to the 2010 Strategic Concept

During the cold war, many thousands of non-strategic nuclear weapons owned by the USA were located in Europe. Some were earmarked for use by US armed forces stationed in Europe and others for release to specially trained and equipped forces of the USA's NATO allies. In addition, the nuclear forces of France and the United Kingdom included a range of different types of nuclear weapon.

After the end of the cold war NATO's nuclear forces underwent a major rationalization. Between 1991 and 1993, NATO reduced the number of US non-strategic weapons located in Europe by roughly 85 per cent, and reduced the categories of deployed weapons from five to just one: a nuclear gravity bomb dropped by a specially equipped combat aircraft.[7] Neither NATO nor the USA release any official information about non-strategic nuclear weapon stockpiles, but in 2009 it was believed that the total number of US non-strategic warheads was roughly 500, including 400 B61 gravity bombs earmarked for delivery by dual-capable combat aircraft (i.e. aircraft capable of carrying both conventional and nuclear weapons) and 100 warheads for the Tomahawk sea-launch cruise missile (SLCM).[8] A significant number of these were stored in continental USA, while the number of locations where US-owned weapons were deployed in Europe continued to diminish. Following their removal from Greece in 2001 and the UK in 2008, by 2009 it was believed that roughly 200 US weapons were deployed at six air bases in five European countries: Belgium, Germany, Italy, the Netherlands and Turkey.[9]

In 2009 two events sparked an internal debate on the role of nuclear weapons in NATO strategy. In April in Prague, Czech Republic, US Presi-

---

[7] NATO, 'NATO's nuclear forces in the new security environment', Fact sheet, June 2004, <http://web.archive.org/web/*/http://www.nato.int/issues/nuclear/sec-environment.htm>. At the same time Russia was independently taking steps to rationalize its nuclear arsenal.

[8] Kile, S. N., Fedchenko, V. and Kristensen, H. M., 'World nuclear forces', *SIPRI Yearbook 2009*, table 8.2 and p. 352.

[9] Kile et al. (note 8), p. 352; and Kristensen, H. M., 'U.S. nuclear weapons removed from the United Kingdom', Strategic Security Blog, Federation of American Scientists, 26 June 2008, <http://blogs.fas.org/security/2008/06/us-nuclear-weapons-withdrawn-from-the-united-kingdom/>. See also chapter 6, section I, in this volume.

dent Barack Obama made a commitment 'to seek the peace and security of a world without nuclear weapons'.[10] In September the German Government led by the newly re-elected Chancellor Angela Merkel included in its coalition agreement a commitment to raise the issue of withdrawing US nuclear weapons from Germany as a step towards realizing Obama's Prague vision.[11]

In most NATO member states, the sudden promotion of the role of nuclear weapons as an issue for discussion by senior leaders was an unwelcome surprise. Most countries were simply not prepared for the debate, having relegated nuclear issues far down their lists of planning priorities. The issue distracted attention from topics considered more urgent and raised potentially divisive questions about alliance cohesion and burden sharing.

During 2010 language was agreed for the NATO Strategic Concept that was sufficiently ambiguous to cover a range of future options, from maintaining the status quo to complete removal of US weapons from Europe. The final document noted that deterrence, 'based on an appropriate mix of nuclear and conventional capabilities, remains a core element of [NATO's] overall strategy' and that NATO members would 'ensure the broadest possible participation of allies in collective defence planning on nuclear roles, in peacetime basing of nuclear forces, and in command, control and consultation arrangements', without clarifying what 'appropriate mix' or 'broadest possible participation' meant in practice.[12] In contrast, the previous Strategic Concept, from 1999, emphasized that a credible nuclear posture required 'widespread participation by European Allies involved in collective defence planning in nuclear roles, in peacetime basing of nuclear forces on their territory and in command, control and consultation arrangements', noted that nuclear forces based in Europe and committed to NATO 'provide an essential political and military link between the European and the North American members of the Alliance' and stated that NATO would therefore 'maintain adequate nuclear forces in Europe'.[13]

While some member states argued that further clarification of the 2010 Strategic Concept was not needed, others disagreed. The DDPR was intended to provide a forum in which allies could continue to discuss some of the issues raised in 2010—not limited to the stationing of US nuclear

[10] White House, 'Remarks by President Barack Obama, Hradcany Square, Prague, Czech Republic', 5 Apr. 2009, <http://www.whitehouse.gov/the_press_office/Remarks-By-President-Barack-Obama-In-Prague-As-Delivered/>.

[11] Growth. Education. Unity. The Coalition Agreement between the CDU, CSU and FDP for the 17th Legislative Period (CDU/CSU/FDP: Berlin, 26 Oct. 2009), pp. 169–70.

[12] NATO, Active Engagement, Modern Defence: Strategic Concept for the Defence and Security of the Members of the North Atlantic Treaty Organization (NATO: Brussels, Nov. 2010), paras 17, 19.

[13] NATO, 'The alliance's strategic concept', Approved at Washington, DC, 24 Apr. 1999, <http://www.nato.int/cps/en/natolive/official_texts_27433.htm>, para. 63.

weapons in Europe, but including NATO declaratory policy on nuclear weapons, the relationship between deterrence and defence in light of the decision to make missile defence a core mission of NATO, and the role of NATO in future arms control talks with Russia (the mandate of which is expected to include non-strategic nuclear weapons).[14]

The 2012 Deterrence and Defence Posture Review

Three aspects of nuclear policy seem to have formed the main focus of the DDPR: harmonizing NATO nuclear declaratory policy with the national positions of nuclear-armed member states; the modernization of non-strategic nuclear capabilities; and the relationship between missile defence and nuclear forces.

Harmonizing NATO nuclear declaratory policy with the national positions of nuclear-armed member states

The 2010 NATO Strategic Concept was preceded by national reviews of nuclear policy in each of the three NATO member states that possesses nuclear weapons—France, the UK and the USA. One issue taken up in each of these reviews was the circumstances under which nuclear weapons might be used. All three countries emphasized that the likelihood of any scenario arising in which nuclear weapons might be used is extremely remote.[15]

Given the benign security environment in the NATO area and the preponderance of allied conventional forces relative to the countries around its periphery, the question arose whether a 'sole purpose' declaration—in which the only scenario for nuclear weapon use in a NATO framework would be as retaliation following a nuclear attack—might be possible. Nevertheless, all of the nuclear-armed NATO members can envisage circumstances where being the first to use nuclear weapons could be justified.

France, the UK and the USA have all given 'negative security assurances', essentially promising not to use nuclear weapons against non-nuclear weapon states parties to the 1968 Treaty on the Non-proliferation of Nuclear Weapons (Non-Proliferation Treaty, NPT) under almost any con-

---

[14] The process by which the DDPR was conducted is described in Lunn, S. and Kearns, I., *NATO's Deterrence and Defence Posture Review: A Status Report*, NATO Policy Brief no. 1 (European Leadership Network: London, Feb. 2012).

[15] French Government, *Défense et sécurité nationale: Le livre blanc* [Defence and national security: the white paper] (Odile Jacob: Paris, June 2008); British Government, *Securing Britain in an Age of Uncertainty: The Strategic Defence and Security Review*, Cm 7948 (Stationery Office: London, Oct. 2010); and US Department of Defense (DOD), *Nuclear Posture Review Report* (DOD: Washington, DC, Apr. 2010).

ditions.[16] Moreover, the language of the negative security assurances offered by the three countries is almost identical. The DDPR acknowledged the importance of these assurances and the guarantee that nuclear weapons 'will not be used or threatened to be used against Non-Nuclear Weapon States that are party to the Non-Proliferation Treaty and in compliance with their nuclear non-proliferation obligations'.[17] However, the decision about whether or not a non-nuclear weapon state is in compliance with its obligations would be taken by the nuclear weapon state concerned, perhaps in consultation with its NATO allies.

The modernization of non-strategic nuclear capabilities

The DDPR underlined that the allies concerned 'will ensure that all components of NATO's nuclear deterrent remain safe, secure, and effective for as long as NATO remains a nuclear alliance'.[18] NATO has enhanced security measures at sites where nuclear weapons are stored, partly in response to the revelation in 2010 that peace activists had repeatedly breached perimeter security undetected.[19] However, according to a senior Polish official the text in the DDPR is apparently 'related primarily to the replacement of aging delivery means'.[20]

The five European countries that currently take part in the nuclear sharing arrangements sustain their participation using dual-capable combat aircraft. They can keep these aircraft in service until approximately 2020, but all are aware that a decision on an eventual replacement (if any) will be needed well before then. In the framework of its 2010 Nuclear Posture Review (NPR), the USA decided to produce a nuclear-capable version of the F-35 (Joint Strike Fighter, JSF) combat aircraft.[21] Of the five, Italy, the Netherlands and Turkey are also part of the international programme to procure the JSF, while Belgium and Germany are not.

Since the USA retired the Tomahawk SLCM in accordance with the NPR, only one type of non-strategic weapon remains in its arsenal—the B61 gravity bomb.[22] Over the coming years the USA plans to consolidate the existing types of B61 into one, designated the B61-12, that can be delivered by both

---

[16] French Permanent Representative to the Conference on Disarmament, Statement concerning security assurances to non-nuclear-weapon states, 6 Apr. 1995, annex to UN document A/50/154-S/1995/264, 6 Apr. 1995; British Government (note 15), para. 3.7; and US Department of Defense (note 15), p. 15. For a summary and other details of the NPT see annex A in this volume.

[17] NATO (note 1), para. 10.

[18] NATO (note 1), para. 11.

[19] E.g. Grossman, E. M., 'More activist intrusions at Belgian nuclear base stoke worries', Global Security Newswire, 22 Oct. 2010, <http://www.nti.org/gsn/article/more-activist-intrusions-at-belgian-nuclear-base-stoke-worries/>.

[20] Quoted in Meier, O., 'NATO sticks with nuclear policy', Arms Control Today, vol. 42, no. 5 (June 2012).

[21] US Department of Defense (note 15), pp. 27–28, 34–35.

[22] See chapter 6, section I, in this volume; and US Department of Defense (note 15), p. 46.

forward-based dual-capable combat aircraft and the long-range B2 strategic bomber.[23] After this consolidation, the need for US nuclear weapons to be located in Europe may be questioned further since the identical munition can be delivered to a target by a B2 strategic bomber based in the USA.[24]

The relationship between missile defence and nuclear forces

At their 2010 summit in Lisbon, NATO leaders decided that, in the light of the on-going proliferation of ballistic missiles with greater range and larger payloads relatively close to the territory of NATO, a ballistic missile defence capacity would strengthen the collective defence commitment. Prior to 2010, NATO states had cooperated on missile defence programmes intended to protect armed forces in the field from attack by short-range missiles. However, in Lisbon the mandate was extended to include full coverage and protection for all NATO European populations, territory and forces against attack by small numbers of ballistic missiles of the type proliferating close to Europe.[25]

In 2012 NATO leaders announced that an interim capability for missile defence had been achieved, based on the US decision to contribute the European Phased Adaptive Approach (EPAA) to NATO missile defence.[26] The EPAA was a 2009 modification to the US national missile defence programme.

In September and October 2011 the first decisions were reached on the future operational elements of the EPAA: that Turkey would host an AN/TPY-2 transportable surveillance radar; that Romania would host the land-based launch site for the RIM-161 Standard Missile 3 (SM-3) system; that the Netherlands would equip four frigates with surveillance radars compatible with the EPAA; that Poland would later also host a land-based launch site for SM-3 missiles; and that Spain would serve as a home port for four US Navy destroyers equipped with the Aegis ballistic missile defence system.[27] After 2015, the EPAA will include a significant land-based

---

[23] See chapter 6, section I, in this volume.

[24] Ted Seay, a former adviser to the US Ambassador to NATO, has noted that in the unlikely event that a nuclear weapon should need to be delivered, the option of using a dual-capable combat aircraft 'would be one of the least preferable for a military commander, and an almost certain suicide mission for the pilots concerned'. Seay, E. E. III, *Theatre Nuclear Weapons and the Next Round of Bilateral New START Treaty Follow-on Talks*, Arms Control Association (ACA), British American Security Information Council (BASIC) and Institute for Peace Research and Security Policy at the University of Hamburg (IFSH) Nuclear Policy Paper no. 12 (ACA/BASI/IFSH: Washington, DC/London/Hamburg, Jan. 2013), p. 4.

[25] NATO (note 12), para. 19.

[26] NATO, 'NATO declares interim missile defence capability', 20 May 2012, <http://www.nato.int/cps/en/natolive/news_87599.htm>; and NATO (note 1), para. 19.

[27] NATO, 'Ballistic missile defence', 8 May 2012, <http://www.nato.int/cps/en/natolive/topics_49635.htm>.

element on the territory of NATO, primarily in the south-eastern part. However, the interim capability depends on the deployment of US ships.[28]

The DDPR emphasized that missile defence should be seen as a complement to—not a substitute for—the role of nuclear weapons in deterrence, first because an adversary with limited missile capabilities might be reluctant to use them if there was no guarantee of success, and second because the possibility of effective defence may reduce the need for a pre-emptive strike on the ballistic missile force of an adversary in a crisis.[29] The review emphasized that this capability 'is not oriented against Russia', and that it does not have technical elements that could undermine Russia's strategic deterrent—although the Russian Government and military remain unconvinced.[30]

In December 2012, in response to a request by Turkey, three members of NATO—Germany, the Netherlands and the USA—agreed to deploy batteries of Patriot short-range missiles to Turkey under the operational command of NATO's Supreme Allied Commander over armed forces in Europe (SACEUR). NATO has described the deployment as forming part of the air defence of Turkey, rather than portraying it as an element of missile defence.[31] However, the US Secretary of Defense, Leon Panetta, noted that one purpose of the deployment was to provide Turkey with some missile defence capability.[32] Anders Fogh Rasmussen, the NATO Secretary General, drew attention to the use of short-range ballistic missiles by the Syrian Government in its ongoing internal conflict as one rationale for support to Turkey.[33]

NATO and the future arms control agenda

The Obama administration has made clear that after the entry into force of the 2010 Russian–US Treaty on Measures for the Further Reduction and Limitation of Strategic Offensive Arms (New START) in 2011, the USA intended to pursue further reductions in strategic, non-strategic and non-

[28] US Department of State, 'United States European Phased Adaptive Approach (EPAA) and NATO Missile Defense', 3 May 2011, <http://www.state.gov/t/avc/rls/162447.htm>.

[29] NATO (note 1), para. 20.

[30] NATO (note 1), para. 21. The Russian Government laid out its objections and concerns about missile defence at an international conference in May 2012 organized by the Russian Ministry of Defence. See RIA Novosti, 'International conference on missile defense in Moscow', May 2012, <http://en.rian.ru/trend/conference_missile_defense_moscow_2012/>; and Russian Ministry of Defence, [Conference on missile defence], 3–4 May 2012, <http://mil.ru/conference_of_pro.htm> (in Russian). On earlier developments see Kile, S. N., 'Russian–US nuclear arms control', *SIPRI Yearbook 2012*, pp. 359–61.

[31] NATO, 'NATO foreign ministers' statement on Patriot deployment to Turkey', 4 Dec. 2012.

[32] Pellerin, C., American Forces Press Service, 'Panetta signs order to deploy 400 U.S. personnel to Turkey', US Department of Defense, 14 Dec. 2012, <http://www.defense.gov/news/newsarticle.aspx?id=118797>.

[33] 'Syria regime firing Scud-type missiles at rebels: NATO', Agence France-Presse, 12 Dec. 2012.

deployed nuclear weapons.[34] If this is the basis for a next phase of bilateral nuclear arms control, then negotiations with Russia will include issues in which NATO allies directly participate.

The DDPR explained that 'NATO is prepared to consider further reducing its requirement for non-strategic nuclear weapons assigned to the Alliance in the context of reciprocal steps by Russia, taking into account the greater Russian stockpiles of non-strategic nuclear weapons stationed in the Euro-Atlantic area.'[35] To that end, NATO will continue to examine the implications of different scenarios, 'including in case NATO were to decide to reduce its reliance on non-strategic nuclear weapons based in Europe'.[36]

NATO is highly unlikely to be a negotiating partner in future talks with Russia. To manage the internal discussion of issues of direct concern to NATO, the DDPR agreed on a new consultative and advisory forum on arms control as a permanent committee, chaired by a member of the NATO International Staff, reporting to the North Atlantic Council—NATO's highest decision-making body. The new committee will allow NATO members to discuss among themselves the possible elements of a future dialogue with Russia on non-strategic nuclear weapons, including confidence- and security-building measures.[37] It will also act as an advisory forum in which the USA can keep other NATO member states informed on the scope and content of bilateral discussions with Russia on various aspects of strategic stability, including nuclear arms control, missile defences and conventional arms control.

As well as linking reductions in the non-strategic nuclear weapons assigned to the alliance to reciprocal steps by Russia, the DDPR offered support and encouragement to the mutual efforts by Russia and the USA to enhance transparency and further reduce their nuclear forces. NATO plans to seek dialogue with Russia on aspects of nuclear arms control in ways that complement the bilateral Russia–USA process. While NATO–Russia dialogue would not have a direct role in determining NATO's nuclear policy or force posture, the DDPR recommended developing transparency and confidence-building ideas in the NATO–Russia Council, 'with the goal of developing detailed proposals on and increasing mutual understanding of NATO's and Russia's non-strategic nuclear force postures in Europe'.[38] During 2012 the NATO allies began to consider initial proposals that may be put to Russia, which are reported to include dialogue about nuclear

[34] Kile (note 30), pp. 361–62; and New START (note 2).

[35] NATO (note 1), para. 26.

[36] NATO (note 1), para. 12.

[37] NATO (note 1), para. 30. The mandate of this forum, known as the Special Advisory and Consultative Arms Control, Disarmament and Non-Proliferation Committee, was agreed on 8 Feb. 2013. Meier, O., 'NATO agrees on new arms control body', Arms Control Now, 26 Feb. 2013, <http://armscontrolnow.org/2013/02/26/nato-agrees-on-new-arms-control-body/>.

[38] NATO (note 1), para. 25.

doctrine and the possibility of reciprocal unilateral actions to relocate or dismantle specified nuclear weapons.[39]

As noted above, the USA continuously raised the issue of next steps in arms control with Russia in 2011–12. While NATO member states began to try to elaborate proposals that they might introduce at some point, it was recognized that any serious engagement with Russia would have to wait until after the result of the US presidential election in November 2012 was known.

Looking forward, the prospects for successful negotiated reductions in non-strategic nuclear weapons will require the USA, together with its NATO allies, and Russia to modify what were, in 2012, incompatible positions. At the end of 2012 there was no indication that such modifications would be forthcoming and it appeared that the future nuclear forces would be shaped less by cooperation through negotiated arms control and more by economic factors combined with evolving internal analyses of the threat environment.

---

[39] Grossman, E. M., 'Seeking Kremlin engagement, NATO weighs next nuclear posture steps', Global Security Newswire, 13 Sep. 2012, <http://www.nti.org/gsn/article/seeking-kremlin-engage ment-nato-weighs-next-nuclear-posture-steps/>.

IV. Measures to combat nuclear terrorism

IAN ANTHONY

On 26–27 March 2012, 53 heads of state and government, as well as representatives of the United Nations, the European Union (EU), the International Atomic Energy Agency (IAEA) and Interpol, took part in a Nuclear Security Summit in Seoul, South Korea.[1] The meeting was the follow-up to the Nuclear Security Summit, convened in Washington, DC, in 2010, in which 47 states and 3 international organizations took part.

Concerns about the possible malicious use of radioactive material have existed since the beginning of the nuclear age, and international standards for nuclear security have been developed from the 1960s onwards.[2] However, the mass impact of the terrorist attacks on the United States of 11 September 2001 provided a catalyst for a significant increase in international attention to the risks of terrorism, including nuclear terrorism. This interest has been reflected in changes to what is called the 'global nuclear security architecture' in the Seoul Summit communiqué.[3]

This section first reviews the current understanding of what nuclear security and nuclear terrorism are. It then summarizes the significant issues discussed at the Seoul Summit—in particular protection of nuclear materials and related facilities, and prevention of trafficking—and the priority issues identified for the next Nuclear Security Summit, to be held in the Netherlands in 2014.

Defining nuclear security and nuclear terrorism

The International Atomic Energy Agency (IAEA) defines nuclear security as 'the prevention and detection of, and response to, theft, sabotage, unauthorized access, illegal transfer or other malicious acts involving nuclear material, other radioactive substances or their associated facilities'.[4] This definition addresses a broader set of concerns than nuclear terrorism, covering other malicious acts such as criminality, acts by psychologically disturbed individuals and acts carried out for political purposes that are not considered to be terrorism—such as opposition to the use of

[1] Nuclear Security Summit Seoul 2012, '2012 Nuclear Security Summit: key facts', <http://www.thenuclearsecuritysummit.org/userfiles/Key Facts on the 2012 Seoul Nuclear Security Summit.pdf>.

[2] Concern about the military use of a bomb containing radioactive material was already present in the 1940s. Ziegler, C. A. and Jacobson, D., *Spying without Spies: Origins of America's Secret Nuclear Surveillance System* (Praeger: Westport, CT, 1995), p. 3.

[3] Nuclear Security Summit Seoul 2012, 'Seoul Communiqué', 27 Mar. 2012, <http://www.thenuclearsecuritysummit.org/userfiles/Seoul Communique_FINAL.pdf>.

[4] IAEA, 'Concepts and terms: meaning of (nuclear) security', 29 May 2012, <http://www-ns.iaea.org/standards/concepts-terms.asp?s=11&l=90>.

nuclear technology to generate electricity. However, while recognizing the need to strengthen all aspects of nuclear security, the Seoul Summit principally focused on the risk of nuclear terrorism.

In 2005, states agreed the text of an amendment to the 1980 Convention on the Physical Protection of Nuclear Material (CPPNM).[5] The CPPNM applies to nuclear material, which is defined in the convention and essentially limited to fissile material (certain isotopes of plutonium, uranium-233 and uranium enriched in the isotopes uranium-235 or -233). The amended convention—which will be renamed the Convention on the Physical Protection of Nuclear Material and Nuclear Facilities when it enters into force—does not mention terrorism, but obliges states to apply physical protection measures to materials and facilities on their own territory, supplementing the measures in the 1980 convention for materials in international transport. When implementing the amended convention, states must criminalize certain acts and ensure that the criminal offences attract the appropriate punishments if proven. The amended CPPNM also recognizes the importance of international cooperation to prevent, detect, respond to and punish malicious acts.

The 2005 International Convention for the Suppression of Acts of Nuclear Terrorism (ICSANT) defined nuclear terrorism in terms of the offences of possession of radioactive material or using radioactive material or a radioactive device, or causing damage to a nuclear facility '(i) With the intent to cause death or serious bodily injury; or (ii) With the intent to cause substantial damage to property or to the environment'.[6] The convention also created offences of conspiracy and aiding and abetting such actions.

The definition of nuclear terrorism in ICSANT is not restricted to the use of fissile material, but covers a wide spectrum of potential malicious acts, including the use of a nuclear explosive or a radioactive 'dirty bomb', the sabotage of a nuclear facility or the use of radioactive material as a poison. However, it differentiates terrorism from, for example, political protests that breach nuclear security but are not intended to injure people or destroy property.

The Seoul Summit

Preparations for the Nuclear Security Summit were affected by the major nuclear incident in Japan that began on 11 March 2011, when an undersea earthquake caused a 15-metre high tidal wave. Together, these events

---

[5] For a summary and other details of the CPPNM see annex A in this volume.
[6] International Convention for the Suppression of Acts of Nuclear Terrorism, adopted 13 Apr. 2005 by UN General Assembly Resolution 59/290, opened for signature 14 Sep. 2005, entered into force 7 July 2007, *United Nations Treaty Series*, vol. 2445 (2007), Article 2.

destroyed critical safety equipment at the Daiichi nuclear power plant in Fukushima, as well as devastating the surrounding area—hindering emergency response. In the first three days of the incident, the cores of three reactors melted down almost completely after electrical power was lost and cooling systems stopped functioning. While the event was natural, it underlined the need to reduce any risk that a deliberate malicious act might lead to sequential failures in the safety systems at a power plant.

At the Seoul Summit, implementation of the voluntary commitments in the Work Plan agreed at the Washington Summit was reviewed on the basis of a document prepared in advance of the meeting itemizing progress.[7] The Seoul Summit also endorsed the findings of the IAEA Nuclear Safety Group on the interface between nuclear safety and nuclear security.[8] The IAEA report recommended a series of measures to promote coordination between safety and security at nuclear installations, including activities such as exercises and seminars; the development of consistent and complementary security guides and safety standards; and combined assistance programmes, as well as review and training missions.

In addition, three issues were highlighted for particular discussion: cooperative measures to combat the threat of nuclear terrorism; the protection of nuclear materials and related facilities; and the prevention of trafficking of nuclear materials.

The protection of nuclear materials and related facilities

The protection of nuclear materials has two dimensions. First, such protection prevents the unauthorized removal of nuclear material (either by theft or diversion). This has been seen historically as an instrument for reducing the risk of proliferation. Second, protection of nuclear materials aims to reduce the risk of sabotage of either nuclear material or a nuclear facility and thereby reduce the risk that a malicious act will create a radiological hazard.

A physical protection system is intended to delay access to vital areas for long enough to allow the appropriate response forces to respond and foil the malevolent action. In developing such a system there are some responsibilities that fall on the state, in particular identifying threats and informing the nuclear facility's operators of what kinds of scenario they need to be prepared for as well as making appropriate response forces available. Some responsibilities fall on the operator, such as identifying the

---

[7] Seoul Nuclear Security Summit Preparatory Secretariat, 'Highlights of achievements and commitments by participating states as stated in national progress reports and national statements', 26 Mar. 2012, <http://www.thenuclearsecuritysummit.org/userfiles/Highlights of the Seoul Nuclear Security Summit(120403).pdf>; and Nuclear Security Summit Washington 2010, 'Work plan', 13 Apr. 2010, <http://www.thenuclearsecuritysummit.org/eng_common/images/fla/12.Work Plan.pdf>.

[8] IAEA, *The Interface Between Safety and Security at Nuclear Power Plants*, Report of the International Nuclear Safety Group (INSAG), INSAG-24 (IAEA, Vienna, 2010).

vital areas for protection and ensuring that necessary personnel, routines and equipment are in place.

In 2011 the IAEA published new recommendations on physical protection as part of its Nuclear Security Series.[9] The recommendations introduced an important change in the categorization of material to be protected. In the past, nuclear material with high radiation levels has been regarded as 'self-protecting' because proximity would seriously injure or kill the handler. The 2011 document recommends applying equal levels of protection to highly radioactive material if the national threat assessment suggests that an adversary is willing to perform a malicious act even if the consequences are fatal.[10] Extremists may be willing to die in order to commit an act of mass impact terrorism, but applying the recommendations could have serious financial and technical implications for countries with large volumes of material currently considered self-protecting. The participants at the Seoul Summit agreed to 'strive to use' the recommendations in their national systems for physical protection but stopped short of making a firm commitment to do so.[11]

The final communiqué of the Seoul Summit urges states in a position to do so to accelerate the process of signing and ratifying the 2005 amendment to the CPPNM, with a view to bringing the amendment into force by 2014. The communiqué encourages states to make use of IAEA activities, such as the International Nuclear Security Advisory Service (INSServ) and the International Physical Protection Advisory Service (IPPAS), to support national efforts to establish and enhance nuclear security.[12] The communiqué also draws attention to the need to use the most modern technical tools in tracking shipments of nuclear materials during transport in order to warn of loss and aid rapid recovery. Five countries—France, Japan, South Korea, the United Kingdom and the United States—promised to take forward a programme of practical activities to promote tighter security in the transport of nuclear and radioactive materials after the Summit.[13]

Preventing trafficking

To help prevent trafficking in nuclear material, the summit focused on what was called 'action-oriented coordination among national capacities' in ways that are consistent with national laws and regulations.[14]

---

[9] IAEA, *Nuclear Security Recommendations on Physical Protection of Nuclear Material and Nuclear Facilities*, INFCIRC/225/Revision 5, IAEA Nuclear Security Series no. 13 (IAEA: Vienna, 2011).

[10] IAEA, INFCIRC/225/Revision 5 (note 9), pp. 19, 21.

[11] Nuclear Security Summit Seoul 2012 (note 3), p. 2.

[12] Nuclear Security Summit Seoul 2012 (note 3), pp. 2, 3.

[13] France, Japan, South Korea, the United Kingdom and the United States, 'Joint Statement on Transport Security', Nuclear Security Summit Seoul 2012, 27 Mar. 2012, <http://www.thenuclear securitysummit.org/eng_media/speeches/speeches_list.jsp>.

[14] Nuclear Security Summit Seoul 2012 (note 3), p. 4.

Enhancing the technical capabilities for radiation detection and portal monitoring, either at the perimeter of a facility or a border-crossing point, has been a priority project in US external assistance since the early 1990s. Through its core programme and the Megaports Initiative, by 2018 the National Nuclear Security Administration in the US Department of Energy will have equipped around 650 sites in roughly 30 countries and more than 100 seaports with radiation detection equipment.[15] The EU has implemented broadly similar projects in 14 countries and is currently expanding its projects to new partner countries in the Middle East and South East Asia.[16]

The participants at the Seoul Summit encouraged wider participation in the IAEA Illicit Trafficking Database programme and to provide necessary information relating to nuclear and other radioactive materials outside of regulatory control.[17] Information on individuals involved in nuclear trafficking is shared, for example, via the Radiological and Nuclear Terrorism Prevention Unit at Interpol.

Identified priority issues for the 2014 Nuclear Security Summit

At the end of the meeting in Seoul, the decision was taken to organize a third Nuclear Security Summit, in 2014, to be hosted by the Netherlands. This summit will address the following issues, among others.

The role of industry in promoting nuclear security

Effective nuclear security is inevitably a partnership between state authorities and industry. State authorities play a key role in prevention by identifying threats, and responding to and recovering from an incident. However, operators must put physical protection and other measures in place at facilities, and they are almost certainly the first to detect an incident and determine its initial scale and the appropriate response.

The Seoul Summit included a side-event at which industry was encouraged to provide its views and positions on legal and technical issues as well as approaches to industry self-governance. Participants were encouraged to present practical measures being implemented and to identify practices and methods that could help improve security at an affordable cost.[18]

---

[15] US National Nuclear Security Administration (NNSA), 'NNSA's Second Line of Defense program', Fact sheet, 1 Feb. 2011, <https://nnsa.energy.gov/mediaroom/factsheets/nnsassecondlineof defenseprogram>.

[16] Abousahl, S. et al., 'Integration of nuclear safeguards and security at the JRC', Paper delivered to the IAEA Safeguards Symposium, Vienna, 1–5 Nov. 2010, no. IAEA-CN-184/225, <http://www.iaea.org/OurWork/SV/Safeguards/Symposium/2010/Documents/Papers.htm>.

[17] Nuclear Security Summit Seoul 2012 (note 3), p. 5.

[18] On the 2012 Seoul Nuclear Industry Summit, 23–24 Mar. 2012, see <http://www.seoulnis.org/>.

At both the Seoul and Washington summits, it was difficult to facilitate a dialogue between political leaders and senior representatives of industry because in each case the summit and the industry side event took place in conjunction. One priority for the 2014 summit will be to find a method to facilitate a dialogue between the government and non-government representatives.

Information security

One issue that was introduced to the discussion at the Seoul Summit was the need to protect sensitive information from unauthorized access. Sensitive information in this context refers to information that reveals vulnerabilities that could be exploited by malicious actors. This might include information about how a nuclear plant is designed and operated, information about the type, quantity, location and containment of nuclear materials at a given facility, or information that could help to organize theft or sabotage—such as access control information or personnel records.

An increasing amount of sensitive information is stored electronically. One important aspect of the discussion of information security was therefore how to enhance cybersecurity. Thirty-one of the countries participating in the Seoul Summit agreed on a statement on information security and decided to keep working on this new topic with a view to bringing specific ideas and proposals to the meeting in 2014.[19]

Sustainability of nuclear security cooperation

Many observers believe that the 2014 Nuclear Security Summit could be the last for the time being. In the Netherlands, participants will discuss how to sustain and measure progress in strengthening nuclear security without biennial summits.

While the IAEA already works extensively on nuclear security issues, one issue that will be discussed in 2014 is the level of priority given to the issue within the overall range of activities being undertaken by the agency. The IAEA senior management has emphasized that, although nuclear security is now regarded as a core activity, implementing agreed nuclear security activities remains 'extensively reliant on uncertain extrabudgetary contributions'.[20] However, the proposal to fund nuclear security activities from the core budget of the IAEA has been, and remains, controversial among the membership.

In October 2012 the Russian Government announced that the legislation governing some cooperative threat reduction (CTR) projects with the USA

---

[19] 'Multinational statement on nuclear information security', Nuclear Security Summit Seoul 2012, Mar. 2012, <http://www.thenuclearsecuritysummit.org/userfiles/Nuclear Information Security.pdf>.

[20] IAEA, *The Agency Programme and Budget 2012–2013*, GC(55)/5 (IAEA: Vienna, Aug. 2011), p. 3.

would not be renewed on expiry in 2013.[21] The 1992 Russia–US CTR Umbrella Agreement had a 7-year lifespan.[22] Subsequent protocols to the original agreement extended its lifetime; the most recent (from 2006) is due to expire in June 2013.[23] The agreement provides the umbrella under which projects managed by the US Department of Defense are implemented in Russia and other countries of the former Soviet Union. The objectives of these projects include consolidating and securing the materials and technologies associated with nuclear weapons, and promoting defence and military cooperation to prevent the proliferation of nuclear weapons.

When announcing the decision, the Russian Ministry of Foreign Affairs underlined that Russia wants to change the basis for bilateral cooperation, not end it. The decision not to renew the CTR Umbrella Agreement when it expires could preclude certain projects, but there are other frameworks for bilateral cooperation on strengthening nuclear security, and Russia and the USA also cooperate in international forums in which both are members.[24]

The main contribution of the nuclear security summits has been to focus high-level political attention on the need to implement programmes and projects that have been in development for many years. While the high-level meetings increased the probability that agreed targets would be met prior to the gathering of heads of state and government, future summits may bring diminishing returns as the focus of discussions moves from agreement on broad objectives to more technical issues and specific projects.

[21] Russian Ministry of Foreign Affairs, 'Comment of the Information and Press Department of the MFA of Russia on the question on term of "Nunn–Lugar Cooperative Threat Reduction"', 10 Oct. 2012, <http://www.mid.ru/brp_4.nsf/0/1AA31F580B2ECD5E44257ADF0033E79D>; and Guarino, D. P., 'Obama team insists security effort with Russia not dead', Global Security Newswire, 12 Oct. 2012, <http://www.nti.org/gsn/article/obama-team-insists-security-effort-russia-not-dead/>.

[22] Agreement between the Russian Federation and the United States of America concerning the Safe and Secure Transportation, Storage, and Destruction of Weapons and the Prevention of Weapons Proliferation (CTR Umbrella Agreement), signed 17 June 1992 at Washington, DC.

[23] Kile, S. N., 'Nuclear arms control and non-proliferation', SIPRI Yearbook 2007, pp. 504–505.

[24] Guarino, D. P., 'White House official: Russian concerns with CTR Agreement are "valid"', Global Security Newswire, 6 Nov. 2012, <http://www.nti.org/gsn/article/white-house-aid-russian-concerns-ctr-agreement-are-valid/>.

8. Reducing security threats from chemical and biological materials

Overview

In 2012 states continued to develop strategies to prevent and remediate the effects of the possible misuse of toxic chemicals and of biological materials. Some of these activities are carried out in the context of environmental and human health, and others in the security and defence spheres. The principal legal instruments against chemical and biological warfare, the 1993 Chemical Weapons Convention (CWC) and the 1972 Biological and Toxin Weapons Convention (BTWC), inform the consideration of chemical and biological threats and responses. These include understanding of past programmes, allegations of the use of biological or chemical weapons, the nature of possible standby programmes, and efforts to ensure that science and technology are not misused as a method of warfare or for other hostile purposes.

In Syria, a government official responded to the numerous reports of suspected chemical weapon stockpiles (see section III in this chapter) by stating that the country possesses such weapons but would only use them against outside forces, not against its own people. Russia noted that, while Syria is not a party to the CWC, it is nevertheless obligated to refrain from using such weapons under the terms of the 1925 Geneva Protocol, to which it is a party. A number of states, including Israel, Jordan, Turkey, the United Kingdom and the United States, reportedly consulted on options to monitor and secure suspected chemical weapon sites in Syria in order to prevent use of these weapons or their falling into the possession of third parties. The United Nations Secretary-General and the Director-General of the Organisation for the Prohibition of Chemical Weapons (OPCW) conferred on the political and technical implications of the possible use of Syrian chemical weapons under their respective mandates.

The states parties to the BTWC met twice during 2012 in the first of a series of four intersessional meetings of experts and parties agreed by the 2011 Seventh Review Conference (see section I). The exercise consists of an exchange of views and information on capacity-building measures, on the implications of developments in science and technology for the regime, on effective national implementation of the convention's provisions, and on enhancing transparency and confidence among the parties. The Implementation Support Unit began implementing a database project to match

366 NON-PROLIFERATION, ARMS CONTROL AND DISARMAMENT, 2012

offers and requests for assistance and cooperation. In comparison to the CWC, however, the regime's institutional capacity remained limited.

Russia and the USA were unable to meet their final April 2012 deadlines for completing the destruction of their declared chemical weapon stockpiles (see section II). In Libya, the OPCW inspected the country's previously undeclared chemical weapons. Elsewhere, the destruction of old and abandoned chemical weapons, including those abandoned by Japan in China during World War II, continued. The states parties to the CWC also discussed the future nature and focus of the regime in the lead-up to the Third CWC Review Conference, to be held in April 2013. The verification of the destruction of chemical weapons nevertheless remained the primary operational focus of the regime.

During 2012 the security and life sciences communities debated the appropriateness of publishing research, completed in 2011, on the transmissibility of avian influenza among ferrets (see section IV). The underlying concern was that such research could be misapplied for hostile purposes, such as by changing avian influenza virus to a form suitable for aerosol transmission between humans. A specially convened World Health Organization (WHO) committee of two research groups—based in the Netherlands and the USA, respectively—also discussed the issue. The Netherlands considered imposing export controls on findings in the research methodology section of the Dutch-based group, but then abandoned the plan. The US National Science Advisory Board for Biosecurity (NSABB) reversed its previous opposition to publication, stating that the researchers had modified the draft findings in a manner that allowed it to support publication. Both papers were published in 2012.

The threats enumerated above will remain important considerations for maintaining international peace and security, and these concerns should be informed by their corresponding political, technical, historical and legal contexts. To do so will help to maintain and strengthen international peace and security. For example, it is important that all allegations of biological or chemical weapon use are authoritatively addressed (e.g. through the UN Secretary-General's authority to investigate alleged use or the OPCW's mandate to investigate CWC violations through on-site inspections). The parties to the BTWC could also attempt to understand better how some advances in science and technology affect the convention. Finally, the parties to both regimes should be alert to paradigm shifts that could require corresponding changes in how the provisions of both are understood, interpreted and implemented.

JOHN HART

I. Biological weapon arms control and disarmament

JOHN HART

The principal activity in 2012 in the biological arms control field was work carried out in connection with the meeting of experts (16–20 July) and the meeting of parties (10–14 December) to the Third Intersessional Process of the 1972 Biological and Toxin Weapons Convention (BTWC).[1] The three standing agenda items for the meetings are (a) cooperation and assistance, (b) science and technology review, and (c) strengthening national implementation.[2] The 2012 and 2013 meetings were mandated to consider 'fuller participation' in the long-standing annual, politically binding information exchanges that are meant to serve as confidence-building measures (CBMs).[3]

One new party joined the convention in 2012: the Marshall Islands. An additional 12 states had signed but not ratified the convention as of 31 December 2012.[4]

The BTWC Implementation Support Unit (ISU) continued to establish a database with offers and requests for assistance in accordance with a decision by the Seventh BTWC Review Conference in 2011.[5] As of 7 November 2012 only 11 offers of assistance had been made, all by one party, while another party had made a single request for assistance. In addition, no matches of offers and requests had been communicated to the ISU.[6] In its assessment of the intersessional process, South Africa called on the meeting of experts to have more in-depth 'technical discussions' that make full use of the time available (which was arguably not the case in the 2012 meetings). South Africa also noted the absence of 'substantive engagement' by the parties on science and technology reviews and that 'no effort was made to discuss' strengthening national implementation, CBMs and pro-

---

[1] For a summary and other details of the Convention on the Prohibition of the Development, Production and Stockpiling of Bacteriological (Biological) and Toxin Weapons and on Their Destruction see annex A in this volume. Documents related to the BTWC are available at <http://www.unog.ch/bwc>. For daily summaries of the meetings see BioWeapons Prevention Project (BWPP), 'Daily reports from BWC meetings', <http://bwpp.org/reports.html>.

[2] Seventh BTWC Review Conference, Final document, BWC/CONF.VII/7, 13 Jan. 2012, para. 8.

[3] Seventh BTWC Review Conference, BWC/CONF.VII/7 (note 2), para. 9.

[4] The states that had signed but not ratified the BTWC were Central African Republic, Côte d'Ivoire, Egypt, Guyana, Haiti, Liberia, Malawi, Myanmar, Nepal, Somalia, Syria and Tanzania. In addition, 17 UN member states had neither signed nor ratified the convention: Andorra, Angola, Cameroon, Chad, Comoros, Djibouti, Eritrea, Guinea, Israel, Kiribati, Mauritania, Micronesia, Namibia, Nauru, Samoa, South Sudan and Tuvalu. See annex A for a full list of parties.

[5] Seventh BTWC Review Conference, BWC/CONF.VII/7 (note 2), para. 20.

[6] Implementation Support Unit (ISU), 'Report of the Implementation Support Unit', [n.d.], para. 28. The report was submitted to the parties prior to the Dec. 2012 Meeting of the States Parties and is available on the ISU website, <http://www.unog.ch/__80256ee600585943.nsf/(httpPages)/f837b6e7a401a21cc1257a150050cb2a?OpenDocument&ExpandSection=1#_Section1>.

motion of universalization 'from a technical point of view'.[7] During the 2012 meeting of parties the participants also considered proposals for self-assessment of national implementation and peer review of scientific research.[8] Five parties called for a conceptual discussion on compliance during the intersessional process, but the final document of the meeting of parties excluded draft language for such a discussion.[9] The experts and parties meetings were both marked by unwillingness to agree substantive text in accordance with the mandate of the final document of the Seventh Review Conference.

The final document of the meeting of parties compiled extracts from the parties' national papers that, among other things, identified seven measures to further national implementation of obligations to facilitate peaceful uses of the life sciences; six types of national measure to increase awareness among life science practitioners of the dual-purpose nature of equipment, technology and know-how; five approaches to strengthen national biorisk-management capacity; and six measures to facilitate submission of data to the ISU.[10] Because the intersessional meetings lack decision-making powers, individual parties are able to decide whether and how to implement the measures discussed.

Discussions of science and technology, for example, offer a potential mechanism for the parties to reach a common understanding on whether and how to ensure that research of concern is used exclusively for peaceful purposes. The World Health Organization (WHO) committee that examined the 2011 H5N1 avian influenza research consisted of scientists who were generally opposed to restrictions.[11] Although the BTWC regime has an inherent security emphasis, the political and technical scope for reaching common understanding on oversight and control of life sciences research remains limited.[12]

---

[7] BTWC, Meeting of the States Parties, 'South Africa: the intersessional process: comments and proposals', BWC/MSP/2012/WP.7, 5 Dec. 2012.

[8] E.g. Revill, J., *A Peer-Review Mechanism for the Biological and Toxin Weapons Convention* (United Nations Institute for Disarmament Research: Geneva, 2013).

[9] BTWC, Meeting of the States Parties, 'Australia, Canada, Japan, New Zealand and Switzerland: We need to talk about compliance', BWC/MSP/2012/WP.11, 12 Dec. 2012.

[10] BTWC, Meeting of the States Parties, 'Report of the Meeting of States Parties', BWC/MSP/2012/5, 19 Dec. 2012; and United Nations Office at Geneva (UNOG), 'Meeting of states parties to Biological Weapons Convention concludes in Geneva', Press Release DC12/038E, 17 Dec. 2012, <http://www.unog.ch/unog/website/news_media.nsf/(httpNewsByYear_en)/D0AF5AE959D406C1C1257AD7005419B5>.

[11] World Health Organization (WHO), 'Technical consultation on H5N1 research issues: consensus points', 16–17 Feb. 2012, <http://www.who.int/influenza/human_animal_interface/consensus_points/en>.

[12] For useful background paper see BTWC, Meeting of the States Parties, 'Making avian influenza aerosol-transmissible in mammals', BWC/MSP/2012/MX/INF.2, 11 June 2012.

II. Chemical weapon arms control and disarmament

JOHN HART

Although the deadline for the final destruction of chemical weapons under the 1993 Chemical Weapons Convention (CWC) passed on 29 April 2012, destruction continued in four states and this remained the primary focus of the CWC regime.[1] No new states joined the CWC in 2012. As of 31 December, 188 states had ratified or acceded to the convention; 2 states had signed but not ratified it; and 6 states had neither signed nor ratified it.[2]

Developments in the OPCW and the Conference of States Parties

The 17th Conference of the States Parties (CSP) approved a 2013 programme and budget of €69 803 800 ($92.7 million) of which €32 166 900 ($42.7 million) is devoted to verification costs.[3] Many delegates at the CSP expressed regret at the lack of full implementation of national obligations by some states parties. As of 27 July 2012, 88 parties (47 per cent) had put in place legislation that covers all key areas of CWC implementation obligations.[4] Since the numbers are self-reported, the actual status may be worse. The Organisation for the Prohibition of Chemical Weapons (OPCW) Technical Secretariat launched a pilot programme to facilitate exchanges between national authorities (e.g. financial support and technical advice) that entails 'twinning' of authorities.[5] The Technical Secretariat continued to develop various model legislation packages for the benefit of parties that are at the start of this process.[6]

As part of efforts to achieve universal membership, the Director-General of the OPCW, Ahmet Üzümcü, held bilateral consultations with officials from four non-parties: Angola, Myanmar, Somalia and South Sudan. Myanmar also agreed to receive a technical assistance visit in early 2013.[7] North

[1] For a summary and other details of the Convention on the Prohibition of the Development, Production, Stockpiling and Use of Chemical Weapons and on Their Destruction see annex A in this volume.
[2] The states that had signed but not ratified the CWC were Israel and Myanmar. The UN member states that had neither signed nor ratified the convention were Angola, Egypt, North Korea, Somalia, South Sudan and Syria.
[3] OPCW, 'Programme and budget of the OPCW for 2013', Decision, C-17/DEC.4, 27 Nov. 2012, para. 3(c). Excluding the line item for the Third CWC Review Conference, the 2013 budget is 1.1% less than that of 2012. Documents relating to the CWC can be found on the website of the Organisation for the Prohibition of Chemical Weapons (OPCW), <http://www.opcw.org/documents-reports/>.
[4] OPCW, Conference of the States Parties, 'Status of implementation of Article VII of the Chemical Weapons Convention', Report by the Director-General, EC-70/DG.4, C-17/DG.7, 28 Aug. 2012, p. 2. See previous editions of the SIPRI Yearbook for corresponding figures in prior years.
[5] OPCW, Conference of the States Parties, 17th Session, Opening statement by the Director-General, C-17/DG.16, 26 Nov. 2012, para. 99.
[6] OPCW, C-17/DG.16 (note 5), para. 101.
[7] OPCW, C-17/DG.16 (note 5), para. 126.

Korea continued to ignore the OPCW's outreach efforts, while prior informal contact with Syria remained in abeyance due to the ongoing civil war in that country. Israel, a signatory to the convention, stated that it 'attaches great importance to the Chemical Weapons Convention and supports its goals' and that it 'look[s] forward to continuing our constructive dialogue with the OPCW'. While Israel generally refrains from issuing official statements regarding its policy on achieving a zone free of weapons of mass destruction (WMD) in the Middle East, it stated at the CSP that its approach to regional security and arms control 'is rooted in its belief that all security concerns of regional members should be considered and addressed within the regional context' and that the prerequisites for a WMD-free zone in the Middle East include 'comprehensive and durable peace between the regional parties, and full compliance by all regional States with their arms control and non-proliferation obligations'.[8] Although an international conference on a WMD-free zone in the Middle East was scheduled to be held in December 2012, hosted by Finland, the co-sponsors announced in November that, since some states in the region had not agreed to participate, it would be delayed.[9] Iran refuses direct negotiations with Israel, and the other states in the region generally wish to agree various preconditions to talks on a WMD-free zone, including by linking nuclear, biological and chemical weapons.

On 27 November 2012 the OPCW and the United Nations Office for the Coordination of Humanitarian Affairs (OCHA) signed 'interface procedures' for, among other things, the coordination of assistance activities during response to emergencies involving the use or threat of use of toxic chemicals as a method of warfare.[10] The OPCW and the UN also concluded a supplementary arrangement to their Relationship Agreement that establishes the 'necessary modalities' for carrying out an investigation of alleged chemical weapon use if requested by the UN Secretary-General.[11] The OPCW carried out one challenge inspection exercise in 2012, in the United Kingdom on 1–4 October (named 'McCavity'). It also carried out an investigation of alleged chemical weapon use on 8–20 October in Serbia.[12] A comprehensively revised inspection manual was also issued in 2012.[13]

---

[8] OPCW, Conference of the States Parties, 17th Session, 'Israel: statement by Mr Eyal Propper, Director arms control policy department, Ministry of Foreign Affairs', C-17/NAT.15, 27 Nov. 2012, pp. 1–3.

[9] E.g. Russian Ministry of Foreign Affairs, 'Press statement on the 2012 conference on the establishment of a Middle East zone free of weapons of mass destruction', 24 Nov. 2012, <http://www.mid.ru/bdomp/brp_4.nsf/0/FDB6A81FF09D276A44257AC2004D9362>.

[10] OPCW, 'OPCW signs interface procedures with UN OCHA', 27 Nov. 2012, <http://www.opcw.org/news/article/opcw-signs-interface-procedures-with-un-ocha/>.

[11] OPCW, C-17/DG.16 (note 5), para. 10.

[12] OPCW, C-17/DG.16 (note 5), para. 64.

[13] OPCW, C-17/DG.16 (note 5), para. 79.

During 2012 the temporary working groups to the OPCW's Scientific Advisory Board (SAB) examined (*a*) sampling and analysis protocols, (*b*) the convergence of biology and chemistry, and (*c*) education and outreach on science and technology.[14] Üzümcü requested the SAB to establish a new temporary working group devoted to reviewing select aspects of the CWC verification regime, including the chemical industry.[15]

A total of 14 international capacity-building activities in the field of assistance and protection were carried out in 2012 by the Technical Secretariat, which also undertook to maintain and strengthen ties with the chemical industry, partly through a dialogue with the International Council of Chemical Associations (ICCA).[16] The OPCW also participated in a variety of outreach and capacity-building meetings and exercises, including an emergency medical assistance training course held at the Ukrainian Scientific and Practical Centre of Emergency Medical and Disaster Medicine.[17] The Technical Secretariat established the Trust Fund for the International Support Network for Victims of Chemical Weapons in accordance with a decision taken by the 16th CSP in 2011.[18] It also continued to work with the World Customs Organization (WCO) and the Green Customs Initiative to develop an electronic learning module on CWC provisions for customs officers, which was completed in 2012 and expected to be available to the WCO in early 2013.[19]

A scientific subcommittee of the WCO has approved changes to the Harmonized Commodity Description and Coding System (HS) codes for the most traded chemicals. While the WCO codes are based on the HS, the CWC coding is based on Chemical Abstracts Service (CAS) numbers. CAS numbers are used as an aid to identify chemicals on the CWC's Annex on Chemicals and can, in practice, be used to exclude a chemical in its salt form. The HS structure, in contrast, is divided into 21 sections and 96 chapters. Such factors are relevant to consideration of whether and how regulatory and treaty regimes cover controlled chemicals and their precursors.[20]

Finally, a number of review and evaluation activities were carried out, partly in preparation for the Third CWC Review Conference—on 7 June 2012 the Working Group for the Preparation of the Third Review Confer-

---

[14] On 10 Dec. the SAB temporary working groups on the convergence of biology and chemistry, and education and outreach on science and technology organized a side event at the BTWC's Meeting of States Parties.

[15] OPCW, C-17/DG.16 (note 5), para. 71. The sampling and analysis working group concluded its work in 2013.

[16] OPCW, C-17/DG.16 (note 5), para. 112.

[17] OPCW, C-17/DG.16 (note 5), para. 110.

[18] OPCW, C-17/DG.16 (note 5), para. 114.

[19] OPCW, C-17/DG.16 (note 5), para. 55.

[20] See OPCW, Executive Council, 'Draft report of the OPCW on the implementation of the Convention on the Prohibition of the Development, Production, Stockpiling and Use of Chemical Weapons and on Their Destruction in 2011', C-17/CRP.1, 11 July 2012, para. 2.18.

ence held its first meeting—and partly to inform longer-term discussions on the balance and focus of activities of the regime as the destruction of declared chemical weapon stockpiles approaches completion.[21]

Destruction of chemical weapons

As of 31 October 2012, 54 258 tonnes of category 1 chemical weapons had been destroyed, representing 78 per cent of the 69 430 tonnes declared.[22] As of December 2012, 13 states had declared 70 former chemical production facilities, of which 43 have been destroyed and 21 converted to peaceful purposes. Seven states have declared chemical weapon stockpiles to the OPCW: Albania, India, Iraq, South Korea, Libya, Russia and the United States. Albania, India and South Korea have destroyed their stockpiles.

Iraq provided additional information on chemical weapons stored in two bunkers at the Al Muthanna Chemical Weapons Complex, including explosive, chemical and physical hazards.[23] On 16 February 2012 the Iraqi Parliament passed the 'Law on the National Monitoring Directorate to prevent chemical, nuclear and biological weapons'.[24]

On 30 July Iraq and the UK signed an agreement whereby specialists from the British Defence Science and Technology Laboratory will train Iraqi personnel at Porton Down, UK, in the safe disposal of the 'remnants of munitions and chemical warfare agents' at the Al Muthanna complex.[25] This will reduce the possibility of exposure during the destruction of Iraqi chemical weapon remnants, which is an ongoing concern. Some suspect that the demolition of an Iraqi weapon depot at Khamisiyah in March 1991,

[21] OPCW, Technical Secretariat, 'Report of the advisory panel on future priorities of the Organisation for the Prohibition of Chemical Weapons' (Ekéus report), S/951/2011, 25 July 2011; OPCW, Conference of the States Parties, 'Report of the Scientific Advisory Board on developments in science and technology for the Third Special Session of the Conference of the States Parties to review the operation of the Chemical Weapons Convention', RC-3/DG.1, 29 Oct. 2012; and Smallwood, K. et al., 'Impact of scientific developments on the Chemical Weapons Convention (IUPAC technical report)', *Pure and Applied Chemistry*, vol. 85, no. 4 (2013). The IUPAC submitted a draft report to the OPCW in late 2012 to help inform its preparations for the 3rd CWC Review Conference. See also OPCW, 'Preparations begin for 3rd Review Conference', 8 June 2012, <http://www.opcw.org/news/article/preparations-begin-for-3rd-review-conference/>.

[22] OPCW, C-17/DG.16 (note 5), para. 18. The CWC's Annex on Chemicals comprises 3 'schedules'. Schedule 1 chemicals consist of chemicals and their precursors judged to have few, if any, peaceful applications. Chemicals listed in schedules 2 and 3 have wider peaceful, including commercial, applications. The definition of chemical weapon categories, which is partly based on what schedule a chemical may be listed under, is given in CWC (note 1), Verification Annex, Part IV(A), para. 16.

[23] OPCW, C-17/DG.16 (note 5), para. 34. For more on the bunkers see Hart, J., 'Chemical weapon arms control and disarmament', *SIPRI Yearbook 2012*, pp. 399–400.

[24] OPCW, Conference of the States Parties, 17th Session, 'Republic of Iraq: statement by H. E. Ambassador Ahmad Bamrani Head of the Department of International Organisations and Cooperation in the Iraqi Ministry of Foreign Affairs, Baghdad', C-17/NAT.32, 26 Nov. 2012, p. 3.

[25] British Embassy Baghdad, 'Chemical weapons disposal', 30 July 2012, <http://ukiniraq.fco.gov.uk/en/news/?view=News&id=794635182>. See also British Defence Science and Technology Laboratory, 'MOD experts to help Iraqis destroy legacy chemical weapons', Press release, 31 July 2012, <https://www.dstl.gov.uk/downloads/Legacy%20Chemical%20Weapons.pdf>.

during the 1990–91 Gulf War, aerosolized the organophosphorus nerve agent sarin and exposed troops in a downwind plume. Some military personnel who fought in the conflict have complained of a variety of ailments, collectively termed Gulf War Syndrome. A 2012 epidemiological study concluded 'current evidence supports long-distance transit', that epidemiologic studies of 'chronic postwar illness' should be reviewed on the basis of whether veterans heard nerve gas alarms as a factor in determining probable exposure and that bombing of the site contributed more to such illness than did post-conflict demolition operations.[26]

As of November 2012 Libya had destroyed 13.5 tonnes (51 per cent of its declared 26 tonnes) of category 1 sulphur mustard chemical weapons.[27] As of the same date, it had destroyed 555.7 tonnes (40 per cent) of its category 2 chemical weapons.[28] In November 2011 Libya revealed the existence of previously undeclared chemical weapons. On 9 February 2012 it formally amended its declaration, which was then verified by OPCW inspectors on 18 April 2012.[29] The destruction of these weapons (mainly empty and sulphur mustard-filled artillery shells) is to start in 2013.[30] The current schedule for Libya is to complete the destruction of category 1 chemical weapons by 31 December 2013, and category 2 chemical weapons by 31 December 2016.[31] Libya will employ a static detonation chamber technology for destruction of the previously undeclared chemical munitions and will hydrolyse the sulphur mustard.[32] Canada announced that it would provide 6 million Canadian dollars ($5.9 million) to support Libya's programme—the largest voluntary offer by a party to the convention since its entry into force in 1997.

As of November 2012 Russia had destroyed 27 653 tonnes (61 per cent) of its declared category 1 chemical weapons and all of its category 2 and 3 chemical weapons. It plans to complete destruction of its stockpile by December 2015.[33] In 2012 four chemical weapon destruction facilities were operating at Leonidovka, Maradykovsky, Pochep and Shchuchye (operations have been completed at Gorny and Kambarka). The last facility, at

---

[26] Haley, R. W. and Tuite, J. J., 'Epidemiologic evidence of health effects from long-distance transit of chemical weapons fallout from bombing early in the 1991 Persian Gulf War', *Neuroepidemiology*, vol. 40, no. 3 (14 Dec. 2012), pp. 178–89; and Tuite, J. J. and Haley, R. W., 'Meteorological and intelligence evidence of long-distance transit of chemical weapons fallout from bombing early in the 1991 Persian Gulf War', *Neuroepidemiology*, vol. 40, no. 3 (14 Dec. 2012), pp. 160–77. See also previous editions of the SIPRI Yearbook.

[27] OPCW, Conference of the States Parties, 17th Session, 'Libya: annual report on progress achieved towards completion of the destruction of the remaining stockpile of chemical weapons', C-17/NAT.2, 1 Nov. 2012, para. 1.

[28] OPCW, C-17/NAT.2 (note 27), para. 2.

[29] OPCW, C-17/NAT.2 (note 27), para. 3.

[30] OPCW, C-17/DG.16 (note 5), paras 19 and 24.

[31] OPCW, C-17/NAT.2 (note 27), para. 5.

[32] OPCW, C-17/NAT.2 (note 27), para. 7.

[33] OPCW, C-17/DG.16 (note 5), para. 27.

Kizner, was scheduled to start operating in 2013.[34] A minor leak of VX nerve agent occurred in July at Pochep. OPCW officials were on site at the time and an organization official stated that 'The leakage/spill occurred within the toxic area and was handled in a very professional and efficient manner by site personnel'.[35]

As of November 2012 the USA had destroyed 24 924 tonnes (90 per cent) of its declared category 1 chemical weapons, and all of its category 2 and 3 chemical weapons.[36] In 2012 it completed destruction operations at Tooele, Utah.[37] Two chemical weapon destruction facilities remain to be constructed and operated at Blue Grass (Richmond), Kentucky, and Pueblo, Colorado, respectively. The former contains 1.7 per cent of the original US stockpile, while the latter contains 8.5 per cent of the original stockpile.[38] Destruction operations are scheduled to begin at Blue Grass in April 2020 and at Pueblo in December 2015.[39] The USA estimated that it would complete destruction at Pueblo in late 2019 and at Blue Grass in 2023.[40]

Old, abandoned and sea-dumped chemical weapons

As of 2012, 3 countries had declared that abandoned chemical weapons (ACW) are present on their territories, and 15 had declared that they have possessed old chemical weapons (OCW) since the CWC's entry into force.[41] In 2012 OCW inspections were carried out in Belgium, Germany, Italy, Japan and the UK.[42]

---

[34] OPCW, C-17/DG.16 (note 5), para. 28.

[35] Winfeld, G., 'Watching the watchmen!', *CBRNe World* (Aug. 2012), p. 36.

[36] OPCW, C-17/DG.16 (note 5), para. 31, p. 6.

[37] The final items destroyed were 10 1-ton containers filled with lewisite, 59 M104 projectiles filled with sulphur mustard and 139 M110 projectiles filled with sulphur mustard. Hopkins, A. T., 'US Department of Defense, United States Chemical Demilitarization Program', Presentation at 17th Conference of the CWC States Parties, Nov. 2012, p. 4. The Tooele facility started operations in 1993.

[38] The Kentucky facility contains sarin, sulphur mustard and VX filled into rockets and projectiles. The agents will be destroyed using a neutralization and supercritical water oxidation process. The Colorado facility has mortars and projectiles filled with sulphur mustard that will be destroyed by a process that uses neutralization followed by biotreatment of hydrolysates. Hopkins (note 37), p. 5.

[39] OPCW, C-17/DG.16 (note 5), para. 32, p. 6.

[40] Hopkins (note 37), p. 17; and US Deputy Assistant Secretary of Defense (Threat Reduction and Arms Control), Presentation to OPCW, Executive Council, 68th Session, 1 May 2012.

[41] The 15 countries that have declared OCW are Austria, Australia, Belgium, Canada, France, Germany, Italy, Japan, Poland, Russia, Slovenia, Solomon Islands, Switzerland, the UK and the USA. China, Iran, Italy and Panama have declared ACW. However, the Technical Secretariat determined that the munitions declared by Iran were conventional. Unconfirmed or unidentified unexploded chemical munitions or their remnants may be present on the territory of Iran.

ACW are defined as chemical weapons that were abandoned by a state after 1 Jan. 1925 on the territory of another state without the permission of the latter. CWC (note 1), Article II, para. 6.

OCW are defined as chemical weapons that were produced before 1925 or chemical weapons produced between 1925 and 1946 that have deteriorated to such an extent that they are no longer usable in the manner for which they were designed. CWC (note 1), Article II, para. 5. On other such cases see previous editions of the SIPRI Yearbook.

[42] OPCW, C-17/DG.16 (note 5), para. 39.

On 14–16 May the Helsinki Commission (HELCOM, the Baltic Marine Environment Protection Commission) ad hoc expert group to update and review the existing information on dumped chemical munitions in the Baltic Sea held its fourth meeting.[43]

France announced in 2012 that it will destroy World War I-era OCW and old conventional munitions at the Suippes military base, starting in 2016.[44]

As of November 2012, approximately 75 per cent of the 48 000 ACW that have been recovered thus far in China had been destroyed.[45] (The ACW were abandoned in China by Japan during World War II.) A total of 300 000–400 000 ACW were estimated to be buried at Haerbaling, Jilin province.[46] Japan allocated approximately €200 million ($266 million) in 2012 for the destruction of ACW in China.[47] Two mobile destruction units were employed at several sites in north-east China, while a fixed chemical weapon destruction facility, consisting of a detonation chamber and a static kiln detonation furnace, was used at Nanjing, Jiangsu province. On 11 June 2012 the mobile destruction facility in Nanjing had completed the destruction of all 35 681 chemical weapons (disposal of contaminated waste had yet to be completed).[48] The Nanjing mobile unit will be deployed to Wuhan, Hubei province. Further destruction operations will occur at Shijiazhuang, Hebei province, while excavation and recovery operations will be carried out in Haerbaling. Excavation and recovery operations were conducted in 2012 at Guangzhou, Guangdong province, and Hunchung and Lianhuapao, both located in Jilin province.[49] X-ray identification work in 2012 was carried out at Longjing, Jilin province, and Shouyang, Shanxi province, while 12 new suspected ACW sites were jointly investigated by China and Japan.[50]

[43] Helsinki Commission, Ad hoc expert group to update and review the existing information on dumped chemical munitions in the Baltic Sea, Fourth Meeting, Kaliningrad, Russia, 14–16 May 2012, HELCOM MUNI 4/2012, <http://meeting.helcom.fi/c/document_library/get_file?p_l_id=18975&folderId=1786543&name=DLFE-49884.pdf>.

[44] Cornevin, C., 'La France va détruire 250 tonnes de bombes chimiques' [France will destroy 250 tonnes of chemical bombs], Le Figaro, 22 Feb. 2012.

[45] OPCW, 17th Conference of the States Parties, 'Japan, abandoned chemical weapons in China: progress in 2012', Poster session, The Hague, Nov. 2012.

[46] OPCW, 'Japan, abandoned chemical weapons in China: progress in 2012' (note 45).

[47] OPCW, 'Japan, abandoned chemical weapons in China: progress in 2012' (note 45).

[48] OPCW (note 45), section 3.1; OPCW, C-17/DG.16 (note 5), para. 36; and OPCW, Conference of the States Parties, 17th Session, 'Japan: statement by H. E. Mr Yasumasa Nagamine, Ambassador and Permanent Representative of Japan', C-17/NAT.22, 26 Nov. 2012.

[49] OPCW (note 45), section 6. The operations at Lianhuapao, which began in 2005, were completed in 2012.

[50] OPCW (note 45), section 6.1.

III. Chemical and biological weapon programmes

JOHN HART

Allegations of chemical and biological weapon programmes and use continued in 2012 with little official or otherwise authoritative reporting to clarify them. Many of these allegations concerned suspected Syrian chemical weapon stockpiles and fears that such stocks would be used in that country's civil war. In addition, new information emerged on the methods used by the Japanese cult Aum Shinrikyo in its 1995 sarin attack on the Tokyo underground, and a definitive account of the Soviet biological weapon programme was published.

Syria[1]

On 23 July 2012 the Syrian Ministry of Foreign Affairs (MFA) stated that Syria possesses chemical weapons and that 'All of these types of weapons are in storage and under security and the direct supervision of the Syrian armed forces and will never be used unless Syria is exposed to external aggression'.[2] On 24 July Syria sought to clarify the press briefing. The spokesman who gave the briefing, Dr Jihad Makdissi, reportedly issued a tweet the following day stating: 'the Foreign Ministry's statement was only "a response to false allegations on [weapons of mass destruction] & explanation of guidelines of defensive policy"'.[3] On 24 July Syrian state media was quoted as stating that

The Ministry said that 'the goal of the statement and the press conference wasn't to declare but rather to respond to a methodical media campaign targeting Syria to prepare world public opinion for the possibility of military intervention under the false premise of weapons of mass destruction (similar to what happened with Iraq) or the possibility of using such weapons against terrorist groups or civilians'.[4]

Ahmet Üzümcü, the Director-General of the Organisation for the Prohibition of Chemical Weapons (OPCW), reacted to the 23 July statement the

---

[1] On other developments in the conflict in Syria see chapter 1, section I, in this volume.

[2] Associated Press, 'Syrian regime makes chemical warfare threat', *The Guardian*, 23 July 2012; and 'Syria: could use chemical arms against "external aggression"', Reuters, <http://www.reuters.com/video/2012/07/23/syria-could-use-chemical-arms-against-ex?videoId=236629771>. For Syrian state television's July broadcast see Makdisi, J. [Foreign and Expatriates Ministry spokesman], 'Terrorists of Arab nationalities killed in Syria', Syria News, 23 July 2012, <http://www.youtube.com/watch?v=8WywYnAIzu4>. For the full MFA statement and questions and answers see Makdisi, J., 'Chemical weapon[s] won't be used unless in case of external aggression', Press conference, 23 July 2012, <http://www.youtube.com/watch?v=fqjWzGfOLlE>.

[3] CNN, 'Syria tries to clarify comments about WMD possession', Phantis, 24 July 2012, <http://www.phantis.com/news/syria-tries-clarify-comments-about-wmd-possession>.

[4] 'Official: reinforcements head to Syria's largest city', CNN, 24 July 2012, <http://www.cnn.com/2012/07/24/world/meast/syria-unrest/>.

following day, stating that chemical weapon use is prohibited under international law and that the reported presence of chemical weapon stockpiles and their possible deployment are a matter of 'grave concern' to the international community.[5] The United Nations Secretary-General, Ban Ki-moon, stated the same day that 'It would be reprehensible if anybody in Syria is contemplating use of such weapons of mass destruction, like chemical weapons'.[6] The Russian MFA reacted by stating that Russia wished to underline that Syria had joined the 1925 Geneva Protocol in 1968 and that Russia 'is confident that the Syrian authorities will henceforth keep to its international commitments'.[7]

That same week the Russian Deputy Foreign Minister, Gennady M. Gatilov, was asked to comment on the Syrian statement on the possibility of the use of chemical weapons in case of external aggression. He responded:

We certainly consider the use of chemical weapon inadmissible. Syria acceded to the Geneva Protocol of 1925 which prohibits the use in war of asphyxiating, poisonous or other gases, and thus, as we consider, it assumed certain obligations to reject such methods of warfare. We consider that Syria has to fulfil its obligations both under the Geneva Protocol of 1925 and the [1993 Chemical Weapons Convention]. On our part, we carried out the respective insistent work with the leaders of Syria to make them ensure reliable protection of the chemical weapon storage sites, and Damascus firmly assured us of absolute safety of these arsenals.[8]

Earlier in 2012, the United States Department of State reportedly sent démarches to Iraq, Jordan, Lebanon and Saudi Arabia in order to express concern about the possibility that weapons could be transported across their respective borders from Syria should President Bashar al-Assad fall from power.[9] Military exercises, code named 'Eager Lion', were purportedly conducted in the Jordanian desert and mountains, including simulation exercises for seizing weapon caches—among them chemical weapons—in at least three Syrian governorates. The spring exercises

[5] OPCW, 'OPCW statement on alleged chemical weapons in Syria', 24 July 2012, <http://www.opcw.org/news/article/opcw-statement-on-alleged-chemical-weapons-in-syria/>.

[6] United Nations News Centre, 'Use of chemical weapons in Syria would be "reprehensible"—UN chief', 23 July 2012, <http://www.un.org/apps/news/story.asp?NewsID=42538&Cr=syria&Cr1=>.

[7] Russian Ministry of Foreign Affairs, [Russian Ministry of Foreign Affairs Department of Information and Press Commentary in connection with a statement by the representative of the Ministry of International Affairs of Syria], 24 July 2012, <http://www.mid.ru/bdomp/brp_4.nsf/0/9a789cac 921b5a9944257a480045059c>. For a summary and other details of the 1925 Protocol for the Prohibition of the Use in War of Asphyxiating, Poisonous or Other Gases, and of Bacteriological Methods of Warfare (1925 Geneva Protocol) see annex A in this volume.

[8] Russian Ministry of Foreign Affairs, [Interview of Deputy Minister of Foreign Affairs G. M. Gatilov to the ITAR-TASS information agency, Moscow, 25 July 2012], 25 July 2012, <http://www.mid.ru/bdomp/brp_4.nsf/0/80f8e1e5e5695fad44257a480028b673/>. For a summary and other details of the Convention on the Prohibition of the Development, Production, Stockpiling and Use of Chemical Weapons and on Their Destruction see annex A in this volume.

[9] Rogin, J., 'Exclusive: State Department quietly warning region on Syrian WMDs', 24 Feb. 2012, Foreign Policy, <http://thecable.foreignpolicy.com/posts/2012/02/24/exclusive_state_department_ quietly_warning_region_on_syrian_wmds>.

attempted to simulate countering al-Qaeda's seizure of chemical weapon caches and other high-end or otherwise strategically significant weapons.[10]

The USA also reportedly told Israel that 'the material' was dispersed among 'many sites' and that it was thus 'doubtful that all these [sites] could be located'.[11] Turkey and the USA consulted each other on Turkish plans to secure sites based on information that Turkey had received from Syrian military officers.

Syria's opposition was decentralized and commanded by a separate committee for each of the country's 14 governorates.[12] An anonymous senior Syrian opposition army defector spoke to the Israeli newspaper *Haaretz* on the opposition forces' plans to take control and stabilize the country as the Assad regime falls. In particular, he stated 'We have divided the aftermath into four periods with different priorities for each day. The first period is the first day, the first hours after Assad's control breaks down, and one of the priorities during those hours is taking control of the chemical weapons so they won't fall in the hands of terrorists'. The defector noted that the chemical weapon stockpiles were controlled by the Air Force Intelligence Directorate and under the overall command of Abdel-Fatah Qudsiyeh (formerly the commander of Air Force Intelligence and head of Syria's secret police since 2009).[13]

General Adnan Silou, a defector from the Syrian Government side, reportedly stated that the rebel forces were forming a special unit to secure chemical weapon sites. Silou oversaw the 2008 creation of emergency plans to help ensure that dangerous weapons remain under government control. He supervised the training of thousands of military personnel in the Damascus and Latakia areas to 'secure what analysts believe are the largest chemical weapons stores in the world, consisting principally of sarin, mustard gas and cyanide'. He stated that there are two principal chemical weapon stockpiles: warehouse 417 in eastern Damascus and warehouse 419 in the Homs area. Traditionally, Syria maintained approximately 1500 soldiers commanded by two or three generals at each site. Silou had met with Assad and other senior leaders numerous times and believed Assad capable of ordering the use of chemical weapons. Silou also stated that he believed government forces had sprayed pesticides over rebel-friendly areas in

---

[10] 'Sources: Eager Lion exercises simulated attempts to seize Syrian arsenals', Al-Quds al-Arabi Online, 30 May 2012, Translation from Arabic, Open Source Center, 30 Apr. 2012.

[11] 'US reportedly tells Israel: unsure all Syrian WMD can be located', *Yedi'ot Aharonot* (Tel Aviv), 12 June 2012, Translation from Hebrew and Abkhazian, Open Source Center, p. 10.

[12] Pfeffer, A., 'Syrian rebel leader to *Haaretz*: Assad's opposition will secure chemical weapons', *Haaretz*, 28 May 2012.

[13] Pfeffer (note 12).

Rastan near Homs.[14] In addition, Syria reportedly has aerial chemical bombs under the control of an air force unit called Unit 450.[15]

On 20 August 2012 US President Barack Obama stated that the issue of Syria's chemical weapons 'doesn't just concern Syria; it concerns our close allies in the region, including Israel', and 'We cannot have a situation where chemical or biological weapons are falling into the hands of the wrong people.'[16] In December 2012 the Secretary General of the North Atlantic Treaty Organization (NATO), Anders Fogh Rasmussen, noted 'The Syrian stockpiles of chemical weapons are a matter of great concern. . . . the possible use of chemical weapons would be completely unacceptable for the whole international community and if anybody resorts to these terrible weapons I would expect an immediate reaction from the international community'.[17] One estimate suggested that 75 000 troops would be required to secure Syrian chemical weapon sites, and the US Secretary of Defense, Leon E. Panetta, stated that Syria's chemical weapon status is '100 times worse' than that of Libya.[18]

Israel has stated that 'Syria still maintains a considerable operational arsenal of chemical weapons and has recently admitted their possession in an official statement'.[19] Iranian and Syrian media made counter-allegations of chemical weapon use by Syrian rebels.[20] Iran stated that Israel possesses a 'clandestine programme to develop chemical weapons' and that the international community should pressure it to join the 1993 Chemical Weapons Convention immediately and without precondition.[21]

Also relevant are the details released by the Panel of Experts on the Democratic People's Republic of Korea (DPRK, North Korea) established by UN Security Council Resolution 1874 concerning two 2009 shipments of

[14] Sherlock, R., 'Rebels forming unit to secure chemical weapons sites', *Daily Telegraph*, 20 July 2012.

[15] Schmitt, E. and Sanger, D. E., 'Hints of Syrian chemical push set off global effort to stop it', *New York Times*, 7 Jan. 2013.

[16] White House, 'Remarks by the President to the White House Press Corps', Press Briefing transcript, 20 Aug. 2012, <http://www.whitehouse.gov/the-press-office/2012/08/20/remarks-president-white-house-press-corps>.

[17] North Atlantic Treaty Organization, 'Doorstep statement by the NATO Secretary General at the start of the Foreign Affairs Ministers meeting', 4 Dec. 2012, <http://www.nato.int/cps/en/natolive/opinions_92785.htm>.

[18] Starr, B., 'Military: thousands of troops needed to secure Syrian chemical sites', CNN, 22 Feb. 2012, <http://security.blogs.cnn.com/2012/02/22/military-thousands-of-troops-needed-to-secure-syrian-chemical-sites/>. Panetta is cited in Nikitin, M. B., Feickert, A. and Kerr, P. K., *Syria's Chemical Weapons: Issues for Congress*, Congressional Research Service (CRS) Report for Congress R42848 (CRS: Washington, DC, 5 Dec. 2012), p. 1.

[19] OPCW, Conference of the States Parties, 17th Session, 'Israel: statement by Mr Eyal Propper, Director arms control policy department, Ministry of Foreign Affairs', C-17/NAT.15, 27 Nov. 2012, p. 2.

[20] 'Report: terrorist groups in Syria armed with chemical weapons', Fars News Agency, 9 June 2012, Open Source Center, document no. IAP20120609950087.

[21] OPCW, Conference of the States Parties, 17th Session, 'Islamic Republic of Iran: Statement by H. E. Kazem Gharib Abadi, Ambassador and Permanent Representative of the Islamic Republic of Iran', C-17/NAT.24, 26 Nov. 2012, p. 3.

chemical protection gear sent by ship from North Korea to Syria.[22] In January 2012 panel members examined the cargo of the November 2009 shipment and confirmed that 13 000 protective coats and 23 600 gas indicator ampoules 'bore clear traces of manufacture in' North Korea and that the coats were identical to those acquired in October 2009 from the MSC *Rachele* (the two shipments with coats were taken in October and November 2009). In March 2012 Syria indicated that the 2009 shipment of protective gear and ampoules was for 'agricultural and laboratory use'. According to shipping documents, the intended recipient was the Environmental Study Centre, which the committee concluded 'appears to be linked with the Higher Institute of Applied Sciences and Technology . . . which provides training to Scientific Studies and Research Centre engineers'. The USA has designated the latter two bodies as suspected of involvement in 'Syrian weapon of mass destruction programmes', while Japan has labelled them 'entities of proliferation concern'.[23]

Aum Shinrikyo

The Japan-based religious cult Aum Shinrikyo is best known for attacking the Tokyo underground with sarin in March 1995. In late 2011 it appeared that all criminal proceedings against members of Aum Shinrikyo were concluded. As of November 2011, 12 of the 13 members prosecuted had been sentenced to death. However, on 31 December 2011 a 14th member of the cult, Makoto Hirata, turned himself over to police. Apparently, he did so in order to delay the executions because all co-defendants to a crime must be tried and sentenced before sentences are carried out. In 2011 Professor Anthony T. Tu, a noted chemist who advised the Tokyo police on technical aspects of their investigation of the 1994 Matsumoto and 1995 Tokyo underground nerve agent attacks, interviewed one of the condemned members, Dr Tomomasa Nakagawa.[24]

According to Nakagawa, two other cult members, Hideo Murai and Masami Tsuchiya, got the idea of using sarin after reading a Japanese translation (by another group member) of *The Story of Poisons*, by D. Vachivarov and G. Nedelchef. Nakagawa said that the idea of using VX came from an article published by Tu in *Chemistry Today*. The specific point of interest was that one of the intermediates the cult was using for the production of sarin to obtain phosphorus trichloride (PCl_3) was a potential VX precursor

---

[22] UN Security Council Resolution 1874, 12 June 2009.

[23] United Nations, Security Council, Letter dated 11 June 2012 from the Coordinator of the Panel of Experts established pursuant to Resolution 1874 (2009) addressed to the President of the Security Council', S/2012/422, 14 June 2012, pp. 27–28.

[24] For Tu's account of his work with the Japanese authorities see Tu, A. T., *Chemical Terrorism: Horrors in Tokyo Subway and Matsumoto City* (Alaken: Fort Collins, CO, 2002). Tu is Professor Emeritus in the Department of Biochemistry and Molecular Biology at Colorado State University.

mentioned in Tu's article. Nakagawa also stated that assistance from Russian actors was confined to supplying pyridostigmine bromide (a pre-treatment prophylactic to protect against nerve agent exposure), respirators, protective gear, a chemical agent monitor, AK-47 blueprints and a helicopter.[25]

Nakagawa indicated that media statements that the Japanese police had found methylphosphonic acid in soil samples taken at the cult's Satyan 7 complex in Kamikuishiki, where the cult engaged in the manufacture of sarin, triggered an effort to destroy all stocks of the precursors (mainly methylphosphonyldifluoride, DF). According to Nakagawa, the news reports caused consternation among religious cult members. He also stated that this reaction 'accelerated the collapse' of the cult and that, without it, 'there would have been more killing by the sect of innocent people'.[26]

The Soviet biological weapon programme

In 2012 Milton Leitenberg and Raymond Zilinskas published what is generally regarded as a definitive study of the Soviet biological weapon programme.[27] Russia dismissed unspecified media reports concerning the fate of the Soviet biological weapon programme (including possible biological weapon stocks) by stating that 'such fabrications do not correspond to reality' and that Russia is fully compliant with the 1972 Biological and Toxin Weapons Convention (BTWC).[28]

[25] Tu, A. T., 'Final death sentences for Aum Shinrikyo's chemical terrorists', *ASA Newsletter*, no. 144 (31 Mar. 2012), p. 10.

[26] Tu (note 25), p. 11.

[27] Leitenberg, M. and Zilinskas, R. A., *The Soviet Biological Weapons Program: A History* (Harvard University Press: Cambridge, MA, 2012). A British participant in the highly secret trilateral British–Soviet (then Russian)–US process to clarify the status of the Soviet violation of the BTWC described the study (in a review that contributes to the literature in its own right) as 'magisterial'. Walker, J. R., 'The Leitenberg–Zilinskas history of the Soviet biological weapons programme', Harvard-Sussex Occasional Paper no. 2, Dec. 2012, <http://www.sussex.ac.uk/Units/spru/hsp/Occ-papers.html>. For extensive interviews of participants in Soviet biological weapon activities in Kazakhstan and related information see Ben Ouagrham-Gormley, S. et al., 'The anthrax diaries: an anthropology of biological warfare', Cornell University, [n.d.], <http://russian.cornell.edu/bio/cfm/home.cfm>.

[28] Russian Ministry for Foreign Affairs, [Department of Information and Publications of the Russian MFA commentary on the matter of the period of operation of 'The Nunn-Lugar Programme'], Press Release 1921–10–10–2012, <http://www.mid.ru/brp_4.nsf/newsline/3B025187C9313ECE4425 7A9300604256> (in Russian).

IV. Oversight of dual-purpose research in the life sciences

PETER CLEVESTIG AND JOHN HART

In 2012 the World Health Organization (WHO) met to consider whether and how to restrict avian influenza research in the midst of a controversy about publishing details on the creation in a laboratory of a strain of influenza that can be transmitted between mammals.[1] Authorities in the United States issued a new policy to mitigate biorisks in life sciences research that attempts to further institutionalize oversight and evaluation procedures in the area of dual-use research of concern in the life sciences. The WHO also confirmed the existence of a novel coronavirus and alerted its members in accordance with the International Health Regulations (IHR).

A novel coronavirus

On 22 September the United Kingdom informed the WHO of the case of a person in London who had presented symptoms of the virus on 3 September and who had previously travelled to Saudi Arabia and Qatar.[2] On 7 September he was admitted to a hospital in Doha, Qatar, and he was transferred to the UK on 11 September.[3]

Professor Maria Zambon's laboratory at the UK's Health Protection Agency (HPA), in consultation with the laboratory at Erasmus Medical Centre in Rotterdam, the Netherlands, and the WHO, evaluated the sample from Qatar. The London strain was '99.5 percent identical with the Dutch team's virus', which had been obtained from a patient travelling from the Arabian peninsula.[4] The HPA then confirmed that the virus matched that obtained from an isolate that was taken from the lung tissue of a 60-year old Saudi national who had died earlier in 2012.[5]

The cases raised concern because of their unknown severity, number and geographic distribution, and the similarity of the virus to another coronavirus which causes severe acute respiratory syndrome (SARS).[6]

---

[1] World Health Organization, 'Technical consultation on H5N1 research issues: consensus points', 16–17 Feb. 2012, <http://www.who.int/influenza/human_animal_interface/consensus_points/en/>.

[2] World Health Organization, 'Novel coronavirus infection: update', Global Alert and Response (GAR), 25 Sep. 2012, <http://www.who.int/csr/don/2012_09_25/en/index.html>.

[3] World Health Organization (note 2).

[4] Kelland, K., 'Finding a new virus: spit, sequencing and serendipity', Reuters, 28 Sep. 2012, <http://www.reuters.com/article/2012/09/28/us-virus-discovery-idUSBRE88R0U620120928>; and World Health Organization (note 2).

[5] World Health Organization (note 2).

[6] See Raveché, B., 'International public health diplomacy and the global surveillance of avian influenza', *SIPRI Yearbook 2008*, pp. 456–69; and Njuguna, J. T., 'The SARS epidemic: the control of infectious diseases and biological weapon threats', *SIPRI Yearbook 2004*, pp. 697–712.

Biorisks oversight

On 29 March 2012 the US National Institutes of Health (NIH) issued a new policy to mitigate biorisks in life sciences research that defines dual-use research of concern as

life sciences research that, based on current understanding, can be reasonably anticipated to provide knowledge, information, products, or technologies that could be directly misapplied to pose a significant threat with broad potential consequences to public health and safety, agricultural crops and other plants, animals, the environment, materiel, or national security.[7]

This definition is based on the US National Science Advisory Board for Biosecurity (NSABB) definition.

The application of this policy is based, in part, on a list of 14 agents and toxins of particular concern, and 7 categories of experiment (based on NSABB categories for research of concern). The 7 categories of experiment are: (*a*) 'enhances the harmful consequences of the agent or toxin'; (*b*) 'disrupts immunity or the effectiveness of an immunization against the agent or toxin without clinical or agricultural justification'; (*c*) 'confers to the agent or toxin resistance to clinically or agriculturally useful prophylactic or therapeutic interventions against that agent or toxin or facilitates their ability to evade detection methodologies'; (*d*) 'increases the stability, transmissibility, or the ability to disseminate the agent or toxin'; (*e*) 'alters the host range or tropism of the agent or toxin'; (*f*) 'enhances the susceptibility of a host population to the agent or toxin'; and (*g*) generates or reconstitutes an eradicated or extinct agent or toxin listed in Section (III.1)' (i.e. on the list of 14 agents and toxins).

The new policy would require funders to review ongoing and future research that falls under these criteria and to establish management criteria for such research, including screening by the Institutional Biosafety Committees (IBC) based on eight questions to be answered by the researchers and on a report by the National Research Council.[8] A positive response to any of the eight questions would prompt a two-phase review by a dual-use research review committee (DURRC).

[7] US Department of Health and Human Services, National Institutes of Health (NIH), 'United States Government policy for oversight of life sciences dual use research of concern', [n.d.], <http://oba.od.nih.gov/oba/biosecurity/pdf/united_states_government_policy_for_oversight_of_durc_final_version_032812.pdf>.

[8] National Institutes of Health, 'Institutional biosafety committees', [n.d.], <http://oba.od.nih.gov/rdna_ibc/ibc.html>; Boston University, 'Dual use research of concern (DURC)', [n.d.], <http://www.bu.edu/orc/durc/>; and National Research Council of the National Academies, *Biotechnology Research in an Age of Terrorism: Confronting the Dual-use Dilemma* (National Academies Press: Washington, DC, 2004).

Avian influenza research controversy[9]

In 2012 important developments in research on highly pathogenic avian influenza A (A/H5N1) occurred following the initial disclosure, at a conference in Malta on 12 September 2011, that influenza capable of airborne transmission between mammals can be derived in the laboratory.[10] The research, funded by the US National Institute of Allergy and Infectious Diseases (NIAID), was performed by two independent groups that were based in the Netherlands and the USA. The two groups submitted their work for publication in *Science* and *Nature* in 2011. However, their publications were delayed and instead initiated international debate on biosecurity versus scientific freedom, especially in regard to the dual-use potential of research on transmissibility of A/H5N1, and led to the further development of research oversight strategies.[11]

Experimental significance

The research originated from a NIAID call for proposals following the 2006 Report of the Blue Ribbon Panel on Influenza Research, which recommended that priority be given to understanding how influenza viruses circulate between animal reservoirs and the evolutionary pressures that lead to new emerging subtypes.[12] In 2009 the WHO also recommended that research on virus-specific factors for transmissibility should be prioritized to allow more rapid identification of emerging influenza strains with pandemic potential.[13]

Both the Dutch and the US research groups set out to evaluate the potential for H5N1 to cause a pandemic, by examining its ability to become transmissible through respiratory droplets, and to identify the required genetic and molecular changes. The researchers genetically modified influenza A strains carrying the H5 hemagglutinine (HA) gene and managed to induce airborne transmissibility through serial passage in ferrets. Serial passage is the process of infecting a series of hosts to either attenuate a

[9] For background see Tucker, J. B. (ed.), *Innovation, Dual-Use and Security: Managing the Risks of Emerging Biological and Chemical Technologies* (MIT Press: Cambridge, MA, 2012).

[10] European Scientific Working Group on Influenza (ESWI), <http://www.eswiconference.org/>.

[11] 'Bridging science and security for biological research: a discussion about dual-use review and oversight at research institutions', Virtual Biosecurity Center, Sep. 2012, <http://virtualbiosecurity center.org/library/bridging-science-and-security-for-biological-research-a-discussion-about-dual-use-review-and-oversight-at-research-institutions>.

[12] US National Institutes of Health, National Institute of Allergy and Infectious Diseases (NIAID), 'Report of the Blue Ribbon Panel on Influenza Research', 11–12 Sep. 2006, <http://www.niaid.nih.gov/topics/flu/documents/influenzablueribbonpanel2006.pdf>, pp. 11–12.

[13] World Health Organization (WHO), Global Influenza Programme, 'WHO public health research agenda for influenza, version 1, 2009', 2010, <http://www.who.int/influenza/resources/research/2010_04_29_global_influenza_research_agenda_version_01_en.pdf>; and Shinya, K. et al., 'Avian flu: influenza virus receptors in the human airway', *Nature*, vol. 440, no. 7083 (23 Mar. 2006), pp. 435–36.

virus or enhance its virulence by forcing mutation via exposure to the host immune system. Ferrets are a common model for influenza research as they are susceptible to both human and avian viruses and develop respiratory disease similar to humans.[14] Influenza A/H5N1 does not naturally possess the ability to transmit through respiratory droplets in humans due to its inefficient replication in the upper respiratory tract. Human and avian influenza viruses differ in their receptor recognition by HA. Thus, avian influenza virus has difficulty replicating efficiently in the upper respiratory tract in humans where virus load is essential for droplet (air) transmission.[15] Avian influenza does not readily transmit between mammals due to this difference in co-receptor preference. The research is significant because very small genetic changes can make avian influenza air-borne transmissible between ferrets, which are mammals—as are humans.

The US research group, headed by Dr Yoshihiro Kawaoka at the University of Wisconsin–Madison, used a reassortant influenza strain with seven gene segments from the 2009 pandemic influenza A/H1N1 (swine flu) and a H5N1-derived H5 subtype HA gene.[16] Ferrets were infected with the virus, which was allowed to reassort between the animals. The air transmissibility of one reassortant virus carrying four mutations in H5 HA was tested by placing the infected animal adjacent to healthy ferrets. Two-thirds of the healthy animals became infected and all of those that were exposed developed antibodies (in a process known as seroconversion).[17]

The Dutch research group, headed by Dr Ron Fouchier, used a wild-type influenza A/H5N1 strain (i.e. the state in nature of the pathogen) sourced from Indonesia to explore potential mutation towards air transmissibility. The Influenza virus A/Indonesia/5/2005, derived from a human patient, was chosen due to its incidence of human infections and high mortality rate. Similar to the US group, the Dutch researchers used site-directed mutagenesis to induce four amino acid substitutions (mutations) in the receptor binding site (RBS) of the H5 subtype HA gene, which has been identified in a human case of H5N1 infection.[18] The researchers aimed at

[14] Smith, W. et al., 'A virus obtained from influenza patients', *The Lancet* (1933), pp. 66–68.

[15] Sorrell, E. M. et al., 'Predicting "airborne" influenza viruses: (trans-) mission impossible?', *Current Opinion in Virology*, vol. 1, no. 6 (Dec. 2011), pp. 635–42.

[16] On reassortment see Neumann, G. et al., 'Generation of influenza A viruses entirely from cloned cDNAs', *Proceedings of the National Academies of Science*, vol. 96, no. 16 (3 Aug. 1999), pp. 9345–50.

[17] Imai, M. et al., 'Experimental adaptation of an influenza H5 HA confers respiratory droplet transmission to a reassortant H5 HA/H1N1 virus in ferrets', *Nature*, vol. 486 (21 June 2012), pp. 420–28.

[18] On site-directed mutagenesis (also known as site-specific mutagenesis) see Flavell, R. A. et al., 'Site-directed mutagenesis: effect of an extracistronic mutation on the in vitro propagation of bacteriophage Qbeta RNA', *Proceedings of the National Academy of Sciences*, vol. 72 no. 1 (Jan. 1975), pp. 67–71. On the RBS of H5 subtype HA gene see also Chutinimitkul S. et al., '*In vitro* assessment of attachment pattern and replication efficiency of H5N1 influenza A viruses with altered receptor specificity', *Journal of Virology*, vol. 84, no. 13 (July 2010), pp. 6825–33; and Russell, C. A. et al., 'The potential for respiratory droplet transmissible A/H5N1 influenza virus to evolve in a mammalian

attaining mutant H5N1 viruses with a specificity towards a receptor that predominates on mammalian upper respiratory tract cells, including in ferrets. The viruses were then 'passaged' 10 times and mutants selected for testing of airborne-transmissibility using the same technique as that used by the US group. The researchers concluded that highly pathogenic avian influenza A virus (HPAI) has the potential to evolve directly into an air-transmissible variant without an intermediate host, as previously assumed, highlighting the risk of such a variant emerging and posing a pandemic threat to humans.[19]

The security implications

All experiments with live viruses were conducted under enhanced bio-safety level 3 (BSL-3+) containment conditions following current standards and guidelines for work.[20] The research was presented before peers prior to submission for publication and concerns about its potential malicious use were not raised at the time. However, both experiments came under much criticism from security specialists following submission to journals, despite the scientists' claiming to have carefully planned the experiments in regard to biosafety and biosecurity and in consultation with experts.[21] In December 2011 the US NSABB, which is tasked with providing advice and guidance on biosecurity oversight of dual-use research, reviewed the potential security implications of the research papers. It concluded that both papers carried potentially sensitive methodological information and recommended to *Nature* and *Science* that, before publishing, the papers be redacted by having key methodological parts removed, that the potential public health benefits be better explained, and that the biosafety and bio-security measures taken during experimentation be detailed. Specifically, the NSABB recommended that 'the manuscripts not include the method-ological and other details that could enable replication of the experiments by those who would seek to do harm'.[22]

---

host', *Science*, vol. 336, no. 6088 (22 June 2012), pp. 1541–47. On the human case of H5N1 infection see Yamada, S. et al., 'Letter, haemagglutinin mutation responsible for the binding of H5N1 influenza A viruses to human-type receptors', *Nature*, 16 Nov. 2006, pp. 378–82.

[19] Herfst, S. et al., 'Airborne transmission of influenza A/H5N1 virus between ferrets', *Science*, vol. 336, no. 6088 (22 June 2012), pp. 1534–41.

[20] BSL-3+ denotes laboratories with appropriate enhancements above the defined containment criteria of BSL-3 containment laboratories. US Department of Health and Human Services (HHS), *Biosafety in Microbiological and Biomedical Laboratories*, 5th edn, HHS publication no. (CDC) 21-1112 (HHS: Washington, DC, Dec.2009), pp. 236–38.

[21] Roos, R., 'Research on contagious H5N1 viruses: space suites needed?', University of Minnesota, Center for Infectious Disease Research & Policy (CIDRAP), 6 Mar. 2012, <http://www.cidrap.umn.edu/cidrap/content/influenza/avianflu/news/mar0612biosafety.html>.

[22] US Department of Health and Human Services, National Institutes of Health (NIH), 'Press statement on the NSABB review of H5N1 research', *NIH News*, 20 Dec. 2011, <http://www.nih.gov/news/health/dec2011/od-20.htm>.

In January 2012 a group of leading influenza researchers reported, through a letter in *Science*, that they had agreed to a 60-day moratorium on sensitive H5N1 research in order to allow international discussion of the future safe and secure communication of such research.[23] The following month the WHO hosted a meeting of 22 influenza experts, public health officials and journal editors from 11 countries to discuss the reports. In contrast to the NSABB, the WHO recommended that they be published in full, after a delay.[24] The meeting concluded, although not unanimously, that the public health benefits and scientific value of improving influenza pandemic preparedness and response—in conjunction with the complexity of attempting to share the full methodology—overshadowed the bioterrorism concerns expressed by the NSABB. Nonetheless, the participants supported delaying publication in accordance with the voluntary 60-day moratorium that expired on 20 March. At the meeting the lead researchers distributed original unredacted versions of the papers and versions redacted in accordance with the NSABB's recommendations; all distributed copies were subsequently destroyed in front of the group.[25]

The export control laws of both the Netherlands and the USA include limits on the export of sensitive information, with exemptions for material that is shared openly and fully in scientific publications. The guidelines of the Australia Group, an informal, non-legally binding, multilateral trade control arrangement, do not restrict research that is basic, although 'applied' research may be subject to transfer controls.[26] Since the NSABB recommended redactions to which the authors also subsequently acceded, export control regulations were in principle applicable to both papers and their immediate publication could have been in violation of the law, carrying criminal penalties.[27]

Ultimately, the NSABB voted unanimously that the Kawaoka group's research be published in full, but it voted 12 to 6 for endorsing publication of the Fouchier group's research. Michael Osterholm, a US virologist, complained that the parameters of the NSABB meeting were 'designed to produce the outcome that occurred'.[28]

---

[23] Fouchier, R. et al., 'Letters: pause on avian flu transmission research', *Science*, vol. 335 (27 Jan. 2012), pp. 400–401.

[24] World Health Organization (WHO), 'Public health, influenza experts agree H5N1 research critical, but extend delay', News release, 17 Feb. 2012, <http://www.who.int/mediacentre/news/releases/2012/h5n1_research_20120217/en/index.html>.

[25] Cohen, J., 'WHO group: H5N1 papers should be published in full', *Science*, vol. 35 , no. 6071 (24 Feb. 2012), pp. 899–900.

[26] For a brief description of the Australia Group see annex B in this volume; and on developments in 2012 see chapter 10, section IV, in this volume.

[27] Greenfieldboyce, N., 'Bird flu studies mired in export control law limbo', National Public Radio, 10 Apr. 2012, <http://www.npr.org/blogs/health/2012/04/10/150311034/bird-flu-studies-mired-in-export-control-law-limbo>; and Ohio State University, Office of Research Compliance, 'Export control', <http://orc.osu.edu/regulations-policies/exportcontrol/>.

[28] 'Jail-bird flu', *The Economist*, vol. 403, no. 8782 (27 Apr.–4 May 2012), p. 69.

On 2 May 2012 *Nature* published the paper by the Kawaoka group, following revision and another review by the NSABB, which reversed its recommendations on redaction, thus removing the export control restriction.[29] The Dutch paper, in principle, remained under Dutch export restrictions until 23 April, when the group received an export licence; *Science* published the paper on 22 June.[30]

---

[29] Roos, R., 'Export controls still blocking publication of Fouchier's H5N1 study', University of Minnesota, Center for Infectious Disease Research & Policy (CIDRAP), 10 Apr. 2012, <http://www.cidrap.umn.edu/cidrap/content/influenza/avianflu/news/apr1012h5n1.html>.

[30] See also explanatory letter submitted by the Dutch Ministry of Societal Health, Well-being and Sport to the Chairman of the Second Chamber of the Dutch Parliament, available at 'Kamerbrief met de stand van zaken onderzoek Erasmus Medisch Centrum naar H5N1' [Letter on the state of H5N1 research at the Erasmus Medical Centre], 7 Mar. 2012, <http://www.rijksoverheid.nl>.

9. Conventional arms control and military confidence building

Overview

In 2012 openness and restraint to provide reassurance that military capabilities will not be used for political gain—which is a broad definition of confidence- and security-building measures (CSBMs)—made a valuable contribution to reducing tensions and preventing the escalation of incidents in several regions of the world. As well as playing their part to prevent specific incidents from escalating into something worse, CSBMs are being developed more broadly in several regions as a positive tool to enhance cooperative relations among states based on partnership, mutual reassurance and transparency. While CSBMs cannot shoulder the burden of promoting cooperative security alone, in several regions they make a useful contribution to promoting and fostering stability and creating the conditions for positive growth and development.

In South Asia the 'hotline' for direct communications between the Directors General of Military Operations (DGMOs) of India and Pakistan was used to reduce the risk that incidents across the line of control in Jammu and Kashmir would escalate into more serious military engagements. In South East Asia the Association of Southeast Asian Nations (ASEAN) established a process for bilateral consultations with China on a binding code of conduct to regulate maritime incidents that have become a significant source of tension in the South China Sea. In the interim period an ASEAN–China dialogue will continue to discuss the Guidelines to Implement the Declaration on the Conduct of Parties in the South China Sea that were agreed in July 2011.

As a contribution to the development of a South American security community, the members of the Union of South American Nations (Unión de Naciones Suramericanas, UNASUR) continued to implement measures agreed in 2011 and to elaborate new CSBMs.

In Europe the states participating in the Organization for Security and Co-operation in Europe (OSCE) agreed on a 'Helsinki+40' process to develop practical measures to implement the 2010 Astana Declaration by 2015. The process will include discussions on the further evolution of the catalogue of CSBMs already undertaken in the framework of the Vienna Document.

As regards arms control—binding commitments to self-restraint in the structure, equipment or operations of armed forces—the situation in 2012 was less encouraging.

In the area of humanitarian arms control (in which states forgo capabilities that have indiscriminate or inhumane effects, regardless of their military utility) the pace of implementation of existing agreements remains slow and uneven. Interested states continue to address the difficulties in finding broad agreement on new measures to restrict landmines other than anti-personnel landmines and cluster munitions. However, in 2012 no consensus was reached on a way forward.

In Africa arms control processes have taken account of the mosaic of different security challenges posed in various subregions. In particular, arms control measures need to take into account the use of conventional arms to commit crimes, the cross-border dimensions of many incidents involving the use of force and the presence of multiple armed factions, some under state control but others acting independently. In contrast to arms control in other regions, which is carried out on a state-to-state basis by the national authorities tasked with providing military security, in Africa efforts have a regional and subregional character and also engage law enforcement communities.

In South Eastern Europe the measures that have successfully reduced the excessive stocks of conventional arms of all kinds over a 20-year period are increasingly under the full ownership and control of local states. The direct engagement of armed forces in the processes of mutual inspection, information exchange and joint implementation effectively eliminates any suspicion that a state will suddenly be surprised by a new and unexpected military development in a neighbour. The value of these measures has been demonstrated to the point where the states in the region continue to support them and participate in them even after integration into institutions, such as the North Atlantic Treaty Organization (NATO), that provide them with a security guarantee.

There was no significant progress in developing arms control at a European level in 2012. Differing views about the objectives of arms control are unresolved. However, at the end of 2012 Ukraine, the incoming OSCE chair, made progress on conventional arms control one of its main priorities for 2013 and put forward ideas that could be the basis for progress. The Ukrainian proposals open the opportunity for a thorough review of the role of conventional arms control in the OSCE area without being tied to finding solutions to unresolved problems that have stopped the momentum in the existing regime.

IAN ANTHONY

I. Humanitarian arms control initiatives

LINA GRIP AND TAMARA PATTON

Developments in the Certain Conventional Weapons Convention: renewed talks to control mines other than anti-personnel mines

During 2012 the main issue for the parties to the 1981 Certain Conventional Weapons (CCW) Convention was the possibility of extending the treaty to cover the use, transfer and clearance obligations for mines other than anti-personnel mines (MOTAPM).[1] Although both Amended Protocol II of the CCW Convention and the 1997 Anti-Personnel Mine Convention address anti-personnel mines (APMs), the former does not specifically regulate MOTAPM and the latter does not include them in the ban on APMs.[2] A number of states parties and civil society organizations have long advocated the creation of a separate protocol on MOTAPM under the CCW Convention; and when the negotiations on controlling cluster munitions in the CCW regime broke down in 2011, they saw an opportunity for this.

No legal definition yet exists for MOTAPM. While the CCW discussions initially sought to tackle all mines left unaddressed in current legal frameworks, they quickly narrowed their scope to anti-vehicle mines (AVMs).[3] In many cases AVMs detonate when a certain pressure is exerted on the trigger system but they cannot differentiate military from civil targets and they may pose a threat to civilians long after a conflict has ended.[4] Contamination of territory by AVMs may deny civilians access to essential items, such as (emergency) aid, food and basic services.

The initiative to control MOTAPM in the CCW Convention was first proposed by Denmark and the United States in 2001, and the states parties subsequently agreed on a mandate to consider a separate CCW protocol for the issue.[5] In 2006 the states parties to the CCW Convention, unable to agree on a protocol to restrict MOTAPM, suspended further negotiation on

---

[1] For a summary and other details of the Convention on Prohibitions or Restrictions on the Use of Certain Conventional Weapons which may be Deemed to be Excessively Injurious or to have Indiscriminate Effects (CCW Convention) and its protocols see annex A in this volume.

[2] For a summary and other details of the Convention on the Prohibition of the Use, Stockpiling, Production and Transfer of Anti-Personnel Mines and on their Destruction (APM Convention) see annex A in this volume.

[3] On AVMs in international law see CCW Convention, Meeting of Experts on Mines other than Anti-personnel Mines, 'Rules of international humanitarian law applicable to anti-vehicle mines', Background paper prepared by the International Committee of the Red Cross (ICRC), 2–4 Apr. 2012. Documents relating to the CCW Convention can be found on the website of the United Nations Office at Geneva, <http://www.unog.ch/ccw/>.

[4] Soldiers of Peace International Association, 'Mines other than the antipersonnel mines, MOTAPM', <http://www.fname.info/aisp/eng/index.php?Itemid=22>.

[5] CCW Convention, Second Review Conference, Final Document, CCW/CONF.II/2, 11–21 Dec. 2001, p. 10.

the issue indefinitely and turned their attention to addressing cluster munitions.[6]

But when the parties to the CCW Convention failed to reach agreement on restricting cluster munitions in 2011, and those negotiations were again suspended, they decided to renew the talks on MOTAPM.[7] An open-ended meeting of experts was convened in April 2012 to submit a report to the 2012 meeting of states parties.[8] At the meeting of experts the issues raised included the irresponsible use of MOTAPM, transfers to non-state actors, the need for mines to incorporate self-destruct mechanisms and detectability, and a specific requirement that AVMs be used exclusively in perimeter-marked areas (i.e. areas marked, fenced and monitored so as to ensure the effective exclusion of civilians).[9]

A consensus among CCW parties on MOTAPM has proved elusive, but their views appear closer on this issue than on cluster munitions.[10] Most states support measures to reduce the risk of indiscriminate and irresponsible use of MOTAPM but do not advocate a total ban, nor is there any global non-governmental organization (NGO) campaign to ban MOTAPM. In its statement in April 2012 the International Committee of the Red Cross (ICRC) underlined the humanitarian consequences of MOTAPM use, but did not advocate a total ban.[11] At the expert meeting on MOTAPM in April the European Union (EU), whose member states had been unable to agree on a common position on cluster munitions in 2011, stated that a balanced approach was needed, taking into consideration humanitarian and military concerns, and acknowledged that 'MOTAPM can still be used as legitimate weapons'.[12] Similarly, Australia, while concerned with the humanitarian consequences of irresponsible use, announced that 'We certainly do not seek or expect to ban all anti-vehicle mines.'[13] Israel also stated its wish for an agreement in the CCW on MOTAPM in order to restrict AVM use outside perimeter-marked areas, to introduce obligations for mechanisms for detection and to prohibit the transfer of MOTAPM to non-state actors, in

---

[6] Lachowski, Z. and Sjögren, M., 'Conventional arms control', *SIPRI Yearbook 2007*, p. 621.

[7] On discussions on cluster munitions in the CCW regime see Grip, L., 'Limiting conventional arms for humanitarian reasons: the case of cluster munitions', *SIPRI Yearbook 2012*.

[8] Geneva International Centre for Humanitarian Demining, 'MOTAPM', <http://www.gichd.org/international-conventions/convention-on-certain-conventional-weapons-ccw/motapm/>.

[9] CCW Convention, Meeting of States Parties, 'Report of the 2012 Meeting of Experts on Mines other than anti-personnel mines (MOTAPM)', CCW/MSP/2012/4, 29 May 2012, p. 2; and CCW Convention (note 3), p. 4.

[10] Cave, R., 'Disarmament as humanitarian action? Comparing negotiations on anti-personnel mines and explosive remnants of war', eds J. Borrie and V. Martin Randin, *Disarmament as Humanitarian Action: From Perspective to Practice* (UN Institute for Disarmament Research: Geneva, May 2006), p. 62.

[11] Statement by the ICRC on the humanitarian impact of MOTAPM, Geneva, Apr. 2012.

[12] CCW Convention, Meeting of Experts on Mines other than Anti-personnel Mines, Statement by the European Union, 2–4 Apr. 2012, p. 1.

[13] CCW Convention, Meeting of Experts on Mines other than Anti-personnel Mines, Statement in General Exchange of Views, P. Kimpton, Australian Permanent Mission to the UN, 2 Apr. 2012, p. 2.

combination with continued legitimate use of this type of weapon.[14] In its initial statement, the Republic of Korea (South Korea) declared that 'under [the] circumstances of its national security, it cannot but depend on the deployment of mines including MOTAPM as a means of defense and deterrence', but it nevertheless supported the balanced regulation of MOTAPM through the CCW regime.[15] Echoing the views of some other AVM-producing and -using states, Brazil stated that it strongly believed that any new obligation with respect to AVMs 'must not imply additional costs in terms of financial and technological requirements, which would impact developing countries disproportionately'.[16]

While many states that use and produce MOTAPM announced support for restrictions on MOTAPM within the CCW regime, a few—notably Russia—did not see a justification for a separate protocol on MOTAPM, citing the lack of evidence that this type of weapon causes more harm to civilians than other explosive devices—such as improvised explosive devices (IEDs).[17] This is the main cause of disagreement between states parties to the CCW Convention on enhancing regulations to cover new weapon types, and a long-standing argument advanced by Russia on the issues of cluster munitions and MOTAPM. Although the aim of the CCW Convention is to prevent conventional weapons that may have indiscriminate effects on civilians, in reality, restrictions on use and production of military strategic weapons have only been introduced once the effects on civilians are well documented.

Based on the various statements made by the states parties in April 2012, there seems to be a consensus that transfers of MOTAPM to non-state actors should be restricted. This issue was highlighted in 2011–12 after reports of AVM use in Libya, the plunder of warehouses allegedly holding AVMs and their subsequent smuggling into the Darfur region of Sudan.[18]

MOTAPM was the main issue discussed at the CCW Convention meeting of states parties in November 2012, although that meeting made no decision to further the preparatory work on MOTAPM during the next intersessional phase. A widely held view at the meeting was that the problems

[14] CCW Convention, Meeting of Experts on Mines other than Anti-personnel Mines, Statement by T. Rahamimoff-Honig, Deputy Permanent Representative of Israel, 2 Apr. 2012, pp. 2–3.

[15] CCW Convention, Meeting of Experts on Mines other than Anti-personnel Mines, Statement by the Republic of Korea, 2–4 Apr. 2012, p. 1.

[16] CCW Convention, Meeting of Experts on Mines other than Anti-personnel Mines, Statement by Brazil, 2 Apr. 2012, p. 1.

[17] CCW Convention, Meeting of Experts on Mines other than Anti-personnel Mines, Statement by Russia, 2 Apr. 2012, p. 1.

[18] Varner, B., 'Libyan arms smuggled into Sudan threaten renewed violence in Darfur region', Bloomberg, 6 Oct. 2011, <http://www.bloomberg.com/news/2011-10-06/libyan-arms-smuggled-into-sudan-threaten-renewed-violence-in-darfur-region.html>; and 'Anti-tank or anti-vehicle mines: perfectly legal and plenty lethal', Landmines in Africa, 11 Oct. 2011, <http://landminesinafrica.wordpress.com/2011/10/11/anti-tank-or-anti-vehicle-mines-perfectly-legal-and-plenty-lethal/>. On the diffusion of weapons from Libya see also chapter 1, section I, in this volume.

have already been identified and the discussions in 2012 were largely a repetition of the findings of the early 2000s. In the absence of a dedicated working group in the CCW regime, there are still a few plausible ways forward in the short term. First, it is clear that the discussions would benefit from new input, including an inclusive global mapping of MOTAPM use, contamination and casualties. States and NGOs that support a CCW protocol on MOTAPM are likely to increase their efforts to produce empirical studies in advance of the 2013 CCW Convention meeting of states parties. The Campaign to Ban Landmines stated in November 2012 that it does not believe in the approach currently taken in the CCW regime and will not support the process; however, it did not present a counter-proposal and there is no open consensus to start a parallel process.[19] Second, in the absence of an AVM protocol to the CCW Convention, states may adopt national moratoriums on the export of AVMs, similar to those adopted on APMs in the 1990s prior to the adoption of Amended Protocol II and on cluster munitions in recent years.[20]

Challenges in national reporting on explosive remnants of war

The CCW Convention's Protocol V on explosive remnants of war (ERW), adopted in November 2003, aims to reduce the impact on civilians of unexploded and abandoned munitions. The protocol requires each party to a conflict to clear ERW from the territory it controls once hostilities have ended. It also requires each party to a conflict to provide technical, material and financial assistance to clear ERW in areas not under its control that resulted from its own operations.

There has been a steady growth in membership since Protocol V entered into force in November 2006, and of the 115 states party to the CCW Convention at the end of 2012, 81 were also party to Protocol V.[21] Five states joined Protocol V in 2012: Burundi, Cuba, Laos, South Africa and Turkmenistan. Burundi was the only new party to the CCW Convention. Membership of both the CCW Convention and its Protocol V remains sparsest in Africa, the Middle East and South East Asia (see figure 9.1).

National reporting remains an important mechanism for creating transparency and building confidence in the implementation of Protocol V. In moving towards the goal of universalization, steady implementation continues to be a key factor in strengthening the legitimacy of the protocol and

---

[19] CCW Meeting of High Contracting Parties, 'ICBL Statement on Antivehicle Mines', 16 Nov. 2012.

[20] E.g. on Bulgaria's moratorium on landmines see First CCW Review Conference, Letter dated 3 May 1996 from the permanent representative of the Republic of Bulgaria to the United Nations at Geneva, CCW/CONF.I/15, 6 May 1996. On Singapore's and the USA's moratoriums on cluster munitions see Grip (note 7), p. 424.

[21] For a full list of parties see annex A in this volume.

encouraging more states to join it in the future. In November 2007 the first conference of the protocol's parties decided to establish a database of national reports on implementation, pursuant to Article 10(2)(b) of the protocol. This database has been made publically available on the official website of the CCW Convention.[22] States are currently requested to submit nine individual forms each year to the CCW Implementation Support Unit (ISU), addressing implementation of articles 3–9 and 11 of Protocol V and other relevant matters.

The number of national reports submitted has steadily increased over the years and 2012 saw the highest number of reports submitted. As of November 2012, the CCW ISU was able to assess reports submitted by 52 states, or 68 per cent of the 76 parties to Protocol V at the start of the year.[23] The CCW ISU continues to encourage more consistent and comprehensive reporting. The coordinator on national reporting at the 2012 Meeting of Experts on Protocol V pointed out that there was a considerable difference between the number of states that provided a response to a form and the number of states that actually provided details on implementation.[24]

The lack of details in national reports on one of articles 3–9 and 11 could indicate a lack of understanding of that article's obligations or an inability to implement it. For example, a particular area of concern for the ISU has been the nature of information reported under Form B on Article 4. To facilitate clearance of ERW, this article calls for states to record and retain information on the use or abandonment of explosive ordnance. While 30 parties submitted Form B in 2012, only 10 reported having established a database for recording munition usage; only 11 provided information on allocation of responsibility for recording the use and abandonment of explosive ordnance; and only 12 reported on whether the relevant authorities and military personnel in the field had been informed about the national database or the Article 4 generic template.[25] These statistics suggest that only a small number of states parties to Protocol V may be implementing Article 4.[26] Many states parties did not provide sufficient infor-

[22] United Nations Office at Geneva, CCW Convention, 'Protocol V database', <http://unog.ch/802 56EE600585943/(httpPages)/B84B4C205835421DC12574230039C42E?OpenDocument>.

[23] CCW Convention, Sixth Conference of Parties to Protocol V, 'Report on national reporting', CCW/P.V/CONF/2012/4, 21 Aug. 2012, p. 2.

[24] CCW Convention, Meeting of Experts on Protocol V, 'Presentation on the assessment of the guide to national reporting and the progress in implementing the provisions of Protocol V', Apr. 2012, p. 1

[25] CCW Convention, CCW/P.V/CONF/2012/4 (note 23), p. 3.

[26] The UN Office for Disarmament Affairs reported in Apr. 2012 at the Protocol V Meeting of Experts that the following states appear to be implementing Article 4: Australia, Belgium, Canada, Czech Republic, France, Germany, Ireland, Italy, Lithuania, New Zealand, Netherlands, Norway, Pakistan, Romania, Russia, Slovakia, Sweden, the United Arab Emirates and the USA. United Nations Office at Geneva, CCW Convention, 'Current status of Article 4 implementation according to the information submitted by states in their national annual reports', <http://unog.ch/80256EDD006B8

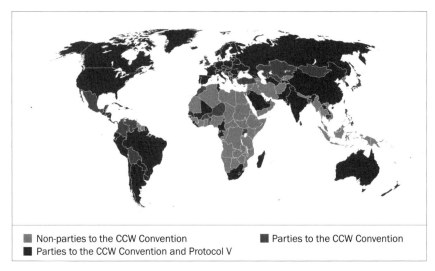

Figure 9.1. Progress towards universalization of Protocol V of the Certain Conventional Weapons Convention on explosive remnants of war

Note: In order to become a party to the 1981 Certain Conventional Weapons (CCW) Convention, a state must ratify at least 2 of its protocols. Of the 54 UN member states in Africa, 22 are party to the CCW Convention and 11 to Protocol V. Of the 35 UN member states in the Americas, 24 are party to the CCW Convention and 19 to Protocol V. Of the 42 UN member states in Asia and Oceania, 19 are party to the CCW Convention and 9 to Protocol V. Of the 48 UN member states in Europe, 42 are party to the CCW Convention and 38 to Protocol V. Of the 14 UN member states in the Middle East, 6 are party to the CCW Convention and 3 to Protocol V. In addition, the Holy See, a non-UN member state, is party to both the CCW Convention and Protocol V.

Source: Annex A in this volume.

mation for the ISU to determine whether they are implementing the article, and the majority did not provide any information at all.

A broader and ongoing national reporting issue of significance involves the differentiation between 'explosive remnants of war' and 'existing explosive remnants of war'. As several key articles in Protocol V apply exclusively to 'explosive remnants of war other than existing explosive remnants of war', the distinction between ERW created before the protocol's entry into force in a state (i.e. existing ERW) and ERW created afterwards is important for determining compliance. For example, issues such as clearance obligations, reporting standards, protection of civilians, and cooperation and assistance only apply to the latter category. Based on reports submitted in 2012, states do not appear to make a clear distinction between ERW and existing ERW. More investigation is required to deter-

954/(httpAssets)/2ECB34574D74A667C12579F20033D8FF/$file/Article+4+Implementation_Rev1_25April.pdf>.

mine whether states are actively integrating this distinction into their national implementation strategies.

In November 2012 the Sixth Conference of parties to Protocol V recommended that the states parties continue to refer to the 'Guide to national reporting', which provides a detailed checklist of items that should, ideally, be included in each reporting form under each article.[27] As the Fourth Conference adopted this guide in 2009, upcoming conferences will be forced to address the continued disparity in reporting standards among states, seeking new ways to incentivize parties to report more thoroughly on implementation of their obligations.

Developments in the Convention on Cluster Munitions

Ten states ratified the 2008 Convention on Cluster Munitions (CCM) in 2012—Australia, Cameroon, Côte d'Ivoire, Honduras, Hungary, Mauritania, Peru, Sweden, Switzerland and Togo—bringing the total number of parties to 77, alongside 34 states that have signed but not ratified the convention.[28] In comparison, 18 states ratified the CCM in 2011—suggesting that, while membership is steadily increasing as signatory states move through their domestic ratification procedure, the CCM did not experience an upsurge of new membership in 2012 after the failure of the parties to the CCW Convention to agree on measures related to cluster munitions in 2011.[29]

In 2012 there were credible reports of the use of cluster munitions by Sudan and Syria—neither of which is a state party to the CCM.[30] In November 2012 Human Rights Watch and others announced that there was compelling evidence that the Syrian armed forces had used cluster munitions against an olive oil-processing facility and in a separate strike on a nearby olive grove, killing at least 12 civilians.[31]

Norway hosted the third meeting of the states parties to the CCM in September 2012, where it encouraged discussion of the role of the CCM in international humanitarian law following the outcome of the discussions in

[27] United Nations Office at Geneva, CCW Convention, Protocol V Sixth Conference, 'Final document, advanced version', Nov. 2012, <http://unog.ch/80256EDD006B8954/(httpAssets)/29E5C7B9932C0A26C1257ADA005884DC/$file/Report_SixthConf_ProtocolV_AdvancedVersion.pdf>, p. 6; and 'Guide to national reporting', <http://unog.ch/80256EE600585943/(httpPages)/C94A2E8E4FB1EF52C12574080055C8CB?>.

[28] For a summary, list of parties and signatories, and other details of the Convention on Cluster Munitions see annex A in this volume.

[29] On discussions on cluster munitions in the CCW regime in 2011 see Grip (note 7), pp. 419–22.

[30] Landmine and Cluster Munition Monitor, *Cluster Munition Monitor 2012* (Cluster Munition Coalition: London, Sep. 2012), p. 5.

[31] Human Rights Watch, 'Syria: evidence shows cluster bombs killed children', 27 Nov. 2012, <http://www.hrw.org/news/2012/11/27/syria-evidence-shows-cluster-bombs-killed-children-0>. On the conflict in Syria see also chapter 1, section I, chapter 2, section II, and chapter 8, section III, in this volume.

the CCW regime in 2011.[32] Many non-parties attended the meeting, but of the main cluster munition-producing states only China was represented. States parties raised the need for universalization of the CCM, but at the meeting Belgium was alone in asking for a realistic strategy to achieve this goal. Several African parties (e.g. Zambia) announced a wish to see Africa become the first 'cluster munitions-free zone'. Representatives of 34 sub-Saharan African countries—including 17 that had signed but not ratified the convention and 3 that had not signed it—took part in a regional conference on the universalization of the convention in Accra, Ghana, in May 2012 at which the Accra Universalization Action Plan was drafted and adopted. Four of the participating states ratified the convention later in 2012 or early 2013.[33]

The CCM meeting took no decision on creating an implementation support unit. On the broader issue of compliance, there was little discussion among states parties at the plenary meeting on the so-called 'interpretative issues' of the convention, namely assistance with prohibited acts (e.g. trade in dual-use weapon components), transit and foreign stockpiling of cluster munitions belonging to non-state parties, and investments in companies producing cluster munitions. However, at the sidelines of the conference, the Cluster Munition Coalition (CMC), a civil society campaign, continued its awareness and advocacy activities to push these issues onto the CCM agenda.[34]

Developments in the Anti-Personnel Mines Convention

The 12th Meeting of the States Parties to the APM Convention was held in Geneva in December 2012. The meeting took place at the 'mid-term review' of the Cartagena Action Plan 2010–14, which seeks to ensure rapid and effective implementation of the APM Convention.[35] Three states ratified the convention in 2012—Finland, Poland and Somalia.

---

[32] CCM, 'Strengthening international humanitarian law', CCM/MSP/2012/3, 9 Aug. 2012; and Norwegian Ministry of Foreign Affairs, Støre, G. J., Former Minister of Foreign Affairs, 'Opening statement at Convention on Cluster Munitions', Oslo, 11 Sep. 2012, <http://www.regjeringen.no/en/dep/ud/whats-new/Speeches-and-articles/speeches_foreign/2012/cluster_convention.html?id=698859>, pp. 7–8.

[33] Dube, G., 'Africa takes the lead in universalising the Convention on Cluster Munitions', Institute for Security Studies, 7 June 2012, <http://www.issafrica.org/iss_today.php?ID=1495-10>; and 'The Accra Universalization Action Plan', Accra, 29 May 2012, <http://www.clusterconvention.org/meetings/regional-meetings/accra-regional-conference-on-the-universalization-of-the-ccm-28-30-may-2012/>. Cameroon, Chad, Côte d'Ivoire and Togo ratified the convention later in 2012 or early 2013. A further 19 sub-Saharan African states have signed but not ratified the treaty. Eritrea, Mauritius and Zimbabwe have neither signed nor ratified the convention.

[34] Landmine and Cluster Munition Monitor (note 30), p. 3.

[35] APM Convention, 12th Meeting of the States Parties, 3–7 Dec. 2012, <http://www.apmineban convention.org/meetings-of-the-states-parties/12msp/>; and APM Convention Second Review Conference, 'Cartagena Action Plan 2010–2014: ending the suffering caused by anti-personnel mines',

During 2012, four states parties requested an extension of the deadline for completing the destruction of APMs in mined areas in accordance with Article 5 of the APM Convention: Afghanistan (requesting an extension for 10 years), Angola (5 years), Cyprus (3 years) and Zimbabwe (2 years). Although the requests—which were all approved—seem modest in time, Angola requested 5 years to complete 'the required activities' after which 'Angola will submit an application more suited to the situation that it identifies'—implying that the country is far from implementing the provisions on clearance.[36] Zimbabwe's request for an extension was its third.[37] In addition, while not requesting an extension, Uganda reported that it would not meet its 1 August 2012 deadline. The Republic of the Congo neither submitted a request for consideration by the meeting of states parties nor indicated whether it would complete implementation by its deadline of 1 January 2013.[38] The president of the 11th Meeting, held in 2011, underlined that some states parties, almost 10 years after entry into force, 'still lacked clarity regarding "the location of all mined areas that contain or are suspected to contain, anti-personnel mines under (their) jurisdiction or control"'.[39] On a positive note several states, including Denmark, Guinea-Bissau and Jordan, declared that they had completed implementation of this obligation in 2012.

The states parties to the APM Convention continue to tackle the issue of how to address newly discovered, previously unknown, mined areas in states parties that signed the convention in the belief that it would not involve any clearance obligations. The convention is silent on this matter.[40]

The state of humanitarian arms control initiatives

In 2012 implementation of the humanitarian arms control-related conventions continued at a typical pace, although each convention also faced unique challenges in terms of its growth and development.

Cartagena, 29 Nov.–4 Dec. 2009. Documents relating to the APM Convention can be found on the website of the UN Office at Geneva, <http://www.unog.ch/aplc/>.

[36] APM Convention, 12th Meeting of the States Parties, 'Request for an extension of the deadline for completing the destruction of anti-personnel mines in accordance with Article 5 of the convention: executive summary', Angola, APLC/MSP.12/2012/WP.7, 9 Oct. 2012, p. 4.

[37] APM Convention, 12th Meeting of the States Parties, 'Request for an extension of the deadline for the fulfilment of the obligations under Article 5 of the Convention on the Prohibition of the Use, Stockpiling, Production and Transfer of Anti-personnel Mines and on their Destruction, Zimbabwe, APLC/MSP.12/2012/WP.11, 22 Oct. 2012, p. 7.

[38] APM Convention, 12th Meeting of the States Parties, 'The analysis of requests for extensions to Article 5 deadlines 2011–2012', APLC/MSP.12/2012/6, 29 Nov. 2012, p. 2.

[39] APM Convention, APLC/MSP.12/2012/6 (note 38), pp. 2–3.

[40] APM Convention, 12th Meeting of the States Parties, 'Proposed rational response to states parties discovering previously unknown mined areas after deadlines have passed', Co-chairs of the Standing Committee on Mine Clearance, Indonesia and Zambia, APLC/MSP.12/2012/7, 26 Nov. 2012.

The convergence of opinion among states that led to adoption of the Cluster Munition and APM conventions has been challenged by the problems of implementation. In the CCM, the seemingly simple issue of establishing an ISU was hampered by differing views on responsibilities for funding implementation. Similarly, questions regarding investments and foreign stockpiles (by non-state parties on the territories of states parties) touch on important national issues, such as financial regulations and military alliances—issues that some states do not want to open to scrutiny under the CCM. A number of states parties face serious challenges in implementing their commitments under the APM Convention within the acceptable time frame. In the medium term, measuring compliance and handling cases of non-compliance will be key tasks for the APM Convention. Within the CCW, although the issue of MOTAPM remains unresolved, the states parties together with the ISU continue to work to improve implementation support mechanisms for existing commitments, especially in the area of national reporting.

Overall, future progress in the humanitarian arms control regime will depend on the unique compositions of states parties to each convention and whether agreement can be reached on financial priorities, on how to deal with compliance challenges, and on the most appropriate means for addressing enduring weapon threats to civilians.

II. Small arms control in Africa

LINA GRIP

Over a period of roughly a decade a framework for the control of small arms and light weapons (SALW) in Africa has gradually been created. This framework has developed, in part, in regional responses to two main United Nations instruments to control small arms: the 2001 UN Programme of Action to Prevent, Combat and Eradicate the Illicit Trade in Small Arms and Light Weapons in All Its Aspects (POA) and the 2001 UN Firearms Protocol.[1] The first steps in the process were made in 2000 when the Organization of African Unity (OAU) compiled a common African position on the trafficking and proliferation of SALW in which African states committed themselves to combating the illicit proliferation, circulation and trafficking of SALW at the regional and subregional levels.[2]

Since then, the African Union (AU), which replaced the OAU in 2002, has been unable to adopt any SALW control measure. While the AU–Regions Steering Committee on SALW, created in 2008, has been tasked with trying to achieve a common African position in advance of UN processes, even this has proved to be difficult. For example, the AU was unable to agree a common position on the arms trade treaty (ATT) negotiations in July 2012, largely due to disagreements between North African states and sub-Saharan African states.[3] In the absence of Africa-wide agreements, interesting developments have been taking place in subregional bodies, and these often surpass global instruments.[4]

Four arms control agreements have been adopted, mainly under the aegis of subregional economic communities (see table 9.1): the 2001 Protocol on the Control of Firearms, Ammunition and other related Materials in the Southern African Development Community (SADC) Region; the 2004 Nairobi Protocol for the Prevention, Control and Reduction of Small Arms and Light Weapons in the Great Lakes Region and the Horn of Africa

---

[1] United Nations, General Assembly, Programme of Action to Prevent, Combat and Eradicate the Illicit Trade in Small Arms and Light Weapons in All Its Aspects, A/CONF.192/15, 20 July 2001, pp. 7–22; and Protocol against the Illicit Manufacturing of and Trafficking in Firearms, their Parts and Components and Ammunition, supplementing the United Nations Convention against Transnational Organized Crime (UN Firearms Protocol), adopted 31 May 2001, entered into force 3 July 2005, *United Nations Treaty Series*, vol. 2326 (2007).

[2] Bamako Declaration on an African Common Position on the Illicit Proliferation, Circulation and Trafficking of Small Arms and Light Weapons, Bamako, 30 Nov. 2000, <http://2001-2009.state.gov/t/ac/csbm/rd/6691.htm>; and Stott, N., 'Implementing the Southern Africa Firearms Protocol: identifying challenges and priorities', Occasional Paper 83, Institute for Security Studies, Nov. 2003, <http://www.iss.co.za/pubs/papers/83/Paper83.html>, p. 2.

[3] Lamb, G., 'African states and ATT negotiations', *Arms Control Today*, vol. 42, no. 7 (Sep. 2012).

[4] Killander, M., 'Legal harmonisation in Africa: taking stock and moving forward', *International Spectator*, vol. 47, no. 1 (2012), pp. 89–90.

Table 9.1. Subregional arms control agreements in Africa

Protocol on the Control of Firearms, Ammunition and other related Materials in the Southern African Development Community (SADC) Region

Signed	14 Aug. 2001, Blantyre
Entered into force	8 Nov. 2004
Depositary	SADC Executive Secretary
Parties as of July 2011	Botswana, Lesotho, Malawi, Mauritius, Mozambique, Namibia, South Africa, Swaziland, Tanzania, Zambia, Zimbabwe
Signed but not ratified	Congo (Democratic Republic of), Seychelles[a]
Not signed, not ratified	Angola, Madagascar
Protocol text	SADC, <http://www.sadc.int/documents-publications/show/796>

[a] Seychelles signed the protocol in 2001 but had not ratified by the time of its withdrawal from the SADC in 2004. It rejoined the SADC in 2008.

Nairobi Protocol for the Prevention, Control and Reduction of Small Arms and Light Weapons in the Great Lakes Region and the Horn of Africa

Signed	21 Apr. 2004, Nairobi
Entered into force:	5 May 2006
Depositary	Regional Centre on Small Arms in the Great Lakes Region, the Horn of Africa and Bordering States (RECSA)
Parties as of July 2012	Burundi, Congo (Democratic Republic of), Djibouti, Eritrea, Ethiopia, Kenya, Rwanda, Sudan, Uganda
Signed but not ratified	Central African Republic, Congo (Republic of), Seychelles, Somalia, South Sudan, Tanzania
Protocol text	RECSA, <http://www.recsasec.org/index.php/publications>

ECOWAS Convention on Small Arms and Light Weapons, their Ammunition and Other Related Materials

Adopted	14 June 2006, Abuja
Entered into force	29 Sep. 2009
Depositary	President of the ECOWAS Commission
Parties as of Dec. 2012	Benin, Burkina Faso, Cape Verde, Ghana, Liberia, Mali, Niger, Nigeria, Senegal, Sierra Leone, Togo
Signed but not ratified	Côte d'Ivoire, Gambia, Guinea, Guinea-Bissau
Convention text	United Nations, Programme of Action, <http://www.poa-iss.org/RegionalOrganizations/7.aspx>

Central African Convention for the Control of Small Arms and Light Weapons, Their Ammunition and All Parts and Components That Can Be Used for Their Manufacture, Repair and Assembly (Kinshasa Convention)

Adopted	30 Apr. 2010, Kinshasa
Opened for signature	19 Nov. 2010, Brazzaville
Entered into force	Not in force
Depositary	UN Secretary-General
Ratifications deposited	Central African Republic, Chad, Congo (Republic of), Gabon as of Dec. 2012
Signed but not ratified	Angola, Burundi, Cameroon, Congo (Democratic Republic of), Equatorial Guinea, Rwanda, Sao Tome and Principe
Convention text	United Nations Treaty Collection, <http://treaties.un.org/Pages/CTCTreaties.aspx?id=26>

(involving the East African Community); the 2006 Economic Community of West African States (ECOWAS) Convention on Small Arms and Light Weapons, their Ammunition and Other Related Materials; and the 2010 Central African Convention for the Control of Small Arms and Light Weapons, their Ammunition, Parts and Components that can be used for their Manufacture, Repair and Assembly, known as the Kinshasa Convention (involving the Communauté économique des États de l'Afrique Centrale, CEEAC, Economic Community of Central African States).[5] These subregional agreements are broad in terms of content: they introduce tighter control over weapon stockpiles and arms transfers; promote the destruction of stocks of surplus weapons; and cover the criminalization of the unauthorized production and possession of SALW. Their scopes are typically more far-reaching than those made on other continents.[6]

The adoption of subregional agreements in Africa is an important confidence- and security-building measure (CSBM) in regions where a number of governments (or factions within governments) stand accused of supplying arms to rebel groups in other states and of violating multilateral arms embargoes. In Central Africa, East Africa and the Horn of Africa, for example, these types of accusation have arisen between the Democratic Republic of the Congo (DRC) and Rwanda, between the DRC and Uganda, and between Ethiopia and Eritrea.[7]

The regional instruments are closely interlinked with state-building and regional integration in Africa. The objective of bringing together different parts of government—such as military services, police and customs agencies—in closer cooperation directly feeds into both these processes. The agreements aim to strengthen the capacities of the state (especially law enforcement capacities), while not imposing restrictions on states' military capabilities. Similarly, as regards transparency, the agreements take a common approach to verifying national implementation, including with regard to transfer controls and stockpile destruction. However, they do not require transparency on defence policy, doctrines or budgets. One consequence of this set-up is the lack of common initiatives to impose controls on major conventional arms in Africa.

Implementation is uneven in terms of how far the states parties have advanced in harmonizing legislation and developing national action plans, and the extent to which the parties have coordinated their national responses and taken responsibility for implementation of the agreements. While positive examples exist at the national level (e.g. in Ghana, Kenya

[5] Lamb, G. and Dye, D., 'African solutions to an international problem: arms control and disarmament in Africa', *Journal of International Affairs*, vol 62, no. 2 (2009), p. 77.

[6] Lamb and Dye (note 5), p. 77.

[7] Lamb and Dye (note 5), p. 80; and Wezeman, P. D., Wezeman, S. T. and Béraud-Sudreau, L., *Arms Flows to Sub-Saharan Africa*, SIPRI Policy Paper no. 30 (SIPRI: Stockholm, Dec. 2011).

and Uganda), the subregional agreements typically face three broad challenges: capacity and resource constraints, fluctuating political momentum from domestic leadership and dependency on external financial support.

Such challenges have been felt in the regional bodies that have been set up to coordinate, facilitate and monitor implementation. Following the adoption of its SALW Convention, ECOWAS established a Small Arms Unit in the ECOWAS Commission as well as a dedicated programme for implementation jointly with the UN Development Programme, the ECOWAS Small Arms Control Programme (ECOSAP). With external support, ECOSAP has supported member states in their implementation (a) by supporting national surveys on the distribution of SALW, stockpile management issues and knowledge, as well as on attitudes to and perception of SALW issues; (b) by holding capacity-building workshops for representatives from member states' armed forces and police on stockpile management, including record keeping and accident prevention; and (c) by consulting on the development of a guide for the harmonization of national SALW legislation in West Africa.[8] In 2011 ECOWAS voted to extend ECOSAP while the donors decided to stop supporting it, causing a deadlock in the programme. Furthermore, the overlapping mandate of the ECOWAS Small Arms Unit and ECOSAP has triggered disputes between the two.

In 2005 the states parties to the Nairobi Protocol established the Regional Centre on Small Arms in the Great Lakes Region, the Horn of Africa and Bordering States (RECSA) to support the implementation of the Protocol. In 2012 RECSA provided assistance to member states in a number of areas, including arms destruction, support to develop national action plans (in the DRC and Malawi), capacity building related to gender mainstreaming and enhanced inter-agency cooperation on SALW, for review of national legislation (in Kenya and Tanzania), development of a manual on public awareness on SALW in local counties (in Kenya), and establishment of a researchers' forum to examine causes and possible solutions for conflicts in the region.[9] RECSA's activities extended to other subregions, where they included purchasing arms-marking machines for four West African countries (Côte d'Ivoire, Ghana, Mali and Togo); organizing arms marking and electronic record keeping in three West African countries (Côte d'Ivoire, Ghana and Togo); capacity building on SALW for law enforcement agencies, civil society, media and parliamentarians (in East, Southern and West Africa); and facilitation of the establishment of joint cross-border task forces on SALW in the RECSA and SADC regions.[10] RECSA's activities have

---

[8] United Nations, Programme of Action, Implementation Support System, PoA-ISS, 'Economic Community of West African States (ECOWAS)', <http://www.poa-iss.org/RegionalOrganizations/7.aspx>.

[9] RECSA official, Communication with author, 21 Dec. 2012.

[10] RECSA official (note 9).

primarily been funded by external partners and all current projects are carried out with the support of the European Union (EU). However, the EU is currently reviewing the programmes that it funds. In the past RECSA has been criticized for inadequate sensitivity to national needs and for lacking a systematic approach, demonstrated by its provision of two weapon-marking machines to Southern Sudan in 2010 that were delivered without the necessary database software, severely limiting the usefulness of the machines.[11]

Unlike the experience in West and East Africa, SADC mainly developed its firearms protocol for crime prevention purposes, following the adoption of the UN Firearms Protocol. The implementing agency is the Southern Africa Regional Police Chiefs Cooperation Organisation (SARPCCO).[12] In November 2012 SADC launched its revised five-year Harmonised Strategic Indicative Plan for the Organ on Politics, Defence and Security Cooperation (SIPO II), which is intended to advance cooperation in five broad sectors: politics, defence, state security, public security and police.[13] The control of SALW could serve as a cross-cutting issue on these five themes.[14]

Although the Kinshasa Convention has not yet entered into force, CEEAC has nonetheless established a unit to provide pre-ratification assistance on the convention's provisions. While financially supported by the EU, CEEAC (and its SALW Unit) is struggling to build the necessary confidence, stability and capacities in the conflict-ridden Central African region to advance cooperation and national implementation. In the meantime, overlapping membership means that at least one of the three other agreements already applies to most signatories to the Kinshasa Convention.

Despite the strong subregional focus on SALW control in Africa, some key external partners, such as the EU, nevertheless still prefer to conduct their strategic dialogue with African states at the continent level.[15] Given the subregional instruments' current dependency on external funds and the difficulty of reaching consensus on SALW-related issues in the AU, finding a way to improve collaboration between subregional instruments and external partners will be crucial in order to ensure implementation.

[11] Bromley, M. et al., 'Transfers of small arms and light weapons to fragile states: strengthening oversight and control', SIPRI Insights on Peace and Security no. 2013/1, Jan. 2013, <http://books.sipri.org/product_info?c_product_id=453>, pp. 13–14.

[12] Stott (note 2), p. 2.

[13] Southern African Development Community (SADC), Harmonised Strategic Indicative Plan for the Organ on Politics, Defence and Security Cooperation (SIPO II), 5 Aug. 2010, <http://www.sadc.int/documents-publications/show/SADC_SIPO_II_Final.pdf>; and Southern African Development Community (SADC), 'Launch of the Strategic Indicative Plan for the Organ (SIPO) II, Arusha, Tanzania', 23 Nov. 2012, <http://www.sadc.int/news-events/news/launch-strategic-indicative-plan-organ-sipo-ii-arusha-tanzan/>.

[14] Motsamai, D., 'SADC 2012 launch of the revised SIPO II: new hopes, old challenges', Institute for Security Studies, 22 Nov. 2012, <http://www.issafrica.org/iss_today.php?ID=1570-2>.

[15] Bagoyoko, N. and Gibert, M. V., 'The linkage between security, governance and development: the European Union in Africa', *Journal of Development Studies*, vol. 45, no. 5 (2009), p. 794.

III. Conventional arms control and confidence- and security-building measures in Europe

IAN ANTHONY AND LINA GRIP

Europe-wide arms control

In 2012 the difficulties in agreeing on further progress on conventional arms control in Europe reported in 2011 continued. However, at the end of 2012 Ukraine, the incoming chair of the Organization for Security and Co-operation in Europe (OSCE) for 2013, initiated a process that might provide a future framework for developing a new approach to conventional arms control.

In November 2011, 24 parties to the 1990 Treaty on Conventional Armed Forces in Europe (CFE Treaty) ceased carrying out certain treaty obligations with regard to Russia as a legal countermeasure to Russia's suspension of implementation of the treaty in late 2007.[1] Russian representatives have stated that no formal talks on next steps in conventional arms control will be possible until the main purpose is agreed.[2]

In the United States the November decision was the catalyst for a 'ground-up' evaluation of conventional arms control, including the future of the CFE Treaty.[3] The USA believes that the original problem the CFE Treaty was intended to address—the destabilizing effect of military capabilities able to seize and hold the territory of another state—has been solved. The review is to identify European security concerns that conventional arms control might help address, and then pinpoint the kinds of measure that could best address the issues identified. In public statements towards the end of 2012 senior US officials gave some indication of the line of thinking the review is expected to contain: arms control is expected to help 'provide confidence regarding the military activities and intentions of neighbors, especially in sensitive areas'.[4]

The USA sees two main objectives for conventional arms control: first, ensuring that there is sufficient predictability and transparency in the development of armed forces to avoid any risk of a 'strategic surprise', and

---

[1] For a summary and other details of the CFE Treaty see annex A in this volume.

[2] Russian Deputy Foreign Minister, Alexander Grushko, quoted in 'Moscow does not expect CFE treaty talks to begin in the near term', RIA Novosti, 5 Apr. 2012, <http://www.russialist.org/russia-cfe-treaty-delayed-787.php>. However, the issue of conventional arms control is still an agenda item during regular but informal bilateral Russian–US consultations.

[3] Gottemoeller, R., US Acting Under Secretary for Arms Control and International Security, Remarks at the US Strategic Command 2012 Deterrence Symposium, Omaha, NE, 9 Aug. 2012, <http://www.state.gov/t/us/196354.htm>.

[4] Gottemoeller, R., US Acting Under Secretary for Arms Control and International Security, 'Revitalizing conventional arms control in Europe', Remarks at SIPRI, Stockholm, 4 Sep. 2012, <http://www.state.gov/t/us/197648.htm>.

second, helping to stabilize the security situation in some subregions of Europe. While no longer a State Department official, Steven Pifer perhaps captured US thinking in a presentation to the 2012 OSCE Security Days when he identified the main problems as: 'lack of political confidence regarding neighbors' intentions coupled with specific concerns that stem from subregions of insecurity or of fragile security plus the fear of localized military tensions or localized offensive operations'.[5]

Russia has focused on the need to establish rules for arms and other items of growing importance to armed forces that are not currently subject to conventional arms control treaties.[6] In this context, Russian officials have referred to ship-borne weapons and armed unmanned aerial vehicles (UAVs).

At the end of 2012 the Ukrainian Government outlined its plans for its chairmanship of the OSCE in 2013, which included revitalizing conventional arms control and making progress on resolving protracted conflicts.[7] The approach proposed by Ukraine offered a possible framework for progress by emphasizing the need to ask fundamental questions about the future of conventional arms control, rather than focusing once again on the difficulties in the existing instruments. In a 'food for thought' paper circulated among OSCE members Ukraine posed a number of possible questions that could be taken up in 2013 on a Europe-wide basis. The questions posed in the paper included:

Can the OSCE play an important role in elaborating fundamental principles of a future conventional arms control regime and developing subsequently new arms control agreement?

If yes, what format can be used for appropriate works: [a] new committee, [an] open-ended ad hoc group, informal consultations, [the Forum for Security Co-operation]?

Does the OSCE require a special mandate for convening this work? . . .

What could be and what could not be expected from any future conventional arms control within the OSCE area? . . .

Should the limitations on categories of armaments be considered as an important element of maintaining security and stability within the OSCE area? [8]

---

[5] Pifer, S., 'Developing a new approach to conventional arms control?', Contribution to OSCE Security Days, Vienna, 25 June 2012, <http://www.brookings.edu/research/speeches/2012/06/25-security-pifer>.

[6] Zellner, W., 'Conventional arms control in Europe: is there a last chance?', Arms Control Today, vol. 42, no. 2 (Mar. 2012).

[7] Organization for Security and Co-operation in Europe (OSCE), 'Protracted conflicts, arms control, trafficking in human beings top agenda as Ukraine takes over OSCE chair', Press release, 1 Jan. 2013, <http://www.osce.org/cio/98443>.

[8] Organization for Security and Co-operation in Europe (OSCE), 'Initiating a dialogue within the OSCE aimed at discussing the role conventional arms control can play in today's and future European security architecture', Ukrainian Food-for-Thought Paper, [n.d.].

These questions are broad enough to be the basis for a thorough assessment of the role of arms control at the European level.

At the OSCE Ministerial Council in December 2012, foreign ministers agreed to launch a process labelled 'Helsinki+40', with the objective of developing practical measures to (among other things) implement the commitment made in the 2010 Astana Commemorative Declaration to overcome the impasse in conventional arms control in Europe and open the way for negotiations on a new agreement.[9] The measures should be elaborated by 2015—four decades after the signing of the Helsinki Final Act. The foreign ministers called on the OSCE'S Forum for Security Co-operation to contribute within its mandate.[10]

South Eastern Europe

The 1996 Agreement on Sub-Regional Arms Control (Florence Agreement) currently limits the armed forces of Bosnia and Herzegovina, Croatia, Montenegro and Serbia.[11] The agreement is one of the political-military components of the Dayton Peace Accords as part of a set of integrated regional stabilization measures. While the weapon holdings of all states parties are now below the treaty-imposed ceilings, the states parties continue to carry out a schedule of inspections, including voluntary inspections beyond their treaty obligations.

Since 2010 the transfer of the Florence Agreement to full local ownership has been under way. Whereas the implementation of the Florence Agreement has involved inspectors from 29 OSCE participating states and the Personal Representative of the OSCE Chairperson-in-Office, the four parties will take full responsibility for implementation in 2014.[12] The inspection process provides the responsible authorities in the region, including the military, with a detailed understanding of the current policies and plans of neighbours and reduces any risk that suspicion might arise over military plans and developments.

From 1996 to the end of October 2012 nearly 10 000 heavy weapons of different kinds were eliminated under the agreement, including roughly 1400 battle tanks, nearly 700 armoured combat vehicles, over 7500 artillery

[9] OSCE, Summit Meeting, Astana 2010, 'Astana Commemorative Declaration: towards a security community', SUM.DOC/1/10/Corr.1*, 3 Dec. 2010, <http://www.osce.org/cio/74985>.

[10] OSCE, 'Decision on the OSCE Helsinki+40 process', MC19EW18, 7 Dec. 2012.

[11] For a summary and other details of the Florence Agreement see annex A in this volume.

[12] 'Interview with Major General Michele Torres, the Personal Representative of the OSCE Chairperson-in-Office for Article IV of Annex 1B of the Dayton Peace Accords', *RACVIAC Newsletter*, no. 30 (July–Dec. 2011), pp. 6–7. In the longer term, the activities are expected to come to an end entirely when all countries in the region become members of the North Atlantic Treaty Organization.

pieces, 167 combat aircraft and 14 helicopters.[13] By the middle of 2012, 670 inspections had been conducted.[14] While the Florence Agreement reduced the volume of major weapons in the region, South Eastern Europe also experienced a tremendous influx of illicit conventional arms of different kinds during the 1990s as well as a significant proliferation of weapons made in the region. In addition, large quantities of arms were lost from state ownership and control in this period as safe and secure stockpiling of existing arsenals was fragile or inadequate.[15] With external support, states in the region set up a number of measures to reduce the excessive accumulations of conventional arms and ammunition. Cooperative and practical approaches were preferred over coercive, strategic measures, including enhancing confidence and integration through setting up regional institutional structures to guide, support and monitor national implementation.

In 2012 the South Eastern and Eastern Europe Clearinghouse for the Control of Small Arms and Light Weapons (SEESAC), launched in May 2002 in Belgrade, passed its 10th anniversary. SEESAC is a regional organization tasked with supporting regional arms control implementation and development and is a component of the Regional Implementation Plan on Combating the Proliferation of Small Arms and Light Weapons (SALW) formulated and adopted by the Stability Pact for South Eastern Europe in November 2001.[16] The Stability Pact was a conflict prevention strategy of the international community set up in 1999 to achieve regional stability by developing and supporting a strong regional framework by which international partners could work closely with states in South Eastern Europe on joint programmes. Since 2006 the Stability Pact has included a Regional Steering Group on SALW.[17]

Under SEESAC states have established national focal points and the Regional Micro-Disarmament Standards and Guidelines. SEESAC's activities focus on SALW destruction, collection, storage management, marking, tracing and registration, and on arms export controls. The organization provides support to governments, institutions and other SALW stakeholders in the form of capacity building, coordination, information

[13] Torres, M. (Maj. Gen.), Personal Representative of the OSCE Chairmanship in Office for Article IV, Annex 1-B, Dayton Peace Accords, 'Post-agreement reflections on the Dayton Peace Accord: the importance of regional arms control agreement', Presentation at the RACVIAC Centre for Security Cooperation Arms Control Symposium, Zagreb, 21 Nov. 2012.

[14] 'Dayton Article IV course conducted', RACVIAC Newsletter, no. 32 (Apr.–June 2012), p. 14.

[15] Regional Approach to Stockpile Reduction (RASR), 'Speech of the Albania Minister of Defence Mr Arben Imami', RASR conference, Durrës, 24 Apr. 2012, <http://www.rasrinitiative.org/pdfs/workshop-5/RASR-Workshop-5-Albania-MOD-Speech.pdf>, p. 2.

[16] South Eastern and Eastern Europe Clearinghouse for the Control of Small Arms and Light Weapons (SEESAC), <http://www.seesac.org/about-seesac/1/>.

[17] Stability Pact for South Eastern Europe, 'Combating the proliferation and impact of small arms and light weapons', Stability Pact for South Eastern Europe Regional Implementation Plan (revised 2006), <http://www.stabilitypact.org/salw/sp_rip_2006.pdf>, p. 1.

management and exchange activities, training and research, and the like.[18] SEESAC's work has enhanced transparency in arms transfers, including through national reports and annual meetings on arms exports. SEESAC's activities in 2012 included the Seventh Meeting of the Regional Arms Export Information Exchange Process, a workshop on gender mainstreaming in security sector reform and a Workshop on Gender and Security for the Women Police Officers Network Council.[19]

The Regional Approach to Stockpile Reduction (RASR) is an initiative of nine states in South Eastern Europe that aims to address the threats posed by stockpiles of conventional weapons and munitions in the region, to prevent proliferation and disastrous explosions.[20] RASR's activities include publications, outreach and capacity building. RASR's fifth annual conference took place in Durrës, Albania, in April 2012, and gathered states and non-governmental organizations (NGOs) to exchange information and best practices on the range of issues under RASR.[21] The Regional Arms Control, Verification and Information Centre (RACVIAC), established in 2000 and based in Zagreb, also holds training programmes on the verification of arms control and confidence-building regimes in the region.

Conventional arms control programmes have been a precondition for European Union (EU) and North Atlantic Treaty Organization (NATO) membership as neither organization could admit members that have large quantities of weapons outside state control and in general circulation.[22] However, states such as Croatia—which joined NATO in 2009 and will join the EU in 2013—have found arms control so useful that they have continued to participate in regional arrangements after integration into wider European institutions. The EU has taken the lead from the United Nations Development Programme in terms of financial support to SALW programmes within the region, and a key objective of the South East European strategy is harmonization with the EU security policies in the field of SALW, thus preparing South East European countries for EU membership.[23]

---

[18] On the 2008 SEESAC Strategy Plan see SEESAC (note 16).

[19] South Eastern and Eastern Europe Clearinghouse for the Control of Small Arms and Light Weapons (SEESAC), 'Events calendar', <http://www.seesac.org/new-events/events-calendar/1/>.

[20] Regional Approach to Stockpile Reduction (RASR), <http://www.rasrinitiative.org/rasr.php>. The 9 states are Albania, Bosnia and Herzegovina, Bulgaria, Croatia, FYR Macedonia, Montenegro, Romania, Serbia and Slovenia.

[21] Regional Approach to Stockpile Reduction (note 15), p. 2.

[22] Grillot, S., 'Guns in the Balkans: controlling small arms and light weapons in seven Western Balkan countries', *Southeast European and Black Sea Studies*, vol. 10, no. 2 (June 2010), p. 148; and Ryabikhin, L. and Jevgenia Viktorova, J., 'Weapons transfers as a soft security issue in Eastern Europe: legal and illicit aspects', *European Security*, vol. 13, nos 1–2 (2004), pp. 78, 80.

[23] Stability Pact for South Eastern Europe (note 17), pp. 6, 10.

IV. Confidence- and security-building measures in Asia

SIEMON T. WEZEMAN

Asia is a region with a significant number of bilateral and subregional tensions, unresolved conflicts that periodically lead to deadly incidents, and disputes over land and sea borders.[1] Nevertheless, although several Asian initiatives include confidence- and security-building measures (CSBMs) as part of their agenda, in general there is no strong mandate or institutional structure supporting CSBMs in Asia.[2] This section describes CSBMs in Asia, with a focus on South and South East Asia. Although there are similar tensions and conflicts in East Asia, the mandates and structures for support of CSBMs are much less developed there than elsewhere in the region.

South Asia

In South Asia, India and Pakistan have agreed on a significant number of CSBMs since their 1971 war, most importantly in the framework of the 1972 Simla Agreement and the 1999 Lahore Declaration.[3] A joint survey conducted in 2012 by Indian and Pakistani experts and former officials identified nine existing military CSBMs as being of primary importance, while six others that have been proposed by either India or Pakistan have not been adopted.[4]

The CSBMs in force include permanent communication channels between the Director General of Military Operations (DGMO) in both countries and between the paramilitary forces responsible for maritime security; advance notification of information on certain military exercises and troop movements, and on ballistic missile tests; joint border patrols on demarcated stretches of the international border; and biannual meetings of the border security forces of each side.[5] However, these CSBMs have not been implemented consistently and have not prevented violent confrontations between Indian and Pakistani military and paramilitary forces in

[1] On the fragile peace in East and South East Asia see chapter 1, section II, in this volume.
[2] CSBMs are defined here as measures undertaken by states to promote confidence and security through military transparency, openness, constraints and cooperation. They are militarily significant, politically binding, verifiable and, as a rule, reciprocal.
[3] Simla Agreement, signed 2 July 1972, entered into force 4 Aug. 1972, <http://www.jammu-kashmir.com/documents/simla.html>; and Lahore Declaration, signed 21 Feb. 1999, <http://cns.miis.edu/inventory/pdfs/aptlahore.pdf>.
[4] Atlantic Council, 'India–Pakistan military CBMs project, phase 1: final report', 25 Sep. 2012, <http://www.acus.org/files/Final Project report - Phase 1_Sept 25.pdf>.
[5] Atlantic Council (note 4); and Creative Associates International, *Preventing and Mitigating Violent Conflicts: A Revised Guide for Practitioners* (Creative Associates: Washington, DC, [1997]), 'Tool category C: military measures, confidence and security-building measures (CSBM)', <http://www.creativeassociatesinternational.com/CAIIStaff/Dashboard_GIROAdminCAIIStaff/Dashboard_CAIIAdminDatabase/resources/ghai/toolbox5.htm>.

the border area.[6] The CSBMs that have not been implemented include a permanent communication channel between the respective air forces and navies and a 2011 agreement in principle to establish a hotline between the interior ministers.[7]

During a sixth round of expert-level talks on conventional CSBMs, in December 2012 in New Delhi, progress was made on one issue: the measures agreed in 2003 to respect the informal ceasefire along the Line of Control separating Indian and Pakistani forces in Kashmir.[8] Since 2008 both sides have complained about the increasing frequency of violations and have stressed the need to check future violations by both sides, and at the December meeting the countries agreed on the need for stricter observance. Together with the use of the direct communication hotline between the DGMOs, the CSBMs have been credited with limiting the consequences of clashes between Indian and Pakistani forces at the end of 2012.[9]

Tensions between China and India over their disputed border have increased in recent years. Few CSBMs have been agreed between the two countries and the small-scale bilateral Chinese–Indian military exercises, which had been held in 2007 and 2008, were cancelled in 2010 by India. The visit of the Chinese Minister of National Defence, Liang Guanglie, to India in September 2012 led to some expectations that such exercises would resume in 2013 and other CSBMs would be agreed.[10] However, by the end of 2012 no progress appeared to have been made.

South East Asia

The elaboration of CSBMs played an important role in the development of the main Asian organization dealing with conflicts and tensions, the Association of Southeast Asian Nations (ASEAN) Regional Forum (ARF). Established in 1994, with participation by 23 Asian countries, Canada, the European Union, Russia and the United States, the ARF focused on discussing CSBMs until 2009.[11] Since that time, preventive diplomacy and conflict

---

[6] Stimson Center, 'Confidence-building and nuclear risk-reduction measures in South Asia', [n.d.], <http://www.stimson.org/research-pages/confidence-building-measures-in-south-asia-/>.

[7] 'Hotline between India-Pak home secys soon', *Hindustan Times*, 13 May 2012.

[8] India and Pakistan also held talks on nuclear CSBMs in 2012. In Feb. 2012 the countries agreed to extend the Agreement on Reducing the Risk from Accidents relating to Nuclear Weapons, which was signed on 21 Feb. 2007, for another 5 years. Sajjad Syed, B., 'Accord on reducing risk of nuclear accidents extended', *Dawn*, 22 Feb. 2012. Although both sides advanced proposals for new nuclear CSBMs at their Dec. 2012 talks, no new agreements were reached. Lodhi, M., 'Balancing hard and soft issues', *The News* (Karachi), 8 Jan. 2013.

[9] See e.g. 'India DGMO speaks to Pakistan counterpart on cross-LoC attack', *Economic Times* (Delhi), 9 Jan. 2013.

[10] Bedi, R., 'Chinese defence minister visits India to improve ties', *Jane's Defence Weekly*, 12 Sep. 2012, p. 16.

[11] For a full list of participants in the ARF see annex B in this volume.

resolution have become core objectives. The ARF meets annually at the level of foreign ministers and has become a framework for organizing working meetings of defence officials and other expert meetings on diverse issues. The ARF has two unofficial support mechanisms—the Council for Security Cooperation in the Asia Pacific (CSCAP) and the ASEAN Institute of Strategic and International Studies (ASEAN-ISIS).[12] While the ARF can itself be considered a CSBM, the catalogue of agreed CSBMs is small despite many proposals put forward by, for example, CSCAP for consideration.[13]

ASEAN asserts that CSBMs are 'important instruments in conflict prevention' both within ASEAN and for relations with non-ASEAN states.[14] However, direct international arbitration or (bilateral or multilateral) negotiations between the states involved have played a more important role in managing or solving intra-regional territorial disputes than has ASEAN.

In recent years a growing number of incidents of various kinds have occurred in the South China Sea that, taken together, have contributed to growing maritime tension among states in the region (see table 9.2). These incidents include patrols and exercises by navies and other maritime security agencies, interference with commercial attempts to exploit maritime resources of various kinds in contested maritime areas, and the establishment of structures on contested islands, reefs and shoals. Recent analyses have drawn attention to the negative impact that the increasing number of such incidents is having on regional security. As more maritime assets (civil and military) are being deployed in the South China Sea, these incidents may continue to increase in number and seriousness and 'over time, the risks are growing of any particular incident leading to miscalculation or the use of force'.[15]

Most of the incidents involve commercial ships or law enforcement authorities from ASEAN member states on the one hand and China on the other, and maritime CSBMs have been discussed in the ASEAN–China

[12] ASEAN Regional Forum (ARF), 'ARF objectives', <http://aseanregionalforum.asean.org/about/arf-objectives.html>; and Australian Department of Foreign Affairs and Trade, 'ASEAN Regional Forum (ARF)', <http://www.dfat.gov.au/arf/index.html>.

[13] E.g. an agreement to publish regular white papers on defence has resulted in only a handful of such documents since 2002. The ARF website lists just 6 papers from 5 countries. ASEAN Regional Forum (ARF), 'ARF defense white papers', <http://aseanregionalforum.asean.org/library/arf-activities/arf-defense-white-papers.html>.

[14] Association of Southeast Asian Nations (ASEAN), ASEAN Political-Security Community Blueprint (ASEAN Secretariat: Jakarta, June 2009).

[15] Medcalf, R., 'Recommendations to boost security in the South China Sea', Paper presented to the Conference on Maritime Security in the South China Sea, Center for Strategic and International Studies, Washington, DC, 28 June 2012, <http://www.lowyinstitute.org/publications/recommendations-boost-security-south-china-sea>; and International Crisis Group (ICG), Stirring up the South China Sea (I), Asia Report no. 223 (ICG: Brussels, 23 Apr. 2012). On transfers of arms to South East Asian states see Wezeman, S. T., 'The maritime dimension of arms transfers to South East Asia, 2007–11', SIPRI Yearbook 2012.

Table 9.2. Main South China Sea incidents, 2011–12

Date	Incident
Mar. 2011	Chinese patrol vessels interfere with a Philippine oil exploration ship near Reed Bank; the Philippine Government announces strengthening of garrison on the Spratly Islands and acquisition of maritime assets
May 2011	Chinese patrol ships interfere with Vietnamese oil exploration ships near the Spratly Islands
Mid-May–31 July 2011	China's annual fishing ban in the South China Sea[a]
June 2011	Chinese naval exercise around the Spratly Islands; the Philippines renames the South China Sea, changing the name to the West Philippine Sea
22 July 2011	China warns Indian warship near southern Viet Nam to stay out of Chinese waters
Apr. 2012–Sep. 2012	China–Philippines confrontation at Scarborough Shoal
Mid-May–31 July 2012	China's annual fishing ban in the South China Sea;[a] Philippines and Viet Nam protest and declare the ban invalid
11 July 2012	Chinese warship runs aground on Half Moon Shoal (Hasa Hasa Shoal), part of the Spratly Islands archipelago
July 2012	The Vietnamese Parliament passes a law on sea borders, including the Spratly and Paracel islands
July 2012	China officially establishes garrison command on the Paracel Islands

[a] Since the late 1990s, China has proclaimed a temporary (mid-May–31 July) ban on all commercial fishing (by both Chinese and foreign vessels) in the South China Sea areas it claims belong to China. Chinese law enforcement agencies harass Philippine and Vietnamese fishing vessels and have arrested crew members. China claims that the ban is to protect fish stocks, but other countries regard it as illegal.

Sources: Buszynski, L., 'The South China Sea: oil, maritime claims, and U.S.–China strategic rivalry', *Washington Quarterly*, spring 2012, pp. 139–56; various media reports; and annex C in this volume.

dialogue since the late 1990s. In 2002 ASEAN and China made a joint political Declaration on the Conduct of Parties in the South China Sea (DOC), which was intended to open the way to agreement on a binding code of conduct.[16] An ASEAN–China joint working group was subsequently established to discuss implementation, and Guidelines to Implement the DOC were agreed in July 2011.[17] However, agreement on a binding code of conduct has proved elusive.

After July 2011, senior ASEAN officials elaborated a draft code of conduct that was circulated in January 2012, but the procedure for developing the code emerged as a contentious issue inside ASEAN in 2012. Prior to the

[16] Declaration on the Conduct of Parties in the South China Sea, signed 4 Nov. 2002, <http://www.asean.org/asean/external-relations/china/item/declaration-on-the-conduct-of-parties-in-the-south-china-sea>.

[17] Guidelines on the implementation of the DOC, July 2011, <http://www.asean.org/portal.asean.org/archive/documents/20185-DOC.pdf>. See also Khalik, A. and Nurhayati, D., 'South China Sea guidelines agreed', *Jakarta Post*, 21 July 2011.

elaboration of a joint ASEAN text, China had argued that maritime issues should be discussed bilaterally by affected states. However, when a joint draft document was circulated, China requested to join the discussion. The Chinese request drew mixed reactions from ASEAN states: some argued for inclusive talks and others argued that a common ASEAN text should first be elaborated and then presented jointly to China.[18] In July ASEAN foreign ministers agreed the Proposed Elements of a Regional Code of Conduct in the South China Sea and also agreed that this document should be offered as the basis for talks with China.[19] In response, China underlined that the main priority was to implement the agreed DOC, while being open to discussing the proposed code of conduct with ASEAN countries. At the end of 2012 Brunei Darussalam, the incoming chair of ASEAN, confirmed that developing a binding code of conduct was a top priority for 2013.[20]

Prospects for CSBMs in Asia

While states in Asia emphasize that disagreement over territory and other matters need to be solved in a peaceful manner, the increasing tensions between them and the military build-up in the region heighten the potential for accidental or planned violent confrontations. CSBMs have been recognized in Asia, as in other regions, as effective mechanisms to prevent, manage and solve such potential violent incidents. However, CSBMs and the infrastructures in which they can be developed are still weak in Asia.

There have been some encouraging recent steps in parts of Asia towards developing CSBMs or mechanisms that can discuss and adopt them. However, most improvement hinges on cooperation among all Asian states, as well as the USA. Considering the current situation, a rather slow incremental process seems to be the most effective path to CSBMs in the region.

[18] For detailed discussion of the process of elaborating the draft code of conduct and an analysis of the content of the text (which is not public) see Thayer, C. A., 'ASEAN'S code of conduct in the South China Sea: a litmus test for community-building?,' *Asia–Pacific Journal*, 20 Aug. 2012.

[19] Severino, R., 'A code of conduct for the South China Sea?', *PacNet*, Pacific Forum CSIS, 17 Aug. 2012.

[20] 'New ASEAN chair Brunei to seek South China Sea code of conduct', GMA news, 14 Jan. 2013, <http://www.gmanetwork.com/news/story/290271/news/world/new-asean-chair-brunei-to-seek-south-china-sea-code-of-conduct>.

V. Confidence- and security-building measures in the Americas

CARINA SOLMIRANO

Unlike other regions of the world, such as Asia, border disputes in the Americas have not led to tensions that have required a military response. The region faces no major external military threat and in the past two decades it has developed an array of confidence- and security-building measures (CSBMs) at both the regional and subregional levels.[1] This section outlines CSBMs with, first, a region-wide application in the framework of the Organization of American States (OAS), then those conducted in subregional forums in South America and in Central America and the Caribbean.

The Organization of American States

The end of the cold war, the transition from authoritarian regimes to democracy in South America and the conclusion of the civil wars in Central America laid the foundation for a new security architecture in the Americas that started to develop in the 1990s. In 1991 the member states of the OAS met in Santiago, Chile, to begin a process of consultation on hemispheric security that would reflect the new international and regional realities.[2] At the First Summit of the Americas in 1994, the OAS member states agreed to support 'actions to encourage a regional dialogue to promote the strengthening of mutual confidence, preparing the way for a regional conference on confidence-building measures in 1995'.[3] The OAS's Committee on Hemispheric Security has led the process and has held a series of conferences on CSBMs that have resulted in the current consolidated list of 36 measures; since 2005 the Committee has organized a series of forums to discuss progress on and implementation of these measures.[4]

OAS member states are asked to submit annual reports on implementation of the consolidated list of CSBMs. A report from the Inter-American Defense Board noted that, between 2001 and 2011, 21 countries

---

[1] CSBMs are defined here as measures undertaken by states to promote confidence and security through military transparency, openness, constraints and cooperation. They are militarily significant, politically binding, verifiable and, as a rule, reciprocal.

[2] Organization of American States (OAS), Permanent Council of the OAS, Committee on Hemispheric Security, 'Confidence and security-building measures', <http://www.oas.org/csh/english/csbmintro.asp>.

[3] Organization of American States (OAS), First Summit of the Americas, 'Summit of the Americas action plan', 9–11 Dec. 1994, <http://www.summit-americas.org/miamiplan.htm>.

[4] Organization of American States (note 2).

had submitted reports at least once, with Brazil, Chile and El Salvador standing out for the regularity of their submissions.[5]

The OAS has emphasized CSBMs that strengthen or promote transparency in military expenditure and arms acquisitions. For example, the Inter-American Convention on Transparency in Conventional Weapons Acquisitions (OAS Transparency Convention) was approved in 1999.[6] In the most recent OAS Forum on Confidence- and Security-building Measures, in 2010, the member states agreed to promote the universalization and full implementation of the convention.[7] As of December 2012, 16 states had ratified the convention, but by January 2012 only 13 had submitted a report on at least one occasion.[8]

South America

Since its establishment was agreed in 2008, the Union of South American Nations (Unión de Naciones Suramericanas, UNASUR) has increasingly become active in peace and security issues in South America. It played an active mediating role in the 2010 diplomatic crisis between Colombia and Venezuela, which legitimized it as a regional security body.[9] In 2009 the UNASUR member states also agreed CSBMs to exchange information and increase transparency.[10]

In May 2012, at a seminar organized by the Ecuadorian Ministry of Defence, the Center for Strategic Defense Studies (CEED) of the South American Defence Council (Consejo de Defensa Suramericano, CDS) presented a 'preliminary' version of the newly created UNASUR register of military expenditure—the first mechanism to compile data on the defence spending of each of the member states of UNASUR from 2006 to 2010.[11] The register, the product of two years of work by a team of defence minis-

---

[5] Organization of American States (OAS), Inter-American Defense Board, 'Confidence building measures: inventory 2012', Mar. 2012, <http://iadb.jid.org/secretaria/confidence-building-meas ures>.

[6] For a summary and other details of the OAS Transparency Convention see annex A in this volume.

[7] Organization of American States (OAS), Permanent Council, Committee on Hemispheric Security, 'IV forum on confidence- and security-building measures, 2010', 15–26 Nov. 2010, <http://www. oas.org/csh/english/Foro.asp>.

[8] See annex A in this volume; Bromley, M. and Solmirano, C., *Transparency in Military Spending and Arms Acquisitions in Latin America and the Caribbean*, SIPRI Policy Paper no. 31 (SIPRI: Stockholm, Jan. 2012), p. 29; and Organization of American States (OAS), Permanent Council of the OAS, Committee on Hemispheric Security, Inter-American Convention on Transparency in Conventional Weapon Acquisition, 'Reports', <http://www.oas.org/csh/english/conventionalweapons.asp>.

[9] Burdman, J., 'UNASUR vs OEA' [UNASUR vs OAS], Infolatam, 15 Aug. 2010, <http://www. infolatam.com/2010/08/16/unasur-vs-oea-julio-burdam/>.

[10] Schmidt, H.-J. and Zellner, W., 'Confidence- and security-building measures', *SIPRI Yearbook 2012*, p. 447.

[11] 'Unasur cuenta con registro de gastos militares' [UNASAR has a register of military expenditure], *El Universo* (Guayaquil), 10 May 2012.

try experts from Argentina, Chile, Ecuador, Peru and Venezuela, employs a common methodology to measure military expenditure using international and regional instruments and experiences. The new register's methodology takes account of the United Nations Standardized Instrument for Reporting Military Expenditures and the common standardized methodology for the measurement of defence expenditure between Argentina and Chile that was conducted by the UN Economic Commission for Latin America and the Caribbean (ECLAC).[12] In June 2012 the CDS agreed to make the UNASUR register public, although that step had yet to be taken at the end of the year.

The UNASUR Action Plan CDS-2012 created a working group tasked with establishing a standard methodology to report on military inventories, including procedures for regular data updates.[13] This instrument will enable information about each country's weapon inventory to be made available to other states, thereby facilitating cooperation in, for example, peace operations.[14] It will also be the first time that countries in South America share information about their current military holdings.[15] The working group met twice in Chile, which chairs the working group, and presented its initial findings to the CDS in Peru in November 2012. While the defence ministers did not achieve consensus on the methodology proposed by the working group, the instrument is expected to be finalized during 2013.[16]

At the same CDS meeting, the defence ministers agreed a new package of CSBMs in an action plan for 2013.[17] The Peruvian Minister of Defence, Pedro Cateriano, noted that these agreed measures would consolidate South America as a zone of peace, adding that 'this confidence should allow

[12] The ECLAC project was the first CSBM aimed at fostering transparency in military expenditure between Argentina and Chile. See UN Economic Commission for Latin America and the Caribbean, *A Common Standardized Methodology for the Measurement of Defence Spending* (United Nations: Santiago, Nov. 2001). On UNASUR's methodology see UNASUR, South American Defence Council, 'Plan de Accion 2010–11, Grupo de Trabajo Informe Final, Diseño de una Metodología Común de Medición de Gastos de Defensa' [Plan of action, 2010–11, working group final report, design of a common methodology for measuring defence spending], La Paz, 29 July 2011, p. 2. On the UN report on military expenditure see chapter 3, section VI, in this volume.

[13] UNASUR, South American Defence Council, Action Plan CDS-2012, <http://www.unasurcds.org/index.php?option=com_content&view=article&id=333&Itemid=261&lang=en>.

[14] 'La Unasur celebra segundo encuentro del Grupo de Trabajo Formulario Suramericano de Inventarios Militares' [UNASAR celebrates second meeting of the South American Military Inventory Form Working Group], Infodefensa, Aug. 28, 2012.

[15] The UN Register of Conventional Arms (UNROCA) invites states to report on their military holdings. Thus, the UNASUR instrument appears to replicate UNROCA, which has been unevenly applied in South America. On states' submissions to UNROCA see Bromley and Solmirano (note 8), pp. 21–27.

[16] 'South American defense ministers meet today in Lima', Andina, 28 Nov. 2012, <http://www.andina.com.pe/ingles/noticia-south-american-defense-ministers-meet-today-in-lima-437638.aspx>.

[17] UNASUR, South American Defence Council, 'Action Plan 2013', <http://www.unasurcds.org/index.php?option=com_content&view=article&id=567&Itemid=270&lang=en>.

standardizing our military forces to deal with potential threats to our nations'.[18]

Central America and the Caribbean

In Central America and the Caribbean, the development of CSBMs has been less structured than in South America, where they fall under the umbrella of UNASUR. Subregional efforts to promote CSBMs are being contemplated in both the Central American Integration System (Sistema de la Integración Centroamericana, SICA) and the Caribbean Community (CARICOM), but little public information is available on the content of these efforts. For example, in 2006 the SICA Security Committee adopted the Central American Permanent Programme on Confidence- and Security-building Measures.[19] To date, it is not known what these CSBMs are and whether they have been developed and implemented more formally.

Trafficking in small arms and light weapons (SALW) has received increased attention as one of the main current security challenges in Central America and the Caribbean. In 2005 the SICA member states adopted the Code of Conduct of Central American States on the Transfer of Arms, Ammunition, Explosives and Other Related Materiel.[20] Similarly, in 2011 the CARICOM member states signed the CARICOM Declaration on Small Arms and Light Weapons in an effort to improve work towards better combating the illicit trade in SALW and their ammunition.[21] These efforts seek to increase the exchange of information and cooperation among states.

Prospects for CSBMs in the Americas

The development and consolidation of CSBMs in the Americas has passed through various stages since the end of the cold war. CSBMs are not only limited to arms control and disarmament issues, but also include cooperation in the fight against terrorism and drug trafficking and in the prevention of, and coordination of response to, natural disasters. While the

[18] 'Estandarizar fuerzas militares plantea Perú a Unasur' [Peru proposes that UNASAR standardizes military forces], Radio Guatapurí, 29 Nov. 2012, <http://www.radioguatapuri.com/index.php?option=com_k2&view=item&id=8389:estandarizar-fuerzas-militares-plantea-per%C3%BA-a-unasur&Itemid=240>.

[19] Villalta Vizcarra, A. E., 'Sistema de la Integración Centroamericana (SICA): aspectos relevantes del año 2006' [Central American Integration System (SICA): highlights of 2006], ASADIP, 24 Mar. 2008, <http://asadip.wordpress.com/2008/03/24/sistema-de-la-integracion-centroamericana-sica-aspectos-relevantes-del-ano-2006/>.

[20] Code of Conduct of Central American States on the Transfer of Arms, Ammunition, Explosives and Other Related Materiel, adopted and entered into force 2 Dec. 2005, <http://www.poa-iss.org/RegionalOrganizations/5.aspx>.

[21] CARICOM Declaration on Small Arms and Light Weapons, signed at the 32nd meeting of the Conference of CARICOM Heads of Government, 30 June–4 July, Basseterre, <http://www.caricom.org/jsp/communications/meetings_statements/declaration_small_arms_light_weapons_2011.jsp>.

OAS continues to be the hemispheric forum for implementation of CSBMs, new subregional bodies, such as UNASUR, have taken steps to develop CSBMs that aim to turn South America into a zone of peace. In just two years a young political entity, the CDS, has proved effective in the creation of a register to measure military expenditure. It remains to be seen whether the level of states' submissions to the register will remain high in future.

10. Dual-use and arms trade controls

Overview

Governments are increasingly aware that controlling flows of conventional arms and items that can be used for both civilian and military purposes—dual-use items—is a complex process involving regulation of exports and associated brokering, transit, trans-shipment and financing activities. This complexity requires effort and cooperation from countries around the world. States, therefore, engage in various multilateral mechanisms and continually create new instruments, or adapt existing ones, to address these challenges.

There were mixed results for multilateral efforts to strengthen trade controls for dual-use items and conventional arms during 2012. With regard to trade controls for conventional arms, the year was characterized by the failure to conclude an arms trade treaty (ATT) in July and to agree a United Nations arms embargo against Syria (see sections I and II in this chapter). Divisions among the five permanent members of the UN Security Council played an important role in both cases. Meanwhile, restrictive measures have been expanded beyond traditional strategic trade controls to regulations and prohibitions regarding items that cannot make a direct contribution to nuclear weapon or missile programmes (see section III). There was more progress in 2012 in the field of trade controls for dual-use items as the multilateral export control regimes agreed to expand the scope of their activities as well as the items subject to controls (see section IV). The European Union also considered strengthening controls on transfers of surveillance technologies through the introduction of a new catch-all clause in its Dual-Use Regulation and it expanded sanctions against Iran and Syria (see section V).

The July 2012 UN Conference on an ATT concluded without agreement on a draft treaty text. Several states, in particular Russia and the United States, called for more time for UN member states to discuss these issues. Advocates for an ATT have sought to universalize principles and standards that already exist in regional and national conventional arms trade control instruments.

Two issues proved particularly challenging for ATT negotiators in 2012. First, it proved difficult to find an agreeable compromise on how to incorporate respect for obligations under international humanitarian and human rights law alongside state security prerogatives for arms transfers, as a number of states feared that the former would have a negative effect on the latter. In contrast, there is an established consensus on principles and international law on the prohibition of the transfer of biological and chemical weapons, and—with some caveats—on the non-proliferation of nuclear weapons. This body of international law provides legitimacy for multilateral supplier regimes and complements UN Security Council Resolution 1540. While the original rationale and stated aim of Resolution 1540 was to prevent supplies to non-state actors, the wording contains generic obligations regarding comprehensive controls that should apply to all actors.

Second, the 2012 draft ATT text defined the scope of items to be subject to transfer controls as encompassing the seven categories of the UN Register of Conventional Arms (UNROCA) plus small arms and light weapons, with some controls on ammunition and parts and components. The scope of the draft was, therefore, narrower than the Munitions List of the Wassenaar Arrangement. In contrast, Resolution 1540 and UN sanctions refer to the control lists agreed by informal supplier regimes when defining dual-use items that are subject to control or prohibition. While much attention focused on the fact that the USA, a member of the Wassenaar Arrangement, took a strong stance on excluding ammunition from the ATT, many other states that are not members of supplier regimes opposed proposals for an ATT to have a broad scope comparable to that of the Wassenaar Arrangement's Munitions List.

The final conference on the ATT took place in March 2013, with UN member states given a final chance to achieve consensus on an international treaty to establish the 'highest possible common international standards for the transfer of conventional arms'.

In 2012 the informal supplier regimes reviewed the scope of items subject to trade controls. The Australia Group highlighted nanoscience as an area for further attention, while the Wassenaar Arrangement expanded existing trade controls to cover certain types of surveillance technology. In the Missile Technology Control Regime, discussions on scope also continue, in particular on the classification of unmanned aerial vehicles (UAVs) for control purposes.

International obligations to establish trade control systems create a legal rationale and policy context for national and international capacity-building efforts. International assistance is essential to the establishment of effective trade control systems, particularly when the instruments establishing obligations do not clearly define standards and leave room for differences in implementation and enforcement. This is the case with Resolution 1540, and an ATT is likely to share this characteristic. One of the advantages for implementing an ATT in this regard is that in many states, the laws, administrative procedures, agencies and staff responsible for controlling transfers of dual-use items overlap with those for conventional arms. Additionally, some categories of goods and technologies appear on control lists for both conventional arms and weapons of mass destruction (WMD), and some conventional arms can also be used to deliver WMD. Enforcement remains a shared challenge for controls on both dual-use items and conventional arms.

SIBYLLE BAUER AND PAUL HOLTOM

I. Arms trade treaty negotiations

PAUL HOLTOM AND MARK BROMLEY

The United Nations process towards an arms trade treaty (ATT) brings together all UN member states in an attempt to negotiate binding international standards in the field of arms transfer controls. The UN process began in 2006 and was expected to conclude in July 2012 with the UN Conference on the ATT. However, the 2012 conference ended without agreement on a treaty text. This section provides an account of the ATT process as well as the two main issues of contention at the 2012 conference: which types of arms the treaty should cover and the types of transfer that it should seek to prevent.

Background to the arms trade treaty process

The UN process towards an ATT began in 2006 when seven co-sponsors—Australia, Costa Rica, Finland, Japan, Kenya and the United Kingdom—circulated a draft resolution, entitled 'Towards an arms trade treaty', among the members of the UN General Assembly First Committee.[1] The draft resolution requested the UN Secretary-General to seek states' views and establish a group of governmental experts (GGE) to examine the 'feasibility, scope and draft parameters for a comprehensive, legally binding instrument establishing common international standards for the import, export and transfer of conventional arms'.[2] In the General Assembly, the resolution was co-sponsored by 77 states, with 153 voting in favour, 24 abstaining (including China, Russia and a large number of Arab states), and only the United States voting against.[3]

By the beginning of 2008, 101 states had submitted their views to the UN Secretary-General.[4] In August 2008 the GGE, chaired by Ambassador Roberto Garcia Moritán of Argentina, recommended further consideration of the issue 'on a step-by-step basis in an open and transparent manner'.[5] In

---

[1] 'Towards an arms trade treaty: establishing common international standards for the import, export and transfer of conventional arms', Draft resolution, A/C.1/61/L.55, 12 Oct. 2006. For more information on the draft resolution see Holtom, P. and Wezeman, S. T., 'Towards an arms trade treaty?', *SIPRI Yearbook 2007*, pp. 431–39.

[2] 'Towards an arms trade treaty' (note 1), paras 1–2.

[3] UN General Assembly Resolution 61/89, 18 Dec. 2006.

[4] United Nations, General Assembly, 'Towards an arms trade treaty: establishing common international standards for the import, export and transfer of conventional arms', Report of the Secretary-General, A/62/278, 17 Aug. 2007 and addenda of 24 Sep. 2007, 19 Oct. 2007, 27 Nov. 2007 and 15 Feb. 2008. See also Parker, S., *Analysis of States' Views on an Arms Trade Treaty* (United Nations Institute for Disarmament Research: Geneva, 2007).

[5] United Nations, General Assembly, 'Report of the Group of Government Experts to examine the feasibility, scope and draft parameters for a comprehensive, legally binding instrument establishing

December 2008, 133 states supported a UN General Assembly resolution asking the UN Secretary-General to establish an open-ended working group (OEWG) and set aside six one-week sessions to carry out the GGE's recommendation.[6] The USA was again the only state to vote against the resolution, with 19 states, including China and Russia, abstaining.

In December 2009 the UN General Assembly decided to convene a UN conference on the ATT in 2012 and tasked it with reaching consensus on a legally binding instrument to establish the 'highest possible common international standards for the transfer of conventional arms'.[7] The remaining four OEWG sessions became preparatory committee (PrepCom) meetings for the conference and a fifth session was added to decide 'all relevant procedural matters'.[8] While 151 states voted in favour of this resolution, China and Russia once again abstained along with 18 other states. Zimbabwe was the only state to vote against the resolution. The USA, having undergone a change of leadership with the election of President Barack Obama, voted in favour of the resolution. However, seeking to retain control over the final text, it made its support for the ATT process conditional on the insertion of language stating that the treaty would be negotiated on the basis of consensus.[9] Moritán, who had chaired the GGE and OEWG, continued in this role during the PrepCom and was named president of the 2012 conference.

The 2012 United Nations conference on an arms trade treaty

When the 2012 conference commenced in New York in July it became apparent that most states could be categorized either as 'progressive' or 'sceptical' in terms of their approach to the negotiations.[10] Progressive states sought to promote a robust ATT that would limit the impact of the illicit arms trade, and that was compatible with the goals of humanitarian arms control treaties. These states—the most vocal being Mexico, Norway, and states from Latin America and the Caribbean—were supported by a coalition of civil society organizations. In contrast, sceptical states sought a treaty that would be limited in terms of the scope of weapons covered, and that would focus on state security concerns. The most vocal of these

common international standards for the import, export and transfer of conventional arms', A/63/334, 26 Aug. 2008, para. 27.

[6] UN General Assembly Resolution 63/240, 24 Dec. 2008.

[7] UN General Assembly Resolution 64/48, 2 Dec. 2009, paras 4, 6, 8.

[8] UN General Assembly (note 7).

[9] US Department of State, 'Secretary of State Hillary Rodham Clinton, U.S. support for the arms trade treaty', 14 Oct. 2009, <http://www.state.gov/secretary/rm/2009a/10/130573.htm>.

[10] The opening of the 2012 conference itself was delayed by a series of procedural disagreements. E.g. the Palestinian Authority, backed by Egypt, demanded full state rights. It agreed to be an observer state, but only after delaying proceedings for 2 days. 'Arms trade talks open after spat over Palestinian status', Deutsche Welle, 4 July 2012, <http://www.dw.de/arms-trade-talks-open-after-spat-over-palestinian-status/a-16071068-1>.

sceptical states were China, Egypt, India and Russia. A third but less signifi-cant group of states—including Cuba, Iran, the Democratic People's Repub-lic of Korea (DPRK, North Korea), Pakistan, Syria, Venezuela and Zim-babwe—consistently opposed the ATT. These states' opposition arguably reflected concerns about the possibility of being subjected to arms embar-goes, as well as their rejection of the human security agenda and its appli-cation to arms export controls.[11] The USA was an outlier, as it took posi-tions that on some issues resembled those of sceptical states and on other issues supported elements proposed by progressive states. Throughout the negotiations, the USA remained the most difficult state to place on the progressive–sceptical spectrum.

As the negotiations progressed, the consensus requirement contributed to a sense that the conference would produce a 'weak' treaty, as it appeared to the progressive states that the demands of the sceptical states were being too readily accommodated.[12] At the end of the third week of the conference, 74 states issued a statement calling for a 'robust' treaty to promote human security.[13] However, on 24 July 2012 Moritán presented a draft text of the whole treaty that appeared heavily skewed towards the demands of the sceptical states.[14] This presentation of a 'weak' treaty is likely to have been a strategic decision by the conference president. When even the most scep-tical states expressed their dissatisfaction with this version, Moritán pre-sented a significantly revised text on 26 July that received much greater support from the progressive states (although many noted that it still needed considerable work).[15] Legal analysts have since highlighted a number of questions regarding terminology and inconsistencies in the draft.[16] While several inconsistencies were a result of the compromises that were made to try and achieve consensus, it was clear that the text produced on 26 July would still require work before it could be adopted.

Nevertheless, there were high hopes that a majority of states, including all five permanent members of the Security Council (China, France, Russia, the UK and the USA), would support a modified version of the 26 July

[11] Bromley, M., Cooper, N. and Holtom, P., 'The UN Arms Trade Treaty: arms export controls, the human security agenda and the lessons of history', International Affairs, vol. 88, no. 5 (Sep. 2012), pp. 1040–44.

[12] 'Germany backs global arms trade treaty, China and Russia abstain', Deutsche Welle, 31 Oct. 2009, <http://www.dw-world.de/dw/article/0,,4842120,00.html?maca=en-en_nr-1893-xml-atom>.

[13] For the full list of states see '74 states stand up for a strong #armstreaty', Control Arms blog, 20 July 2012, <http://controlarmsblog.posterous.com/60-states-stand-up-for-a-strong-armstreaty>.

[14] Moritán had also presented a discussion paper at the start of the conference but the rest of the conference was spent dealing only with discrete sections of the text.

[15] United Nations, General Assembly, 'The draft of the arms trade treaty', A/CONF.217/CRP.1, 26 July 2012.

[16] Casey-Maslen, S. and Parker, S., 'The draft arms trade treaty', Geneva Academy of International Humanitarian Law and Human Rights Briefing no. 2, Oct. 2012, <http://www.geneva-academy.ch/academy-publications/academy-briefings>.

text.[17] However, on 27 July—the final day of the conference—the US delegation stated that it needed more time to work on the text and proposed convening another conference to conclude negotiations.[18] Cuba, North Korea, Russia and Venezuela echoed this call.[19]

Barriers to consensus in the negotiations

Although the draft ATT of 26 July was flawed and could have benefited from being circulated to UN member states earlier, the US delegation's call for more negotiations probably owed more to political considerations than the actual content of the draft. Support for an ATT could have been used by the Republican Party to misrepresent the potential impact of an ATT on the USA, and portray President Obama as an opponent of the rights of US citizens to keep and bear arms.[20]

The 2012 conference demonstrated the persistence of crucial dividing lines between states on the main objectives of an ATT, in particular on the issue of weighing state security interests against human security concerns. This division lay at the heart of discussions on defining prohibited transfers, mitigating the risks associated with particular transfers, and deciding when to authorize or deny arms exports. Another issue that consumed considerable time during the PrepCom meetings and the 2012 conference was the scope of the items to be covered by the ATT, particularly whether small arms and light weapons (SALW) and ammunition should be included. Other issues that remained unresolved at the close of negotiations included (a) whether gifts should be excluded from the scope of the treaty; (b) whether regional integration organizations—such as the European Union (EU)—should be allowed to sign and ratify the treaty; (c) the number of state signatories needed before entry into force; and (d) the types of transparency mechanism that should be included in the treaty.[21]

Immediately after the 2012 conference, a number of states and non-governmental organizations (NGOs) identified the USA as the main cause of the failure to conclude an ATT.[22] While it is questionable whether the USA was exclusively to blame for the failure of the 2012 conference, the

[17] 'U.N. states fail to reach global arms trade treaty', Associated Press, 28 July 2012.

[18] US Department of State, 'Arms trade treaty conference', Press release, 27 July 2012, <http://www.state.gov/r/pa/prs/ps/2012/07/195622.htm>.

[19] Acheson, R., 'Editorial: A pause for reflection', Arms Trade Treaty Monitor, vol. 5, no. 16 (July 2012), pp. 1–2.

[20] Holtom, P., 'The UN conference on an arms trade treaty: no treaty . . . yet?', IPI Global Observatory, 16 Aug. 2012, <http://theglobalobservatory.org/analysis/339-the-un-conference-o>.

[21] Article 16 of the draft treaty stipulated the entry into force of the ATT '90 days after the deposit of the 65th instrument of ratification, acceptance, approval or accession with the depositary'. United Nations, A/CONF.217/CRP.1 (note 15), Article 16. The 1993 Chemical Weapons Convention also required ratification by 65 states before it entered into force.

[22] 'U.N. states fail to reach global arms trade treaty' (note 17).

process nonetheless served to demonstrate that the USA remains the predominant force in discussions on multilateral arms transfer controls. The fact that long-term advocates of an ATT were willing to make concessions and compromises in order to accommodate US concerns further illustrates this reality. Importantly, US concerns and views were at the centre of discussions on the two most contentious issues: (*a*) prohibited transfers and arms export risk assessments, and (*b*) the definition of the scope of an ATT.

Prohibited transfers and arms export risk assessments

Long-standing proponents of an ATT have emphasized that it should have a positive impact on human security, and that it should oblige states to consider international human rights and humanitarian law as well as other human security impacts before authorizing arms exports.[23] However, the sceptical states questioned the proposition that human security considerations have a place in arms export decision making.[24] Therefore, the inclusion of human security considerations in the 26 July text was particularly significant.

To a certain extent the 26 July text's three categories of prohibited transfers merely re-codified existing obligations in international law: (*a*) Chapter VII of the UN Charter (particularly the provisions relating to arms embargoes); (*b*) relevant obligations relating to arms transfers and trafficking; and (*c*) international law relating to genocide, crimes against humanity and war crimes as defined in Common Article 3 of the Geneva Conventions of 1949. It has been argued that the text's formulations regarding this third category of international obligations provide a narrow definition of war crimes and include a very high threshold for denials and should therefore be replaced by a knowledge-based approach.[25]

The idea of including a prohibition on transfers to non-state actors that had not been authorized to receive arms by the state in which they were located had a broad group of supporters among both progressive and sceptical states.[26] Such language has been strongly opposed by the USA in other settings, in particular in discussions relating to the Programme of Action to Prevent, Combat and Eradicate the Illicit Trade in Small Arms and Light Weapons in All Its Aspects (POA).[27] While the USA never men-

---

[23] For a discussion of this issue see Bromley et al. (note 11), pp. 1034–43.

[24] Bromley et al. (note 11), pp. 1040–41. For brief descriptions and lists of members of ASEAN, the CSTO and the Arab League see annex B in this volume.

[25] United Nations, A/CONF.217/CRP.1 (note 15), Article 3; and Casey-Maslen and Parker (note 16), p. 23.

[26] This group included the African Group of UN member states; Brazil, Russia, India and China (the BRIC states); the Caribbean Community (CARICOM); the Economic Community of West African States (ECOWAS); and Turkey.

[27] Holtom, P., *Prohibiting Arms Transfers to Non-state Actors and the Arms Trade Treaty* (United Nations Institute for Disarmament Research: Geneva, 2012).

428 NON-PROLIFERATION, ARMS CONTROL AND DISARMAMENT, 2012

tioned the issue explicitly during public negotiations, its central concern was its desire to retain the ability to supply arms to non-state actors to allow them to defend themselves against armed violence committed by repressive state forces, or where the USA's own security concerns were seen to be at stake.[28] The 26 July text made no explicit reference to a ban on arms transfers to unauthorized non-state actors.

The 26 July text would also oblige states to carry out a risk assessment before authorizing an export. The assessment would focus on the risk that the proposed export could be used to commit or facilitate a serious violation of international humanitarian law or human rights law or an offence under international conventions and protocols relating to terrorism, but would also include a general assessment of 'whether the proposed export would contribute to or undermine peace and security'. Measures undertaken by the supplier and recipient states to mitigate these risks would be considered in the assessment, but if the exporting state finds an 'overriding risk', then it should not authorize the export.[29] In addition to the risk assessment, each state party would be required to

consider taking feasible measures, including joint actions with other States involved in the transfer, to avoid the arms:
   a. being diverted to the illicit market or for unauthorized end use;
   b. being used to commit or facilitate gender-based violence or violence against children;
   c. being used for transnational organized crime;
   d. becoming subject to corrupt practices; or
   e. adversely impacting the development of the importing State.[30]

In order to help ensure the primacy of state security, the USA supported the inclusion of language that would require exporting states to consider the potential effect of an arms export on peace and security. However, the clearest example of the way in which the 26 July text privileges state security interests is contained in Article 5(2), which states that 'This Treaty shall not be cited as grounds for voiding contractual obligations under defence cooperation agreements concluded by States Parties to this Treaty'.[31] India insisted on including this clause in the treaty, presumably as a means of ensuring 'security of supply' for itself and other recipients.[32]

Defining the scope of the arms trade treaty

A considerable amount of time during the ATT process has been spent discussing the categories of items to be covered by the treaty. Some states

---

[28] Greene, O., Kirkham, E. and Watson, C., *Developing International Norms to Restrict SALW Transfers to Non-state Actors* (Biting the Bullet Project: London, Jan. 2006), p. 2.
[29] United Nations, A/CONF.217/CRP.1 (note 15), articles 4 and 6.
[30] United Nations, A/CONF.217/CRP.1 (note 15), Article 4.
[31] United Nations, A/CONF.217/CRP.1 (note 15), Article 5(2).
[32] Casey-Maslen and Parker (note 16), p. 27.

have called for the scope of the ATT to be limited to the seven categories of the UN Register of Conventional Arms (UNROCA).[33] Others have called for the scope to match that of the Wassenaar Arrangement Munitions List and encompass all military equipment as well as associated parts and technologies.[34] The 26 July draft treaty text used the narrow '7 + 1 formula'—that is, its scope was limited to the seven categories of the UNROCA and an additional category for SALW. Notably, according to an unpublished document presented at the conference, several sceptical states accepted the inclusion of SALW in the scope of an ATT after previously opposing it.

Several states pushed for the inclusion of a prohibition on circumventing the treaty via licensed production arrangements and technology transfers in order to expand the range of items that would be covered by the treaty's provisions. Such language was not included in the 26 July draft. However, the draft required states to establish national export control lists and to exchange these lists with other states parties to the ATT. The sharing of these lists could support the practice of controlling a far broader range of items than is covered by the '7 + 1 formula', since this is a common practice among states that have transfer control systems in place.[35]

The most contested issue relating to scope was the way in which the 26 July draft addressed ammunition. While the USA was not alone in opposing the inclusion of ammunition in the ATT, most attention on this issue focused on the US position. Before the 2012 conference, the USA had identified reporting or marking ammunition as a symbolic line that it would not cross.[36] During the conference, US negotiators stated that 'ammunition is a fundamentally different commodity than everything else we have discussed including within the scope of an ATT' and strongly objected to its inclusion within the scope of the treaty.[37] While technical concerns relating to the monitoring of the large volume of ammunition transfers could help to explain this position, so too could political concerns about the US National Rifle Association's ability to misrepresent to the US electorate a treaty that explicitly mentioned controls on ammunition transfers.[38]

Many states from the Caribbean, Central and Western Europe, Latin America and sub-Saharan Africa regard ammunition as an important element for the scope of the ATT and pushed hard for the USA to shift its

[33] On UNROCA see chapter 5, section IV, in this volume.

[34] On the Wassenaar Arrangement see section IV below; and annex B, section III, in this volume.

[35] United Nations, A/CONF.217/CRP.1 (note 15), Article 2.

[36] US Department of State, Bureau of International Security and Nonproliferation, 'Elements of an arms trade treaty', 4 June 2010, <http://www.state.gov/t/isn/rls/fs/148314.htm>.

[37] Pecquet, J., 'Obama administration: UN arms trade treaty shouldn't regulate ammunition', The Hill, 10 July 2012, <http://thehill.com/blogs/global-affairs/un-treaties/236969-us-says-un-arms-trade-treaty-shouldnt-cover-ammunition>.

[38] Goodman, C., 'Why is the United States opposing small arms ammunition in an ATT?', Arms Trade Insider, 1 Mar. 2011, <http://armstradeinsider.com/2011/03/01/why-the-united-states-is-obstinate-on-small-arms-ammunition-in-an-att>.

position. The 26 July text offered an alternative solution that was widely regarded as unacceptable by the progressive states. It proposed that 'Each State Party shall establish and maintain a national control system to regulate the export of ammunition for conventional arms under the scope of this Treaty'. It would also require that exports of ammunition not be authorized if they would be classed as 'prohibited transfers' or if there were a risk that they would be used to commit or facilitate a serious violation of international humanitarian law, human rights law or an offence under international conventions and protocols relating to terrorism.[39] However, states parties to the ATT would not be required to consider taking feasible measures to prevent risks relating to (*a*) diversion; (*b*) use in gender-based violence or violence against children; (*c*) transnational organized crime; (*d*) corruption in the deal; or (*e*) a negative impact on the development of the importing state. In addition, they would not be required to keep records or submit reports on their respective transfers.

The 2013 United Nations conference on an arms trade treaty

Following the 2012 conference, negotiators faced three broad options for further action: (*a*) make minor amendments to the 26 July draft ATT and table it for a vote in the UN General Assembly in late 2012; (*b*) convene another UN negotiating conference to further consider the draft ATT; or (*c*) take the process outside the UN framework, strengthen the human security references in the draft ATT and include ammunition in its scope.[40]

During the General Assembly First Committee meetings in the autumn of 2012, the seven original co-sponsors of the General Assembly resolutions for the ATT tabled a resolution to hold a final conference in early 2013, in line with the requests of Russia and the USA.[41] As a whole, the resolution was adopted by a vote of 157 to none, with 18 abstentions (including Russia). Separate votes approved the use of the same rules of procedure for the 'final conference', and the use of the 26 July text as the basis for future work. Only Iran voted against these proposals, although Russia abstained. The draft resolution called for a report on the final outcome to be presented 'as soon as possible after 28 March 2013'.[42]

The vote on the resolution in the UN General Assembly on 24 December 2012 was adopted by 133 votes to none, with 17 abstentions.[43] The 2013

[39] Parts and components were also dealt with in the same manner. United Nations, A/CONF.217/CRP.1 (note 15), Article 6.

[40] Bromley et al. (note 11), pp. 1029–48.

[41] United Nations, General Assembly, First Committee, 'The arms trade treaty', A/C.1/67/L.11, 18 Oct. 2012.

[42] United Nations, A/C.1/67/L.11 (note 41), para. 7.

[43] UN General Assembly Resolution 67/234, 24 Dec. 2012.

conference, which was due to commence on 18 March, was therefore considered an extension of 2012 conference. One of the key changes would be that Moritán would not be the president of the 2013 conference. Despite widespread support from the international community to continue in this role, he did not have the support of the Argentinian Government. In December 2012 Ambassador Peter Woolcott of Australia was confirmed as president-designate of the conference.[44]

[44] 'Australian Department of Foreign Affairs and Trade, Ministers welcome the adoption of the UN Resolution on the Final Conference on the Arms Trade Treaty', Press release, 24 Dec. 2012, <http://www.dfat.gov.au/media/releases/department/2012/dfat-release-20121224.html>.

II. Multilateral arms embargoes

PIETER D. WEZEMAN AND CHRISTINA BUCHHOLD

Unlike in 2011, there were few substantial developments in multilateral arms embargoes in 2012. Whereas the United Nations Security Council was able to agree swiftly on an arms embargo on Libya in 2011 in response to violent repression of peaceful demonstrators, it could not agree on similar sanctions against Syria despite the worsening of the conflict there during 2012.[1] Violations of UN embargoes continued to be reported during the year, with the investigating panels of experts expressing frustration at some states' lack of cooperation.

During 2012, 13 UN arms embargoes, 19 European Union (EU) arms embargoes, and one League of Arab States arms embargo were in force (see table 10.1).[2] Of the EU's 19 embargoes, 9 implemented UN decisions directly, 3 implemented UN embargoes with modified scope or coverage, and 7 had no UN counterpart.[3] The Arab League embargo (on Syria) had no UN counterpart.

No new embargo was imposed or lifted by the UN Security Council, the EU or any other multilateral organization in 2012.

Syria

After efforts in 2011 to threaten or impose UN arms embargoes against Syria failed, no similar draft resolutions were presented to the UN Security Council during 2012. In particular, Russia remained an outspoken opponent of any UN sanctions against Syria and continued to supply arms to Syria.[4] In July 2012 Russia, together with China, vetoed a draft Security Council resolution that threatened economic sanctions against the Syrian

---

[1] Wezeman, P. D. and Kelly, N., 'Multilateral arms embargoes', *SIPRI Yearbook 2012*, pp. 431–35.

[2] In addition, 1 voluntary multilateral embargo was still in force in 2012: in 1992 the Conference on Security and Co-operation in Europe (CSCE, now renamed the Organization for Security and Co-operation in Europe) requested that all participating states impose an embargo on arms deliveries to Armenian and Azerbaijani forces engaged in combat in the Nagorno-Karabakh area. The request has never been repealed but a number of OSCE participating states have supplied arms to Armenia and Azerbaijan since 1992. Conference on Security and Co-operation in Europe, Committee of Senior Officials, Statement, annex 1 to Journal no. 2 of the Seventh Meeting of the Committee, Prague, 27–28 Feb. 1992. See also Holtom, P., 'Arms transfers to Armenia and Azerbaijan, 2007–11', *SIPRI Yearbook 2012*, pp. 286–92.

[3] The 3 that differed from equivalent UN embargoes were those on Iran and North Korea, which covered more weapon types than the UN embargo, and on Sudan, which covered the whole country whereas the UN embargo applied only to the Darfur region. The 7 with no UN counterpart were those on Belarus, China, Guinea, Myanmar, South Sudan, Syria and Zimbabwe. The 9 that implement UN embargoes are indicated in table 10.1.

[4] See e.g. 'Russia to veto Syria arm embargo-envoy', RIA Novosti, 1 Feb. 2012, <http://en.rian.ru/russia/20120201/171072768.html>. On arms supplies to Syria see chapter 5, section III, in this volume. On other developments in the conflict see chapter 1, section I, in this volume

Government in response to the escalation of violence, including the increase in the use of heavy weapons by the government and its failure to implement a UN peace plan.[5]

The EU had imposed sanctions on Syria in May 2011 that included an arms embargo. Questions arose in 2012 about its implementation in cases (a) where embargoed goods from non-EU states are transported to Syria through EU territory or (b) that involve companies and individuals based in the EU. In January 2012 Cypriot authorities inspected a ship with a military cargo from Russia at a port in Cyprus. After receiving assurances from the shipping company that the ship was not going to Syria, Cyprus allowed it to leave port. The ship promptly delivered the cargo to Syria.[6] The European Commission found that Cyprus had not breached the EU sanctions.[7] However, to address the transport of embargoed items through the EU to Syria, the Council of the EU decided in July 2012 that EU member states should inspect all vessels and aircraft bound, or believed to be bound, for Syria within their territories, with the consent of the flag state, if they have reasonable grounds to believe that the cargo may include sanctioned items.[8] It remains unclear what actions EU member states are able, or required, to take if embargoed goods are found on Syria-bound craft or if the flag state refuses to consent to inspection.

France and the United Kingdom made repeated calls during 2012 for the embargo on Syria to be amended to enable direct support to armed opposition groups. This contrasted with developments in 2011 concerning the arms embargoes on Libya. There had been debate about whether a certain amendment to the UN embargo permitted the supply of arms to the rebels fighting the Libyan regime of Muammar Gaddafi.[9] In the Libyan case, while several EU member states, including France and the UK, interpreted the amendment as allowing the supply of military equipment to the rebels, they did not attempt to amend the EU embargo on Syria, which clearly banned supply to both sides.

From August 2012 the UK expanded what it termed 'non-lethal practical assistance' (which included providing communication equipment and body

[5] United Nations, Security Council, 6810th meeting, S/PV.6810, 19 July 2012; and United Nations, Security Council, Draft resolution, S/2012/538, 19 July 2012.

[6] 'Cyprus releases suspected Syrian arms ship', Voice of America, 10 Jan. 2012, <http://www.voanews.com/content/cyprus-releases-suspected-syrian-arms-ship-137092243/173361.html>; and Brantner, F. K., 'Actions of the Republic of Cyprus in relation to the conflict in Syria', Question for written answer to the Commission (Vice-President/High Representative), European Parliament, 15 Mar. 2012, <http://www.europarl.europa.eu/sides/getDoc.do?type=WQ&reference=P-2012-002 870&language=EN>.

[7] Ashton, C., High Representative/Vice-President, Answer given on behalf of the Commission, 7 May 2012, <http://www.europarl.europa.eu/sides/getAllAnswers.do?reference=P-2012-002870& language=EN>.

[8] Council Decision 2012/420/CFSP of 23 July 2012 amending Decision 2011/782/CFSP concerning restrictive measures against Syria, *Official Journal of the European Union*, L196, 24 July 2012.

[9] Wezeman and Kelly (note 1), p. 433.

armour) to unarmed parts of the Syrian opposition, arguing that it was in compliance with the EU embargo.[10] After officially recognizing the newly established Syrian National Coalition as the sole representative of the Syrian people on 13 November 2012, France called for a review of the arms embargo to enable the delivery of 'defensive arms' to opposition forces.[11] In late November, as the EU sanctions against Syria came up for renewal, the UK asked for more frequent reviews of the arms embargo and a significantly shorter renewal term, which would allow the EU to consider amendments that would allow the supply of non-lethal training and equipment to armed Syrian rebels.[12] The EU then extended the existing sanctions against Syria for three months, from 1 December 2012 to 1 March 2013, rather than the usual period of one year.[13]

The Arab League had imposed sanctions—its first ever—against Syria in December 2011, including an arms embargo.[14] Discussions within the Arab League about the possibility of arming the Syrian opposition surfaced soon afterwards.[15] On 12 February 2012 the Arab League reaffirmed the economic sanctions of December 2011 but added that it had decided to provide the Syrian opposition with 'all forms of political and material support'—language that could be interpreted as changing the scope of the arms embargo.[16] Arab League diplomats confirmed that 'material support' could include arms transfers to the opposition.[17] Despite this change, there was no official acknowledgement that Arab League states were involved in such transfers.[18]

[10] British Foreign and Commonwealth Office, 'Foreign Secretary statement on Syria', 10 Aug. 2012, <http://www.gov.uk/government/news/foreign-secretary-statement-on-syria?id=798971582>; and British Foreign and Commonwealth Office, 'Foreign Secretary written ministerial statement on Syria', 7 Nov. 2012, <http://www.gov.uk/government/news/foreign-secretary-written-ministerial-statement-on-syria?id=832340182>.

[11] 'Laurent Fabius sur la Syrie: "Paris va demander à l'UE la levée de l'embargo sur les armes défensives"' [Laurent Fabius on Syria: 'Paris will ask the EU to lift the embargo on defensive arms'], RTL, 15 Nov. 2012, <http://www.rtl.fr/actualites/info/politique/article/video-laurent-fabius-sur-la-syrie-paris-va-demander-a-l-ue-la-levee-de-l-embargo-sur-les-armes-defensives-7754703699>; and 'France proposes defensive weapons for Syria rebels', Agence France-Presse, 15 Nov. 2012.

[12] 'EU cuts sanctions term to possibly help rebels', Reuters, 28 Nov. 2012.

[13] Council Decision 2012/739/CFSP of 29 November 2012 concerning restrictive measures against Syria, *Official Journal of the European Union*, L330, 30 Nov. 2012.

[14] Wezeman and Kelly (note 1), p. 435.

[15] League of Arab States, Council, Statement on the situation in Syria, 3 Dec. 2011, <http://www.lasportal.org/wps/wcm/connect/c38cc58049521706877cef7abaae88c3/البيان+النهائي.doc,,.pdf?MOD=AJPERES> (in Arabic).

[16] League of Arab States, Council, Resolution 7446, 12 Feb. 2012, <http://www.lasportal.org/wps/wcm/connect/b093ad804a246c8985c59d526698d42c/7446.pdf?MOD=AJPERES> (in Arabic), para. 9 (authors' translation).

[17] 'Conflict flares across Syria, Arabs mull arms support', Reuters, 14 Feb. 2012.

[18] On arms transfers to Syrian rebel groups see chapter 5, section III, in this volume.

Other multilateral arms embargoes

In October 2012 the African Union (AU) Peace and Security Council called for 'urgent steps to be taken to restructure and empower' the Somali defence and security sector, including the lifting of the UN arms embargo on Somali Government forces, while maintaining it against non-state actors.[19] The AU's motivations were unclear, as the existing arms embargo on Somalia allowed arms supplies aimed at strengthening Somali Government forces if they were reported to the UN Sanctions Committee on Somalia. In March 2013 the UN Security Council decided that for 12 months it would place no restrictions on deliveries of weapons, military equipment, assistance or training intended solely for the development of the Security Forces of the Federal Government of Somalia, and to provide security for the Somali people.[20]

The UN Security Council Group of Experts on the Democratic Republic of the Congo (DRC) concluded that, despite the UN embargo on supplies of arms to non-governmental forces in the DRC, a variety of groups continued to procure small arms and light weapons (SALW) and ammunition during 2011–12.[21] In particular, it concluded that the Rwandan Government continued to support the 23 March Movement (M23) rebel group, including by providing weapons. In response, the Security Council threatened targeted sanctions against those providing external support to M23 or those who otherwise violated the arms embargo.[22]

In reaction to a military coup in April 2012, in May the UN Security Council threatened to impose sanctions against Guinea-Bissau, including an arms embargo.[23] However, despite its concerns about stability in Guinea-Bissau, the Security Council deemed the subsequent political developments sufficiently positive and did not carry through with the threat.[24]

In October 2012 the EU extended its embargo on Guinea for another year without public explanation, even though the political situation had improved considerably since the embargo was imposed in 2009 and the

---

[19] African Union, Peace and Security Council, 337th meeting, Press statement, 11 Oct. 2012 <http://www.peaceau.org/en/article/press-statement-of-the-337th-meeting-of-the-peace-and-security-council-on-somalia/>.

[20] United Nations, Security Council, 6854th meeting, S/PV.6854, 7. Nov. 2012, p. 3.

[21] United Nations, Security Council, Interim report of the Group of Experts on the Democratic Republic of the Congo, 18 May 2012, annex to S/2012/348, 21 June 2012, pp. 6–15; Addendum, annex to S/2012/348/Add.1, 27 June 2012; and United Nations, Security Council, Final report of the Group of Experts on the Democratic Republic of the Congo, 12 Oct. 2012, annex to S/2012/843,15 Nov. 2012, p. 3.

[22] UN Security Council Resolution 2078, 28 Nov. 2012, para. 9.

[23] UN Security Council Resolution 2048, 18 May 2012, para. 12.

[24] UN Security Council Resolution 2092, 22 Feb 2013.

country had returned to civilian rule in 2010.[25] In April and May 2012 the EU suspended certain sanctions against the Government of Myanmar but extended the arms embargo for a year.[26]

Multilateral embargoes are sometimes refined before they are due for renewal or review based on new insights related to the relevance of certain technologies. In 2012 the EU amended its arms embargo on Iran to include surveillance equipment, following a similar amendment to its arms embargo on Syria in 2011 (see also section V below).

Violations of United Nations embargoes

In 2012, as in previous years, several significant violations of UN arms embargoes were reported, primarily by the UN panels of experts tasked with monitoring the embargoes.[27]

Two leaked reports by two separate panels of experts on Sudan in early 2012 described how the Sudanese Government had continued to move recently imported arms and military equipment into the Darfur region in 2011 and 2012.[28] These movements violated the UN embargo and contradicted assurances given by the Sudanese Government to the suppliers of the equipment.

The UN Sanctions Committee on Libya established that significant quantities of weapons, in particular SALW, plundered from Libyan stockpiles, had left the country.[29] This was in violation of the UN embargo on arms exports from Libya but, more importantly, these weapon flows fuelled conflicts in neighbouring countries, in particular Mali.[30]

---

[25] Council Decision 2012/665/CFSP of 26 October 2012 amending Decision 2010/638/CFSP concerning restrictive measures against the Republic of Guinea, *Official Journal of the European Union*, L299, 27 Oct. 2012.

[26] Council Decision 2012/225/CFSP of 26 April 2012 amending Decision 2010/232/CFSP renewing restrictive measures against Burma/Myanmar, *Official Journal of the European Union*, L115, 27 Apr. 2012.

[27] In 2012 panels existed for all UN arms embargoes except those on non-governmental forces in Iraq and Lebanon. Reports by panels of experts can be found on the websites of the UN Security Council sanctions committees, <http://www.un.org/sc/committees/>.

[28] 'Letter dated 24 January 2012 from the Panel of Experts on the Sudan established pursuant to resolution 1591 (2005) addressed to the Chairman of the Security Council committee established pursuant to Resolution 1591 (2005) concerning the Sudan'; and 'Letter dated 24 January 2011 [sic] from former members of the Panel of Experts on the Sudan established pursuant to Resolution 1591 (2005) and renewed pursuant to resolution 1945 (2010) addressed to the Chairman of the Security Council committee established pursuant to resolution 1591 (2005) concerning the Sudan', 24 Jan. 2012. Both reports were leaked in Apr. 2012. 'UN clash over Beijing bullets claim', Africa Confidential, 13 Apr. 2012, <http://www.africaconfidential.com/index.aspx?pageid=7&articleid=4417>.

[29] United Nations, Security Council, Sanctions Committee on Libya, Consolidated working document on the implementation of paragraph 5 of Security Council Resolution 2017 (2011), 23 Mar. 2012, annex to S/2012/178, 26 Mar. 2012, p. 4.

[30] See chapter 1, section I, in this volume.

The Democratic People's Republic of Korea (DPRK, North Korea) continued to build and launch ballistic missiles in 2012 in violation of UN Security Council demands. Some of the components of these missiles are foreign-sourced. For example, the transporter erector launchers (TELs) for a new type of ballistic missile shown for the first time during a military parade in April 2012 use a Chinese chassis. Six of these chassis were supplied to North Korea in 2011 by a Chinese company reportedly under the assurance that they would be used in the logging industry.[31]

According to a 2012 report of the UN Panel of Experts on Iran, the interception in 2011 of two batches of arms en route to Syria confirmed the panel's earlier conclusion that Syria was the main recipient of Iranian arms exported in violation of the UN embargo on arms exports from Iran.[32]

In July 2012 the UN Monitoring Group on Somalia and Eritrea concluded that arms markets in Yemen remained the principal external source of SALW for non-state groups in Somalia, but that the role of Eritrea as a source of military support appeared to have declined.[33] The group noted with concern that during the second half of 2011 and the first half of 2012 Ethiopia, France, Sudan, Turkey, the United Arab Emirates, the United States, several private companies and the UN itself all provided support to Somali Government security forces without the mandatory prior notification to the Sanctions Committee.[34] In a separate report on the UN arms embargo on Eritrea, the group concluded that, although the embargo had an adverse effect on the operational readiness of the Eritrean Air Force, there were indications that there had been imports of spare parts and external assistance in servicing aircraft during the first half of 2012.[35]

In previous years, assessing trends in violations of arms embargoes had been hindered by efforts of UN Security Council members to prevent or delay the publication of reports by UN panels of experts.[36] However, in 2012 only one new report—on Sudan—was not released to the public,

[31] United Nations, Security Council, Report of the Panel of Experts established pursuant to Resolution 1874 (2009), 11 May 2012, annex to S/2012/422, 14 June 2012, p. 19; and 'U.N. panel probing how North Korea acquired mobile missile launchers', Global Security Newswire, 15 Nov. 2012, <http://www.nti.org/gsn/article/securtity-council-probing-how-north-korea-acquired-large-missile-launchers/>.
[32] United Nations, Security Council, Final report of the Panel of Experts established pursuant to Resolution 1929 (2010), 4 June 2012, annex to S/2012/395, 12 June 2012, pp. 4, 27–29.
[33] United Nations, Security Council, Report of the Monitoring Group on Somalia and Eritrea pursuant to Security Council Resolution 2002 (2011), 27 June 2012, annex to S/2012/544, 13 July 2012, paras 51–53.
[34] United Nations, S/2012/544 (note 33), paras 51–78.
[35] United Nations, Security Council, Report of the Monitoring Group on Somalia and Eritrea pursuant to Security Council Resolution 2002 (2011), 27 June 2012, annex to S/2012/545, 13 July 2012, para. 64.
[36] On efforts to change or block reports in 2010 and 2011 see Wezeman, P. D. and Kelly, N., 'Multilateral arms embargoes, 2010', SIPRI Yearbook 2011, pp. 449–51; and Wezeman and Kelly (note 1), p. 437.

although it was leaked.[37] In a positive development, in 2012 a report by the UN Panel of Experts on Iran was published after the first two had not.[38] The third annual report by the Panel of Exports on North Korea was published in 2012 after the second report, in 2011, had not been released.[39]

However, as in previous years, several of the panels expressed concern about absent or incomplete responses to requests for information from certain governments. Former members of the UN Panel of Experts on Sudan complained about the complete lack of cooperation from Sudan and the poor responses from China and Russia in the investigation of violations of the embargo on movements of arms to Darfur.[40] The groups on Côte d'Ivoire, the DRC, and Somalia and Eritrea also noted or expressed concern about the poor responses to their requests for information.[41] The Group of Experts on the DRC reported that its efforts to investigate sanctions violations in Rwanda were obstructed by the Rwandan Government.[42]

[37] Panel of Experts on the Sudan (note 28).

[38] United Nations, S/2012/395 (note 32).

[39] United Nations, S/2012/422 (note 31).

[40] Former members of the Panel of Experts on the Sudan (note 28), pp. 21–23.

[41] United Nations, Security Council, Final report of the Group of Experts on Côte d'Ivoire, 16 Mar. 2012, annex to S/2012/196, 14 Apr. 2012, paras 29–43, pp. 12–14; United Nations, S/2012/196 (note 31), para. 14; United Nations, S/2012/544 (note 33), pp. 30–31; and United Nations, S/2012/348 (note 21), p. 56.

[42] United Nations, S/2012/348 (note 21), p. 56.

Table 10.1. Multilateral arms embargoes in force during 2012

Target[a]	Date embargo first imposed	Principal instruments establishing or amending the embargo[b]	Key developments during 2012
United Nations arms embargoes			
Al-Qaeda and associated individuals and entities	16 Jan. 2002	SCRs 1390, 1989	
Congo, Democratic Republic of the (NGF)	28 July 2003	SCRs 1493, 1596, 1807	Extended until 1 Feb. 2014 by SCR 2078, 28 Nov. 2012
Côte d'Ivoire	15 Nov. 2004	SCRs 1572, 1946	Amended and extended until 30 Apr. 2013 by SCR 2045, 26 Apr. 2012[c]
Eritrea	23 Dec. 2009	SCR 1907	
Iran	23 Dec. 2006	SCRs 1737, 1747, 1929	
Iraq (NGF)	6 Aug. 1990	SCRs 661, 1483, 1546	
Korea, North	15 July 2006	SCRs 1695, 1718, 1874	
Lebanon (NGF)	11 Aug. 2006	SCR 1701	
Liberia (NGF)	22 Dec. 2003[d]	SCRs 1521, 1683, 1903	Extended until 12 Dec. 2013 by SCR 2079, 12 Dec. 2012
Libya (NGF)	26 Feb. 2011	SCRs 1970, 1973, 2009	
Somalia	23 Jan. 1992	SCRs 733, 1725	
Sudan (Darfur)	30 July 2004	SCRs 1556, 1591, 1945	
Taliban	16 Jan. 2002	SCRs 1390, 1988	
European Union arms embargoes			
Al-Qaeda, the Taliban and associated individuals and entities*	17 Dec. 1996	CPs 96/746/CFSP, 2001/154/CFSP, 2002/402/CFSP	
Belarus	20 June 2011	CD 2011/357/CFSP	Extended until 31 Oct. 2013 by CD 2012/642/CFSP, 15 Oct. 2012
China	27 June 1989	European Council declaration	
Congo, Democratic Republic of the (NGF)*	7 Apr. 1993	Declaration, CPs 2003/680/CFSP, 2005/440/CFSP, 2008/369/CFSP	
Côte d'Ivoire*	13 Dec. 2004	CP 2004/852/CFSP, 2010/656/CFSP	Amended by CD 2012/371/CFSP, 10 July 2012[e]
Eritrea*	1 Mar. 2010	CD 2010/127/CFSP	

Target[a]	Date embargo first imposed	Principal instruments establishing or amending the embargo[b]	Key developments during 2012
Guinea	27 Oct. 2009	CPs 2009/788/CFSP, 2009/1003/CFSP	Extended until 27 Oct. 2013 by CD 2012/665/CFSP 26 Oct. 2012
Iran	27 Feb. 2007	CPs 2007/140/CFSP, 2007/246/CFSP	Amended by CD 0212/168/CFSP, 23 March 2012[f]
Iraq (NGF)*	4 Aug. 1990	Declaration, CPs 2003/495/CFSP, 2004/553/CFSP	
Korea, North	20 Nov. 2006	CPs 2006/795/CFSP, 2009/573/CFSP	
Lebanon (NGF)*	15 Sep. 2006	CP 2006/625/CFSP	
Liberia (NGF)*	7 May 2001	CPs 2001/357/CFSP, 2004/137/CFSP, 2006/518/CFSP, 2010/129/CFSP	
Libya (NGF)*	28 Feb. 2011	CD 2011/137/CFSP, 2011/625/CFSP	
Myanmar	29 July 1991[g]	GAC declaration, CPs 96/635/CFSP, 2003/297/CFSP, 2010/232/CFSP	Extended until 30 Apr. 2013 by CD 2012/225/CFSP, 26 Apr. 2012
Somalia (NGF)*	10 Dec. 2002	CPs 2002/960/CFSP, 2009/138/CFSP, 2010/231/CFSP	
South Sudan	18 July 2011	CD 2011/423/CFSP	
Sudan	15 Mar. 1994	CPs 94/165/CFSP, 2004/31/CFSP, 2005/411/CFSP, CD 2011/423/CFSP	
Syria	9 May 2011	CD 2011/273/CFSP	Amended by CR 36/2012, 18 Jan. 2012, CR 509/2012, 16 June 2012, and CD 2012/420/CFSP, 23 July 2012, and extended until 1 Mar. 2013 by CD 2012/739/CFSP, 29 Nov. 2012[h]
Zimbabwe	18 Feb. 2002	CP 2002/145/CFSP	Extended until 20 Feb. 2013 by CD 2012/97/CFSP, 17 Feb. 2012
League of Arab States arms embargo			
Syria	3 Dec. 2011	Arab League Council statement	Amended by Arab League Council Resolution 7446, 12 Feb. 2012[i]

* = EU embargo implementing a UN embargo; CD = Council Decision; CP = Council Common Position; CR = Council Regulation; GAC = General Affairs Council; NGF = non-governmental forces; SCR = UN Security Council Resolution.

[a] The target may have changed since the first imposition of the embargo. The target stated here is as at the end of 2012.
[b] The earlier instruments may have been amended or repealed by subsequent instruments.

[c] UN Security Council Resolution 2045 lifted all restrictions on the provision of training, advice and expertise related to security and military activities and on supplies of civilian vehicles to the Ivorian security forces.

[d] Liberia has been the target of UN arms embargoes since 1992, with related but different objectives.

[e] CD 2012/371/CFSP implemented the changes of UNSCR 2045 (see note c).

[f] CD 0212/168/CFSP prohibited the supply of equipment or software intended primarily for monitoring by the Iranian Government of Internet and telephone communications in Iran.

[g] The EU and its member states first imposed an arms embargo on Myanmar in 1990.

[h] Council Regulation 36/2012 prohibited the export of telecommunications monitoring equipment and service for use by the Syrian Government. Council Regulation 509/2012 prohibited the supply of equipment, goods or technology which might be used for internal repression or for the manufacture and maintenance of products which might be used for internal repression. Council Decision 2012/420/CFSP stated that EU member states should inspect all vessels and aircraft bound for Syria within their territories and with the consent of the flag state if they have reasonable grounds to believe that the cargo may include sanctioned items.

[i] Resolution 7446 could be interpreted as permitting the provision of arms to the Syrian opposition.

Sources: United Nations, Security Council, 'UN Security Council sanctions committees', <http://www.un.org/sc/committees/>; and European Union External Action, 'Sanctions or restrictive measures', 18 Jan. 2013, <http://eeas.europa.eu/cfsp/sanctions/index_en.htm>.

III. Financial sanctions and other restrictive measures

IAN ANTHONY

A variety of restrictive measures have been used to prevent proliferation of nuclear, biological and chemical weapons, and missile systems for their delivery. These measures include restrictions on trade, financial sanctions and restrictions on travel. Restrictions on trade can be either general or targeting particular goods. Financial sanctions can include, for example, the freezing of funds or economic resources, prohibitions on financial transactions or requirements for prior approval before entering into such transactions, and restrictions on the provision of export credits or investment funds. Examples of restrictions on travel include flight bans and restrictions on the admission of named individuals. In 2012 an important understanding was reached among the states that play a central role in managing the international financial system on how to use financial sanctions to support non-proliferation. In addition, new and expanded measures were adopted to attempt to bring about a change in the national nuclear policy of Iran.

The Financial Action Task Force

The Financial Action Task Force (FATF) is an intergovernmental body established in 1989 by the Group of Seven (G7) to combat money laundering and block financing that might facilitate terrorist acts.[1] The number of states participating in the FATF has subsequently expanded and the task force has broadened its agenda to take account of other illicit activities—including the proliferation of nuclear, biological and chemical weapons—that could be considered threats to the integrity of the international financial system.

While the FATF first investigated recommendations related to proliferation financing in 2008, it was not until February 2012 that it published revised recommendations that addressed proliferation financing for the first time.[2] The recommendations have two objectives in relation to proliferation: (a) ensuring consistent and effective implementation of targeted financial sanctions when these are called for by the United Nations Security

---

[1] On FATF see annex B, section III, in this volume; and the FATF website, <http://www.fatf-gafi.org>.

[2] Financial Action Task Force (FATF), *International Standards on Combating Money Laundering and the Financing of Terrorism & Proliferation: The FATF Recommendations* (FATF/Organisation for Economic Co-operation and Development: Paris, 2012), <http://www.fatf-gafi.org/media/fatf/documents/recommendations/pdfs/FATF_Recommendations.pdf>. See also Bauer, S., Dunne, A. and Mićić, I., 'Strategic trade controls: countering the proliferation of weapons of mass destruction', *SIPRI Yearbook 2011*, pp. 441–43.

Council; and (b) helping countries implement effective national mechanisms to enable their authorities to 'cooperate, and, where appropriate, coordinate domestically with each other concerning the development and implementation of policies and activities to combat money laundering, terrorist financing and the financing of proliferation of weapons of mass destruction'.[3] At the same time, the FATF published a detailed guidance document that described the most effective ways to implement the recommendations at the national level.[4]

In 2012 the FATF's membership comprised 34 participating states (including almost all of the important financial centres) as well as two regional organizations: the European Commission and the Gulf Cooperation Council.[5] The FATF also has both associated partners and observers. Associated partners are mostly specialized regional networks of financial regulators responsible for overseeing anti-money laundering measures. The group of observers is a heterogeneous mix of banks, UN bodies, European Union (EU) agencies and specialized intergovernmental networks (e.g. those involved in combating drug trafficking). In order to become an associated partner or an observer, entities must promise to implement FATF recommendations. Therefore, the recommendations on proliferation financing should 'cascade' through FATF cooperation networks to virtually all parts of the world in coming years.

Strengthening restrictive measures against Iran

Between 2006 and 2010 the UN Security Council adopted a series of resolutions that introduced a range of restrictive measures on Iran as part of an attempt to persuade Iran to modify its national nuclear programme to reduce proliferation risks.[6] The restrictive measures mandated in the resolutions were relatively narrow, primarily directly linked to the supply of goods or services that could make a direct contribution to a nuclear weapon programme or a programme to develop a ballistic missile delivery system for a nuclear weapon.

In June 2010 the UN Security Council recommended (but did not require) that states take broader steps—for example, inspecting all air and sea cargo bound for Iran, preventing financial services that may be used for sensitive nuclear activities and generally subjecting the Iranian banking

---

[3] Financial Action Task Force (note 2), page 11.
[4] Financial Action Task Force (FATF), *Best Practices Paper on Recommendation 2: Sharing Among Domestic Competent Authorities Information Related to the Financing of Proliferation* (FATF: Paris, 2012).
[5] For a full list of FATF members see annex B in this volume.
[6] On recent developments with regard to Iran see chapter 7, section I, in this volume.

sector to closer scrutiny.[7] However, unlike previous measures, the resolution did not gain the support of all members of the Security Council, with two non-permanent members (Brazil and Turkey) voting against it. Public statements by China and Russia, which both have a veto on Security Council decisions, suggested that future proposals to introduce additional restrictive measures would be unlikely to gain the necessary support.[8]

Since 2010 a number of states and the EU have adopted restrictive measures against Iran that go far beyond what can be agreed in the UN Security Council. Some features of these sanctions are particularly noteworthy. First, after an extended period in which states sought restrictive measures that were narrowly targeted, in 2012 the scope of sanctions was expanded to the point where widespread damage would inevitably be caused to the Iranian economy. Second, a number of the measures also apply to any legal entity incorporated or constituted under the law of a state other than that which has put the measures in place. For example, under the terms of a number of the measures enacted in the United States, restrictive measures apply to foreign subsidiaries of a US company even if they are incorporated or constituted under the laws of another country.[9]

Traditionally, the extraterritorial application of restrictive measures has been controversial, to the point where some European governments have instructed companies incorporated under their laws to disobey US restrictive measures.[10] However, in the case of restrictive measures applied to Iran this feature appears to be increasingly accepted. Cooperation among likeminded states to implement measures and share information on enforcement appears to be expanding.[11] These developments suggest that the

[7] UN Security Council Resolution 1929, 9 June 2010; and Wezeman, P. D. and Kelly, N., 'Multilateral arms embargoes, 2010', *SIPRI Yearbook 2011*, pp. 447–48.

[8] Melnikov, V., 'U.S. Iran sanctions threaten ties with Russia—official', RIA Novosti, 13 Aug. 2012, <http://en.rian.ru/russia/20120813/175189517.html>; and 'China slams new US–Iran sanctions as "serious violation of intl rules"', Russia Today, 1 Aug. 2012, <http://rt.com/news/iran-fresh-sanctions-obama-552/>.

[9] In Aug. 2012 the Iran Threat Reduction and Syria Human Rights Act of 2012 applied US sanctions on Iran to US–controlled offshore subsidiaries. In Oct. 2012 the executive order implementing the sanctions on Iran established a 'grace period', until 13 Feb. 2013, during which time offshore subsidiaries could wind down their commercial relations with Iran. White House, 'Executive Order from the President regarding authorizing the implementation of certain sanctions set forth in the Iran Threat Reduction and Syria Human Rights Act of 2012 and additional sanctions with respect to Iran', 9 Oct. 2012, <http://www.whitehouse.gov/the-press-office/2012/10/09/executive-order-president-regarding-authorizing-implementation-certain-s>.

[10] In 1996 the EU introduced legislation instructing companies not to implement extraterritorial dimensions of the US Iran and Libya Sanctions Act of 1996. Council Regulation (EC) no. 2271/96 of 22 Nov. 1996 protecting against the effects of the extra-territorial application of legislation adopted by a third country, and actions based thereon or resulting therefrom, *Official Journal of the European Union*, L309, 29 Nov. 1996, pp. 1–6.

[11] Australia, Canada, Japan, South Korea and Switzerland have also adopted some or all of the restrictive measures enacted by the EU and the USA. See Katzman, K., *Iran Sanctions*, Congressional Research Service (CRS) Report for Congress RS20871 (US Congress, CRS: Washington, DC, 15 Oct. 2012); Autonomous Sanctions Regulations 2011, Australian Select Legislative Instrument 2011 no. 247 as amended, 21 Aug. 2012, <http://www.comlaw.gov.au/Details/F2012C00562>; and Swiss

urgent need to address the proliferation concerns arising from Iran's nuclear programme have generated a growing consensus, at least within the Euro-Atlantic community, on the need for restrictive measures.

European Union decisions on restrictive measures

In addition to actions intended to implement decisions of the UN Security Council more effectively, the EU introduced several new and important restrictive measures in 2012.

In January 2012 the Council of the EU decided that, in the light of the potential use of revenues derived from the energy sector to fund pro-liferation-sensitive nuclear activities, new investment in the petrochemical sector in Iran would be prohibited. In March the scope of the restrictive measures was expanded significantly to prohibit the purchase of oil and petroleum products from Iran.[12] In December this was extended to cover natural gas.[13]

A second new element in EU restrictive measures was the decision to impose restrictive measures against the Central Bank of Iran, in the light of evidence that it was involved in activities to circumvent existing UN and EU sanctions.[14]

In March 2012 the Council took a new decision to deny specialized financial messaging services—which are used to exchange financial data—to specified Iranian entities and individuals.[15] Immediately after the EU decision, the Society for Worldwide Interbank Financial Telecommuni-cation (SWIFT), which is incorporated in Belgium and subject to EU law, announced that it would discontinue its communications services to Iranian financial institutions subject to EU sanctions. SWIFT's chief execu-tive officer noted that 'disconnecting banks is an extraordinary and unpre-cedented step for SWIFT. It is a direct result of international and multilateral action to intensify financial sanctions against Iran'.[16] Trans-

State Secretariat for Economic Affairs, 'Iran: Federal Council takes steps to improve legal certainty and prevent possible evasion', Press release, 19 Jan. 2011, <http://www.seco.admin.ch/aktuell/00277/01164/01980/?lang=en&msg-id=37283>.

[12] Council of the European Union, Council Regulation (EU) no. 267/2012 of 23 March 2012 concerning restrictive measures against Iran and repealing Regulation (EU) no. 961/2010, *Official Journal of the European Union*, L88, 24 Mar. 2012.

[13] Council of the European Union, Council Regulation (EU) no. 1263/2012 of 21 December 2012 amending Regulation (EU) no. 267/2012 concerning restrictive measures against Iran, *Official Journal of the European Union*, L356, 22 Dec. 2012.

[14] Council of the European Union, Council Implementing Regulation (EU) no. 54/2012 of 23 Jan. 2012 implementing Regulation (EU) no. 961/2010 on restrictive measures against Iran, *Official Journal of the European Union*, L19, 24 Jan. 2012, pp. 1–5.

[15] Council of the European Union, Council Council Decision 2012/152/CFSP of 15 Mar. 2012 amending Decision 2010/413/CFSP concerning restrictive measures against Iran, *Official Journal of the European Union*, L77, 16 Mar. 2012, p. 18.

[16] SWIFT is the digital network through which more than 10 000 financial institutions and corporations in 212 countries exchange financial information. Society for Worldwide Interbank

actions involving gold, diamonds and other precious metals, which could provide an alternative means of payment once access to financial systems was restricted, were subsequently prohibited.

In November 2012 the responsible financial authority within the Bank of France imposed penalties on the manager of a Paris branch of an Iranian bank.[17] This was the first instance of an imposition of sanctions on an individual bank manager based on a breach of the restrictive measures in an EU regulation on Iran. In France, the decision was interpreted as a strategic signal from the responsible authorities to the banking sector about the need for vigilance and compliance.

The actions taken by the EU were part of a wider effort by a number of like-minded states to apply more restrictive financial measures against Iran. For example, under previous restrictive measures, while US persons were instructed not to execute transactions involving the Iranian Government, they could simply reject them rather than being required to freeze the related assets. However, after the US administration's adoption in February 2012 of new restrictions, all financial transactions involving any Iranian financial institution must be blocked by all US persons (including financial institutions).[18]

The progressive introduction of new and more restrictive financial sanctions has made it more difficult for Iranian entities to gain access to the international financial system. This has reportedly led Iran to receive payments in local currency through a domestic bank in some trading partners when implementing foreign trade transactions.[19] This effectively forces Iran to buy goods in the local market to the equivalent value of items it exports—a form of barter arrangement.

Financial Telecommunication (SWIFT), 'SWIFT instructed to disconnect sanctioned Iranian banks following EU Council decision', Press release, 15 Mar. 2012, <http://www.swift.com/about_swift/shownews?param_dcr=news.data/en/swift_com/2012/press_releases_SWIFT_disconnect_Iranian_banks.xml>.

[17] Autorité de Contrôle Prudentiel, Commission des Sanctions, 'Bank Tejarat Paris, M. Mohammad Mahdian, M. Hossein Fazeli', Procédure n° 2011-03, 27 Nov. 2012, <http://www.acp.banque-france.fr/fileadmin/user_upload/acp/publications/registre-officiel/20121127-Decision-de-la-commission-des-sanctions.pdf>.

[18] US President, 'Blocking property of the Government of Iran and Iranian financial institutions', Executive Order no. 13 599, 5 Feb. 2012, Federal Register, vol. 77, no. 26, 8 Feb. 2012.

[19] Parent, V. and Hafezi, P., 'Iran turns to barter for food as sanctions cripple imports', Reuters, 9 Feb. 2012.

IV. Export control regimes

SIBYLLE BAUER AND ANDREA VISKI

In 2012 four informal, consensus-based export control regimes—the Australia Group, the Missile Technology Control Regime (MTCR), the Nuclear Suppliers Group (NSG) and the Wassenaar Arrangement on Export Controls for Conventional Arms and Dual-use Goods and Technologies—worked within their specific fields to strengthen trade control cooperation.[1] One cross-regime trend throughout the year involved ongoing efforts to expand the scope of discussions and guidelines about activities and items to be subject to controls, in particular regarding brokering, transit and trans-shipment, intangible transfers of technology, and proliferation financing. Although export controls remain the regimes' main organizing principle, associated trade activities are increasingly becoming the focus of control efforts.

The Australia Group

The Australia Group was established in the light of international concern about the use of chemical weapons in the 1980–88 Iran–Iraq War.[2] The 41 participating states now seek to prevent the intentional or inadvertent supply of materials, equipment and technology to chemical or biological weapon programmes.

During its annual plenary in Paris in June 2012, the Australia Group took a specific step towards strengthening controls of brokering services by amending the group's guidelines.[3] For the past decade the international debate, policy decisions and legal provisions regarding strategic trade controls have gradually been expanded to include a range of activities related to export controls—notably brokering, transit, trans-shipment and financing. Before 2012, however, international export control regimes had not moved beyond discussions and exchanges of experience on these issues. The Australia Group's amendment of its guidelines, therefore, marks a significant step towards it becoming a trade control regime, rather than a regime limited to export controls. According to the new wording,

Australia Group members should have in place or establish measures against illicit activities that allow them to act upon brokering services related to items mentioned

---

[1] For brief descriptions and lists of participating states of each of these regimes see annex B, section III, in this volume.

[2] Australia Group, 'The origins of the Australia Group', [n.d.], <http://www.australiagroup.net/en/origins.html>.

[3] Australia Group, 'Media Release 2012 Australia Group Plenary', Paris, 15 June 2012, <http://www.australiagroup.net/en/media_june2012.html>.

in the Australia Group control lists which could contribute to CBW activities. Australia Group members will make every effort to implement those measures in accordance with their domestic legal framework and practices.

In addition, the group amended the assessment criteria for evaluating export applications to include

the role of distributors, brokers or other intermediaries in the transfer, including, where appropriate, their ability to provide an authenticated end-user certificate specifying both the importer and ultimate end-user of the item to be transferred, as well as the credibility of assurances that the item will reach the stated end-user.[4]

The group also made several changes to its control list at the plenary.[5] In particular, five pathogens were added to the List of Plant Pathogens for Export Control, and the List of Biological Agents for Export Control was amended.[6] In December 2012 an inter-sessional meeting convened in Bonn, Germany, made further recommendations, including suggestions to strengthen the language on agitators, impellers and blades; clarify the scope of the *Clostridium perfringens* toxin entry; and strengthen controls on single-use bioreactors.[7]

At the plenary, the Australia Group also discussed new areas that may warrant attention in the future, such as the relevance of life sciences and nanotechnology to the control list, intangible transfers of technology and threats posed by non-state actors.[8] States noted the possibility of the use of biological or chemical weapons by the Syrian Government and the methods used to import control list items and other dual-use items for proliferation purposes. Participants agreed to exercise increased vigilance with regard to dual-use exports to Syria.[9]

Another outcome of the plenary was an agreement to enhance cooperation within the group in a number of areas, through the sharing of information on 'enforcement capabilities, approaches to visa vetting, [and] experience in the implementation of catch-all provisions'.[10] The group reiterated its commitment to outreach, having conducted outreach briefings for over 50 countries in 2012, as well as visits to China, Colombia,

---

[4] Australia Group, 'Guidelines for transfers of sensitive chemical or biological items', June 2012, <http://www.australiagroup.net/en/guidelines.html>.

[5] Tilemann, J., 'Preventing CW and BW proliferation: the Australia Group', 20th Asian Export Control Seminar, Tokyo, 26–28 Feb. 2013, <http://www.simul-conf.com/outreach/2012/asian_ec/>.

[6] The 5 plant pathogens are *Peronosclerospora philippinensis* (*P. sacchari*), *Sclerophthora rayssiae* var. *Zeae*, *Synchytrium endobioticum*, *Tilletia indica* and *Thecaphora solani*. Australia Group, 'List of plant pathogens for export control', June 2012, <http://www.australiagroup.net/en/plants.html>.

[7] Tilemann (note 5).

[8] On dual uses of nanotechnology see Eggleson, K., 'Dual-use nanoresearch of concern: recognizing threat and safeguarding the power of nanobiomedical research advances in the wake of the H5N1 controversy', *Nanomedicine: Nanotechnology, Biology and Medicine*, vol. 9, no. 3 (Apr. 2013), pp. 316–21.

[9] Australia Group (note 3).

[10] Australia Group (note 3).

Malaysia, Pakistan, Thailand and Viet Nam in 2012 and early 2013.[11] Furthermore, the group noted the importance of increasing awareness of intangible transfers and brokering in relevant sectors, such as academia.

In March 2012, a Wilton Park conference on the Australia Group discussed the group's membership, the challenges of constant scientific advancement, and engagement with non-government actors.[12] Recommendations from the conference were considered at the Australia Group annual plenary.[13] This demonstrated the Australia Group's ongoing efforts to explore ways to engage with non-participating states, industry and academia. However, no new states were admitted in 2012, although applications and expressions of interest from several countries remain pending. The last countries to have been admitted to the Australia Group were Ukraine (in 2005) and Croatia (in 2007).[14]

The Missile Technology Control Regime

The MTCR, which celebrated its 25th anniversary in 2012, was created to prevent the proliferation of unmanned systems capable of delivering weapons of mass destruction (WMD).[15] Its 26th plenary meeting was held in October 2012 in Berlin, with Germany assuming the rotating chair.[16] Approximately 250 representatives from the 34 partner states participated.[17] At the opening of the plenary, Guido Westerwelle, the German Foreign Minister identified several key issues that the MTCR needs to address, including advanced delivery systems and new technologies such as lighter-than-air vehicles; as well as concerns about the missile programmes of Iran, the Democratic People's Republic of Korea (North Korea) and Syria.[18]

Westerwelle also referred to membership expansion, mentioning that 'important technology supplier states that are not yet in this group are

---

[11] Tilemann (note 5).

[12] 'The Australia Group: challenges and future directions', Wilton Park, 29–31 Mar. 2012, <http://www.wiltonpark.org.uk/conference/wp1143/>.

[13] Australia Group (note 3).

[14] See Anthony, I. and Bauer, S., 'Transfer controls', *SIPRI Yearbook 2006*, pp. 780–81; Anthony, I., Bauer, S. and Wetter, A., 'Controls on security-related international transfers', *SIPRI Yearbook 2008*, p. 494; and Bauer, S., Dunne, A. and Mićić, I., 'Strategic trade controls: countering the proliferation of weapons of mass destruction', *SIPRI Yearbook 2011*.

[15] For further detail see the MTCR website, <http://www.mtcr.info>.

[16] Missile Technology Control Regime, 'Chair's statement on the plenary meeting of the Missile Technology Control Regime', Berlin, 24–26 Oct. 2012, <http://www.mtcr.info/english/press.html>. No plenary statement was issued in 2012. Argentina held the chair in 2011. Italy will chair the MTCR and host its plenary in 2013 and Norway will do so in 2014.

[17] German Foreign Office, 'Verbreitung von Raketentechnologie verhindern' [Preventing proliferation of missile technology], 24 Oct. 2012, <http://www.auswaertiges-amt.de/DE/Aussenpolitik/Aussenwirtschaftsfoerderung/121024-MTCR-Plenum.html>.

[18] German Foreign Office, 'Speech by Foreign Minister Guido Westerwelle to open the Missile Technology Control Regime (MTCR) meeting', 24 Oct. 2012, <http://www.auswaertiges-amt.de/EN/Infoservice/Presse/Reden/2012/121024-BM_MTCR.html>.

knocking at the door, for example India' and stating that admission of the eight EU member states that remain outside the regime was 'long over-due'.[19] The USA publicly stated its support for Indian membership.[20] Despite this, no membership decisions were taken at the 2012 plenary, although individual applications were discussed.[21] However, the MTCR engaged in outreach activities in a range of non-participating countries to increase transparency of the regime and to promote its objectives, including visits to United Arab Emirates (UAE) and Pakistan in early 2013.[22] The engagement with the UAE indicates the importance of trans-shipment hubs, not just producing and exporting countries. Furthermore, MTCR members reiterated their willingness to assist other countries in applying MTCR guidelines and control lists. Westerwelle also discussed missile issues more broadly, stating that MTCR 'efforts must also include encour-aging more countries to sign up to the Hague Code of Conduct'.[23]

As usual, three expert groups met in advance of the plenary: the Licensing and Enforcement Experts Meeting (LEEM), the Information Exchange Meeting (IEM), and the Technical Experts Meeting (TEM).[24]

At the 2012 plenary, partner states agreed on updates to the MTCR control list that were designed to keep up with technological changes in the equipment, materials, software and technology needed for missile develop-ment, production and operation. In addition, the plenary discussed a number of issues relating to missile proliferation, including rapid tech-nological change; intangible transfers of technology, including transfers by parties with access to sensitive scientific knowledge; catch-all controls for unlisted items based on end-use; and brokering, transit and trans-shipment. However, since no new documents were added to the MTCR website, it appears that these discussions did not lead to any agreements on new guidelines or principles.

The MTCR plenary discussed concerns about missile programmes in the Middle East, North East Asia and South Asia, including Iran and North Korea. The chair's statement at the conclusion of the plenary highlighted

[19] German Foreign Office (note 18). The 8 EU member states outside the MTCR at the end of 2012 were Cyprus, Estonia, Latvia, Lithuania, Malta, Romania, Slovakia and Slovenia.

[20] Davenport, K., Horner, D. and Kimball, D. G., 'Missile control: an interview with Deputy Assistant Secretary of State Vann Van Diepen', Arms Control Today, vol. 42, no. 6 (June/Aug. 2012).

[21] Missile Technology Control Regime (note 16).

[22] Ranau, J., 'Arms Trade Treaty und internationale Entwicklungen' [Arms trade treaty and international developments], Presentation at Exportkontrolltag (Export Control Day), Münster, 1 Mar. 2013.

[23] German Foreign Office (note 18). As of 1 Jan. 2013 there were 134 signatories to the Hague Code of Conduct against Ballistic Missile Proliferation (HCOC). For a list of signatories and a sum-mary of the HCOC see annex B, section III, in this volume; and the HCOC website, <http://www.hcoc.at/>. South Korea took over the chair from Romania at the 11th regular plenary meeting, held from 31 May to 1 June 2012. Japan was elected as chair for the period 2013–14. The Republic of the Congo and Singapore both subscribed during Romania's chairmanship.

[24] Missile Technology Control Regime (note 16).

the relevance of United Nations Security Council resolutions 1874 and 1929—which imposed sanctions on North Korea and Iran, respectively, in response to their nuclear and missile programmes—to the MTCR's activities.[25]

Unmanned aerial vehicles

The issue of unmanned aerial vehicles (UAVs) has been contentious within the MTCR for a number of years, primarily because many larger UAVs are capable of delivering WMD. The UAV dilemma—which also applies to other regimes and to national trade controls more broadly—reflects the difficulties inherent in seeking to keep up with changing proliferation-related trends while protecting trade and market competitiveness.

Unmanned UAVs have been defined by the US Department of Defense as 'powered aerial vehicles sustained in flight by aerodynamic lift over most of their flight path and guided without an onboard crew'.[26] While UAVs have widely recognized civilian applications, their use for military applications such as intelligence gathering and reconnaissance has grown in recent years. UAV technology is also part of the development of unmanned combat air vehicles (UCAVs), which are seen as a probable future replacement for manned combat aircraft and other aircraft.[27] The MTCR does not differentiate between reconnaissance UAVs and UCAVs because the restrictions are based on the assumption that a UAV payload (conventional ammunition or reconnaissance equipment) could be replaced with a WMD payload.

The scope of the MTCR was expanded in 1992 to include UAVs in the MTCR's Category I of most sensitive items. Regardless of their purpose, Category I items can only be authorized for export on rare occasions and under specified conditions. Further, the transfer of Category I production facilities is not to be authorized at all.[28] Category I items include systems capable of delivering a payload of at least 500 kilograms to a minimum range of 300 kilometres, as well as the production facilities and major subsystems for such items. For their export, 'particular restraint' is to be exercised and a 'strong presumption to deny' applies based on MTCR guidelines. In contrast, Category II systems, which are items capable of flying at least 300 km but below Category I's payload size parameters, require an

---

[25] Missile Technology Control Regime (note 16).
[26] US Department of Defense, 'Introduction of the unmanned aerial vehicle', 3 June 2003, <http://www.defense.gov/specials/uav2002/>.
[27] The MTCR Annex Handbook includes cruise missile systems in the UAV category but also states that, unlike a cruise missile, a UAV will return and can be re-used. Missile Technology Control Regime, *MTCR Annex Handbook*, 23 Oct. 2012, MTCR/TEM/2012/Annex, <http://www.mtcr.info/english/annex.html>.
[28] Missile Technology Control Regime, 'Guidelines for sensitive missile-relevant transfers', [n.d.], <http://www.mtcr.info/english/guidetext.htm>, para. 2.

export licence based on criteria specified in the guidelines, but are not subject to Category I's presumption to deny.[29]

In the early 1990s UAVs were only used in small numbers, had very limited capabilities and played a minor role compared to manned military aircraft. This situation has changed considerably. UAVs are now widely used, and it is generally expected that they will increasingly replace manned aircraft. There is also growing interest in using UAVs for civilian surveillance and earth observation roles. Additionally, the development of long-range UAVs is expensive and technologically challenging, meaning that states have sought international partnerships to develop them, as well as export deals to achieve economies of scale.[30]

The growth in the acquisition and use of UAVs and associated technology has led to increasing military and economic pressures to re-evaluate the current MTCR restrictions on transfers of larger UAVs. Many exporting companies see MTCR controls as a market obstacle and, therefore, design systems for exports that are just below the minimum threshold to be designated as a Category I item. Companies have also been lobbying governments to favour changing the MTCR guidelines in order to reclassify some Category I UAV goods as Category II, which would facilitate UAV export.[31]

In the period 2008–12 non-MTCR partners ordered large numbers of UAVs from MTCR states. However, most of these vehicles have ranges of less than 300 km and potential payloads of much less than 500 kg and therefore fall outside the scope of the MTCR. The only UAVs falling within the MTCR were 11 MQ-9s transferred from the USA to the UK; 4 MQ-9s transferred from the USA to Italy; and 5 RQ-4E Euro Hawks transferred from the USA to Germany. Several other countries, including non-MTCR partners, have shown an interest in the MQ-9 and the RQ-4. In addition, Canada has supplied engines to Israel (which is not an MTCR partner) for the Israeli-produced Heron-TP, which also has a range and payload far above the MTCR limits.[32]

A 2012 report by the US Government Accountability Office (GAO) refers to approximately 70 diplomatic cables that the US Department of State sent to 20 governments and the MTCR in the period 2005–11 addressing UAV-related concerns. Over 75 per cent of these cables were in response to 'efforts by a small number of countries of concern to obtain controlled and uncontrolled technologies for use in their UAV programs'.[33] The GAO con-

[29] Missile Technology Control Regime (note 28), para. 3.

[30] See e.g. Jackson, S. T., 'Key developments in the main arms-producing countries', *SIPRI Yearbook 2012*, pp. 224–27.

[31] British Parliament, 'Arms export controls 2013: written evidence from Drone Wars UK', 22 Oct. 2012, <http://www.publications.parliament.uk/pa/cm201213/cmselect/cmquad/writev/689/m01.htm>.

[32] SIPRI Arms Transfers Database, <http://www.sipri.org/databases/armstransfers>.

[33] US Government Accountability Office (GAO), *Nonproliferation*, GAO-12 536 (GAO: Washington, DC, July 2012), p. 22.

cluded that 'although UAV proliferation poses risks, the U.S. government has determined that selected transfers of UAV technology can further national security objectives'.[34] The USA has sponsored six UAV-related proposals in the MTCR, of which one was adopted. The other five would have moved some UAVs from Category I to Category II, but no consensus was reached, and the proposals were taken off the agenda after 2008.[35]

In the wake of North Korea's test of the Unha-3 rocket on 12 December 2012, the US Government offered to sell reconnaissance UAVs to the Republic of Korea (South Korea).[36] In 2008 the US Secretary of Defense had mentioned the need to overcome issues related to obligations under the MTCR in order to make such a sale to South Korea.[37]

The Nuclear Suppliers Group

The NSG aims to prevent the proliferation of nuclear weapons by controlling transfers of nuclear and nuclear-related material, equipment, software and technology.[38] NSG members are also able to access information on best practices and specific data that can be put into the risk-management systems of licensing and customs authorities. The group's June 2012 plenary in Seattle, USA, brought together the 46 participating states, as well as the European Commission and the Chair of the Zangger Committee (both of which are permanent observers).[39] The USA took over the NSG chair from the Netherlands, a position it will hold until the 2013 plenary.

At its 2010 plenary meeting in Christchurch, New Zealand, the NSG initiated a fundamental review of its control lists, an ongoing process that is being undertaken in order to keep up with technological developments. The 2012 plenary agreed changes to the control lists in relation to nuclear

---

[34] US Government Accountability Office (note 33), p. 19.

[35] US Government Accountability Office (note 33), pp. 20–21.

[36] South Korean experts concluded that the North Korean rocket did not contain any items violating the MTCR guidelines, although some components had been imported. The expert team also concluded that this test had served to test North Korea's intercontinental ballistic missile programme. Kim, E., 'Rocket debris reveals N. Korea's intention to test ICBM technology', Yonhap News Agency, 23 Dec. 2012, <http://english.yonhapnews.co.kr/national/2012/12/22/99/0301000000AEN2 0121222002300315F.HTML>. See also chapter 6, section IX, and chapter 7, section II, in this volume.

[37] 'U.S. moves to sell advanced spy drones to South Korea', Reuters, 25 Dec. 2012; and Hardy, J., 'New eyes in the Asian skies', The Diplomat, 4 Jan. 2013. An official request for the Global Hawk UAV had also been made in 2005.

[38] On the NSG see Bauer, S., 'Developments in the Nuclear Suppliers Group', SIPRI Yearbook 2012, pp. 376–86; Viski, A., 'The revised Nuclear Suppliers Group guidelines: a European Union perspective', Non-proliferation Papers no. 15, EU Non-proliferation Consortium, May 2012, <http://www.nonproliferation.eu/activities/activities.php>; Anthony, I., Ahlström, C. and Fedchenko, V., Reforming Nuclear Export Controls: The Future of the Nuclear Suppliers Group, SIPRI Research Report no. 22 (Oxford University Press: Oxford, 2007); annex B, section III, in this volume; and the NSG website, <http://www.nuclearsuppliersgroup.org/>.

[39] For a brief description of the Zangger Committee see annex B, section III, in this volume; and the Zangger Committee website, <http://www.zanggercommittee.org>.

reactors, heavy water production, lithium isotope separation and uranium enrichment. However, the participating states agreed to wait until the completion of the review process before issuing revised versions of the control lists.[40]

The plenary approved an amendment to part I of the NSG Guidelines in relation to access to nuclear material for peaceful purposes:

Suppliers should, in accordance with the objective of these guidelines, facilitate access to nuclear material for the peaceful uses of nuclear energy, and encourage, within the scope of Article IV of the [1968 Non-Proliferation Treaty], recipients to take the fullest possible advantage of the international commercial market and other available international mechanisms for nuclear fuel services while not undermining the global fuel market.[41]

A paper approved by the plenary to guide the NSG's outreach programme noted the importance of engaging industry and 'approved revising the guidance on such efforts'.[42] The group further discussed establishing closer links with other bodies such as the UN Security Council's 1540 Committee, the World Institute for Nuclear Security and the World Nuclear Association.[43] While brokering and transit were discussed, no decisions were announced on these issues. As usual, information and best practices on licensing and enforcement were discussed and exchanged. As in 2011, the plenary statement mentioned proliferation concerns raised by the nuclear programmes of Iran and North Korea.[44]

Mexico and Serbia were invited to the 2012 plenary as observers.[45] Mexico was admitted to the NSG in November 2012 after gaining the unanimous approval of the 46 participants. In 2011 Mexico exported over $1 billion worth of goods on the NSG control lists.[46] By joining the NSG Mexico can now contribute to discussions and help shape consensus-based decisions. Throughout the year, India continued to seek support for its membership bid via diplomatic channels.[47] Several NSG members—

[40] Nuclear Suppliers Group (NSG), 'NSG public statement', NSG Plenary, Seattle, 21–22 June 2012, <http://www.nuclearsuppliersgroup.org/A_test/01-eng/10-docu.php>; and Nuclear Suppliers Group, 'NSG Fundamental List Review', June 2012, <http://www.nuclearsuppliersgroup.org/Leng/08-list.htm>.

[41] International Atomic Energy Agency, 'Communication received from the Permanent Mission of the United States of America to the International Atomic Energy Agency regarding certain member states' guidelines for the export of nuclear material, equipment and technology', INFCIRC 254/Rev.11/Part I, 12 Nov. 2012, para. 12.

[42] Nuclear Suppliers Group, 'NSG public statement', (note 40).

[43] Stratford, R., 'Nuclear Suppliers Group: Evolution, transformation and future outlook', 20th Asian Export Control Seminar, Tokyo, 26–28 Feb. 2013.

[44] Nuclear Suppliers Group, 'NSG public statement' (note 40).

[45] Nuclear Suppliers Group, 'NSG public statement' (note 40).

[46] Mexican Ministry of Foreign Affairs, 'Mexico formally enters the Nuclear Suppliers Group (NSG)', Press release, [n.d.], <http://www.sre.gob.mx/en/index.php?option=com_content&view=article&id=1740>.

[47] 'India seeks South Korean support for NSG bid', Zee News, 15 Sep. 2012, <http://zeenews.india.com/news/nation/india-seeks-south-korean-support-for-nsg-bid_766062.html>.

including Australia, Belgium, France, Russia and Ukraine—expressed support for India's membership in 2012.[48] Countries that have previously expressed support include the UK and the USA.[49] At the 2011 plenary, the US delegation circulated a 'food for thought' paper arguing against conditioning India's NSG membership on its accession to the 1968 Non-Proliferation Treaty (NPT).[50] However, while the paper was discussed further at the 2012 plenary, the group's public statement remained unchanged from that of the 2011 plenary, which noted continued consideration of Indian membership.[51] This suggests implications for cooperation with other countries suspected of having nuclear weapon programmes.

While the ongoing issue of China supplying two more reactors to Pakistan without asking for an NSG waiver was also discussed at the plenary, no progress seems to have been made.[52]

The Wassenaar Arrangement

While the Australia Group, the MTCR and the NSG focus on WMD and their delivery systems, the Wassenaar Arrangement promotes transparency and the exchange of information and views on transfers of conventional arms and related dual-use goods and technologies.[53] It encourages responsible behaviour and seeks to prevent 'destabilising accumulations' of such items.[54]

The December 2012 Wassenaar Arrangement plenary was held, as usual, in Vienna, Austria, with Germany as the chair. (Denmark became the new chair on 1 January 2013.) In preparation for the plenary, the General Working Group discussed policy matters; the Experts Group discussed control list-related issues; the annual Licensing and Enforcement Officers Meeting (LEOM) was held; and the ad hoc Group of Security and Intelligence

[48] Dikshit, S., 'India, Ukraine ink defence cooperation agreement', *The Hindu*, 10 Dec. 2012; 'Belgium backs India for NSG, seeks economic cooperation', SME Times, 9 Aug. 2012, <http://www.smetimes.in/smetimes/news/indian-economy-news/2012/Aug/09/belgium-backs-India-NSG-seeks-economic-cooperation74194.html>; Dhasmana, I., 'Russia supports India's membership in NSG', *Business Standard* (New Delhi), 21 June 2012; and 'Australia commits NSG support for India', *New York Daily News*, 3 May, 2012.

[49] Bauer (note 38).

[50] US State Department, 'United States communication—"food for thought" paper on Indian NSG membership', 23 May 2011, <http://www.armscontrol.org/system/files/nsg1130.pdf>. For a brief description and other details of the 1968 Treaty on the Non-Proliferation of Nuclear Weapons (Non-Proliferation Treaty, NPT) see annex A, section I, in this volume.

[51] Horner, D., 'NSG still mulling Indian membership', *Arms Control Today*, vol. 42, no. 6 (July/Aug. 2012).

[52] Dahl, F., 'West worried by China–Pakistan atomic ties: sources', Reuters, 27 July 2012; and Bauer (note 38).

[53] For a brief description of the Wassenaar Arrangement see annex B, section III, in this volume; and the Wassenaar Arrangement website, <http://www.wassenaar.org/>.

[54] Wassenaar Arrangement, 'Guidelines and procedures, including the initial elements', Dec. 2011, <http://www.wassenaar.org/guidelines/>.

Experts met. The plenary statement welcomed Philip Wallace Griffiths from New Zealand as the new head of the Wassenaar Secretariat. Sune Danielsson from Sweden had held this position for 10 years up until June 2012.[55]

As in 2011, the plenary agreed to continue outreach to non-member states, industry and other interested groups during 2013 through post-plenary briefings, interaction and bilateral dialogue with non-participating states, and to offer a technical briefing on recent control list changes to a number of non-participating states. The aim of the technical briefing is to promote the Wassenaar Arrangement and encourage voluntary adherence to its standards by non-participating states.[56] While regime outreach activities have in the past focused on generic presentations or obtaining countries' voluntary commitments to regime guidelines and principles, there have been some efforts to add more technical elements.

Mexico became the 41st Wassenaar Arrangement member in January 2012.[57] This was the first expansion of the group since South Africa joined in 1996. Applications from several other states are pending.

The Wassenaar Arrangement control list was amended in a number of areas including spacecraft and passive counter-surveillance equipment of mobile telecommunications.[58] As a result, the control list now covers transfers of off-the-air interception devices, such as international mobile subscriber identity (IMSI) catchers.[59] Controls for gas turbine engines and machine tools were relaxed, and the cryptography note was revised. Participating states decided to conduct a comprehensive and systematic review of the dual-use and munitions list.[60] They also agreed to 'make further use of the Regional Views exercise, implementing a rotating focus on geographic regions'.[61]

An updated version of the compilation of all Wassenaar Arrangement documents was made available in January 2013.[62]

[55] Wassenaar Arrangement, 'Wassenaar Arrangement public statement', Vienna, 11–12 Dec. 2012, <http://www.wassenaar.org/publicdocuments/index_PS_PS.html>.

[56] Wassenaar Arrangement (note 55).

[57] Wassenaar Arrangement (note 55); and US State Department, 'U.S congratulates Mexico on accession to Wassenaar Arrangement', Media note, PRN: 2012/122, 25 Jan. 2012, <http://www.state.gov/r/pa/prs/ps/2012/01/182499.htm>.

[58] On export controls for surveillance technology in the EU see section V below.

[59] On the types of technology involved see Privacy International, 'Surveillance Industry Index: Cobham', [n.d.], <https://www.privacyinternational.org/sii/cobham/>.

[60] Wassenaar Arrangement (note 55). On the agreed Experts Group amendments see Wassenaar Arrangement, 'Summary of changes, list of dual-use goods and technologies and munitions list', 12 Dec. 2012, <http://www.wassenaar.org/controllists/>.

[61] Wassenaar Arrangement (note 55).

[62] Wassenaar Arrangement, 'Basic documents: compilation', Jan. 2013, <http://www.wassenaar.org/publicdocuments/index_BD.html>.

V. Export control developments in the European Union

SIBYLLE BAUER AND MARK BROMLEY

During 2012 the ongoing review of the European Union (EU) Common Position defining common rules governing control of exports of military technology and equipment led to no major developments regarding EU-wide rules for the control of arms exports, brokering, trans-shipment and transit. However, EU member states moved ahead with the implementation of a new regulation governing intra-community trade in defence goods. The range of dual-use items subject to control was expanded in line with agreements in the multilateral control regimes, albeit with a substantial delay due to the new requirement to involve the European Parliament. The European Parliament's efforts to expand the coverage of EU controls on dual-use items to include transfers of surveillance technology formed part of a range of initiatives in this area in the wake of the events of the Arab Spring in 2011 and 2012. The European Parliament is thus emerging as a new actor shaping dual-use trade controls in the EU.

The review of the European Union's Common Position on arms exports

Since the early 1990s there have been ongoing efforts at the EU level to strengthen and harmonize member states' arms export policies.[1] The most important element of these efforts is the 2008 EU Common Position defining common rules governing control of exports of military technology and equipment.[2] Article 15 of the Common Position states that the instrument 'shall be reviewed three years after its adoption'. In mid-2011, the European External Action Service (EEAS)—as chair of the Council Working Group on Conventional Arms Exports (COARM), which oversees implementation of the Common Position—began preparations for the review. A questionnaire was distributed seeking EU member states' views on the potential scope and coverage of the review and substantive dis-

[1] See Bauer, S., 'The Europeanisation of arms export policies and its impact on democratic accountability', Doctoral thesis, Université libre de Bruxelles and Freie Universität Berlin, May 2003; and Bromley, M., *The Impact on Domestic Policy of the EU Code of Conduct on Arms Exports: The Czech Republic, the Netherlands and Spain*, SIPRI Policy Paper no. 21 (SIPRI: Stockholm, May 2008).

[2] Council of the European Union, Council Common Position 2008/944/CFSP of 8 Dec. 2008 defining common rules governing control of exports of military technology and equipment, *Official Journal of the European Union*, L335, 8 Dec. 2008. The 2008 Common Position superseded the 1998 Code of Conduct on Arms Exports. Council of the European Union, 'European Union Code of Conduct on Arms Exports', 8675/2/98 Rev. 2, 5 June 1998.

cussions on the topic took place in COARM throughout 2012.[3] Discussions were also held with the European Parliament, non-governmental organizations (NGOs) and defence industry representatives.[4]

The review took place against a background of widespread criticism by NGOs and parliamentarians concerning the implementation of EU arms export controls at the national level, largely due to revelations about transfers to states in the Middle East and North Africa prior to the Arab Spring uprisings.[5] However, in late 2012 the EU and its member states announced that the EU Common Position continued to 'properly serve the objectives set by the Council in 2008 and to provide a solid basis for the coordination of member states' arms export policies'.[6] This means the review will not result in any changes to the text of the Common Position itself. However, the EU also announced that 'further progress is achievable in the implementation of the Common Position and in ensuring maximum convergence among Member States in the field of exports of conventional arms'.[7] The EU and its member states have tasked themselves with updating, as appropriate, 'the User's Guide and EU Common Military List, notably in the light of the results of the review process of the Common Position'.[8] It is likely that several sections of the User's Guide—which provides guidance on the implementation of the Common Position—will be revised and updated, particularly those sections that deal with the implementation of the Common Position's eight criteria as well as the mechanisms for information exchange, denial notification and consultation.[9]

Implementation of the directive on intra-community transfers

During 2012, EU member states continued to transpose the directive on intra-community transfers of defence related products (ICT Directive) into

---

[3] Council of the European Union, 'Council conclusions on the review of Council Common Position 2008/944/CFSP defining common rules governing control of exports of military technology and equipment', 3199th Foreign Affairs Council Meeting, Brussels, 19 Nov. 2012.

[4] Council of the European Union (note 3).

[5] See e.g. A. Vranckx, F. Slijper and R. Isbister (eds), 'Lessons from MENA: appraising EU transfers of military and security equipment to the Middle East and North Africa', Academia Press, Nov. 2011, <http://www.saferworld.org.uk/smartweb/resources/view-resource/596>.

[6] Council of the European Union (note 3).

[7] Council of the European Union (note 3).

[8] Council of the European Union, Fourteenth Annual Report according to Article 8(2) of Council Common Position 2008/944/CFSP defining common rules governing control of exports of military technology and equipment, *Official Journal of the European Union*, C386, 14 Dec. 2012, p. 3.

[9] Council of the European Union (note 4); and EU official, Communication with author, 28 Jan. 2013. For the current version of the User's Guide see Council of the European Union, 'User's guide to Council Common Position 2008/944/CFSP defining common rules governing the control of exports of military technology and equipment', 9241/09, 29 Apr. 2009 <http://register.consilium.europa.eu/pdf/en/09/st09/st09241.en09.pdf>.

their national legislation on arms transfer controls.[10] The ICT Directive forms part of a wider package of EU efforts aimed at reducing barriers to intra-EU cooperation in the defence industry.[11] It requires EU member states to grant general or global licences that would allow their recipient to carry out certain intra-EU exports of defence-related products without needing additional authorizations. These exports could include transfers to the national armed forces of another member state, transfers that are part of a cooperative armament programme within the EU, or transfers to a 'certified company' in another member state. The process of certifying a company will be handled, in accordance with common criteria agreed at the EU level, by the national authorities of the member state where the company is headquartered.[12] The ICT Directive also abolishes require-ments for transit and trans-shipment licences for defence-related products originating in another EU member state (although reasons of public secur-ity can justify retaining such requirements).

EU member states were given until 30 June 2011 to transpose the directive and until 30 June 2012 to apply it.[13] As of June 2012, 20 states had officially notified the Commission of their transposition of the ICT Direct-ive into national legislation, indicating that 'timely transposition seemed to have been difficult for several Member States'.[14] The Commission has launched infringement proceedings against member states that have failed to communicate the national rules transposing the Directive.

Developments in dual-use trade controls

In 2011 the European Commission launched a green paper on reviewing the EU's trade controls on dual-use products, contained in the 2009 Dual-

---

[10] Directive 2009/43/EC of the European Parliament and of the Council of 6 May 2009 simplify-ing terms and conditions of transfers of defence-related products within the Community, *Official Journal of the European Union*, L146, 10 June 2009.

[11] Anthony, I. and Bauer, S., 'Controls on security-related international transfers', *SIPRI Yearbook 2009*, pp. 476–78.

[12] Commission Recommendation of 11 Jan. 2011 on the certification of defence undertakings under Article 9 of Directive 2009/43/EC of the European Parliament and of the Council simplifying terms and conditions of transfers of defence-related products within the Community, *Official Journal of the European Union*, L11, 15 Jan. 2011, pp. 62–74. Information about which companies have been certified at the national level is made available via the CERTIDER database maintained by the European Commission, <http://ec.europa.eu/enterprise/sectors/defence/certider/index.cfm>.

[13] European Commission, Directorate-General for Enterprise and Industry, 'Defence industries: reference documents', 2 Feb. 2012, <http://ec.europa.eu/enterprise/sectors/defence/documents/index_en.htm>.

[14] European Commission, Report from the Commission to the European Parliament and the Council on transposition of Directive 2009/43/EC simplifying terms and conditions for transfer of defence-related products within the EU, 29 June 2012, <http://eur-lex.europa.eu/LexUriServ/LexUriServ.do?uri=COM:2012:0359:FIN:EN:PDF>, p. 5.

use Regulation.[15] The paper was part of a public consultation process that aimed to initiate a discussion about how the EU's current dual-use trade control system functions. A wide range of submissions from civil society organizations, industry, academia and the governments of member states were summarized in a staff working document published in January 2013.[16] This document, in turn, is expected to form the basis of a document to be submitted to the European Parliament and the Council of the EU during 2013.[17]

The staff working document reflects the diversity of perspectives in the submissions, which covered a broad range of issues including challenges related to the practical implementation of the new transit and brokering controls; the uniform implementation of catch-all controls across the EU; and the appropriateness of activities and items subject to control in the current trade, political and technological environment. A Swedish Government report stated that the 'result of the joint consultation will ... contribute to identifying strengths and weaknesses in the current system and to map out a long-term vision of the EU's export control framework'. According to the report, 'the ambition is that the results will contribute to concrete changes in the current system and to the preparation of a long-term strategy for developing the EU's export controls'.[18]

In April 2012 the EU amended its control list for dual-use items, which is an annex to the Dual-use Regulation.[19] Changes routinely add, remove or

[15] European Commission, 'The dual-use export control system of the European Union: ensuring security and competitiveness in a changing world', Green Paper COM(2011) 393, 30 June 2011. EU Regulation 428/2009 regulating the export, brokering and transit of dual-use items, including software and technology, entered into force on 27 Aug. 2009. The law substantially expanded the scope of dual-use trade activities subject to control, in line with the requirements of UN Security Council Resolution 1540 regarding brokering, transit and trans-shipment controls. Council Regulation (EC) no. 428/2009 of 5 May 2009 setting up a Community regime for the control of exports, transfer, brokering and transit of dual-use items, *Official Journal of the European Union*, L134, 29 May 2009. This regulation updates and expands previous EU-wide control provisions for dual-use items, the first of which go back as far as 1995. Anthony, I. et al., 'Multilateral weapon-related export control measures', *SIPRI Yearbook 1995*, pp. 616–19.

[16] European Commission, 'Strategic export controls: enduring security and competiveness in a changing world. A report on the public consultation launched under the Green Paper COM(2011) 393', European Commission staff working document, SWD(2013) 7 final, Brussels, 17 Jan. 2013, <http://trade.ec.europa.eu/doclib/docs/2013/february/tradoc_150459.pdf>.

[17] Some of the organizations consulted made their submissions public. See e.g. British Department for Business Innovation and Skills, Export Control Organisation, 'Response from Her Majesty's Government to the European Commission Green Paper on the dual-use export control system of the European Union', Jan. 2012, <http://www.bis.gov.uk/assets/biscore/eco/docs/12-509-eco-response-eu-green-paper-dual-use.pdf>.

[18] Swedish Government, 'Strategic export controls in 2011: military equipment and dual-use products', Skr. 2011/12:114, 15 Mar. 2011, <http://www.isp.se/sa/node.asp?node=528>, p. 48.

[19] Regulation (EU) no. 388/2012 of the European Parliament and of the Council of 19 Apr. 2012 amending Council Regulation (EC) no. 428/2009 of 5 May 2009 setting up a Community regime for the control of exports, transfer, brokering and transit of dual-use items, *Official Journal of the European Union*, L129, 16 May 2012; and British Export Control Organisation, 'Annex 1: Comprehensive change note summary for Council Regulation (EU) no. 428/2009', 25 May 2012, <http://trade.ec.europa.eu/doclib/docs/2012/may/tradoc_149517.pdf>.

reduce controls on certain items, and revise definitions and descriptions in the control list. The most recent control list amendments (approximately 250 in total) entered into force on 15 June 2012, bringing the EU list in line with changes agreed in the Australia Group, the Missile Technology Control Regime (MTCR), the Nuclear Suppliers Group (NSG) and the Wassenaar Arrangement during 2010. The implementation of multilaterally agreed changes always takes time due to technical consultations and translation processes. In addition, for practical reasons, while changes are made on an annual basis they are agreed at different points in the year depending on the regime.

Parliaments are not normally involved in control list changes, which are generally of a technical nature and, in many cases, implement international obligations taken on by governments. The unusually long delay in the implementation of the 2010 changes was due to the adoption of the 2007 Lisbon Treaty, which gave the European Parliament a co-decision right in the Dual-use Regulation.[20] The delay is significant because such changes must be made swiftly in order to keep up with technological developments and evolving procurement methods. The implications of the delayed update of the EU list are compounded by the fact that an increasing number of European countries outside the EU and countries in other regions, particularly Asia, base their control list updates on the EU changes, since the EU list simply consolidates and structures the various international regime requirements.[21]

To help prevent such delays in the future, in late 2011 the European Commission presented a proposal for changes in the EU Dual-use Regulation that would empower it to update Annex I in line with control list amendments adopted by the four regimes. The proposal would also have allowed the Commission to swiftly exclude specific destinations or products from the scope of the EU's general export licences.[22] The Commission would therefore be empowered to adopt delegated acts, as foreseen in the Lisbon

---

[20] Treaty of Lisbon amending the Treaty on European Union and the Treaty establishing the European Community, signed 13 Dec. 2007, entered into force 1 Dec. 2009, <http://europa.eu/lisbon_treaty/>.

[21] Countries that use the same control list structure as the EU include the accession and potential accession countries in South Eastern Europe—Albania, Bosnia and Herzegovina, Croatia, FYR Macedonia, Montenegro and Serbia—as well as countries in Asia including Singapore and Malaysia. See e.g. Singapore Customs, 'Strategic Goods Control List: overview', 28 Feb. 2013, <http://www.customs.gov.sg/stgc/leftNav/str/>; and Malaysian Government, Ministry of International Trade and Industry, 'Strategic Trade Act 2010', [n.d.], <http://www.miti.gov.my/cmspreview/content.jsp?id=com.tms.cms.article.Article_a84fac8e-c0a81573-f5a0f5a0-57df60c6>. For more information see Holtom, P. and Mićić, I., 'European Union arms export control outreach activities in Eastern and South Eastern Europe', Non-proliferation Papers no. 14, EU Non-proliferation Consortium, Apr. 2012, <http://nonproliferation.eu/activities/activities.php>.

[22] European Commission, Proposal for a regulation of the European Parliament and of the Council amending Regulation (EC) no. 428/2009 setting up a Community Regime for the control of exports, transfer, brokering and transit of dual use items, COM(2011) 704 final, 7 Nov. 2011.

Treaty.[23] At its plenary session of 23 October 2012, the European Parliament adopted its position on the Commission's proposal. The Parliament proposed amendments that would (a) provide for delegated powers in those areas for tacitly extendable five-year periods and (b) require the Commission to provide 'full information and documentation on its meetings with national experts within the framework of its work on the preparation and implementation of delegated acts'.[24]

The European Parliament also proposed other amendments to the Commission's proposal, in relation to surveillance and interception technology (see below) and the so-called catch-all provision. The catch-all provision, or end-use control mechanism, allows the competent EU member state authorities to impose an authorization requirement if items are or may be intended for end-use in a weapon of mass destruction (WMD) programme, or in relation to a listed conventional military item in a destination subject to an arms embargo. However, other member states do not have to follow suit, even when informed. This had previously resulted in the creation of different authorization requirements within the EU's common market for dual-use items. The Parliament's proposal, therefore, would oblige all EU member states to 'impose the same authorisation requirement' if one member state decides to apply a catch-all control to a certain unlisted item.[25]

A proposal to create five new EU general export authorizations (GAEs) was agreed by the European Parliament and the Council at the end of 2011 and entered into force in January 2012. These GAEs provide for some facilitation of the export of certain dual-use items to certain destinations; export after repair or replacement; temporary export for an exhibition or fair; exports of telecommunications systems; and exports of chemicals. For certain specified items and destinations, no individual export licence is required from the EU.[26]

In terms of implementation efforts, a database of notifications of export licence application denials and catch-all decisions by member states was launched in 2011.[27] The database is available to authorized enforcement officers and licensing officers.

---

[23] Treaty of Lisbon (note 20), Article 290.

[24] European Parliament, European Parliament legislative resolution of 23 Oct. 2012 on the proposal for a regulation of the European Parliament and of the Council amending Regulation (EC) no. 428/2009 setting up a Community regime for the control of exports, transfer, brokering and transit of dual-use items (COM(2011)0704–C7-0395/2011–2011/0310 (COD)), Strasbourg, 23 Oct. 2012.

[25] European Parliament (note 24), amendment 12.

[26] Regulation no. 1232/2011 of the European Parliament and of the Council of 16 Nov. 2011 amending Regulation (EC) no. 428/2009 setting up a Community regime for the control of exports, transfer, brokering and transit of dual-use items, *Official Journal of the European Union*, L326, 8 Dec. 2011.

[27] Swedish Government (note 18).

Controls on transfers of surveillance technology

During 2011, companies based in the EU (as well as companies based in other parts of Europe and North America) were revealed to have been involved in the supply of security, surveillance and censorship technologies and services to states in the Middle East and North Africa.[28] In many cases, these technologies were used by national security forces in the commission of violations of international human rights law. Existing EU and Wassenaar Arrangement strategic trade control lists do not cover many of the technologies involved, which include systems for monitoring or censoring Internet activity or mobile phone-based communications. During 2011 and 2012 the EU explored ways in which existing systems for controlling transfers of strategic goods could be expanded to encompass and control these items. The issue was also raised and discussed within the Wassenaar Arrangement (see section IV above). Several European governments— including the United Kingdom—have explored the issue of how to exert control in this area through the implementation of existing national laws and regulations.[29] There have also been attempts to exert stronger controls on the export of surveillance technologies through the development of improved industry standards, such as via the US-based Global Network Initiative (GNI).[30]

In late 2011 and early 2012, the EU arms embargoes on Iran and Syria (see section II above) were both updated to include prohibitions on the sale of surveillance technologies. In December 2011, the EU embargo on Syria was updated to include a ban on the 'sale, supply, transfer or export of equipment or software intended primarily for use in the monitoring or interception by the Syrian regime, or on its behalf, of the Internet and of telephone communications on mobile or fixed networks', as well as the provision of associated services.[31] In March 2012 equivalent language was inserted into the EU embargo on Iran.[32] The EU also specified the list of

---

[28] Grey, S., 'UK firm denies "cyber-spy" deal with Egypt', BBC News, 20 Sep. 2011, <http://www.bbc.co.uk/news/technology-14981672>; Elgin, B. and Silver, V., 'Syria crackdown gets Italy firm's aid with U.S.–Europe spy gear', Bloomberg, 4 Nov. 2011, <http://www.bloomberg.com/news/2011-11-03/syria-crackdown-gets-italy-firm-s-aid-with-u-s-europe-spy-gear.html>; Elgin, B. and Silver, V., 'The surveillance market and its victims', Bloomberg, 20 Dec. 2011, <http://www.bloomberg.com/data-visualization/wired-for-repression/>; and Wagner, B., 'Exporting censorship and surveillance technology', Humanist Institute for Co-operation with Developing Countries (Hivos), Jan. 2012, <http://www.academia.edu/2133607/Exporting_Censorship_and_Surveillance_Technology#>, p. 7. See also Bromley, M. and Wezeman, P. D., 'Policies on exports of arms to states affected by the Arab Spring', *SIPRI Yearbook 2012*.

[29] Topping, A., 'Customs urged to investigate UK spyware firm', *The Guardian*, 26 Dec. 2012.

[30] For more detail see the GNI website, <http://www.globalnetworkinitiative.org>.

[31] Council Decision 2011/782/CFSP of 1 Dec. 2011 concerning restrictive measures against Syria and repealing Decision 2011/273/CFSP, *Official Journal of the European Union*, 2 Dec. 2012.

[32] Council Decision 2012/168/CFSP of 23 March 2012 amending Decision 2011/235/CFSP concerning restrictive measures directed against certain persons and entities in view of the situation in Iran, *Official Journal of the European Union*, 24 Mar. 2012, p. 85.

technologies covered by the expanded embargoes on Iran and Syria, including deep packet inspection equipment, semantic processing engine equipment, speaker recognition or processing equipment, pattern recognition and pattern profiling equipment, semantic processing engine equipment, and wired equivalent privacy (WEP) and Wi-Fi protected access (WPA) code-breaking equipment.[33] This language represented the first time that the EU has specified the types of surveillance technology that are of concern with regard to potential violations of international human rights law.

The EU has also investigated ways of extending controls on transfers of surveillance technologies to countries that are not subject to EU arms embargoes, particularly through the expansion of controls on transfers of dual-use items. In May 2012 the European Parliament adopted a non-legislative resolution deploring 'the role of European companies in the exporting of arms and dual-use items to repressive regimes, and in complying with technological disruptions organised by the dictatorships'. The resolution called on the European Commission to 'produce guidelines for EU companies to act in a manner consistent with the Union's fundamental principles in such situations'.[34] In October 2012 the European Parliament included relevant language in its list of proposed amendments to the European Commission proposal to amend the 2009 Dual-use Regulation. Specifically, the Parliament proposed the inclusion of a requirement for authorization of exports of unlisted dual-use items if the exporter has been informed by either its national authorities or the Commission that the items may be used in connection with violations of human rights, democratic principles or freedom of speech through the use of 'interception technologies and digital data transfer devices for monitoring mobile phones and text messages and targeted surveillance of internet use'.[35] If this wording were included (which is unlikely, due to competence issues and the division of responsibilities) the amendment would potentially increase the involvement of the Commission in the implementation of controls on transfers of dual-use items by giving it the right to

---

[33] Council Regulation (EU) no. 36/2012 of 18 Jan. 2012 concerning restrictive measures in view of the situation in Syria and repealing Regulation (EU) no. 442/2011, *Official Journal of the European Union*, L16, 19 Jan. 2012, Annex V; and Council Regulation (EU) no. 264/2012 of 23 Mar. 2012 amending Regulation (EU) no. 359/2011 concerning restrictive measures directed against certain persons, entities and bodies in view of the situation in Iran, *Official Journal of the European Union*, L87, 3 Mar. 2012, Annex IV.

[34] European Parliament, 'Trade for change: the EU Trade and Investment Strategy for the Southern Mediterranean following the Arab Spring revolutions (2011/2113(INI))', Resolution, 10 May 2012, <http://www.europarl.europa.eu/sides/getDoc.do?pubRef=-//EP//TEXT+TA+P7-TA-2012-0201+0+DOC+XML+V0//EN>.

[35] European Parliament, Legislative resolution on the proposal for a regulation of the European Parliament and of the Council amending Regulation (EC) no. 428/2009 setting up a Community regime for the control of exports, transfer, brokering and transit of dual-use items (COM(2011)0704 – C7-0395/2011 – 2011/0310(COD)), 23 Oct. 2012.

directly inform exporters of the need for an authorization. A similar legal catch-all construction is already in place for dual-use items with a WMD end-use or a conventional military use in connection with listed items in an embargoed destination. However, the Commission has no information role in those instances.

European Union cooperation programmes on dual-use and arms trade control

A number of actors have been involved in the development of cooperative measures to establish and strengthen systems to control cross-border flows of arms and dual-use items. These cooperative measures initially focused on export controls but now also encompass associated activities of transit, trans-shipment, brokering and financing. The major dedicated programmes with international scope are the EU-funded Cooperation in Export Control of Dual-use Goods programme and the US Department of State's Export Control and Related Border Security (EXBS) programme, as well as complementary programmes funded by other US Government agencies, such as the Department of Energy.[36] While the US programme is larger, the EU programme now involves countries in Africa, Asia and the Middle East as well as Europe.[37] Due to the internal division of competences, the EU's dual-use and arms trade control programmes are funded by different financial instruments.

During the 1990s the EU provided technical assistance on chemical, biological, radiological and nuclear (CBRN) issues such as detecting the trafficking of nuclear materials.[38] However, such assistance was ad hoc and primarily focused on the former Soviet Union. Furthermore, it was not underpinned by a common strategy and did not focus on establishing dual-use export control systems. Before 2005 certain EU member states also provided bilateral export control cooperation that was limited in scope. In 2004–2005 the realization grew in EU circles that export control was one area where EU funding could support the implementation of the 2003 EU

---

[36] German Office of Economics and Export Control (BAFA), 'EU cooperation in dual-use export control', [n.d.], <http://www.eu-outreach.info/eu_outreach/>; US Department of State, Export Control and Related Border Security (EXBS) programme, 'The EXBS Program', <http://www.state. gov/t/isn/ecc/c27911.htm>; and US Department of Energy, National Nuclear Security Administration, 'Second Line of Defence Program', <http://nnsa.energy.gov/aboutus/ourprograms/non proliferation/programoffices/internationalmaterialprotectionandcooperation/se>.

[37] A number of other states, including Japan and to a lesser extent Australia, focus on WMD-related trade control capacity building at the regional level. See Bauer, S., 'Enhancing export control-related CTR (cooperative threat reduction) programmes: options for the EU', Background Paper no. 6, Conference on Strengthening European Action on WMD Non-proliferation and Disarmament, Brussels, 7–8 Dec. 2005; and Bauer, S., 'Arms trade control capacity building: lessons from dual-use trade controls', SIPRI Insights on Peace and Security no. 2013/2, Mar. 2013, <http://books.sipri.org/ product_info?c_product_id=454>.

[38] Bauer, 'Enhancing export control-related CTR programmes' (note 37).

Strategy against the Proliferation of WMD, and United Nations Security Council Resolution 1540.[39] In 2006 the EU created the Instrument for Stability (IFS) to respond to global issues, including the threats outlined in the WMD Strategy, by providing financial support for capacity-building measures in non-EU countries.[40]

The IFS allocated about €13 million ($17.8 million) to dual-use export control capacity building for the period 2007–13.[41] The EU Cooperation in Export Control of Dual-use Goods programme is implemented by the German Federal Office of Economics and Export Control (Bundesamt für Wirtschaft und Ausfuhrkontrolle, BAFA), with a pool of legal, licensing, industry outreach and enforcement practitioners drawn from across the EU.[42] While substantial technical assistance on CBRN issues has also been provided by EU member states, in particular Germany and the UK, capacity building in the area of strategic trade controls has been delivered almost exclusively within the EU programmes. The programmes evolved from an export control component of an EU pilot project on cooperative threat reduction and two pilot projects specifically dedicated to technical assistance on dual-use export controls. While only 4 countries were involved in the first pilot project in 2005, the geographical scope of the long-term programme has since expanded to include nearly 30 countries. The EU programme conducts activities across five specific pillars: legal, awareness of industry and other stakeholders, licensing, the role of customs, and investigation and prosecution of export control-related offences.[43]

During 2010 the EU began to broaden the substantial, geographical and financial scope of its CBRN- and proliferation-related cooperation programmes. The EU CBRN Risk Mitigation Centres of Excellence (CBRN

[39] Council of the European Union, 'Fight against the proliferation of weapons of mass destruction: EU Strategy against Proliferation of Weapons of Mass Destruction', 15708/03, 10 Dec. 2003, <http://europa.eu/legislation_summaries/foreign_and_security_policy/cfsp_and_esdp_implementati on/l33234_en.htm>; and UN Security Council Resolution 1540, 15 Apr. 2004.

[40] Council Regulation (EC) no. 1717/2006 of the European Parliament and of the Council of 15 Nov. 2006 establishing an Instrument for Stability, *Official Journal of the European Union*, L327, 24 Nov. 2006; and European Commission, 'Instrument for Stability', <http://ec.europa.eu/europe aid/how/finance/ifs_en.htm>.

[41] The total IFS budget is approximately €2.1 billion ($2.8 billion) and includes funding for crisis management, conflict prevention and disaster response. The IFS has assigned €320 million ($438 million) for non-proliferation and chemical, biological, radiological and nuclear (CBRN) risk-mitigation activities for the period 2007–13.

[42] German Office of Economics and Export Control (note 36).

[43] The 1st pilot project (led by SIPRI) contained a field validation exercise designed to explore ways to deliver effective export control assistance. The 2nd and 3rd (led by BAFA and implemented in cooperation with SIPRI) were dedicated to expanding and developing this work. BAFA also implemented a European Commission export control cooperation programme with Russia. See German Office of Economics and Export Control (note 36); and SIPRI Dual-use and Arms Trade Control, 'Current projects', <http://www.sipri.org/research/disarmament/dualuse/capacity-build ing/current>.

COEs) are funded through the IFS budget.[44] Programmes are now carried out in North Africa; the 'African Atlantic façade'; the Middle East; South Eastern Europe, the Southern Caucasus, Moldova and Ukraine; and South East Asia.[45] The CBRN COE initiative aims to build on and expand regional expertise on CBRN issues, complemented by expertise from the EU, other regions, and regional and international organizations. Partner countries and regions can propose the scope, type and issue area of EU-funded projects implemented through this conceptual and financial framework. The COE concept seeks to expand the discussion and action on CBRN issues beyond WMD and export control to include issues such as 'criminal (proliferation, theft, sabotage and illicit trafficking), accidental (industrial catastrophes, in particular chemical or nuclear, waste treatment and transport) or natural (mainly pandemics)'.[46]

Limited funding is currently provided for complementary EU capacity-building activities in the conventional arms transfers area, although an expansion of activities is foreseen from 2013.[47] In November 2012 the Council adopted a Decision in support of continued EU activities to promote the control of conventional arms exports and the principles and criteria of the EU Common Position on arms exports outside the EU.[48] The 2012 Decision will fund regional seminars in South Eastern Europe, North Africa, Eastern Europe and the Caucasus during 2013 and 2014 to support licensing and enforcement officials in the effective control of exports of military technology and equipment. The initiative will also support staff exchanges between partner countries in these regions and export control

[44] On the EU CBRN Risk Mitigation Centres of Excellence initiative see the CBRN COE website, <http://www.cbrn-coe.eu/>. The estimated budget for the CBRN COEs in 2007–13 is €95 million ($130 million). UN Interregional Crime and Justice Research Institute, 'CBRN Risk Mitigation and Security Governance Programme: CBRN Centres of Excellence', [n.d.], <http://www.unicri.it/topics/cbrn/coe/>.

[45] The COE African Atlantic façade region potentially includes Benin, Gabon, Guinea, Côte d'Ivoire, Liberia, Mauritania, Morocco and Senegal.

[46] EU CBRN Risk Mitigation Centres of Excellence initiative, 'A coordinated strategy for CBRN risk mitigation', [n.d.], <http://www.cbrn-coe.eu/ReadMore.aspx>.

[47] Holtom, P. and Bromley, M., 'Implementing an arms trade treaty: mapping assistance to strengthen arms transfer controls', SIPRI Insights on Peace and Security no. 2012/2, July 2012, <http://books.sipri.org/product_info?c_product_id=447>; and Council Decision 2012/711/CFSP of 19 Nov. 2012 on support for Union activities in order to promote, among third countries, the control of arms exports and the principles and criteria of Common Position 2008/944/CFSP, *Official Journal of the European Union*, L321, 20 Nov. 2012.

[48] Council Decision 2012/711/CFSP provides €1.86 million ($2.4 million) for 24 months (2013–14) and follows on from 2 previous Council decisions: 1 in Dec. 2009 providing €787 000 ($1.1 million) for conventional outreach initiatives for 2010–11, and a 2nd in Mar. 2008 providing €500 500 ($733 000) towards conventional outreach initiatives for 2008–2009. Council Decision 2009/1012/CFSP of 22 Dec. 2009 on support for EU activities in order to promote the control of arms exports and the principles and criteria of Common Position 2008/944/CFSP among third countries, *Official Journal of the European Union*, L348, 29 Dec. 2009, pp. 16–20; and Council Joint Action 2008/230/CFSP of 17 Mar. 2008 on support for EU activities in order to promote the control of arms exports and the principles and criteria of the EU Code of Conduct on arms exports among third countries, *Official Journal of the European Union*, L75, 18 Mar. 2008, pp. 81–85.

authorities in EU member states and the drafting, implementation and enforcement of legislation. In contrast to previous Council decisions, the 2012 Decision also introduced two new activities: individual country assistance and the development of a web portal for access to technical resources and information. The two-year project will be implemented by BAFA, which is the implementing agent for EU-funded capacity-building programmes for export control of dual-use items and conventional arms.[49]

---

[49] Holtom and Mićić (note 21).

Annexes

Annex A. Arms control and disarmament agreements

Annex B. International security cooperation bodies

Annex C. Chronology 2012

Annex A. Arms control and disarmament agreements

NENNE BODELL

This annex lists multi- and bilateral treaties, conventions, protocols and agreements relating to arms control and disarmament. Unless otherwise stated, the status of agreements and of their parties and signatories is as of 1 January 2013.

Notes

1. The agreements are divided into universal treaties (i.e. multilateral treaties open to all states; section I), regional treaties (i.e. multilateral treaties open to states of a particular region; section II) and bilateral treaties (section III). Within each section, the agreements are listed in the order of the date on which they were adopted, signed or opened for signature (multilateral agreements) or signed (bilateral agreements). The date on which they entered into force and the depositary for multilateral treaties are also given.

2. The main source of information is the lists of signatories and parties provided by the depositaries of the treaties. In lists of parties and signatories, states whose name appears in italics ratified, acceded or succeeded to, or signed the agreement during 2012.

3. States and organizations listed as parties have ratified, acceded to or succeeded to the agreements. Former non-self-governing territories, upon attaining statehood, sometimes make general statements of continuity to all agreements concluded by the former governing power. This annex lists as parties only those new states that have made an uncontested declaration on continuity or have notified the depositary of their succession. The Russian Federation continues the international obligations of the Soviet Union. Serbia continues the international obligations of the State Union of Serbia and Montenegro.

4. Unless stated otherwise, the multilateral agreements listed in this annex are open to all states or to all states in the respective zone (or region) for signature, ratification, accession or succession. Not all the signatories and parties are United Nations members. Taiwan, while not recognized as a sovereign state by many countries, is listed as a party to the agreements that it has ratified.

5. Where possible, the location (in a printed publication or online) of an accurate copy of the treaty text is given. This may be provided by a treaty depositary, an agency or secretariat connected with the treaty, or in the *United Nations Treaty Series* (available online at <http://treaties.un.org/>).

I. Universal treaties

Protocol for the Prohibition of the Use in War of Asphyxiating, Poisonous or Other Gases, and of Bacteriological Methods of Warfare (1925 Geneva Protocol)

Signed at Geneva on 17 June 1925; entered into force on 8 February 1928; depositary French Government

The protocol prohibits the use in war of asphyxiating, poisonous or other gases and of bacteriological methods of warfare. The protocol remains a fundamental basis of the international prohibition against chemical and biological warfare, and its principles, objectives and obligations are explicitly supported by the 1972 Biological and Toxin Weapons Convention and the 1993 Chemical Weapons Convention.

Parties (139): Afghanistan, Albania, Algeria, Angola, Antigua and Barbuda, Argentina, Australia, Austria, Bahrain, Bangladesh, Barbados, Belgium, Benin, Bhutan, Bolivia, Brazil, Bulgaria, Burkina Faso, Cambodia, Cameroon, Canada, Cape Verde, Central African Republic, Chile, China, Costa Rica, Côte d'Ivoire, Croatia, Cuba, Cyprus, Czech Republic, Denmark, Dominican Republic, Ecuador, Egypt, El Salvador, Equatorial Guinea, Estonia, Ethiopia, Fiji, Finland, France, Gambia, Germany, Ghana, Greece, Grenada, Guatemala, Guinea-Bissau, Holy See, Hungary, Iceland, India, Indonesia, Iran, Iraq, Ireland, Israel, Italy, Jamaica, Japan, Jordan, Kenya, Korea (North), Korea (South), Kuwait, Laos, Latvia, Lebanon, Lesotho, Liberia, Libya, Liechtenstein, Lithuania, Luxembourg, Madagascar, Malawi, Malaysia, Maldives, Malta, Mauritius, Mexico, Moldova, Monaco, Mongolia, Morocco, Nepal, Netherlands, New Zealand, Nicaragua, Niger, Nigeria, Norway, Pakistan, Panama, Papua New Guinea, Paraguay, Peru, Philippines, Poland, Portugal, Qatar, Romania, Russia, Rwanda, Saint Kitts and Nevis, Saint Lucia, Saint Vincent and the Grenadines, Saudi Arabia, Senegal, Serbia, Sierra Leone, Slovakia, Slovenia, Solomon Islands, South Africa, Spain, Sri Lanka, Sudan, Swaziland, Sweden, Switzerland, Syria, Taiwan, Tanzania, Thailand, Togo, Tonga, Trinidad and Tobago, Tunisia, Turkey, Uganda, UK, Ukraine, Uruguay, USA, Venezuela, Viet Nam, Yemen

Note: On joining the protocol, some states entered reservations which upheld their right to employ chemical or biological weapons against non-parties to the protocol, against coalitions which included non-parties or in response to the use of these weapons by a violating party. Many of these states have withdrawn these reservations, particularly after the conclusion of the 1972 Biological and Toxin Weapons Convention and the 1993 Chemical Weapons Convention since the reservations are incompatible with their obligation under the conventions.

In addition to these, 'explicit', reservations, a number of states that made a declaration of succession to the protocol on gaining independence inherited 'implicit' reservations from their respective predecessor states. For example, these implicit reservations apply to the states that gained independence from France and the UK before the latter states withdrew or amended their reservations. States that acceded (rather than succeeded) to the protocol did not inherit reservations in this way.

Protocol text: French Ministry of Foreign Affairs, <http://www.diplomatie.gouv.fr/traites/affichetraite.do?accord=TRA19250001>

Convention on the Prevention and Punishment of the Crime of Genocide (Genocide Convention)

Adopted at Paris by the UN General Assembly on 9 December 1948; entered into force on 12 January 1951; depositary UN Secretary-General

Under the convention any commission of acts intended to destroy, in whole or in part, a national, ethnic, racial or religious group as such is declared to be a crime punishable under international law.

Parties (142): Afghanistan, Albania*, Algeria*, Andorra, Antigua and Barbuda, Argentina*, Armenia, Australia, Austria, Azerbaijan, Bahamas, Bahrain*, Bangladesh*, Barbados, Belarus*, Belgium, Belize, Bolivia, Bosnia and Herzegovina, Brazil, Bulgaria*, Burkina Faso, Burundi, Cambodia, Canada, *Cape Verde*, Chile, China*, Colombia, Comoros, Congo (Democratic Republic of the), Costa Rica, Côte d'Ivoire, Croatia, Cuba, Cyprus, Czech Republic, Denmark, Ecuador, Egypt, El Salvador, Estonia, Ethiopia, Fiji, Finland, France, Gabon, Gambia, Georgia, Germany, Ghana, Greece, Guatemala, Guinea, Haiti, Honduras, Hungary*, Iceland, India*, Iran, Iraq, Ireland, Israel, Italy, Jamaica, Jordan, Kazakhstan, Korea (North), Korea (South), Kuwait, Kyrgyzstan, Laos, Latvia, Lebanon, Lesotho, Liberia, Libya, Liechtenstein, Lithuania, Luxembourg, Macedonia (Former Yugoslav Republic of), Malaysia*, Maldives, Mali, Mexico, Moldova, Monaco, Mongolia*, Montenegro*, Morocco*, Mozambique, Myanmar*, Namibia, Nepal, Netherlands, New Zealand, Nicaragua, Nigeria, Norway, Pakistan, Panama, Papua New Guinea, Paraguay, Peru, Philippines*, Poland*, Portugal*, Romania*, Russia*, Rwanda*, Saint Vincent and the Grenadines, Saudi Arabia, Senegal, Serbia*, Seychelles, Singapore*, Slovakia, Slovenia, South Africa, Spain*, Sri Lanka, Sudan, Sweden, Switzerland, Syria, Tanzania, Togo, Tonga, Trinidad and Tobago, Tunisia, Turkey, Uganda, UK, Ukraine*, United Arab Emirates, Uruguay, USA*, Uzbekistan, Venezuela*, Viet Nam*, Yemen*, Zimbabwe

* With reservation and/or declaration.

Signed but not ratified (1): Dominican Republic

Convention text: United Nations Treaty Collection, <http://treaties.un.org/Pages/CTCTreaties. aspx?id=4>

Geneva Convention (IV) Relative to the Protection of Civilian Persons in Time of War

Signed at Geneva on 12 August 1949; entered into force on 21 October 1950; depositary Swiss Federal Council

The Geneva Convention (IV) establishes rules for the protection of civilians in areas covered by war and in occupied territories. This convention was formulated at the diplomatic conference held from 21 April to 12 August 1949. Other conventions adopted at the same time were: Convention (I) for the Amelioration of the Condition of the Wounded and Sick in Armed Forces in the Field; Convention (II) for the Amelioration of the Condition of the Wounded, Sick and Shipwrecked Members of Armed Forces at Sea; and Convention (III) Relative to the Treatment of Prisoners of War.

Parties (194): Afghanistan, Albania*, Algeria, Andorra, Angola*, Antigua and Barbuda, Argentina, Armenia, Australia*, Austria, Azerbaijan, Bahamas, Bahrain, Bangladesh*, Barbados*, Belarus, Belgium, Belize, Benin, Bhutan, Bolivia, Bosnia and Herzegovina, Botswana, Brazil, Brunei Darussalam, Bulgaria, Burkina Faso, Burundi, Cambodia, Cameroon,

Canada, Cape Verde, Central African Republic, Chad, Chile, China*, Colombia, Comoros, Congo (Democratic Republic of the), Congo (Republic of the), Cook Islands, Costa Rica, Côte d'Ivoire, Croatia, Cuba, Cyprus, Czech Republic*, Denmark, Djibouti, Dominica, Dominican Republic, Ecuador, Egypt, El Salvador, Equatorial Guinea, Estonia, Eritrea, Ethiopia, Fiji, Finland, France, Gabon, Gambia, Georgia, Germany*, Ghana, Greece, Grenada, Guatemala, Guinea, Guinea-Bissau*, Guyana, Haiti, Holy See, Honduras, Hungary, Iceland, India, Indonesia, Iran*, Iraq, Ireland, Israel*, Italy, Jamaica, Japan, Jordan, Kazakhstan, Kenya, Kiribati, Korea (North)*, Korea (South)*, Kuwait*, Kyrgyzstan, Laos, Latvia, Lebanon, Lesotho, Liberia, Libya, Liechtenstein, Lithuania, Luxembourg, Macedonia (Former Yugoslav Republic of)*, Madagascar, Malawi, Malaysia, Maldives, Mali, Malta, Marshall Islands, Mauritania, Mauritius, Mexico, Micronesia, Moldova, Monaco, Mongolia, Montenegro, Morocco, Mozambique, Myanmar, Namibia, Nauru, Nepal, Netherlands, New Zealand*, Nicaragua, Niger, Nigeria, Norway, Oman, Pakistan*, Palau, Panama, Papua New Guinea, Paraguay, Peru, Philippines, Poland, Portugal*, Qatar, Romania, Russia*, Rwanda, Saint Kitts and Nevis, Saint Lucia, Saint Vincent and the Grenadines, Samoa, San Marino, Sao Tome and Principe, Saudi Arabia, Senegal, Serbia, Seychelles, Sierra Leone, Singapore, Slovakia, Slovenia, Solomon Islands, Somalia, South Africa, Spain, Sri Lanka, Sudan, Suriname*, Swaziland, Sweden, Switzerland, Syria, Tajikistan, Tanzania, Thailand, Timor-Leste, Togo, Tonga, Trinidad and Tobago, Tunisia, Turkey, Turkmenistan, Tuvalu, Uganda, UK*, Ukraine*, United Arab Emirates, Uruguay*, USA*, Uzbekistan, Vanuatu, Venezuela, Viet Nam*, Yemen*, Zambia, Zimbabwe

* With reservation and/or declaration.

Note: In 1989 the Palestine Liberation Organization (PLO) informed the depositary that it had decided to adhere to the four Geneva conventions and the protocols of 1977.

Convention text: Swiss Federal Department of Foreign Affairs, <http://www.eda.admin.ch/eda/fr/home/topics/intla/intrea/chdep/warvic/gvaciv.html>

Protocol I Additional to the 1949 Geneva Conventions, and Relating to the Protection of Victims of International Armed Conflicts

Protocol II Additional to the 1949 Geneva Conventions, and Relating to the Protection of Victims of Non-International Armed Conflicts

Opened for signature at Bern on 12 December 1977; entered into force on 7 December 1978; depositary Swiss Federal Council

The protocols confirm that the right of parties that are engaged in international or non-international armed conflicts to choose methods or means of warfare is not unlimited and that the use of weapons or means of warfare that cause superfluous injury or unnecessary suffering is prohibited.

Parties to Protocol I (172) and Protocol II (166): Afghanistan, Albania, Algeria*, Angola[1]*, Antigua and Barbuda, Argentina*, Armenia, Australia*, Austria*, Bahamas, Bahrain, Bangladesh, Barbados, Belarus*, Belgium*, Belize, Benin, Bolivia*, Bosnia and Herzegovina*, Botswana, Brazil*, Brunei Darussalam, Bulgaria*, Burkina Faso*, Burundi, Cambodia, Cameroon, Canada*, Cape Verde*, Central African Republic, Chad, Chile*, China*, Colombia*, Comoros, Congo (Democratic Republic of the)*, Congo (Republic of the), Cook Islands*, Costa Rica*, Côte d'Ivoire, Croatia, Cuba, Cyprus*, Czech Republic*, Denmark*, Djibouti, Dominica, Dominican Republic,

Ecuador, Egypt*, El Salvador*, Equatorial Guinea, Estonia, Ethiopia, Fiji, Finland*, France*, Gabon, Gambia, Georgia, Germany*, Ghana, Greece*, Grenada, Guatemala, Guinea*, Guinea-Bissau, Guyana, Haiti, Holy See, Honduras, Hungary*, Iceland*, Iraq[1], Ireland*, Italy*, Jamaica, Japan*, Jordan, Kazakhstan, Kenya, Korea (North)[1], Korea (South)*, Kuwait, Kyrgyzstan, Laos*, Latvia, Lebanon, Lesotho, Liberia, Libya, Liechtenstein*, Lithuania*, Luxembourg*, Macedonia (Former Yugoslav Republic of)*, Madagascar*, Malawi, Maldives, Mali*, Malta*, Mauritania, Mauritius*, Mexico[1], Micronesia, Moldova, Monaco, Mongolia*, Montenegro, Morocco, Mozambique, Namibia*, Nauru, Netherlands*, New Zealand*, Nicaragua, Niger, Nigeria, Norway*, Oman, Palau, Panama*, Paraguay*, Peru, *Philippines**, Poland*, Portugal*, Qatar*, Romania*, Russia*, Rwanda*, Saint Kitts and Nevis, Saint Lucia, Saint Vincent and the Grenadines, Samoa, San Marino, Sao Tome and Principe, Saudi Arabia*, Senegal*, Serbia*, Seychelles*, Sierra Leone, Slovakia*, Slovenia*, Solomon Islands, South Africa, Spain*, Sudan, Suriname, Swaziland, Sweden*, Switzerland*, Syria*[1], Tajikistan*, Tanzania, Timor-Leste, Togo*, Tonga*, Trinidad and Tobago*, Tunisia, Turkmenistan, Uganda, UK*, Ukraine*, United Arab Emirates*, Uruguay*, Uzbekistan, Vanuatu, Venezuela, Viet Nam[1], Yemen, Zambia, Zimbabwe

* With reservation and/or declaration.
[1] Party only to Protocol I.

Note: The Philippines ratified Protocol I on 30 Mar. 2012. It had ratified Protocol II on 11 Dec. 1986.

Protocol texts: Swiss Federal Department of Foreign Affairs, <http://www.eda.admin.ch/eda/fr/home/topics/intla/intrea/chdep/warvic.html>

Antarctic Treaty

Signed at Washington, DC, on 1 December 1959; entered into force on 23 June 1961; depositary US Government

The treaty declares the Antarctic an area to be used exclusively for peaceful purposes. It prohibits any measure of a military nature in the Antarctic, such as the establishment of military bases and fortifications, and the carrying out of military manoeuvres or the testing of any type of weapon. The treaty bans any nuclear explosion as well as the disposal of radioactive waste material in Antarctica. The treaty provides a right of on-site inspection of all stations and installations in Antarctica to ensure compliance with its provisions.

In accordance with Article IX, consultative meetings are convened at regular intervals to exchange information and hold consultations on matters pertaining to Antarctica, as well as to recommend to the governments measures in furtherance of the principles and objectives of the treaty.

The treaty is open for accession by UN members or by other states invited to accede with the consent of all the parties entitled to participate in the consultative meetings provided for in Article IX. States demonstrating their interest in Antarctica by conducting substantial scientific research activity there, such as the establishment of a scientific station or the dispatch of a scientific expedition, are entitled to become consultative members.

Parties (50): Argentina*, Australia*, Austria, Belarus, Belgium*, Brazil*, Bulgaria*, Canada, Chile*, China*, Colombia, Cuba, Czech Republic, Denmark, Ecuador*, Estonia, Finland*, France*, Germany*, Greece, Guatemala, Hungary, India*, Italy*, Japan*, Korea (North), Korea

(South)*, Malaysia, Monaco, Netherlands*, New Zealand*, Norway*, *Pakistan*, Papua New Guinea, Peru*, Poland*, Portugal, Romania, Russia*, Slovakia, South Africa*, Spain*, Sweden*, Switzerland, Turkey, UK*, Ukraine*, Uruguay*, USA*, Venezuela

> * This state is a consultative member under Article IX of the treaty.

Treaty text: Secretariat of the Antarctic Treaty, <http://www.ats.aq/e/ats.htm>

The Protocol on Environmental Protection (**1991 Madrid Protocol**) entered into force on 14 January 1998.

Protocol text: Secretariat of the Antarctic Treaty, <http://www.ats.aq/e/ep.htm>

Treaty Banning Nuclear Weapon Tests in the Atmosphere, in Outer Space and Under Water (Partial Test-Ban Treaty, PTBT)

Signed at Moscow by three original parties on 5 August 1963 and opened for signature by other states at London, Moscow and Washington, DC, on 8 August 1963; entered into force on 10 October 1963; depositaries British, Russian and US governments

The treaty prohibits the carrying out of any nuclear weapon test explosion or any other nuclear explosion: (*a*) in the atmosphere, beyond its limits, including outer space, or under water, including territorial waters or high seas; and (*b*) in any other environment if such explosion causes radioactive debris to be present outside the territorial limits of the state under whose jurisdiction or control the explosion is conducted.

Parties (126): Afghanistan, Antigua and Barbuda, Argentina, Armenia, Australia, Austria, Bahamas, Bangladesh, Belarus, Belgium, Benin, Bhutan, Bolivia, Bosnia and Herzegovina, Botswana, Brazil, Bulgaria, Canada, Cape Verde, Central African Republic, Chad, Chile, Colombia, Congo (Democratic Republic of the), Costa Rica, Côte d'Ivoire, Croatia, Cyprus, Czech Republic, Denmark, Dominican Republic, Ecuador, Egypt, El Salvador, Equatorial Guinea, Fiji, Finland, Gabon, Gambia, Germany, Ghana, Greece, Guatemala, Guinea-Bissau, Honduras, Hungary, Iceland, India, Indonesia, Iran, Iraq, Ireland, Israel, Italy, Jamaica, Japan, Jordan, Kenya, Korea (South), Kuwait, Laos, Lebanon, Liberia, Libya, Luxembourg, Madagascar, Malawi, Malaysia, Malta, Mauritania, Mauritius, Mexico, Mongolia, Montenegro, Morocco, Myanmar, Nepal, Netherlands, New Zealand, Nicaragua, Niger, Nigeria, Norway, Pakistan, Panama, Papua New Guinea, Peru, Philippines, Poland, Romania, Russia, Rwanda, Samoa, San Marino, Senegal, Serbia, Seychelles, Sierra Leone, Singapore, Slovakia, Slovenia, South Africa, Spain, Sri Lanka, Sudan, Suriname, Swaziland, Sweden, Switzerland, Syria, Taiwan, Tanzania, Thailand, Togo, Tonga, Trinidad and Tobago, Tunisia, Turkey, Uganda, UK, Ukraine, Uruguay, USA, Venezuela, Yemen, Zambia

Signed but not ratified (11): Algeria, Burkina Faso, Burundi, Cameroon, Ethiopia, Haiti, Mali, Paraguay, Portugal, Somalia, Viet Nam

Treaty text: *United Nations Treaty Series*, vol. 480 (1963)

Treaty on Principles Governing the Activities of States in the Exploration and Use of Outer Space, Including the Moon and Other Celestial Bodies (Outer Space Treaty)

Opened for signature at London, Moscow and Washington, DC, on 27 January 1967; entered into force on 10 October 1967; depositaries British, Russian and US governments

The treaty prohibits the placing into orbit around the earth of any object carrying nuclear weapons or any other kind of weapons of mass destruction, the installation of such weapons on celestial bodies, or the stationing of them in outer space in any other manner. The establishment of military bases, installations and fortifications, the testing of any type of weapon and the conducting of military manoeuvres on celestial bodies are also forbidden.

Parties (110): Afghanistan, Algeria, Antigua and Barbuda, Argentina, Australia, Austria, Bahamas, Bangladesh, Barbados, Belarus, Belgium, Benin, Brazil, Brunei Darussalam, Bulgaria, Burkina Faso, Canada, Chile, China, Cuba, Cyprus, Czech Republic, Denmark, Dominica, Dominican Republic, Ecuador, Egypt, El Salvador, Equatorial Guinea, Estonia, Fiji, Finland, France, Germany, Greece, Grenada, Guinea-Bissau, Hungary, Iceland, India, Indonesia, Iraq, Ireland, Israel, Italy, Jamaica, Japan, Kazakhstan, Kenya, Korea (North), Korea (South), Kuwait, Laos, Lebanon, Libya, Luxembourg, Madagascar, Mali, Mauritius, Mexico, Mongolia, Montenegro, Morocco, Myanmar, Nepal, Netherlands, New Zealand, Niger, Nigeria, Norway, Pakistan, Papua New Guinea, Peru, Poland, Portugal, Romania, Russia, Saint Kitts and Nevis, Saint Lucia, Saint Vincent and the Grenadines, San Marino, Saudi Arabia, Seychelles, Sierra Leone, Singapore, Slovakia, Solomon Islands, South Africa, Spain, Sri Lanka, Swaziland, Sweden, Switzerland, Syria, Taiwan, Thailand, Togo, Tonga, Tunisia, Turkey, Uganda, UK, Ukraine, United Arab Emirates, Uruguay, USA, Venezuela, Viet Nam, Yemen, Zambia

Signed but not ratified (27): Bolivia, Botswana, Burundi, Cameroon, Central African Republic, Colombia, Congo (Democratic Republic of the), Congo (Republic of the), Ethiopia, Gambia, Ghana, Guyana, Haiti, Holy See, Honduras, Iran, Jordan, Lesotho, Macedonia (Former Yugoslav Republic of), Malaysia, Nicaragua, Panama, Philippines, Rwanda, Serbia, Somalia, Trinidad and Tobago

Treaty text: *United Nations Treaty Series*, vol. 610 (1967)

Treaty on the Non-Proliferation of Nuclear Weapons (Non-Proliferation Treaty, NPT)

Opened for signature at London, Moscow and Washington, DC, on 1 July 1968; entered into force on 5 March 1970; depositaries British, Russian and US governments

The treaty prohibits the transfer by a nuclear weapon state—defined in the treaty as those which have manufactured and exploded a nuclear weapon or other nuclear explosive device prior to 1 January 1967—to any recipient whatsoever of nuclear weapons or other nuclear explosive devices or of control over them, as well as the assistance, encouragement or inducement of any non-nuclear weapon state to manufacture or otherwise acquire such weapons or devices. It also prohibits the receipt by non-nuclear weapon states from any transferor whatsoever, as well as the manufacture or other acquisition by those states, of nuclear weapons or other nuclear explosive devices.

The parties undertake to facilitate the exchange of equipment, materials and scientific and technological information for the peaceful uses of nuclear energy and to ensure that potential benefits from peaceful applications of nuclear explosions will be made available to non-nuclear weapon parties to the treaty. They also undertake to pursue negotiations in good faith on effective measures relating to cessation of the nuclear arms race at an early date and to nuclear disarmament, and on a treaty on general and complete disarmament.

Non-nuclear weapon states undertake to conclude safeguard agreements with the International Atomic Energy Agency (IAEA) with a view to preventing diversion of nuclear energy from peaceful uses to nuclear weapons or other nuclear explosive devices. A Model Protocol Additional to the Safeguards Agreements, strengthening the measures, was approved in 1997; additional safeguards protocols are signed by states individually with the IAEA.

A Review and Extension Conference, convened in 1995 in accordance with the treaty, decided that the treaty should remain in force indefinitely.

Parties (190): Afghanistan*, Albania*, Algeria*, Andorra*, Angola*, Antigua and Barbuda*, Argentina*, Armenia*, Australia*, Austria*, Azerbaijan*, Bahamas*, Bahrain*, Bangladesh*, Barbados*, Belarus*, Belgium*, Belize*, Benin, Bhutan*, Bolivia*, Bosnia and Herzegovina*, Botswana*, Brazil*, Brunei Darussalam*, Bulgaria*, Burkina Faso*, Burundi*, Cambodia*, Cameroon*, Canada*, Cape Verde, Central African Republic*, Chad*, Chile*, China*†, Colombia*, Comoros*, Congo (Democratic Republic of the)*, Congo (Republic of the)*, Costa Rica*, Côte d'Ivoire*, Croatia*, Cuba*, Cyprus*, Czech Republic*, Denmark*, Djibouti, Dominica*, Dominican Republic*, Ecuador*, Egypt*, El Salvador*, Equatorial Guinea, Eritrea, Estonia*, Ethiopia*, Fiji*, Finland*, France*†, Gabon*, Gambia*, Georgia*, Germany*, Ghana*, Greece*, Grenada*, Guatemala*, Guinea, Guinea-Bissau, Guyana*, Haiti*, Holy See*, Honduras*, Hungary*, Iceland*, Indonesia*, Iran*, Iraq*, Ireland*, Italy*, Jamaica*, Japan*, Jordan*, Kazakhstan*, Kenya*, Kiribati*, Korea (South)*, Kuwait*, Kyrgyzstan*, Laos*, Latvia*, Lebanon*, Lesotho*, Liberia, Libya*, Liechtenstein*, Lithuania*, Luxembourg*, Macedonia (Former Yugoslav Republic of)*, Madagascar*, Malawi*, Malaysia*, Maldives*, Mali*, Malta*, Marshall Islands*, Mauritania*, Mauritius*, Mexico*, Micronesia, Moldova*, Monaco*, Mongolia*, Montenegro*, Morocco*, Mozambique*, Myanmar*, Namibia*, Nauru*, Nepal*, Netherlands*, New Zealand*, Nicaragua*, Niger*, Nigeria*, Norway*, Oman*, Palau*, Panama*, Papua New Guinea*, Paraguay*, Peru*, Philippines*, Poland*, Portugal*, Qatar*, Romania*, Russia*†, Rwanda*, Saint Kitts and Nevis*, Saint Lucia*, Saint Vincent and the Grenadines*, Samoa*, San Marino*, Sao Tome and Principe, Saudi Arabia*, Senegal*, Serbia*, Seychelles*, Sierra Leone*, Singapore*, Slovakia*, Slovenia*, Solomon Islands*, Somalia, South Africa*, Spain*, Sri Lanka*, Sudan*, Suriname*, Swaziland*, Sweden*, Switzerland*, Syria*, Taiwan*, Tajikistan*, Tanzania*, Thailand*, Timor-Leste, Togo*, Tonga*, Trinidad and Tobago*, Tunisia*, Turkey*, Turkmenistan*, Tuvalu*, Uganda*, UK*†, Ukraine*, United Arab Emirates*, Uruguay*, USA*†, Uzbekistan*, Vanuatu, Venezuela*, Viet Nam*, Yemen*, Zambia*, Zimbabwe*

* Party with safeguards agreements in force with the IAEA, as required by the treaty, or concluded by a nuclear weapon state, as defined in the treaty, on a voluntary basis.

† Nuclear weapon state.

Treaty text: International Atomic Energy Agency, INFCIRC/140, 22 Apr. 1970, <http://www.iaea.org/Publications/Documents/Treaties/npt.html>

Additional safeguards protocols in force (120): Afghanistan, Albania, Andorra, Angola, Armenia, Australia, Austria, Azerbaijan, Bahrain, Bangladesh, Belgium, Botswana, Bulgaria, Burkina Faso, Burundi, Canada, Central African Republic, Chad, Chile, China, Colombia, Comoros, Congo (Democratic Republic of the), Congo (Republic of), Costa Rica, Croatia, Cuba, Cyprus, Czech Republic, Denmark, Dominican Republic, Ecuador, El Salvador, Estonia, Euratom, Fiji, Finland, France, Gabon, Gambia, Georgia, Germany, Ghana, Greece, Guatemala, Haiti, Holy See, Hungary, Iceland, Indonesia, *Iraq*, Ireland, Italy, Jamaica, Japan, Jordan, Kazakhstan, Kenya, Korea (South), Kuwait, Kyrgyzstan, Latvia, Lesotho, Libya, Lithuania, Luxembourg, Macedonia (Former Yugoslav Republic of), Madagascar, Malawi, Mali, Malta, Marshall Islands, Mauritania, Mauritius, Mexico, *Moldova*, Monaco, Mongolia, Montenegro, Morocco, Mozambique, *Namibia*, Netherlands, New Zealand, Nicaragua, Niger, Nigeria, Norway, Palau, Panama, Paraguay, Peru, Philippines, Poland, Portugal, Romania, Russia, Rwanda, Seychelles, Singapore, Slovakia, Slovenia, South Africa, Spain, Swaziland, Sweden, Switzerland, Tajikistan, Tanzania, *Togo*, Turkey, Turkmenistan, Uganda, UK, Ukraine, United Arab Emirates, Uruguay, USA, Uzbekistan, *Viet Nam*

Notes: On 6 Feb. 2007 Iran informed the IAEA that it would no longer act in accordance with the provisions of its unratified additional safeguards protocol. Taiwan has agreed to apply the measures contained in the 1997 Model Additional Protocol.

Model Additional Safeguards Protocol text: International Atomic Energy Agency, INFCIRC/540 (corrected), Sep. 1997, <http://www.iaea.org/Publications/Factsheets/English/sg_over view.html>

Treaty on the Prohibition of the Emplacement of Nuclear Weapons and other Weapons of Mass Destruction on the Seabed and the Ocean Floor and in the Subsoil thereof (Seabed Treaty)

Opened for signature at London, Moscow and Washington, DC, on 11 February 1971; entered into force on 18 May 1972; depositaries British, Russian and US governments

The treaty prohibits implanting or emplacing on the seabed and the ocean floor and in the subsoil thereof beyond the outer limit of a 12-mile (19-kilometre) seabed zone any nuclear weapons or any other types of weapon of mass destruction as well as structures, launching installations or any other facilities specifically designed for storing, testing or using such weapons.

Parties (97): Afghanistan, Algeria, Antigua and Barbuda, Argentina, Australia, Austria, Bahamas, Belarus, Belgium, Benin, Bosnia and Herzegovina, Botswana, Brazil*, Bulgaria, Canada*, Cape Verde, Central African Republic, China, Congo (Republic of the), Côte d'Ivoire, Croatia, Cuba, Cyprus, Czech Republic, Denmark, Dominican Republic, Equatorial Guinea, Ethiopia, Finland, Germany, Ghana, Greece, Guatemala, Guinea-Bissau, Hungary, Iceland, India*, Iran, Iraq, Ireland, Italy*, Jamaica, Japan, Jordan, Korea (South), Laos, Latvia, Lesotho, Libya, Liechtenstein, Luxembourg, Malaysia, Malta, Mauritius, Mexico*, Mongolia, Montenegro, Morocco, Nepal, Netherlands, New Zealand, Nicaragua, Niger, Norway, Panama, Philippines, Poland, Portugal, Qatar, Romania, Russia, Rwanda, Saint Kitts and Nevis, Saint Vincent and the Grenadines, Sao Tome and Principe, Saudi Arabia, Serbia*, Seychelles, Singapore, Slovakia, Slovenia, Solomon Islands, South Africa, Spain, Swaziland, Sweden, Switzerland, Taiwan, Togo, Tunisia, Turkey*, UK, Ukraine, USA, Viet Nam*, Yemen, Zambia

* With reservation and/or declaration.

Signed but not ratified (20): Bolivia, Burundi, Cambodia, Cameroon, Colombia, Costa Rica, Gambia, Guinea, Honduras, Lebanon, Liberia, Madagascar, Mali, Myanmar, Paraguay, Senegal, Sierra Leone, Sudan, Tanzania, Uruguay

Treaty text: *United Nations Treaty Series*, vol. 955 (1974)

Convention on the Prohibition of the Development, Production and Stockpiling of Bacteriological (Biological) and Toxin Weapons and on their Destruction (Biological and Toxin Weapons Convention, BTWC)

Opened for signature at London, Moscow and Washington, DC, on 10 April 1972; entered into force on 26 March 1975; depositaries British, Russian and US governments

The convention prohibits the development, production, stockpiling or acquisition by other means or retention of microbial or other biological agents or toxins whatever their origin or method of production of types and in quantities that have no justification of prophylactic, protective or other peaceful purposes, as well as weapons, equipment or means of delivery designed to use such agents or toxins for hostile purposes or in armed conflict. The destruction of the agents, toxins, weapons, equipment and means of delivery in the possession of the parties, or their diversion to peaceful purposes, should be effected not later than nine months after the entry into force of the convention for each country.

The parties hold annual political and technical meetings to strengthen implementation of the convention. A three-person Implementation Support Unit (ISU), based in Geneva, supports the parties in implementing the treaty, including facilitating the collection and distribution of annual confidence-building measures and supporting their efforts to achieve universal membership.

Parties (167): Afghanistan, Albania, Algeria, Antigua and Barbuda, Argentina, Armenia, Australia, Austria*, Azerbaijan, Bahamas, Bahrain*, Bangladesh, Barbados, Belarus, Belgium, Belize, Benin, Bhutan, Bolivia, Bosnia and Herzegovina, Botswana, Brazil, Brunei Darussalam, Bulgaria, Burkina Faso, Burundi, Cambodia, Canada, Cape Verde, Chile, China*, Colombia, Congo (Democratic Republic of the), Congo (Republic of the), Cook Islands, Costa Rica, Croatia, Cuba, Cyprus, Czech Republic*, Denmark, Dominica, Dominican Republic, Ecuador, El Salvador, Equatorial Guinea, Estonia, Ethiopia, Fiji, Finland, France, Gabon, Gambia, Georgia, Germany, Ghana, Greece, Grenada, Guatemala, Guinea-Bissau, Holy See, Honduras, Hungary, Iceland, India*, Indonesia, Iran, Iraq, Ireland*, Italy, Jamaica, Japan, Jordan, Kazakhstan, Kenya, Korea (North), Korea (South)*, Kuwait*, Kyrgyzstan, Laos, Latvia, Lebanon, Lesotho, Libya, Liechtenstein, Lithuania, Luxembourg, Macedonia (Former Yugoslav Republic of), Madagascar, Malaysia*, Maldives, Mali, Malta, *Marshall Islands*, Mauritius, Mexico*, Moldova, Monaco, Mongolia, Montenegro, Morocco, Mozambique, Netherlands, New Zealand, Nicaragua, Niger, Nigeria, Norway, Oman, Pakistan, Palau, Panama, Papua New Guinea, Paraguay, Peru, Philippines, Poland, Portugal, Qatar, Romania, Russia, Rwanda, Saint Kitts and Nevis, Saint Lucia, Saint Vincent and the Grenadines, San Marino, Sao Tome and Principe, Saudi Arabia, Senegal, Serbia, Seychelles, Sierra Leone, Singapore, Slovakia*, Slovenia, Solomon Islands, South Africa, Spain, Sri Lanka, Sudan, Suriname, Swaziland, Sweden, Switzerland*, Taiwan, Tajikistan, Thailand, Timor-Leste, Togo, Tonga, Trinidad and Tobago, Tunisia, Turkey, Turkmenistan, Uganda, UK*, Ukraine, United

Arab Emirates, Uruguay, USA, Uzbekistan, Vanuatu, Venezuela, Viet Nam, Yemen, Zambia, Zimbabwe

* With reservation and/or declaration.

Signed but not ratified (12): Central African Republic, Côte d'Ivoire, Egypt, Guyana, Haiti, Liberia, Malawi, Myanmar, Nepal, Somalia, Syria, Tanzania

Note: In addition to the 167 parties as of 1 Jan. 2013, Cameroon acceded to the convention on 18 Jan. 2013 and Nauru on 5 Mar. 2013.

Treaty text: United Nations Treaty Series, vol. 1015 (1976)

Convention on the Prohibition of Military or Any Other Hostile Use of Environmental Modification Techniques (Enmod Convention)

Opened for signature at Geneva on 18 May 1977; entered into force on 5 October 1978; depositary UN Secretary-General

The convention prohibits military or any other hostile use of environmental modification techniques having widespread, long-lasting or severe effects as the means of destruction, damage or injury to states parties. The term 'environmental modification techniques' refers to any technique for changing—through the deliberate manipulation of natural processes—the dynamics, composition or structure of the earth, including its biota, lithosphere, hydrosphere and atmosphere, or of outer space. Understandings reached during the negotiations, but not written into the convention, define the terms 'widespread', 'long-lasting' and 'severe'.

Parties (76): Afghanistan, Algeria, Antigua and Barbuda, Argentina, Armenia, Australia, Austria, Bangladesh, Belarus, Belgium, Benin, Brazil, Bulgaria, Cameroon, Canada, Cape Verde, Chile, China*, Costa Rica, Cuba, Cyprus, Czech Republic, Denmark, Dominica, Egypt, Estonia, Finland, Germany, Ghana, Greece, Guatemala, Honduras, Hungary, India, Ireland, Italy, Japan, Kazakhstan, Korea (North), Korea (South)*, Kuwait, Lithuania, Laos, Malawi, Mauritius, Mongolia, Netherlands*, New Zealand, Nicaragua, Niger, Norway, Pakistan, Panama, Papua New Guinea, Poland, Romania, Russia, Saint Lucia, Saint Vincent and the Grenadines, Sao Tome and Principe, Slovakia, Slovenia, Solomon Islands, Spain, Sri Lanka, Sweden, Switzerland, Tajikistan, Tunisia, UK, Ukraine, Uruguay, USA, Uzbekistan, Viet Nam, Yemen

* With declaration.

Signed but not ratified (16): Bolivia, Congo (Democratic Republic of the), Ethiopia, Holy See, Iceland, Iran, Iraq, Lebanon, Liberia, Luxembourg, Morocco, Portugal, Sierra Leone, Syria, Turkey, Uganda

Convention text: United Nations Treaty Collection, <http://treaties.un.org/Pages/CTCTreaties.aspx?id=26>

Convention on the Physical Protection of Nuclear Material

Original convention opened for signature at New York and Vienna on 3 March 1980; entered into force on 8 February 1987; convention amended in 2005; depositary IAEA Director General

The original convention obligates the parties to protect nuclear material for peaceful purposes while in international transport.

The amended convention—renamed the **Convention on the Physical Protection of Nuclear Material and Nuclear Facilities**—will obligate the parties to protect nuclear facilities and material used for peaceful purposes while in storage as well as transport. The amendments will take effect 30 days after they have been ratified, accepted or approved by two-thirds of the states parties to the convention.

Parties to the original convention (148): Afghanistan, Albania, Algeria*, Andorra*, Antigua and Barbuda, Argentina*, Armenia, Australia, Austria*, Azerbaijan*, Bahamas, Bahrain*, Bangladesh, Belarus, Belgium*, Bolivia, Bosnia and Herzegovina, Botswana, Brazil, Bulgaria, Burkina Faso, Cambodia, Cameroon, Canada, Cape Verde, Central African Republic, Chile, China*, Colombia, Comoros, Congo (Democratic Republic of the), Costa Rica, *Côte d'Ivoire*, Croatia, Cuba*, Cyprus*, Czech Republic, Denmark, Djibouti, Dominica, Dominican Republic, Ecuador, El Salvador*, Equatorial Guinea, Estonia, Euratom*, Fiji, Finland*, France*, Gabon, Georgia, Germany, Ghana, Greece*, Grenada, Guatemala*, Guinea, Guinea-Bissau, Guyana, Honduras, Hungary, Iceland, India*, Indonesia*, Ireland*, Israel*, Italy*, Jamaica, Japan, Jordan*, Kazakhstan, Kenya, Korea (South)*, Kuwait*, Laos*, Latvia, Lebanon, Lesotho, Libya, Liechtenstein, Lithuania, Luxembourg*, Macedonia (Former Yugoslav Republic of), Madagascar, Mali, Malta, Marshall Islands, Mauritania, Mexico, Moldova, Monaco, Mongolia, Montenegro, Morocco, Mozambique*, Namibia, Nauru, Netherlands*, New Zealand, Nicaragua, Niger, Nigeria, Niue, Norway*, Oman*, Pakistan*, Palau, Panama, Paraguay, Peru*, Philippines, Poland, Portugal*, Qatar*, Romania*, Russia*, Rwanda, Saint Kitts and Nevis, *Saint Lucia**, Saudi Arabia*, Senegal, Serbia, Seychelles, Slovakia, Slovenia, South Africa*, Spain*, Sudan, Swaziland, Sweden*, Switzerland*, Tajikistan, Tanzania, Togo, Tonga, Trinidad and Tobago, Tunisia, Turkey*, Turkmenistan, Uganda, UK*, Ukraine, United Arab Emirates, Uruguay, USA, Uzbekistan, *Viet Nam**, Yemen

* With reservation and/or declaration.

Signed but not ratified (1): Haiti

Convention text: International Atomic Energy Agency, INFCIRC/274/Rev.1, May 1980, <http://www.iaea.org/Publications/Documents/Conventions/cppnm.html>

Ratifications, acceptances or approvals of the amended convention deposited (61): Algeria, Antigua and Barbuda, Argentina, Australia, Austria, Bahrain, Bosnia and Herzegovina, Bulgaria, Chile, China, Croatia, Czech Republic, Denmark*, Estonia, Fiji, Finland, Gabon, *Georgia*, Germany, *Ghana*, Greece, Hungary, India, Indonesia, *Israel**, Jordan, Kazakhstan, Kenya, Latvia, *Lesotho*, Libya, Liechtenstein, Lithuania, *Luxembourg*, Macedonia (Former Yugoslav Republic of), Mali, Mauritania, *Mexico*, Moldova, Nauru, Netherlands, Niger, Nigeria, Norway, Poland, Portugal, Romania, Russia, *Saint Lucia*, Saudi Arabia, Seychelles, Slovenia, Spain, *Sweden*, Switzerland, Tunisia, Turkmenistan, UK, Ukraine, United Arab Emirates, *Viet Nam*

* With reservation and/or declaration.

Amendment text: International Atomic Energy Agency, Board of Governors, GOV/INF/2005/ 10-GC(49)/INF/6, 6 Sep. 2005, <http://www.iaea.org/Publications/Documents/Conventions/ cppnm.html>

Convention on Prohibitions or Restrictions on the Use of Certain Conventional Weapons which may be Deemed to be Excessively Injurious or to have Indiscriminate Effects (CCW Convention, or 'Inhumane Weapons' Convention)

The convention, with protocols I, II and III, opened for signature at New York on 10 April 1981; entered into force on 2 December 1983; depositary UN Secretary-General

The convention is an 'umbrella treaty', under which specific agreements can be concluded in the form of protocols. In order to become a party to the convention a state must ratify at least two of the protocols.

The amendment to Article I of the original convention was opened for signature at Geneva on 21 November 2001. It expands the scope of application to non-international armed conflicts. The amended convention entered into force on 18 May 2004.

Protocol I prohibits the use of weapons intended to injure by fragments which are not detectable in the human body by X-rays.

Protocol II prohibits or restricts the use of mines, booby-traps and other devices.

Amended Protocol II, which entered into force on 3 December 1998, reinforces the constraints regarding anti-personnel mines.

Protocol III restricts the use of incendiary weapons.

Protocol IV, which entered into force on 30 July 1998, prohibits the employment of laser weapons specifically designed to cause permanent blindness to unenhanced vision.

Protocol V, which entered into force on 12 November 2006, recognizes the need for measures of a generic nature to minimize the risks and effects of explosive remnants of war.

Parties to the original convention and protocols (115): Albania, Antigua and Barbuda[1], Argentina*, Australia, Austria, Bangladesh, Belarus, Belgium, Benin[2], Bolivia, Bosnia and Herzegovina, Brazil, Bulgaria, Burkina Faso, *Burundi*[4], Cambodia, Cameroon, Canada*, Cape Verde, Chile[2], China*, Colombia, Costa Rica, Croatia, Cuba, Cyprus*, Czech Republic, Denmark, Djibouti, Dominican Republic, Ecuador, El Salvador, Estonia[2], Finland, France*, Gabon[2], Georgia, Germany, Greece, Guatemala, Guinea-Bissau, Holy See*, Honduras, Hungary, Iceland, India, Ireland, Israel*[1], Italy*, Jamaica[2], Japan, Jordan[2], Kazakhstan[2], Korea (South)[3], Laos, Latvia, Lesotho, Liberia, Liechtenstein, Lithuania[2], Luxembourg, Macedonia (Former Yugoslav Republic of), Madagascar, Maldives[2], Mali, Malta, Mauritius, Mexico, Moldova, Monaco[3], Mongolia, Montenegro, Morocco[4], Nauru, Netherlands*, New Zealand, Nicaragua[2], Niger, Norway, Pakistan, Panama, Paraguay, Peru[2], Philippines, Poland, Portugal, Qatar[2], Romania*, Russia, Saint Vincent and the Grenadines[1], Saudi Arabia[2], Senegal[5], Serbia, Seychelles, Sierra Leone[2], Slovakia, Slovenia, South Africa, Spain, Sri Lanka, Sweden, Switzerland, Tajikistan, Togo, Tunisia, Turkey*[3], Turkmenistan[1], Uganda, UK*, Ukraine, United Arab Emirates[2], Uruguay, USA*, Uzbekistan, Venezuela

* With reservation and/or declaration.

[1] Party only to 1981 protocols I and II.
[2] Party only to 1981 protocols I and III.
[3] Party only to 1981 Protocol I.
[4] Party only to 1981 Protocol II.
[5] Party only to 1981 Protocol III.

Signed but not ratified the original convention and protocols (5): Afghanistan, Egypt, Nigeria, Sudan, Viet Nam

Parties to the amended convention and original protocols (76): Albania, Argentina, Australia, Austria, Belarus, Belgium, Bosnia and Herzegovina, Brazil, Bulgaria, Burkina Faso, Canada, Chile, China, Colombia, Costa Rica, Croatia, Cuba, Czech Republic, Denmark, Dominican Republic, Ecuador, El Salvador, Estonia, Finland, France, Georgia, Germany, Greece, Guatemala, Guinea-Bissau, Holy See*, Hungary, Iceland, India, Ireland, Italy, Jamaica, Japan, Korea (South), Latvia, Liberia, Liechtenstein, Lithuania, Luxembourg, Macedonia (Former Yugoslav Republic of), Malta, Mexico*, Moldova, Montenegro, Netherlands, New Zealand, Nicaragua, Niger, Norway, Panama, Paraguay, Peru, Poland, Portugal, Romania, Russia, Serbia, Sierra Leone, Slovakia, Slovenia, *South Africa*, Spain, Sri Lanka, Sweden, Switzerland, Tunisia, Turkey, UK, Ukraine, Uruguay, USA

* With reservation and/or declaration.

Parties to Amended Protocol II (98): Albania, Argentina, Australia, Austria*, Bangladesh, Belarus*, Belgium*, Bolivia, Bosnia and Herzegovina, Brazil, Bulgaria, Burkina Faso, Cambodia, Cameroon, Canada, Cape Verde, Chile, China*, Colombia, Costa Rica, Croatia, Cyprus, Czech Republic, Denmark*, Dominican Republic, Ecuador, El Salvador, Estonia, Finland*, France*, Gabon, Georgia, Germany*, Greece*, Guatemala, Guinea-Bissau, Holy See, Honduras, Hungary*, Iceland, India, Ireland*, Israel*, Italy*, Jamaica, Japan, Jordan, Korea (South)*, Latvia, Liberia, Liechtenstein*, Lithuania, Luxembourg, Macedonia (Former Yugoslav Republic of), Madagascar, Maldives, Mali, Malta, Moldova, Monaco, Montenegro, Morocco, Nauru, Netherlands*, New Zealand, Nicaragua, Niger, Norway, Pakistan*, Panama, Paraguay, Peru, Philippines, Poland, Portugal, Romania, Russia*, Saint Vincent and the Grenadines, Senegal, Serbia, Seychelles, Sierra Leone, Slovakia, Slovenia, South Africa*, Spain, Sri Lanka, Sweden, Switzerland, Tajikistan, Tunisia, Turkey, Turkmenistan, UK*, Ukraine*, Uruguay, USA*, Venezuela

* With reservation and/or declaration.

Parties to Protocol IV (101): Albania, Antigua and Barbuda, Argentina, Australia*, Austria*, Bangladesh, Belarus, Belgium*, Bolivia, Bosnia and Herzegovina, Brazil, Bulgaria, Burkina Faso, Cambodia, Cameroon, Canada*, Cape Verde, Chile, China, Colombia, Costa Rica, Croatia, *Cuba*, Cyprus, Czech Republic, Denmark, Dominican Republic, Ecuador, El Salvador, Estonia, Finland, France, Gabon, Georgia, Germany*, Greece*, Guatemala, Guinea-Bissau, Holy See, Honduras, Hungary, Iceland, India, Ireland*, Israel*, Italy*, Jamaica, Japan, Kazakhstan, Latvia, Liberia, Liechtenstein*, Lithuania, Luxembourg, Macedonia (Former Yugoslav Republic of), Madagascar, Maldives, Mali, Malta, Mauritius, Mexico, Moldova, Mongolia, Montenegro, Morocco, Nauru, Netherlands*, New Zealand, Nicaragua, Niger, Norway, Pakistan, Panama, Paraguay, Peru, Philippines, Poland*, Portugal, Qatar, Romania, Russia, Saint Vincent and the Grenadines, Saudi Arabia, Serbia, Seychelles, Sierra Leone, Slovakia, Slovenia, South Africa*, Spain, Sri Lanka, Sweden*, Switzerland*, Tajikistan, Tunisia, Turkey, UK*, Ukraine, Uruguay, USA*, Uzbekistan

* With reservation and/or declaration.

Parties to Protocol V (81): Albania, Argentina*, Australia, Austria, Belarus, Belgium, Bosnia and Herzegovina, Brazil, Bulgaria, *Burundi*, Cameroon, Canada, Chile, China*, Costa Rica, Croatia, *Cuba*, Cyprus, Czech Republic, Denmark, Dominican Republic, Ecuador, El Salvador, Estonia, Finland, France, Gabon, Georgia, Germany, Guatemala, Guinea-Bissau, Holy See*, Honduras,

Hungary, Iceland, India, Ireland, Italy, Jamaica, Korea (South), *Laos*, Latvia, Liberia, Liechtenstein, Lithuania, Luxembourg, Macedonia (Former Yugoslav Republic of), Madagascar, Mali, Malta, Moldova, Netherlands, New Zealand*, Nicaragua, Norway, Pakistan, Panama, Paraguay, Peru, Poland, Portugal, Qatar, Romania, Russia, Saint Vincent and the Grenadines, Saudi Arabia, Senegal, Sierra Leone, Slovakia, Slovenia, *South Africa*, Spain, Sweden, Switzerland, Tajikistan, Tunisia, *Turkmenistan*, Ukraine, United Arab Emirates, Uruguay, USA*

* With reservation and/or declaration.

Convention and protocol texts (original and amendments): United Nations Treaty Collection, <http://treaties.un.org/Pages/CTCTreaties.aspx?id=26>

Convention on the Prohibition of the Development, Production, Stockpiling and Use of Chemical Weapons and on their Destruction (Chemical Weapons Convention, CWC)

Opened for signature at Paris on 13 January 1993; entered into force on 29 April 1997; depositary UN Secretary-General

The convention prohibits the development, production, acquisition, transfer, stockpiling and use of chemical weapons. The CWC regime consists of four 'pillars': disarmament, non-proliferation, assistance and protection against chemical weapons, and international cooperation on the peaceful uses of chemistry.

Each party undertook to destroy its chemical weapon stockpiles by 29 April 2012. By that date, of the seven parties that had declared stocks of chemical weapons, three had destroyed them; Iraq, Libya, Russia and the USA continue to destroy their stocks. Old and abandoned chemical weapons will continue to be destroyed as they are uncovered from, for example, former battlefields.

Parties (188): Afghanistan, Albania, Algeria, Andorra, Antigua and Barbuda, Argentina, Armenia, Australia, Austria, Azerbaijan, Bahamas, Bahrain, Bangladesh, Barbados, Belarus, Belgium, Belize, Benin, Bhutan, Bolivia, Bosnia and Herzegovina, Botswana, Brazil, Brunei Darussalam, Bulgaria, Burkina Faso, Burundi, Cambodia, Cameroon, Canada, Cape Verde, Central African Republic, Chad, Chile, China, Colombia, Comoros, Congo (Democratic Republic of the), Congo (Republic of the), Cook Islands, Costa Rica, Côte d'Ivoire, Croatia, Cuba, Cyprus, Czech Republic, Denmark, Djibouti, Dominica, Dominican Republic, Ecuador, El Salvador, Equatorial Guinea, Eritrea, Estonia, Ethiopia, Fiji, Finland, France, Gabon, Gambia, Georgia, Germany, Ghana, Greece, Grenada, Guatemala, Guinea, Guinea-Bissau, Guyana, Haiti, Holy See, Honduras, Hungary, Iceland, India, Indonesia, Iran, Iraq, Ireland, Italy, Jamaica, Japan, Jordan, Kazakhstan, Kenya, Kiribati, Korea (South), Kuwait, Kyrgyzstan, Laos, Latvia, Lebanon, Lesotho, Liberia, Libya, Liechtenstein, Lithuania, Luxembourg, Macedonia (Former Yugoslav Republic of), Madagascar, Malawi, Malaysia, Maldives, Mali, Malta, Marshall Islands, Mauritania, Mauritius, Mexico, Micronesia, Moldova, Monaco, Mongolia, Montenegro, Morocco, Mozambique, Namibia, Nauru, Nepal, Netherlands, New Zealand, Nicaragua, Niger, Nigeria, Niue, Norway, Oman, Pakistan, Palau, Panama, Papua New Guinea, Paraguay, Peru, Philippines, Poland, Portugal, Qatar, Romania, Russia, Rwanda, Saint Kitts and Nevis, Saint Lucia, Saint Vincent and the Grenadines, Samoa, San Marino, Sao Tome and Principe, Saudi Arabia, Senegal, Serbia, Seychelles, Sierra Leone, Singapore, Slovakia, Slovenia, Solomon Islands, South Africa, Spain, Sri Lanka, Sudan, Suriname, Swaziland, Sweden, Switzerland, Tajikistan, Tanzania, Thailand, Timor-Leste, Togo, Tonga, Trinidad and

Tobago, Tunisia, Turkey, Turkmenistan, Tuvalu, Uganda, UK, Ukraine, United Arab Emirates, Uruguay, USA, Uzbekistan, Vanuatu, Venezuela, Viet Nam, Yemen, Zambia, Zimbabwe

Signed but not ratified (2): Israel, Myanmar

Convention text: United Nations Treaty Collection, <http://treaties.un.org/Pages/CTCTreaties. aspx?id=26>

Comprehensive Nuclear-Test-Ban Treaty (CTBT)

Opened for signature at New York on 24 September 1996; not in force; depositary UN Secretary-General

The treaty would prohibit the carrying out of any nuclear weapon test explosion or any other nuclear explosion, and urges each party to prevent any such nuclear explosion at any place under its jurisdiction or control and refrain from causing, encouraging or in any way participating in the carrying out of any nuclear weapon test explosion or any other nuclear explosion.

The treaty will enter into force 180 days after the date of the deposit of the instruments of ratification of the 44 states listed in an annex to the treaty. All 44 states possess nuclear power reactors and/or nuclear research reactors.

States whose ratification is required for entry into force (44): Algeria, Argentina, Australia, Austria, Bangladesh, Belgium, Brazil, Bulgaria, Canada, Chile, China*, Colombia, Congo (Democratic Republic of the), Egypt*, Finland, France, Germany, Hungary, India*, Indonesia, Iran*, Israel*, Italy, Japan, Korea (North)*, Korea (South), Mexico, Netherlands, Norway, Pakistan*, Peru, Poland, Romania, Russia, Slovakia, South Africa, Spain, Sweden, Switzerland, Turkey, UK, Ukraine, USA*, Viet Nam

* Has not ratified the treaty.

Ratifications deposited (157): Afghanistan, Albania, Algeria, Andorra, Antigua and Barbuda, Argentina, Armenia, Australia, Austria, Azerbaijan, Bahamas, Bahrain, Bangladesh, Barbados, Belarus, Belgium, Belize, Benin, Bolivia, Bosnia and Herzegovina, Botswana, Brazil, Bulgaria, Burkina Faso, Burundi, Cambodia, Cameroon, Canada, Cape Verde, Central African Republic, Chile, Colombia, Congo (Democratic Republic of the), Cook Islands, Costa Rica, Côte d'Ivoire, Croatia, Cyprus, Czech Republic, Denmark, Djibouti, Dominican Republic, Ecuador, El Salvador, Eritrea, Estonia, Ethiopia, Fiji, Finland, France, Gabon, Georgia, Germany, Ghana, Greece, Grenada, *Guatemala*, Guinea, Guyana, Haiti, Holy See, Honduras, Hungary, Iceland, *Indonesia*, Ireland, Italy, Jamaica, Japan, Jordan, Kazakhstan, Kenya, Kiribati, Korea (South), Kuwait, Kyrgyzstan, Laos, Latvia, Lebanon, Lesotho, Liberia, Libya, Liechtenstein, Lithuania, Luxembourg, Macedonia (Former Yugoslav Republic of), Madagascar, Malawi, Malaysia, Maldives, Mali, Malta, Marshall Islands, Mauritania, Mexico, Micronesia, Moldova, Monaco, Mongolia, Montenegro, Morocco, Mozambique, Namibia, Nauru, Netherlands, New Zealand, Nicaragua, Niger, Nigeria, Norway, Oman, Palau, Panama, Paraguay, Peru, Philippines, Poland, Portugal, Qatar, Romania, Russia, Rwanda, Saint Kitts and Nevis, Saint Lucia, Saint Vincent and the Grenadines, Samoa, San Marino, Senegal, Serbia, Seychelles, Sierra Leone, Singapore, Slovakia, Slovenia, South Africa, Spain, Sudan, Suriname, Sweden, Switzerland, Tajikistan, Tanzania, Togo, Trinidad and Tobago, Tunisia, Turkey, Turkmenistan, Uganda, UK, Ukraine, United Arab Emirates, Uruguay, Uzbekistan, Vanuatu, Venezuela, Viet Nam, Zambia

Note: In addition to the 157 parties as of 1 Jan. 2013, Brunei Darussalam deposited its instrument of ratification on 14 Jan. 2013 and Chad on 11 Feb. 2013.

Signed but not ratified (25): Angola, Brunei Darussalam, Chad, China, Comoros, Congo (Republic of the), Egypt, Equatorial Guinea, Gambia, Guinea-Bissau, Iran, Iraq, Israel,

Myanmar, Nepal, Papua New Guinea, Sao Tome and Principe, Solomon Islands, Sri Lanka, Swaziland, Thailand, Timor-Leste, USA, Yemen, Zimbabwe

Treaty text: United Nations Treaty Collection, <http://treaties.un.org/Pages/CTCTreaties. aspx?id=26>

Convention on the Prohibition of the Use, Stockpiling, Production and Transfer of Anti-Personnel Mines and on their Destruction (APM Convention)

Opened for signature at Ottawa on 3–4 December 1997 and at New York on 5 December 1997; entered into force on 1 March 1999; depositary UN Secretary-General

The convention prohibits anti-personnel mines (APMs), which are defined as mines designed to be exploded by the presence, proximity or contact of a person and which will incapacitate, injure or kill one or more persons.

Each party undertakes to destroy all its stockpiled APMs as soon as possible but not later that four years after the entry into force of the convention for that state party. Each party also undertakes to destroy all APMs in mined areas under its jurisdiction or control not later than 10 years after the entry into force of the convention for that state party.

Parties (161): Afghanistan, Albania, Algeria, Andorra, Angola, Antigua and Barbuda, Argentina*, Australia*, Austria*, Bahamas, Bangladesh, Barbados, Belarus, Belgium, Belize, Benin, Bhutan, Bolivia, Bosnia and Herzegovina, Botswana, Brazil, Brunei Darussalam, Bulgaria, Burkina Faso, Burundi, Cambodia, Cameroon, Canada*, Cape Verde, Central African Republic, Chad, Chile*, Colombia, Comoros, Congo (Democratic Republic of the), Congo (Republic of the), Cook Islands, Costa Rica, Côte d'Ivoire, Croatia, Cyprus, Czech Republic*, Denmark, Djibouti, Dominica, Dominican Republic, Ecuador, El Salvador, Equatorial Guinea, Eritrea, Estonia, Ethiopia, Fiji, *Finland*, France, Gabon, Gambia, Germany, Ghana, Greece*, Grenada, Guatemala, Guinea, Guinea-Bissau, Guyana, Haiti, Holy See, Honduras, Hungary, Iceland, Indonesia, Iraq, Ireland, Italy, Jamaica, Japan, Jordan, Kenya, Kiribati, Kuwait, Latvia, Lesotho, Liberia, Liechtenstein, Lithuania*, Luxembourg, Macedonia (Former Yugoslav Republic of), Madagascar, Malawi, Malaysia, Maldives, Mali, Malta, Mauritania, Mauritius*, Mexico, Moldova, Monaco, Montenegro*, Mozambique, Namibia, Nauru, Netherlands, New Zealand, Nicaragua, Niger, Nigeria, Niue, Norway, Palau, Panama, Papua New Guinea, Paraguay, Peru, Philippines, *Poland*, Portugal, Qatar, Romania, Rwanda, Saint Kitts and Nevis, Saint Lucia, Saint Vincent and the Grenadines, Samoa, San Marino, Sao Tome and Principe, Senegal, Serbia*, Seychelles, Sierra Leone, Slovakia, Slovenia, Solomon Islands, *Somalia*, South Africa*, South Sudan, Spain, Sudan, Suriname, Swaziland, Sweden*, Switzerland*, Tajikistan, Tanzania, Thailand, Timor-Leste, Togo, Trinidad and Tobago, Tunisia, Turkey, Turkmenistan, Tuvalu, Uganda, UK*, Ukraine, Uruguay, Vanuatu, Venezuela, Yemen, Zambia, Zimbabwe

* With reservation and/or declaration.

Signed but not ratified (1): Marshall Islands

Convention text: United Nations Treaty Collection, <http://treaties.un.org/Pages/CTCTreaties. aspx?id=26>

Convention on Cluster Munitions

Adopted at Dublin on 30 May 2008; opened for signature at Oslo on 3 December 2008; entered into force on 1 August 2010; depositary UN Secretary-General

The convention's objectives are to prohibit the use, production, transfer and stockpiling of cluster munitions that cause unacceptable harm to civilians, and to establish a framework for cooperation and assistance that ensures adequate provision of care and rehabilitation for victims, clearance of contaminated areas, risk reduction education and destruction of stockpiles. The convention does not apply to mines.

Parties (77): Afghanistan, Albania, Antigua and Barbuda, *Australia*, Austria, Belgium*, Bosnia and Herzegovina, Botswana, Bulgaria, Burkina Faso, Burundi, *Cameroon*, Cape Verde, Chile, Comoros, Cook Islands, Costa Rica, *Côte d'Ivoire*, Croatia, Czech Republic, Denmark, Dominican Republic, Ecuador, El Salvador*, Fiji, France, Germany, Ghana, Grenada, Guatemala, Guinea-Bissau, Holy See*, *Honduras*, *Hungary*, Ireland, Italy, Japan, Laos, Lebanon, Lesotho, Lithuania, Luxembourg, Macedonia (Former Yugoslav Republic of), Malawi, Mali, Malta, *Mauritania*, Mexico, Moldova, Monaco, Montenegro, Mozambique, Netherlands, New Zealand, Nicaragua, Niger, Norway, Panama, *Peru*, Portugal, Samoa, Saint Vincent and the Grenadines, San Marino, Senegal, Seychelles, Sierra Leone, Slovenia, Spain, Swaziland, *Sweden*, *Switzerland*, *Togo*, Trinidad and Tobago, Tunisia, UK, Uruguay, Zambia

* With reservation and/or declaration.

Signed but not ratified (34): Angola, Benin, Bolivia, Canada, Central African Republic, Chad, Colombia, Congo (Democratic Republic of the), Congo (Republic of the), Cyprus, Djibouti, Gambia, Guinea, Haiti, Iceland, Indonesia, Iraq, Jamaica, Kenya, Liberia, Liechtenstein, Madagascar, Namibia, Nauru, Nigeria, Palau, Paraguay, Philippines, Rwanda, Sao Tome and Principe, Somalia, South Africa, Tanzania, Uganda

Convention text: United Nations Treaty Collection, <http://treaties.un.org/Pages/CTCTreaties.aspx?id=26>

II. Regional treaties

Treaty for the Prohibition of Nuclear Weapons in Latin America and the Caribbean (Treaty of Tlatelolco)

Original treaty opened for signature at Mexico City on 14 February 1967; entered into force on 22 April 1968; treaty amended in 1990, 1991 and 1992; depositary Mexican Government

The treaty prohibits the testing, use, manufacture, production or acquisition by any means, as well as the receipt, storage, installation, deployment and any form of possession of any nuclear weapons by Latin American and Caribbean countries.

The parties should conclude agreements individually with the IAEA for the application of safeguards to their nuclear activities. The IAEA has the exclusive power to carry out special inspections.

The treaty is open for signature by all the independent states of the Latin American and Caribbean zone as defined in the treaty.

Under *Additional Protocol I* states with territories within the zone (France, the Netherlands, the UK and the USA) undertake to apply the statute of military denuclearization to these territories.

Under *Additional Protocol II* the recognized nuclear weapon states—China, France, Russia, the UK and the USA—undertake to respect the statute of military denuclearization of Latin America and the Caribbean and not to contribute to acts involving a violation of the treaty, nor to use or threaten to use nuclear weapons against the parties to the treaty.

Parties to the original treaty (33): Antigua and Barbuda, Argentina[1], Bahamas, Barbados[1], Belize[2], Bolivia, Brazil[1], Chile[1], Colombia[1], Costa Rica[1], Cuba[1], Dominica, Dominican Republic[3], Ecuador[1], El Salvador[1], Grenada[4], Guatemala[1], Guyana[1], Haiti, Honduras, Jamaica[1], Mexico[1], Nicaragua[3], Panama[1], Paraguay[1], Peru[1], Saint Kitts and Nevis, Saint Lucia, Saint Vincent and the Grenadines, Suriname[1], Trinidad and Tobago, Uruguay[1], Venezuela[1]

[1] Has ratified the amendments of 1990, 1991 and 1992.
[2] Has ratified the amendments of 1990 and 1992 only.
[3] Has ratified the amendment of 1992 only.
[4] Has ratified the amendment of 1990 only.

Parties to Additional Protocol I (4): France*, Netherlands, UK*, USA*

Parties to Additional Protocol II (5): China*, France*, Russia*, UK*, USA*

* With reservation and/or declaration.

Original treaty text: *United Nations Treaty Series*, vol. 634 (1968)

Amended treaty text: Agency for the Prohibition of Nuclear Weapons in Latin America and the Caribbean, <http://www.opanal.org/opanal/Tlatelolco/P-Tlatelolco-i.htm>

South Pacific Nuclear Free Zone Treaty (Treaty of Rarotonga)

Opened for signature at Rarotonga on 6 August 1985; entered into force on 11 December 1986; depositary Secretary General of the Pacific Islands Forum Secretariat

The treaty prohibits the manufacture or acquisition of any nuclear explosive device, as well as possession or control over such device by the parties anywhere inside or outside the zone defined in an annex. The parties also undertake not to supply nuclear material or equipment, unless subject to IAEA safeguards, and to prevent in their territories the stationing as well as the testing of any nuclear explosive device and undertake not to dump, and to prevent the dumping of, radioactive waste and other radioactive matter at sea anywhere within the zone. Each party remains free to allow visits, as well as transit, by foreign ships and aircraft.

The treaty is open for signature by the members of the Pacific Islands Forum.

Under *Protocol 1* France, the UK and the USA undertake to apply the treaty prohibitions relating to the manufacture, stationing and testing of nuclear explosive devices in the territories situated within the zone for which they are internationally responsible.

Under *Protocol 2* China, France, Russia, the UK and the USA undertake not to use or threaten to use a nuclear explosive device against the parties to the treaty or against any territory within the zone for which a party to Protocol 1 is internationally responsible.

Under *Protocol 3* China, France, Russia, the UK and the USA undertake not to test any nuclear explosive device anywhere within the zone.

Parties (13): Australia, Cook Islands, Fiji, Kiribati, Nauru, New Zealand, Niue, Papua New Guinea, Samoa, Solomon Islands, Tonga, Tuvalu, Vanuatu

Parties to Protocol 1 (2): France, UK; *signed but not ratified (1)*: USA

Parties to Protocol 2 (4): China, France*, Russia, UK*; *signed but not ratified (1)*: USA

Parties to Protocol 3 (4): China, France, Russia, UK; *signed but not ratified (1)*: USA

* With reservation and/or declaration.

Treaty text: *United Nations Treaty Series*, vol. 1445 (1987)

Treaty on Conventional Armed Forces in Europe (CFE Treaty)

Original treaty signed at Paris on 19 November 1990; entered into force on 9 November 1992; depositary Dutch Government

The treaty sets ceilings on five categories of treaty-limited equipment (TLE)— battle tanks, armoured combat vehicles, artillery of at least 100-mm calibre, combat aircraft and attack helicopters—in an area stretching from the Atlantic Ocean to the Ural Mountains (the Atlantic-to-the-Urals, ATTU).

The treaty was negotiated and signed by the member states of the Warsaw Treaty Organization and NATO within the framework of the Conference on Security and Co-operation in Europe (from 1995 the Organization for Security and Co-operation in Europe, OSCE).

The **1992 Tashkent Agreement**, adopted by the former Soviet republics with territories within the ATTU area of application (with the exception of Estonia, Latvia and Lithuania) and the **1992 Oslo Document** (Final Document of the Extraordinary Conference of the States Parties to the CFE Treaty) introduced modifications to the treaty required because of the emergence of new states after the break-up of the USSR.

Parties (30): Armenia, Azerbaijan, Belarus, Belgium[2], Bulgaria[2], Canada[2], Czech Republic[2], Denmark[2], France, Georgia, Germany[2], Greece, Hungary[2], Iceland[2], Italy[2], Kazakhstan, Luxembourg[2], Moldova[2], Netherlands[2], Norway, Poland, Portugal[2], Romania, Russia[1], Slovakia[2], Spain, Turkey[2], UK[2], Ukraine, USA[2]

[1] On 14 July 2007 Russia declared its intention to suspend its participation in the CFE Treaty and associated documents and agreements, which took effect on 12 Dec. 2007.

[2] In Nov.–Dec. 2011, these countries notified the depositary that they will cease to perform their obligations under the treaty with regard to Russia.

The first review conference of the CFE Treaty adopted the **1996 Flank Document**, which reorganized the flank areas geographically and numerically, allowing Russia and Ukraine to deploy TLE in a less constraining manner.

Original (1990) treaty text: Organization for Security and Co-operation in Europe, <http://www.osce.org/library/14087>

Consolidated (1993) treaty text: Dutch Ministry of Foreign Affairs, <http://wetten.overheid.nl/BWBV0002009/>

Flank Document text: Organization for Security and Co-operation in Europe, <http://www.osce.org/library/14099>, annex A

Concluding Act of the Negotiation on Personnel Strength of Conventional Armed Forces in Europe (CFE-1A Agreement)

Signed by the parties to the CFE Treaty at Helsinki on 10 July 1992; entered into force simultaneously with the CFE Treaty; depositary Dutch Government

The politically binding agreement sets ceilings on the number of personnel of the conventional land-based armed forces of the parties within the ATTU area.

Agreement text: Organization for Security and Co-operation in Europe, <http://www.osce.org/library/14093>

Agreement on Adaptation of the Treaty on Conventional Armed Forces in Europe

Signed by the parties to the CFE Treaty at Helsinki on 19 November 1999; not in force; depositary Dutch Government

The agreement would replace the CFE Treaty bloc-to-bloc military balance with regional balance, establish individual state limits on TLE holdings, and provide for a new structure of limitations and new military flexibility mechanisms, flank sub-limits and enhanced transparency. It would open the CFE regime to all other European states. It will enter into force when it has been ratified by all of the signatories. The **1999 Final Act**, with annexes, contains politically binding arrangements with regard to Georgia, Moldova and Central Europe and to withdrawals of armed forces from foreign territories.

Ratifications deposited (3): Belarus, Kazakhstan, Russia*[1]

* With reservation and/or declaration.
[1] On 14 July 2007 Russia declared its intention to suspend its participation in the CFE Treaty and associated documents and agreements, which took effect on 12 Dec. 2007.
Note: Ukraine has ratified the 1999 Agreement on Adaptation of the CFE Treaty but has not deposited its instrument with the depositary.

Agreement text: Organization for Security and Co-operation in Europe, <http://www.osce.org/library/14108>

Treaty text as amended by 1999 agreement: SIPRI Yearbook 2000, pp. 627–42

Final Act text: Organization for Security and Co-operation in Europe, <http://www.osce.org/library/14114>

Treaty on Open Skies

*Opened for signature at Helsinki on 24 March 1992; entered into force on
1 January 2002; depositaries Canadian and Hungarian governments*

The treaty obligates the parties to submit their territories to short-notice
unarmed surveillance flights. The area of application stretches from Vancouver,
Canada, eastward to Vladivostok, Russia.

The treaty was negotiated between the member states of the Warsaw Treaty
Organization and NATO. It was opened for signature by the NATO member
states, former member states of the Warsaw Treaty Organization and the states
of the former Soviet Union (except for Estonia, Latvia and Lithuania). For six
months after entry into force of the treaty, any other participating state of the
Organization for Security and Co-operation in Europe could apply for
accession to the treaty, and from 1 July 2002 any state can apply to accede to
the treaty.

Parties (34): Belarus, Belgium, Bosnia and Herzegovina, Bulgaria, Canada, Croatia, Czech
Republic, Denmark, Estonia, Finland, France, Georgia, Germany, Greece, Hungary, Iceland,
Italy, Latvia, Lithuania, Luxembourg, Netherlands, Norway, Poland, Portugal, Romania,
Russia, Slovakia, Slovenia, Spain, Sweden, Turkey, UK, Ukraine, USA

Signed but not ratified (1): Kyrgyzstan

Treaty text: Canada Treaty Information, <http://www.treaty-accord.gc.ca/text-texte.aspx?id=
102747>

Treaty on the Southeast Asia Nuclear Weapon-Free Zone (Treaty of Bangkok)

*Signed at Bangkok on 15 December 1995; entered into force on 27 March 1997;
depositary Thai Government*

The treaty prohibits the development, manufacture, acquisition or testing of
nuclear weapons inside or outside the zone as well as the stationing and
transport of nuclear weapons in or through the zone. Each state party may
decide for itself whether to allow visits and transit by foreign ships and aircraft.
The parties undertake not to dump at sea or discharge into the atmosphere
anywhere within the zone any radioactive material or waste or dispose of
radioactive material on land. The parties should conclude an agreement with
the IAEA for the application of full-scope safeguards to their peaceful nuclear
activities.

The zone includes not only the territories but also the continental shelves
and exclusive economic zones of the states parties.

The treaty is open for signature by all states of South East Asia.

Under a *Protocol* to the treaty, China, France, Russia, the UK and the USA are
to undertake not to use or threaten to use nuclear weapons against any state
party to the treaty. They should further undertake not to use nuclear weapons
within the South East Asia nuclear weapon-free zone. The protocol will enter
into force for each state party on the date of its deposit of the instrument of
ratification.

Parties (10): Brunei Darussalam, Cambodia, Indonesia, Laos, Malaysia, Myanmar, Philippines, Singapore, Thailand, Viet Nam

Protocol: no signatures, no parties

Treaty and protocol texts: ASEAN Secretariat, <http://www.asean.org/news/item/treaty-on-the-southeast-asia-nuclear-weapon-free-zone>

African Nuclear-Weapon-Free Zone Treaty (Treaty of Pelindaba)

Signed at Cairo on 11 April 1996; entered into force on 15 July 2009; depositary Secretary-General of the African Union

The treaty prohibits the research, development, manufacture and acquisition of nuclear explosive devices and the testing or stationing of any nuclear explosive device. Each party remains free to allow visits and transit by foreign ships and aircraft. The treaty also prohibits any attack against nuclear installations. The parties undertake not to dump or permit the dumping of radioactive waste and other radioactive matter anywhere within the zone. Each party should individually conclude an agreement with the IAEA for the application of comprehensive safeguards to their peaceful nuclear activities.

The zone includes the territory of the continent of Africa, island states members of the African Union (AU) and all islands considered by the AU to be part of Africa.

The treaty is open for signature by all the states of Africa.

Under *Protocol I* China, France, Russia, the UK and the USA are to undertake not to use or threaten to use a nuclear explosive device against the parties to the treaty.

Under *Protocol II* China, France, Russia, the UK and the USA are to undertake not to test nuclear explosive devices within the zone.

Under *Protocol III* states with territories within the zone for which they are internationally responsible are to undertake to observe certain provisions of the treaty with respect to these territories. This protocol is open for signature by France and Spain.

The protocols entered into force simultaneously with the treaty for those protocol signatories that had deposited their instruments of ratification.

Parties (36): Algeria, Benin, Botswana, Burkina Faso, Burundi, Cameroon, *Chad, Comoros*, Côte d'Ivoire, Equatorial Guinea, Ethiopia, Gabon, Gambia, Ghana, Guinea, *Guinea-Bissau*, Kenya, Lesotho, Libya, Madagascar, Malawi, Mali, Mauritania, Mauritius, Mozambique, *Namibia*, Nigeria, Rwanda, Senegal, South Africa, Swaziland, Tanzania, Togo, Tunisia, Zambia, Zimbabwe

Signed but not ratified (18): Angola, Cape Verde, Central African Republic, Congo (Democratic Republic of the), Congo (Republic of the), Djibouti, Egypt, Eritrea, Liberia, Morocco, Niger, Sahrawi Arab Democratic Republic (Western Sahara), Sao Tome and Principe, Seychelles, Sierra Leone, Somalia, Sudan, Uganda

Parties to Protocol I (4): China, France*, Russia*, UK*; *signed but not ratified (1)*: USA*

Parties to Protocol II (4): China, France, Russia*, UK*; *signed but not ratified (1)*: USA*

Parties to Protocol III (1): France

  * With reservation and/or declaration.

Treaty text: African Union, <http://au.int/en/treaties>

Agreement on Sub-Regional Arms Control (Florence Agreement)

Adopted at Florence and entered into force on 14 June 1996

The agreement was negotiated under the auspices of the OSCE in accordance with the mandate in Article IV of Annex 1-B of the 1995 General Framework Agreement for Peace in Bosnia and Herzegovina (Dayton Agreement). It sets numerical ceilings on armaments of the former warring parties. Five categories of heavy conventional weapons are included: battle tanks, armoured combat vehicles, heavy artillery (75 mm and above), combat aircraft and attack helicopters. The limits were reached by 31 October 1997; by that date 6580 weapon items, or 46 per cent of pre-June 1996 holdings, had been destroyed. By 1 January 2010, a further 2650 items had been destroyed voluntarily.

The implementation of the agreement is monitored and assisted by the OSCE's Personal Representative of the Chairman-in-Office and the Contact Group (France, Germany, Italy, Russia, the UK and the USA) and supported by other OSCE states. Under a two-phase action plan agreed in November 2009, responsibility for the implementation of the agreement will be transferred to the parties by the end of 2014.

Parties (4): Bosnia and Herzegovina, Croatia, Montenegro, Serbia

Agreement text: OSCE Mission to Bosnia and Herzegovina, <http://www.oscebih.org/Down load.aspx?id=100>

Inter-American Convention Against the Illicit Manufacturing of and Trafficking in Firearms, Ammunition, Explosives, and Other Related Materials (CIFTA)

Adopted at Washington, DC, on 13 November 1997; opened for signature at Washington, DC, on 14 November 1997; entered into force on 1 July 1998; depositary General Secretariat of the Organization of American States

The purpose of the convention is to prevent, combat and eradicate the illicit manufacturing of and trafficking in firearms, ammunition, explosives and other related materials; and to promote and facilitate cooperation and the exchange of information and experience among the parties.

Parties (30): Antigua and Barbuda, Argentina*, Bahamas, Barbados, Belize, Bolivia, Brazil, Chile, Colombia, Costa Rica, Dominica, Dominican Republic, Ecuador, El Salvador, Grenada, Guatemala, Guyana, Haiti, Honduras, Mexico, Nicaragua, Panama, Paraguay, Peru, Saint Kitts and Nevis, Saint Lucia, Suriname, Trinidad and Tobago, Uruguay, Venezuela

  * With reservation.

Signed but not ratified (4): Canada, Jamaica, Saint Vincent and the Grenadines, USA

Convention text: Organization of American States, <http://www.oas.org/juridico/english/treaties/a-63.html>

Inter-American Convention on Transparency in Conventional Weapons Acquisitions

Adopted at Guatemala City on 7 June 1999; entered into force on 21 November 2002; depositary General Secretariat of the Organization of American States

The objective of the convention is to contribute more fully to regional openness and transparency in the acquisition of conventional weapons by exchanging information regarding such acquisitions, for the purpose of promoting confidence among states in the Americas.

Parties (16): Argentina, Barbados, Brazil, Canada, Chile, Costa Rica, Dominican Republic, Ecuador, El Salvador, Guatemala, Mexico, Nicaragua, Paraguay, Peru, Uruguay, Venezuela

Signed but not ratified (6): Bolivia, Colombia, Dominica, Haiti, Honduras, USA

Convention text: Organization of American States, <http://www.oas.org/juridico/english/treaties/a-64.html>

Protocol on the Control of Firearms, Ammunition and other related Materials in the Southern African Development Community (SADC) Region

Signed at Blantyre on 14 August 2001; entered into force on 8 November 2004; depositary SADC Executive Secretary

The objectives of the protocol include the prevention, combating and eradication of the illicit manufacturing of firearms, ammunition and other related materials, and prevention of their excessive and destabilizing accumulation, trafficking, possession and use in the region.

Parties as of July 2011 (11): Botswana, Lesotho, Malawi, Mauritius, Mozambique, Namibia, South Africa, Swaziland, Tanzania, Zambia, Zimbabwe

Signed but not ratified (2*): Congo (Democratic Republic of the), Seychelles**

* Two member states of SADC, Angola and Madagascar, have neither signed nor ratified the protocol.
** Seychelles signed the protocol in 2001, but did not ratify it before withdrawing from SADC in 2004. It rejoined in 2008.

Protocol text: SADC, <http://www.sadc.int/documents-publications/show/796>

Nairobi Protocol for the Prevention, Control and Reduction of Small Arms and Light Weapons in the Great Lakes Region and the Horn of Africa

Signed at Nairobi on 21 April 2004; entered into force on 5 May 2006; depositary Regional Centre on Small Arms in the Great Lakes Region, the Horn of Africa and Bordering States (RECSA)

The objectives of the protocol include the prevention, combating and eradication of the illicit manufacture of, trafficking in, possession and use of small arms and light weapons in the subregion.

496 SIPRI YEARBOOK 2013

Parties (9): Burundi, Congo (Democratic Republic of the), Djibouti, Eritrea, Ethiopia, Kenya, Rwanda, Sudan, Uganda

Signed but not ratified (6): Central African Republic, Congo (Republic of the), Seychelles, Somalia, South Sudan, Tanzania

Protocol text: RECSA, <http://www.recsasec.org/publications/Nairobi_Protocal.pdf>

ECOWAS Convention on Small Arms and Light Weapons, their Ammunition and Other Related Materials

Adopted by the member states of the Economic Community of West African States (ECOWAS) at Abuja, on 14 June 2006; entered into force on 29 September 2009; depositary President of the ECOWAS Commission

The convention obligates the parties to prevent and combat the excessive and destabilizing accumulation of small arms and light weapons in the 15 ECOWAS member states.

Parties (11): Benin, Burkina Faso, Cape Verde, Ghana, Liberia, Mali, Niger, Nigeria, Senegal, Sierra Leone, Togo

Signed but not ratified (4): Côte d'Ivoire, Gambia, Guinea, Guinea-Bissau

Convention text: United Nations, Programme of Action Implementation Support System, <http://www.poa-iss.org/RegionalOrganizations/7.aspx>

Treaty on a Nuclear-Weapon-Free Zone in Central Asia (Treaty of Semipalatinsk)

Signed at Semipalatinsk on 8 September 2006; entered into force on 21 March 2009; depositary Kyrgyz Government

The treaty obligates the parties not to conduct research on, develop, manufacture, stockpile or otherwise acquire, possess or have control over any nuclear weapons or other nuclear explosive device by any means anywhere.

Under a *Protocol* China, France, Russia, the UK and the USA are to undertake not to use or threaten to use a nuclear explosive device against the parties to the treaty. This protocol will enter into force for each party on the date of its deposit of its instrument of ratification.

Parties (5): Kazakhstan, Kyrgyzstan, Tajikistan, Turkmenistan, Uzbekistan

Protocol: no signatures, no parties

Treaty text: United Nations, Office for Disarmament Affairs, Status of Multilateral Arms Regulation and Disarmament Agreements, <http://disarmament.un.org/treaties/t/canwfz/text>

Central African Convention for the Control of Small Arms and Light Weapons, Their Ammunition and All Parts and Components That Can Be Used for Their Manufacture, Repair and Assembly (Kinshasa Convention)

Adopted at Kinshasa on 30 April 2010; opened for signature at Brazzaville on 19 November 2010; not in force; depositary UN Secretary-General

The objectives of the convention are to prevent, combat and eradicate illicit trade and trafficking in small arms and light weapons (SALW) in Central Africa (defined to be the territory of the 10 members of the Economic Community of Central African States and Rwanda); to strengthen the control in the region of the manufacture, trade, transfer and use of SALW; to combat armed violence and ease the human suffering in the region caused by SALW; and to foster cooperation and confidence among the states parties. The convention will enter into force 30 days after the date of deposit of the sixth instrument of ratification.

Ratifications deposited (4): Central African Republic, Chad, Congo (Republic of the), Gabon

Signed but not ratified (7): Angola, Burundi, Cameroon, Congo (Democratic Republic of the), Equatorial Guinea, Rwanda, Sao Tome and Principe

Treaty text: United Nations Treaty Collection, <http://treaties.un.org/Pages/CTCTreaties.aspx?id=26>

Vienna Document 2011 on Confidence- and Security-Building Measures

Adopted by the participating states of the Organization for Security and Co-operation in Europe at Vienna on 30 November 2011; entered into force on 1 December 2011

The Vienna Document 2011 builds on the 1986 Stockholm Document on Confidence- and Security-Building Measures (CSBMs) and Disarmament in Europe and previous Vienna Documents (1990, 1992, 1994 and 1999). The Vienna Document 1990 provided for annual exchange of military information, military budget exchange, risk reduction procedures, a communication network and an annual CSBM implementation assessment. The Vienna Document 1992 and the Vienna Document 1994 extended the area of application and introduced new mechanisms and parameters for military activities, defence planning and military contacts. The Vienna Document 1999 introduced regional measures aimed at increasing transparency and confidence in a bilateral, multilateral and regional context and some improvements, in particular regarding the constraining measures.

The Vienna Document 2011 incorporated revisions on such matters as the timing of verification activities and demonstrations of new types of weapon and equipment system, and established a procedure for updating the Vienna Document every five years.

Document text: Organization for Security and Co-operation in Europe, <http://www.osce.org/fsc/86597>

III. Bilateral treaties

Treaty on the Limitation of Anti-Ballistic Missile Systems (ABM Treaty)

Signed by the USA and the USSR at Moscow on 26 May 1972; entered into force on 3 October 1972; not in force from 13 June 2002

The parties—Russia and the USA—undertook not to build nationwide defences against ballistic missile attack and to limit the development and deployment of permitted strategic missile defences. The treaty prohibited the parties from giving air defence missiles, radars or launchers the technical ability to counter strategic ballistic missiles and from testing them in a strategic ABM mode.

The **1974 Protocol** to the ABM Treaty introduced further numerical restrictions on permitted ballistic missile defences.

In 1997, Belarus, Kazakhstan, Russia, Ukraine and the USA signed a memorandum of understanding designating Belarus, Kazakhstan and Ukraine as parties to the treaty along with Russia as successor states of the USSR and a set of Agreed Statements specifying the demarcation line between strategic missile defences (which are not permitted under the treaty) and non-strategic or theatre missile defences (which are permitted under the treaty). The set of 1997 agreements on anti-missile defence were ratified by Russia in April 2000, but because the USA did not ratify them they did not enter into force. On 13 December 2001 the USA announced its withdrawal from the treaty, which came into effect on 13 June 2002.

Treaty and protocol texts: United Nations Treaty Series, vol. 944 (1974)

Treaty on the Limitation of Underground Nuclear Weapon Tests (Threshold Test-Ban Treaty, TTBT)

Signed by the USA and the USSR at Moscow on 3 July 1974; entered into force on 11 December 1990

The parties—Russia and the USA—undertake not to carry out any underground nuclear weapon test having a yield exceeding 150 kilotons. The 1974 verification protocol was replaced in 1990 with a new protocol.

Treaty and protocol texts: United Nations Treaty Series, vol. 1714 (1993)

Treaty on Underground Nuclear Explosions for Peaceful Purposes (Peaceful Nuclear Explosions Treaty, PNET)

Signed by the USA and the USSR at Moscow and Washington, DC, on 28 May 1976; entered into force on 11 December 1990

The parties—Russia and the USA—undertake not to carry out any individual underground nuclear explosion for peaceful purposes having a yield exceeding 150 kilotons or any group explosion having an aggregate yield exceeding 150 kilotons; and not to carry out any group explosion having an aggregate yield exceeding 1500 kilotons unless the individual explosions in the group could be identified and measured by agreed verification procedures. The 1976 verification protocol was replaced in 1990 with a new protocol.

Treaty and protocol texts: *United Nations Treaty Series*, vol. 1714 (1993)

Treaty on the Elimination of Intermediate-Range and Shorter-Range Missiles (INF Treaty)

Signed by the USA and the USSR at Washington, DC, on 8 December 1987; entered into force on 1 June 1988

The treaty obligated the original parties—the USA and the USSR—to destroy all ground-launched ballistic and cruise missiles with a range of 500–5500 kilometres (intermediate-range, 1000–5500 km; and shorter-range, 500–1000 km) and their launchers by 1 June 1991. A total of 2692 missiles were eliminated by May 1991. In 1994 treaty membership was expanded to include Belarus, Kazakhstan and Ukraine. For 10 years after 1 June 1991 on-site inspections were conducted to verify compliance. The use of surveillance satellites for data collection continued after the end of on-site inspections on 31 May 2001.

Treaty text: *United Nations Treaty Series*, vol. 1657 (1991)

Treaty on the Reduction and Limitation of Strategic Offensive Arms (START I)

Signed by the USA and the USSR at Moscow on 31 July 1991; entered into force on 5 December 1994; expired on 5 December 2009

The treaty obligated the original parties—the USA and the USSR—to make phased reductions in their offensive strategic nuclear forces over a seven-year period. It set numerical limits on deployed strategic nuclear delivery vehicles (SNDVs)—intercontinental ballistic missiles (ICBMs), submarine-launched ballistic missiles (SLBMs) and heavy bombers—and the nuclear warheads they carry. In the Protocol to Facilitate the Implementation of START (**1992 Lisbon Protocol**), which entered into force on 5 December 1994, Belarus, Kazakhstan and Ukraine also assumed the obligations of the former USSR under the treaty.

A follow-on treaty, New START, entered into force on 5 February 2011.

Treaty and protocol texts: US Department of State, <http://www.state.gov/t/avc/trty/146007.htm>

Treaty on Further Reduction and Limitation of Strategic Offensive Arms (START II)

Signed by Russia and the USA at Moscow on 3 January 1993; not in force

The treaty obligated the parties to eliminate their MIRVed ICBMs and reduce the number of their deployed strategic nuclear warheads to no more than 3000–3500 each (of which no more than 1750 may be deployed on SLBMs) by 1 January 2003. On 26 September 1997 the two parties signed a *Protocol* to the

treaty providing for the extension until the end of 2007 of the period of implementation of the treaty.

Note: START II was ratified by the US Senate and the Russian Parliament, but the two signatories
never exchanged the instruments of ratification. The treaty thus never entered into force. On 14 June
2002, as a response to the taking effect on 13 June of the USA's withdrawal from the ABM Treaty,
Russia declared that it would no longer be bound by START II.

Treaty and protocol texts: US Department of State, <http://www.state.gov/t/avc/trty/102887.
htm>

Treaty on Strategic Offensive Reductions (SORT, Moscow Treaty)

*Signed by Russia and the USA at Moscow on 24 May 2002; entered into force on
1 June 2003; not in force from 5 February 2011*

The treaty obligated the parties to reduce the number of their operationally
deployed strategic nuclear warheads so that the aggregate numbers did not
exceed 1700–2200 for each party by 31 December 2012. The treaty was superseded by New START on 5 February 2011.

Treaty text: *United Nations Treaty Series*, vol. 2350 (2005)

Treaty on Measures for the Further Reduction and Limitation of Strategic Offensive Arms (New START, Prague Treaty)

*Signed by Russia and the USA at Prague on 8 April 2010; entered into force on
5 February 2011*

The treaty obligates the parties—Russia and the USA—to each reduce their
number of (*a*) deployed ICBMs, SLBMs and heavy bombers to 700; (*b*) warheads on deployed ICBMs and SLBMs and warheads counted for deployed
heavy bombers to 1550; and (*c*) deployed and non-deployed ICBM launchers,
SLBM launchers and heavy bombers to 800. The reductions must be achieved
by 5 February 2018; a Bilateral Consultative Commission resolves questions
about compliance and other implementation issues. A protocol to the treaty
contains verifications mechanisms.

The treaty follows on from START I and supersedes SORT. It will remain in
force for 10 years unless superseded earlier by a subsequent agreement.

Treaty and protocol texts: US Department of State, <http://www.state.gov/t/avc/newstart/
c44126.htm>

Annex B. International security cooperation bodies

NENNE BODELL

This annex describes the main international organizations, intergovernmental bodies, treaty-implementing bodies and transfer control regimes whose aims include the promotion of security, stability, peace or arms control and lists their members or participants as of 1 January 2013. The bodies are divided into three categories: those with a global focus or membership (section I), those with a regional focus or membership (section II) and those that aim to control strategic trade (section III).

The member states of the United Nations and organs within the UN system are listed first, followed by all other bodies in alphabetical order. Not all members or participants of these bodies are UN member states. States that joined or first participated in the body during 2012 are shown in italics. The address of an Internet site with information about each organization is provided where available. On the arms control and disarmament agreements mentioned here, see annex A.

I. Bodies with a global focus or membership

United Nations (UN)

The UN, the world intergovernmental organization, was founded in 1945 through the adoption of its Charter. Its headquarters are in New York, USA. The six principal UN organs are the General Assembly, the Security Council, the Economic and Social Council (ECOSOC), the Trusteeship Council (which suspended operation in 1994), the International Court of Justice (ICJ) and the secretariat.

The General Assembly has six main committees. The First Committee (Disarmament and International Security Committee) deals with disarmament and related international security questions; the Fourth Committee (Special Political and Decolonization Committee) deals with a variety of subjects including decolonization, Palestinian refugees and human rights, peacekeeping, mine action, outer space, public information, atomic radiation and the University for Peace.

The UN Office for Disarmament Affairs (UNODA), a department of the UN Secretariat, promotes disarmament of nuclear, biological, chemical and conventional weapons. The UN also has a large number of specialized agencies and other autonomous bodies.

UN member states (193) and year of membership

Afghanistan, 1946
Albania, 1955
Algeria, 1962
Andorra, 1993
Angola, 1976
Antigua and Barbuda, 1981
Argentina, 1945
Armenia, 1992
Australia, 1945
Austria, 1955
Azerbaijan, 1992
Bahamas, 1973
Bahrain, 1971
Bangladesh, 1974
Barbados, 1966
Belarus, 1945
Belgium, 1945
Belize, 1981
Benin, 1960
Bhutan, 1971
Bolivia, 1945
Bosnia and Herzegovina, 1992
Botswana, 1966
Brazil, 1945
Brunei Darussalam, 1984
Bulgaria, 1955
Burkina Faso, 1960
Burundi, 1962
Cambodia, 1955
Cameroon, 1960
Canada, 1945
Cape Verde, 1975
Central African Republic, 1960
Chad, 1960
Chile, 1945
China, 1945
Colombia, 1945
Comoros, 1975
Congo, Democratic Republic of the, 1960
Congo, Republic of the, 1960
Costa Rica, 1945
Côte d'Ivoire, 1960
Croatia, 1992
Cuba, 1945
Cyprus, 1960
Czech Republic, 1993
Denmark, 1945
Djibouti, 1977
Dominica, 1978
Dominican Republic, 1945

Ecuador, 1945
Egypt, 1945
El Salvador, 1945
Equatorial Guinea, 1968
Eritrea, 1993
Estonia, 1991
Ethiopia, 1945
Fiji, 1970
Finland, 1955
France, 1945
Gabon, 1960
Gambia, 1965
Georgia, 1992
Germany, 1973
Ghana, 1957
Greece, 1945
Grenada, 1974
Guatemala, 1945
Guinea, 1958
Guinea-Bissau, 1974
Guyana, 1966
Haiti, 1945
Honduras, 1945
Hungary, 1955
Iceland, 1946
India, 1945
Indonesia, 1950
Iran, 1945
Iraq, 1945
Ireland, 1955
Israel, 1949
Italy, 1955
Jamaica, 1962
Japan, 1956
Jordan, 1955
Kazakhstan, 1992
Kenya, 1963
Kiribati, 1999
Korea, Democratic People's Republic of (North Korea), 1991
Korea, Republic of (South Korea), 1991
Kuwait, 1963
Kyrgyzstan, 1992
Laos, 1955
Latvia, 1991
Lebanon, 1945
Lesotho, 1966
Liberia, 1945
Libya, 1955
Liechtenstein, 1990

Lithuania, 1991
Luxembourg, 1945
Macedonia, Former Yugoslav Republic of, 1993
Madagascar, 1960
Malawi, 1964
Malaysia, 1957
Maldives, 1965
Mali, 1960
Malta, 1964
Marshall Islands, 1991
Mauritania, 1961
Mauritius, 1968
Mexico, 1945
Micronesia, 1991
Moldova, 1992
Monaco, 1993
Mongolia, 1961
Montenegro, 2006
Morocco, 1956
Mozambique, 1975
Myanmar, 1948
Namibia, 1990
Nauru, 1999
Nepal, 1955
Netherlands, 1945
New Zealand, 1945
Nicaragua, 1945
Niger, 1960
Nigeria, 1960
Norway, 1945
Oman, 1971
Pakistan, 1947
Palau, 1994
Panama, 1945
Papua New Guinea, 1975
Paraguay, 1945
Peru, 1945
Philippines, 1945
Poland, 1945
Portugal, 1955
Qatar, 1971
Romania, 1955
Russia, 1945
Rwanda, 1962
Saint Kitts and Nevis, 1983
Saint Lucia, 1979
Saint Vincent and the Grenadines, 1980
Samoa, 1976
San Marino, 1992
Sao Tome and Principe, 1975

Saudi Arabia, 1945
Senegal, 1960
Serbia, 2000
Seychelles, 1976
Sierra Leone, 1961
Singapore, 1965
Slovakia, 1993
Slovenia, 1992
Solomon Islands, 1978
Somalia, 1960
South Africa, 1945
South Sudan, 2011
Spain, 1955
Sri Lanka, 1955
Sudan, 1956

Suriname, 1975
Swaziland, 1968
Sweden, 1946
Switzerland, 2002
Syria, 1945
Tajikistan, 1992
Tanzania, 1961
Thailand, 1946
Timor-Leste, 2002
Togo, 1960
Tonga, 1999
Trinidad and Tobago, 1962
Tunisia, 1956
Turkey, 1945
Turkmenistan, 1992

Tuvalu, 2000
Uganda, 1962
UK, 1945
Ukraine, 1945
United Arab Emirates, 1971
Uruguay, 1945
USA, 1945
Uzbekistan, 1992
Vanuatu, 1981
Venezuela, 1945
Viet Nam, 1977
Yemen, 1947
Zambia, 1964
Zimbabwe, 1980

Website: <http://www.un.org/>

UN Security Council

Permanent members (the P5): China, France, Russia, UK, USA

Non-permanent members (10): Argentina**, Australia**, Azerbaijan*, Guatemala*, Korea (South)**, Luxembourg**, Morocco*, Pakistan*, Rwanda**, Togo*

> *Note*: Non-permanent members are elected by the UN General Assembly for two-year terms.
> * Member in 2012–13.
> ** Member in 2013–14.

Website: <http://www.un.org/en/sc/>

Conference on Disarmament (CD)

The CD is a multilateral arms control negotiating body that is intended to be the single multilateral disarmament negotiating forum of the international community. It has been enlarged and renamed several times since 1960. It is not a UN body but reports to the UN General Assembly. It is based in Geneva, Switzerland.

Members (65): Algeria, Argentina, Australia, Austria, Bangladesh, Belarus, Belgium, Brazil, Bulgaria, Cameroon, Canada, Chile, China, Colombia, Congo (Democratic Republic of the), Cuba, Ecuador, Egypt, Ethiopia, Finland, France, Germany, Hungary, India, Indonesia, Iran, Iraq, Ireland, Israel, Italy, Japan, Kazakhstan, Kenya, Korea (North), Korea (South), Malaysia, Mexico, Mongolia, Morocco, Myanmar, Netherlands, New Zealand, Nigeria, Norway, Pakistan, Peru, Poland, Romania, Russia, Senegal, Slovakia, South Africa, Spain, Sri Lanka, Sweden, Switzerland, Syria, Tunisia, Turkey, UK, Ukraine, USA, Venezuela, Viet Nam, Zimbabwe

Website: <http://www.unog.ch/disarmament/>

International Atomic Energy Agency (IAEA)

The IAEA is an intergovernmental organization within the UN system. It is endowed by its Statute, which entered into force in 1957, to promote the peaceful uses of atomic energy and ensure that nuclear activities are not used to further any military purpose. Under the 1968 Non-Proliferation Treaty and the nuclear weapon-free zone treaties, non-nuclear weapon states must accept IAEA nuclear safeguards to demonstrate the fulfilment of their obligation not to manufacture nuclear weapons. Its headquarters are in Vienna, Austria.

Members (158): Afghanistan, Albania, Algeria, Angola, Argentina, Armenia, Australia, Austria, Azerbaijan, Bahrain, Bangladesh, Belarus, Belgium, Belize, Benin, Bolivia, Bosnia and Herzegovina, Botswana, Brazil, Bulgaria, Burkina Faso, Burundi, Cambodia, Cameroon, Canada, Central African Republic, Chad, Chile, China, Colombia, Congo (Democratic Republic of the), Congo (Republic of the), Costa Rica, Côte d'Ivoire, Croatia, Cuba, Cyprus, Czech Republic, Denmark, *Dominica*, Dominican Republic, Ecuador, Egypt, El Salvador, Eritrea, Estonia, Ethiopia, *Fiji*, Finland, France, Gabon, Georgia, Germany, Ghana, Greece, Guatemala, Haiti, Holy See, Honduras, Hungary, Iceland, India, Indonesia, Iran, Iraq, Ireland, Israel, Italy, Jamaica, Japan, Jordan, Kazakhstan, Kenya, Korea (South), Kuwait, Kyrgyzstan, Laos, Latvia, Lebanon, Lesotho, Liberia, Libya, Liechtenstein, Lithuania, Luxembourg, Macedonia (Former Yugoslav Republic of), Madagascar, Malawi, Malaysia, Mali, Malta, Marshall Islands, Mauritania, Mauritius, Mexico, Moldova, Monaco, Mongolia, Montenegro, Morocco, Mozambique, Myanmar, Namibia, Nepal, Netherlands, New Zealand, Nicaragua, Niger, Nigeria, Norway, Oman, Pakistan, Palau, Panama, *Papua New Guinea*, Paraguay, Peru, Philippines, Poland, Portugal, Qatar, *Rwanda*, Romania, Russia, Saudi Arabia, Senegal, Serbia, Seychelles, Sierra Leone, Singapore, Slovakia, Slovenia, South Africa, Spain, Sri Lanka, Sudan, Sweden, Switzerland, Syria, Tajikistan, Tanzania, Thailand, *Togo*, *Trinidad and Tobago*, Tunisia, Turkey, Uganda, UK, Ukraine, United Arab Emirates, Uruguay, USA, Uzbekistan, Venezuela, Viet Nam, Yemen, Zambia, Zimbabwe

Notes: North Korea was a member of the IAEA until June 1994. In addition to the above-named states, Cape Verde, San Marino, Swaziland and Tonga have had their membership approved by the IAEA General Conference; it will take effect once the state deposits the necessary legal instruments with the IAEA.

Website: <http://www.iaea.org/>

International Court of Justice (ICJ)

The ICJ was established in 1945 by the UN Charter and is the principal judicial organ of the UN. The court's role is to settle legal disputes submitted to it by states and to give advisory opinions on legal questions referred to it by authorized UN organs and specialized agencies. The Court is composed of 15 judges, who are elected for terms of office of nine years by the UN General Assembly and the Security Council. Its seat is at The Hague, the Netherlands.

Website: <http://www.icj-cij.org/>

Bilateral Consultative Commission (BCC)

The BCC is a forum established under the 2010 Russian–US New START treaty to discuss issues related to the treaty's implementation. It replaced the Joint Compliance and Inspection Commission (JCIC) of the 1991 START treaty. The

BCC is required to meet at least twice each year in Geneva, Switzerland, unless the parties agree otherwise. Its work is confidential.

Website: US Department of Defense, <http://www.acq.osd.mil/tc/treaties/NST/BCC_state ments.htm>

Commonwealth of Nations

Established in its current form in 1949, the Commonwealth is an organization of developed and developing countries whose aim is to advance democracy, human rights, and sustainable economic and social development within its member states and beyond. Its secretariat is in London, UK.

Members (54): Antigua and Barbuda, Australia, Bahamas, Bangladesh, Barbados, Belize, Botswana, Brunei Darussalam, Cameroon, Canada, Cyprus, Dominica, Fiji*, Gambia, Ghana, Grenada, Guyana, India, Jamaica, Kenya, Kiribati, Lesotho, Malawi, Malaysia, Maldives, Malta, Mauritius, Mozambique, Namibia, Nauru, New Zealand, Nigeria, Pakistan, Papua New Guinea, Rwanda, Saint Kitts and Nevis, Saint Lucia, Saint Vincent and the Grenadines, Samoa, Seychelles, Sierra Leone, Singapore, Solomon Islands, South Africa, Sri Lanka, Swaziland, Tanzania, Tonga, Trinidad and Tobago, Tuvalu, Uganda, UK, Vanuatu, Zambia

  * Fiji's membership of the Commonwealth was suspended on 1 Sep. 2009.

Website: <http://www.thecommonwealth.org/>

Comprehensive Nuclear-Test-Ban Treaty Organization (CTBTO)

The CTBTO will become operational when the 1996 Comprehensive Nuclear-Test-Ban Treaty (CTBT) has entered into force. It will resolve questions of compliance with the treaty and act as a forum for consultation and cooperation among the states parties. A Preparatory Commission was established to prepare for the work of the CTBTO, in particular by establishing the International Monitoring System, consisting of seismic, hydro-acoustic, infrasound and radionuclide stations from which data is transmitted to the CTBTO International Data Centre. Its seat is in Vienna, Austria.

Signatories to the CTBT (182): See annex A

Website: <http://www.ctbto.org/>

Group of Eight (G8)

The G8 is a group of (originally seven) leading industrialized countries that have met informally, at the level of head of state or government, since the 1970s. The G8 Global Partnership against the Spread of Weapons and Materials of Mass Destruction was launched in 2002 to address non-proliferation, disarmament, counterterrorism and nuclear safety issues. It was extended for an unspecified period in May 2011.

Members (8): Canada, France, Germany, Italy, Japan, Russia, UK, USA

Website: <http://www.g8.gc.ca/>

International Criminal Court (ICC)

The ICC is an independent, permanent international criminal court dealing with questions of genocide, war crimes and crimes against humanity. The court's statute was adopted in Rome in 1998 and entered into force on 1 July 2002. Its seat is at The Hague, the Netherlands.

Parties (121): Afghanistan, Albania, Andorra, Antigua and Barbuda, Argentina, Australia, Austria, Bangladesh, Barbados, Belgium, Belize, Benin, Bolivia, Bosnia and Herzegovina, Botswana, Brazil, Bulgaria, Burkina Faso, Burundi, Cambodia, Canada, Cape Verde, Central African Republic, Chad, Chile, Colombia, Comoros, Congo (Democratic Republic of the), Congo (Republic of the), Cook Islands, Costa Rica, Croatia, Cyprus, Czech Republic, Denmark, Djibouti, Dominica, Dominican Republic, Ecuador, Estonia, Fiji, Finland, France, Gabon, Gambia, Georgia, Germany, Ghana, Greece, Grenada, *Guatemala*, Guinea, Guyana, Honduras, Hungary, Iceland, Ireland, Italy, Japan, Jordan, Kenya, Korea (South), Latvia, Lesotho, Liberia, Liechtenstein, Lithuania, Luxembourg, Macedonia (Former Yugoslav Republic of), Madagascar, Malawi, Maldives, Mali, Malta, Marshall Islands, Mauritius, Mexico, Moldova, Mongolia, Montenegro, Namibia, Nauru, Netherlands, New Zealand, Niger, Nigeria, Norway, Panama, Paraguay, Peru, Philippines, Poland, Portugal, Romania, Saint Kitts and Nevis, Saint Lucia, Saint Vincent and the Grenadines, Samoa, San Marino, Senegal, Serbia, Seychelles, Sierra Leone, Slovakia, Slovenia, South Africa, Spain, Suriname, Sweden, Switzerland, Tajikistan, Tanzania, Timor-Leste, Trinidad and Tobago, Tunisia, Uganda, UK, Uruguay, Vanuatu, Venezuela, Zambia

Website: <http://www.icc-cpi.int/>

Non-Aligned Movement (NAM)

NAM was established in 1961 as a forum for consultations and coordination of positions in the United Nations on political, economic and arms control issues among non-aligned states. The 16th NAM Summit was held in Tehran, Iran, in August 2012. The 17th summit will be hosted by Venezuela in 2015.

Members (120): Afghanistan, Algeria, Angola, Antigua and Barbuda, Azerbaijan, Bahamas, Bahrain, Bangladesh, Barbados, Belarus, Belize, Benin, Bhutan, Bolivia, Botswana, Brunei Darussalam, Burkina Faso, Burundi, Cambodia, Cameroon, Cape Verde, Central African Republic, Chad, Chile, Colombia, Comoros, Congo (Democratic Republic of the), Congo (Republic of the), Côte d'Ivoire, Cuba, Djibouti, Dominica, Dominican Republic, Ecuador, Egypt, Equatorial Guinea, Eritrea, Ethiopia, Fiji, Gabon, Gambia, Ghana, Grenada, Guatemala, Guinea, Guinea-Bissau, Guyana, Haiti, Honduras, India, Indonesia, Iran, Iraq, Jamaica, Jordan, Kenya, Korea (North), Kuwait, Laos, Lebanon, Lesotho, Liberia, Libya, Madagascar, Malawi, Malaysia, Maldives, Mali, Mauritania, Mauritius, Mongolia, Morocco, Mozambique, Myanmar, Namibia, Nepal, Nicaragua, Niger, Nigeria, Oman, Pakistan, Palestine Liberation Organization, Panama, Papua New Guinea, Peru, Philippines, Qatar, Rwanda, Saint Kitts and Nevis, Saint Lucia, Saint Vincent and the Grenadines, Sao Tome and Principe, Saudi Arabia, Senegal, Seychelles, Sierra Leone, Singapore, Somalia, South Africa, Sri Lanka, Sudan, Suriname, Swaziland, Syria, Tanzania, Thailand, Timor-Leste, Togo, Trinidad and Tobago, Tunisia, Turkmenistan, Uganda, United Arab Emirates, Uzbekistan, Vanuatu, Venezuela, Viet Nam, Yemen, Zambia, Zimbabwe

Website: <http://www.nam.gov.ir/>

Organisation for Economic Co-operation and Development (OECD)

Established in 1961, the OECD's objectives are to promote economic and social welfare by coordinating policies among the member states. Its headquarters are in Paris, France.

Members (34): Australia, Austria, Belgium, Canada, Chile, Czech Republic, Denmark, Estonia, Finland, France, Germany, Greece, Hungary, Iceland, Ireland, Israel, Italy, Japan, Korea (South), Luxembourg, Mexico, Netherlands, New Zealand, Norway, Poland, Portugal, Slovakia, Slovenia, Spain, Sweden, Switzerland, Turkey, UK, USA

Website: <http://www.oecd.org/>

Organisation for the Prohibition of Chemical Weapons (OPCW)

The OPCW was established by the 1993 Chemical Weapons Convention to oversee implementation of the convention and resolve questions of compliance. Its seat is in The Hague, the Netherlands.

Parties to the Chemical Weapons Convention (188): See annex A

Website: <http://www.opcw.org/>

Organization of the Islamic Conference (OIC)

The OIC was established in 1969 by Islamic states to promote cooperation among the members and to support peace, security and the struggle of the people of Palestine and all Muslim people. Its secretariat is in Jeddah, Saudi Arabia.

Members (57): Afghanistan, Albania, Algeria, Azerbaijan, Bahrain, Bangladesh, Benin, Brunei Darussalam, Burkina Faso, Cameroon, Chad, Comoros, Côte d'Ivoire, Djibouti, Egypt, Gabon, Gambia, Guinea, Guinea-Bissau, Guyana, Indonesia, Iran, Iraq, Jordan, Kazakhstan, Kuwait, Kyrgyzstan, Lebanon, Libya, Malaysia, Maldives, Mali, Mauritania, Morocco, Mozambique, Niger, Nigeria, Oman, Pakistan, Palestine, Qatar, Saudi Arabia, Senegal, Sierra Leone, Somalia, Sudan, Suriname, Syria, Tajikistan, Togo, Tunisia, Turkey, Turkmenistan, Uganda, United Arab Emirates, Uzbekistan, Yemen

Website: <http://www.oic-oci.org/>

Special Verification Commission (SVC)

The Commission was established by the 1987 Soviet–US Treaty on the Elimination of Intermediate-Range and Shorter-Range Missiles (INF Treaty) as a forum to resolve compliance questions and measures necessary to improve the viability and effectiveness of the treaty.

Parties to the INF Treaty (5): See annex A

II. Bodies with a regional focus or membership

African Union (AU)

The AU was formally established in 2001 and in 2002 it replaced the Organization for African Unity. Membership is open to all African states. The AU promotes unity, security and conflict resolution, democracy, human rights, and political, social and economic integration in Africa. The Peace and Security Council (PSC) is a standing decision-making organ for the prevention, management and resolution of conflicts. The AU's headquarters are in Addis Ababa, Ethiopia.

Members (54): Algeria, Angola, Benin, Botswana, Burkina Faso, Burundi, Cameroon, Cape Verde, Central African Republic, Chad, Comoros, Congo (Democratic Republic of the), Congo (Republic of the), Côte d'Ivoire, Djibouti, Egypt, Equatorial Guinea, Eritrea, Ethiopia, Gabon, Gambia, Ghana, Guinea, Guinea-Bissau*, Kenya, Lesotho, Liberia, Libya, Madagascar**, Malawi, Mali, Mauritania, Mauritius, Mozambique, Namibia, Niger, Nigeria, Rwanda, Western Sahara (Sahrawi Arab Democratic Republic, SADR), Sao Tome and Principe, Senegal, Seychelles, Sierra Leone, Somalia, South Africa, South Sudan, Sudan, Swaziland, Tanzania, Togo, Tunisia, Uganda, Zambia, Zimbabwe

* Guinea-Bissau was suspended from the AU in Apr. 2012.
** Madagascar was suspended from the AU in Mar. 2009.

Website: <http://www.au.int/>

Asia–Pacific Economic Cooperation (APEC)

APEC was established in 1989 to enhance open trade and economic prosperity in the Asia–Pacific region. Security and political issues, including combating terrorism, non-proliferation of weapons of mass destruction and effective transfer control systems, have been increasingly discussed in this forum since the mid-1990s. Its seat is in Singapore.

Member economies (21): Australia, Brunei Darussalam, Canada, Chile, China, Hong Kong, Indonesia, Japan, Korea (South), Malaysia, Mexico, New Zealand, Papua New Guinea, Peru, Philippines, Russia, Singapore, Taiwan, Thailand, USA, Viet Nam

Website: <http://www.apec.org/>

Association of Southeast Asian Nations (ASEAN)

ASEAN was established in 1967 to promote economic, social and cultural development as well as regional peace and security in South East Asia. The seat of the secretariat is in Jakarta, Indonesia.

Members (10): Brunei Darussalam, Cambodia, Indonesia, Laos, Malaysia, Myanmar, Philippines, Singapore, Thailand, Viet Nam

Website: <http://www.asean.org/>

ASEAN Regional Forum (ARF)

The ARF was established in 1994 to address security issues.

Participants (27): The ASEAN member states and Australia, Bangladesh, Canada, China, European Union, India, Japan, Korea (North), Korea (South), Mongolia, New Zealand, Pakistan, Papua New Guinea, Russia, Sri Lanka, Timor-Leste, USA

Website: <http://aseanregionalforum.asean.org/>

ASEAN Plus Three (APT)

The APT cooperation began in 1997, in the wake of the Asian financial crisis, and was institutionalized in 1999. It aims to foster economic, political and security cooperation and financial stability among its participants.

Participants (13): The ASEAN member states and China, Japan, Korea (South)

Website: <http://www.asean.org/asean/external-relations/asean-3>

East Asia Summit (EAS)

The East Asia Summit started in 2005 as a regional forum for dialogue on strategic, political and economic issues with the aim of promoting peace, stability and economic prosperity in East Asia. The annual meetings are held in connection with the ASEAN summits.

Participants (18): The ASEAN member states and Australia, China, India, Japan, Korea (South), New Zealand, Russia, USA

Website: <http://www.asean.org/asean/external-relations/east-asia-summit-eas/>

Collective Security Treaty Organization (CSTO)

The CSTO was formally established in 2002–2003 by six signatories of the 1992 Collective Security Treaty. It aims to promote cooperation among its members. An objective is to provide a more efficient response to strategic problems such as terrorism and narcotics trafficking. Its seat is in Moscow, Russia.

Members (6): Armenia, Belarus, Kazakhstan, Kyrgyzstan, Russia, Tajikistan

Website: <http://www.odkb-csto.org/>

Note: Uzbekistan suspended its membership in June 2012.

Commonwealth of Independent States (CIS)

The CIS was established in 1991 as a framework for multilateral cooperation among former Soviet republics. Its headquarters are in Minsk, Belarus.

Members (11): Armenia, Azerbaijan, Belarus, Kazakhstan, Kyrgyzstan, Moldova, Russia, Tajikistan, Turkmenistan, Ukraine, Uzbekistan

Website: <http://www.cis.minsk.by/>

Communauté économique d'États de l'Afrique Centrale (CEEAC, Economic Community of Central African States, ECCAS)

CEEAC was established in 1983 to promote political dialogue, create a customs union and establish common policies in Central Africa. Its secretariat is in Libreville, Gabon. The Council for Peace and Security in Central Africa (COPAX) is a mechanism for promoting joint political and military strategies for conflict prevention, management and resolution in Central Africa.

Members (10): Angola, Burundi, Cameroon, Central African Republic, Chad, Congo (Democratic Republic of the), Congo (Republic of the), Equatorial Guinea, Gabon, Sao Tome and Principe

Website: <http://www.ceeac-eccas.org/>

Conference on Interaction and Confidence-building Measures in Asia (CICA)

Initiated in 1992, CICA was formally established in 1999 as a forum to enhance security cooperation and confidence-building measures among the member states. It also promotes economic, social and cultural cooperation. Its secretariat is in Almaty, Kazakhstan.

Members (24): Afghanistan, Azerbaijan, Bahrain, Cambodia, China, Egypt, India, Iran, Iraq, Israel, Jordan, Kazakhstan, Korea (South), Kyrgyzstan, Mongolia, Pakistan, Palestine, Russia, Tajikistan, Thailand, Turkey, United Arab Emirates, Uzbekistan, Viet Nam

Website: <http://www.s-cica.org/>

Council of Europe (COE)

Established in 1949, the Council is open to membership of all European states that accept the principle of the rule of law and guarantee their citizens' human rights and fundamental freedoms. Its seat is in Strasbourg, France. Among its organs are the European Court of Human Rights and the Council of Europe Development Bank.

Members (47): Albania, Andorra, Armenia, Austria, Azerbaijan, Belgium, Bosnia and Herzegovina, Bulgaria, Croatia, Cyprus, Czech Republic, Denmark, Estonia, Finland, France, Georgia, Germany, Greece, Hungary, Iceland, Ireland, Italy, Latvia, Liechtenstein, Lithuania, Luxembourg, Macedonia (Former Yugoslav Republic of), Malta, Moldova, Monaco, Montenegro, Netherlands, Norway, Poland, Portugal, Romania, Russia, San Marino, Serbia, Slovakia, Slovenia, Spain, Sweden, Switzerland, Turkey, UK, Ukraine

Website: <http://www.coe.int/>

Council of the Baltic Sea States (CBSS)

The CBSS was established in 1992 as a regional intergovernmental organization for cooperation among the states of the Baltic Sea region. Its secretariat is in Stockholm, Sweden.

Members (12): Denmark, Estonia, European Commission, Finland, Germany, Iceland, Latvia, Lithuania, Norway, Poland, Russia, Sweden

Website: <http://www.cbss.org/>

Economic Community of West African States (ECOWAS)

ECOWAS was established in 1975 to promote trade and cooperation and contribute to development in West Africa. In 1981 it adopted the Protocol on Mutual Assistance in Defence Matters. Its executive secretariat is in Lagos, Nigeria.

Members (15): Benin, Burkina Faso, Cape Verde, Côte d'Ivoire, Gambia, Ghana, Guinea, Guinea-Bissau, Liberia, Mali, Niger, Nigeria, Senegal, Sierra Leone, Togo

Website: <http://www.ecowas.int/>

European Union (EU)

The EU is an organization of European states that cooperate in a wide field, including a single market with free movement of people, goods, services and capital, a common currency for some members, and a Common Foreign and Security Policy (CFSP). Its main bodies are the European Council, the Council of the European Union, the European Commission and the European Parliament. The CFSP and the Common Security and Defence Policy (CSDP) are coordinated by the High Representative of the Union for Foreign Affairs and Security Policy, assisted by the European External Action Service (EEAS). The 2007 Treaty of Lisbon, which modernizes the way in which the EU functions, entered into force on 1 December 2009. The EU's seat is in Brussels, Belgium.

Members (27): Austria, Belgium, Bulgaria, Cyprus, Czech Republic, Denmark, Estonia, Finland, France, Germany, Greece, Hungary, Ireland, Italy, Latvia, Lithuania, Luxembourg, Malta, Netherlands, Poland, Portugal, Romania, Slovakia, Slovenia, Spain, Sweden, UK

Website: <http://europa.eu/>

European Atomic Energy Community (Euratom, or EAEC)

Euratom was created by the 1957 Treaty Establishing the European Atomic Energy Community (Euratom Treaty) to promote the development of nuclear energy for peaceful purposes and to administer (in cooperation with the IAEA) the multinational regional safeguards system covering the EU member states. The Euratom Supply Agency, located in Luxembourg, has the task of ensuring a regular and equitable supply of ores, source materials and special fissile materials to EU member states.

Members (27): The EU member states

Website: <http://ec.europa.eu/euratom/>

European Defence Agency (EDA)

The EDA is an agency of the EU, under the direction of the Council. It was established in 2004 to help develop European defence capabilities, to promote European armaments cooperation and to work for a strong European defence technological and industrial base. The EDA's decision-making body is the Steering Board, composed of the defence ministers of the participating member states and the EU's High Representative for Foreign Affairs and Security Policy (as head of the agency). The EDA is located in Brussels, Belgium.

Participating member states (26): Austria, Belgium, Bulgaria, Cyprus, Czech Republic, Estonia, Finland, France, Germany, Greece, Hungary, Ireland, Italy, Latvia, Lithuania, Luxembourg, Malta, Netherlands, Poland, Portugal, Romania, Slovakia, Slovenia, Spain, Sweden, UK

Website: <http://eda.europa.eu/>

Gulf Cooperation Council (GCC)

Formally called the Cooperation Council for the Arab States of the Gulf, the GCC was created in 1981 to promote regional integration in such areas as economy, finance, trade, administration and legislation and to foster scientific and technical progress. The members also cooperate in areas of foreign policy and military and security matters. The Supreme Council is the highest GCC authority. Its headquarters are in Riyadh, Saudi Arabia

Members (6): Bahrain, Kuwait, Oman, Qatar, Saudi Arabia, United Arab Emirates

Website: <http://www.gcc-sg.org/>

Intergovernmental Authority on Development (IGAD)

Initiated in 1986 as the Intergovernmental Authority on Drought and Development, IGAD was formally established in 1996 to promote peace and stability in the Horn of Africa and to create mechanisms for conflict prevention, management and resolution. Its secretariat is in Djibouti.

Members (7): Djibouti, Ethiopia, Kenya, Somalia, South Sudan, Sudan, Uganda

Note: Eritrea suspended its membership in 2007 in response to IGAD's support of Ethiopia's intervention in Somalia. Eritrea attempted to reactivate its membership in 2011, but this was not accepted by the other members.

Website: <http://www.igad.int/>

International Conference on the Great Lakes Region (ICGLR)

The ICGLR, which was initiated in 2004, works to promote peace and security, political and social stability, and growth and development in the Great Lakes region. In 2006 the member states adopted the Pact on Peace, Stability and Development in the Great Lakes Region, which entered into force in 2008. The executive secretariat of the ICGLR is in Bujumbura, Burundi.

Members (11): Angola, Burundi, Central African Republic, Congo (Republic of the), Congo (Democratic Republic of the), Kenya, Uganda, Rwanda, Sudan, Tanzania, Zambia

Website: <http://www.icglr.org/>

Joint Consultative Group (JCG)

The JCG was established by the 1990 Treaty on Conventional Armed Forces in Europe (CFE Treaty) to promote the objectives and implementation of the treaty by reconciling ambiguities of interpretation and implementation. Its seat is in Vienna, Austria.

Parties to the CFE Treaty (30): See annex A

Website: <http://www.osce.org/jcg/>

League of Arab States

Also known as the Arab League, it was established in 1945. Its principal object-ive is to form closer union among Arab states and foster political and economic cooperation. An agreement for collective defence and economic cooperation among the members was signed in 1950. Its permanent headquarters are in Cairo, Egypt.

Members (22): Algeria, Bahrain, Comoros, Djibouti, Egypt, Iraq, Jordan, Kuwait, Lebanon, Libya, Mauritania, Morocco, Oman, Palestine, Qatar, Saudi Arabia, Somalia, Sudan, Syria*, Tunisia, United Arab Emirates, Yemen

  * Syria was suspended from the organization on 16 Nov. 2011.

Website: <http://www.lasportal.org/>

North Atlantic Treaty Organization (NATO)

NATO was established in 1949 by the North Atlantic Treaty (Washington Treaty) as a Western defence alliance. Article 5 of the treaty defines the members' commitment to respond to an armed attack against any party to the treaty. Its headquarters are in Brussels, Belgium.

Members (28): Albania, Belgium, Bulgaria, Canada, Croatia, Czech Republic, Denmark, Estonia, France, Germany, Greece, Hungary, Iceland, Italy, Latvia, Lithuania, Luxembourg, Netherlands, Norway, Poland, Portugal, Romania, Slovakia, Slovenia, Spain, Turkey, UK, USA

Website: <http://www.nato.int/>

Euro-Atlantic Partnership Council (EAPC)

The EAPC brings together NATO and its Partnership for Peace (PFP) partners for dialogue and consultation. It is the overall political frame-work for the bilateral PFP programme.

Members (50): The NATO member states and Armenia, Austria, Azerbaijan, Belarus, Bosnia and Herzegovina, Finland, Georgia, Ireland, Kazakhstan, Kyrgyzstan,

Macedonia (Former Yugoslav Republic of), Malta, Moldova, Montenegro, Russia, Serbia, Sweden, Switzerland, Tajikistan, Turkmenistan, Ukraine, Uzbekistan

Website: <http://www.nato.int/cps/en/natolive/topics_49276.htm>

NATO–Georgia Commission (NGC)

The NGC was established in September 2008 to serve as a forum for political consultations and for practical cooperation to help Georgia achieve its goal of membership in NATO.

Participants (29): The NATO member states and Georgia

Website: <http://www.nato.int/cps/en/natolive/topics_52131.htm>

NATO–Russia Council (NRC)

The NRC was established in 2002 as a mechanism for consultation, consensus building, cooperation, and joint decisions and action on security issues. It focuses on areas of mutual interest identified in the 1997 NATO–Russia Founding Act on Mutual Relations, Cooperation and Security and new areas, such as terrorism, crisis management and non-proliferation.

Participants (29): The NATO member states and Russia

Website: <http://www.nato-russia-council.info/>

NATO–Ukraine Commission (NUC)

The NUC was established in 1997 for consultations on political and security issues, conflict prevention and resolution, non-proliferation, arms transfers and technology transfers, and other subjects of common concern.

Participants (29): The NATO member states and Ukraine

Website: <http://www.nato.int/cps/en/natolive/topics_50319.htm>

Open Skies Consultative Commission (OSCC)

The OSCC was established by the 1992 Treaty on Open Skies to resolve questions of compliance with the treaty.

Parties to the Open Skies Treaty (34): See annex A

Website: <http://www.osce.org/oscc/>

Organisation Conjointe de Coopération en matière d'Armement (OCCAR, Organisation for Joint Armament Cooperation)

OCCAR was established in 1996, with legal status since 2001, by France, Germany, Italy and the UK. Its aim is to provide more effective and efficient arrangements for the management of specific collaborative armament pro-grammes. Its headquarters are in Bonn, Germany.

Members (6): Belgium, France, Germany, Italy, Spain, UK

Website: <http://www.occar.int/>

Organismo para la Proscripción de las Armas Nucleares en la América Latina y el Caribe (OPANAL, Agency for the Prohibition of Nuclear Weapons in Latin America and the Caribbean)

OPANAL was established by the 1967 Treaty of Tlatelolco to resolve, together with the IAEA, questions of compliance with the treaty. Its seat is in Mexico City, Mexico.

Parties to the Treaty of Tlatelolco (33): See annex A

Website: <http://www.opanal.org/>

Organization for Democracy and Economic Development–GUAM

GUAM is a group of four states, established to promote stability and strengthen security, whose history goes back to 1997. The organization was established in 2006. The members cooperate to promote social and economic development and trade in eight working groups. Its secretariat is in Kyiv, Ukraine.

Members (4): Azerbaijan, Georgia, Moldova, Ukraine

Website: <http://guam-organization.org/>

Organization for Security and Co-operation in Europe (OSCE)

The Conference on Security and Co-operation in Europe (CSCE), which had been initiated in 1973, was renamed the OSCE in 1995. It is intended to be the primary instrument of comprehensive and cooperative security for early warn-ing, conflict prevention, crisis management and post-conflict rehabilitation in its area. Its headquarters are in Vienna, Austria. The OSCE Troika consists of the chairperson-in-office and the previous and succeeding chairpersons. The Forum for Security Co-operation (FSC) deals with arms control and con-fidence- and security-building measures. The OSCE comprises several institu-tions, all located in Europe.

Participants (57): Albania, Andorra, Armenia, Austria, Azerbaijan, Belarus, Belgium, Bosnia and Herzegovina, Bulgaria, Canada, Croatia, Cyprus, Czech Republic, Denmark, Estonia, Finland, France, Georgia, Germany, Greece, Holy See, Hungary, Iceland, Ireland, Italy, Kazakhstan, Kyrgyzstan, Latvia, Liechtenstein, Lithuania, Luxembourg, Macedonia (Former Yugoslav Republic of), Malta, Moldova, Monaco, *Mongolia*, Montenegro, Netherlands, Norway, Poland, Portugal, Romania, Russia, San Marino, Serbia, Slovakia, Slovenia, Spain, Sweden, Switzerland, Tajikistan, Turkey, Turkmenistan, UK, Ukraine, USA, Uzbekistan

Website: <http://www.osce.org/>

Minsk Group

The Minsk Group supports the Minsk Process, an ongoing forum for negotiations on a peaceful settlement of the conflict in Nagorno-Karabakh.

Members: Armenia, Azerbaijan, Belarus, Finland, France*, Germany, Italy, Russia*, Sweden, Turkey, USA*, OSCE Troika

   * The representatives of these 3 states co-chair the group.

Website: <http://www.osce.org/mg/>

Organization of American States (OAS)

The OAS is a group of states in the Americas that adopted its charter in 1948, with the objective of strengthening peace and security in the western hemisphere. The general secretariat is in Washington, DC, USA.

Members (35): Antigua and Barbuda, Argentina, Bahamas, Barbados, Belize, Bolivia, Brazil, Canada, Chile, Colombia, Costa Rica, Cuba*, Dominica, Dominican Republic, Ecuador, El Salvador, Grenada, Guatemala, Guyana, Haiti, Honduras, Jamaica, Mexico, Nicaragua, Panama, Paraguay, Peru, Saint Kitts and Nevis, Saint Lucia, Saint Vincent and the Grenadines, Suriname, Trinidad and Tobago, Uruguay, USA, Venezuela

   * By a resolution of 3 June 2009, the 1962 resolution that excluded Cuba from the OAS ceased to have effect; according to the 2009 resolution, Cuba's participation in the organization 'will be the result of a process of dialogue'. Cuba has declined to participate in OAS activities.

Website: <http://www.oas.org/>

Organization of the Black Sea Economic Cooperation (BSEC)

BSEC was established in 1992. Its aims are to ensure peace, stability and prosperity and to promote and develop economic cooperation and progress in the Black Sea region. Its permanent secretariat is in Istanbul, Turkey.

Members (12): Albania, Armenia, Azerbaijan, Bulgaria, Georgia, Greece, Moldova, Romania, Russia, Serbia, Turkey, Ukraine

Website: <http://www.bsec-organization.org/>

Pacific Islands Forum

The forum was founded in 1971 by a group of South Pacific states that proposed the South Pacific Nuclear-Free Zone, embodied in the 1985 Treaty of Rarotonga. As well as monitoring implementation of the treaty, the forum provides a venue for informal discussions on a wide range of issues. The secretariat is in Suva, Fiji.

Members (16): Australia, Cook Islands, Fiji, Kiribati, Marshall Islands, Micronesia, Nauru, New Zealand, Niue, Palau, Papua New Guinea, Samoa, Solomon Islands, Tonga, Tuvalu, Vanuatu

Website: <http://www.forumsec.org/>

Regional Cooperation Council

The RCC was launched in 2008 as the successor of the Stability Pact for South Eastern Europe that was initiated by the EU at the 1999 Conference on South Eastern Europe. It promotes mutual cooperation and European and Euro-Atlantic integration of South Eastern Europe in order to inspire development in the region for the benefit of its people. It focuses on six priority areas: economic and social development, energy and infrastructure, justice and home affairs, security cooperation, building human capital, and parliamentary cooperation. Its secretariat is based in Sarajevo and its Liaison Office in Brussels.

Members (46): Albania, Austria, Bosnia and Herzegovina, Bulgaria, Canada, Council of Europe, Council of Europe Development Bank, Croatia, Czech Republic, Denmark, European Bank for Reconstruction and Development, European Investment Bank, European Union, Germany, Finland, France, Greece, Hungary, International Organization for Migration, Ireland, Italy, Latvia, Macedonia (Former Yugoslav Republic of), Moldova, Montenegro, North Atlantic Treaty Organization, Norway, Organisation for Economic Co-operation and Development, Organization for Security and Co-operation in Europe, Poland, Romania, Serbia, Slovakia, Slovenia, South East European Cooperative Initiative, Spain, Sweden, Switzerland, Turkey, UK, United Nations, UN Economic Commission for Europe, UN Development Programme, UN Interim Administration Mission in Kosovo, USA, World Bank

Website: <http://www.rcc.int/>

Shanghai Cooperation Organisation (SCO)

The SCO's predecessor group, the Shanghai Five, was founded in 1996; it was renamed the SCO in 2001 and opened for membership of all states that support its aims. The member states cooperate on confidence-building measures and regional security and in the economic sphere. The SCO secretariat is in Beijing, China.

Members (6): China, Kazakhstan, Kyrgyzstan, Russia, Tajikistan, Uzbekistan

Website: <http://www.sectsco.org/>

Sistema de la Integración Centroamericana (SICA, Central American Integration System)

SICA was founded in 1991 with the signing of the Tegucigalpa Protocol. One of the organization's purposes is to set up a new model of regional security based on the reasonable balance of forces; the strengthening of civilian authority; the overcoming of extreme poverty; the promotion of sustainable development; the protection of the environment; and the eradication of violence, corruption, terrorism, and drug and arms trafficking. The SICA headquarters are located in San Salvador, El Salvador.

Members (7): Belize, Costa Rica, El Salvador, Guatemala, Honduras, Nicaragua, Panama

Website: <http://www.sica.int/>

Six-Party Talks

The talks are a forum for multilateral negotiations on North Korea's nuclear programme. They are held in Beijing and are chaired by China.

Participants (6): China, Japan, Korea (North), Korea (South), Russia, USA

Southern African Development Community (SADC)

SADC was established in 1992 to promote regional economic development and the fundamental principles of sovereignty, peace and security, human rights and democracy. The Organ on Politics, Defence and Security Cooperation (OPDS) is intended to promote peace and security in the region. The secretariat is in Gaborone, Botswana.

Members (15): Angola, Botswana, Congo (Democratic Republic of the), Lesotho, Madagascar*, Malawi, Mauritius, Mozambique, Namibia, Seychelles, South Africa, Swaziland, Tanzania, Zambia, Zimbabwe

 * Madagascar was suspended from all organs of the SADC in Mar. 2009.

Website: <http://www.sadc.int/>

Sub-Regional Consultative Commission (SRCC)

The SRCC was established by the 1996 Agreement on Sub-Regional Arms Control (Florence Agreement) as the forum in which the parties resolve questions of compliance with the agreement.

Parties to the Florence Agreement (4): See annex A

Website: <http://www.osce.org/item/43725>

Unión de Naciones Suramericanas (UNASUR, Union of South American Nations)

UNASUR is an intergovernmental organization with the aim of strengthening regional integration, political dialogue, economic development and coordination in defence matters among its member states. Its 2008 Constitutive Treaty entered into force on 11 March 2011 and it will gradually replace the Andean Community and the Mercado Común del Sur (MERCOSUR, Southern Common Market). Its headquarters are in Quito, Ecuador.

Members (12): Argentina, Bolivia, Brazil, Chile, Colombia, Ecuador, Guyana, Paraguay, Peru, Suriname, Uruguay, Venezuela

Website: <http://www.unasursg.org/>

Consejo de Defensa Suramericano (CDS, South American Defence Council)

The CDS was approved by the UNASUR member states in December 2008 and had its first meeting in March 2009. The objectives of the CDS are to consolidate South America as a zone of peace and to create a regional identity and strengthen regional cooperation in defence issues.

Members (12): The UNASUR members

Website: <http://www.unasurcds.org/>

III. Strategic trade control regimes

Australia Group (AG)

The AG is a group of states, formed in 1985, that seeks to prevent the intentional or inadvertent supply of materials or equipment to chemical or biological weapon programmes by sharing information on proliferation cases and strategies to manage them, including the harmonization of transfer controls.

Participants (41): Argentina, Australia, Austria, Belgium, Bulgaria, Canada, Croatia, Cyprus, Czech Republic, Denmark, Estonia, European Commission, Finland, France, Germany, Greece, Hungary, Iceland, Ireland, Italy, Japan, Korea (South), Latvia, Lithuania, Luxembourg, Malta, Netherlands, New Zealand, Norway, Poland, Portugal, Romania, Slovakia, Slovenia, Spain, Sweden, Switzerland, Turkey, UK, Ukraine, USA

Website: <http://www.australiagroup.net/>

Financial Action Task Force (FATF)

The FATF is an intergovernmental policymaking body whose purpose is to establish international standards and develop and promote policies, at both national and international levels. It was established in 1989 by the Group of Seven (G7), initially to examine and develop measures to combat money laundering; its mandate was expanded in 2001 to incorporate efforts to combat terrorist financing and again in 2008 to include the financing of weapon of mass destruction (WMD) proliferation efforts. Its secretariat is in Paris, France.

Members (36): Argentina, Australia, Austria, Belgium, Brazil, Canada, China, Denmark, European Commission, Finland, France, Germany, Greece, Gulf Cooperation Council, Hong Kong (China), Iceland, India, Ireland, Italy, Japan, Korea (South), Luxembourg, Mexico, Netherlands, New Zealand, Norway, Portugal, Russia, Singapore, South Africa, Spain, Sweden, Switzerland, Turkey, UK, USA

Website: <http://www.fatf-gafi.org/>

Hague Code of Conduct against Ballistic Missile Proliferation (HCOC)

The 2002 HCOC is subscribed to by a group of states that recognize its principles, primarily the need to prevent and curb the proliferation of ballistic missile systems capable of delivering weapons of mass destruction and the importance of strengthening multilateral disarmament and non-proliferation mechanisms. The Austrian Ministry of Foreign Affairs, Vienna, Austria, acts as the HCOC secretariat.

Subscribing states (134): Afghanistan, Albania, Andorra, Argentina, Armenia, Australia, Austria, Azerbaijan, Belarus, Belgium, Benin, Bosnia and Herzegovina, Bulgaria, Burkina Faso,

Burundi, Cambodia, Cameroon, Canada, Cape Verde, Central African Republic, Chad, Chile, Colombia, Comoros, Congo (Republic of), Cook Islands, Costa Rica, Croatia, Cyprus, Czech Republic, Denmark, Dominican Republic, Ecuador, El Salvador, Eritrea, Estonia, Ethiopia, Fiji, Finland, France, Gabon, Gambia, Georgia, Germany, Ghana, Greece, Guatemala, Guinea, Guinea-Bissau, Guyana, Haiti, Holy See, Honduras, Hungary, Iceland, Iraq, Ireland, Italy, Japan, Jordan, Kazakhstan, Kenya, Kiribati, Korea (South), Latvia, Liberia, Libya, Liechtenstein, Lithuania, Luxembourg, Macedonia (Former Yugoslav Republic of), Madagascar, Malawi, Maldives, Mali, Malta, Marshall Islands, Mauritania, Micronesia, Moldova, Monaco, Mongolia, Montenegro, Morocco, Mozambique, Netherlands, New Zealand, Nicaragua, Niger, Nigeria, Norway, Palau, Panama, Papua New Guinea, Paraguay, Peru, Philippines, Poland, Portugal, Romania, Russia, Rwanda, Samoa, San Marino, Senegal, Serbia, Seychelles, Sierra Leone, Singapore, Slovakia, Slovenia, South Africa, Spain, Sudan, Suriname, Sweden, Switzerland, Tajikistan, Tanzania, Timor-Leste, Tonga, Tunisia, Turkey, Turkmenistan, Tuvalu, Uganda, UK, Ukraine, Uruguay, USA, Uzbekistan, Vanuatu, Venezuela, Zambia

Website: <http://www.hcoc.at/>

Missile Technology Control Regime (MTCR)

The MTCR is an informal group of countries that seek to coordinate national export licensing efforts aimed at preventing the proliferation of missile systems capable of delivering weapons of mass destruction. The countries apply the Guidelines for Sensitive Missile-Relevant Transfers.

Partners (34): Argentina, Australia, Austria, Belgium, Brazil, Bulgaria, Canada, Czech Republic, Denmark, Finland, France, Germany, Greece, Hungary, Iceland, Ireland, Italy, Japan, Korea (South), Luxembourg, Netherlands, New Zealand, Norway, Poland, Portugal, Russia, South Africa, Spain, Sweden, Switzerland, Turkey, UK, Ukraine, USA

Website: <http://www.mtcr.info/>

Nuclear Suppliers Group (NSG)

The NSG, formerly also known as the London Club, was established in 1975. It coordinates national transfer controls on nuclear materials according to its Guidelines for Nuclear Transfers (London Guidelines, first agreed in 1978), which contain a 'trigger list' of materials that should trigger IAEA safeguards when they are to be exported for peaceful purposes to any non-nuclear weapon state, and the Guidelines for Transfers of Nuclear-Related Dual-Use Equipment, Materials, Software and Related Technology (Warsaw Guidelines).

Participants (47): Argentina, Australia, Austria, Belarus, Belgium, Brazil, Bulgaria, Canada, China, Croatia, Cyprus, Czech Republic, Denmark, Estonia, Finland, France, Germany, Greece, Hungary, Iceland, Ireland, Italy, Japan, Kazakhstan, Korea (South), Latvia, Lithuania, Luxembourg, Malta, *Mexico*, Netherlands, New Zealand, Norway, Poland, Portugal, Romania, Russia, Slovakia, Slovenia, South Africa, Spain, Sweden, Switzerland, Turkey, UK, Ukraine, USA

Website: <http://www.nuclearsuppliersgroup.org/>

Proliferation Security Initiative (PSI)

Based on a US initiative announced in 2003, the PSI is a multilateral forum focusing on law enforcement cooperation for the interdiction and seizure of illegal weapons of mass destruction, missile technologies and related materials when in transit on land, in the air or at sea. The PSI Statement of Interdiction Principles was issued in 2003. The PSI has no secretariat, but its activities are coordinated by an Operational Experts Group.

Participants (102): Afghanistan, Albania, Andorra, Angola, Antigua and Barbuda, Argentina*, Armenia, Australia*[†], Austria, Azerbaijan, Bahamas, Bahrain, Belarus, Belgium, Belize, Bosnia and Herzegovina, Brunei Darussalam, Bulgaria, Cambodia, Canada*, Chile, Colombia, Croatia[†], Cyprus, Czech Republic[†], Denmark*, Djibouti[†], *Dominica, Dominican Republic*, El Salvador, Estonia, Fiji, Finland, France*[†], Georgia, Germany*[†], Greece*, Holy See, Honduras, Hungary, Iceland, Iraq, Ireland, Israel, Italy*[†], Japan*[†], Jordan, Kazakhstan, Korea (South)*[†], Kyrgyzstan, Kuwait, Latvia, Liberia, Libya, Liechtenstein, Lithuania[†], Luxembourg, Macedonia (Former Yugoslav Republic of), Malta, Marshall Islands, Moldova, Mongolia, Montenegro, Morocco, Netherlands*[†], New Zealand*[†], Norway*[†], Oman, Panama, Papua New Guinea, Paraguay, Philippines, Poland*[†], Portugal*[†], Qatar, Romania, Russia*, *Saint Lucia*, Saint Vincent and the Grenadines, Samoa, San Marino, Saudi Arabia, Serbia, Singapore*[†], Slovakia, Slovenia[†], Spain*[†], Sri Lanka, Sweden, Switzerland, Tajikistan, *Thailand*, Tunisia, Turkey*[†], Turkmenistan, Ukraine[†], United Arab Emirates[†], UK*[†], USA*[†], Uzbekistan, Vanuatu, Yemen

* Member of the Operational Experts Group.
[†] PSI exercise host, 2003–12.

Website: US Department of State, <http://www.state.gov/t/isn/c10390.htm>

Wassenaar Arrangement (WA)

The Wassenaar Arrangement on Export Controls for Conventional Arms and Dual-Use Goods and Technologies was formally established in 1996. It aims to prevent the acquisition of armaments and sensitive dual-use goods and technologies for military uses by states whose behaviour is cause for concern to the member states. Its secretariat is in Vienna, Austria.

Participants (41): Argentina, Australia, Austria, Belgium, Bulgaria, Canada, Croatia, Czech Republic, Denmark, Estonia, Finland, France, Germany, Greece, Hungary, Ireland, Italy, Japan, Korea (South), Latvia, Lithuania, Luxembourg, Malta, *Mexico*, Netherlands, New Zealand, Norway, Poland, Portugal, Romania, Russia, Slovakia, Slovenia, South Africa, Spain, Sweden, Switzerland, Turkey, UK, Ukraine, USA

Website: <http://www.wassenaar.org/>

Zangger Committee

Established in 1971–74, the Nuclear Exporters Committee, called the Zangger Committee, is a group of nuclear supplier countries that meets informally twice a year to coordinate transfer controls on nuclear materials according to its regularly updated trigger list of items which, when exported, must be subject to IAEA safeguards. It complements the work of the Nuclear Suppliers Group.

Members (38): Argentina, Australia, Austria, *Belarus*, Belgium, Bulgaria, Canada, China, Croatia, Czech Republic, Denmark, Finland, France, Germany, Greece, Hungary, Ireland, Italy, Japan, Kazakhstan, Korea (South), Luxembourg, Netherlands, Norway, Poland, Portugal, Romania, Russia, Slovakia, Slovenia, South Africa, Spain, Sweden, Switzerland, Turkey, UK, Ukraine, USA

Website: <http://www.zanggercommittee.org/>

Annex C. Chronology 2012

NENNE BODELL

This chronology lists the significant events in 2012 related to armaments, disarmament and international security. The dates are according to local time. Keywords are indicated in the right-hand column. Definitions of the abbreviations are given on pp. xviii–xxi.

1 Jan.	The Atomic Energy Organization of Iran announces that it has manufactured Iran's first domestically produced nuclear fuel rod. On 2 Jan. Iran test-fires medium- and long-range ballistic missiles during naval exercises in the Gulf. The tension in the region grows following the new US sanctions targeting Iran's Central Bank and financial sector, imposed on 31 Dec. 2011.	Iran; USA
3 Jan.	A 6000–8000-strong group of armed Lou Nuer fighters attacks the town of Pibor, Jonglei state, South Sudan. Personnel from the UN Mission in South Sudan (UNMISS) and the South Sudanese Army (the Sudan People's Liberation Army) deployed in the area claim that they are outnumbered by the fighters. Ethnic violence between the Lou Nuer and Murle tribes since Dec. has left several thousand civilians dead and has displaced thousands more.	South Sudan
5 Jan.	US President Barack Obama presents a new strategic guidance document for the Department of Defense to articulate priorities for US defence in the 21st century, including strengthening the US presences in the Asia–Pacific region and the Middle East, reducing nuclear arsenals, and strengthening intelligence, surveillance and reconnaissance, and counterterrorism capabilities.	USA; Military strategy
8 Jan.	The Iranian newspaper *Kayhan* reports that Iran has begun uranium enrichment at a new underground site at Fordow, close to the city of Qom. The Fordow facility is smaller but more efficient than the main enrichment site at Natanz.	Iran; Nuclear programme
11 Jan.	An Iranian nuclear scientist dies in Tehran in what is termed a 'terrorist bomb blast', when a magnetic explosive device attached to his car explodes. This is the fourth killing of an Iranian nuclear scientist; officials indicate that they believe that Israel is responsible.	Iran; Nuclear programme; Terrorism
20 Jan.	At least 200 people are killed in a series of bombings and attacks carried out by the militant Islamist group Boko Haram ('Western education is forbidden') in Kano, Nigeria. The group has killed hundreds of people since its bombing of the UN headquarters in Abuja in Aug. 2011.	Nigeria; Terrorism

22 Jan.	The Arab League presents a proposal for a peace plan to end the 10-month-long conflict in Syria. Under the agreement, President Bashar al-Assad would transfer power to a deputy and start negotiations with the opposition, and a government of national unity would be formed within 2 months, followed by presidential and parliamentary elections. On 23 Jan. Syria rejects the plan and calls it an infringement of its sovereignty.	Arab League; Syria
24 Jan.	The UN Political Office for Somalia re-establishes a presence in Mogadishu, after being based in Nairobi, Kenya, since 1995.	UN; Somalia
28 Jan.	The Arab League suspends its monitoring mission in Syria. This follows days of escalating violence across the country, with the army launching an offensive against opposition fighters in the suburbs of Damascus, and President Bashar al-Assad's refusal to step down and hand power to a government of national unity.	Arab League; Syria
3–4 Feb.	Syrian Government forces attack Homs with artillery, reportedly killing about 300 people, in the most deadly attack since anti-government protests began in Mar. 2011. On 4 Feb. the UN Security Council fails to agree on a resolution to back the Arab League's proposed peace plan. Thirteen of the Council's members vote in favour of the resolution, but it is vetoed by China and Russia.	UN; Syria
6 Feb.	The UK and the USA recall their ambassadors to Syria in protest at the Syrian Government's violence against the civilian population. Government forces renew shelling Homs on 6–7 Feb.; the Syrian National Council, the main opposition group, claims that at least 50 people are killed.	Syria; UK; USA
8 Feb.	The Darfur Regional Authority (DRA) is inaugurated in the regional capital, Al Fashir. The DRA is intended to stimulate development and facilitate peace in Darfur; it is part of the implementation of the Doha Peace Document, signed by the Sudanese Government and a rebel group, the Liberation and Justice Movement (LJM), on 14 July 2011.	Sudan; Darfur
10 Feb.	Officials of the governments of South Sudan and Sudan sign, in Addis Ababa, Ethiopia, a Memorandum of Understanding (MOU) on Non-aggression and Cooperation, at a meeting of the Joint Political and Security Mechanism (JPSM). The MOU calls for mutual respect of the two countries' sovereignty and territorial integrity, non-interference in each other's internal affairs and no use of force in their relations. Both the African Union and the UN welcome the agreement.	South Sudan; Sudan
16 Feb.	The UN General Assembly adopts, by a vote of 137–12 (China and Russia voting against) with 17 abstentions, a resolution strongly condemning the continuing 'widespread and systematic' human rights violations by the Syrian authorities and calling on all parties in Syria 'to stop all violence or reprisals immediately'.	UN; Syria

22 Feb.	The UN Security Council unanimously adopts Resolution 2036, requesting the African Union (AU) to increase the strength of the AU Mission in Somalia (AMISOM) to a maximum of 17 731 uniformed personnel until 31 Oct. 2012, and deciding to expand the UN logistic support package for AMISOM.	UN; AU; Somalia
22–27 Feb.	Following the burning of copies of the Quran at Bagram Airfield, Afghanistan, by soldiers of the NATO-led International Security Assistance Force (ISAF) on 22 Feb., violent protests spread throughout Afghanistan and more than 20 people are killed, including ISAF soldiers. On 23 Feb. US President Barack Obama expresses his 'deep regret' to Afghan President Hamid Karzai in a personal letter, in which he vows to hold to account those responsible for the Bagram incident.	ISAF; Afghanistan; USA; Islam
23 Feb.	The UN and the Arab League appoint Kofi Annan, a former UN Secretary-General, as their Joint Special Envoy for Syria. The envoy will provide good offices aimed at bringing an end to all violence and human rights violations in Syria and promoting a peaceful solution to the Syrian crisis.	UN; Arab League; Syria
23 Feb.	Meeting at the London Conference on Somalia, delegates from Somalia, 38 other countries and the international community agree to support the Somali political process; to strengthen the African Union Mission in Somalia (AMISOM) and help Somalia develop its own security forces; to help build stability at the local level; and to step up action against pirates and terrorism.	Somalia
24 Feb.	Meeting in Tunis, Tunisia, foreign ministers from about 60 countries attend the International Conference of the Friends of the Syrian People. The participants agree on a declaration calling for an immediate ceasefire and halt to all violence in Syria; in response the Syrian Government allows humanitarian aid organizations to enter the country.	Syria
29 Feb.	Following talks in Beijing, China, between North Korean and US officials, North Korea agrees to suspend its nuclear weapon tests and uranium enrichment and to allow inspectors from the International Atomic Energy Agency (IAEA) to verify and monitor activities at its main nuclear reactor, in Yongbyon, North Pyongan. North Korea also agrees to a moratorium on launches of long-range missiles. The North Korean concessions are part of a larger deal including 240 000 tonnes of US food aid.	North Korea; USA; Nuclear programme
4 Mar.	Militants from Ansar al-Sharia (Partisans of Islamic Law), which is linked to al-Qaeda in the Arabian Peninsula (AQAP), launch a suicide attack on military bases in Zinjibar, Yemen, killing over 100 soldiers and wounding many more. During the attack the militants also take soldiers hostage and capture heavy weapons. Around 30 rebels are killed.	Yemen; al-Qaeda

11 Mar.	A US soldier murders and burns 16 Afghan civilians in a night-time attack in two villages close to the Zangabad military base, in the south of Afghanistan. The Taliban vow revenge for the 'inhumane attack'. Anti-US sentiment in Afghanistan has escalated since the burning of the Quran on 22 Feb.	USA; Afghanistan
14 Mar.	In its first verdict since it was set up in 2002, the International Criminal Court (ICC) in The Hague, Netherlands, finds the leader of the Union of Congolese Patriots (Union des Patriotes Congolais, UPC), Thomas Lubanga Dyilo, guilty of war crimes. The crimes consist of enlisting and conscripting children under the age of 15 years and using them to participate actively in hostilities in the Democratic Republic of the Congo (DRC) between 2002 and 2003. Lubanga Dyilo was arrested in 2006 and went on trial in 2009. On 10 July the ICC sentences him to 14 years in prison.	ICC; DRC; War crimes
22 Mar.	Following violent clashes between government forces and Tuareg rebels from the National Movement for the Liberation of Azawad (Mouvement National de Liberation de l'Azawad, MNLA) in northern Mali since mid-Jan., President Amadou Toumani Touré is overthrown in a military coup d'état. The international community condemns the coup.	Mali
26 Mar.	The UN–Arab League Joint Special Envoy for Syria, Kofi Annan, receives the formal acceptance from the Syrian Government of a six-point proposal to end the ongoing violence in the country. The plan, which was unanimously endorsed by the UN Security Council on 21 Mar., includes a UN-monitored ceasefire and the withdrawal of Syrian Government forces and artillery from population centres.	UN; Arab League; Syria
26–27 Mar.	The second Nuclear Security Summit is held in Seoul, South Korea, with more than 53 heads of states and international organizations participating. The summit focuses on cooperative measures to combat the threat of nuclear terrorism, the protection of nuclear materials and related facilities, and the prevention of trafficking in nuclear materials. The next Nuclear Security Summit will be held in the Netherlands in 2014.	Nuclear security
8 Apr.	Following reports of Chinese fishing boats in the area of Scarborough Shoal, South China Sea, the Philippine Navy sends its largest vessel, which engages in a stand-off with Chinese maritime surveillance ships. Both countries claim that the shoal is 'an integral part' of their territory. The dispute continues into Dec.; the Philippines calls for international support to resolve it in multilateral talks.	China; Philippines
12 Apr.	A military coup d'état ousts the civilian government of Guinea-Bissau. (See also *11 May*.)	Guinea-Bissau

12 Apr.	The ceasefire under the peace plan of Kofi Annan, the UN–Arab League Joint Special Envoy for Syria, takes effect, after escalated violence throughout Syria during the past week. The UN estimates that more than 9000 people have been killed during the past year's fighting. The Syrian Government claims that the rebels have killed more than 2600 security personnel.	UN; Arab League; Syria
13 Apr.	To celebrate the 100th anniversary of the birth of Kim Il Sung, the country's founder, North Korea launches a rocket that is intended to send a satellite into orbit. The rocket explodes less than two minutes after lift-off and falls into the Yellow Sea. The launch is condemned by the international community, which claims that it violates UN Security Council resolutions. Following North Korea's announcement of the planned launch, the USA had suspended planned food aid on 28 Mar.	North Korea
14 Apr.	The UN Security Council unanimously adopts Resolution 2042, authorizing the deployment of an advance team of up to 30 unarmed military observers to Syria. The team is to report on the implementation of a full cessation of armed violence, pending the deployment of a UN supervision mission to monitor the ceasefire. (See also *21 Apr.*)	UN; Syria
15 Apr.	Taliban militants launch a coordinated attack on the diplomatic quarter and the parliament in Kabul, Afghanistan, and in three eastern provinces. A spokesman for the Taliban states that the attack is the opening of the movement's spring offensive.	Afghanistan; Terrorism
19 Apr.	India successfully carries out a test flight of the Agni V, a long-range ballistic missile capable of carrying a nuclear warhead. The missile has a range of 5000 kilometres, and so is capable of reaching Beijing and Shanghai in China.	India; Missiles
20 Apr.	Following weeks of increasing violence over the disputed oil town of Heglig on the border between South Sudan and Sudan, South Sudan withdraws its troops from the area. South Sudan claims Heglig as part of its territory, but the international community has condemned the actions in the area.	South Sudan; Sudan
21 Apr.	The UN Security Council unanimously adopts Resolution 2043, authorizing the establishment of the UN Supervision Mission in Syria (UNSMIS), for an initial period of 90 days, to monitor the cessation of violence and to monitor and support the full implementation of the six-point UN peace plan. UNSMIS will comprise up to 300 unarmed military observers and 'an appropriate civilian component'.	UN; Syria

26 Apr.	After 4 years of hearings, the Special Court for Sierra Leone, based in the Hague, Netherlands, finds former Liberian President Charles Taylor guilty of 11 charges of aiding and abetting war crimes in Sierra Leone's 1991–2002 civil war. Taylor is the first former head of state to be convicted in an international court on war crimes since World War II. On 30 May he is sentenced to 50 years imprisonment.	Special Court for Sierra Leone; Liberia; Sierra Leone; War crimes
1 May	Meeting in Kabul, Afghanistan, US President Barack Obama and Afghan President Hamid Karzai sign the Afghan–US Enduring Strategic Partnership Agreement, a legally binding executive agreement defining how the partnership between the two countries will continue after the withdrawal of US troops in 2014.	Afghanistan; USA
2 May	Following the lifting of a hold on publication, *Nature* publishes an article by a US research group on laboratory-derived influenza strains airborne transmissible between mammals. *Science* publishes a similar article by a Dutch research group on 22 June after the Netherlands issues an export licence. The question of publishing the research, which had been announced on 12 Sep. 2011, had prompted debate in the security and life science communities about whether bioterrorism concerns outweighed the value for public health and influenza pandemic preparedness.	Biosecurity; Export control; Terrorism
5 May	The trial of Khalid Sheikh Mohammed, the alleged planner of al-Qaeda's attacks on the USA on 11 Sep. 2001, and four other accused terrorists begins before a military tribunal at the US base at Guantánamo Bay, Cuba. The five men are charged with the murder of almost 3000 people, terrorism, hijacking, conspiracy and destruction of property.	USA; Terrorism
10 May	Two successive explosions in Damascus kill 55 people and injure nearly 400. The Syrian Government blames what it terms 'terrorists'; the opposition accuses the government of staging the blasts. Since the ceasefire brokered by the UN–Arab League Joint Special Envoy, Kofi Annan, began in Apr. numerous violations have been reported on both sides.	Syria
11 May	Following the military coup d'état in Guinea-Bissau on 12 Apr., the Economic Community of West African States (ECOWAS) brokers a deal setting up a transitional government. On 18 May the ECOWAS Mission in Guinea-Bissau (ECOMIB) is deployed to lead the transition back to civilian rule after the elections to be held in Apr. 2013, assist in security sector reform and facilitate the withdrawal of the Angolan Technical and Military Assistance Mission in Guinea-Bissau (MISSANG).	ECOWAS; Guinea-Bissau

16 May	The trial of Ratko Mladić, a Bosnian Serb military leader, begins at the International Criminal Tribunal for the former Yugoslavia (ICTY), based in The Hague, Netherlands. Mladić was arrested in May 2011 and has been charged over the 1995 Srebrenica massacre and other war crimes during the 1992–95 Bosnian War.	ICTY; Bosnia and Herzegovina; War crimes
18–19 May	Meeting in Camp David, Maryland, USA, the leaders of the Group of Eight (G8) industrialized states adopt the Camp David Declaration, which addresses the question of food security and reaffirms that non-proliferation and disarmament are top priorities for the group.	G8
20–21 May	At its 2012 summit, held in Chicago, Illinois, USA, the North Atlantic Treaty Organization (NATO) adopts a declaration on defence capabilities, 'Toward NATO Forces 2020'; approves and makes public the results of the Deterrence and Defence Posture Review; declares that an 'interim' NATO ballistic missile defence (BMD) capability has been achieved; endorses NATO's Policy Guidelines on Counter-Terrorism; and reiterates that the ISAF combat mission in Afghanistan will close by the end of 2014, and starts planning for a post-2014 mission to assist Afghan security forces.	NATO; Afghanistan; BMD; Terrorism
21 May	A suicide bomb attack targets soldiers rehearsing for a military parade in Sana'a, Yemen, killing over 100 people and injuring hundreds more. Ansar al-Sharia (Partisans of Islamic Law), a militant group linked to al-Qaeda in the Arabian Peninsula (AQAP), claims responsibility for the attack in a Facebook posting, calling it a retaliation for the government campaign against al-Qaeda that began in early May.	Yemen; al-Qaeda
25 May	Over 100 people are killed, including more than 30 children, and hundreds are injured in an artillery attack by government forces on the village of Houla, Homs Governorate, Syria. On 27 May the UN Security Council unanimously condemns the killings and demands that the Syrian Government immediately ceases the use of heavy weapons in population centres.	Syria
16 June	The UN Supervision Mission in Syria (UNSMIS) suspends its activities because of the escalation of violence across the country over the past 10 days. The monitors will remain at their locations in Syria until further notice but will not conduct patrols.	UN; Syria
22 June	A Turkish F-4 combat aircraft is shot down by Syrian forces over the Mediterranean while conducting a training flight. Syria claims that the aircraft was flying over its territorial waters. The European Union condemn Syria for downing the aircraft. Turkey calls a NATO meeting on 26 June to discuss the incident.	Syria; Turkey

30 June   Meeting in Geneva, Switzerland, the Action Group for   Syria
               Syria, chaired by the UN–Arab League Joint Special Envoy
               for Syria, Kofi Annan, agrees on steps and measures to be
               taken by the parties to the Syrian conflict in order to secure
               full implementation of the six-point UN peace plan and UN
               Security Council resolutions 2042 and 2043. The steps
               include an immediate cessation of violence in all its forms.
               The Action Group also agrees on principles and guidelines
               for a Syrian-led transition. Opposition groups react nega-
               tively to the agreement.

30 June   The mandate of the European Union Police Mission in   EU; Bosnia and
               Bosnia and Herzegovina (EUPM) ends. The EUPM was   Herzegovina;
               deployed in Jan. 2003 as the first EU civil crisis manage- Crisis
               ment mission within the framework of the European   management
               Security and Defence Policy (ESDP, now known as the
               Common Security and Defence Policy).

2–27 July   The UN Conference on the Arms Trade Treaty (ATT) is   Arms trade treaty
               held at the UN headquarters in New York, USA. It ends
               without reaching consensus on a treaty text. On 24 Dec. the
               UN General Assembly decides to hold a follow-on confer-
               ence on the treaty in Mar. 2013.

12 July   In an attack with mortars and artillery, Syrian Government Syria
               troops and shabiha pro-regime militia groups kill more
               than 200 people, mostly civilians, in the village of Tremseh,
               near Hamah, Syria.

16 July   The Council of the European Union (EU) establishes the   EU; Niger; Peace
               EU Capacity Building Mission in Niger (EUCAP Sahel   operations
               Niger) under the Common Security and Defence Policy
               (CSDP) to improve the capacities of the Nigerien security
               forces (Gendarmerie, National Police and National Guard)
               to fight terrorism and organized crime in an effective and
               coordinated manner. The Council had approved a crisis
               management concept for a potential civilian mission in the
               Sahel region on 23 Mar. Deployment of the mission starts
               in Aug.

16 July   The Council of the European Union (EU) establishes the   EU; Horn of
               EU Mission on Regional Maritime Capacity Building in the Africa; Indian
               Horn of Africa (EUCAP Nestor) under the Common Secur-   Ocean; Peace
               ity and Defence Policy (CSDP). The mission, which was   operations
               approved in Dec. 2011, will be a civilian mission and will
               complement the EU Naval Force Somalia (EUNAVFOR
               Somalia, Operation Atalanta) and the EU Training Mission
               Somalia (EUTM Somalia). Deployment of the mission
               starts in early Sep.

18 July   A bomb detonates at the National Security Building,   Syria
               Damascus, killing three top officials, including the defence
               minister, and injures many more. Rebels claim responsi-
               bility for the attack, which comes after several days of
               heavy violence in the city.

23 July   A spokesman of the Syrian Ministry of Foreign Affairs   Syria; CBW
acknowledges for the first time that Syria possesses
'weapons of mass destruction', and in particular chemical
weapons, when he states that 'All of these types of weapons
are in storage and under security and the direct supervision
of the Syrian armed forces and will never be used unless
Syria is exposed to external aggression'. The statement was
made as Syria faces international isolation and threats by
Israel to invade to prevent such weapons from falling into
the hands of the rebels.

23 July   At least 116 people are killed and around 300 injured in a   Iraq; al-Qaeda;
series of coordinated gun and bomb attacks across Iraq.   Terrorism
The Islamic State of Iraq (ISI), al-Qaeda's affiliate in Iraq,
claims responsibility for the attacks, which were mostly
targeted at Shia Muslims.

2 Aug.   The UN–Arab League Joint Special Envoy for Syria, Kofi   UN; Arab League;
Annan, announces his resignation after failing to achieve a   Syria
temporary ceasefire in the 6 months since his appointment.
He claims that his peace mission has become a 'mission
impossible'. On 17 Aug. Lakhdar Brahimi, an Algerian
diplomat and former UN special representative, is
appointed as Annan's replacement as Joint Special Envoy.

8 Aug.   Following an attack by Islamists on an Egyptian checkpoint   Egypt; Sinai;
on the border between Sinai and Israel on 5 Aug., which   Terrorism
killed 16 Egyptian soldiers, the Egyptian military launches
air and ground operations against the suspected perpetrators. Egypt also closes the Rafah border crossing with
the Gaza Strip until further notice, leaving the Gaza Strip
largely cut off from the outside world. This is the first time
since the 1973 war with Israel that the Egyptian Army fires
missiles in Sinai. On 11 Aug. Egyptian President Muhamed
Morsy orders tanks to be deployed at posts along the
border in Sinai.

19 Aug.   Following a decision on 16 Aug. by the UN Security Council   UN; Syria
to create a liaison office to support efforts for a political
solution in Syria, the UN Supervision Mission in Syria
(UNSMIS) ends at midnight. The 150 observers leave the
country.

27 Aug.–7 Sep. The second UN Conference to Review Progress Made   UN; SALW
in the Implementation of the Programme of Action to
Prevent, Combat and Eradicate the Illicit Trade in Small
Arms and Light Weapons in All Its Aspects is held in New
York, USA. The parties adopt by consensus an outcome
document highlighting that the international community
renews its commitment to preventing, combating and
eradicating the illicit trade in small arms and light
weapons.

11–14 Sep.	Protesters against a film seen as insulting the Islamic prophet Muhammad attack the US Embassy in Cairo, Egypt. On 12 Sep. the US Consulate in Benghazi, Libya, is attacked by gunmen and US diplomatic personnel are killed. The protests spread across the Arab world, and Western embassies are attacked in several countries on 14 Sep.	USA; Islam
11 –17 Sep.	Following the Japanese Government's announcement that it has bought three of the Senkaku Islands (called the Diaoyu Islands in China) in the East China Sea from a private owner, the territorial dispute between China and Japan over the islands escalates. Chinese marine patrol ships enter Japanese-claimed waters around the islands. Large demonstrations against Japan take place across China, and on 17 Sep. Japanese companies in China close factories and offices.	China; Japan
13 Sep.	The Conference on Disarmament (CD) concludes its 2012 session without any substantive negotiations on a fissile material cut-off treaty (FMCT).	CD; Arms control
27 Sep.	Meeting in Addis Ababa, Ethiopia, under the auspices of the African Union High-level Implementation Panel and the UN Security Council, the presidents of South Sudan and Sudan sign a cooperation agreement, the Addis Ababa Agreement. The agreement commits the two countries to implementing a series of arrangements dealing with issues including security, the management of oil resources and border demarcation.	South Sudan; Sudan
28 Sep.	Kenyan troops, operating as part of the African Union Mission in Somalia (AMISOM), launch an air and sea attack on Kismayo, Somalia, the last stronghold of the Islamist movement al-Shabab. After heaving fighting, al-Shabab withdraws from the city.	Kenya; Somalia; Peace operations
3–4 Oct.	After a mortar bomb is fired across the border from Syria into Turkish territory, killing Turkish civilians, the Turkish military strikes target inside Syria. In an emergency meeting held later that day to discuss the escalating Syrian conflict, NATO ambassadors condemn the Syrian attack and Turkey makes a formal complaint to the UN. On 4 Oct. the UN Security Council unanimously approves a statement condemning Syria's shelling of a Turkish town. On the same day, the Turkish Parliament gives its military legal authority to launch cross-border strikes into Syria in response to the attack.	Syria; Turkey

7 Oct.	Meeting in Kuala Lumpur, Malaysia, the Philippine Government and the Moro Islamic Liberation Front (MILF) reach a framework peace agreement under which a new region, named Bangsamoro, on part of the island of Mindanao with a mainly Muslim population, will be given considerably autonomy. The Philippine Government will retain control over defence, foreign policy and broad economic policy. The deal ending a 40-year conflict is signed in Manila, Philippines, on 15 Oct.	Philippines
10 Oct.	The Russian Government announces that it will not renew the Cooperative Threat Reduction (CTR) programme (also known as the Nunn–Lugar programme) when it expires in early 2013. The programme, under which Russia and the USA safeguard and dismantle nuclear and chemical weapons in the former USSR, has been running since 1992.	Russia; USA; Disarmament
10 Oct.	A Syrian passenger aircraft travelling from Moscow, Russia, to Damacus, Syria, and suspected of carrying military equipment is intercepted by Turkish combat aircraft and forced to land at Ankara Airport. In 2011 Turkey stated that it would be willing to take measures to 'stop and confiscate' any shipment of military supplies, by air or sea, to Syria in contravention of Turkey's unilateral arms embargo.	Syria; Turkey
12 Oct.	The UN Security Council requests that the Africa Union, the Economic Community of West African States (ECOWAS) and the UN Secretary-General present a plan within 45 days to deploy a military force to counter the Islamist rebellion in northern Mali, should diplomacy fail. (See also *11 Nov.*)	UN; AU; ECOWAS; Mali; Peace operations
18 Oct.	Meeting in Hurdal, Norway, the Colombian Government and the Revolutionary Armed Forces of Colombia (Fuerzas Armadas Revolucionarias de Colombia, FARC) formally start negotiations aiming at ending the conflict that began in 1964. Three earlier attempts have failed.	Colombia
24 Oct.	The Yarmouk military-industrial complex in Khartoum, Sudan, is bombed by four aircraft, causing a huge explosion. Sudanese officials blame Israel for the attack and state that 'Sudan reserves the right to strike back at Israel'. Israel does not comment on the accusations.	Israel; Sudan
11 Nov.	At an emergency meeting in Abuja, Nigeria, the leaders of the Economic Community of West African States (ECOWAS) member states agree to deploy a 3300-strong military force to counter the Islamist rebellion in northern Mali. The Africa Union approves the plan on 13 Nov. Although the UN Security Council had requested that such a plan be presented by 25 Nov., on 28 Nov. the UN Secretary-General, Ban Ki-moon, states that the plan needs to be developed further on 'fundamental questions' on how the force will be led, trained and equipped; nonetheless, he recommends that the Security Council approves the deployment. (See also *20 Dec.*)	UN; AU; ECOWAS; Mali; Peace operations

12 Nov.	The members of the Gulf Cooperation Council (GCC) recognize the National Coalition of Syrian Revolutionary and Opposition Forces as the legitimate representative of the Syrian people. France, the first Western country to recognize the coalition, does so on 13 Nov. and states that it is considering providing arms to the rebel group. On 15 Nov. Turkey also officially recognizes the coalition.	GCC; France; Turkey; Syria
14–21 Nov.	Israel launches aerial attacks on the Gaza Strip, killing among others Ahmed Jabari, Hamas's top military commander. The attack follows continued Palestinian rocket fire into Israel from the Gaza Strip since Hamas withdrew from its unilateral ceasefire in Oct. The Israeli attack escalates the hostilities with Hamas, and Israel prepares for a ground invasion of the Gaza Strip. The violence is condemned by the international community, and the UN Secretary-General, Ban Ki-moon, calls for an immediate ceasefire. Following intensive negotiations in Cairo, Egypt, mediated by Egyptian President Muhamed Morsy, a ceasefire agreement between Israel and Hamas is announced on 21 Nov. More than 160 people are killed during the eight days of fighting.	Israel; Gaza Strip
15–20 Nov.	Fighting between the Congolese armed forces (Forces armées de la République démocratique du Congo, FARDC) and the 23 March Movement (Mouvement du 23 mars, M23) rebel group erupts in eastern Democratic Republic of the Congo (DRC), breaking a 3-month ceasefire. Rwanda and Uganda are accused of aiding M23 but strongly deny it. After the UN Organization Stabilization Mission in the DRC (MONUSCO) fails to stop the rebels from advancing, M23 captures Goma, the largest city in eastern DRC, on 20 Nov., without resistance. M23 was formed in April 2012 by soldiers deserting from the FARDC.	UN; DRC
18 Nov.	At the 21st ASEAN Summit, held in Phnom Penh, Cambodia, the leaders of the Association of Southeast Asian Nations (ASEAN) launch the ASEAN Institute for Peace and Reconciliation (AIPR). The institute will review ASEAN's cooperation on conflict resolution and aims to contribute to peace and reconciliation in South East Asia.	ASEAN
28 Nov.	Dozens of people, mostly civilians, are killed in four consecutive explosions in Damascus, Syria. The Syrian Government and the opposition blame each other for the attacks.	Syria
29 Nov.	The UN General Assembly adopts, by a vote of 138–9 with 41 abstentions, a resolution granting Palestine non-member state status at the UN. Israel and the USA are among those voting against. Previously, the Palestine Liberation Organization (PLO) held permanent observer status. Palestine's enhanced status as a non-member state will permit it to participate, but not vote, in UN General Assembly debates and to apply to join UN agencies and the International Criminal Court (ICC).	UN; Palestine

3 Dec.	An international peace initiative for a resumption of dialogue between the government and Kurds in Turkey is launched in Brussels, Belgium. The initiative is supported by Archbishop Emeritus Desmond Tutu and a list of leading international figures, including Nobel Peace Prize winners and former heads of states. The launch coincides with the end of a hunger strike by more than 700 Kurdish prisoners.	Turkey; Kurds
7 Dec.	At a meeting in Dublin, Ireland, of the OSCE Ministerial Council, the foreign ministers of the OSCE participating states launch the Helsiniki+40 process, a strategic road map addressing security challenges more effectively by developing practical measures to implement the commitments agreed in the 2010 Astana Commemorative Declaration 'Towards a Security Community' by 2015, 40 years after the signing of the Helsinki Final Act.	OSCE; CSBMs
10 Dec.	The rebel coalition Séléka launches an offensive with the aim of overthrowing President François Bozizé of the Central African Republic. On 11 Jan. 2013, after several days of negotiations, a ceasefire agreement is signed in Libreville, Gabon, under which a government of national unity is to be created.	Central African Republic
12 Dec.	North Korea successfully launches a Unha-3 rocket. According to the Canadian–US North American Aerospace Defense Command (NORAD), the rocket 'deployed an object that appeared to achieve orbit'. The launch is immediately condemned by the international community. The UN Secretary-General, Ban Ki-moon, states that it is a violation of UN Security Council Resolution 1874 (2009), which demands that North Korea conducts no launch using ballistic missile technology. North Korea has previously made four failed attempts to launch long-range missiles. (See also *13 Apr.*)	North Korea; Missiles
17–19 Dec.	Nine health workers on a polio vaccination programme are shot dead in a series of attacks in Karachi and Peshawar, Pakistan. Rumours that immunization campaigns are cover for spies have circulated since Pakistani vaccination workers were used to gather intelligence prior to the USA's assassination of Osama bin Laden in Abbottabad on 1 May 2011. The polio vaccination programme is suspended in Sindh and Khyber Pakhtunkhwa provinces.	Pakistan; Health; Terrorism
20 Dec.	The UN Security Council unanimously adopts Resolution 2085, under Chapter VII of the UN Charter, authorizing the deployment of an African-led International Support Mission in Mali (AFISMA), as agreed by the Economic Community of West African States (ECOWAS) on 11 Nov., 'to provide coordinated and coherent support to the ongoing political and security processes in the country'. The Council also emphasizes 'the need to further refine planning before the start of an offensive military operation'.	UN; ECOWAS; Mali; Peace operations

31 Dec.   The UN Security Council Sanctions Committee on the UN; DRC; Arms Democratic Republic of the Congo (DRC) adds the embargoes 23 March Movement (Mouvement du 23 mars, M23) rebel group and its alleged Rwandan allies, the FDLR (Forces démocratiques de libération du Rwanda, Democratic Forces for the Liberation of Rwanda), to the list of groups subject to an arms embargo and other sanctions in eastern DRC.

31 Dec.   The United Nations Integrated Mission in Timor-Leste UN; Timor-Leste; (UNMIT) completes its mandate. UNMIT, a multi- Peace operations dimensional, integrated UN peace operation, was established in 2006 in the wake of a major political, humanitarian and security crisis in the country.

About the authors

Wael Abdul-Shafi (Germany/Palestine) was an intern with the SIPRI Military Expenditure and Arms Production Programme in 2012. He is studying for a masters degree at the University of Gothenburg.

Marie Allansson (Sweden) is a Research Assistant and Information Officer with the Uppsala Conflict Data Program (UCDP) at the Uppsala University Department of Peace and Conflict Research. Prior to joining the UCDP, she conducted an internship at the United Nation Development Programme (UNDP) Iraq Country Office, based in Jordan, focusing on small arms and light weapons. She has contributed to the SIPRI Yearbook since 2012.

Dr Ian Anthony (United Kingdom) is Director of the SIPRI Arms Control and Non-proliferation Programme. His publications include *Reforming Nuclear Export Controls: The Future of the Nuclear Suppliers Group*, SIPRI Research Report no. 22 (2007, co-author), and *The Future of Nuclear Weapons in NATO* (Friedrich-Ebert-Stiftung, 2010, co-author). He has contributed to the SIPRI Yearbook since 1988.

Dr Sibylle Bauer (Germany) is Director of the SIPRI Dual-use and Arms Trade Control Programme. Before joining SIPRI in 2003, she was a Researcher with the Institute for European Studies (ULB), Brussels. Since 2005 she has designed and implemented capacity-building activities in Europe and South East Asia, with a focus on legal and enforcement issues related to the enhancement of transit, brokering and export controls. Her publications include 'Arms trade control capacity building: lessons from dual-use trade controls', SIPRI Insights on Peace and Security no. 2013/2 (Mar. 2013). She has contributed to the SIPRI Yearbook since 2004.

Dr Elin Bjarnegård (Sweden) is Assistant Professor at the Uppsala University Department of Government and is a member of the core group of the East Asian Peace programme at the Uppsala University Department of Peace and Conflict Research. She has authored or co-authored a number of publications on issues related to gender and conflict, as well as to Thai politics. Her recent publications include *Gender, Informal Institutions and Political Recruitment* (Palgrave Macmillan, 2013) and 'Revisiting representation: communism, women in politics, and the decline of armed conflict in East Asia', *International Interactions* (forthcoming, co-author).

Nenne Bodell (Sweden) is Director of the SIPRI Library and Documentation Department and of the SIPRI Arms Control and Disarmament Documentary Survey. She has contributed to the SIPRI Yearbook since 2003.

Vincent Boulanin (France) has been a Visiting Research Fellow at SIPRI since 2008, working with the SIPRI Arms Production Project. He is a doctoral student at l'École des hautes études en sciences sociales (EHESS), Paris, looking at the development of the European defence industry in the realm of security. His other interests include the development of military and security technologies and their impact on the practice of security professionals and the social construction of threats and risks. He has also conducted research and published on the Swedish defence industry and Swedish defence policy.

Mark Bromley (United Kingdom) is a Senior Researcher with the SIPRI Arms Transfers Programme, where his work focuses on European arms exports and arms export controls, South American arms acquisitions and efforts to regulate the international arms trade. Previously, he was a policy analyst for the British American Security Information Council (BASIC). His recent publications include *Transparency in Military Spending and Arms Acquisitions in Latin America and the Caribbean*, SIPRI Policy Paper no. 31 (Jan. 2012, co-author), and 'The review of the EU Common Position on arms exports: prospects for strengthened controls', Non-proliferation Papers no. 7 (Jan. 2012). He has contributed to the SIPRI Yearbook since 2004.

Professor Tilman Brück (Germany) is Director of SIPRI. He is a development economist with research interests in the interrelationship between peace, security and development (especially at the micro-level), the economics of post-war reconstruction, and the economics of terrorism and security policy. He also collects and analyses household-level surveys to study poverty and employment and how they relate to conflict. He is a co-founder and co-director of the Households in Conflict Network and a founding member of the Global Young Academy. He was previously a full professor of development economics at Humboldt-University of Berlin and a head of department at the German Institute for Economic Research (DIW).

Christina Buchhold (Germany) is a Research Assistant for the Director and the SIPRI Dual-use and Arms Trade Control Programme. Before joining SIPRI she was a Research Assistant at the Kroc Institute for International Peace Studies and at a Ugandan non-governmental organization.

Dr Peter Clevestig (Sweden) is Senior Researcher with the Chemical and Biological Security Project of the SIPRI Arms Control and Non-proliferation Programme. He specializes in safety and security of biological materials, biotechnology and related policies. He has authored several articles and book chapters on bioterrorism, security aspects of the life sciences and the threats posed by infectious diseases, as well as *Handbook of Applied Biosecurity for Life Science Laboratories* (2009). He has contributed to the SIPRI Yearbook since 2008

Jane Dundon (Ireland) is an Associate Researcher with the SIPRI Armed Conflict and Conflict Management Programme. Prior to joining SIPRI she worked with Transparency International and has volunteered with Amnesty International for several years. Her research interests include peace operations, crisis management and international human rights law.

Vitaly Fedchenko (Russia) is a Senior Researcher with the SIPRI Arms Control and Non-proliferation Programme, with responsibility for nuclear security issues and the political, technological and educational dimensions of nuclear arms control and non-proliferation. Previously, he was a visiting researcher at SIPRI and worked at the Center for Policy Studies in Russia and the Institute for Applied International Research in Moscow. His publications include *Reforming Nuclear Export Controls: The Future of the Nuclear Suppliers Group*, SIPRI Research Report no. 22 (2007, co-author). He has contributed to the SIPRI Yearbook since 2005.

Dr Alexander Glaser (Germany) is Assistant Professor at the Woodrow Wilson School of Public and International Affairs and in the Department of Mechanical and Aerospace Engineering at Princeton University. He is a participant in the university's Program on Science and Global Security and works with the International Panel on Fissile Materials, which publishes the annual Global Fissile Material Report. He works on nuclear energy and security policy with a focus on nuclear non-proliferation and arms control. He is co-editor of *Science & Global Security*. He has contributed to the SIPRI Yearbook since 2007.

Lina Grip (Sweden) is a Researcher with the SIPRI Arms Control and Non-proliferation Programme and is SIPRI's coordinator for the EU Non-proliferation Consortium. She is also a doctoral candidate in political science at Helsinki University. Her research interests include regional and multilateral non-proliferation and arms control policies and processes, with a focus on the European Union. Her recent publications include 'Assessing selected European Union external assistance and cooperation projects on WMD non-proliferation', Non-proliferation Papers no. 6 (Dec. 2011) and 'The role of the European Union in delivering Resolution 1540 implementation assistance', Non-proliferation Paper No. 22 (Oct. 2012)

John Hart (United States) is a Senior Researcher and Head of the Chemical and Biological Security Project of the SIPRI Arms Control and Non-proliferation Programme. He is a doctoral candidate in military sciences at the at the Finnish National Defence University. His recent publications include *The Future of the Chemical Weapons Convention: Policy and Planning Aspects*, SIPRI Policy Paper no. 35 (Apr. 2013, co-author). He has contributed to the SIPRI Yearbook since 1997.

Dr Paul Holtom (United Kingdom) is Director of the SIPRI Arms Transfers Programme. Previously, he was a Research Fellow with the University of Glamorgan Centre for Border Studies. His research interests include the monitoring of international conventional arms transfers, promoting transparency in international arms transfers and initiatives to strengthen conventional arms transfer controls to prevent trafficking. His most recent publications include 'The UN Arms Trade Treaty: arms export controls, the human security agenda and the lessons of history', *International Affairs* (2012, co-author). He has contributed to the SIPRI Yearbook since 2007.

Dr Susan T. Jackson (United States) was Head of the SIPRI Arms Production Project until May 2013. She is currently Assistant Professor of International Relations at Malmö University. Her work focuses on the links between militarization and globalization and she has published on the national security exception and the marketing of militarism. She has contributed to the SIPRI Yearbook since 2010.

Shannon N. Kile (United States) is a Senior Researcher and Head of the Nuclear Weapons Project of the SIPRI Arms Control and Non-proliferation Programme. His principal areas of research are nuclear arms control and non-proliferation, with a special interest in Iran and regional security issues. His publications include *Europe and Iran: Perspectives on Non-proliferation*, SIPRI Research Report no. 21 (2005, editor), and *Verifying a Fissile Materials Cut-off Treaty: Technical and Organizational Considerations*, SIPRI Policy Paper no. 33 (2012). He has contributed to the SIPRI Yearbook since 1993.

Hans M. Kristensen (Denmark) is Director of the Nuclear Information Project at the Federation of American Scientists (FAS). He is a frequent consultant to the news media and institutes on nuclear weapon matters and is co-author of the 'Nuclear notebook' column in the *Bulletin of the Atomic Scientists*. His recent publications include *Non-Strategic Nuclear Weapons* (FAS, 2012), *Trimming Nuclear Excess: Options for Further Reductions of U.S. and Russian Nuclear Forces* (FAS, 2012), and *Reducing Alert Rates of Nuclear Weapons* (UNIDIR, 2012, co-author). He has contributed to the SIPRI Yearbook since 2001.

Dr Jaïr van der Lijn (Netherlands) is a Senior Researcher with the SIPRI Armed Conflict and Conflict Management Programme, where he leads research on peacekeeping, peacebuilding and conflict management. Previously he was a Senior Research Fellow at the Netherlands Institute of International Relations 'Clingendael' and an Assistant Professor at Radboud University Nijmegen. His research interests include the future of peace operations, evaluation and factors for success and failure of peace operations, and comprehensive approaches in missions. His most recent publications include 'Afghanistan post-2014: groping in the dark?' (Clingendael, May 2013) and 'The future of peace operations', (Clingendael, Jan. 2013).

Professor Erik Melander (Sweden) is a professor at the Uppsala University Department of Peace and Conflict Research. He is the Deputy Program Leader of the East Asian Peace programme and Deputy Director of the Uppsala Conflict Data Program (UCDP). His research interests include patterns of armed conflict, gender and war, geographic aspects of ethnic conflict, and prevention of genocide.

Dr Neil Melvin (United Kingdom) is Director of the SIPRI Armed Conflict and Conflict Management Programme. Prior to joining SIPRI he held senior adviser positions in the Energy Charter Secretariat and the Organization for Security and Co-operation in Europe (OSCE). He has worked at a variety of leading policy institutes in Europe and published widely on issues of conflict. His recent publications include 'Don't oversell "overspill": Afghanistan and emerging conflicts in Central Asia', Central Asia Policy Brief no. 6 (Elliott School of International Affairs, Dec. 2012). He contributed to the SIPRI Yearbook in 2006–2007 and 2011–2012.

Zia Mian (Pakistan/United Kingdom) is a physicist with Princeton University's Program on Science and Global Security, where he directs the Project on Peace and Security in South Asia. He is co-deputy chair of the International Panel on Fissile Materials and co-editor of *Science & Global Security*. His work focuses on nuclear weapons, arms control and disarmament, and nuclear energy issues in India and Pakistan. He contributed to the SIPRI Yearbook in 2003 and since 2007.

Tamara Patton (United States) is a Researcher with the SIPRI Arms Control and Non-proliferation Programme. Her research interests include non-proliferation and disarmament issues related to both nuclear and conventional weapons, with a particular focus on technologies for transparency and verification. Her recent publications include *A New START Model for Transparency in Nuclear Disarmament* (UNIDIR, 2013, co-author), and 'Using 3D modeling for verification design', *Trust & Verify* (Apr.–June 2012).

Dr Sam Perlo-Freeman (United Kingdom) is Director of the SIPRI Military Expenditure and Arms Production Programme. Previously, he was a Senior Lecturer at the University of the West of England, working on defence and peace economics. His recent publications include 'Military expenditure and the global culture of militarism' in *The Marketing of War in the Age of Neo-Militarism* (Routledge, 2012) and 'Budgetary priorities in Latin America: military, health and education spending', SIPRI Insights on Peace and Security no. 2011/2 (Dec. 2011). He has contributed to the SIPRI Yearbook since 2003.

Susanne Schaftenaar (Netherlands) is a Research Assistant with the East Asian Peace programme at the Uppsala University Department of Peace and Conflict Research. Her main research interests are unarmed insurrections and post-war democratization.

Phillip Schell (Germany) is a Researcher with the SIPRI Arms Control and Non-Proliferation Programme. His research focuses on security issues related to the arms control, disarmament and non-proliferation of weapons of mass destruction, with a regional specialization on East Asia and South Asia. His recent publications include *A New START Model for Transparency in Nuclear Disarmament* (UNIDIR, 2013, co-author). He has contributed to the SIPRI Yearbook since 2012

Dr Elisabeth Sköns (Sweden) is Head of the SIPRI Africa Security and Governance Project. Her recent publications include 'The private military services industry', SIPRI Insights on Peace and Security no. 2008/1 (Sep. 2008, co-author), 'The economics of arms production' in *Encyclopedia of Violence, Peace and Conflict* (Elsevier, 2008, co-author), 'The military-industrial complex' in *The Global Arms Trade* (Routledge, 2010, co-author) and 'The US defence industry after the cold war' in *The Global Arms Trade* (Routledge 2010). She has contributed to the SIPRI Yearbook since 1983.

Dr Margareta Sollenberg (Sweden) is a Researcher with the Uppsala Conflict Data Program (UCDP) and an Assistant Professor at the Uppsala University Department of Peace and Conflict Research. She worked as a Project Leader at UCDP in 1994–2003 and has co-authored a number of articles and book chapters on armed conflicts. She contributed to the SIPRI Yearbook in 1995–2003.

Carina Solmirano (Argentina) is a Senior Researcher with the SIPRI Military Expenditure and Arms Production Programme, responsible for monitoring military expenditure in Latin America, the Middle East and South Asia. Previously, she worked at the Josef Korbel School of International Studies at the University of Denver, Colorado. Her recent publications include *Transparency in Military Spending and Arms Acquisitions in Latin America and the Caribbean*, SIPRI Policy Paper no. 31 (Jan. 2012, co-author) and 'The politics of military spending and arms acquisitions in Latin America', *Export Vooruzheny* (July/ Aug. 2012). She has contributed to the SIPRI Yearbook since 2010.

Isak Svensson (Sweden) is Associate Professor at the Uppsala University Department of Peace and Conflict Research. He was previously Director of Research at the National Centre for Peace and Conflict Studies, University of Otago. His areas of expertise are international mediation in civil wars and religious aspects of conflict-resolution processes. His most recent books are *The Go-between: Ambassador Jan Eliasson and the Styles of International Mediation,* (USIP Press, 2010, co-author), and *Ending Holy Wars: Religion and Conflict Resolution in Civil Wars* (University of Queensland Press, 2012).

Lotta Themnér (Sweden) is a Research Coordinator with the Uppsala Conflict Data Program (UCDP) at the Uppsala University Department of Peace and Conflict Research. She has edited nine editions of the UCDP's *States in Armed Conflict* and has co-authored a number of articles and book chapters on armed conflicts. She has contributed to the SIPRI Yearbook since 2005.

Dr Stein Tønnesson (Norway) is a Research Professor at the Peace Research Institute Oslo (PRIO) and Adjunct Professor at Uppsala University, where he leads the East Asian Peace programme. His publications are mainly about nationalism and nation building, the history of war and revolution in Indochina, and the disputes in the South China Sea.

Dr Andrea Viski (Hungary) is a researcher with the SIPRI Non-proliferation and Arms Control Programme and the SIPRI Dual-use and Arms Trade Control Programme. She is the author of several publications on export controls, international nuclear law, trade control regimes and other areas, including 'The Missile Technology Control Regime 25 years on', *World Export Controls Review* (June 2012), and 'International law and nuclear export controls', *International Journal of Nuclear Law* (2011).

Professor Peter Wallensteen (Sweden) has been Senior Professor of Peace and Conflict Research at Uppsala University since 2012 and Richard G. Starmann Senior Research Professor of Peace Studies at the University of Notre Dame since 2006. He held the Dag Hammarskjöld Chair of Peace and Conflict Research at Uppsala University in 1985–2012. He directs the Uppsala Conflict Data Program (UCDP) and the Special Program on International Targeted Sanctions (SPITS). His publications include *Understanding Conflict Resolution: War, Peace and the Global System* (Sage, 3rd edn, 2012) and *Peace Research: Theory and Practice* (Routledge, 2011). He has contributed to the SIPRI Yearbook since 1988.

Pieter D. Wezeman (Netherlands) is a Senior Researcher with the SIPRI Arms Transfers Programme. Prior to rejoining SIPRI in 2006 he was a Senior Analyst for the Dutch Ministry of Defence in the field of proliferation of conventional and nuclear weapon technology. His recent publications include *Arms Flows to Sub-Saharan Africa*, SIPRI Policy Paper no. 30 (Dec. 2011, co-author). He has contributed to the SIPRI Yearbook since 1995.

Siemon T. Wezeman (Netherlands) is a Senior Fellow with the SIPRI Arms Transfers Programme. His areas of research include the monitoring of arms transfers, with a particular focus on the Asia–Pacific region and North America, the use of weapons in conflicts, and transparency in arms transfers. His recent publications include *Arms Flows to Sub-Saharan Africa*, SIPRI Policy Paper no. 30 (Dec. 2011, co-author). He has contributed to the SIPRI Yearbook since 1993.

Helén Wilandh (Sweden) was a Research Assistant with the SIPRI Military Expenditure and Arms Production Programme and worked on the SIPRI Project on Security, Democratization and Good Governance in Africa. Her main research interest is African security issues.

Errata

SIPRI Yearbook 2012: Armaments, Disarmament and International Security

Page 331   For 'H-6 fighter-bomber' *read* 'H-6 bomber'

SIPRI Yearbook 2013: Armaments, Disarmament and International Security

Errata for this printed version of *SIPRI Yearbook 2013* will appear at <http://www.sipri.org/yearbook/> and in *SIPRI Yearbook 2014*. The online version of *SIPRI Yearbook 2013* at <http://www.sipriyearbook.org/> will be updated as errors are discovered.

Index